Lecture Notes in Computer Science 680

Edited by G. Goos and J. Hartmanis

Berthold Hoffmann
Bernd Krieg-Brückner (Eds.)

Program Development by Specification and Transformation

The PROSPECTRA Methodology, Language Family, and System

Springer-Verlag
Berlin Heidelberg New York
London Paris Tokyo
Hong Kong Barcelona
Budapest

Series Editors

Gerhard Goos
Universität Karlsruhe
Postfach 69 80
Vincenz-Priessnitz-Straße 1
D-76131 Karlsruhe, FRG

Juris Hartmanis
Cornell University
Department of Computer Science
4130 Upson Hall
Ithaca, NY 14853, USA

Volume Editors

Berthold Hoffmann
Bernd Krieg-Brückner
FB 3 Mathematik und Informatik, Universität Bremen
Postfach 33 04 40, D-28334 Bremen, Germany

CR Subject Classification (1991):D.2.1, D.2.3, D.2.4, D.2.6, D.2.10, D.2.m

ISBN 3-540-56733-X Springer-Verlag Berlin Heidelberg New York
ISBN 0-387-56733-X Springer-Verlag New York Berlin Heidelberg

Printed in Germany

Typesetting: Camera ready by author
45/3140-543210 - Printed on acid-free paper

Preface

The PROSPECTRA project has been partially funded by the Commission of the European Communities under the ESPRIT Programme, ref. #390 and #835, from March 1985 to March 1990. Many people have contributed to the project (see *The PROSPECTRA Consortium* and *The PROSPECTRA Teams* on the next pages). The Consortium also very gratefully acknowledges the constructive contributions of the project officers from the Commission for PROSPECTRA, Dr. Pierre-Yves Cunin and Jack Metthey, and, last but not least, the Reviewers, Robert F. Maddock (IBM, Hursley), Professor Peter Pepper (Technische Universität Berlin), and Professor John Darlington (Imperial College, London), who have carefully, critically and benevolently guided the project through easy and hard times.

The objective of this documentation is a coherent presentation of the outcome of the project PROSPECTRA (PROgram development by SPECification and TRAnsformation) that aimed to provide a rigorous methodology for developing *correct* software and a comprehensive support system. The results are substantial: a theoretically well-founded *methodology* covering the whole development cycle, a very high-level specification and transformation *language family* allowing meta-program development and formalisation of the development process itself, and a prototype development *system* supporting structure editing, incremental static-semantic checking, interactive, context-sensitive transformation and verification, development of transformation (meta-) programs, version management, etc., with an initial library of some specifications and a sizeable collection of implemented transformations.

One intended audience for this documentation is clearly the academic community working in the areas of formal methods for software (and hardware) development, specification languages, theory of computation, semantics and verification, implementation of functional languages, structure editors, attribute grammars, advanced software engineering environments, etc. An even more important audience is the industrial community interested in the use of formal methods. It is still a long way to the widespread use of production-quality systems employing formal methods to increase correctness, reliability, and safety of systems, and productivity of developers. The PROSPECTRA Consortium has made a conscious effort of technology transfer, trying to implement the state-of-the-art, in a realistic setting. The prototype system, a "PROSPECTRA workstation", allows serious experimentation to enable feedback for extensions and improvements (that are undoubtedly needed). Eventually, we see various classes of PROSPECTRA users, with potentially distinct abilities and educational background: the PROSPECTRA system developers, the developers of transformations and development methods, the developers of (generically re-usable) specifications, and the software developers (end users). At the moment, the system is really only usable externally for benevolent experimenters due to its size and complexity of integration (coming from many development sites). We hope for a new version in the near future, however, based on the extensive experience with PROSPECTRA, as related work at Universität Bremen is presently funded by the Bundesministerium für Forschung und Technologie in the national project KORSO („Korrekte Software").

This volume contains three Parts. Part I contains a description of the PROSPECTRA Methodology of specification, transformation and verification, including the catalogue of presently available transformations. Part II contains a description of the PROSPECTRA Language Family: a rationale for the language subsets and their relationship, reference manuals for concrete syntax, informal semantics, abstract syntax and static semantic attributes, and a formal definition of the semantics of the specification subset. Part III contains a description of the PROSPECTRA System: a rationale for the uniform system structure, a short overall users´ guide, and reference manuals for the various system components.

Bremen, March 1993 Bernd Krieg-Brückner, Berthold Hoffmann

The PROSPECTRA Consortium

Professor Bernd Krieg-Brückner
(Project Director)
FB3 Mathematik und Informatik
Universität Bremen
Postfach 330 440
D- 28334 Bremen

Universität Bremen *(Prime Contractor)*

Professor Harald Ganzinger
now at:
Max-Planck-Institut für Informatik
Im Stadtwald
D- 66123 Saarbrücken

Universität Dortmund

Professor Manfred Broy
now at: Institut für Informatik
Technische Universität München
Arcisstraße 21
D- 80290 München

Universität Passau

Professor Reinhard Wilhelm
FB14 - Informatik
Universität des Saarlandes
Postfach 1150
D- 66041 Saarbrücken

Universität des Saarlandes

Professor Andrew D. McGettrick
Computer Science Department
University of Strathclyde
Livingstone Tower, 26 Richmond St.
UK- Glasgow G1 1XH

University of Strathclyde

Dr. Emmanuel Fermaut
Syseca Logiciel
315 Bureaux de la Colline
F- 92213 St Cloud Cedex

Syseca Logiciel

Einar W. Karlsen
CASE Division
Computer Resources International A/S
(Dansk Datamatik Center)
Bregenerødvej 144
DK- 3460 Birkerød

Computer Resources International

Angel Perez Riesco
Research Center
Alcatel Standard Eléctrica, S. A.
Ramirez de Prado, 5
E- 28045 Madrid

Alcatel Standard Eléctrica SA

Professor Fernando Orejas
Departamento de Lenguajes
y Systemas Informáticas
Universitat Politécnica de Catalunya
Pau Gargallo 5
E- 08028 Barcelona

Universitat Politécnica de Catalunya
(Subcontractor)

The PROSPECTRA Teams

Prof. Bernd Krieg-Brückner, Dr. Berthold Hoffmann, Bernd Gersdorf,
Frank Drewes, Yulin Feng, Jörn von Holten, Stefan Kahrs, Wei Li, Junbo Liu,
Detlef Plump, Zhenyu Qian, Richard Seifert, Elisabeth Swart

Universität Bremen

Prof. Harald Ganzinger, Hubert Bertling,
Dr. Michael Hanus, Renate Schäfers

Universität Dortmund

Prof. Manfred Broy, Thomas Grünler, Dr. Friederike Nickl,
Michael Breu, Frank Dederichs, Rainer Weber

Universität Passau

Prof. Reinhard Wilhelm, Reinhold Heckmann, Dr. Ulrich Möncke,
Martin Alt, Andreas Fecht, Christian Ferdinand, Andreas Hense,
Peter Lipps, Stefan Pistorius, Georg Sander, Beatrix Weisgerber

Universität des Saarlandes

Prof. Andrew D. McGettrick, Owen Traynor,
Charles Chen, David Duffy, Joseph McLean

University of Strathclyde

Dr. Emmanuel Fermaut, Alain Marcuzzi,
Hérvé Bazin, Pierre Boulle, Ian Campbell, Dominique Girard, Dominique Houdier, Dr. Amaury Legait,
Bernard Mathae, Elaine Morcos, Dr. Olivier Roubine, Jean-Luc Saouli, Chantal Vilhet

Syseca Logiciel

Dr. Georg Winterstein,
Peter Dencker, León Treff, Erich Zimmermann

Systeam KG Dr. Winterstein*

Einar W. Karlsen,
Jesper Andersen, Nicola Botta, Jesper Jørgensen
Steen Lynenskjøld, Claus Bendix Nielsen

Computer Resources International A/S

Angel Perez Riesco, Pedro de la Cruz Ramos,
Maria Dolores Hinojal, Alicia Lopez, Juan Antonio de Miguel, José Luis Mañas,
Carlos Muñoz, Miguel Muñoz†, Rafael Perez Gonzales, José Manuel del Prado, José Miguel Pinilla

Alcatel Standard Eléctrica SA

Prof. Fernando Orejas,
Marisa Navarro, Maria Pilar Nivela, Roberto Nieuvenhuis, Ricardo Peña

Universitat Politécnica de Catalunya

---

* past member team

Contents

PART I: METHODOLOGY

PART II: LANGUAGE FAMILY

PART III: SYSTEM

Author Index

PROgram Development by SPECification and TRAnsformation

Part I

Methodology

1. Introduction

Bernd Krieg-Brückner, Universität Bremen

This chapter gives a tutorial introduction to the Methodology. It serves as an overall rationale for the PROSPECTRA Project and relates this part to those on the Language Family and the System. In the methodology of PROgram development by SPECification and TRAnsformation, algebraic specifications are the basis for constructing *correct* and efficient programs by gradual transformation. The combination of algebraic specification and functionals increases abstraction, reduces development effort, and allows reasoning about correctness and direct optimisations. The uniformity of the approach to program and meta-program development is stressed (cf. also the chapter on Uniform Transformational Development in part III chapter 1).

1.1. Overview

The project PROSPECTRA ("PROgram development by SPECification and TRAnsformation") aims to provide a rigorous methodology for developing *correct* software and a comprehensive support system. From 1985 to 1990, it was sponsored by the Commission of the European Communities in the ESPRIT Programme, ref. #390 and #835, as a cooperative project between Universität Bremen (Prime Contractor), Universität Dortmund, Universität Passau, Universität des Saarlandes (all D), University of Strathclyde (GB), SYSECA Logiciel (F), Computer Resources International (DK), Alcatel Standard Eléctrica S.A. (E), and Universitat Politécnica de Catalunya (E) (cf. [Krieg-Brückner 88a, 89a, b, 90], [Krieg-Brückner 91b] (of which this combined volume is a revised edition), [Krieg-Brückner et al. 91], [Karlsen, Krieg-Brückner, Traynor 91], [Liu, Traynor, Krieg-Brückner 92], and the bibliography in part III chapter 7).

The Methodology of Program Development by Transformation (based on the CIP approach of TU München, see e.g. [Bauer 79], [Bauer et al. 85-89]) integrates program construction and verification during the development process. User and implementor start with a formal specification, the interface or "contract". This initial specification is then gradually transformed into an optimised machine-oriented executable program. The final version is obtained by stepwise application of transformation rules. These are applied by the system, with interactive guidance by the implementor, or automatically by compact transformation scripts. Transformations form the nucleus of an extendible knowledge base. Any kind of activity is conceptually and technically regarded as a transformation of a "program" in one of the system components. This provides for a uniform user interface, reduces system complexity, allows the construction of system components in a highly generative way, and is the basis for generalisation of specification, transformation, and command language, even library access, into a single framework.

Overall, PROSPECTRA has achieved a powerful specification *and* transformation *language* with well-defined semantics that reflects the state-of-the-art in algebraic specification combined with higher order functions. In addition, a comprehensive *methodology* covering the complete life-cycle (including re-development after revisions), integrating verification in a realistic way, supporting the development process as a computer-aided activity, and giving hope for a comprehensive formalisation of programming knowledge. A *prototype system* is operational, with a uniform user interface and library management including version and configuration control, that gives complete support and control of language and methodology to ensure correctness.

1.1.1. Overview of Part I

This book contains three Parts. Part I contains a description of the PROSPECTRA Methodology of specification, transformation and verification, including the catalogue of presently available transformations. Part II contains a description of the PROSPECTRA Language Family: a rationale for the language subsets and their relationship, reference manuals for concrete syntax, informal semantics, abstract syntax and static semantic attributes, and a formal definition of the semantics of the specification subset. Part III contains a description of the PROSPECTRA System: a rationale for the uniform system structure, a short overall users guide, and reference manuals for the various system components.

The intended audience for part I, on the PROSPECTRA Methodology, is the program developer.

Chapter 1 gives a tutorial introduction to the methodology, including a small representative example for program development by transformation. It serves as an overall rationale for the PROSPECTRA Project and relates this part I to those on the Language Family and the System.

Chapter 2 describes the specification approach used. It is written for a reader who is familiar with the general concepts of algebraic specification and wants to learn about the particular approach used in the PROSPECTRA Project and its extensions over more conventional approaches, such as loose specifications, partial, higher-order and non-strict functions, notably for the description of distributed systems.

Chapter 3 contains a Reference Manual of the Transformations that are presently available in the System, intended for the program developer. The individual transformations are described in a tutorial style using a semi-formal notation, with some examples. The catalogue is not complete but rather a collection of representative transformations. It will become more complete over time.

Chapter 4 is a tutorial introduction to the methodology of verification.

1.1.2. PROSPECTRA

Within chapter 1, the *objectives* of the PROSPECTRA methodology, its development model, algebraic specification and transformational program development are briefly summarised in section 1.2; the following subsections concentrate on particular extensions to classical algebraic specification and their relation to the methodology. An example illustrating the transformational approach, as supported by the PROSPECTRA system, is given in section 1.3.

1.1.3. Algebraic Specification and Functionals

Section 1.4 describes the combined advantages of functional programming and algebraic specification: a considerably higher degree of abstraction, avoiding much repetitive development effort, the use of homomorphic extension functionals as "program generators". The importance of the *combination* of algebraic specification with higher order functions should be stressed. The ability to specify *partial* higher-order functions (i.e. with conditions on functional parameters; see part II chapter 3) has been an important contribution of PROSPECTRA to the theory of algebraic specifications. The algebraic properties of functionals allow a high level of reasoning *about* functional programs, and permit general and powerful optimisations, supported by the PROSPECTRA approach.

1.1.4. Transformational Meta Program Development

The approach for meta-program development in PROSPECTRA, described in section 1.5, is to regard transformation rules as equations in an algebra of programs, to derive basic transformation operations from these rules, to allow composition and functional abstraction, and to regard transformation *scripts* as (compositions of) such transformation operations. Using all the results from program development based on algebraic specifications and functionals we can then reason about the development of *meta-programs*, i.e. transformation programs or development scripts, in the same way as about programs. Homomorphic extension functionals are important for the concise definition of program development tactics.

Although section 1.5 focusses on meta-program development, it should be clear that the combined advantages of algebraic specification and higher order functions (described in section 1.4) apply to program and meta-program development in the same way. Similarly, all the transformation technology developed for program development can be carried over to meta-program development.

The meta-program development paradigm leads naturally to a *formalisation of the software development process* itself, described in section 1.6. A program development is a sequence of transformations. The system automatically generates a transcript of a development "history". A *development script* is a formal object that does not only represent a documentation of the past but is a plan for future developments. It can be used to abstract from a particular development to a class of similar developments, a *development method*, incorporating a certain strategy.

1.2. PROgram Development by SPECification and TRAnsformation

1.2.1. Objectives

Current software developments are characterised by ad-hoc techniques, chronic failure to meet deadlines because of inability to manage complexity, and unreliability of software products. The major objective of the PROSPECTRA project is to provide a technological basis for developing *correct* programs. This is achieved by a methodology that starts from a formal specification and integrates verification into the development process.

The initial *formal requirement specification* is the starting point of the methodology. It is sufficiently rigorous, on a solid formal basis, to allow verification of correctness during the complete development process thereafter. The methodology is deemed to be more realistic than the conventional style of *a posteriori* verification: the construction process and the verification process are broken down into managable steps; both are coordinated and integrated into an implementation process by *stepwise transformation* that guarantees *a priori* correctness with respect to the original specification. Programs need no further debugging; they are correct by construction. Testing is performed as early as possible by *validation* of the formal specification against the informal requirements (e.g. using a prototyping tool).

Complexity is managed by abstraction, modularisation and stepwise transformation. Efficiency considerations and machine-oriented implementation detail come in by conscious design decisions from the implementor when applying pre-conceived transformation rules. A long-term research aim is the incorporation of goal orientation into the development process. In particular, the crucial selection in large libraries of rules has to reflect the reasoning process in the development.

Engineering Discipline for Correct SW. The PROSPECTRA project aims at making software development an engineering discipline. In the development process, ad hoc techniques are replaced by the proposed uniform and coherent methodology, covering the complete development cycle. Programming knowledge and expertise are formalised as transformation rules and methods with the same rigour as engineering calculus and construction methods, on a solid theoretical basis.

Individual transformation *rules*, compact automated transformation *scripts* and advanced transformation *methods* are developed to form the kernel of an extendible knowledge base, the Method Bank, analogously to a handbook of physics. Transformation rules in the method bank are proved to be correct and thus allow a high degree of confidence. Since the methodology completely controls the system, reliability is significantly improved and higher quality can be expected.

Specification. Formal specification provides the foundation which enables the use of formal methods. High-level development of specifications and abstract implementations (a variation of "logic programming") is seen as the central "programming" activity in the future. In particular, the development of methods for "program synthesis", the derivation of constructive design specifications from non-constructive requirement specifications, is a present focus of research.

The abstract formal (algebraic) specification of requirements, interfaces and abstract designs (including concurrency) relieves the programmer from unnecessary detail at an early stage. Detail comes in by gradual optimising transformation, but only where necessary for efficiency reasons. Specifications are the basis for adaptations in evolving systems, with possible replay of the implementation from development histories that have been stored automatically.

The semantics of the specification language is based on the theory of algebraic specification (with looseness, partial functions, higher-order functions etc., see chapter 2), extended by constructs for predicative specification (pre- and post-conditions of functions).

A transformation is a development step producing a new program version by application of an individual transformation rule, or, more generally, a compact transformation "program" ("meta-" program, see sections 1.4, 1.5 below). Transformations preserve correctness and therefore maintain a tighter and more formalised relationship to prior versions. Their classical application is the construction of optimised implementations by transformation of an initial design that has been proved correct against the formal requirement specification. Further design activity then requires the selection of an appropriate rule, oriented by development goals, for example machine-oriented optimisation criteria.

Programming Language Spectrum: Ada and Anna. Targetting the general methodology and the support system to Ada [ADA 83] (with Anna as its complement for formal specification, see [Luckham et al. 87]) make it realistic for systems development. $PA^{nn}dA$, the PROSPECTRA (Anna/Ada subset) specification and programming language, covers the complete spectrum of language levels from formal specifications and applicative implementations to imperative and machine-dependent representations.

The target language has been Ada in the PROSPECTRA project, but the approach can be generalised to cover other targets as well (a translator to C is available). Stepwise transformations synthesise Ada programs such that many detailed language rules necessary to achieve reliability in direct Ada programming are obeyed *by construction* and need not concern the program developer. In this respect, the PROSPECTRA methodology makes a contribution to managing the complexity of Ada.

Research Consolidation and Technology Transfer. The PROSPECTRA project aims at contributing to the technology transfer from academia to industry by consolidating converging research in formal methods, specification and non-imperative "logic" programming, stepwise verification, formalised implementation techniques, transformation systems, and human interfaces.

Industry of Software Components. The portability of Ada allows pre-fabrication of software components. This is explicitly supported by the methodology. A component is catalogued on the basis of its interface.

Formal specification gives the semantics as required by and made visible to the user; the implementation is hidden and remains a (company) secret.

The methodology emphasises the *pre-fabrication* of generic, universally *(re-)usable* components that can be instantiated according to need. This will invariably cut down production costs by avoiding duplicate efforts. The production of perhaps small but universally marketable (Ada) components on a common technology base can also assist smaller companies in Europe.

Tool Environment. Emphasis on the development of a comprehensive support system is mandatory to make the methodology realistic. The system can be seen as an integrated set of advanced tools based on a minimal support environment, e.g. the ESPRIT Portable Common Tool Environment (PCTE). Because of the generative nature of system components, adaptation to future languages is comparatively easy.

The support of correct and efficient transformations is seen as a major advance in programming environment technology. The central concept of system activity is the application of transformations to trees. Generator components are employed to construct transformers for individual transformation rules and to incorporate the hierarchical approach of PA^{nn}dA (PROSPECTRA Anna/Ada), TrafoLa (the language of transformation descriptions), and ControLa (the command language); in fact, these turn out to be all sublanguages of the same language, for user program, transformation, proof, and system development. This integration and uniformity is seen as one of the major results of the PROSPECTRA project (cf. [Krieg-Brückner 88-92], [Karlsen, Krieg-Brückner, Traynor 91], [Krieg-Brückner et al. 91], [Liu, Traynor, Krieg-Brückner 92] and see part III chapter 1). Generators, in particular the Synthesizer Generator (cf. [Reps, Teitelbaum 88]), increase flexibility and avoid duplication of efforts; thus the overall system complexity is significantly reduced.

1.2.2. The Development Model

Consider a simple model of the major development activities in the life of a program:

Requirements Analysis

- Informal Problem Analysis
- Informal Requirement Specification

Development ⇑ *Validation*

- **Formal** Requirement Specification ⇑ *Verification*
- **Formal** Design Specification ⇑ *Verification*
- **Formal** Construction *by Transformation*

Evolution

- Changes in Requirements ⇒ **Re-Development** ⇑

The *informal requirements analysis* phase precedes the phases of the *development* proper, at the level of formal specifications and by transformation into and at the level(s) of a conventional programming language such as Ada. After the program has been installed at the client, no maintenance in the sense of conventional testing needs to be done; "testing" is perfomed *before* a program is constructed, at the very early stages, by validation of the formal requirement specification against the informal requirements.

The *evolution* of a program system over its lifetime, however, is likely to economically outweigh the original development by an order of magnitude. Changes in the informal requirements lead to re-development, starting with changes in the requirement specification. This requires re-design, possibly by *replay* of the original development (which has been archived by the system) and adaptation of previous designs or re-consideration of previously discarded design variants.

1.2.3. Specification

A requirement specification defines *what* a program should do, a design specification *how* it does it. The motivations and reasons for design decisions, the *why*'s, are recorded along with the developments.

Requirement specifications are, in general, non-constructive; there may be no clue for an algorithmic solution of the problem or for a mapping of abstract to concrete (i.e. predefined) data types. It is essential that the requirement specification should not define more than the *necessary* properties of a program to leave room for design decisions. It is intentionally vague or *loose* in areas where the further specification of detail is irrelevant or impossible, i.e. it denotes a set of models (cf. [Krieg-Brückner 90]). In this sense, loose specification replaces non-determinacy, for example to specify an unreliable transmission medium in a concurrent, distributed situation [Broy 87d, 88, 89], [Dederichs 89].

From an economic point of view, overspecification may lead to substantial increase in development costs and inefficiency of execution of the program since easier solutions are not admissable. If the requirement specification is taken as the formal *contract* between client and software developer, then there should perhaps be a new profession of an independent *software notary* who negotiates the contract, advises the client on consequences by answering questions, checks for inconsistencies, resolves unintentional ambiguities, but guards against overspecification in the interest of both, client and developer. The answer of questions about properties of the formal requirement specification correspond to a *validation* of the informal requirement specification using a prototyping tool.

As an example take the specification of Booleans in (2-1), as it might appear for the standard Ada type. Some axioms (such as associativity, commutativity, distributivity) specify important properties of Booleans, but they are non-operational, whereas other equations can be interpreted as operational rewrite rules, see also (5-3) below.

Note that BOOLEAN is an algebraically specified Abstract Data Type (as the others below) such that its values can be manipulated in user-defined functions, etc., whereas axioms in the specifications are of a built-in type LOGICAL that denotes two-valued logic (without undefined). For better readability, the LOGICAL operators are written in the usual mathematical notation, e.g. $\vee$ instead of **or**. A symbolic style rather than a more conventional Ada oriented notation is used, e.g. —> instead of **return**, and, to exhibit the use of functionals, a notation with explicit Curry-ing to allow partial parameterisation.

In the example for natural numbers in (2-1), some general, non-operational properties are given first (more are needed to characterise the natural numbers completely). Then two alternative sets of rewrite rules are given (corresponding to the two boxes side by side; only a few rules are shown as an example): one for a linear presentation based on zero and succ as constructors, the other for a binary presentation based on zero, dble and dble1 as constructors. They play an important role for (automatic) simplification during transformation below. Each set represents a different design decision. Using the Conditional Equational Completion subsystem (cf. [Ganzinger 87]), each set of rewrite rules has been made terminating and confluent. The general properties are the basis for derivation of the more technical rewrite rules: cf. e.g. sqr x = x * x and the sets of corresponding rewrite rules for sqr.

(2-1) Specification: Booleans and Natural Numbers

```
package BOOLS is
  type BOOLEAN is private;
  false, true:    BOOLEAN;
  "not":          BOOLEAN —> BOOLEAN;
  "and", "or":    BOOLEAN × BOOLEAN —> BOOLEAN;
axiom for all x, y, z: BOOLEAN =>
  true ≠ false,          not false = true,      not true = false,       not not x = x,
  x and false = false,   x or true = true,      x and true = x,         x or false = x,
  x and (y and z) = (x and y) and z,            x and y = y and x,      x and x = x,
  x or (y or z) = (x or y) or z,                x or y = y or x,        x or x = x,
  x and (y or z) = (x and y) or (x and z),      x or (y and z) = (x or y) and (x or z),
  x or not x = true,     x and not x = false,
  x or y = not (not x and not y),               x and y = not (not x or not y);
end BOOLS;
```

```
package NATS is
  type NAT is private;
  zero:    NAT;
  succ:    NAT —> NAT;                    dble, dble1:   NAT —> NAT;     -- *2, *2+1
  ---------------------------------------------------------------------------------
  one,:    NAT;
  "+", "*":  NAT × NAT —> NAT;
  "<=",">":  NAT × NAT —> BOOLEAN;
  "–":       (x: NAT) × (y: NAT:: y <= x) —> NAT;
  sqr,div2:  NAT —> NAT;
axiom for all x, y, z: NAT =>
  x + y = y + x,        x + (y + z) = (x + y) + z,     x + zero = x,     x * one = x,   ...
  (x + y) – x = y,      x <= y → x + (y – x) = y,
  succ x = x + one,     dble x = x + x,     dble1 x = (dble x) + one,     (x + one) + x = dble1 x,
  div2 (dble x) = x,    div2 (dble1 x) = x,                          (sqr x) – (sqr y) = (x + y) * (x – y),
  sqr x = x * x,        sqr (x + y) = sqr x + dble (x * y) + sqr y,  sqr (x + one) = sqr x + dble x + one,  ...
  ---------------------------------------------------------------------------------
  one = succ zero,                                   || one = dble1 zero,
  ---------------------------------------------------||----------------------------------------
  x + zero = x,      zero + y = y,                   || x + zero = x,      zero + y = y,
  (succ x) + y = succ (x + y),                       || dble(x) + dble(y)   = dble(x + y),
  x + (succ y) = succ (x + y),                       || dble(x) + dble1(y)  = dble1(x + y),
                                                     || dble1(x) + dble(y)  = dble1(x + y),
  (succ x) + (succ y) = succ (succ (x + y)), -- derivable || dble1(x) + dble1(y) = dble((one + x) + y),
  ---------------------------------------------------||----------------------------------------
  sqr zero = zero,                                   || sqr(zero)       = zero,
  sqr (succ x) = sqr x + x + x + one,                || sqr(dble(x))    = dble(dble (sqr x)),
  ...                                                || sqr(dble1(x))   = dble1(dble((sqr x) + x)),  ...   ;
end NATS;
```

An example of a non-operational requirement specification is that of a *concept* which may be used in other specifications, cf. (2-2) and (2-3). As another example of a specification consider lists in (2-3). Note that we may have two views of lists: either constructed by empty and cons or by empty, "&" and single (one of the views is, of course, enough as a requirement specification). Depending on the view, lists have different algebraic properties; in the second case those of a monoid (associativity and neutral element empty). Such strong properties become important for reasoning about optimisations, as we will see below. The definition of the selectors head and tail ensures uniqueness of models up to isomorphism.

Partial Functions are only defined if the pre-condition on the parameter holds (see [Broy, Wirsing 82], [Broy 87], [Nickl et al. 88], part II chapter 3), cf. head and tail. Similarly, a pre-condition on cons could be introduced, stating, for example, that the length should be less than some number MAX_SIZE. cons becomes a *partial constructor function,* LISTS defines bounded lists (cf. [Krieg-Brückner 88a]); corresponding definedness premisses must then also be included in the equations.

When introducing limitations such as bounds in a methodological step, it is desirable not to have to introduce the definedness premises explicitly; they should be included implicitly by a transformation. In fact it can be argued that they should not be shown explicitly in the text of the specification at all (see [Owe 85]) so that they will not clutter the definition of the "normal cases". The cluttering problem can be solved by subtypes used to abbreviate such conditions, potentially leading to a more efficient way of checking for definedness; see also [Krieg-Brückner 87a, 88b] for the introduction of exceptions that arise from partialities in the operations and have their counterpart in the delay conditions of monitor tasks.

(2-2) Parameterised Specification: Concept of a Monoid

```
generic
  type M is private;
package IS_MONOID is
  predicate isMonoid:   M —> (M × M —> M);
  axiom for all n: M; "⊕": M × M —> M =>
    isMonoid n "⊕" <-> for all x, y, z: M => x ⊕ n = x,  n ⊕ x = x,  (x ⊕ y) ⊕ z = x ⊕ (y ⊕ z);
end IS_MONOID;
```

(2-3) Requirement Specification: Lists

```
with IS_MONOID;
generic
  type ITEM is private;
package LISTS is
  type LIST is private;
  empty:    LIST;
  cons:     ITEM —> LIST —> LIST;
  "&":      LIST × LIST —> LIST;
  single:   ITEM —> LIST;
  package LIST_IS_MONOID is new IS_MONOID (LIST);
axiom  isMonoid empty "&";
  isEmpty: LIST —>                            BOOLEAN;
  head:     (x: LIST :: ¬ isEmpty x) —> ITEM;
  tail:     (x: LIST :: ¬ isEmpty x) —> LIST;
axiom for all e: ITEM; l: LIST =>
  isEmpty empty = true,     isEmpty (cons e l) = false,
  head (cons e l) = e,      tail (cons e l) = l,      (single e) & l = cons e l;
end LISTS;
```

The specification of sets and ordered sets given in (2-4, 2-5) is an even better example of a non-constructive requirement specification. It is also an example of a loose specification. If several elements in a sequence of $\cup$'s are equivalent, these elements may or may not be multiply represented; sets and multisets ("bags") are allowed as models. This may be desirable: the semantics of some algortihm using sets may not depend on the existence of multiple elements. The user may know that multiple elements in a set are unlikely for the application and would not matter. In this case, the implementation freedom and potential efficiency should not be unnecessarily restricted. If we want to insist on multiple occurrences, we must add some function to be able to distinguish, such as a counting of elements; for true sets, we may add an axiom $x \cup x = x$ that forces absorption. (Omitting the commutativity and absorption axioms in ordered sets with the design specification of (2-6) yields priority queues, cf. [Krieg-Brückner 88a]).

(2-4) Requirement Specification: Sets

```
generic
  type ITEM is private;
package LSETS is
  type SET is private;
  empty:        SET;
  singleton:    ITEM —> SET;
  "∪":          SET × SET —> SET;
  "∈":          ITEM × SET —> BOOLEAN;
axiom for all a, b: ITEM; x, y, z: SET =>
  x ∪ empty = x,  x ∪ (y ∪ z) = (x ∪ y) ∪ z,  x ∪ y = y ∪ x,
  a ∈ empty = false,   a ∈ (singleton a),   a ∈ (x ∪ y) = (a ∈ x) ∨ (a ∈ y);
end LSETS;
```

(2-5) Requirement Specification: (Partially) Ordered Sets

```
generic
  type ITEM is private;
  "<=": ITEM × ITEM —> BOOLEAN::
  for all x, y, z: ITEM => x <= x,  x <= y ∧ y <= x → x = y,  x <= y ∧ y <= z → x <= z,  x <= y ∨ y <= x;
package ORD_SETS is
  type SET is private;
  ... as for LSETS above
  isEmpty:   SET —>                      BOOLEAN;
  min:       (s: SET:: ¬ isEmpty s) —>   ITEM;
  rest:      (s: SET:: ¬ isEmpty s) —>   SET;
axiom for all a: ITEM; x: SET; s: SET:: ¬ isEmpty s =>
  isEmpty empty,       a ∈ x → ¬ isEmpty x,          (min s) ∈ s,     a ∈ s → (min s) <= a,
  a ∈ (rest s) → a ∈ s,   a ∈ s ∧ ¬ a <= (min s) → a ∈ (rest s);
end ORD_SETS;
```

Design specifications denote abstract implementations. They are constructive, both in terms of more basic specifications and in the algorithmic sense. For a loose requirement specification, the design specification will usually restrict the set of models, eventually to one. (2-6, 2-7) show parts of a design specification for sets to multisets and true sets, resp.

(2-6) Design Specification for Ordered Multisets (partial)

```
                   min (singleton a )        = a,
 ¬ (min s <= a) →  min (s ∪ singleton a)     = a,
   min s <= a →    min (s ∪ singleton a)     = min s,
                   rest (singleton a )       = empty,
 ¬ (min s <= a) →  rest (s ∪ singleton a)    = s,
   min s <= a →    rest (s ∪ singleton a)    = rest s ∪ singleton a;      -- only one is removed
```

(2-7) Design Specification for Ordered Sets (partial)

```
 x ∪ x = x,                      min as above
   a <= min s ∧ ¬ a ∈ s →        rest (s ∪ singleton a)    = s,
   a <= min s ∧   a ∈ s →        rest (s ∪ singleton a)    = rest s,
 ¬ (a <= min s) →                rest (s ∪ singleton a)    = rest s ∪ singleton a;
```

Implementation: What remains for abstract specifications is a mapping onto some suitable specification at a lower level of the system hierarchy, i.e. a standard one or one that has already been implemented. Certain abstract types (schemata) that correspond to predefined Ada types (constructors, selectors, other auxiliary functions and their algebraic specification), for example **record**, or the usual recursive variant (or union) types (free term constructions for lists, trees etc.) are standard in PA^{nn}dA, cf. part II chapter 5. They are turned into an Ada text automatically as an alternative (standard Ada) notation for the package defining the abstract type. We assume that a standard Ada implementation using access types (pointers) and allocators is still considered to be "applicative" at this level of abstraction and that side-effects of allocation will be eliminated during the development process by explicit storage allocation if required.

Consider sets implemented as lists (see [Krieg-Brückner 88a]). In one implementation, all terms building one set using ∪ are represented by distinct lists:

x ∪ y and y ∪ x or x ∪ x and x

have distinct representations and a search is performed when ∈ is applied. In the other extreme, all such terms are represented by a list without duplicates; elements are ordered canonically and a search has to be made to eliminate elements from y that already occur in x upon ∪. Between the two extremes lie other admissible implementations, for example ordering but not eliminating multiple occurrences (or vice-versa), or one using a hash table. It should also be emphasised that not only list-like implementations are possible, of course. An implementation of an ordered set using, for example, a binary or balanced tree representation is also admissable. Similarly, any search algorithm, for example binary search, will do. Note the analogy between binary search and a binary search tree: the same idea is once represented in the algorithm and once in the data structure.

Integration of Construction and Verification: Not only is the program construction process formalised and structured into individual mechanisable steps, but the verification process is structured as well and becomes more manageable. If transformation rules are correctness-preserving, then only the applicability of each individual rule has to be verified at each step. Thus a major part of the verification, the verification of the correctness of each rule, need not be repeated. Verification then reduces to verification of the applicability of a rule, and program versions are correct by construction (with respect to the original requirement specification). This interactive, stepwise proof, aided by the system, is expected to be much easier than a corresponding proof of the final version.

As an alternative to proving the applicability conditions as they arise, the system can keep track of the verification conditions generated and accumulate them till the (successful) end of the development. This way, no proofs are necessary for "blind alleys", with the danger that the supposedly correct development sequence leading to the final version turns out to be a "blind alley" itself, if the proof fails. But even if we consider all proofs required from the developer (with assistance from the system) together, they are still much less complicated than a monolithic proof of the final version.

Transformations for verification (simplification of verification conditions to true) and an interactive Proof Editor are incorporated in the PROSPECTRA system. They use the PROSPECTRA paradigm for their implementation: inference rules are regarded as transformation rules, and proof strategies can be added by the user in analogy to transformation strategies (see chapter 4 and part III section 4.4). The Conditional Equational Completion subsystem (see [Ganzinger 87] and part III section 4.3) can also be used for verification; its major use is a kind of "program synthesis" for deriving construcive design specifications.

Development-in-the-large is supported by strictly *hierarchical decomposition of modules* following the algebraic notion of hierarchy-consistency, and is compatible with the notion of (generic) Ada packages and with-clauses. Moreover, for any given hierarchy of requirement specifications (visible package interfaces with associated specification of semantics) there is a *one-to-one correspondence* of a *requirement specification* to a particular, hidden *implementation* (package private part and body). This implementation has been formally developed by transformational refinement following the semantic notion of algebraic implementation (cf. section 2.2). The methodology and system also support the notion of revision of a requirement specification (variation that does not necessarily retain a semantic relationship) and of variant implementations for a given requirement specification, with associated version and configuration control in the library (see part III section 3.2).

1.2.4. Transformational Program Development

Each transition from one program version to another can be regarded as a transformation in an abstract sense. It has a more technical meaning here: a transformation is a development step producing a new program version by application of an individual transformation rule, a compact transformation script, or, more generally, a transformation method invoking these. Before we come to the latter two, the basic approach will be described in terms of the transformation rule concept.

A transformation rule (e.g. (2-8)) is a schema for an atomic development step that has been pre-conceived and is universally trusted (modulo some applicability conditions), analogously to a theorem in mathematics. It embodies a grain of expertise that can be transferred to a new development. Its application realises this transfer and formalises the development process.

Language Levels: We can distinguish various language levels at which the program is developed or into which versions are transformed, corresponding to phases of the development:

- formal requirement specification: loose equational or predicative specifications
- formal design specification: specification of abstract implementation
- applicative implementation: recursive functions
- imperative implementation: variables, procedures, iteration by loops

All these language levels are covered by PAnndA.

Many developments at lower levels can also be expressed at the specification level, for example "recursion removal" methods transforming into tail-recursive functions [Huet, Lang 78], [Bauer, Wössner 82], [Krieg-Brückner 87a], see section 3.4.6. As an example, consider the special case that ⊕ and n form a Monoid, where ⊕ is an arbitrary associative operation, expressed here at the specification level. The rule in (2-8) could be generalised and adapted further to apply to equations with constructors on the left instead of selectors on the right-hand sides. Assume that we want to derive a body for length (see 2-9). It is not in tail-recursive form: the addition of 1 still has to be made upon return from the recursion. By applying the transformation rule in (2-8), however, we can embed the addition into a function len that is tail-recursive, see (2-9). len can thus be transformed into a local loop, see (2-10).

In general, the applicability condition, namely that ⊕ is an associative operation with neutral element 0, has to be proved with the aid of the Proof Subsystem (cf. part III section 4.4). However, the system keeps track of user-defined axioms and conditions that are valid in a particular context in a special attribute, the so-called local theory (cf. part III section 1.2.5). This attribute is available in the Proof Subsystem; it is also available during transformation such that an automatic search for a required property can be made and no interaction from the user is required when it is successful. This would, for example, be the case when the monoid property is stated on a parameter of a function as in section 1.4.

Transformation Rules, Scripts, and Methods. Individual transformation rules are generalised to transformation *scripts*: sets of transformations rules applied together, possibly with local tactics that increase the efficiency. The long term research goal is to develop transformation *methods* that relieve the programmer from considerations about individual rules to concentrate on the goal-oriented design activity. A transformation method is thus a set of rules or scripts with a global application strategy.

(2-8) Transformation Rule: Linear Recursion with Assoc. Operation to Tail Recursion

```
f: S —> M;

axiom for all x: S =>
   B x →    f x = T x,
¬ B x →    f x = f (H x) ⊕ K x;

such that
  f does not occur in B, T, H, K
  n: M;
  axiom for all x, y, z: M =>
     (x ⊕ y) ⊕ z = x ⊕ (y ⊕ z),   x ⊕ n = x;
```

=

```
 f:  S —> M;
 g:  S —> M —> M;
axiom for all x: S; y: M =>
                f x = g x n,
    B x →   g x y = (T x) ⊕ y,
  ¬ B x →   g x y = g (H x) ((K x) ⊕ y);
```

(2-9) Transformation: Linear Recursion to Tail Recursion: length

```
 length:  LIST —>   INTEGER;

axiom for all x: LIST =>

  isEmpty x →   length x = 0,
¬ isEmpty x →   length x = length (tail x) + 1;
```

```
 length:  LIST —> INTEGER;
 len:     LIST —> INTEGER —> INTEGER;
axiom for all x: LIST ; r: INTEGER =>
                 length x = len x 0,
  isEmpty x →    len x r = 0 + r,
¬ isEmpty x →    len x r = len (tail x) (1 + r);
```

```
Matches:                     ⊕   ≈  +  - - INTEGER
  B x  ≈  isEmpty x,         T x ≈  0,
  H x  ≈  tail x,            K x ≈  1

Parameters:                  n   ≈  0
```

(2-10) Ada Program: Applicative and Imperative Body of length (with Unfold of len)

```
function LENGTH (X: LIST) return INTEGER is
begin
  if IS_EMPTY (X) then
     return 0;
  else
     return LENGTH (TAIL (X)) + 1;
  end if;
end LENGTH;
```

```
function LENGTH (X: LIST) return INTEGER is
  V: LIST:= X;  R: INTEGER := 0;
begin
  while not IS_EMPTY(V) loop
     V := TAIL(V);    R := 1+R;
  end loop;
  return R;
end LENGTH;
```

Catalogues of Transformations: Some catalogues of transformation rules have been assembled for various high-level languages. Of particular interest is the structured approach of the CIP group. The program development language CIP-L is formally defined by transformational semantics (see [Bauer et al. 85, 87]), mapping all constructs in the wide spectrum of the language to a language kernel. The PROSPECTRA catalogue is compiled in chapter 3.

Calculus of Transformational Development: In analogy to an algebraic "calculus of data", a transformation rule is an axiom or theorem in a calculus of transformation. In fact we can regard the basic transformation rules as equations in the semantic algebra of program terms, using algebraic semantics [Broy et al. 87], [Krieg-Brückner 87b-89b, 91a]; see section 1.5. Alternatively, we can prove the correctness of a basic rule against a given semantics of the (kernel) language. More complex derived transformation rules actually used in development can then either be proved as equational or inductive theorems or, if the basic rules are loose (or the given semantics is, for example with respect to the order of evaluation), then transformation rules may introduce design decisions in analogy to design specifications, and are robustly correct. They must, of course, be consistent with the basic rules. Current research is concerned with such a calculus of transformation rules and their composition to complex development terms, representation of development strategies etc, see [Krieg-Brückner 87b-89b, 91a] and section 1.6.

1.2.5. Modularisation

The concepts for modularisation shall only be touched briefly here. The concept of hierarchical decomposition using the **with**-clause (cf. [ADA 83]) corresponds to the algebraic concept of hierarchy-preservation or conservative extension (cf. chapter 2): the semantics of the specification referred to is left unchanged and definitions are only added. Note that all objects from the visible part are directly visible by a **with**-clause (the **use** of Ada is implicit).

The notion of a parameterised specification comes also in a form inherited from Ada: the generic package. The concept of a Monoid is defined in (2-2), for example, and can be instantiated with an actual type according to need (e.g. in (4-2)). After instantiation, a predicate with two parameters (a neutral element and a binary operation) is available on the actual type.

In the presence of overloading, a function(al) that is locally defined to a parameterised specification has an analogous effect to a polymorphic function(al). Analogously, the predicate isMonoid could have been defined as a polymorphic predicate, if this concept was available. The lack of implicit polymorphism in the specification language (as in most functional languages, cf. e.g. [Gordon et al. 78, Bird 88]) is often felt and should be re-considered in future versions. It is cumbersome, for example, to have to instantiate functional composition for each necessary combination of parameters.Some limitations of Ada have also been inherited: for example, generics (such as IS_MONOID) cannot be instantiated in a generic parameter. Similarly, generic parameters can only be types, functions etc., but not packages. Thus it is not possible to state a whole specification as a parameter of another, one has to repeat all components and axioms needed, see e.g. (2-11). Note that local instantiation of LISTS in LIST_OPS does not help since multiple instantiations are considered to be distinct in the application context and are therefore undesireable.

The subtype TOTAL_ORDER in (2-11) is another example of the abbreviation of a "concept" (cf. Monoid in (2-2)), defined as a restriction on the set of binary predicates. LexLe is a typical example of a precise and compact but not operational requirement specification.

(2-11) Parameterised Specification: Functions on Lists

```
generic
  type ITEM is private;
  type LIST is private;
  empty:  LIST;
  "&":      LIST × LIST —>   LIST;
  axiom for all x, y, z: LIST => x & empty = x,   empty & x = x,   (x & y) & z = x & (y & z);
  single:  ITEM —>   LIST;
package LIST_OPS is
  subtype TOTAL_ORDER is
     "<": ITEM × ITEM —> BOOLEAN::
     for all x, y, z: ITEM =>  ¬ (x < x),  x < y ∧ y < z → x < z,  x = y ∨ x < y ∨ y < x;
  LexLe:  TOTAL_ORDER —>  (LIST × LIST —>  BOOLEAN);              - - lexicographic order
  axiom for all "<": TOTAL_ORDER; l, l1, l2: LIST ; x1, x2: ITEM  =>
     LexLe("<") (l, l & l2),        x1 < x2 → LexLe("<") (l & (single x1) & l1, l & (single x2) & l2);
end LIST_OPS ;
```

1.3. An Example of Transformational Development

Let us have a look at a more comprehensive example illustrating the transformational approach, as supported by the PROSPECTRA system (another example is given in the Guided Tour of the PROSPECTRA system in part III chapter 2). The example is rather academic due to space limitations, but several design decisions yielding non-trivial solutions can be illustrated. The transformation rules used in this introduction are slightly simplified versions of those described for the system in chapter 3, where the notation is also explained.

1.3.1. From Requirement to Design Specification: Split of Postcondition

First consider a transformation rule that is representative for the class of *"program synthesis"* or *"problem solving"* transformations. The transformation is applicable to a whole class of problems that can be solved by iteration in the classical style of predicative programming promoted by [Hoare 69], [Dijkstra 76], [Gries 81] and others. If the characteristic predicate ("postcondition") specifying the result of a function f can be split into a conjunct of an invariant ***Inv*** and a terminating condition *B*, and if a starting value *E* and a recursion function *H* are provided as parameters to the transformation, then a recursive version of f can be generated, and the precise conditions for its correctness can be stated. These conditions are given as applicability conditions on the rule in (3-1); they are instantiated automatically and need to be proved before the rule is applied (with the aid of the Proof Editor), or delayed and proved during replay.

(3-1) Split of Postcondition

```
axiom for all x: S; z: R =>
   z = f(x) → Inv(x,z) ∧ B(x,z);
-----------------------------------------
let  START:= E(x),
     REC:=   H(x,y)
-----------------------------------------
such that
   |= defined ( E(x)),  defined ( H(x, y)),
   |= Inv(x,E(x)),
   |= Inv(x,y) ∧ ¬ B(x,y) → Inv(x,H(x,y)),
   |= exist i: NAT => B(x, term (x, E(x), i))
-----------------------------------------
where
   term: S × R × NAT —> BOOLEAN;
axiom for all x: S; y: R; i: NAT =>
   i = 0 →   term (x, y, i) = y,
   i > 0 →   term (x, y, i) = term (x, H(x, y), i–1);
```

≡

```
   g: S × R —> R;
axiom for all x: S; y: R =>
                  f(x) = g(x, E(x)),
   B(x, y) →      g(x, y) = y,
 ¬ B(x, y) →      g(x, y) = g(x, H(x, y));
```

(3-2) shows the application to the square root of natural numbers. It is based on the specification in (2-1). We made a particular design decision here in the order of the conjuncts for ***Inv*** and *B* and in the choice (or "invention") of *E* and *H*. By reversing the order as in (3-3), the interpretation of invariant and terminating condition is interchanged; the "loop" corresponding to the tail-recursive function then runs "down" instead of "up"; *H* can be chosen to decrement from n.

We can even choose a better starting value n **div** 2; note that one has to be careful about 1 in the presence of integer division (by 2); this error was actually discovered using the system to do the proof of the invariant for the starting value. A non-trivial termination function *H* is given in version 2: Newton's algorithm adapted to integer division. The invariant condition is harder to prove than it looks because of integer division here; it took several pages with the Proof Editor.

(3-2) Split of Postcondition: Integer Squareroot, version 1

```
sqrt:     (n: NAT) —>
          (k: NAT :: sqr k ≤ n ∧ sqr (succ k) > n);

axiom for all n,k: NAT =>
    k = sqrt n → sqr k ≤ n ∧ sqr (succ k) > n;
```

Matches:

```
Inv(n, k) ≈ sqr k ≤ n
B(n, k)   ≈ sqr (succ k) > n
```

Parameters:

```
E(n)      ≈ zero
H(n, k)   ≈ succ k
```

```
sqrt:     (n: NAT) —>
               (k: NAT :: sqr k ≤ n ∧ sqr (succ k) > n);
sqrt1:    NAT × NAT —> NAT;
axiom for all n, k: NAT =>
      sqrt n = sqrt1 (n, zero),
    sqr (succ k) > n → sqrt1 (n, k) = k,
  ¬ sqr (succ k) > n → sqrt1 (n, k) = sqrt1 (n, succ k);
```

Applicability Conditions:

```
  defined zero,    defined succ k,
  sqr zero ≤ n,
  sqr k ≤ n ∧ ¬ sqr (succ k) > n → sqr (succ k) ≤ n,
  exist i: NAT => sqr (succ (term (n, zero, i) ) > n
where
  term: NAT × NAT × NAT —> BOOLEAN;
axiom for all n: NAT; k: NAT; i: NAT =>
  i = zero → term (n, k,i) = k,
  i > zero → term (n, k,i) = term (n, succ k, i - 1)
```

(3-3) Split of Postcondition: Integer Squareroot, version 2

```
axiom for all n,k: NAT =>
    k = sqrt n → sqr (succ k) > n ∧ sqr k ≤ n;
```

Matches:

```
Inv(n, k) ≈ sqr (succ k) > n
B(n, k)   ≈ sqr k ≤ n
```

Parameters:

```
E(n)      ≈ max (div2 n, one),
H(n, k)   ≈ div2 (k + (div n k))
```

```
sqrt1: NAT × NAT —> NAT;
axiom for all n, k: NAT =>
      sqrt n = sqrt1 (n, max (div2 n, one).),
    sqr k ≤ n → sqrt1 (n, k) = k,
  ¬ sqr k ≤ n → sqrt1 (n, k) =
                     sqrt1 (n, div2 (k + (div n k)) );
```

Applicability Conditions:

```
  defined max (div2 n, one),
  defined div2 (k + (div n k)),
  sqr (succ max (div2 n, one) ) > n,
  sqr (succ k) > n ∧ ¬ sqr k ≤ n →
        sqr (succ (div2 (k + (div n k)) ) > n,
  exist i: NAT =>
      sqr (term (n, max (div2 n, one), i) ≤ n
where
  term: NAT × NAT × NAT —> BOOLEAN;
axiom for all n: NAT; k: NAT; i: NAT =>
  i = zero → term (n, k,i) = k,
  i > zero → term (n, k,i) =
                  term (n, div2 (k + (div n k)), i-1)
```

1.3.2. Optimisation by Transformation: Embedding and Finite Differencing

Embedding is a method that can very often be applied to improve efficiency: to embed into a more general function that can be (re-)used for other purposes, to avoid multiple computations ("common subexpression elimination"), to prepare for Finite Differencing ("strength reduction", see the next section), etc. We find a "costly" subexpression E and embed into a second function with an extra parameter.

The version of rule (3-4) is special for recursion with one terminating case; it can be generalised. Note also that the property $y = E(x)$ is maintained as an invariant in this version. Most of the applicability conditions can be derived automatically from available static semantic attributes. It is applied to the example in (3-5).

The choice of a "costly" subexpression $\mathbb{E}$ is given as a parameter to the transformation, thus it is an explicit design-decision; an automatic choice would require some notion of relative efficiency or complexity analysis.

(3-4) Embedding

f: S ---> R; **axiom for all** x: S => $\mathbb{B}$(x, $\mathbb{E}$(x)) → f(x) = $\mathbb{H}$1(x, $\mathbb{E}$(x)), ¬ $\mathbb{B}$(x, $\mathbb{E}$(x)) → f(x) = $\mathbb{H}$2(x, $\mathbb{E}$(x), f($\mathbb{L}$(x, $\mathbb{E}$(x)))); **let** CE: T :: CE = $\mathbb{E}$(x) **where** [see part I section 3.4.4.2]	=	f: S —> R; g: S × T —> R; **axiom for all** x: S; y: T :: y = $\mathbb{E}$(x) => f(x) = g(x, $\mathbb{E}$(x)), $\mathbb{B}$(x, y) → g(x, y) = $\mathbb{H}$1(x, y), ¬ $\mathbb{B}$(x, y) → g(x, y) = $\mathbb{H}$2(x, y, g($\mathbb{L}$(x, y), $\mathbb{E}$($\mathbb{L}$(x, y)));

(3-5) Embedding: Integer Squareroot

sqrt1: NAT × NAT —> NAT;
axiom for all n, k: NAT =>
sqr (succ k) > n → sqrt1 (n, k) = k,
¬ sqr (succ k) > n → sqrt1 (n, k) = sqrt1 (n, succ k);

Matches:

$\mathbb{E}$(n, k)	≈ sqr (succ k)
$\mathbb{B}$(n, k, $\mathbb{E}$(n, k))	≈ $\mathbb{E}$(n, k) > n,
$\mathbb{H}$1(n, k, $\mathbb{E}$(n, k))	≈ k,
$\mathbb{H}$2(n, k, $\mathbb{E}$(n, k), f($\mathbb{L}$(n,k)))	≈ f($\mathbb{L}$(n, k)),
$\mathbb{L}$(n, k))	≈ (n, succ k),
$\mathbb{E}$($\mathbb{L}$(n, k)) ≈ $\mathbb{E}$(n, k+1)	≈ sqr (succ (succ k))

sqrt1: NAT × NAT —> NAT;
sqrt2: NAT × NAT × NAT —> NAT;
axiom for all n, k: NAT;
sq: NAT:: sq = sqr (succ k) =>
sqrt1 (n, k) = sqrt2 (n, k, sqr (succ k)),
sq > n → sqrt2 (n, k, sq) = k,
¬ sq > n → sqrt2 (n, k, sq) = sqrt2(n, succ k, sqr (succ (succ k)));

Finite Differencing

Finite Differencing (cf. (3-6), after previous embedding) is representative for the class of *optimising* transformations. Application areas are: generalization of strength reduction, Early's "iterator inversion", algorithms on sets or graphs such as Schorr-Waite's garbage collection algorithm, Habermann's banker's algorithm, knapsack problems, or optimised completion techniques (see [Sharir 82], [Paige, Koenig 82]). The idea is to avoid that the "costly" subexpression of the embedding is computed over and over again in each recursion; instead, only the increment is computed each time. This increment is supposedly an expression that is less "costly" to compute, for example using addition instead of multiplication; this corresponds to "strength reduction" in compiler optimisations.

(3-6) Finite Differencing

$\mathbb{E}$(x) ⊕ Δ$\mathbb{E}$ (x, y) **such that** ⊨ y = $\mathbb{E}$(x)	=	y ⊕ Δ$\mathbb{E}$ (x, y)

After embedding, we need to find an arbitrary operation ⊕ (this could be any binary numeric operation, e.g. integer addition or set union, for example) and an increment Δ$\mathbb{E}$ such that

$\mathbb{E}$($\mathbb{L}$(x, y)) = $\mathbb{E}$(x) ⊕ Δ$\mathbb{E}$ (x, y)

This can be done interactively by using other transformations to bring the expression into this form ("conditioning" for the subsequent transformation), e.g. by applying equations available in the context as rewrite rules, cf. (3-7). We can then apply the finite differencing transformation rule of (3-6), see (3-8);

the applicability condition holds since the property $y = \mathbb{E}(x)$ [sq = sqr (succ k)] was maintained as an invariant.

Goal-Oriented Transformation

(3-7) Goal-Oriented Rewriting with Equation

sqr (succ (succ k))		*sqr (succ k) + dble (succ k) + one*

Parameter: - sqr (succ a) = sqr a + dble a + one

(3-8) Finite Differencing: Integer Squareroot

```
sqrt2:   NAT × NAT × NAT —> NAT;
axiom for all n, k: NAT; sq: NAT:: sq=sqr(succ k) =>
  sq > n → sqrt2 (n, k, sq) = k,
¬ sq > n → sqrt2 (n, k, sq) = sqrt2 (n, succ k,
                  sqr (succ k) + dble (succ k) + one));
```

```
sqrt2:   NAT × NAT × NAT —> NAT;
axiom for all n,k: NAT; sq: NAT:: sq=sqr(succ k)=>
  sq > n → sqrt2 (n, k, sq) = k,
¬ sq > n → sqrt2 (n, k, sq) = sqrt2 (n, succ k,
                  sq + (dble (succ k) + one));
```

Matches: ⊕ ≈ + --*on NAT*
𝔼(x) ⊕ Δ𝔼 (x, y) ≈
sqr (succ k) + 2 (succ k) + one)*

Simplification

After this transformation, $\Delta\mathbb{E}(x, y)$ should be simplified and is then expected to be "cheaper" than the original expression $\mathbb{E}(\mathbb{L}(x, y))$. The simplification (3-9) uses a set of rewrite rules provided as a parameter. [The implemented transformation, cf. section 3.4.2, combines the effect of Goal-Oriented Rewriting, Finite Differencing, and Simplification.]

(3-9) Simplification using Equations as Rewrite Rules

dble (succ k) + one		*succ (succ (succ (k + k)))*

Parameter: dble a = a + a,
(succ a) + (succ b) = succ (succ (a + b)),
a + one = succ a

Towards Automated Development Methods: Finite Differencing with Inverse Operation

As a second strategy, finite differencing can be done automatically by simplifying $\Delta\mathbb{E}(x) = \mathbb{E}(\mathbb{L}(x, y)) \ominus \mathbb{E}(x)$, if an inverse operation $\ominus$ exists such that $\mathbb{E}(x) \oplus (\mathbb{E}(\mathbb{L}(x, y)) \ominus \mathbb{E}(x)) = \mathbb{E}(\mathbb{L}(x, y))$ holds, see (3-10). Note that $\oplus$ and $\ominus$ may be abitrary operations of the type of $\mathbb{E}$, for example union and set difference. The equation relating the operations is conditional on some predicate $\mathbb{P}$; $\ominus$ (or $\oplus$) is often only partially defined, such as – on naturals numbers, cf. (3-11). For sets, *b* must be contained in *a*, for lists with concatenation and a (properly defined) list difference, *isHeadOf b a* must hold. This predicate must be proved for the instantiated expressions. Applied to the example in (3-11), the result is, of course, the same as in (3-8, 9) above.

(3-10) Finite Differencing with Inverse Operation

𝔼(𝕃(x, y))	=	*y ⊕ (𝔼(𝕃(x, y)) ⊖ 𝔼(x))*
let *y:T,* *INV:= ℙ (a, b) → a ⊕ (b ⊖ a) = b*		
such that ⊨ *ℙ (𝔼(𝕃(x, y), 𝔼(x)), y = 𝔼(x), INV*		

(3-11) Finite Differencing with Inverse Operation: Integer Squareroot

```
sqrt2:   NAT × NAT × NAT —> NAT;
axiom for all n, k: NAT; sq: NAT:: sq=sqr(succ k) =>
  sq > n →  sqrt2 (n, k, sq) = k,
¬ sq > n →  sqrt2 (n, k, sq) = sqrt2 (n, succ k,
                              sqr (succ (succ k)) );
```

Matches: ⊕ ≈ + Θ ≈ − *-- on NAT*

E(L(n, k)) ≈ sqr (succ (succ k))

E(L(n, k)) Θ E(n, k)

≈ sqr (succ (succ k)) – sqr (succ k)

```
sqrt2:   NAT × NAT × NAT —> NAT;
axiom for all n,k: NAT; sq: NAT:: sq=sqr(succ k)=>
  sq > n →  sqrt2(n, k, sq) = k,
¬ sq > n →  sqrt2(n, k, sq) = sqrt2(n, succ k,
            sq + (sqr (succ (succ k)) – sqr (succ k) ) );
```

Parameters:

y ≈ sq,

INV ≈ x ≤ y → x + (y – x) = y,

Applicability Conditions:

x ≤ y → x + (y – x) = y,

sqr (succ k) ≤ sqr (succ (succ k))

(3-12) Finite Differencing with Inverse Operation: Binary Operations

```
sqrt2:   NAT × NAT × NAT —> NAT;
axiom for all n, k: NAT; sq: NAT:: sq=sqr(succ k) =>
  sq > n →  sqrt2 (n, k, sq) = k,
¬ sq > n →  sqrt2 (n, k, sq) = sqrt2 (n, succ k,
                              sqr (succ (succ k)) );
```

Matches: ⊕ ≈ + Θ ≈ − *-- on NAT*

E(L(n, k)) ≈ sqr (succ (succ k))

E(L(n, k)) Θ E(n, k)

≈ sqr (succ (succ k)) – sqr (succ k)

≈ (sqr (succ k) + (dble (succ k) + one)) – sqr (succ k)

≈ dble (succ k) + one

≈ dbl1 (succ k)

```
sqrt2:   NAT × NAT × NAT —> NAT;
axiom for all n,k: NAT; sq: NAT:: sq=sqr(succ k)=>
  sq > n →  sqrt2(n, k, sq) = k,
¬ sq > n →  sqrt2(n, k, sq) = sqrt2(n, succ k,
                               sq + dbl1 (succ k) );
```

Parameters:

y ≈ sq,

INV ≈ x ≤ y → x + (y – x) = y,

EQS ≈ sqr (succ a) = sqr a + dble a + one,

(a + b) – a = b,

dble (succ k) + one = dbl1 a

Applicability Conditions:

x ≤ y → x + (y – x) = y,

sqr (succ k) ≤ sqr (succ (succ k))

(3-13) Embedding and Finite Differencing: Integer Squareroot

```
sqrt2:   NAT × NAT × NAT —> NAT;

axiom for all n, k: NAT; sq: NAT:: sq=sqr(succ k) =>
  sq > n →  sqrt2 (n, k, sq) = k,
¬ sq > n →  sqrt2 (n, k, sq) = sqrt2 (n, succ k,
                    sq + succ (succ (succ (k + k))) );
```

Matches: ⊕ ≈ + Θ ≈ − *-- on NAT*

E(n, k)) ≈ succ (succ (succ (k + k)))

y ⊕ E(L(n, k)) Θ E(n, k)

≈ su + succ (succ (succ ((succ k)+ (succ k))))

  – succ (succ (succ (k + k)))

≈ su + succ (succ (succ (succ (succ (k + k)))))

  – succ (succ (succ (k + k)))

≈ su + succ (succ zero)

≈ succ (succ su)

```
sqrt2:   NAT × NAT × NAT —> NAT;
sqrt3:   NAT × NAT × NAT × NAT —> NAT;
axiom for all n,k: NAT; sq: NAT:: sq = sqr (succ k);
        su: NAT :: su = succ (succ (succ (k + k))) =>
     sqrt2 (n, k, sq) = sqrt3 (n, k, sq,
                          succ (succ (succ (k + k))) ),
  sq > n →  sqrt3(n, k, sq, su) = k,
¬ sq > n →  sqrt3(n, k, sq, su) =
            sqrt3(n, succ k, sq + su, succ (succ su) );
```

Parameters:

y ≈ sq,

INV ≈ x ≥ y → y + (x - y) = x,

EQS ≈ (succ x) + (succ y) = succ (succ (x + y)),

succ (succ x) – x = succ (succ zero)

x + succ (succ zero) = succ (succ x)

Applicability Conditions:

x ≥ y → y + (x - y) = x,

succ (succ (succ ((succ k)+ (succ k)))) ≥

  succ (succ (succ (k + k)))

As an example of a composition of two transformations into one (cf. also section 1.5), the implemented transformation combines finite differencing with automatic simplification (similarly, embedding and finite differencing could be combined into one compact transformation, a development method). For this purpose, a set of (conditional) equations is provided as an additional parameter; it is the user's risk, that this set of rewrite rules is terminating. The result is, of course, the same as above (cf. sections 3.4.5.1, 3.4.5.3).

Using the combined transformation, we can provide equations for natural numbers based on zero and succ or on the binary constructors zero and dble, dble1 (i.e. *2, *2+1), achieving different results in (3-9), (3-11), and (3-12).

Applying this method of Finite Differencing, combined with Embedding, again (3-13), we achieve a progressively longer list of parameters that can be evaluated in parallel, with less and less complex operations.

Converting Depth to Breadth of Computation

Another possibility is an unfold of the recursive function on itself (expanding or "unrolling" the recursion, see 3-14)): the number of recursions is halved, but, at the end, some computations may have been superfluous. Such a transformation could be applied several times, bounded by pragmatic considerations; this would correspond to a cache in hardware, trading chip space for speed. One would also apply Finite Differencing to the thus newly created "costly" expressions, e.g. sq+su or even comparisons such as sq+su > n, thereby converting depth of recursion into cascades of conditionals, program length and complexity of computation within one recursion, and complexity of computation into breadth of parallel evaluation in the parameters (supposedly corresponding to one parallel "cycle" in hardware). Combining an efficient algorithm (by some complexity measure), such as version 2 in (3-3), and an efficient implementation of basic types, we could thus derive algorithms to be used for (semi-automatic) VLSI implementation. "Silicon compilers" only deliver a result that is (hopefully) as correct as their input; therefore the derivation of correct and efficient algorithms at the software level should be of prime importance. Note that the target of the development (i.e. the complexity or "machine" model of the underlying operational semantics and the basic types), such as binary arithmetic and parallel evaluation (of parameter tuples) significantly determine the design decisions.

Partial Evaluation

A collapse of the chain of embeddings can be achieved by *partial evaluation*, a combination of unfold and simplification, see (3-15).

C Program

Finally, an Ada or C program (see (3-16)) can be generated; the C program still contains the basic operations of the data type (cf. (2-1)) such as succ or (succ zero) instead of +1 or 1. A representation of NAT by the predefined integer type would eventually make this replacement by unfolding the basic operations by their implementation. This representation is still a crucial step since it implies a transition from unbounded natural numbers to bounded integers; the operations all become partial.

(3-14) Unfold of Recursive Call: Integer Squareroot

```
    sqrt3:     NAT × NAT × NAT × NAT —> NAT;
axiom for all n,k: NAT; sq: NAT:: sq = sqr (succ k);
            su: NAT :: su = succ (succ (succ (k + k))) =>
       sqrt2(n, k, sq) = sqrt3(n, k, sq,
                                   succ (succ (succ (k + k))) ),
  sq > n →   sqrt3(n, k, sq, su) = k,
¬ sq > n →   sqrt3(n, k, sq, su) =
             sqrt3(n, succ k, sq + su, succ (succ su) );
```

Parameter:

```
  sq > n →   sqrt3(n, k, sq, su) = k,
¬ sq > n →   sqrt3(n, k, sq, su) =
             sqrt3(n, succ k, sq + su, succ (succ su) )
```

```
    sqrt3:     NAT × NAT × NAT × NAT —> NAT;
axiom for all n,k: NAT; sq: NAT:: sq = sqr (succ k);
            su: NAT :: su = succ (succ (succ (k + k))) =>
  sq > n →sqrt3(n, k, sq, su) = k,
¬ sq > n →( sq+su > n → sqrt3(n, k, sq, su) = succ k,
            ¬ sq+su > n → sqrt3(n, k, sq, su) =
                sqrt3 (n, succ (succ k),
                       (sq+su)+(succ (succ su)),
                       succ (succ (succ (succ su))))  );
```

(3-15) Partial Evaluation: Integer Squareroot

```
    sqrt:      (n: NAT) —>
               (k: NAT :: sqr k ≤ n ∧ sqr (succ k) > n);
    sqrt1:     NAT × NAT —> NAT;
    sqrt2:     NAT × NAT × NAT —> NAT;
    sqrt3:     NAT × NAT × NAT × NAT —> NAT;
axiom for all n,k: NAT; sq: NAT:: sq = sqr (succ k);
            su: NAT :: su = succ (succ (succ (k + k))) =>
       sqrt n = sqrt1 (n, zero),
       sqrt1 (n, k) = sqrt2 (n, k, sqr (succ k) ),
       sqrt2 (n, k, sq) = sqrt3 (n, k, sq,
                                   succ (succ (succ (k + k))) ),
  sq > n →   sqrt3(n, k, sq, su) = k,
¬ sq > n →   sqrt3(n, k, sq, su) =
             sqrt3(n, succ k, sq + su, succ (succ su) );
```

```
    sqrt:      (n: NAT) —>
               (k: NAT :: sqr k ≤ n ∧ sqr (succ k) > n);


    sqrt3:     NAT × NAT × NAT × NAT —> NAT;
axiom for all n,k: NAT; sq: NAT:: sq = sqr (succ k);
            su: NAT :: su = succ (succ (succ (k + k))) =>


       sqrt n = sqrt3 (n, zero, succ zero,
                               succ (succ (succ zero))) ),
  sq > n →   sqrt3(n, k, sq, su) = k,
¬ sq > n →   sqrt3(n, k, sq, su) =
             sqrt3(n, succ k, sq + su, succ (succ su) );
```

(3-16) C Program: Integer Squareroot

```
    sqrt:      (n: NAT) —>
               (k: NAT :: sqr k ≤ n ∧ sqr (succ k) > n);
    sqrt3:     NAT × NAT × NAT × NAT —> NAT;
axiom for all n,k: NAT; sq: NAT:: sq = sqr (succ k);
            su: NAT :: su = succ (succ (succ (k + k))) =>
       sqrt n = sqrt3 (n, zero, succ zero,
                               succ (succ (succ zero))) ),
  sq > n →   sqrt3(n, k, sq, su) = k,
¬ sq > n →   sqrt3(n, k, sq, su) =
             sqrt3(n, succ k, sq + su, succ (succ su) );
```

```
 NAT sqrt (n)
   NAT n;
{ return sqrt3 (n, zero, succ (zero),
                       succ (succ (succ (zero))); }
 NAT sqrt3 (n, k, sq, su)
   NAT n; NAT k; NAT sq; NAT su;
{ if (sq > n)    return k;
  if (!(sq > n)) return sqrt3 (n, succ (k), sq + su,
                                      succ (succ (su)) );}
```

1.4. Functionals

This section describes the combined advantages of functional programming and algebraic specification: a considerably higher degree of abstraction, avoiding much repetitive development effort by the use of homomorphic extension functionals as "program generators". The importance of the *combination* of algebraic specification with higher order functions should be stressed. The ability to specify *partial* higher-order functions (i.e. with conditions on functional parameters) has been an important contribution of PROSPECTRA to the theory of algebraic specifications. The algebraic properties of functionals allow a high level of reasoning *about* functional programs, and permit general and powerful optimisations, supported by the PROSPECTRA approach. The combined advantages of algebraic specification and higher order functions apply to program and meta-program development in the same way, cf. section 1.5.

1.4.1. Methodological Advantages

Higher order functions (with functions as parameters and/or results, cf. e.g. [Bird, Wadler 88], [Bird 89], [Möller 87a]), allow a substantial reduction of re-development effort, in the early specifications and all subsequent developments. This aspect of functional abstraction is analogous to parameterised data type specifications such as generics in Ada. (4-1) shows some examples. Note that the type parameters are still stated as generic parameters (corresponding to parameterised specifications). The need to instantiate these parameters explicitly (cf. **new** IS_MONOID (LIST) in (2-3)) is sometimes tedious; polymorphic functions would be a help here.

(4-1) Generic Functionals

```
generic
   type S is private;
   type T is private;
package UP is
   Up:          (T×T—>T)—> (S—>T)—> (S—>T)—> S—> T;
axiom for all "⊕" T×T—>T; f, g: S—>T; x: S =>
   Up "⊕" f g x = (f x) ⊕ (g x);
end UP;
```

```
generic
   type S is private;
   type T is private;
package PAIR is
   PairHom:    (T×T—>T)—> (S—>T)—> S×S —> T;
axiom for all "⊕" T×T—>T; f, g: S—>T; x, y: S =>
   PairHom "⊕" f (x, y) = (f x) ⊕ (f y);
end PAIR;
```

It is an interesting observation that many definitions of functionals have a restricted form: the functional argument is unchanged in recursive calls. A functional together with its (fixed) function parameters can then always be explicitly expanded by transformation. Thus the major advantage of functionals appears, at first glance, to be "merely" one of abbreviation. In contrast to generics, tedious explicit instantiation is avoided for functional parameters, in particular for partial parameterisation ("Curry'ing"). However, working with functionals quickly leads to a new style of programming (i.e. specification and development) at a considerably higher degree of abstraction. As we shall see below, much repetitive development can be reduced to the application of homomorphic extension functionals; these can be considered as kinds of "program generators".

It is this aspect, that many functions should have the property of being homomorphisms, that goes beyond the correctness properties expressible in standard functional programming (in Miranda, for example). There, one tends to think only in terms of free term algebras (lists, trees etc.). Here, we have the whole power of algebraic specification available to state, for example, that the properties of a monoid hold and are preserved by a (homomorphic) function, indeed by a functional for a whole class of applications. Development (optimising transformations etc.) need be made only once for the functional. In fact, the recursion schema of homomorphic extension (see [von Henke 76], [Böhm, Berarducci 85]) provides a program development strategy ("divide and conquer", cf. [Smith 85]) and an induction schema for proofs.

In meta-programming, these homomorphic extension functionals are important for the concise definition of program development tactics (see section 1.5.4). The algebraic properties of functionals allow a high level of reasoning *about* functional programs (postulated in [Bird, Wadler 88], [Bird 89]) that is supported by the PROSPECTRA system.

1.4.2. Homomorphisms and Homomorphic Extension Functionals

The functionals Map, Filter, Reduce of [Bird, Wadler 88], [Bird 89] and others are special cases of a more general homomorphic extension functional, see (4-2). Hom corresponds to the Monoid view of list construction (cf. section 1.2.3 above) and thus to a program development strategy by (binary) partitioning. An analogous homomorphic extension functional corresponds to the linear view and thus to a linear "divide and conquer" strategy. Map can be defined as an automorphism (i. e. a homomorphism to the same structure); in fact it can be defined more generally to map between two lists of different component types.

Note the use of nested generics in (4-2), corresponding to a parameterised specification that can first be (partially) parameterised by the source (this could be a list but also, say, a stack or queue having the same (sub-) specification), and then sometime later by different target monoids as actual parameters for M. Again, at this stage only the target type is given, and at yet a later stage, a neutral element and a binary operation are supplied along with the other parameters of Hom.

As an example for the instantiation of a homomorphic extension functional, existential and universal quantification of a predicate over a list can be defined by homomorphic extension of the predicate over lists, using the algebraic properties of Booleans. Map and Filter are defined as automorphisms from LIST to LIST; this is a simplification of the general case, where lists of x's are mapped to lists of y's.

Note that Hom requires that the target algebraic structure has the properties of a monoid (the function composition operator • and the identity function id are assumed to be universally defined in this chapter). In this case we can transform Hom using the monoid properties of lists and employ the recursion removal transformation of (2-8) that is only applicable, if ⊕ and n form a monoid (cf. [Bauer 82], [Bird, Wadler 88], [Bird 89], [Krieg-Brückner 89, a, 90]). With the aid of an auxiliary Function H2, a linear, tail-recursive version is obtained. In functional programming, such a global optimisation is not possible since we could not be sure that the binary operation is associative in general; there is no way to state such a requirement in a standard functional programming language. In conventional programming or algebraic specification without functionals we would have to separately prove the property and optimise for each case (each instance of the functional).

(4-2) Homomorphic Extension Functionals over Lists

```
with IS_MONOID;
generic
   type ITEM is private;
   type LIST is private;
   empty:    LIST;
   "&":      LIST × LIST —>  LIST;
   axiom for all x, y, z: LIST => x & empty = x,   empty & x = x,   (x & y) & z = x & (y & z);
   single:   ITEM —>  LIST;
   isEmpty: LIST —>  BOOLEAN;
   head:     (x: LIST :: ¬ isEmpty x) —> ITEM;
   tail:     (x: LIST :: ¬ isEmpty x) —> LIST;
   axiom for all e: ITEM; l: LIST =>
      isEmpty empty = true,                head ((single e) & l) = e,
      isEmpty ((single e) & l) = false,     tail ((single e) & l) = l;
package LIST_HOMS is
   generic
      type M is private;
   package HOM_TO is
      package M_IS_MONOID is new IS_MONOID (M);
      Hom:    (n: M) —> ("⊕": M × M —> M:: isMonoid n "⊕") —> (ITEM —> M) —> LIST —> M;
      axiom for all n: M; "⊕": M × M —> M:: isMonoid n "⊕"; h: ITEM —> M; e: ITEM; x, y: LIST; r: M =>
         Hom n "⊕" h empty          = n,
         Hom n "⊕" h (x & y)        = (Hom n "⊕" h x) ⊕ (Hom n "⊕" h y),
         Hom n "⊕" h (single e)     = h e;
      H2:     (n: M) —> ("⊕": M × M —> M:: isMonoid n "⊕") —> (ITEM —> M) —> M —> LIST —> M;
      axiom for all n: M; "⊕": M × M —> M:: isMonoid n "⊕"; h: ITEM —> M; e: ITEM; x, y: LIST; r: M =>
         Hom n "⊕" h z              = H2 n "⊕" h n z,  - - embedding for tail-recursive definition
         H2  n "⊕" h r empty        = r,
         H2  n "⊕" h r (single e & y) = H2 n "⊕" h (r ⊕ (h e)) y;
   end HOM_TO;
   package AUTO is new HOM_TO (LIST);
   Map:     (ITEM —> ITEM) —>       LIST —>  LIST;
   Filter:  (ITEM —> BOOLEAN) —> LIST —>  LIST;
   Filt:    (ITEM —> BOOLEAN) —> ITEM —>  LIST;
axiom for all f: ITEM —> ITEM; p: ITEM —> BOOLEAN; x: ITEM =>
   Map f    = Hom empty "&" (single • f),
   Filter p = Hom empty "&" (Filt p),    p x → Filt p x = single x,    ¬ p x → Filt p x = empty;
   package toITEMS is new HOM_TO (ITEM);
   Reduce:   (n: ITEM) —> ("⊕": ITEM × ITEM —> ITEM:: isMonoid n "⊕") —> LIST —> ITEM;
axiom for all n: ITEM; "⊕": ITEM × ITEM —> ITEM:: isMonoid n "⊕" =>
   Reduce n "⊕" = Hom n "⊕" id;
   package toBOOL is new HOM_TO (BOOLEAN);
   Exist, ForAll:   (ITEM —> BOOLEAN) —> LIST —>   BOOLEAN;
axiom for all x: ITEM; a, b: LIST =>
   Exist = Hom false "or",            ForAll = Hom true "and";
end LIST_HOMS;
```

1.5. Formalisation of Program Transformation

The Meta-Development Methodology

The methodology for program development based on the concept of algebraic specification of data types, and program transformation can be applied to the development of transformation algorithms, i.e. for program-manipulating programs (or *meta*-programs). Starting from small elementary transformation rules, we can apply the usual equational and inductive reasoning to derive complex rules. All the methodology and transformation technology for program development is carried over to meta-program development.

In Program Development by Transformation [Bauer, Wössner 82], [Bauer et al. 85-89], [Partsch, Steinbrüggen 83], an elementary development step is a *program transformation*: the application of a transformation rule that is generally applicable; a particular development is then a sequence of rule applications. The question is how to best formalise rules and application (or inference) strategies, in general how to develop program transformation programs or *meta*-programs.

The approach taken in PROSPECTRA is to regard transformation rules as equations in an algebra of programs, to derive basic transformation operations from these rules, to allow composition and functional abstraction, and to regard transformation scripts as (compositions of) such transformation operations. Using all the results from program development based on algebraic specifications and functionals we can then reason about the development of meta-programs, i.e. transformation programs or development scripts, in the same way as about programs: we can define requirement specifications (development goals) and implement them by various design strategies; in short, we can develop *correct*, efficient, complex transformation operations from elementary rules stated as algebraic equations. Homomorphic extension functionals are important for the concise definition of program development tactics.

1.5.1. The Syntactic Algebra of Programs

We can define the Abstract Syntax of a programming language such as PAnndA by an algebraically specified Abstract Data Type: trees in the Abstract Syntax correspond to terms in this algebra of (PAnndA) programs, non-terminals to sorts, tree constructor operations to constructor operations, etc., see (5-1). Most constructor operations are free, except for & corresponding to list concatenation.

(5-1) Abstract Syntax for Expressions and Expression Lists

```
with NAMES, LISTS;
package EXPS is
   type EXP is private;
   package EXP_LISTS is new LISTS(EXP);   subtype EXP_LIST is EXP_LISTS.LIST;
   mkName:    NAME —>       EXP;           -- concrete phrase: ⌈ n ⌋
   mkTuple:   EXP_LIST —> EXP;             -- concrete phrase: ⌈ el ⌋  if empty or single, otherwise: ⌈ ( el ) ⌋
   mkCall:    EXP × EXP —> EXP;            -- concrete phrase: ⌈ e1 e2 ⌋
   ... a definition of selectors and their axioms is omitted for brevity; for homomorphisms etc. see below
end EXPS;
```

(5-2) Concrete Syntax Phrase and Abstract Syntax Term

```
axiom for all x, y: EXP =>
   ⌈ not x and not y ⌋ =
   mkCall (mkName boolAnd) (mkTuple   (   (single (mkCall (mkName boolNot) x)) &
                                          (single (mkCall (mkName boolNot) y))    )  );
```

Although we are interested in the operations of the *abstract* syntactic algebra of programs, it is often more convenient to use a notation for *phrases* (program fragments with schema variables) of the *concrete syntax* corresponding to appropriate terms (with variables) in the algebra. Phrases provide a concise notation for large terms, cf. (5-2) for a small example (boolAnd, boolNot stand for further subterms denoting special names). The brackets ⌈ ⌋ are used whenever a (nested) phrase of the concrete syntax is introduced. In this paper, we are not concerned with notational issues at the concrete syntax level nor with the (non-trivial) translation of phrases from concrete to abstract syntax. Specifications of abstract types such as in (5-1), including selectors and other auxiliary operations, are automatically constructed from a given abstract syntax specification in the PROSPECTRA system.

1.5.2. Transformation Rules: Equations in the Semantic Algebra

In the approach of the algebraic definition of the semantics of a programming language (cf. [Broy et al. 87]), an evaluation function or interpretation function from syntactic to semantic domains is axiomatised. The equational axioms of such functions induce equivalence classes on (otherwise free) constructor terms. In other words, we can prove that two (syntactic) terms are *semantically equivalent,* in a context-free way or possibly subject to some syntactic or semantic pre-conditions. Such a proof can of course also be made with respect to some other style of semantic definition for the language. Thus we obtain a *semantic algebra* of programs in which transformation rules are equations as a quotient algebra of the *abstract syntactic algebra* in which only equations for & exist.

(5-3) shows examples of transformation rules for Boolean expressions, i.e. of type EXP, analogous to the algebraic properties of Booleans, i.e. of type BOOLEAN. These examples are, of course, very simple-minded; in general, one has large syntactic phrases and complex context conditions as applicability conditions.

(5-3) Transformation Rules (in the Semantic Algebra): Boolean expressions

```
axiom for all x, y: EXP =>
  ⌈not x and not y⌋ = ⌈not (x or y)⌋,        ⌈not x or not y⌋ = ⌈not (x and y)⌋;
```

The major kind of transformation rules we are interested in is the *bi-directional transformation rule*, a pair of semantically equivalent terms: an *equation* in the semantic algebra of programs that is provable by deductive or inductive reasoning against the semantics. The rules in this chapter are of this kind. All considerations about interpreting equations as rewrite rules apply (confluence, termination, etc.).

A *uni-directional* transformation rule corresponds to a relation between semantic models such that each model in the range is a robustly correct implementation of some model in the domain; thus it corresponds to a semantic inclusion relation in a model-oriented sense. Again this notion is taken from the theory of algebraic specification (cf. [Broy, Wirsing 82] for the converse relation as the approximation relation ≤ on (transformation) functions in [Möller 87a]). It formalises the notion of correctness with respect to some implementation decision that narrows implementation flexibility or chooses a particular implementation. These rules are of course not invertible (a decision cannot be reversed) and, interpreted as rewrite rules, are not confluent in general. In this paper, we restrict our attention to bi-directional rules although most considerations generalise.

We can apply all the power of the algebraic framework to transformation rules specified in this way, for example the deduction of new rules using equational or inductive reasoning, even completion techniques (cf. [Ganzinger 87], part III section 4.3).

1.5.3. Basic Transformations: Operations in the Syntactic Algebra

From each transformation rule or set of related rules, i.e. equations in the semantic algebra, an elementary transformation operation can be constructed in a straightforward way as a partial function in the *abstract syntactic algebra*, see (5-4): it maps to a normal form in the quotient algebra corresponding to the equations. Each equation is considered as a rewrite rule from left to right (or from right to left), and, if the system of rewrite rules is confluent, yields a corresponding normal form. The function corresponds to an identity in the semantic algebra and achieves a kind of normalisation in the syntactic algebra.

(5-4) shows an example of a basic transformation function derived from a single transformation rule: deMorgan applies deMorgan's laws in expressions. Similarly, a basic applicability predicate (5-5) can be derived from the transformation rule (possibly including contextual or semantic applicability conditions in addition to the syntactic ones). Note that the **others** can be expanded using simple syntactic predicates (to be defined jointly with the Abstract Syntax). Other basic transformation functions and predicates are defined analogously. More simplification rules could of course be used on Booleans, cf. [Krieg-Brückner 89, a, 90].

(5-4) Basic Transformation Function: *deMorgan*

```
 deMorgan:     (e: EXP:: is_deMorgan e) —> EXP;
axiom for all x, y: EXP =>
 deMorgan ⌈ not x and not y ⌋ = ⌈ not (x or y) ⌋,   deMorgan ⌈ not x or not y ⌋ = ⌈ not (x and y) ⌋;
```

(5-5) Basic Applicability Predicate: *is_deMorgan*

```
 is_deMorgan:  EXP —> BOOLEAN;
axiom for all x, y: EXP =>
 (is_deMorgan ⌈ not x and not y ⌋ = true,          is_deMorgan ⌈ not x or not y ⌋ = true,
 others → is_deMorgan x = false);
```

1.5.4. Transformation Functionals: Homomorphic Extensions and Tactics

In analogy to tacticals in [Gordon et al. 78], we might call some transformation functionals *transformals* since they embody application tactics or strategies for applying elementary transformations over a larger context. Consider for example (5-6): if some transformation function *f* and its applicability condition *p* are given, then *Try* provides a totalisation (extension to identity) if *p* does not hold.

(5-6) Functional: *Try*

```
 Try:          (p: EXP —> BOOLEAN) —>  (f: (x: EXP:: p x) —> EXP) —>  EXP —>  EXP;
axiom for all    p: EXP —> BOOLEAN;  f: (x: EXP:: p x) —> EXP;  x: EXP =>
 p x →  Try p f x = f x      ¬ p x →  Try p f x = x,
---
 tdeMorgan:    EXP —>  EXP;
axiom tdeMorgan = Try is_deMorgan deMorgan;
```

More important for application tactics are *homomorphic extension* functionals, in this case the structural extension of the effect of a (local) transformation or predicate over larger terms. This is an extension of the basic case for lists in section 1.4.2. In (5-7), Hom extends a function on names over expressions. This version is rather simple-minded (but general, as we shall see below in (5-10)), it does not apply the homomorphism recursively to the constituent parts of an expression automatically; one has to supply this recursion ("from the outside") in the call. For automorphisms, (5-8) shows such a version.

(5-7) Basic Homomorphic Extension for Expressions and Expression Lists

```
generic
  type E is private;
package EXP_HOM is
  Hom:        (NAME —> E) —>  (EXP_LIST —> E) —>  (EXP × EXP —> E) —>  EXP —>  E;
  axiom for all fName: NAME —> E; fTuple: EXP_LIST —> E; fCall: EXP × EXP —> E;
                  n: NAME; e1, e2: EXP; el: EXP_LIST =>
    Hom fName fTuple fCall (mkName n)       =  fName n,
    Hom fName fTuple fCall (mkTuple el)     =  fTuple el,
    Hom fName fTuple fCall (mkCall (e1, e2)) =  fCall (e1, e2);
  end EXP_HOM;
```

(5-8) Derived Homomorphic Extension (with recursive application)

```
  package EXP_LIST_HOMS is new LIST_HOMS (EXP, EXP_LIST, empty, "&", single, isEmpty, head, tail);
  package AUTO is new EXP_HOM (EXP);
  package EXP_PAIR_EXP is new PAIR (EXP, EXP);
• RHom:   (NAME —> EXP) —>  (EXP_LIST —> EXP) —>  (EXP × EXP —> EXP) —>  EXP —>  EXP;
axiom for all fName: NAME —> EXP; fTuple: EXP_LIST —> EXP; fCall: EXP × EXP —> EXP =>
  RHom fName fTuple fCall  =  Hom fName  (fTuple • Map (RHom fName fTuple fCall))
                                          (PairHom fCall (RHom fName fTuple fCall));
```

(5-9) Transformation Tactics for Expressions: *AtLeaves* and *Sweep*

```
  AtLeaves:  (NAME —> EXP) —>  EXP —>  EXP;
axiom for all fn: NAME —> EXP =>
  AtLeaves fn   = RHom fn id id;
  Sweep:     (EXP —> EXP) —>  EXP —>  EXP;
axiom for all f: EXP —> EXP =>
  Sweep f       = RHom (f • mkName) f f;
```

```
  everydeMorgan:  EXP —>  EXP;
axiom  everydeMorgan = Sweep tdeMorgan;
```

(5-10) Homomorphic Predicates for Expressions

```
  package toBOOL is new EXP_HOM (BOOLEAN);
  package UP_EXP_LIST_BOOL is new UP (EXP_LIST, BOOLEAN);
  package UP_EXP_PAIR_BOOL is new UP (EXP × EXP, BOOLEAN);
  package EXP_PAIR_BOOL is new PAIR (EXP, BOOLEAN);
```

```
  SweepP:   (n: BOOLEAN) —>  ("⊕": BOOLEAN × BOOLEAN —> BOOLEAN:: isMonoid n "⊕") —>
            (EXP —> BOOLEAN) —>  EXP —>  BOOLEAN;
axiom for all n: BOOLEAN; "⊗": BOOLEAN × BOOLEAN —> BOOLEAN; p: EXP —> BOOLEAN =>
  SweepP n "⊗" p = Hom (p • mkName)
                       (Up "⊗") (p • mkTuple, Hom n "⊗" (SweepP n "⊗" p))  - - Hom on lists
                       (Up "⊗") (p • mkCall, PairHom "⊗" (SweepP n "⊗" p));
```

```
  Exist, ForAll:   (EXP —> BOOLEAN) —>  EXP —>  BOOLEAN;
axiom for all p: EXP —> BOOLEAN; e: EXP =>
  Exist p      =  SweepP false "or" p,
  ForAll p     =  SweepP true "and" p;
```

As an example for application tactics, consider (5-9): AtLeaves applies a basic function to all leaves of an expression (names in this case); Sweep applies the basic function f to every subexpression. SweepP is a similar (pseudo-)homomorphic extension functional for predicates, see (5-10). Analogous definitions can be made for more complex expressions, statements etc. (cf. [Krieg-Brückner 88, 89a, b]). In fact, general definitions of homomorphic extension functionals could be constructed automatically for a given abstract syntax, in the same way as the construction of an algebraically specified type for an abstract syntax in the PROSPECTRA system.

1.6. Formalisation of Transformational Program Development

Various authors have stressed the need for a formalisation of the software development process: the need for an automatically generated development "history" [Wile 86a]. Approaches to formalise development descriptions contain a kind of development program [Wile 86a], functional abstraction [Feijs et al. 87] and composition of logical inference rules [Sintzoff 87], [Jähnichen et al. 86].

The meta-program development paradigm of PROSPECTRA leads naturally to a *formalisation of the software development process* itself. A program development is a sequence (more generally: a term) of transformations. The system automatically generates a transcript of a development "history"; it allows re-play upon re-development when requirements have changed, containing goals of the development, design decisions taken, and alternatives discarded but relevant for re-development.

1.6.1. Development Scripts: Composite Transformation Functions

In Program Development by Transformation, we can regard every elementary program development step as a transformation; we may conversely define a *development script* to be a composition of transformation operations (including application strategies for sets of elementary transformation operations). In this view we regard a development script as a *development transcript* (of some constant program term) that formalises a concrete development history, possibly to be re-played. A *development script* is, in general, a formal object that does not only represent a documentation of the past but is a plan for future developments (cf. also its use in the command language ControLa, see part III section 1.2 and part III chapters 2 and 3). It can be used to abstract from a particular development to a class of similar developments, a *development method*, incorporating a certain strategy.

The abstraction from concrete developments to development methods, incorporating formalised development tactics and strategies, and the formalisation of programming knowledge as "transformation rules + development methods" will be a challenge for the future.

1.6.2. Development Goals: Requirement Specifications

A *development goal* is a requirement specification for a development script, i.e. a transformation function employing a certain transformation strategy, yet to be designed. It can be a characteristic predicate for the respective transformation function or the post-condition of the application of some set of transformation rules. For example, we can state the (converse of the) desired goal for normalisation of Boolean expressions as in (6-1); this would be generalised for several sets of rules.

(6-1) Development Goals: Normalisation of Expressions

```
  not_normExp: EXP —> BOOLEAN;
axiom for all x: EXP =>
  not_normExp = Exist is_deMorgan;
```

Often, the application of some set of rules requires the satisfaction of some pre-condition established by (previous exhaustive application of) some other set of rules, i.e. as the post-condition of this set of rules. Note that such intermediate conditions never need to be checked operationally as long as it can be shown that they are established by previous application of other rules. If these conditions can be defined structurally (or "syntactically"), as in our example, then they characterise certain normal forms. This leads to a substantial improvement in the modularisation of sets of rules and separation of concerns, consequently easing verification. Transformation functions, having structural normal forms as applicability conditions, correspond to Wile's syntax directed experts [Wile 86b].

1.6.3. Development Tactics: Transformals

Exhaustive application of some set of rules can be expressed by suitable transformals. While can be used to apply a transformation function f as long as some condition p holds. Similarly, Iterate iterates a local transformation function f as long as some local condition p holds somewhere, see (6-2). These transformals correspond to a kind of "Markov algorithm" tactics when generalised to sets of rules.

(6-2) Development Tactics: *While, Iterate*

```
   While, Every, Iterate:  (EXP —> BOOLEAN) —>  (EXP —> EXP) —>  EXP —>  EXP;
axiom for all p: EXP —> BOOLEAN;  f: EXP —> EXP;  x: EXP =>
   ¬p x → While p f x = x,              p x →  While p f x = While p f (f x),
   Every p f x = Sweep (Try p f) x,            Iterate p f x = While (Exist p) (Every p f) x;
```

(6-3) Application of Development Tactics: *iter_normExp*

```
   iter_deMorgan:    EXP —> EXP;
axiom for all x: EXP =>
   iter_deMorgan x  = Iterate is_deMorgan deMorgan x;
```

1.6.4. Development Rules: Equations over Tactics

We would like to improve the transformation tactics even further. As far as possible, we would like to achieve the same strategic effect (the same development goal) by different, increasingly more efficient, application tactics. A transformation from one tactic to another is possible by development rules, see (6-5). *Development rules,* i.e. equational properties of development scripts, allow us to express and to reason about design alternatives or *alternative development tactics*, and to *simplify developments* by considering them as algebraic terms in the usual way. (6-6) shows the development of a derived rule by equational reasoning. It may be used to simplify iterated application into a single bottom-up one-sweep application. This rule is used in (6-7) to simplify our example since we can prove the premise.

(6-5) Development Rule: Elimination of *While*

```
axiom for all p: EXP —> BOOLEAN;  f: EXP —> EXP;  x: EXP =>
   p x ∧ ¬p (f x) →  While p f x = f x
```

(6-6) Development Rule Derivation: *Iterate ⇔ Every ⇔ Sweep*

```
                                           Iterate  p f x = While (Exist p) (Every p f) x,   -- definition of While
   Exist p x ∧ ¬ Exist p (Every p f x) →  Iterate  p f x = Every p f x ,                   -- elimination of While
   Exist p x ∧ ¬ Exist p (Every p f x) →  Iterate  p f x = Sweep (Try p f) x;              -- definition of Every
```

(6-7) Derivation: *iter_normExp*

```
axiom   iter_deMorgan = Sweep (Try is_deMorgan deMorgan);
```

1.7. Conclusion

Transformational Program Development

An overview of the PROSPECTRA methodology and its objectives was given. The power of compact development methods using the transformational approach was illustrated by an example in section 1.3.

Algebraic Specification and Functionals

The importance of the combination of algebraic specification with higher order functions was stressed in section 1.4. The functional programming paradigm leads to a considerably higher degree of abstraction and avoids much repetitive development effort, in particular through the use of homomorphic extension functionals. Only the combination with algebraic specification allows reasoning about correctness. For example, the statement of properties for parameters of a functional (such as those of a monoid) are not possible in conventional functional programming languages. The (first order) algebraic properties of types with the (higher order) algebraic properties of functionals allow general and powerful optimisations.

Meta-Development and Formalisation of Program Development

An important aspect of the PROSPECTRA approach is its use for *meta-development* and formalisation of developments (sections 1.5, 1.6). The methodology and transformation technology for program development is carried over to the development of *transformation programs*. Moreover, an automatically generated transscript of a development "history" allows re-play upon re-development when requirements have changed, containing goals of the development, design decisions taken, and alternatives discarded but relevant for re-development. A *development script* is thus a formal object that does not only represent a documentation of the past but is also a plan for future developments. It can be used to abstract from a particular development to a class of similar developments, a *development method*, incorporating a certain strategy.

The approach of PROSPECTRA is to regard transformation rules as equations in an algebra of programs, to derive basic transformation operations from these rules, to allow composition and functional abstraction, and to regard development scripts as (compositions of) such transformation operations. Using all the results from program development based on algebraic specifications and functionals, we can then reason about the development of meta-programs, i.e. transformation programs or development scripts, in the same way as about programs. We can define requirement specifications (development goals) and implement them by various design strategies, and we can simplify development terms, re-play developments by interpretation, and abstract to development methods, incorporating formalised development tactics and strategies. In short, we can develop *correct*, efficient, complex transformation programs and development methods from elementary rules stated as algebraic equations.

Uniformity of the Approach

The uniform approach to program, meta-program, proof and meta-proof development has had some major practical consequences. Since any system interaction can be formalised as a transformation of some "program" (term), the PROSPECTRA approach leads to a uniform treatment of programming language, program manipulation and transformation language, proof and proof development language, also command language and even library access. This uniformity has been exploited in the PROSPECTRA system, see part III chapter 1.

The essence of the uniform approach is the use of the specification language PAnndA-S as the transformation specification language TrafoLa-S. In this case, an abstract type schema to define Abstract Syntax is predefined, and translation to the applicative tree manipulation language of the Synthesizer Generator [Reps, Teitelbaum 88] (used both as an Editor and as a Transformer Generator in the system) is automatic. ControLa, the command language of the system, is also a subset of PAnndA-S: development histories can be treated as formal objects, developed, translated to executable scripts, and (re-)played.

There is a close analogy to the development of efficient proof tactics for given proof or inference rules (transformation rules in the algebra of proofs). This is the basis for the development of the Proof Subsystem in PROSPECTRA, cf. part III section 4.4.

Context-Sensitive Transformation, Filtering of Proof Obligations

Experience with the transformational approach and the implementation of non-trivial transformations has shown that context-sensitivity of transformations is essential. Transformations need complex applicability conditions; thus the first requirement is that such conditions can be specified. As has been demonstrated in the examples, the combination of algebraic specification and restrictions on parameters (such as the monoid property) is quite powerful in this sense. Objects (and terms) can be "lifted" to meta-objects (and terms) and thus can become subject to manipulation during transformation and proof.

Furthermore, complex applicability conditions give rise to complex proof obligations. It is crucial to discard as many of them as possible automatically. The use of static semantic attributes, representing, for example, type information, allows the automatic check of static semantic conditions. A special context attribute, the "local theory"(cf. part III section 1.2.5), contains the set of all applicable axioms and theorems, accessible during proof. It also permits a search, during transformation, for some implicit parameters with certain restrictions (e.g. an associative operation and the corresponding neutral element), or some limited automatic theorem proving, leaving those conditions that need user interaction during proof as a residue. Thus a combination of compiler technology, theorem proving and a knowledge-based approach achieve the required filtering of proof obligations and need for interaction. This is one reason why the integration of construction and verification in the transformational approach of PROSPECTRA becomes practical.

Another use of attributes is the filtering of available transformations in the menue. It is quite important that those transformations that cannot be applied to a given term do not clutter the menue; they should be suppressed and not shown. Structural applicability is checked by the built-in pattern matching; (static) semantic applicability conditions can be defined and checked automatically before the transformation is shown to be (potentially) applicable in the menue; others are only checked when the user has selected a transformation or are filtered out as residual proof obligations.

The Synthesizer Generator [Reps, Teitelbaum 88], one of the major tools used to implement the system, provides trees with attributes and incremetal re-evaluation. However, parameters with interaction from the user, static applicability conditions, interaction with the Proof Editor, re-computation of the context when moving about in trees, recording of the development history etc. all had to be added to the Synthesizer Generator to adapt it to the needs of PROSPECTRA (cf. part III chapter 6).

Comparison with Other Approaches

From all the approaches and systems for transformational program development (cf. [Partsch, Steinbrüggen 83]), two should be mentioned here for comparison: CIP (cf. [Bauer et al. 85 - 87]) and KIDS (cf. [Smith, Lowry 90], [Smith 91]). Both support requirement specification and stepwise refinement with correctness-preserving transformations in a kind of wide-spectrum language. CIP is oriented towards a Pascal or Algol-like target language, KIDS towards REFINE. Neither system supports higher-order functions (but cf. [Möller 87a]). Non-determinism as in CIP is not included in PROSPECTRA since it complicates the notion of equivalence of programs and therefore transformation; instead, it is replaced in PROSPECTRA (for most purposes) by a choice of model in a loose specification, even when specifying distributed systems with the aid of non-strict functions; this aspect is not treated here due to lack of space (cf. [Weber 91], [Broy 87-89]).

The KIDS system is mainly aimed at the algorithm design phase, from non-operational specifications. It is quite automatic but lacks a certain generality. The proof system is separate and not so smoothly integrated into the approach as in PROSPECTRA. Due to the use of the Synthesizer Generator, the PROSPECTRA system has a user-friendly interface (suppressing, e.g., non-applicable transformations from the menue) compared with CIP. The Library Manager in the PROSPECTRA system can save and retrieve development histories; this makes re-development possible.

The major difference in the approaches is the treatment of meta-development of compact transformations and methods. CIP allows composition of transformation rules etc. based on a notion of transformational expression; this is general and permits easy extension of transformation knowledge but does not allow the development of efficient transformation programs and compact abstract methods. KIDS has some powerful built-in design tactics, but no tactics definition facility is provided for the user.

Research Perspectives

Considerably more work is needed in the areas of automating the transformational process, development of efficient, compact context-sensitive transformations (using, e.g., incremental attribute evaluation), of a classification and categorisation of transformations in the system to allow specific sets of transformations to be used more effectively in a goal directed development situation, and of goal-orientation during transformation, driven by efficiency considerations and target systems, trying to assist the user in the choice of transformations and methods. The abstraction from concrete developments to development methods, incorporating formalised development tactics and strategies, and the formalisation of programming knowledge as *transformation rules + development methods*, will be a challenge for the future. Current research focusses on methods for the early stages of development to aid the finding of problem solutions and the synthesis of operational versions.

The experience of PROSPECTRA shows that more research is needed in specification language design, concerning, in particular, the structuring of specifications, programs, proofs and developments, i.e. development in-the-large. Structuring, e.g. by powerful mechanisms for abstraction and genericity, is crucial for the re-usability of specifications, programs, proofs and developments and thus a foundation for the development of libraries and standardisation of specifications etc. A starting point for the design of SPECTRAL ([Krieg-Brückner, Sannella 91]) was to combine the mutually complementary experiences of PROSPECTRA and Extended ML (for aspects of development in-the-large). SPECTRAL is very general and quite compact. It will be the basis for future work on a methodology and system, incorporating the aspects of uniformity described above (cf. also part III chapter 1).

Acknowledgements

I wish to thank the other members of the PROSPECTRA project for their contributions, and Stefan Sokolowski for his suggestions.

2. Specification

2.1. Algebraic Specification

*Thomas Grünler, Universität Passau**

This section describes the approach to algebraic specification within the PROSPECTRA project. It serves as an introduction to the semantic concepts of PA^{nn}dA-S. We try to motivate the specialities of this specification language with the application of these features to examples.

2.1.1. Introduction

Nowadays, the merits of algebraic specification of abstract data types and software systems is widely acknowledged in the computer science community. This section cannot and does not want to serve as an introduction to the theory of algebraic specifications. For this purpose the reader is referred to introductory text books [Ehrich et al. 89], [Ehrig, Mahr 85], and [Wirsing 89]. This section is meant to be a tutorial introduction to the specification approach and to the specification language used in the PROSPECTRA project.

The algebraic specification language PA^{nn}dA-S extends the classical algebraic first order specification framework by higher order functions and non-monotonic predicates. The first are useful for describing both concurrent systems and schematic algorithms such as generic tree-traversals. The latter are needed to characterize objects and functions satisfying certain conditions and for the description of non-monotonic properties. Full first order logic is supplied for, but in many applications one will confine oneself to writing axioms which are positive Horn formulas. The predefined equality is strong, that is, besides its obvious meaning for defined elements, undefined elements are also equal to each other. We extend every carrier set by a special element $\perp$ which stands for that undefined element.

The language PA^{nn}dA-S, the syntax as well as the semantics, changed significantly during the PROSPECTRA project as can be seen by the different versions of the abstract syntax and the semantics. However, we tried to present algebraic specification in PA^{nn}dA-S as close as possible to former attempts of its description. The underlying papers are [Grünler, Broy 88], [Nickl et al. 88], and, of course, part II chapter 3, the final version of the semantics.

2.1.2. Algebras

A specification of an abstract data type consists of two parts: its syntactic structure given by a signature, and its properties. These are given by axioms which describe the relations between syntactic entities.

We start by giving the definition of a higher order signature.

2.1.2.1. Higher Order Signatures

We use a framework in which it is possible to specify higher order functions. For that purpose we also need the notion of a higher order sort. We take a set of atomic sorts and construct tuple sorts and functional sorts inductively (cf. also [Broy 87], [Möller 87], [Möller et al. 88], and [Grünler 90]).

---

* *Author's current address*: Philips Kommunikations Industrie AG, Thurn-und-Taxis-Straße 14, D-8500 Nürnberg

Definition: Let S be a set of sorts. The set H(S) of *higher order sorts* is defined to be the least set (w.r.t. inclusion) that satisfies the following conditions:

(i) (*atomic sort*)
if $s \in S$ then $s^{\perp} \in H(S)$,

(ii) (*tuple sort*)
if $n \in \mathbb{N}$, $n \geq 2$ and $t_1, t_2, \ldots, t_n \in H(S)$ then $(t_1 \times t_2 \times \ldots \times t_n) \in H(S)$,

(iii) (*functional sort*)
if $t, t' \in H(S)$ then $(t' \dashrightarrow t) \in H(S)$.

The signature of an algebraic specification consists of the atomic sorts and of names for functions and predicates over the corresponding higher order sorts.

Definition: A *higher order signature* $\Sigma = (S, F, P, fct)$ consists of

a set S of *sorts*,
a set F of *function symbols*, and
a set P of *predicate symbols*,

together with a function $fct: F \cup P \rightarrow H(S)$. $fct(f)$ is called the *functionality* of f ($f \in F \cup P$). We assume that the sets F and P are disjoint.

Example:

```
package NAT_EX is
   type NAT is private;
   zero: NAT⊥;
   succ: NAT⊥ --> NAT⊥;
   predicate iszero: NAT⊥;
end NAT_EX;
```

The higher order signature corresponding to the "package" NAT_EX can be derived straightforwardly. Names enclosed between the keywords **type** and **is private** are names for atomic sorts, names without a keyword stand for function symbols, and names following the keyword **predicate** correspond to predicate symbols. In this case we get S = {NAT}, F = {zero, succ}, and P = {iszero}. The functionality of a function or predicate symbol is the sort which follows the colon after that name. In the concrete syntax of PA^{nn}dA-S a plus-sign is appended to a sort, s+. We will use $s^{\perp}$ instead of the notation s+ since consider it to be more suggestive. Accordingly we obtain the function $fct: F \cup P \rightarrow H(S)$ given by

fct (zero) = $NAT^{\perp}$,
fct (succ) = ($NAT^{\perp}$ --> $NAT^{\perp}$), and
fct (iszero) = $NAT^{\perp}$.

2.1.2.2. Function Space Algebras

We are going to explain the notion of a function space algebra. As carrier sets for higher order sorts we admit complete partially ordered sets (cpo's). These are partially ordered sets with a least element $\perp$ where every directed subset has a least upper bound. A set is called directed if there exists an upper bound for each two elements in it. The carrier set of a tuple sort is the cartesian product of its constituents with the componentwise ordering. The carrier set of a functional sort is the full set of continuous functions between the carriers of its constituents ordered by the pointwise ordering.

We denote the set of continuous functions between cpo's D' and D by $[\,D' \rightarrow D\,]$. Then a function *f* is less than or equal to *g* ($f \sqsubseteq g$) if for all $x \in D'$ it holds that $f(x) \sqsubseteq g(x)$. $[\,D' \rightarrow D\,]$ is again a cpo with the totally undefined function as its least element.

Definition: Let $\Sigma = (S, F, P, fct)$ be a higher order signature. A *Σ-function space algebra* A consists of

(i) a family $(t^A)_{t\in H(S)}$ of *carrier sets* with the following properties:
for all $s \in S$
$((s^{\perp})^A, \sqsubseteq^A)$ is a complete partially ordered set with a least element $\perp$,

for $n\in \mathbb{N}, n \geq 2$ and $t_1,\ldots, t_n \in H(S)$
$(t_1 \times \ldots \times t_n)^A := t_1{}^A \times \ldots \times t_n{}^A$,

for all $t, t' \in H(S)$
$(t' \dashrightarrow t)^A := [\,t'^A \rightarrow t^A\,]$,

(ii) a family $(f^A)_{f\in F}$ of functions (or constants) such that $f^A \in fct(f)^A$ for all $f \in F$,

(iii) a family $(p^A)_{p\in P}$ of relations such that $p^A \subseteq fct(p)^A$ for all $p \in P$.

Example: Continuing the last example we indicate an algebra $\mathbb{N}$ for the higher order signature ({NAT}, {zero, succ}, {iszero}, fct). According to (i) above it suffices to define carrier sets $((s^{\perp})^N, \sqsubseteq^N)$ for all $s \in S$ (since the others are constructed from these). We set

$(NAT^{\perp})^N := \mathbb{N} \cup \{\perp\}$,

the set of natural numbers augmented by an "undefined" element. The partial order $\sqsubseteq^N$ is the *flat* order, i.e. for all $a, b \in \mathbb{N} \cup \{\perp\}$

$a \sqsubseteq^N b$ if and only if $a = \perp$ or $a = b$.

According to (ii) and (iii) we have to define $zero^N$, $succ^N$, and $iszero^N$ such that their functionalities are respected. We set

$zero^N := 0 \in \mathbb{N} \subseteq (NAT^{\perp})^N = fct(zero)^N$,

and define

$succ^N \in [\,(NAT^{\perp})^N \rightarrow (NAT^{\perp})^N\,] = fct(succ)^N$

by

$succ^N(a) := a + 1$ for all $a \in \mathbb{N}$,
$succ^N(\perp) := \perp$.

This function is continuous. In general, every strict function *f* from a flat cpo into an arbitrary cpo is continuous. A function $f\colon D' \rightarrow D$ between cpo's D and D' is called *strict* if $f(\perp) = \perp$.
Finally we set

$iszero^N := \{0\} \subseteq (NAT^{\perp})^N = fct(iszero)^N$.

This concludes the definition of the function space algebra $\mathbb{N}$.

2.1.2.3. *Homomorphisms*

In order to compare different Σ-function space algebras one needs morphisms. The following concept of a morphism is chosen especially with respect to our notion of algebraic implementation (see part I section 2.2). There one needs a morphism from the implementing algebra into the algebra that is to be implemented. We take the view that the functions of the implementing algebra may be more defined than those of the given one. This corresponds to the notion of robust implementation.

Definition: Let A and B be Σ-function space algebras with signature $\Sigma = (S, F, P, fct)$. A *weakening higher order* (Σ-) *homomorphism* $h: A \to B$ is a family $h = (h_t: t^A \to t^B)_{t \in H(S)}$ of continuous mappings h_t satisfying

(i) for $n \in \mathbb{N}$, $n \geq 2$ and $t_1, \ldots, t_n \in H(S)$

$h_{(t_1 \times \ldots \times t_n)}(a_1, \ldots, a_n) = (h_{t_1}(a_1), \ldots, h_{t_n}(a_n))$ for all $a_i \in t_i^A$, $1 \leq i \leq n$,

for all $t, t' \in H(S)$

$h_t(a(a')) \sqsupseteq h_{(t' \dashrightarrow t)}(a)(h_{t'}(a'))$ for all $a \in (t' \dashrightarrow t)^A$, $a' \in t'^A$,

(ii) for all $f \in F$

$h_{fct(f)}(f^A) \sqsupseteq f^B$.

We do not impose any conditions on the families $(p^A)_{p \in P}$ and $(p^B)_{p \in P}$ corresponding to the predicate symbols of Σ.

Example: Regarding our example we indicate a second algebra $\mathbb{Z}$ for the higher order signature ({NAT}, {zero, succ}, {iszero}, fct). We define

$$(NAT^{\perp})^{\mathbb{Z}} := \mathbf{Z} \cup \{\perp\},$$

the set of the integers augmented by an "undefined" element. The rest of the definition is the same as that of N with the exception that every occurrence of N, resp. IN must be replaced by $\mathbb{Z}$, resp. **Z**.

In order to construct a homomorphism h from $\mathbb{Z}$ to N we need to define continuous mappings $h_t: t^{\mathbb{Z}} \to t^N$ for all $t \in H(S)$. For this purpose it is very convenient to define continuous mappings in the other direction, too. Therefore we now consider the embedding projection pair $(i_{NAT\perp}, h_{NAT\perp})$ which is given by

$i_{NAT\perp}: (NAT^{\perp})^N \to (NAT^{\perp})^{\mathbb{Z}}$ and $h_{NAT\perp}: (NAT^{\perp})^{\mathbb{Z}} \to (NAT^{\perp})^N$

$$n \mapsto \begin{cases} n \text{ if } n \in \mathbb{N} \\ \perp \text{ if } n = \perp \end{cases} \qquad z \mapsto \begin{cases} z \text{ if } z \in \mathbb{N} \\ \perp \text{ otherwise} \end{cases}$$

We obtain the characteristic properties $h_{NAT\perp} \circ i_{NAT\perp} = id_{(NAT\perp)^N}$ and $i_{NAT\perp} \circ h_{NAT\perp} \sqsubseteq id_{(NAT\perp)^{\mathbb{Z}}}$, where id_X denotes the identity function on a set X and where ∘ denotes function composition. Starting with these we define embedding projection pairs $(i_t: t^N \to t^{\mathbb{Z}}, h_t: t^{\mathbb{Z}} \to t^N)$ for all $t \in H(S)$. If for $n \in \mathbb{N}$, $n \geq 2$ and $t_1, \ldots, t_n \in H(S)$ embedding projection pairs (i_{t_k}, h_{t_k}), $1 \leq k \leq n$ are already constructed then we set

$i_{(t_1 \times \ldots \times t_n)}(a_1, \ldots, a_n) := (i_{t_1}(a_1), \ldots, i_{t_n}(a_n))$ for all $a_k \in t_k^N$, $1 \leq k \leq n$, and

$h_{(t_1 \times \ldots \times t_n)}(z_1, \ldots, z_n) := (h_{t_1}(z_1), \ldots, h_{t_n}(z_n))$ for all $z_k \in t_k^{\mathbb{Z}}$, $1 \leq k \leq n$.

For $t, t' \in H(S)$ and embedding projection pairs (i_t, h_t) and $(i_{t'}, h_{t'})$ we define $i_{(t' \dashrightarrow t)}: (t' \dashrightarrow t)^{\mathbf{N}} \to (t' \dashrightarrow t)^{\mathbf{Z}}$ and $h_{(t' \dashrightarrow t)}: (t' \dashrightarrow t)^{\mathbf{Z}} \to (t' \dashrightarrow t)^{\mathbf{N}}$ by

$$i_{(t' \dashrightarrow t)}(a) := i_t \circ a \circ h_{t'} \quad \text{for all } a \in (t' \dashrightarrow t)^{\mathbf{N}}, \text{ and}$$

$$h_{(t' \dashrightarrow t)}(z) := h_t \circ z \circ i_{t'} \quad \text{for all } z \in (t' \dashrightarrow t)^{\mathbf{Z}}.$$

One shows inductively that $i_t: t^{\mathbf{N}} \to t^{\mathbf{Z}}$ and $h_t: t^{\mathbf{Z}} \to t^{\mathbf{N}}$ are continuous for all $t \in H(S)$, and also that they satisfy the embedding projection pair properties, i. e.

$$h_t \circ i_t = id_{t^{\mathbf{N}}} \quad \text{and} \quad i_t \circ h_t \sqsubseteq id_{t^{\mathbf{Z}}} \quad \text{for all } t \in H(S).$$

With these definitions of h_t, $t \in H(S)$ the first part of (i) in the definition of Σ-homomorphism is trivially fulfilled. As to the second part we consider for $t, t' \in H(S)$ and for $z \in (t' \dashrightarrow t)^{\mathbf{Z}}$, $z' \in t'^{\mathbf{Z}}$ the computation

$$\begin{aligned} h_{(t' \dashrightarrow t)}(z)(h_{t'}(z')) &= (h_t \circ z \circ i_{t'})(h_{t'}(z')) = \\ &= (h_t \circ z)((i_{t'} \circ h_{t'})(z')) \\ &\sqsubseteq (h_t \circ z)(id_{t'^{\mathbf{Z}}}(z')) \\ &= h_t(z(z')). \end{aligned}$$

This proves the second part of (i). It remains to prove condition (ii). The only function symbols are zero and succ. According to (ii) we have to prove $h_{NAT\perp}(zero^{\mathbf{Z}}) \sqsupseteq zero^{\mathbf{N}}$ and $h_{(NAT\perp \dashrightarrow NAT\perp)}(succ^{\mathbf{Z}}) \sqsupseteq succ^{\mathbf{N}}$. The first inequation is trivially true because both sides are equal to 0. The second holds because of the computation

$$\begin{aligned} h_{(NAT\perp \dashrightarrow NAT\perp)}(succ^{\mathbf{Z}})(n) &= (h_{NAT\perp} \circ succ^{\mathbf{Z}} \circ i_{NAT\perp})(n) = \\ &= (h_{NAT\perp} \circ succ^{\mathbf{Z}})(n) \\ &= h_{NAT\perp}(n+1) \\ &= n+1 \\ &= succ^{\mathbf{N}}(n) \quad \text{for all } n \in \mathbb{N}. \end{aligned}$$

Altogether we proved that $h = (h_t: t^{\mathbf{Z}} \to t^{\mathbf{N}})_{t \in H(S)}$ is indeed a weakening higher order (Σ-) homomorphism. If one reconsiders the proof one becomes aware of the fact that the main part of the work lies in the definition of the homomorphisms h_t for all higher order sorts t. This is one of the technical difficulties which come with the use of higher order functions.

2.1.2.4. Terms over Higher Order Signatures

Every higher order signature defines a set of syntactically correct expressions which can be formed from its function symbols.

Definition: For a higher order signature $\Sigma = (S, F, P, fct)$ and an H(S)-sorted family of variables $X = (X_t)_{t\in H(S)}$ the sets of (Σ-) *terms* $T_{\Sigma,t}(X)$ of higher order sorts $t \in H(S)$ with free variables from X are defined as the least sets having the following properties:

(i) $x \in T_{\Sigma,t}(X)$ for all variables $x \in X_t$,

(ii) $f \in T_{\Sigma,fct(f)}(X)$ for all function symbols $f \in F$,

(iii) if $n \in \mathbb{N}$, $n \geq 2$ and $u_i \in T_{\Sigma,t_i}(X)$ for $1 \leq i \leq n$ then $(u_1,\ldots, u_n) \in T_{\Sigma,(t_1 \times \ldots \times t_n)}(X)$,

(iv) if $u \in T_{\Sigma,(t' \dashrightarrow t)}(X)$, $u' \in T_{\Sigma,t'}(X)$ then $u(u') \in T_{\Sigma,t}(X)$.

We assume that the F, P, and X_t, $t \in H(S)$ are pairwise disjoint.
A *ground term* is a Σ-term without (free) variables. The sets of ground terms of sort $t \in H(S)$ are denoted by $T_{\Sigma,t}$.

Example: For the above higher order signature ({NAT}, {zero, succ}, {iszero}, fct) =: Σ let the following sets of variables be given $X_{NAT\perp} := \{x, \ldots\}$, $X_{(NAT\perp \times NAT\perp)} := \{y, \ldots\}$, and $X_{(NAT\perp \dashrightarrow NAT\perp)} := \{z, \ldots\}$ then the following terms are examples for terms of the indicated sorts.

x, zero, succ(zero), succ(x), z(zero), z(x) $\in T_{\Sigma,NAT\perp}(X)$,

y, (zero, x), (succ(succ(zero)), zero), (x, z(x)) $\in T_{\Sigma,(NAT\perp \times NAT\perp)}(X)$,

z, succ $\in T_{\Sigma,(NAT\perp \dashrightarrow NAT\perp)}(X)$.

Terms without x, y, or z are ground terms of the respective sorts.

2.1.2.5. Interpretation of Terms in Function Space Algebras

Any Σ-term can be interpreted in a Σ-function space algebra. If terms contain (free) variables from X then we must first assign values to these variables. For this purpose let $\beta = (\beta_t: X_t \rightarrow t^A)_{t\in H(S)}$ be a family of maps associating an element $\beta_t(x) \in t^A$ with every free variable x of sort t. Such a β is called a *valuation of* X *in* A (β: X $\rightarrow$ A). Now we are able to assign a value to any term.

Definition: Let $\Sigma = (S, F, P, fct)$ be a higher order signature, X an H(S)-sorted family of variables, and β a valuation of X in A. Then the *interpretation* $u^A[\beta]$ of a term u in A w.r.t. the valuation β is defined inductively as follows:

(i) $x^A[\beta] := \beta_t(x)$ for all variables $x \in X_t$,

(ii) $f^A[\beta] := f^A$ for all function symbols $f \in F$,

(iii) if $n \in \mathbb{N}$, $n \geq 2$ and $u_i \in T_{\Sigma,t_i}(X)$ for $1 \leq i \leq n$ then $(u_1,\ldots, u_n)^A[\beta] := (u_1{}^A[\beta],\ldots, u_n{}^A[\beta])$,

(iv) if $u \in T_{\Sigma,(t' \dashrightarrow t)}(X)$, $u' \in T_{\Sigma,t'}(X)$ then
$u(u')^A[\beta] := u^A[\beta]\,(u'^A[\beta])$.

If u is a ground term its interpretation does not depend on the valuation β. In this case we write u^A for the interpretation of u w.r.t. any valuation.

***Example*:** In continuation of our example we take the signature Σ, variables X, and the algebra $\mathbb{N}$ as above and give the interpretation in $\mathbb{N}$ of the terms of the example in the last section with respect to the following valuation $\beta: X \to \mathbb{N}$. For that purpose we only need these three mappings:

$\beta_{NAT\perp}: X_{NAT\perp} \to (NAT\perp)^{\mathbb{N}}$,
$\beta_{NAT\perp}(x) := 5, \ldots$

$\beta_{(NAT\perp \times NAT\perp)}: X_{(NAT\perp \times NAT\perp)} \to (NAT\perp)^{\mathbb{N}} \times (NAT\perp)^{\mathbb{N}}$,
$\beta_{(NAT\perp \times NAT\perp)}(y) := (93, 27), \ldots$

$\beta_{(NAT\perp \dashrightarrow NAT\perp)}: X_{(NAT\perp \dashrightarrow NAT\perp)} \to [\,(NAT\perp)^{\mathbb{N}} \to (NAT\perp)^{\mathbb{N}}\,]$,
$\beta_{(NAT\perp \dashrightarrow NAT\perp)}(z) := fac, \ldots$
where fac is the faculty function.

Then the interpretations of those terms are as follows.

$x^{\mathbb{N}}[\beta] = \beta_{NAT\perp}(x) = 5$, $zero^{\mathbb{N}}[\beta] = zero^{\mathbb{N}} = 0$,
$succ(zero)^{\mathbb{N}}[\beta] = succ^{\mathbb{N}}[\beta]\,(zero^{\mathbb{N}}[\beta]) = succ^{\mathbb{N}}(0) = 0 + 1 = 1$,
$succ(x)^{\mathbb{N}}[\beta] = succ^{\mathbb{N}}(5) = 6$, $z(zero)^{\mathbb{N}}[\beta] = fac(0) = 1$,
$z(x)^{\mathbb{N}}[\beta] = fac(5) = 120$,
$y^{\mathbb{N}}[\beta] = (93, 27)$, $(zero, x)^{\mathbb{N}}[\beta] = (zero^{\mathbb{N}}[\beta], x^{\mathbb{N}}[\beta]) = (0, 5)$,
$(succ(succ(zero)), zero)^{\mathbb{N}}[\beta] = (2, 0)$, $(x, z(x))^{\mathbb{N}}[\beta] = (5, 120)$,
$z^{\mathbb{N}}[\beta] = fac$, $succ^{\mathbb{N}}[\beta] = succ^{\mathbb{N}}$.

***Remark*:** Let $\Sigma = (S, F, P, fct)$ be a higher order signature. Let $h = (h_t: t^A \to t^B)_{t \in H(S)}$ be a weakening higher order (Σ-) homomorphism between Σ-function space algebras A and B. By induction on the term structure it is not difficult to prove that for all ground terms $u \in T_{\Sigma,t}$, $t \in H(S)$ it holds that

$$h_t(u^A) \sqsupseteq u^B.$$

2.1.2.6. Term-generatedness

In general, the class of all Σ-function space algebras is too rich for practical computations. Usually one concentrates one's attention to term-generated algebras (cf. [Bauer et al. 85], [Wirsing et al. 83], and [Wirsing 89]). This restriction is sufficient for the first order case but it won't work here:

Due to the fact that the functionalities of function symbols are not restricted to the first order case it is not straightforward what the meaning of term-generated is to be. Of course, there is no way to obtain a generation principle for the carrier sets of higher order functional sorts since these are the whole sets of continuous functions. As even the carrier sets of atomic sorts are (non-flat) cpo's in general we won't get a hold on the infinite objects (e.g. infinite streams). Thus the best we can hope for is a generation principle for the finite elements of the zero order carrier sets. This principle is explained in this chapter.

Definition: Let $\Sigma = (S, F, P, fct)$ be a higher order signature. A zero order sort is an atomic sort or a tuple sort built from zero order sorts. Thus the set $H_0(S)$ of *zero order sorts* is defined to be the least set (w.r.t. inclusion) that satisfies the following conditions:

(i) if $s \in S$ then $s^{\perp} \in H_0(S)$,

(ii) if $n \in \mathbb{N}$, $n \geq 2$ and $t_1, \ldots, t_n \in H_0(S)$ then $(t_1 \times \ldots \times t_n) \in H_0(S)$.

$H_0(S) \subseteq H(S)$ is the subset of the higher order sorts which is constructed without the possibility to build functional sorts.

We demand that the carrier sets of zero order sorts are generated by the interpretations of the first order ground terms. The precise meaning of these notions is the following.

Definition: A cpo $(C, \sqsubseteq)$ is said to be *generated by a subset* $U \subseteq C$ iff there is no proper subset Γ of C such that

(i) $\{\perp\} \cup U \subseteq \Gamma$, and

(ii) Γ is closed under least upper bounds of directed subsets.

Hence if C is a flat cpo, then C is generated by U iff $\{\perp\} \cup U = C$.

Because of the possibility to express an n-ary first order function as curried higher order version, the first order ground terms are not only composed of zero and first order function symbols but also of the curried equivalents of the latter.

Definition: For $s \in S$ we call a ground term $u \in T_{\Sigma,s^{\perp}}$ a *first order ground term* if all function symbols occurring in u are of a zero order or an essentially first order functionality. Here a functional sort $ft \in H(S)$ is called *essentially first order* if

(i) $ft = (t \text{ --> } t')$ with $t, t' \in H_0(S)$ or

(ii) $ft = (t \text{ --> } ft')$ where $t \in H_0(S)$ and ft' is essentially first order again.

Definition: Now a Σ-function space algebra A is called *first order term-generated* if for every $s \in S$ the carrier $(s^{\perp})^A$ is generated by the set

$\{u^A \mid u \in T_{\Sigma,s^{\perp}}$ is a first order ground term$\}$

Hence $(s^{\perp})^A$ is generated by the interpretation of all first order ground terms of sort $s^{\perp}$.

Example: The algebra N is first order term-generated. As the carrier $(\text{NAT}^{\perp})^N = \mathbb{N} \cup \{\perp\}$ is a flat cpo, it is generated by the set $\mathbb{N}$. From the facts that

$T_{\Sigma,\text{NAT}^{\perp}} = \{$zero, succ(zero), succ(succ(zero)), ...$\}$

and that the interpretations of these first order ground terms are 0, 1, 2, ..., we conclude

$\mathbb{N} = \{u^N \mid u \in T_{\Sigma,\text{NAT}^{\perp}}$ is a first order ground term$\}$.

Thus $(\text{NAT}^{\perp})^N$ is generated by the set

$\{u^N \mid u \in T_{\Sigma,\text{NAT}^{\perp}}$ is a first order ground term$\}$

whence the assertion follows.

2.1.3. Specifications

The signature fixes the sorts, and the number and syntactic structure of the function and relation symbols. It does not talk about their intended meanings. These, namely the relations between syntactic entities, are given by axioms. The latter are arbitrary closed formulas which we are now going to define.

2.1.3.1. Formulas over Higher Order Signatures

As we said in the introduction, PA^{nn}dA-S allows us to express full first order logic. Thus we are completely free to combine atomic formulas by the logical operators $\neg$, $\wedge$, $\vee$, $\rightarrow$, $\leftrightarrow$, $\forall$, $\exists$. The atomic formulas are not only equations. These can also be constructed by applying a predicate symbol to a suitable term. Finally, it is possible to express the definedness of a term by means of a predefined predicate.

***Definition*:** Let Σ = (S, F, P, fct) be a higher order signature and X an H(S)-sorted family of variables. The set of (Σ-) *formulas* is defined as the least set having the following properties:

(i) if u is a term then

defined u

is a formula,

(ii) if u and u' are terms of the same higher order sort then

u = u'

is a formula,

(iii) if $p \in P$ is a predicate symbol and $u \in T_{\Sigma,fct(p)}(X)$ then

p(u)

is a formula,

(iv) if φ and ψ are formulas and $x \in X_t$ then

$\neg\,\varphi$

$\varphi \wedge \psi$

$\forall$ x:t $\Rightarrow \varphi$

are formulas.

$\varphi \vee \psi$ is an abbreviation for $\neg(\neg\varphi \wedge \neg\psi)$,
$\varphi \rightarrow \psi$ is an abbreviation for $\neg\varphi \vee \psi$,
$\varphi \leftrightarrow \psi$ is an abbreviation for $(\varphi\rightarrow\psi) \wedge (\psi\rightarrow\varphi)$, and
$\exists$ x:t $\Rightarrow \varphi$ is an abbreviation for $\neg(\forall$ x:t $\Rightarrow \neg\varphi)$.

In $\forall$ x:t $\Rightarrow \varphi$ we call φ the *range* of the quantifier $\forall$ x:t. A variable $x \in X_t$ occurring in a formula ψ is called *bound* if it is in the range of a quantifier $\forall$ x:t in ψ. Any other occurrence of x in ψ is called *free*.

A formula is called *closed* if all variables occurring in it are bound.

***Example*:** Again we refer to our example. For that higher order signature Σ and that family of variables X we obtain the following examples for formulas.

defined zero, x = succ(x), $\neg$ iszero(succ(zero)), $\exists$x:NAT$^{\perp}$ $\Rightarrow$ z(x) = x,
$\forall$x:NAT$^{\perp}$ $\Rightarrow$ x = zero $\rightarrow$ z(x) = succ(zero).

2.1.3.2. Validity of Formulas

In the following we make sure that each of our symbols means what we want it to mean. We define the validity of a formula as usual.

***Definition*:** Let $\Sigma = (S, F, P, fct)$ be a higher order signature, X an H(S)-sorted family of variables, A a Σ-function space algebra, and β be a valuation of X in A. Then a formula φ is *valid in* A w.r.t. β, denoted by $A, \beta \models \varphi$, iff the following holds:

(i) if u is a term then
$A, \beta \models$ **defined** u iff $u^A[\beta] \neq \bot$,

(ii) if u and u' are terms of the same higher order sort then
$A, \beta \models (u = u')$ iff $u^A[\beta] = u'^A[\beta]$
(*strong equality*),

(iii) if $p \in P$ is a predicate symbol and $u \in T_{\Sigma,fct(p)}(X)$ then
$A, \beta \models p(u)$ iff $u^A[\beta] \in p^A$,

(iv) if φ and ψ are formulas and $x \in X_t$ then

$A, \beta \models \neg\varphi$ iff φ is not valid in A w.r.t. β,

$A, \beta \models \varphi \wedge \psi$ iff $A, \beta \models \varphi$ and $A, \beta \models \psi$,

$A, \beta \models \forall x{:}t \Rightarrow \varphi$ iff $A, \beta[a/x] \models \varphi$ for all $a \in t^A$,
where

$$\beta[a/x]_{t'} = \beta_{t'} \text{ for } t' \neq t \text{ and}$$

$$\beta[a/x]_t(y) = \begin{cases} \beta_t(y) & \text{for } y \in X_t,\ y \neq x \\ a & \text{for } y = x \end{cases}$$

If φ is not valid in A w.r.t. β we also write $A, \beta \not\models \varphi$.

Let A be a Σ-algebra and φ be a closed formula. Then the validity of φ in A does not depend on the choice of a valuation β. Therefore, for a closed formula φ we define

$A \models \varphi$ iff there exists a valuation β such that $A, \beta \models \varphi$.

***Example*:** We take the signature Σ, variables X, the algebra $\mathbb{N}$, and the valuation $\beta: X \to \mathbb{N}$ of section 2.1.2.5 and check whether the formulas of the last paragraph are valid or not. We obtain

$\text{zero}^{\mathbb{N}}[\beta] = 0 \neq \bot$, thus $\mathbb{N}, \beta \models$ **defined** zero.

Further

$x^{\mathbb{N}}[\beta] = 5 \neq 6 = \text{succ}(x)^{\mathbb{N}}[\beta]$, and therefore $\mathbb{N}, \beta \not\models x = \text{succ}(x)$.

We have got $\text{succ(zero)}^{\mathbb{N}}[\beta] = 1 \notin \{0\} = \text{iszero}^{\mathbb{N}}$; hence

$\mathbb{N}, \beta \not\models \text{iszero(succ(zero))}$ which is equivalent to $\mathbb{N}, \beta \models \neg\, \text{iszero(succ(zero))}$.

The validity $\mathbb{N}, \beta \models \exists x{:}\text{NAT}^{\bot} \Rightarrow z(x) = x$ is satisfied if and only if there exists an $a \in (\text{NAT}^{\bot})^{\mathbb{N}}$ such that $\mathbb{N}, \beta[a/x] \models z(x) = x$ holds. But this is true if we choose $a = 1$:

$z(x)^{\mathbb{N}}[\beta[a/x]] = z^{\mathbb{N}}[\beta[a/x]]\,(x^{\mathbb{N}}[\beta[a/x]]) = z^{\mathbb{N}}[\beta]\,(a) = \text{fac}(1) = 1 = x^{\mathbb{N}}[\beta[a/x]]$.

As a last example we examine the validity $\mathbb{N}, \beta \models \forall x{:}\mathsf{NAT}^{\perp} \Rightarrow x = \mathsf{zero} \rightarrow z(x) = \mathsf{succ(zero)}$. This is equivalent to $\mathbb{N}, \beta[a/x] \models x = \mathsf{zero} \rightarrow z(x) = \mathsf{succ(zero)}$ for all $a \in (\mathsf{NAT}^{\perp})^{\mathbb{N}}$ which in turn holds if and only if for all $a \in (\mathsf{NAT}^{\perp})^{\mathbb{N}}$

$$\mathbb{N}, \beta[a/x] \models z(x) = \mathsf{succ(zero)} \quad \text{whenever} \quad \mathbb{N}, \beta[a/x] \models x = \mathsf{zero}.$$

For the last condition it is sufficient and necessary that

$$a = x^{\mathbb{N}}[\beta[a/x]] = \mathsf{zero}^{\mathbb{N}}[\beta[a/x]] = \mathsf{zero}^{\mathbb{N}} = 0.$$

But in that case we also get

$$z(x)^{\mathbb{N}}[\beta[a/x]] = \mathrm{fac}(0) = 1 = \mathsf{succ(zero)}^{\mathbb{N}}[\beta[a/x]]$$

whence the validity $\mathbb{N}, \beta \models \forall x{:}\mathsf{NAT}^{\perp} \Rightarrow x = \mathsf{zero} \rightarrow z(x) = \mathsf{succ(zero)}$ follows.

2.1.3.3. Higher Order Specifications and Their Models

Now we are in a position to define the central notion of this paper, a higher order specification. Such a specification consists of a syntactic and a semantic part. The latter is described by axioms.

***Definition*:** A *higher order specification* $T = (\Sigma, E)$ consists of a higher order signature Σ and a set E of axioms, i.e. of arbitrary closed formulas.

The axioms are to characterize the essential properties of a data type. A specification should both enable a programmer to implement the data type and enable a user to use it at the same time. The only but important conditions are that the implementation is a model of the specification and that the user does not restrict the model class by assuming further axioms for its usage.

The class of all models is defined as follows.

***Definition*:** A Σ-function space algebra A is called a *model* of T iff $A \models \varphi$ holds for all $\varphi \in E$. The class of all models of T is denoted by MOD(T). (Note that MOD(T) may be empty. In this case T is said to be *inconsistent*.

In order to stay close to the familiar framework of denotational semantics, we consider only first order term-generated Σ-algebras as candidates for models of T. We explained this notion in the chapter on term-generatedness. The definition of the relevant models of a specification (which is the basis for our further considerations) reads as follows.

***Definition*:** A first order term-generated Σ-algebra A is called a *first order term-generated model* of T iff $A \models \varphi$ holds for all $\varphi \in E$. The class of all first order term-generated models of T is denoted by GEN(T).

***Example*:** We extend the higher order signature of our little example by a set of axioms in the following way.

```
package NAT_EX is
   type NAT is private;
   zero: NAT⊥;
   succ: NAT⊥ --> NAT⊥;
   predicate iszero: NAT⊥;
axiom for all x:NAT⊥; x1:NAT⊥ ⇒
   defined zero,
   defined x ↔ defined succ(x),
   succ(x) = succ(x1) → x = x1,
   iszero(zero),
   not ( iszero(succ(x)) );
end NAT_EX;
```

A few remarks on the syntax used: The axioms in a higher order specification are marked by the keyword **axiom**. Instead of the logical symbols $\neg$, $\wedge$, $\vee$, $\forall$, $\exists$ we use the keywords **not**, **and**, **or**, **for all**, **exist**, respectively. An axiom of the form

$$\forall x_1{:}t_1; \dots ; x_n{:}t_n \Rightarrow \varphi_1, \dots , \varphi_m$$

where $x_1, \dots , x_n$ are different variables and $\varphi_1, \dots , \varphi_m$ are formulas is an abbreviation for the formula

$$\forall x_1{:}t_1 \Rightarrow (\dots \Rightarrow (\forall x_n{:}t_n \Rightarrow \varphi_1 \wedge \dots \wedge \varphi_m) \dots).$$

The higher order specification NAT_EX consists of the signature

$$\Sigma_{NAT\_EX} = (\{NAT\}, \{zero, succ\}, \{iszero\}, fct)$$

end the set of axioms (only one in this example)

$$E_{NAT\_EX} = \{ \forall x{:}NAT^{\perp} \Rightarrow \forall x1{:}NAT^{\perp} \Rightarrow \textbf{defined}\ zero \wedge \textbf{defined}\ x \leftrightarrow \textbf{defined}\ succ(x) \wedge succ(x) = succ(x1) \rightarrow x = x1 \wedge iszero(zero) \wedge \neg\, iszero(succ(x)) \}$$

2.1.3.4. Hierarchical Specifications

While a specification grows it becomes more and more unreadable. Sooner or later the pure amount of axioms becomes incomprehensible to a human reader. Therefore, we need a means to structure specifications. "Structuring of specifications leads to hierarchies of types: A hierarchical abstract type contains a designated primitive subtype (which may again be a hierarchical type) that can be understood, analysed, and implemented on its own, that is, without using any information about the overall type. On the other hand, the enclosing type can be viewed as a 'black box' the behavior of which is given by the effects in the primitive type. This reflects a basic method in computer science: Nonprimitive objects are semantically explained by the effects they have within arbitrary primitive contexts ('visible' or 'observable' behavior, 'input-output' behavior)" ([Wirsing et al. 83]).

***Definition*:** A *hierarchical* (*higher order*) *specification* T is either a higher order specification (Σ, E) or a triple (Σ, E, T_P) where the hierarchical specification T_P with signature Σ_P and axioms E_P is a subspecification of T, i.e. it is contained in T: $\Sigma_P \subseteq \Sigma$, $E_P \subseteq E$.

T_P is called the *primitive subspecification* of T, and the sorts as well as the function and predicate symbols in Σ_P are called *primitive*.

As models of hierarchical specifications we consider only hierarchical models which are defined as follows (cf. [Wirsing et al. 83]).

Definition: Let $T = (\Sigma, E, T_P)$ be a hierarchical specification. A Σ-algebra A is called a *hierarchical model* of T if A is a first-order term-generated model of (Σ, E) and its Σ_P-reduct $A|_{\Sigma_P}$ is a hierarchical model of T_P.

Example: We base the specification of stacks on that of natural numbers.

```
with NAT_EX;
package STACK_EX is
   type STACK is private;
   empty: STACK⊥;
   push: NAT⊥ x STACK⊥ --> STACK⊥;
   pop: STACK⊥ --> STACK⊥;
   top: STACK⊥ --> NAT⊥;
   predicate isempty: STACK⊥;
axiom for all x:NAT⊥; s:STACK⊥ ⇒
   defined empty,
   defined x and defined s ↔ defined push(x,s),
   pop(push(x,s)) = s,
   top(push(x,s)) = x,
   isempty(empty),
   not isempty(push(x,s));
end STACK_EX;
```

The primitive part of a specification is marked by the keyword **with**. Hence in the example the higher order specification NAT_EX is the primitive subspecification of the hierarchical specification STACK_EX = (Σ_{STACK_EX}, E_{STACK_EX}, NAT_EX). Its signature is

Σ_{STACK_EX} =

({NAT, STACK}, {zero, succ, empty, push, pop, top}, {iszero, isempty}, fct)

where the functionalities are defined according to the package STACK_EX. The set of axioms E_{STACK_EX} is the axiom of NAT_EX together with the one of the package STACK_EX.

2.1.3.5. Parameterized Specifications

Strongly connected with the structuring of specifications is the concept of parameterized specifications. One reason for introducing parameters to specifications is again to structure large specifications and to divide them into smaller parts. This is, of course, not the whole story since we already posess a means to structure specifications by hierarchies. The more important reason for parameterized specifications is that with this notion we are able to build specifications without the explicit knowledge of the underlying structure. It is possible to construct stacks, queues, lists, streams, and so on over a formal parameter which can lateron be instantiated with an actual parameter. By this means one is able to specify streams of booleans, of the natural numbers, of actions, and of whatever has previously been specified.

The semantics of a parameterized specification is the class of all algebras which are relatively first-order term-generated w.r.t. the formal parameter sorts. For the technical details we refer to the formal semantics in part II chapter 3.

The keyword in PA^{nn}dA-S that indicates the definition of a parameterized specification is **generic**. We give an example for its usage.

***Example*:** We base the above specification of stacks on a formal parameter ITEM instead of a previously fixed specification like that of natural numbers.

```
generic
   type ITEM is private;
package PAR_STACK is
   type STACK is private;
   empty: STACK⊥;
   push: ITEM⊥ × STACK⊥ --> STACK⊥;
   pop: STACK⊥ --> STACK⊥;
   top: STACK⊥ --> ITEM⊥;
   predicate isempty: STACKV;
axiom for all i:ITEM⊥; s:STACK⊥ ⇒
   defined empty,
   defined i and defined s ↔ defined push(i,s),
   pop(push(i,s)) = s,
   top(push(i,s)) = i,
   isempty(empty),
   not isempty(push(i,s));
end PAR_STACK;
```

For the solution of concrete problems one will instantiate a parameterized specification with actual parameters. Let us assume that all actual parameter sorts are zero-order sorts. Then the semantics of a generic instantiation is exactly the hierarchical model of the specification which is obtained by textual substitution (for the technical details see the formal semantics in part II chapter 3).

The construct in PA^{nn}dA-S that indicates a generic instantiation is

package p **is new** g(act_pars);

Here g is the name of the generic package, act_pars is a list of actual parameters that correspond to the formal parameters, and p is the name of the instantiated package.

***Example*:** As example we instantiate the parameterized stack specification with the actual parameter sort NAT. By textual substitution we thus obtain a package with exactly the same semantics as STACK_EX.

```
with NAT_EX;
package STACK_EX2 is new PAR_STACK(NAT);
```

2.1.4. The Expressive Power of PA^{nn}dA-S

Up to now we described the kernel language of PA^{nn}dA-S. This language is very powerful due to the possibilities to use higher order functions as well as full first order logic. On the other hand, if one is mainly interested in specifying, say, first order functions by Horn clauses, programming can become pretty tedious. This stems from the fact that in these cases most of the formulas are valid only for defined elements, that the functions should be strict, and that the domains of functions are often restricted. To express all these properties in axioms requires lots of extra formulas. Due to this handling of the undefined cases even simple specifications become rather large. In order to cope with this situation we now present concepts which were introduced into PA^{nn}dA-S to ease programmers' lives.

2.1.4.1. *Characteristic Predicates*

In PA^{nn}dA-S we have the possibility to restrict the domain and the range of functions by characteristic predicates. This should be considered only as a shorthand notation as explained below. The need for this arises from the fact that a programmer often uses a function merely for parts of the involved domains.

Let t and t1 be higher order sorts and f a function symbol with functionality (t --> t1). Let P(x) and Q(y) be formulas wherein only the variables x:t and y:t1 occur. The axiom

axiom for all x:t $\Rightarrow$ P(x) $\rightarrow$ Q(f(x));

means that the function value f(x) is only guaranteed to satisfy property Q if x satisfies P. An axiom of this kind can be expressed within the specification of f by means of

f: (x:t :: P(x)) --> y:t1 :: Q(y);

***Example*:** We modify the specification of stacks of the last example. The behavior of the functions pop and top is relevant for stacks which are defined and not empty. In that case the result of these operations should be defined, too. We describe this behavior by specifying

pop: (s:STACK$^{\perp}$:: **defined** s **and not** isempty(s)) --> s:STACK$^{\perp}$:: **defined** s;
top: (s:STACK$^{\perp}$:: **defined** s **and not** isempty(s)) --> x:NAT$^{\perp}$:: **defined** x;

In the above example one usually demands even more, that is one wants to express that the application of pop and top is not defined if the stack itself is undefined or empty. Actually, such a situation occurs frequently in specification practice.

Consider f: t --> t1 and formulas P(x) and Q(y) again. It is very often the case that one expects an undefined result whenever P(x) is not fulfilled. That is, one often wishes to express an axiom like

axiom for all x:t $\Rightarrow$ P(x) $\rightarrow$ Q(f(x)) $\wedge$
not P(x) $\rightarrow$ **not defined** f(x);

This can be specified by another kind of arrow, ==>, which we call the "strong" version of the function arrow. It corresponds exactly to the above axiom if we use it in the function declaration of f in the following manner:

f: (x:t :: P(x)) ==> y:t1 :: Q(y);

***Example*:** We continue the above example. The result of applying the operations pop and top should be undefined whenever the argument itself (the stack) is undefined <u>or</u> empty. We can specify this behavior by

pop: (s:STACK$^{\perp}$:: **defined** s **and not** isempty(s)) ==> s:STACK$^{\perp}$:: **defined** s;
top: (s:STACK$^{\perp}$:: **defined** s **and not** isempty(s)) ==> x:NAT$^{\perp}$:: **defined** x;

Abstracting from these trivial examples, one can imagine that for first order functions a programmer is only interested in the specification of the defined elements very often. In order to cope with this wish there exists the possibility to mark the defined elements of a basic sort. If $s \in S$ then $s^{\perp} \in H(S)$ (i. e. s+ in the concrete syntax) stands for all elements whereas the bare sort name s denotes the defined elements only.

***Example*:** Now we are in a position to express the function declarations of the last example very elegantly. They read as follows.

```
pop: (s:STACK::not isempty(s)) ==> STACK;
top: (s:STACK::not isempty(s)) ==> NAT;
```

The domain in which a constant takes its value can be restricted in exactly the same manner. On predicates, however, a domain restriction does not have any meaning. That is, the specification

predicate p: (x:t :: P(x));

is transformed into the specification

predicate p: t;

Therefore we will not restrict their domains in the following examples. We now give a few basic examples which use these concepts extensively.

***Example*:** We present the specification of the natural numbers where we use all these possibilities.

```
package NAT_S is
   type NAT is private;
   zero: NAT;
   succ: NAT ==> NAT;
   pred: (x:NAT:: not iszero(x)) ==> NAT;
   predicate iszero: NAT⊥;
axiom for all x:NAT⊥ ⇒
   iszero(zero),
   not iszero(succ(x)) ,
   pred(succ(x)) = x;
end NAT_S;
```

Here the definedness of zero and the strictness of succ and pred is expressed by the function declarations. Further the totality of succ and the definedness of pred(x) for all natural numbers x different from zero can easily be deduced. Moreover the undefinedness of pred(zero) follows immediately.

Before we come to the next example we explain the notion of restricted quantification. Sometimes it is convenient to quantify not over all elements of a sort but only over those satisfying a certain formula. This will happen especially in the first order case when most of the formulas are valid only for defined elements. Then we can apply the above abbreviations in much the same way as we did there. That is, the axiom

axiom for all x:t :: P(x) $\Rightarrow$ ϕ;

(where ϕ is any formula) is an abbreviation for

axiom for all x:t $\Rightarrow$ P(x) $\rightarrow$ ϕ;

For basic sorts $s \in S$ and an axiom like

axiom for all x:s :: P(x) $\Rightarrow$ ϕ;

this means that the unabbreviated version reads as

axiom for all x:$s^{\perp}$ $\Rightarrow$ **defined** x **and** P(x) $\rightarrow$ ϕ;

We will make use of this in the next example.

***Example*:** The second specification is that of queues of a formal parameter sort ITEM. Note that in these examples the quantification is over the bare sorts s only (i. e. without ⊥).

```
generic
   type ITEM is private;
package QUEUES is
   type QUEUE is private;
   emptyq: QUEUE;
   stock: QUEUE × ITEM ==> QUEUE;
   rest: (q:QUEUE::not isemptyq(q)) ==> QUEUE;
   first: (q:QUEUE::not isemptyq(q)) ==> ITEM;
   predicate isemptyq: QUEUE⊥;
axiom for all i:ITEM; q:QUEUE ⇒
   isemptyq(emptyq),
   not isemptyq(stock(q,i)),
   rest(stock(emptyq,i)) = emptyq,
   first(stock(emptyq,i)) = i,
   not isemptyq(q) → rest(stock(q,i)) = stock(rest(q),i),
   not isemptyq(q) → first(stock(q,i)) = first(q);
end QUEUES;
```

***Example*:** The last example in this section is the specification of trees over a formal parameter sort ITEM.

```
generic
   type ITEM is private;
package TREES is
   type TREE is private;
   etree: TREE;
   node: TREE × ITEM × TREE ==> TREE;
   left: (t:TREE::not isetree(t)) ==> TREE;
   right: (t:TREE::not isetree(t)) ==> TREE;
   root: (t:TREE::not isetree(t)) ==> ITEM;
   predicate isetree: TREE⊥;
axiom for all i:ITEM; t1,t2:TREE ⇒
   isetree(etree),
   not isetree(node(t1,i,t2)),
   left(node(t1,i,t2)) = t1,
   right(node(t1,i,t2)) = t2,
   root(node(t1,i,t2)) = i;
end TREES;
```

Note that all these examples contain only first order functions. Then the use of the strong arrow in connection with the bare atomic sorts throughout leads to specifications with strict first order functions only. In these cases the resulting domains are all flat.

Therefore first order specifications can be dealt with as usual!

2.1.4.2. Subtypes

Often one uses the same characteristic predicates as restrictions for sorts over and over again, e. g.

```
x: INTEGER:: x>0 = TRUE;
```

In these cases it is very convenient to have a name for such a restricted sort. This is handled in PA^{nn}dA-S by the notion of a subtype. These are abbreviations for type expressions and they are declared by

```
subtype st is (x:t :: P(x));
```

If one uses the name st in type expressions or in quantifications thereafter, then st is replaced by its declaration. For example,

```
axiom for all x:st ⇒ ϕ;
```

will be transformed into a restricted quantification, namely

```
axiom for all x:t :: P(x) ⇒ ϕ;
```

Example: We specify finite and infinite sequences together in one sort. As usual we represent infinite sequences $(a_n)_{n\in\mathbb{N}}$ of items as total mappings from the natural numbers into these items (let´s call them $\mathbb{I}$), s: $\mathbb{N}^\perp \rightarrow \mathbb{I}^\perp$, such that $s(n) = a_n$, $n \in \mathbb{N}$. Finite sequences $(a_0,\ldots, a_m)$ are going to be represented by partial mappings from the naturals into those items. That is, the sequence $(a_0,\ldots, a_m)$ is represented by the function s: $\mathbb{N}^\perp \rightarrow \mathbb{I}^\perp$ with

$$s(n) = \begin{cases} a_n \text{ if } 0 \leq n \leq m \\ \perp \text{ else.} \end{cases}$$

Thus the indices which are not used are mapped to the undefined element.

Now we can combine the representations of finite and infinite sequences by the observation that these are functions s: $\mathbb{N}^\perp \rightarrow \mathbb{I}^\perp$ with the following property. If $s(n_0)$ is undefined for some $n_0 \in \mathbb{N}$ then s(n) is undefined for all $n \geq n_0$, too. By induction it is easy to see that this follows already if we demand merely that $s(n_0 + 1)$ is undefined. In PA^{nn}dA-S this property can be expressed by the formula

```
for all n:NAT ⇒ not defined s(n) → not defined s(succ(n)) ;
```

Positively formulated this reads as

```
for all n:NAT ⇒ defined s(succ(n)) → defined s(n);
```

With these considerations the specification of sequences consists essentially of one subtype declaration.

```
with NAT_S;
generic
   type ITEM is private;
package SEQUENCES is
   subtype SEQUENCE is s:NAT⊥ --> ITEM⊥ :: for all n:NAT => defined s(succ(n)) → defined s(n);
end SEQUENCES;
```

2.1.4.3. An Example of a Higher Order Specification

We conclude this chapter with an example that makes use of higher order functions. Many more examples can be found in [Dederichs, Grünler 88].

***Example*:** Using the last example of section 2.1.4.1, the specification of labelled binary trees, we specify a package MAPS. For every function f from items to items we specify a function from trees to trees that acts like f on the labels of the trees.

```
with TREES;
generic
   type ITEM is private;
package MAPS is
   package TS is new TREES(ITEM);
   map: (ITEM⊥ --> ITEM⊥) --> (TREE⊥ --> TREE⊥);
axiom for all i:ITEM⊥; f:(ITEM⊥ --> ITEM⊥); t1,t2:TREE⊥ ⇒
   map(f)(etree) = etree,
   map(f)(node(t1,i,t2)) = node(map(f)(t1),f(i),map(f)(t2));
end MAPS;
```

Note that we did not use strong function arrows nor domain restrictions in this example. This was done for good reasons. For example, think of map specified with a strong arrow. This would imply that the totally undefined function from items to items is mapped onto the totally undefined function from trees to trees. The latter function would map the empty tree, etree, onto the undefined element of $\text{TREE}^{\perp}$, especially. On the other hand the first axiom above tells us that this result must be the empty tree again. We would thus arrive at a contradiction (Note that etree is defined by declaration in TREE).

Again the consequence must be that one uses strong function arrows and domain restrictions for higher order functions with great care. A special section on this topic may be found in the semantics. It is part II section 3.4.3, entitled "Some Methodological Advice on the Use of the Strong Arrow".

2.2. Development of Implementations

*Michael Breu, Universität Passau**

Program development in the framework of PROSPECTRA is done by a gradual transformation of specifications. A transformation of a specification is correct, if the resulting specification is in the implementation relation with respect to the starting specification. The proposed implementation relation is a combination of model class inclusion, model simulation by standard homomorphisms and robust model simulation by weakening homomorphisms. These notions are extended to an implementation relation on higher order algebras.

In the methodological part of this chapter, it is demonstrated how to obtain an implementing specification from an abstract specification using standard homomorphisms in the framework of PA^{nn}dA-S. The presented method is then generalized to develop robust implementations, first by allowing more defined functions, then by allowing arbitrary orderings on types and using weakening homomorphisms. The main aim of the introduced methodology is the ability to carry out a step by step development together with the required correctness proofs within the framework of PA^{nn}dA-S.

2.2.1. Introduction

The rich expressiveness of PA^{nn}dA-S allows the description of an ADA-like package from the first formal requirement specification down to an algorithm-like functional specification. The development process includes several typical intermediate steps like

- changing the representation of elements of a type,
- refining the specification of a function and introducing auxiliary functions,
- proving properties of an intermediate specification.

The transition between intermediate specifications is done by a collection of transformations. Such a transformation from a specification A to a specification B is correct only if B is in the implementation relation with A.

The first purpose of this chapter therefore is, to give a formalization of the notion of implementation. A second aim pursued, is the methodological support for implementation development.

In the following we will call a specification that is to be implemented an *abstract* specification and an implementing specification a *concrete* specification (even if the specifications are only "more" abstract or "more" concrete relative to each other). The attributes abstract and concrete will also be applied to types, functions, models and elements of the carrier sets of the respective specifications.

The implementation relation will combine the three major issues *model class inclusion*, *simulation* and *robustness* already studied separately in several approaches. It is based on the following concepts

- Not all models of an abstract specification must be supported by a chosen implementation. *Model class inclusion* allows the restriction of the class of considered models in a development step. This was e.g. chosen for the algebraic specification language ASL [Sannella, Wirsing 83].

---

* *Author's current address*: Siemens-Nixdorf AG, EMSC AP 432, Otto-Hahn-Ring 6, D-8000 München 83

- The transition from one data representation to another is achieved by the concept of *simulation*. Concrete functions simulate the behaviour of the abstract functions on the chosen representation. This concept is mainly due to [Hoare 72] and was first applied to algebraic specifications by the ADJ-group [ADJ 78]. [Ehrig et al. 82] used the closely related *forget-restrict-identify* concept to describe an implementation of an abstract equational specification by an implementing specification. [Ganzinger 83] generalized it to parameterized specifications with observable sorts. A further generalization to observational concepts can be found in [Schoett 87].

  For the simulation concept we use the classical approach of homomorphisms to relate each concrete model with some abstract model. As already introduced in section 2.1.2.3 a homomorphism is a family of (partial) functions that map elements of the concrete carriers to the represented elements of the abstract carriers. Thus a homomorphism allows to change the representation of elements of a type, and to tag unused representations (i.e. elements in the implementing type that do not represent a certain defined element in the abstract type) by mapping them to $\perp$.

- The treatment of errors in implementations leads to the notion of *robustness*. In general computations with undefined result should not lead to nontermination, but rather return an error message (*error detection*) or even a reasonable result (*error correction*). For this [Broy 85] coined the notion of *robust* correctness. Robust (and also partial) implementations of algebraic specifications were also discussed in [Nipkow 87].

  Robustness is handled as a generalization of the simulation concept. Standard homomorphisms are generalized to weakening homomorphisms. With this notion functions can be robustly implemented by stronger defined functions, i.e. they may yield defined results outside the domain specified in the abstract specification. There are several applications of such an implementation relation in the program development process:

  - Specifications can be enhanced to *error specifications* by implementing a diverging function call (i.e. an application of a function to arguments outside its specified domain) by returning some error value.

  - The specification of a concrete function may cover special cases which are left undefined by the abstract specification. (Assume for instance a theorem proving function that "computes" the validity of a logical formula and is specified to return the result *true* in the positive case, and is undefined otherwise. Recall, this problem is semi-decidable. It may be implemented by a function that returns a correct result also in some negative cases.)

  - On types with a non-flat ordering functions are allowed to return more defined (i.e. stronger) results, e.g. the implementation of a continuous stream processing function may return "longer" outputs in cases, where the next output values are independent of the input values.

It turns out that the notion of robust implementation by weakening homomorphisms can easily be extended to higher order algebras and specifications.

Since (weakening) homomorphisms are families of continuous functions as any other functions in a specification, (robust) simulation can be seen as a special case of model class inclusion. Thus a development method can be given that treats implementation development as specification development by specifying homomorphisms. The starting specification is refined into an implementing specification by adding auxiliary functions and axioms and transforming axioms into theorems. Such a methodological framework for implementing algebraic specifications was already proposed in [Broy 89a]. In the framework of institutions, similar implementation strategies were already presented in [Beierle, Voß 87].

For readers who are just interested in an informal introduction to the implementation relation and method, an overview with an detailed example is given in the next subsection. Subsection 2.2.2 introduces some notations and gives the connection to the formal PA^{nn}dA-S semantics. The following subsection introduces the notions of standard and weakening homomorphisms. Subsection 2.2.4 then defines the standard and the robust implementation relation on algebras and specifications. Subsection 2.2.5 finally discusses methodological issues for developing standard and robust implementations.

2.2.2. Informal Description of the Implementation Methodology

In the following informal introduction we shall explain the notion of standard implementation, robust implementation and the methodology to develop implementations and demonstrate it with an accompanying example.

The development of an implementation can be viewed as a series of design decisions applied to an abstract specification. The developer starts with a specification that may have several models. This specification is then manipulated step by step (by e.g. excluding some inadequate models, or introducing additional sorts and functions), in order to get a concrete specification that is better adapted to the computational model of a target machine and/or allows a more efficient evaluation.

We use the example of a data type describing stacks of natural numbers that is to be implemented in a random access memory. Thus our aim is the development of an implementation for the following package:

```
with NAT, BOOL;
package STACKS is

    type STACK is private;
    est: STACK;
    push: STACK × NAT ==> STACK;
    isest: STACK ==> BOOL;
    pop: (s: STACK :: not isest(s)) ==> STACK;
    top: (s: STACK :: not isest(s)) ==> NAT;

axiom for all s: STACK; n: NAT ⇒
    isest(est) = true,
    isest(push(s, n)) = false,
    pop(push(s, n)) = s,
    top(push(s, n)) = n

end STACKS;
```

An abstract specification may have several models. When taking a certain design decision, in general some models of the specification are excluded.

In the STACKS-example it can be shown that all models are structurally equal, i.e. all models fulfil the same equations. We call such packages *monomorphic*. Hence in the following development no models will be excluded, but the specification will be revised: Some auxiliary types and functions will be introduced and the axioms will be manipulated.

A major design decision is in general a change of the representation of some type. In this case the abstract functions must be redefined to operate on the new representations.

In the following we present a design in four steps that carries out such a change in representation.

Step A

First, the basic types and concrete functions required by the implementation are introduced.

In the STACKS example we decide to represent a stack by an area in a memory that starts at location 0 and ends at address N. The elements of the stack are stored successively in this area. The value N+1 is stored in a register *stackpointer*. If the stackpointer contains 0, this encodes the empty stack.

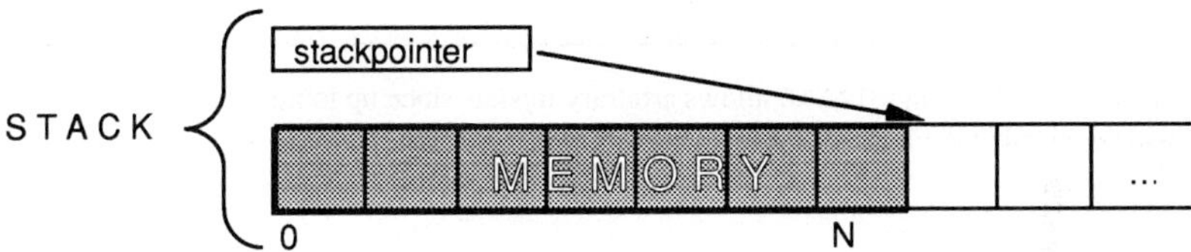

The memory itself can be viewed as a function mapping addresses (natural numbers) to the contents (natural numbers) of the respective cells in the memory. Thus we decide to represent a stack by elements of a type ISTACK, which is a tuple type ((NAT$^\perp$ --> NAT$^\perp$) $\times$ NAT$^\perp$) of a memory and a stackpointer. Also the concrete counterparts of the abstract functions

```
Iest: ISTACK;
Ipush: ISTACK × NAT --> ISTACK;
Iisest: ISTACK --> BOOL;
Ipop:  ISTACK --> ISTACK;
Itop:  ISTACK --> ISTACK;
```

operating on ISTACK are introduced. In PA^{nn}dA-S we can import the signature of the implementing package ISTACKS into STACKS with a **with**-clause:

```
with NAT, BOOL;
package ISTACKS is
   subtype ISTACK is (NAT⊥ --> NAT⊥) × NAT;
   Iest: ISTACK;
   Ipush: ISTACK × NAT --> ISTACK;
   Iisest: ISTACK --> BOOL;
   Ipop: ISTACK --> ISTACK;
   Itop: ISTACK --> ISTACK;
end ISTACKS;
```

```
with NAT, BOOL;  with ISTACKS;
package STACKS is

   type STACK is private;
   est: STACK;
   push: STACK × NAT ==> STACK;
   isest: STACK ==> BOOL;
   pop: (s: STACK :: not isest(s)) ==> STACK;
   top: (s: STACK :: not isest(s)) ==> NAT;

axiom for all s: STACK; n: NAT ⇒
   isest(est) = true,
   isest(push(s, n)) = false,
   pop(push(s, n)) = s,
   top(push(s, n)) = n;

end STACKS;
```

Note that the specification ISTACKS allows arbitrary models since up to now no axioms are included. They will be added in the further development step.

Step B

The second step now introduces the formal relation between the abstract and the concrete specification.

To relate abstract types and functions with implementing types and functions a mapping α from the symbols of the abstract specification to the symbols of the implementation must be given. This mapping is called a *signature morphism.* (A precise definition of signature morphisms can be found in subsection 3.3.3.2.8.)

As the chosen symbols suggest, the function est will be implemented by Iest, push by Ipush, isest by Iisest, pop by Ipop and top by Itop. I.e. α(STACK) = ISTACK, α(est) = Iest and so on.

After fixing the implementation relation on the syntactic level of signatures we must also give an relation between the abstract and concrete elements of the carrier sets on the semantic level of models.

Every element in the carrier set of an implementing type $\alpha(s)$ represents a certain element in the carrier set of the abstract type s. In general an abstract element may even have several representations. This can obviously be characterized by a function φ_s that maps representations to abstract elements. Such a function is called an *abstraction function.*

In the STACKS example the empty stack is represented by each tuple with 0 in the second component (the stackpointer) and an arbitrary value in the first component. Moreover every pair (f, N+1) represents a stack constructed by the term push(...push (push (est, f(0)), f(1)),..., f(N)).

This abstraction functions should have the properties of a homomorphism. To give a precise definition of homomorphisms let us retreat for a moment from specifications to models. Let A be a model of the abstract specification and C be some model of the implementing specification aimed to. For every carrier set $s^{\perp A}$ there exists a carrier $\alpha(s)^{\perp C}$. For every function f^A: $s_1, \ldots, s_n \rightarrow s$ in model A there exists a function $\alpha(f)^C$: $\alpha(s_1), \ldots, \alpha(s_n) \rightarrow \alpha(s)$ in model C.

The family $\varphi = (\varphi_s)$ of abstraction functions $\varphi_s:\alpha(s)^C \to s^A$ for all abstract types s map the representations to the represented elements. There may be objects in the implementing type that do not represent (defined) abstract objects. Those elements are mapped to $\perp$ by φ_s.

We say C is a *standard implementation* of A, if for every function f: $s_1, \ldots, s_n \to s$ from the signature of A and for all representations $a_1 \in \alpha(s_1)^{\perp C}, \ldots, a_n \in \alpha(s_n)^{\perp C}$, the property

$$\varphi_s(\alpha(f)^C(a_1,\ldots,a_n)) = f^A(\varphi_{s1}(a_1),\ldots, \varphi_{sn}(a_n)) \qquad (*)$$

is fulfilled.

In other words, the result of the concrete function $\alpha(f)^C$ applied to concrete representations of abstract objects yields a representation of the application of the abstract function f^A to the abstract objects. I.e. $\alpha(f)^C$ simulates f^A on representations. Given fixed algebras A and C, a family of functions φ_s fulfilling the laws (*) above is called a *standard homomorphism.*

A standard homomorphism is surjective on the term generated part of a model. That means, for every defined object we can find a representation.

Since in many applications we wish to implement functions by functions that return more defined results, the definition (*) above is too strong. Thus it is weakened to the following notion:

C *robustly implements* A, if for every function f: $s_1, \ldots, s_n \to s$ from the signature of A and for all representations $a_1 \in \alpha(s_1)^{\perp C}, \ldots, a_n \in \alpha(s_n)^{\perp C}$, the property

$$\varphi_s(\alpha(f)^C(a_1,\ldots,a_n)) \sqsupseteq f^A(\varphi_{s1}(a_1),\ldots, \varphi_{sn}(a_n)) \qquad (**)$$

is fulfilled.

In other words, the result of the implementing function $\alpha(f)^C$ applied to concrete representations of abstract objects represents a *stronger* object than the application of the abstract function f^A to the abstract objects. A family of functions φ_s fulfilling the laws (**) above is called a *weakening* homomorphism.

If the ordering on s is flat (i.e. $x \sqsubseteq y$ iff $x=\perp$ or $x=y$ for all $x,y \in s^{\perp A}$), the homomorphism property (**) can be simplified to

$$\textbf{defined}\ f^A(\varphi_{s1}(a_1),\ldots, \varphi_{sn}(a_n)) \to \varphi_s(\alpha(f)^C(a_1,\ldots,a_n)) = f^A(\varphi_{s1}(a_1),\ldots, \varphi_{sn}(a_n)) \qquad (***)$$

Lemma 3.2 in subsection 2.2.3 will show that on flat types for every defined abstract element there exists a concrete representation.

Condition (**) guarantees for any ground term t of type s

$$\varphi_s(\alpha(t)^C) \sqsupseteq t^A,$$

where $\alpha(t)$ is the translation of t by the signature morphism α. Often some carrier sets (especially primitive ones as BOOL or NAT) will coincide in A and C. Then φ_s will in general be the identity on those types s. If the ground term t is of such a type s, we get the property

$$\alpha(t)^C \sqsupseteq t^A .$$

I.e. the interpretation of a ground term yields in the concrete implementation C a value that is stronger than in the abstract model A, provided φ_s is the identity.

Now we can switch back to the specification level. The family of homomorphism functions can be specified as auxiliary functions in the package, mapping elements of concrete types to elements of the abstract types. If homomorphism functions are chosen as identities, they need not to be declared explicitly. The definition of the homomorphism and its homomorphism properties are added to the signature and axioms, resp.

The homomorphism function from type ISTACK to STACK is called *abstr*. The homomorphism functions on the basic types NAT and BOOL are assumed to be identities.

We want to use a weakening homomorphism to construct a robust implementation. Since the type STACK is flat, the simplified weakening homomorphism property (***) can be used:

```
with NAT, BOOL; with ISTACKS;
package STACKS is

   type STACK is private;
   est: STACK;
   push: STACK × NAT ==> STACK;
   isest: STACK ==> BOOL;
   pop: (s: STACK :: not isest(s)) ==> STACK;
   top: (s: STACK :: not isest(s)) ==> NAT;

axiom for all s: STACK; n: NAT ⇒
   isest(est) = true,
   isest(push(s, n)) = false,
   pop(push(s, n)) = s,
   top(push(s, n)) = n;

- -: abstr: ISTACK --> STACK⊥;                    - - auxiliary definition of the homomorphism abstr

axiom for all f: (NAT⊥ --> NAT⊥);  n:  NAT⊥ ⇒
      abstr((f, 0)) = est,
      abstr((f, n+1)) = push(abstr((f, n)), f(n));

axiom for all s: ISTACK⊥; n: NAT⊥ ⇒               - - homomorphism properties
   defined est →                  est = abstr(Iest),
   defined push(abstr(s), n) →    push(abstr(s), n) = abstr(Ipush(s, n)),
   defined isest(abstr(s)) →      isest(abstr(s)) = Iisest(s),
   defined pop(abstr(s)) →        pop(abstr(s)) = abstr(Ipop(s)),
   defined top(abstr(s)) →        top(abstr(s)) = Itop(s);

end STACKS;
```

The axioms added at the bottom of STACKS can be viewed as specifications for the introduced concrete functions Iest, Ipush etc. in ISTACKS. Note that the actual version of STACKS is not hierarchy conservative in the sense of chapter 4.10.1 (or hierarchy persistent in the terms of [Wirsing et al. 83]). I.e. not every model of the primitive package ISTACKS can be used to construct a model of the package STACKS. This deficiency will be healed in the following steps by refining the class of models of ISTACKS.

Note that the functions in ISTACKS are not specified uniquely. For instance it is not specified, whether Ipop should leave the freed cell unchanged or reinitialize it to 0.

Adding new axioms to a package P yields an implementation of this package, because every model of the resulting package is a model of P. Some models not supported by this implementation may be excluded.

Since we add only auxiliary functions, term-generation properties are not affected (see section 2.1.2.6 and 3.3.3.2.6). Hence every model of the constructed specification is a model of the starting specification.

Step C

In this step additional design decisions about the implementing functions are taken. In general the decision for a specific abstraction function already includes the basic design of the concrete functions. But as explained for the function Ipop, still some minor alternatives are open.

Now we add axioms to the package that define the implementing functions more explicitly (and perhaps more precisely). In general it may also be necessary to introduce some additional auxiliary functions. The addition of axioms may again restrict the class of models.

```
with NAT, BOOL;
package ISTACKS is

    subtype ISTACK is (NAT⊥ --> NAT⊥) × NAT;
    Iest: ISTACK;
    Ipush: ISTACK × NAT --> ISTACK;
    Iisest: ISTACK --> BOOL;
    Ipop: ISTACK --> ISTACK;
    Itop: ISTACK --> ISTACK;

--: undef: --> (NAT⊥ --> NAT⊥);                          -- additional auxiliary functions
--: upd: ((NAT⊥ --> NAT⊥) × NAT × NAT)   --> (NAT⊥ --> NAT⊥);

axiom for all f: NAT⊥ --> NAT⊥; n, d, m: NAT ⇒
    Iest = (undef, 0),                                  -- (1)
    Ipush ((f , n), d) = (upd(f, n, d), n+1),           -- (2)
    Iisest (f, 0) = true,                               -- (3)
    Iisest (f, n+1) = false,                            -- (4)
    Ipop (f, n+1) = (f, n),                             -- (5)
    Itop (f, n+1) = f(n),                               -- (6)

-- error correction:
    Ipop (f, 0) = (f, 0),                               -- (7)
    Itop (f, 0) = 0,                                    -- (8)

-- auxiliary functions
    not defined undef(n),                               -- (9)
    upd(f, n, d)(n) = d,                                -- (10)
    not n=m → upd(f, n, d)(m) = f(m);                   -- (11)

end ISTACKS;
```

Here an error correcting stack is developed that returns defined results, if Itop and Ipop are applied to a representation of an empty stack. Iest returns the pair of the everywhere undefined function and 0. Ipush adds an element to the cell pointed to by the stackpointer and increments the stackpointer.

Additionally we need the everywhere undefined function *undef* and a functional *upd* which updates the memory at a certain address. upd takes a function f, an argument n for this function and a result d. It returns a function that coincides with f on all points but n, where it returns d. These properties are expressed by the axioms (1) to (11).

Step D

In steps A, B and C we just tailored the class of models by adding axioms and auxiliary functions. Now we have to show that from every model of the implementation an implemented model of the abstract specification can be constructed. That means, in step D we have to show that the constructed specification is indeed a *conservative extension* of the implementing specification. To see this, the original axioms must be simplified significantly.

In our example we have to show that the original axioms of STACKS are derivable by the new added axioms, i.e. they are theorems based on the axioms added in steps A, B and C. This is not completely true, since the definedness information of the abstract functions gets lost when using weakening homomorphisms. Therefore we have to add axioms that specify the definedness of the abstract functions.

Then we can prove

a) *isest(est) = true*

```
isest(est)
  = isest(abstr(lest))          (homomorphism property and defined est )
  = lisest(lest)                (homomorphism property and defined isest(est) )
  = lisest (undef, 0)           (1)
  = true                        (3)
```

b) *isest(push(s, n)) = false*

Since we know that abstr is surjective on all defined elements of STACK, there is a representation (f, m) of s with abstr (f, m) = s. Hence

```
isest(push(s, n))
  = isest(push(abstr(f, m), n))
  = isest(abstr(lpush((f, m), n)))    (homomorphism property and defined push(s, n))
  = lisest(lpush((f, m), n))          (homomorphism property and defined isest(push(s, n)))
  = lisest(upd(f, m, n), m+1)         (2)
  = false                             (4)
```

c) *pop(push(s, n)) = s*

For this proof we need the lemma abstr(upd(f, m, n), m) = abstr(f, m), which can easily be proven by induction on m.

```
pop(push(s, n))
  = pop(push(abstr(f, m), n))
  = pop(abstr(lpush((f, m), n)))      (homomorphism property and defined push(s, n))
  = abstr(lpop(lpush((f, m), n)))     (homomorphism property and defined pop(push(s, n)))
  = abstr(lpop(upd(f, m, n), m+1))    (2)
  = abstr(upd(f, m, n), m)            (5)
  = abstr(f, m)
  = s
```

d) *top(push(s, n)) = n*

```
top(push(s, n))
  = top(push(abstr(f, m), n))
  = top(abstr(lpush((f, m), n)))     (homomorphism property and defined push(s, n))
  = ltop(lpush((f, m), n))           (homomorphism property and defined top(push(s, n)))
  = ltop(upd(f, m, n), m+1)          (2)
  = upd(f, m, n)(m)                  (6)
  = n                                (10)
```

If the definition of the homomorphism and the concrete functions are too loose, the abstract axioms may not be derivable. Then the homomorphism and the concrete functions must be specified more precisely.

The signature of the starting package may also contain implicit axioms that describe the domain of a function, e.g.

```
top: (s: STACK :: not isest(s)) ==> STACK;
```

contains the implicit axiom

```
isest(s) → not defined top(s);
```

Also those axioms must be proved that guarantee the correctness of the constructed implementation.

In our example, we have to add six axioms that show the definedness of est, push, pop and top. Then the final specification is

```
with NAT, BOOL; with ISTACKS;
package STACKS is

    type STACK is private;
    est: STACK;
    push: (STACK × NAT) ==> STACK;
    isest: STACK ==> BOOL;
    pop: (s: STACK :: not isest(s)) ==> STACK;
    top: (s: STACK :: not isest(s)) ==> NAT;

-- the following axioms can be derived from the remaining axioms
-- axiom for all s: STACK; n: NAT ⇒
--  isest(est) = true,
--  isest(push(s, n)) = false,
--  pop(push(s, n)) = s,
--  top(push(s, n)) = n;

    abstr: ISTACK⊥ --> STACK⊥;                    -- definition of the homomorphism abstr
axiom for all f: (NAT⊥ —> NAT⊥); n: NAT⊥ ⇒
        abstr((f, 0)) = est,
        abstr((f, n+1)) = push(abstr((f, n)), f(n));

axiom for all s: ISTACK⊥, n: NAT⊥ ⇒              -- homomorphism properties
    defined est() → est() = abstr(lest),
    defined push(abstr(s), n) → push(abstr(s), n) = abstr(lpush(s, n)),
    defined isest(abstr(s)) → isest(abstr(s)) = lisest(s),
    defined pop(abstr(s)) → pop(abstr(s)) = abstr(lpop(s)),
    defined top(abstr(s)) → top(abstr(s)) = ltop(s);
```

```
axiom for all s: STACK, n: NAT ⇒
   defined est,
   defined isest(s),
   defined push(s, n),
   defined top(push(s, n)),
   defined pop(push(s, n)),
   not defined pop(est),
   not defined top(est);

end STACKS;
```

For the specification above it is easy to show that it is hierarchy conservative w.r.t. ISTACKS.

Thus we end up in two specifications. The abstract specification (STACKS) was gradually transformed into an interface specification that constructs abstract models from concrete models. In parallel another specification (ISTACKS) was developed that contains the concrete implementation of the abstract specification.

Conclusion of the Informal Part

The sketched development of an implementation can be completely carried out in the framework of PA^{nn}dA-S. Design decisions are expressed simply by adding new axioms which specify the new properties. Introducing homomorphisms can be seen as adding some auxiliary functions fulfilling the homomorphism properties. The correctness of the implementation can be shown by simplifying the abstract axioms, i.e. converting them into theorems and proving the hierarchy conservation of the resulting specification.

2.2.3. Basic Notations

Since for the implementation development the use of auxiliary (hidden) functions is essential, we introduce here the notion of a hidden signature. The hidden signature contains besides the elements of the visible signature also the identifiers and functionality of the auxiliary functions.

In the following a package is denoted as a triple (Σ, HΣ, E), where Σ denotes the visible signature, HΣ denotes the hidden signature and E is the set of all axioms of the package. The connection with the formal semantics of PA^{nn}dA-S (see part II chapter 3) is as follows:

A package **package** p **is** ds **end** denotes a specification SP = (Σ, HΣ, E), with

$\Sigma =_{def} DC[ds]$

$H\Sigma =_{def} AUX\text{-}DC[ds]$

E is the set of all (explicit and implicit) axioms in ds.

The class of models of such a specification SP is defined as

MOD(SP) $=_{def}$ {val(σ, **pack**, p); DL_σ[**package** p **is** ds **end**](σ), where σ is an environment}.

Note that the model class only contains Σ-algebras, not HΣ-algebras.

Definition 3.0 (signature morphism)

A *signature morphism* α from a higher order signature $\Sigma_1 = (S_1, F_1, P_1, fct_1)$ into a higher order signature $\Sigma_2 = (S_2, F_2, P_2, fct_2)$ is a triple $(\alpha_S, \alpha_F, \alpha_P)$ of mappings $\alpha_S: S_1 \rightarrow H(S_2)$, $\alpha_F: F_1 \rightarrow F_2$ and $\alpha_P: P_1 \rightarrow P_2$ such that

$fct_2(\alpha_F(f)) = \alpha_S^*(fct_1(f))$ for all $f \in F$

$fct_2(\alpha_P(p)) = \alpha_S^*(fct_1(p))$ for all $p \in P$

(where $\alpha_S^*: H(S_1) \rightarrow H(S_2)$ is the pointwise renaming of the type identifiers by α_S).

Remark: With this definition of signature morphisms an atomic type may be mapped onto a higher order type, but not vice versa. Since we do not develop implementations for predicates, the predicate part α_P of the signature morphism is not used in the following.

Let $\alpha: \Sigma_1 \rightarrow \Sigma_2$ be a signature morphism and A a Σ_2-algebra. Then $A|_\alpha$ denotes the *reduct* of A w.r.t. α, i.e. the Σ_1-algebra B with

$s^B =_{def} \alpha(s)^A$ for all atomic types s in Σ_1,

$f^B =_{def} \alpha(f)^B$ for all functions and predicates f in Σ_1.

The symbol $\sqsubseteq \subseteq s^{\perp A} \times s^{\perp A}$ denotes the complete partial ordering on the cpo $s^{\perp A}$. The infix operation $\sqcap$: $s^{\perp A} \times s^{\perp A} \rightarrow s^{\perp A}$ denotes the greatest lower bound of two elements, if it exists. □

2.2.4. Homomorphisms

Definition 3.1 (Σ-homomorphism)

Let $\Sigma = (S, F, P, fct)$ be a signature only containing first order functions. For two Σ-algebras A and B a family $\varphi = (\varphi_s)_{s \in S}$ of continuous mappings

$\varphi_s : s^{\perp A} \rightarrow s^{\perp B}$

is called a *weakening* Σ-homomorphism, iff for every $f: s_1 \times \ldots \times s_n \dashrightarrow s \in F$ the following condition is fulfilled:

$\forall\, a_1 \in s_1^{\perp A}, \ldots, a_n \in s_n^{\perp A}$:

(*) $\varphi_s(f^A(a_1,\ldots,a_n)) \sqsupseteq f^B(\varphi_{s1}(a_1),\ldots, \varphi_{sn}(a_n))$

φ is called a weakening epimorphism, if all φ_s are surjective.

A weakening Σ-homomorphism φ is called *standard*, iff for every $f: s_1 \times \ldots \times s_n \dashrightarrow s \in F$ the following condition is fulfilled:

$\forall\, a_1 \in s_1^{\perp A}, \ldots, a_n \in s_n^{\perp A}$:

$\varphi_s(f^A(a_1,\ldots,a_n)) = f^B(\varphi_{s1}(a_1),\ldots, \varphi_{sn}(a_n))$

□

To ease readability, we omit the type index s of φ_s in the following, if it can be determined from the context.

Remark: Standard homomorphisms were first defined in [Broy, Wirsing 82] (but called *weak* homomorphisms there).

In general a weakening homomorphism φ from A to B does not define a congruence relation on A. But a standard homomorphism does.

Lemma 3.2 (surjectivity of homomorphisms on term generated algebras)
Let $\Sigma = (S, F, P, fct)$ be a signature only containing first order functions and A, AI two Σ-algebras.
a) A standard homomorphism φ:AI→A is surjective on the term generated part of A.
b) Let $M_s =_{def} \{ x \in s^{\perp A}; \neg\exists\, y \in s^{\perp A}\ x \neq y$ and $x \sqsubseteq y$ and x is first-order term generated$\}$ for $s \in S$, i.e. the set of all first order term generated maxima of $s^{\perp A}$. Then a weakening homomorphism φ: AI→A is surjective on M_s.

Proof

a) Let x be a first order term generated object in A, i.e. there exists a ground term $t \in T_{\Sigma,s}$ with $t^A = x$. By a simple induction on the term structure we can show: $\varphi(t^{AI}) = t^A$. Hence x is in the range of φ.
b) Let $x \in M_s$, then there exists a ground term $t \in T_{\Sigma,s}$ with $t^A = x$. By a simple induction on the term structure we can show: $\varphi(t^{AI}) \sqsupseteq t^A$. Since $x = t^A$ is a maximum in $s^{\perp A}$, we have $\varphi(t^{AI}) = t^A$. Hence there exists the element $t^{AI} \in s^{\perp AI}$ with $\varphi(t^{AI}) = x$.

□

Up to now, we assumed that the carrier sets of the target algebra of a homomorphism are just related by functions (and predicates) in the signature. A higher order algebra does also implicitly contain the apply operator and constructors for tuples. A homomorphism has to handle these implicit operators, too. To implement higher order functions we therefore need a notion of a homomorphism that maps objects of higher order types from one algebra to another algebra.

Definition 3.3 (homomorphisms between higher order algebras)
Let A and AI be higher order Σ-algebras, where $\Sigma = (S, F, P, fct)$ is an arbitrary signature. Let $\varphi = (\varphi_s)_{s \in H(S)}$ be a family of continuous mappings from A to AI with φ_s: $s^{\perp AI} \rightarrow s^{\perp A}$. Then φ is called a *weakening higher order homomorphism*, iff

$\varphi_{(s1 \times \ldots \times sn)}(x_1, \ldots, x_n) = (\varphi_{s1}(x_1), \ldots, \varphi_{sn}(x_n))$
for $(s1 \times \ldots \times sn) \in H(S)$ and $x_1 \in s_1^{\perp AI}, \ldots, x_n \in s_n^{\perp AI}$

$\varphi_{s2}(g(x)) \sqsupseteq \varphi_{s1\rightarrow s2}(g)\varphi_{s1}(x)$
for $s_1 \text{-->} s_2 \in H(S)$, $g \in (s_1 \rightarrow s_2)^{AI}$ and $x \in s_1^{\perp AI}$

$\varphi_s(f^A(x_1,\ldots,x_n)) \sqsupseteq f^B(\varphi_{s_1}(x_1),\ldots, \varphi_{s_n}(x_n))$
for every $f \in F$ and all $x_1 \in s_1^{\perp A}, \ldots, x_n \in s_n^{\perp A}$.

□

Note: No notion of a *"standard" higher order homomorphism* has been defined, because in general, the existence of a standard homomorphism on the atomic types does not imply the existence of a standard higher order homomorphism. We will give a counterexample 4.5 in subsection 2.2.4. For a weakening higher order homomorphism the following lemma shows that is is not necessary to construct infinitely many homomorphism functions. It is sufficient to define the homomorphism functions only for those types that are atomic or appear in the functionality of an abstract function. All other homomorphism functions can be supplemented implicitly such that they fulfil the properties of a weakening higher order homomorphism. This result is vital for the following methodological part, because only a finite number of auxiliary functions must be declared.

Lemma 3.4

Let $\Sigma = (S, F, P, fct)$ be a higher order signature and A and AI Σ-algebras.

Let $U \subseteq H(S)$ be a set of types with

$S \subseteq U$, $fct(f) \in U$ for all $f \in F$,

and if $s_1 \rightarrow s_2 \in U$ or $(s_1 \times \ldots \times s_n) \in U$ then also $s_1, s_2, \ldots, s_n \in U$.

If $\varphi = (\varphi_s)_{s \in U}$ a family of continuous mappings from A to AI with φ_s: $s^{\perp AI} \rightarrow s^{\perp A}$ with

$\varphi_{(s1 \times \ldots \times sn)}(x_1, \ldots, x_n) = (\varphi_{s1}(x_1), \ldots, \varphi_{sn}(x_n))$

for $(s1 \times \ldots \times sn) \in U$ and $x_1 \in s_1{}^{\perp AI}, \ldots, x_n \in s_n{}^{\perp AI}$

$\varphi_{s2}(g(x)) \sqsupseteq \varphi_{s1 \rightarrow s2}(g)\varphi_{s1}(x)$

for $s_1 \text{-->} s_2 \in U$, $g \in (s_1 \rightarrow s_2)^{AI}$ and $x \in s_1{}^{\perp AI}$

$\varphi_s(f^A(x_1, \ldots, x_n)) \sqsupseteq f^B(\varphi_{s1}(x_1), \ldots, \varphi_{sn}(x_n))$

for every $f \in F$ and all $x_1 \in s_1{}^{\perp A}, \ldots, x_n \in s_n{}^{\perp A}$

then it can be extended to a weakening higher order homomorphism $\underline{\varphi} = (\underline{\varphi}_s)_{s \in H(S)}$ from AI to A with $\underline{\varphi}_s = \varphi_s$ for $s \in U$.

Proof

Since there are no function $f \in F$, we can define the remaining $\underline{\varphi}_s$ with $s \notin U$ as the following mappings:

$\underline{\varphi}_{(s1 \times \ldots \times sn)}(x_1, \ldots, x_n) =_{def} (\varphi_{s1}(x_1), \ldots, \varphi_{sn}(x_n))$

for $(s1 \times \ldots \times sn) \in H(S) \setminus U$ and $x_1 \in s_1{}^{\perp AI}, \ldots, x_n \in s_n{}^{\perp AI}$

$\underline{\varphi}_{(s1 \rightarrow s2)}(x) =_{def} \perp$, where $\perp$ is the least element of $(s1 \rightarrow s2)^A$

for $(s1 \rightarrow s2) \in H(S) \setminus U$ and $x \in (s1 \rightarrow s2)^{AI}$.

It is easy to show that $\underline{\varphi}$ is a weakening higher order homomorphism.

□

2.2.5. The Implementation Relation

First we will investigate the implementation of Σ-algebras, where Σ only contains first order functions. We say that two Σ-algebras A and AI are in the (*robust*) implementation relation, if there is a weakening homomorphism from AI to A. In general it is more convenient to allow additional renaming of functions and type symbols, i.e. to use a signature morphism α from the signature Σ of A to the signature ΣI of AI. This also allows the implementation of atomic types by tuples or functional types. The homomorphism is then a mapping from the Σ-algebra $AI|_\alpha$ to A.

Definition 4.1 (robust implementation relation between algebras)

Let Σ be a signature only containing first order functions and ΣI an arbitrary signature. A ΣI-algebra AI is a *robust implementation* of a Σ-algebra A with respect to a signature morphism α: $\Sigma \rightarrow \Sigma I$ iff

there exists a weakening Σ-homomorphism φ: $AI|_\alpha \rightarrow A$.

This implementation relation on algebras is denoted by $AI \rightsquigarrow_\alpha A$.

If φ is a standard homomorphism, then AI is called a *standard* implementation of A w.r.t. α.

□

With this definition the result of a first order function applied to arguments outside its specified domain is left open for the implementation. In the implementation the respective function may return any defined value, some junk or error messages, or the call may even not terminate (i.e. may also be undefined).

Definition 4.2 (implementation of packages)

A specification SPI with signature ΣI implements a specification SP with signature Σ w.r.t. a signature morphism α: $\Sigma \to \Sigma I$, iff

for all AI ∈ MOD(SPI) there exists some A ∈ MOD(SP) such that AI $\rightsquigarrow_\alpha$ A .

This fact is denoted by SPI $\rightsquigarrow_\alpha$ SP.

SPI is a *standard* implementation of SP, iff

for all AI ∈ MOD(SPI) there exists some A ∈ MOD(SP) such that AI is a standard implementation of A .

□

Note: With this definition of implementation an inconsistent specification of a package (whose class of models is empty) implements every abstract specification if only the signatures can be related by a signature morphism. Therefore one could think of extending this definition to disallow inconsistent implementations. But why should the development of an implementation be burdened with an additional proof obligation? It is assumed that the chain of implementations ends in a machine executable set of function definitions (i.e. a monomorphic specification that allows exactly one model). This guarantees the consistency of the implementing specification and of every intermediate specification. It is left to the implementor to prove the consistency at some intermediate steps, in order to ensure the existence of a final (constructive) implementation.

Theorem 4.3 (Vertical composition, vertical composition of implementations)

Given three signatures Σ_1, Σ_2 and Σ_3, two signature morphisms α_1: $\Sigma_1 \to \Sigma_2$, α_2: $\Sigma_2 \to \Sigma_3$, a Σ_1-algebra A_1, a Σ_2-algebra A_2 and a Σ_3-algebra A_3. Σ_1 and Σ_2 do not contain higher order functions.

If $A_3 \rightsquigarrow_{\alpha_2} A_2$ and $A_2 \rightsquigarrow_{\alpha_1} A_1$ then $A_3 \rightsquigarrow_{\alpha_1 \cdot \alpha_2} A_1$.

Proof

Since $A_3 \rightsquigarrow_{\alpha_2} A_2$ and $A_2 \rightsquigarrow_{\alpha_1} A_1$ we know that there exist two weakening homomorphisms φ_1:$A_2|_{\alpha_1} \to A_1$ and φ_2: $A_3|_{\alpha_2} \to A_2$. We will prove that the composition $\varphi =_{def} \varphi_2 \cdot \varphi_1$ also yields a weakening homomorphism φ_3: $A_3|_{\alpha_1 \cdot \alpha_2} \to A_1$.

For all f: $s_1 \times \ldots \times s_n$ --> s ∈ Σ_1 the following holds by the definition 3.1 of weakening homomorphisms.

$\forall\, a_1 \in \alpha_1 \cdot \alpha_2(s_1)^{\perp A_3}, \ldots, a_n \in \alpha_1 \cdot \alpha_2(s_n)^{\perp A_3}$:

$\varphi(\alpha_1 \cdot \alpha_2)(f)^{A_3}(a_1,\ldots,a_n))$

$= \varphi_2 \cdot \varphi_1((\alpha_1 \cdot \alpha_2)(f)^{A_3}(a_1,\ldots,a_n))$

$\sqsupseteq \varphi_1(\alpha_1(f)^{A_2}(\varphi_2(a_1), \ldots, \varphi_2(a_n))$ (φ_2 is a weakening homomorphism and φ_1 is monotone)

$\sqsupseteq f^{A_1}(\varphi_2 \cdot \varphi_1(a_1), \ldots, \varphi_2 \cdot \varphi_1(a_n))$ (φ_1 is a weakening homomorphism)

$= f^{A_1}(\varphi(a_1), \ldots, \varphi(a_n))$

□

Remark: The same holds in particular for standard homomorphisms.

Example 4.4 (implementing stacks in a random access memory)
We will illustrate the explicit handling of homomorphisms with the example of the informal introduction. Let the package STACKS be as specified at the beginning of subsection 2.2.1. It will be proved that this package is implemented by ISTACKS as specified in step C of subsection 2.2.1.

Both packages are monomorphic. Let S be a model of STACKS, and IS a model of ISTACKS. We assume that the interpretation of the primitive packages NAT and BOOL coincide with the standard interpretation of natural numbers and boolean values. The signature morphism α is already indicated by the names of the types and functions: α(STACK) = ISTACK, α(est) = Iest, α(push) = Ipush and so on.

We have to find a weakening homomorphism φ from $IS|_\alpha$ to S. We assume that φ_{NAT} and φ_{BOOL} are identities and have to find a suitable mapping φ_{STACK}: $STACK^{SI|\alpha} \rightarrow STACK^S$.

Let for $f \in \mathbb{N}^\perp \rightarrow \mathbb{N}^\perp$ and $n \in \mathbb{N}$

$\varphi_{STACK}(\ (f, 0)\ ) =_{def} est^S$,

$\varphi_{STACK}(\ (f, n+1)\ ) =_{def} push^S(\ \varphi_{STACK}((f, n)), \varphi_{NAT}(f(n))),$

$\varphi_{STACK}(\ (f, \perp)\ ) =_{def} \perp$.

I.e. the pair (f,n) represents the stack containing the elements f(0), f(1), …, f(n-1).

We will now prove that this is a weakening homomorphism. It can be shown easily by induction on n that the lemma $\varphi((upd^{SI}(f, n, d), n)) = \varphi((f, n))$ holds. Thus we can derive the homomorphism properties by the axioms of STACKS and ISTACKS and the definition of the homomorphism φ.

Proof of $\varphi(Ipush^{SI}(\ (f, n\ ), d)\ ) \sqsupseteq push^S(\varphi(f, n), d)$ for all $f \in \mathbb{N}^\perp \rightarrow \mathbb{N}^\perp$ and $n, d \in \mathbb{N}^\perp$.

$$\begin{aligned}\varphi(Ipush^{SI}(\ (f, n), d)\ ) &= \varphi((upd^{SI}(f, n, d), n+1))\\ &= push^S(\varphi((upd^{SI}(f, n, d), n)), \varphi(upd^{SI}(f,n,d)(n)))\\ &= push^S(\varphi((upd^{SI}(f, n, d), n)), d) = push^S(\varphi((f, n)), d)\\ &\sqsubseteq push^S(\varphi((f, n)), d)\end{aligned}$$

Proof of $\varphi(Ipop^{SI}(f, n)\ ) \sqsupseteq pop^S(\varphi(f, n)\ )$ for all $f \in \mathbb{N}^\perp \rightarrow \mathbb{N}^\perp$ and $n \in \mathbb{N}^\perp$.

$\varphi(Ipop^{SI}(f, 0)\ ) = \varphi(f, 0) = est^S \sqsupseteq \perp = pop^S(est^S) = pop^S(\ \varphi(f, 0))$

$\varphi(Ipop^{SI}(f, n+1)) = \varphi(f, n) = pop^S(push^S(\varphi(f, n), f(n))) = pop^S(\varphi(f, n+1))$

$\varphi(Ipop^{SI}(f, \perp)) \sqsupseteq \perp = pop^S(\perp) = pop^S(\varphi(f, \perp))$

$\varphi(Itop^{SI}(f, n)) \sqsupseteq top^S(\varphi(f, n))$ can be proved analogously.

Proof of $\varphi(Iest^{SI}) \sqsupseteq est^S$.

$\varphi(Iest^{SI}) = \varphi(\ (undef^{SI}, 0)\ ) = est^S$,

Proof of $Iisest^{SI}(\ (f, n)\ ) \sqsupseteq isest^S(\ \varphi((f,n))\ )$

$Iisest^{SI}(\ (f, 0)\ ) = true^{SI} = isest^S(\ \varphi((f,0))\ )$

$Iisest^{SI}(\ (f, n+1)\ ) = false^{SI} = isest^S(push^S(\ \varphi(f, n), f(n)\ ) = isest^S(\ \varphi((f,n+1))\ )$

$Iisest^{SI}(\ (f, \perp)\ ) = \perp = isest^S(\ \varphi((f,\perp))\ )$

□

Note: Here we proved that φ is a weakening homomorphism, whereas in subsection 2.2.1 we proved that the axioms of STACK are theorems in the resulting package. These proof techniques are complementary.

We will now give a counterexample that a "standard" higher order homomorphisms between algebras with higher order carrier sets does not exist in general (cf. definition 3.3), even if there exists a homomorphism between atomic types.

Counter-Example 4.5

Let the algebras IS and S be as in example 4.4 and let $f \in [\text{ISTACK}^{\perp} \rightarrow \text{NAT}^{\perp}]^{\text{IS}}$ with $f((m, n)) = m(n)$ for $(m,n) \in \text{ISTACK}^{\text{IS}}$.

The tuples (m', 0) and (m'', 0), with $m', m'' \in [\text{NAT}^{\perp} \rightarrow \text{NAT}^{\perp}]^{\text{IS}}$

$$m'(n) =_{def} \perp \text{ for all } n \in \text{NAT}^{\perp}$$

$$m''(n) =_{def} \begin{cases} 0 & \text{for n = 0} \\ \perp & \text{else} \end{cases}$$

both represent the empty stack in IS. But, f acts different on these representations.

Let $\underline{\varphi}$ be a weakening higher order homomorphism that is an extension of φ (as defined in example 4.4), that has the properties of a standard homomorphism also on functional types. I.e.

$\underline{\varphi}_s = \varphi_s$ for $s \in S$, where S is the set of atomic types

and $\varphi_{(s_1 \times \ldots \times s_n)}(x_1, \ldots, x_n) = (\varphi_{s_1}(x_1), \ldots, \varphi_{s_n}(x_n))$

for $(s_1 \times \ldots \times s_n) \in H(S)$, and $x_1 \in s_1^{AI}, \ldots, x_n \in s_n^{AI}$

and $\varphi_{s_1 \rightarrow s_2}(g)\varphi_{s_1}(x) = \varphi_{s_2}(g(x))$

for $s_1 \rightarrow s_2 \in H(S)$, and $g \in [s_1 \rightarrow s_2]^{AI}$, and $x \in s_1^{AI}$.

Then we get

$$\varphi(f(m', 0)) = \varphi(\perp) \neq \varphi(0) = \varphi(f(m'', 0))$$

$$\quad \| \qquad\qquad\qquad\qquad \|$$

but $\varphi(f)\varphi(m', 0) = \varphi(f)(\text{est}^S) = \varphi(f)\varphi(m'', 0)$. This is a contradiction.

Hence in general we cannot get a homomorphism with

$\varphi(f)(\varphi(x)) = \varphi(f(x))$ with $f \in [\text{ISTACK}^{\perp} \rightarrow \text{NAT}^{\perp}]^{\text{IS}}$, and $x \in \text{ISTACK}^{\perp \text{IS}}$.

□

With the notion of weakening higher order homomorphism we can now define the implementation relation between general higher order Σ-algebras.

Definition 4.6 (robust implementation relation between algebras containing higher order sorts)

Let Σ and ΣI be arbitrary signatures. A (higher order) ΣI-algebra AI robustly implements a Σ-algebra A with respect to a signature morphism $\alpha: \Sigma \rightarrow \Sigma I$ iff

there exists a weakening higher order Σ-homomorphism $\varphi: AI|_{\alpha} \rightarrow A$.

This implementation relation on algebras is denoted by $AI \rightsquigarrow_{\alpha} A$.

□

Definition 4.7 (implementation of higher order packages)
A (concrete, implementing) specification SPI of a package implements an (abstract) specification SP of a package with respect to a signature morphism $\alpha: \Sigma \rightarrow \Sigma I$, iff

for all AI $\in$ MOD(SPI) there exists some A $\in$ MOD(SP) such that AI $\rightsquigarrow_\alpha$ A .

This fact is denoted by SPI $\rightsquigarrow_\alpha$ SP.
If even

for all AI $\in$ MOD(SPI) $AI|_\alpha \in$ MOD(SP),

SPI is an implementation of SP *by model inclusion* (i.e. the homomorphism is standard and the identity).

□

Note: By the notation SPI $\rightsquigarrow_\alpha$ SP we do not explicitly distinguish between higher order and first order implementations. This can be determined by the signature of SP.

We illustrate definition 4.7 by an example that specifies the apply operator explicitly. This operator is implemented by a functional *Iapply* that treats the application of a function f to the undefined data $\perp$ in a special way: if f is constant on all defined data, Iapply(f, $\perp$) returns this constant. Otherwise it returns f($\perp$).

Example 4.8 (implementing higher order functions)
Assume a primitive package DATA that contains a specification of a flat type DATA.

```
with DATA;
package APPLY is

   apply: (DATA⊥ --> DATA⊥) × DATA --> DATA⊥;

axiom for all f: (DATA⊥ --> DATA⊥); d: DATA⊥ ⇒
   apply(f, d) = f(d);

end APPLY;
```

```
with DATA;
package IAPPLY is

   Iapply: ((DATA⊥ --> DATA⊥) × DATA⊥) --> DATA⊥;
   undef: --> DATA⊥;

axiom for all f: (DATA⊥ --> DATA⊥); d: DATA ⇒
   not defined undef,
   for all c: DATA⊥ ⇒ ( for all x: DATA ⇒ f(x) = c ) → Iapply(f,undef) = c,
   (not exist c: DATA⊥ ⇒ for all x: DATA ⇒ f(x) = c) → Iapply(f,undef) = f(undef),
   Iapply(f, d) = d;

end APPLY;
```

Note that the definition of Iapply still leads to a continuous function, i.e. IAPPLY is consistent. APPLY and IAPPLY are both monomorphic specifications. Let A and AI be models of APPLY and IAPPLY respectively. We can assume that φ is a bijective function on the atomic type DATA, because APPLY and IAPPLY use the same primitive package. Then we can define $\varphi_{DATA \to DATA}$ by

$$\varphi_{DATA \to DATA}(f)\varphi(d) = \varphi(f(d)) \quad \text{for } f \in [DATA \to DATA]^{AI} \text{ and } d \in DATA^{\perp AI}$$

and analogously for all other functional types and tuples. Now φ is a bijective homomorphism on the function space:

$$\varphi(\mathrm{Iapply}^{AI}(f,\perp)) = \left\{ \begin{array}{ll} c & \text{if for all } x \in DATA^{AI}\ f(x)=c \\ f(\perp) & \text{else} \end{array} \right\} \sqsupseteq f(\perp) = \mathrm{apply}^{A}(\varphi(f), \perp),$$

$\varphi(\mathrm{Iapply}^{AI}(f, d)) = f(d) = \mathrm{apply}^{A}(f, d)$,

$\varphi(g(x)) \sqsupseteq \varphi(g)\varphi(x)$ for all $g \in (s_1 \to s_2)^{AI}$ and $x \in s_1{}^{AI}$ and the homomorphism property for tuples are clear.

□

2.2.6. A Methodology for the Development of Implementations

This chapter gives an outline for the development of implementations. The development is done by a gradual refinement and enrichment of a given (abstract) specification. This view of implementation development is an adaption of the method presented in [Broy 89a] to the framework of PAnndA-S. The philosophy of this methodology is to keep the logic. which is used to prove the correctness of implementations, simple. This mainly means to view a homomorphism just as a family of some auxiliary functions in the signature of a package. The properties of a homomorphism can be expressed in the logic of PAnndA-S. Thus the development of robust implementation is a by-product of implementation by model class inclusion. This allows the developer of an implementation to use PAnndA-S itself to carry out correctness proofs for the implementation relation. This is supported by the tools of the PROSPECTRA-system.

The general development idea is based on instantiations of the following three atomic development techniques that can be viewed as transformations of specifications:

1. Adding a set of new axioms **Ax** to a package:

   The developer may add new axioms to make a loose specification more specific or to change the definition of a given function (e.g. to make it a constructive definition).

   Since PAnndA-S has a monotone logic, the following relation between the model classes holds:

   $$\mathrm{MOD}((\Sigma, H\Sigma, E)) \supseteq \mathrm{MOD}((\Sigma, H\Sigma, E \cup \mathbf{Ax}))$$

   Hence

   $(\Sigma, H\Sigma, E \cup \mathbf{Ax})$ is an implementation of $(\Sigma, H\Sigma, E)$ by model class inclusion w.r.t. the identity as signature morphism.

2. Removing a set of axioms **Ax** that can be derived from the remaining axioms:

   Axioms that are derivable by other axioms may be deleted (more exactly: they can be converted to theorems in the theory of the other axioms).

   If $MOD((\Sigma, H\Sigma, E \setminus \mathbf{Ax})) \models \mathbf{Ax}$ *then* $MOD((\Sigma, H\Sigma, E \setminus \mathbf{Ax})) = MOD((\Sigma, H\Sigma, E))$

   Hence we have again

   $(\Sigma, H\Sigma, E \setminus \mathbf{Ax})$ is an implementation of $(\Sigma, H\Sigma, E)$ by model class inclusion w.r.t. the identity as signature morphism.

3. Adding new functions and types together with their axioms:

   It is allowed to import additional types and declare auxiliary functions together with some axioms. These additional types are not included in the visible signature, only the hidden signature is changed.

   Let $H\Sigma$ be a subsignature of $H\Sigma'$ and let E' be additional axioms over $H\Sigma'$.

   Again we have

   $(\Sigma, H\Sigma', E \cup E')$ is an implementation of $(\Sigma, H\Sigma, E)$ by model class inclusion w.r.t. the identity as signature morphism.

   Technique 3 is a generalization of technique 1.

These three techniques are used in the following to develop implementations. Since every technique restricts the class of models the following lemma holds:

Lemma 5.1 (correctness of basic development techniques)
A specification SPI derived from a specification SP by a series of development techniques 1, 2, or 3 is a *implementation by model class inclusion* of SP w.r.t. the identity as signature morphism.

□

2.2.6.1. Standard Implementations

To begin with the simplest case, first an implementation development with a standard homomorphism is demonstrated. We are starting with a specification ABSTR = $(\Sigma, H\Sigma, E)$.

```
package ABSTR is
   HΣ ;
   E ;
end ABSTR;
```

Step A

Create a new package CONCRETE that contains the signature ΣI of the implementing types and functions. We assume that ΣI and Σ only coincide on identifiers of common primitive packages.

```
package CONCRETE is
   ΣI ;
end ABSTR;
```

This package is included in ABSTR with a **with**-clause.

```
with CONCRETE;
package ABSTR is
   Σ ;
   E ;
end ABSTR;
```

This is a development technique of type 3.

Step B

The respective signature morphism $\alpha:\Sigma \rightarrow \Sigma I$ relating the signatures Σ and ΣI must be fixed. Function and type identifiers in Σ are mapped to function identifiers and type expressions declared in CONCRETE. The auxiliary declarations and axioms E" for the definition of a standard homomorphism φ are added. Elements in the concrete types that do not represent a correct object in the abstract type should be mapped to undefined.

```
with CONCRETE;
package ABSTR is
   Σ ;
   E ;

   φs:α(s) --> s ;                          - - for every atomic type s
   E" ;                                     - - axioms specifying the homomorphism

                                            - - for every function f with fct(f) = s1 × ... × sn --> s in Σ:
axiom for all x1:α(s1); ...; xn:α(sn) ⇒
   φs(α(f)(x1,...,xn)) = f(φs1(x1),...,φsn(xn));

end ABSTR;
```

This is again an application of a development technique of type 3. At this point we have a *specification* of the concrete functions in CONCRETE. In general this package ABSTR is not hierarchy conservative.

Step C

Now the development of the implementing functions can start. The package CONCRETE is augmented by additional axioms E' describing the semantics of the implementing functions.

```
package CONCRETE is
   ΣI;
   E';                                      - - axioms defining the implementation
end ABSTR;
```

Since the homomorphism φ is already fixed, the axioms in E" may give some hints, how to specify the concrete functions explicitly.

Step D

According to definition 4.2 every model of CONCRETE must implement a model of ABSTR. This leads to a proof obligation for hierarchy conservation of ABSTR w.r.t. CONCRETE. To facilitate this proof, the axioms enclosed in ABSTR should be transformed to simpler axioms. Therefore the axioms in E should be eliminated (or at least replaced by a set of simpler axioms).

For the simple case of standard implementation it is indeed possible to eliminate all axioms in E: The homomorphism properties

$$\textbf{for all } x_1{:}\alpha(s_1); \ldots; x_n{:}\alpha(s_n) \Rightarrow \varphi_s(\alpha(f)(x_1,\ldots,x_n)) = f(\varphi_{s1}(x_1),\ldots,\varphi_{sn}(x_n)) \qquad (*)$$

serve as an alternative definition of the abstract functions f. Therefore the specification of f in the axioms of E must be derivable from axiom (*), the specification of φ and the specification of α(f), provided CONCRETE is indeed a standard implementation of ABSTR.

```
with CONCRETE;
package ABSTR is
  Σ ;
-- E;     (these axioms are derivable from the axioms below and in CONCRETE)

  φs:α(s) --> s;                          -- for every atomic type s

  E" ;                                    -- axioms specifying the homomorphism

                                          -- for every function    f:s1x ...xsn-->s ∈ F(Σ):
axiom for all x1:α(s1); ...; xn:α(sn) ⇒
  φs(α(f)(x1,...,xn)) = f(φs1(x1),...,φsn(xn));

end ABSTR;
```

This step is a development technique of type 2. Additionally the hierarchy conservation of ABSTR must be proven. Appropriate proof methods are explained in chapter 4.10.

Note that the main design decisions are made in step A and C. There it is documented, how abstract types and functions are implemented. Step B supplies the definition of the homomorphism. In step D the correctness proof is done.

The development steps A to D lead to a specification ABSTR' that is an implementation by model class inclusion of the starting specification ABSTR. On the other hand the developed specification CONCRETE is an standard implementation of both ABSTR and ABSTR'.

Theorem 5.2 (correctness of implementation steps)

If the specifications ABSTR' and CONCRETE are developed from a specification ABSTR via the previous steps A to D and a signature morphism α, then

a) ABSTR' is an implementation of ABSTR by model class inclusion,

b) CONCRETE $\rightsquigarrow_{\alpha}$ ABSTR' $\rightsquigarrow_{id}$ ABSTR.

Proof

a) This is an immediate consequence of lemma 5.1.

b) Let AI be a model of CONCRETE. Since ABSTR' is hierarchy conservative, there exists a model A of ABSTR'. Then there must exist the hidden auxiliary functions φ_s that fulfil the properties of a standard homomorphism from AI to A. Since a standard homomorphism is also a weakening homomorphism, AI $\leadsto_\alpha$ A holds. By a), A is also a model of ABSTR. Hence CONCRETE $\leadsto_\alpha$ ABSTR' $\leadsto_{id}$ ABSTR.

□

2.2.6.2. Robust Implementation with Flat Types and Strict Functions

Now the development method is generalized in order to allow also weakening homomorphisms. This means that in step C "more defined" functions (compared with the original package) may be introduced. For simplicity we assume that for every function f: $s_1 \times \ldots \times s_n$ --> s $\in F(\Sigma)$ we have a domain predicate $dom_f\ s_1 \times \ldots \times s_n$ with

$$\textbf{for all } x_1{:}s_1;\ldots;x_n{:}s_n \Rightarrow dom_f(x_1,\ldots,x_n) \leftrightarrow \textbf{defined } f(x_1,\ldots,x_n)\ .$$

On flat types we can deduce:

$$\textbf{for all } x_1{:}s_1^{\perp};\ldots;x_n{:}s_n^{\perp} \Rightarrow \varphi(\alpha(f)(x_1,\ldots,x_n) \sqsupseteq f(\varphi(x_1), \ldots , \varphi(x_n))$$

is equivalent to

$$\textbf{for all } x_1{:}s_1^{\perp};\ldots;x_n{:}s_n^{\perp}\ dom_f\ (\varphi(x_1), \ldots , \varphi(x_n)) \rightarrow \varphi(\alpha(f)(x_1,\ldots,x_n) = f(\varphi(x_1), \ldots , \varphi(x_n))$$

if f is strict. Thus the homomorphism properties can be expressed without using the predicate $\sqsubseteq$. Step B is therefore changed to

Step B'

Instead of a standard homomorphism, a weakening homomorphism is specified by adding the transformed axioms above.

```
with CONCRETE;
package ABSTR is
   Σ;
   E;

   φs: (α(s)) --> s;                        -- for every atomic type s
   E"                                       -- axioms for φs

                                            -- for every function f with fct(f) = s1 × ... × sn --> s in Σ:
axiom  for all x1:α(s1); ...; xn:α(sn) ⇒
   domf x1,...,xn → φs(α(f)(x1,...,xn)) = f(φs1(x1),...,φsn(xn)),
   not domf x1,...,xn → not defined f(φs1(x1),...,φsn(xn));

end ABSTR;
```

To apply step D again (i.e. to deduce the axiom E by the properties of the implementing functions and the homomorphism) we need more information about the definedness of f. Since the homomorphism property only allows to deduce the behaviour of the abstract function if it is defined, we have to add

for all $x_1{:}s_1;\ldots;x_n{:}s_n \Rightarrow dom_f(x_1,\ldots,x_n) \leftrightarrow$ **defined** $f(x_1,\ldots,x_n)$.

The steps A and C remain unchanged.

Theorem 5.3 (correctness of implementation steps)

If the specifications ABSTR' and CONCRETE are developed from a specification ABSTR via the previous steps A, B', C and D and a signature morphism α, then

a) ABSTR' is an implementation of ABSTR by model class inclusion,

b) CONCRETE $\rightsquigarrow_\alpha$ ABSTR' $\rightsquigarrow_{id}$ ABSTR

Proof

a) This is immediately clear by lemma 5.1.

b) Let AI be a model of CONCRETE. Since ABSTR' is hierarchy conservative, there exists a model A of ABSTR'. Then there must exist the the family of auxiliary functions φ_s that fulfils the properties of a weakening homomorphism from AI to A. Hence AI $\rightsquigarrow_\alpha$ A. By a) A is also a model of ABSTR. Hence CONCRETE $\rightsquigarrow_\alpha$ ABSTR' $\rightsquigarrow_{id}$ ABSTR.

□

2.2.6.3. Robust Implementation with Non-Flat Types

The general method to develop robust implementations is by far more complicated, because the predicate $\sqsubseteq$ is not a built-in predicate in PA^{nn}dA-S. Therefore it must be defined explicitly. Step B' has now to be divided into two steps B_1 and B_2. In step B_1 the predicate $\sqsubseteq$ is defined on atomic types and extended to tuples and function spaces. We need the predicate $\sqsubseteq$ only for those types that appear in the codomains of the functionality of the functions in the signature. In step B_2 the weakening homomorphism φ is introduced into the specification. By Lemma 3.4 it is sufficient to define the homomorphism functions only for those types that appear in the functionality of any function in Σ.

Step B_1

We have to declare the predicate $\sqsubseteq$ for atomic types, and for every type appearing in the functionality of any function symbol in Σ

predicate $\sqsubseteq : (s \times s)$;

\+ defining axioms for $\sqsubseteq$ on atomic types

(e.g. on a flat type s:
for all $x, y : s^\perp \Rightarrow x \sqsubseteq y \leftrightarrow$ ((**not defined** x) **or** x = y))

\+ defining axioms for $\sqsubseteq$ on higher order types.

for all $f,f'{:}(s_1 \times \ldots \times s_n) \rightarrow s \Rightarrow$
(**for all** $x_1{:}s_1; \ldots ; x_n{:}s_n \Rightarrow f(x_1,\ldots,x_n) \sqsubseteq f'(x_1,\ldots,x_n)$) $\leftrightarrow f \sqsubseteq f'$

for all $x_1, y_1{:}s_1; \ldots ; x_n, y_n{:}s_n \Rightarrow$
$(x_1,\ldots,x_n) \sqsubseteq (y_1,\ldots,y_n) \leftrightarrow x_1 \sqsubseteq y_1$ **and** ... **and** $x_n \sqsubseteq y_n$

Step B2

In step B_2 now the weakening homomorphism and its defining axioms can be introduced:

```
with CONCRETE;
package ABSTR is
   Σ ;
   E ;

                                                  - - for every atomic type s and every type occuring in the
                                                  - - codomain of the functionality of a function in Σ
predicate ⊑ : (s × s);
                                                  - - + axioms for specifying ⊑ for every type s

   φs : (α(s)) --> s;        - - for every atomic type s
   E" ;                      - - axioms for φs

                                                  - - for every function f with fct(f) = s1 × ... × sn --> s in Σ:
axiom for all x1:α(s1); ...; xn:α(sn) ⇒
      φs(α(f)(x1,...,xn)) ⊑ f(φs1(x1),...,φsn(xn));
                                                  - - + homomorphism properties for function types and tuples

end ABSTR;
```

Steps A and C remain again unchanged.

Step D

In general the axioms E cannot be derived by the axioms for φ and the concrete functions, because the homomorphism laws $\varphi_s(\alpha(f)(x_1,\ldots,x_n)) \sqsubseteq f(\varphi_{s1}(x_1),\ldots,\varphi_{sn}(x_n))$ are too weak. But the axioms in E may be simplified significantly to facilitate the proof of hierarchy conservation.

Theorem 5.4 (correctness of implementation steps)

If the specifications ABSTR' and CONCRETE are developed from a specification ABSTR via the previous steps A, B', C and D and a signature morphism α, then

a) ABSTR' is an implementation of ABSTR by model class inclusion,

b) If in all models A of ABSTR' the interpretation of ⊑ coincides with the partial ordering on types, then CONCRETE $\rightsquigarrow_\alpha$ ABSTR' $\rightsquigarrow_{id}$ ABSTR .

Proof

a) This is immediately clear by the correctness preservation of every single step (lemma 5.1).

b) Let AI be a model of CONCRETE. Since ABSTR' is hierarchy conservative, there exists a model A of ABSTR'. Since in A the predicate ⊑ coincides with the partial ordering on types, there must the hidden auxiliary function φ that fulfils the properties of a weakening homomorphism from AI to A. Hence AI $\rightsquigarrow_\alpha$ A. By a), A is also a model of ABSTR. Hence CONCRETE $\rightsquigarrow_\alpha$ ABSTR' $\rightsquigarrow_{id}$ ABSTR. □

This method is very general. It has the drawback that the requirements to develop step B_1 and to prove the consistency of the implementation in step D can become rather complicated.

2.2.7. Conclusion

The basis of the presented implementation method is to view the development of an implementation as transforming a requirement specification step by step and proving properties of intermediate and resulting specifications.

The basic implementation relation is implementation by model class inclusion. It is well supported by the loose semantics approach of PA^{nn}dA-S. By adding new (auxiliary) functions and packages or axioms the implementation designer can reduce the associated model class of a specification, to that model class that is best suited for implementation. By proving axioms as redundant, package specifications can be simplified. The proof of theorems is supported by the verification system (chapter 4).

As demonstrated, also other implementation relations based on homomorphism concepts can be realised on top of model class inclusion, by specifying homomorphism functions as auxiliary functions. Generalizing classical homomorphisms to weakening homomorphisms allows error handling, especially error correcting functions. Implementations based on weakening homomorphisms can easily be extended to higher order types and functions. Employing these implementation relations also leads to the verification of hierarchy conservation.

One general disadvantage of this implementation method was exhibited in subsection 2.2.5.3: to use robust implementations in its full power forces the developer to use a very heavy and complicated logic calculus involving the partial ordering on types. Further investigations are necessary to supply tailor-made methods for certain kinds of orderings and specifications.

2.3. Distributed Systems

*Rainer Weber, Universität Passau**

We show how distributed systems can be described on different levels of abstraction using the specification language PA^{nn}dA-S developed in the PROSPECTRA project. The underlying formalisms are streams and stream processing agents. In particular we treat the question how to use these description formalisms in a methodologically sound way.

2.3.1. Motivation

With the increasing usage of parallel computing systems (multiprocessors, computer networks, etc.), questions concerning the development of programs for these systems have become more and more important. Therefore a practical approach to software development should also be able to tackle these problems.

We present the PROSPECTRA approach to distributed systems. It integrates a well-developed theory and methodology into PROSPECTRA: the streams and stream processing agents by M. Broy's group (cf. e.g. [Broy 89]).

So the purpose of this paper is twofold:

Firstly we show that distributed systems can be *described* using PA^{nn}dA-S with the different description formalisms by M. Broy, which vary in degree of abstractness. Thus the results achieved by his group can be applied within PROSPECTRA.

Secondly we provide an introduction for the reader who is not very familiar with distributed systems and wants to use PA^{nn}dA-S for specifying some particular system. In particular, we demonstrate how the formalisms for the description of distributed systems can be used in a *methodologically* sound way.

Transformations between the different description formalisms, however, are not treated here. We believe that in complicated cases transitions between these formalisms can hardly be done by transformations (for the topic of transformation cf. [Grünler, Dederichs 89]). We do not treat one complete program development process for distributed systems (for this topic cf. [Dederichs 89]), but we restrict ourselves to small examples illustrating the general techniques.

We assume that the reader has some general knowledge of fixpoint theory (e.g. consult [Loeckx, Sieber 84], chapter 4) and is familiar with the language PA^{nn}dA-S (its syntax and semantics, cf. part II chapter 3).

Section 2.3. is organized as follows: in section 2.3.2. we introduce the notions of the field "distributed systems" informally. Section 2.3.3. gives an overview of a design methodology for distributed systems, comprising different description formalisms. Sections 2.3.4. and 2.3.5. form the core of section 2.3. They describe the phases of requirement specification and design specification respectively, using the so-called stream formalism. In section 2.3.6. we touch on program notations for distributed systems. Section 2.3.7. contains concluding remarks.

---

* *Author's current address*: IBM, Europäisches Zentrum für Netzwerksforschung, Tiergartenstraße 8, D-6900 Heidelberg

2.3.2. Some General Remarks About Distributed Systems

What is a distributed system? There is no commonly accepted definition for this notion. Terms in the area of distributed systems are used in more or less different ways, like the terms *agent*, *communication network*, *process* or even the term *distributed system* itself. We introduce general notions in the field of distributed systems informally and clarify them by specific description formalisms in later sections.

Reflecting different aspects of distributed systems, terms like *concurrent systems*, *parallel systems*, *reactive systems* and *parallel programs* are widespread. Some people use the term distributed systems only for physically distributed systems (cf. below). We, however, will use them synonymously, because on the specification level this physical aspect is irrelevant .

There are several reasons for the use of distributed systems. The first is to achieve higher *performance* when running several computers in parallel, the second is to obtain *fault tolerance* by running several identical processes in parallel. A third reason is the need or wish to *communicate*. This concerns telecommunication, but more general also communication between several machines and users, like in factory automation or office automation.

A distributed system consists of a number of active entities, called *agents*, *processes* or *tasks*. They may be separated *physically* (e.g. in multiprocessor systems) or *logically* (e.g. several processes in an operating system). The agents operate in parallel, but in general not independently. Their aim is to fulfil a certain task in cooperation. To accomplish cooperation the agents *communicate*: they exchange data and they *synchronize*. Exchanging data can be done by *message passing* or by *shared memory*. Synchronization is necessary, because the concurrently operating agents may at some time request resources that cannot be used by all of them at the same time. There are various ways in which synchronization can be provided for, a possiblity again is message passing.

It is convenient to regard the environment, i.e. those components that give input and receive output by the system, as one part of the distributed system. For example, in a process control system the devices that are controlled by some control program and which give feedback signals to it are this program's environment. Often *environment components* are highly *nondeterministic*, a typical feature in modelling distributed systems. Thus we may regard a distributed system as a *closed system* where its components, the agents, do some "computing" independently, receive data or signals from other components, and send data or signals to other components. This mutual interdependence between the components justifies the term *reactive system*. Moreover, *real-time* aspects have to be included in certain applications. Then formalisms dealing explicitly with time are needed. We do not treat this topic here, but cf. [Broy 90] for the inclusion of real-time aspects into the stream formalism.

A variety of formalisms for the description of distributed systems is given in the literature. They can be classified by the way in which they treat certain topics. One feature has already been mentioned: the way in which communication is achieved (shared storage vs. message passing). Message passing can either be *asynchronous*, i.e. the sender transmits data at some time, the receiver reads them some time later, or *synchronous*, i.e. to enable communication, sender and receiver must be ready at the same time for this communication and perform a "joint action". Other topics are the way how the buffering is done, how information flows, the process dynamics (dynamic process creation vs. static process creation) and many more. For an overview cf. [Filman, Friedman 84], where a variety of models and programming languages for distributed systems is discussed and classifications are given. We just mention some of the models: *Petri nets* (cf. for example [Peterson 77]), various *process algebras* ([Milner 80], [Hoare 85], [Bergstra, Klop 86]), *communicating automata* [Bochmann, Sunshine 80], *stream processing agents* [Broy 89].

Furthermore there are programming languages designed for distributed systems, e.g. *Ada* [Ada 83], *Occam* [INMOS 84], *Lucid* [Ashcroft 77].

When several activities happen in parallel and affect each other, the behaviour of a system becomes much more difficult to understand. This problem became especially critical when distributed systems became larger, like those in telecommunications. For the description of such systems, structuring mechanisms like *modularisation* and *hierarchical decomposition* are used. A prominent example is the *ISO/OSI model* in telecommunication. Furthermore the need for formal specification languages was recognized. Due to the fact that telecommunication systems cross national boundaries (in high level networks), an unambigous description is mandatory for standardization purposes. The ISO languages ESTELLE (based on automata) and LOTOS (based on process algebra and algebraic specification) emerged as well as the CCITT language SDL (based on automata). Their application area is the specification of protocols used for telecommunication systems.

As well as for an unambiguous description, formal specification techniques are well-suited and indispensable for the correct design of distributed systems. The correctness of distributed systems is vital due to their application areas: they are used in production control systems, flight control systems, traffic control systems and many other areas where an incorrect behaviour would be disastrous. So methods used for designing distributed systems must be carefully chosen and theoretically sound.

2.3.3. Describing Distributed Systems

We present ways to describe distributed systems in different degrees of abstractness. The idea is to use these description formalisms in a *design methodology* as is usual in software engineering. This design methodology is due to M. Broy [Broy 89], and its applicability has been tested and proved in a variety of case studies, that in turn gave feedback to the development of this methodology. The case studies comprise a railway system [Broy 87a], protocol specifications [Broy 87b], [Streicher 87], a serializable database interface [Broy 87c], shared resource arbitration [Broy, Streicher 87], a lift controller [Broy 88a] and the specification of a gas station [Weber 91]. However, the design methodology does not depend on the PA^{nn}dA-S language. In fact it can be used in any algebraic specification formalism with sufficient expressive power. One representative case study has been translated into PA^{nn}dA-S [Dederichs 89].

In contrast to many life cycle models, we use for each phase a description *formalism* (with the stress on *formal*). In order to facilitate the development, we have to ensure that these formalisms are such that the transitions between the corresponding phases do not become too complicated. A certain *coherence* is important to meet this goal. The phases of this methodology are:

0. informal problem description
1. requirement specification
2. design specification
3. abstract program
4. concrete program

Actually, the informal problem description, as a starting point for our specification, is not part of the methodology. It is translated into a formal requirement specification.

There is a slight deviation from the terminology used in the PROSPECTRA methodology for the development of sequential programs (cf. the introduction in vol. I). Here we use non-constructive formal specifications both in a requirement specification and in a design specification. A design means identifying agents, for which there is no counterpart in the development model of vol. I. In our terminology a design specification comes close to a "requirement specification", an abstract program corresponds to the "design specification". We use this slightly different development model, because we think it is more appropriate for distributed systems and because it is also used in case studies done with our approach.

In the following we will explain the development phases and, more importantly, show how to use PA^{nn}dA-S for these phases.

2.3.4. Nonfunctional Specification: Requirement Specification

On this first level we describe the behaviour of a distributed system in an abstract and problem-oriented, but nevertheless formal way. As a first modelling decision we determine which *actions* can be observed in the whole distributed system. The actions are considered to have no duration, hence they are also called *atomic actions*. "Actions" that have a certain duration may be modelled by two actions, representing its start and its end respectively. We have chosen the *action oriented view*, but mention that in our description formalisms states can also be explicitly introduced whenever this is convenient in some application.

After having described the actions ocurring in the distributed system, we describe its behaviour as the set of possible sequences of actions.

In the following sections we demonstrate how to describe actions, sequences (streams) of actions and finally sets of streams of actions:

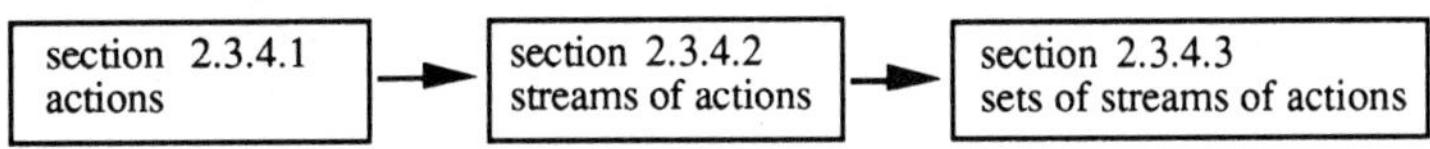

2.3.4.1. Describing Actions

Actions can be described using algebraic specification. The result is a package that includes the type ACTION.

Example: Actions at a gas station

When considering a gas station as a distributed system, we may regard the following observable actions:

- the arrival of a car at a certain line (queue),
- the acceptance of this car at the line if the queue is not full,
- the rejection of this car at the line if the queue is full,
- the start of the service of a car from a certain line at a certain pump and
- the stop of the service of this car at the pump.

In PA^{nn}dA-S this can be done in the following way, where we assume that cars, pumps and lines have already been described in the packages CARS, PUMPS and LINES respectively:

```
with CARS, PUMPS, LINES;
package ACTIONS is
   type ACTION is private;
   arrive: (CAR;LINE) ==> ACTION;
   accept: (CAR;LINE) ==> ACTION;
   reject: (CAR;LINE) ==> ACTION;
   accept: (c: CAR; p: PUMP; l: LINE :: not (p = A and l = L3) and not (p = B and l = L1) ) ==> ACTION;
   stop: (CAR; PUMP) ==> ACTION;
end ACTIONS;
```

In this simple package no axioms are given. We assume that the pumps A and B are declared in the package PUMPS and that the lines L1, L2 and L3 are declared in the package LINES. For the action accept an applicabilty condition (or precondition) is given. Accordingly, it does not hold that for every combination of a car c, a pump p and a line l accept(c,p,l) is a permitted action (cf. Fig. 2.3-1).

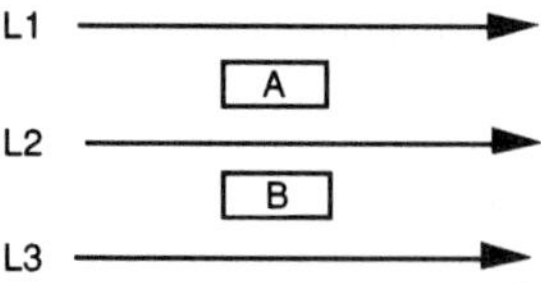

Fig. 2.3-1 A gas station

2.3.4.2. Describing Streams of Actions

Streams and Some Basic Functions on Streams

After having determined which actions are considered observable, we describe the *behaviours* of the distributed system. A behaviour can be observed when a run of the distributed system is made. A run consists of actions occuring in some order. Again we have to take a modelling decision: Can an observer notice whether two atomic actions are happening at the same time, and if this is so, is it useful to express this in our model? If we want to model that actions may happen at the same time, we use partially ordered multisets of events (also called *action structures* in [Broy 89]). This concept is called the *true concurrency viewpoint* of modelling distributed systems. Alternatively we may use sequences of actions (also called *streams* or *traces*) in the *interleaving view*. Here we can imagine that an observer writes in his notebook the order of the actions occurring in a run of the distributed system. When two actions occur simultaneously, he records one at first, then the other; the order in which he records them does not matter (This is also the CSP-viewpoint, cf. [Hoare 85]).

We decide to take the interleaving viewpoint, but point out that the following considerations can also be applied in the model of action structures, although the treatment becomes more complicated. The experience gained in the case studies shows that for our purposes (i.e. modelling and reasoning about the functional behaviour) interleaving is sufficient. Then the behaviour of the distributed system we have in mind is described by a set of streams.

Distributed systems often show unbounded or even *infinite behaviour*. Since we consider it mandatory to model also infinite behaviour explicitly, we include infinite streams in our description formalism.

The following package STREAMS, parameterized by the type ITEM, describes streams and some basic operations on them. In our applications this package is usually instantiated by the type ACTION or by some subclass of actions like input actions and output actions.

In [Dederichs 89] and [Grünler, Dederichs 89] a specification that differs from the one below is given. Nonetheless both specifications are equivalent. The difference is that in the former specification some information (concerning strictness for example) is provided within the functionalities of the functions and predicates whereas we prefer to include *all* information in the axioms. The former specification is shorter, but we think ours is more transparent.

```
generic
   type ITEM is private;
package STREAMS is
   type STREAM is private;
   es: STREAM⊥;
   ap : (ITEM⊥; STREAM⊥) ==> STREAM⊥;
   rt: STREAM⊥ ==> STREAM⊥;
   ft: STREAM⊥ ==> ITEM⊥;
   predicate is_prefix: (STREAM⊥;STREAM⊥);
axiom for all s:STREAM⊥; t:STREAM⊥; i:ITEM⊥ ⇒
   ft(ap(i,s)) = i,
   defined i → rt(ap(i,s)) = s,
   defined ap(i,s) ↔ defined i,
   defined rt(s) → defined s,
   not defined es,
   is_prefix(s,t) ↔ s = t or s = es or (ft(s) = ft(t) and is_prefix(rt(s),rt(t)))
end STREAMS;
```

By the semantics of PA^{nn}dA-S, every type is interpreted as a *complete partial order (cpo)*. This facilitates the specification of streams. They build a cpo with the *empty stream* as least element (the bottom element) and the prefix ordering as the intended ordering. Thus we have a non-flat cpo. For the question of the semantic consistency cf. the appendix of this section.

es denotes the empty stream. It is the first constructor operation for streams and the "least defined" element of sort $STREAM^{\perp}$. The second constructor is ap (ap stands for append). With an item i and a stream s it produces the stream where i is followed by s. The axioms and the semantics of PA^{nn}dA-S imply that whenever there is an undefined item in the stream, then the stream can be considered to end at this item. Thus whenever x is undefined, then

ap(1,ap(2,ap(3,ap(x,ap(4,...))))) = ap(1,ap(2,ap(3,es)))

for streams of natural numbers.

ft and rt are projection functions, yielding the first item of a stream and the rest of the stream when the first item is deleted, respectively.

The predicate is_prefix is true exactly if the stream s is a prefix of the stream t. Note that the empty stream is a prefix of every stream. If both s and t are infinite, then is_prefix(s,t) holds exactly if $s = t$. Because if $s \neq t$, then there exists a natural number i such that $ft(rt^i(s)) \neq ft(rt^i(t))$, and therefore is_prefix(s,t) does not hold. (In general for functions f, f^i is defined by $f^0(x) = x$, $f^{i+1}(x) = f(f^i(x))$).

Infinite streams can be obtained for instance by recursion. This is possible because ap is nonstrict in its second argument when this is of type STREAM (i.e. not equal to es). Thus s = ap(1,s) describes an equation with the (smallest) solution s = ap(1,ap(1,ap(1,...))) (which would be an *infinite* term; this is of course not allowed in PA^{nn}dA-S), the stream consisting of an infinite number of 1's.

Further Operations on Streams

For description purposes (like in a requirement specification) it is convenient to have some additional operations on streams. We include the following commonly used operators and predicates in the package STREAMS:

1) The predicate is_in:

```
predicate is_in: (ITEM;STREAM⊥);
```

Axiom:

```
axiom for all s: STREAM⊥; a: ITEM ⇒
    is_in(a,s) ↔ exist i: NAT ⇒ ft(iterate(rt,i)(s)) = a;
```

Here we use a higher-order function iterate. For an (endo-)function f and a natural number i, iterate(f,i) results in f^i. A definition of iterate is given in the appendix.

is_in(a,s) is true exactly if the item a occurs somewhere in the stream s. Note that a is a "real" item, not an undefined one.

2) The function filter:

```
filter: (ITEM;STREAM⊥) ==>STREAM⊥;
```

Axioms:

```
axiom for all s: STREAM⊥; a: ITEM; b: ITEM ⇒
    a = b → filter(a,ap(b,s)) = ap(b,filter(a,s)),
    not (a = b) → filter(a, ap(b,s)) = filter(a,s),
    filter(a,es) = es;
```

For an item a and a stream s, filter(a,s) filters the substream of s consisting only of a-actions. For example, filter(1,(ap(1,ap(2,ap(1,ap(3,es))))) = ap(1,ap(1,es)).

This function can easily be extended to SET(ITEM) instead of ITEM:

```
filter: (SET;STREAM⊥) ==>STREAM⊥;
```

Axioms:

```
axiom for all s: STREAM⊥; b: ITEM; m: SET ⇒
    is_el(b,m) → filter(m,ap(b,s)) = ap(b,filter(m,s)),
    not is_el(b,m) → filter(m,ap(b,s)) = filter(m,s),
    filter(m,es) = es
```

In this declaration we have used the type SET; we assume to have a generic SETS with parameter ITEM for this purpose. We will instantiate it for a specific application, e.g. with ACTION for ITEM, and define further axioms for specific sets of actions, in particular also for infinite sets of actions.

For an example, let us return to the example of the "Actions of a gas station" and define the set of stop actions (i.e. stop_actions = {stop(c,p) | c∈CAR, p∈PUMP}, which is infinite if CAR or PUMP are infinite). In PA^{nn}dA-S this can be written as follows:

```
with ACTIONS, SETS;
package STOP_ACTIONS is
    package A_SETS is new SETS(ACTION);
    stop_actions: A_SETS.SET;
axiom for all c: CAR; p: PUMP; a: ACTION ⇒
    is_el(stop(c,p),stop_actions) = true,
    (not (exist: c: CAR; p: PUMP ⇒ a = stop(c,p))) →
        is_el(a,stop_actions) = false
end STOP_ACTIONS;
```

3) The predicate is_finite:

```
predicate is_finite: (STREAM⊥);
```

Axiom:

```
axiom for all s: STREAM⊥ ⇒
is_finite(s) ↔ exist i: NAT fi iterate(rt,i)(s) = es
```

is_finite(s) tells whether the stream s is finite.

4) The operator length:

```
length: STREAM⊥ ==> NAT_INF;
```

Axiom:

```
axiom for all s: STREAM⊥; a: ITEM ⇒
    not is_finite(s) → length(s) = omega,
    defined a → length(ap(a,s)) = 1 + length(s),
    length(es) = 0;
```

length(s) gives the length of the stream s. The empty stream has length 0. An infinite stream has the length "omega". "omega" is defined in the package NAT_INF, a specification of the set of natural numbers plus a number ("omega") that is greater than all natural numbers.

```
with BOOL;
package NAT_INF is
    type NAT_INF is private;
    pred le: (NAT_INF,NAT_INF);
    zero: NAT_INF;
    succ: NAT_INF ==> NAT_INF;
    pred: (x: NAT_INF :: not x=zero) ==> NAT_INF;
    add: (NAT_INF; NAT_INF)==> NAT_INF;
    sub: (x,y: NAT_INF :: not (x = omega) and not (y = omega) )==> NAT_INF;
    omega: NAT_INF;
axiom for all x: NAT_INF; y: NAT_INF⇒
    pred(succ(x)) = x,
    le(zero,x),
    not le(succ(x),zero),
    le(succ(x),succ(y)) ↔ le(x,y),
    le(omega,omega),
    succ(omega) = omega,
    add(x,zero) = x,
    add(x,succ(y)) = succ(add(x,y)),
    sub(x,zero) = x,
    le(x,y) → sub(x,y) = zero,
    not le(x,y)) → sub(x,y) = pred(sub(x,pred(y)))
end NAT_INF;
```

5) The predicate is_concat:

We would like to have the operation of concatenation for streams. Unfortunately we cannot specify it in PA^{nn}dA-S as a function, because it is not monotonic and thus also not continuous. So we model concatenation by the predicate is_concat, using PROLOG style.

predicate is_concat: (STREAM$^{\perp}$;STREAM$^{\perp}$;STREAM$^{\perp}$);

Axiom:

```
axiom for all x: STREAM⊥; y: STREAM⊥; z: STREAM⊥ ⇒
    is_concat(x,y,z) ↔          - - z is the concatenation of x and y
        ( x = es and z = y
        or not (x = es and ft(x) = ft(z) and is_concat(rt(x),y,rt(z)))
        or not (is_finite(x)) and z = x )
```

2.3.4.3. Describing Sets of Streams of Actions

The streams of actions that may occur when a run of the system is made are also called the *traces* of the distributed system. We specify sets of streams by predicates of the form P(t) where t is a trace variable. This can be interpreted: the stream t is a "correct" trace of the system exactly if it fulfils P.

From a methodological point of view it is convenient to provide a number of requirements on the behaviour, i.e. on the traces, of the system. These separate requirements can be given as predicates, all of them the traces must fulfil.

So the predicate P(t) will in general be given as a conjunction of "simpler" predicates $P_i(t)$:

$P(t) = P_1(t)$ **and** ... **and** $P_n(t)$

In PA^{nn}dA-S this can be done by declaring and defining predicates of the form

predicate p: (STREAM$^{\perp}$);

with axioms of the form

```
axiom for all t: STREAM⊥ ⇒
    p(t) ↔ ...
```

In the axioms we shall use the operations on streams introduced in the last sections. Using the algebraic approach it becomes easy to define new operations on streams when needed. We have only introduced those that were frequently used in the case studies.

Example: A safety property of semaphores

We consider a very simple system with an action set that contains (at least) the actions p and v. We formulate a requirement that says that the actions p and v alternate. So if only the actions p and v could happen in the system, merely streams of the kind ⟨p,v,p,v,p,v,...⟩ were allowed; if also other actions are possible, we may intersperse them arbitrarily, but only a finite number between a p and the following v (and between a v and the following p). The reader will have noticed that this is the way how semaphores work. The restriction to intersperse only a finite number of actions between a p and the corresponding v requires that all critical sections (that is what happens between a p and the corresponding v in one process) terminate.

We formalize this requirement:

predicate sem: (A.STREAM$^\perp$);

(Here A is the package STREAMS(ACTION).)

Axiom:

```
axiom for all t: A.STREAM⊥ ⇒
    sem(t) ↔ (for all s: A.STREAM⊥ ⇒
                 is_finite(s) and is_prefix(s,t) →
                         le( sub( length(filter(p,s)),  length(filter(v,s)) ), succ(zero) )
                  and    le( zero, sub( length(filter(p,s)), length(filter(v,s)) ) )
```

This formula says: t is a correct semaphore trace exactly if for all finite prefixes s of t (this could be interpreted as: for all moments s up to t) the number of p-actions (i.e. length(filter(p,s))) minus the number of v-actions always varies from 0 to 1. Note that the length of a finite stream is finite, i.e. not equal to omega. Therefore in the axiom above the case sub(omega,omega) does not arise.

This is a typical *safety property*. A safety property states that nothing incorrect can be observed in finite time. An incorrect behaviour would be that the p- and v-actions do not alternate.

Note however that it is not required that something happens at all: also the empty stream es fulfills the condition. □

Example: A liveness property of semaphores

The counterpart of safety properties are *liveness properties:* these state that "something" will happen eventually. So the conjunction of the safety properties and the liveness properties of the system state that exactly the "good things" happen.

predicate v_after_p: (A.STREAM$^\perp$);

(Again A is the package STREAMS(ACTION).)

Axiom:

```
axiom for all t: STREAM⊥ ⇒
    v_after_p(t) ↔ (exist r: STREAM⊥; s: STREAM⊥ ⇒
        is_finite(r) and is_concat(r, ap(p,s),t) → is_in(v,s))
```

The "good thing" that happens here is that every p-action is followed by a v-action. □

In general, liveness properties refer to infinite observations. Unlike safety properties, for liveness properties it cannot be observed at every moment (i.e. for every finite prefix of the behaviour) whether the property is fulfilled. In our example we cannot give a bound *when* the v-action does happen after a p-action has happened.

The need for infinite observations is the reason why infinite streams are necessary. It is not enough to talk about infinite behaviour in terms of its finite approximations. Consider for instance the set of finite sequences $\{a^i \mid i \in Nat\}$, where Nat denotes the set of natural numbers and a^i is the stream consisting of exactly i a-actions. This set can be the set of (finite) traces of a process that can do an arbitrary but finite number of a-actions. However, it is also an approximation of the infinite process that does infinitely many a-actions. We could not distinguish these two processes, though the first one always terminates whereas the second one never does.

So by giving specifications both in terms of safety *and* liveness properties, we need finite *and* infinite streams.

2.3.5. Functional Specification: Design Specification

2.3.5.1. Motivation

Here the word "functional" refers to two aspects. Firstly, functional specification just means "description of the *input/output behaviour*" of the agents in a network. This is in contrast to the requirement specification where we do not classify actions as input- or output actions of some agent. Secondly, we describe a distributed system using *functions*. As we will see, we can describe each agent by a (stream processing) function in its simplest case, by sets of stream processing functions when we have to treat "more complicated" agents.

There are two advantages when using a functional specification. Firstly, it is a natural way to modularize a system. This is simply done using the composition principles which are common in functional calculus. Secondly, we can use existing theories and methods of computer science and mathematics: fixpoint theory, functional calculus and functional programming.

The functional approach is both suited for the design specification and the abstract program. In the design specification the agents may be described in an "abstract", non-executable way, whereas the abstract program is a kind of functional program. So the means to give abstract programs is just a subset of the means used in design specifications.

2.3.5.2. The Basic Idea of Stream Processing

The concepts go back to G. Kahn [Kahn 74]. We briefly review his computational model: some autonomous computing stations (called *agents* or *processes*) are connected to each other in a network by communication lines (called *channels*). The agents exchange information through these channels. Each agent computes on data coming along its input channels, using some memory of its own, to produce output on some or all of its output channels. We furthermore assume that channels are the only way by which the agents may communicate and that the channels transmit information within an impredictable but finite amount of time. Kahn imposes some further restrictions that guarantee that the agents behave *deterministically*. We, however, drop this restriction, because nondeterminism is a typical phenomenon found in distributed systems. It becomes especially important when we model environment components. So the output of the agents just depends on (possibly) all inputs and on internal decisions of the agents (modelled by nondeterminism).

A small network might look like this:

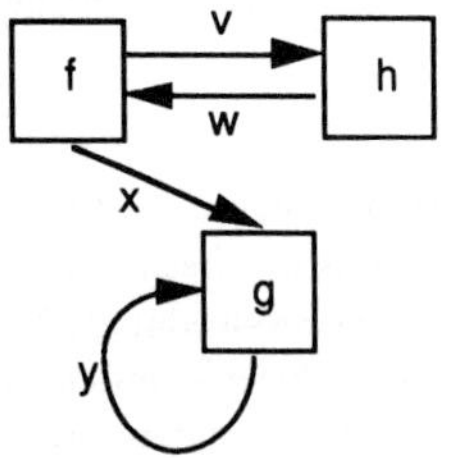

Fig. 2.3-2 A small network

f, g and h are agents, v, w, x and y are (directed) channels.

We describe a behaviour of an agent by *stream processing functions*. This is a function that has a tuple of input streams as argument and produces a tuple of output streams. Furthermore we require that the function is monotonic and continuous w.r.t. the cpo of streams. Monotonicity means that receiving more input can only result in more output. Consequently the agent need not have all of its input to start computing, since future input concerns only future output. This enables parallel operation of the agents. Furthermore continuity prevents an agent from deciding to send some output only after it has received an infinite amount of input.

If an agent behaves nondeterministically, we say that it has several behaviours. As we model each behaviour by one stream processing function, we can model the behaviour of a nondeterministic agent by a *set* of stream processing functions.

The composition of agents (i.e. linking them by channels) then becomes composition of functions, which is a well-understood subject. We have the composition principles depicted in the following pictures:

a) Sequential composition

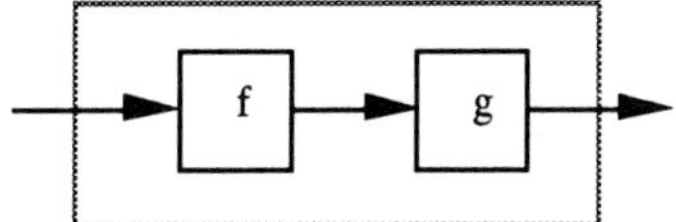

Fig. 2.3-3 Sequential composition

b) Parallel composition

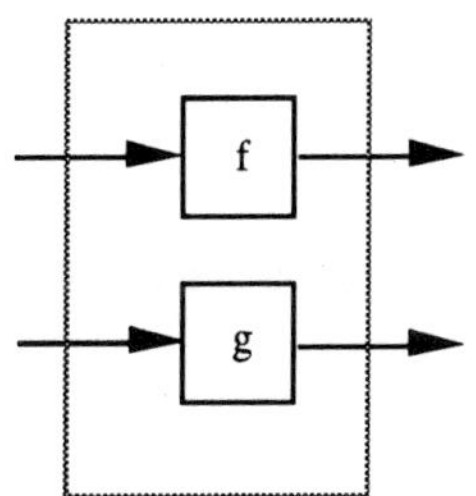

Fig. 2.3-4 Parallel composition

c) Feedback

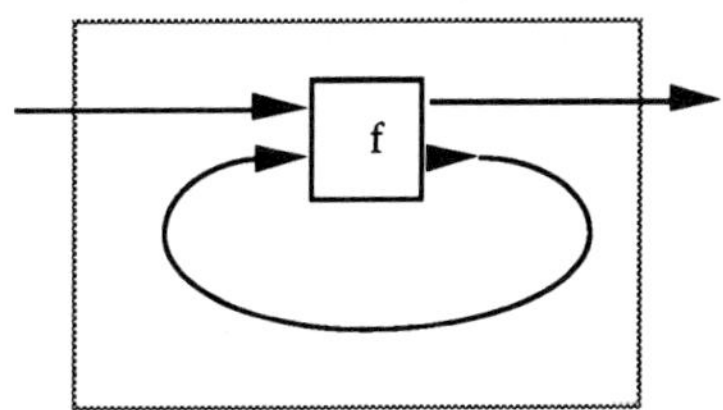

Fig. 2.3-5 Feedback

Every network of agents can then be described by a composition of the corresponding (sets of) stream processing functions. The main advantage of the stream processing agent approach is that we get *compositionality* in a straightforward way.

2.3.5.3. *Describing Stream Processing Agents with PA^nndA-S*

We now demonstrate how we can describe stream processing functions and sets thereof with the language PAnndA-S. In this section we look at "atomic" processes, i.e. we do not describe an agent by a *network* (of other agents), we just specify the nodes of such networks. We use the algebraic specification formalism of PAnndA-S with its cpo-based semantics. As stream processing functions are continuous mappings from the cpo of streams to the cpo of streams (or cartesian products of these cpo's respectively), the description in PAnndA-S is easy.

Deterministic Agents

Let us first look at *deterministic agents*, which can be described by just one stream processing function.

Example: Copying (identity function)

This agent reads a datum from its input channel and writes it on its output channel.

Assume we have declared a package IN defining actions of the form r(d) and a package OUT defining actions of the form w(d), meaning the reading of datum d from the input channel and the writing of datum d on the output channel. Let furthermore denote IS the package STREAMS(IN), OS the package STREAMS(OUT). Then we can define

```
copy: (IS.STREAM⊥) ==> OS.STREAM⊥;
```

by the axiom

```
axiom for all d: DATA⊥; s: I.STREAM⊥ ⇒
    copy(IS.ap(r(d),s)) = OS.ap(w(d),buffer(s));
```

Note that we have to prefix the function ap by the corresponding package (IS or OS), because there is no polymorphism in PAnndA-S. □

Example: Summation of a stream

We specify a function that computes the stream of the (momentary) sum of the items of the input stream. With N = STREAMS(NAT) we have:

```
sum: (N.STREAM⊥) ==> N.STREAM⊥;
```

with the axiom

```
axiom for all s: N.STREAM⊥ ⇒
    sum(s) = help(0,s);
```

Here we use a help function help that is defined as follows:

```
help: (NAT; N.STREAM⊥) ==> N.STREAM⊥;
```

with the axiom

```
axiom for all n: NAT; s: N.STREAM⊥ ⇒
help(n,s) = ap(n,help(add(n,first(s)),rest(s)))
```

This example illustrates a useful method of specifying stream processing functions: we introduce a *help function* that has a *state component* in addition to the input stream , here it is a natural number. The state component can be seen as a condensed form of the input history. In our example it is the sum of items of the input stream read up to a certain moment. At the beginning (no input element has been read) this sum equals 0.

The method of flexibly introducing a state component is important for specifying more complex functions easily. □

Nondeterministic Agents

Nondeterminism is a typical feature of distributed systems. It means that an agent has a choice between several possibilities in some situations.

Nondeterminism could be described by considering *relations* instead of functions. However then compositionality is lost, as the so-called Brock-Ackerman-anomaly shows [Brock, Ackerman 81]. Many proposals have been made to overcome this difficulty, e.g. by describing a nondeterministic agent by a *set* of stream processing functions [Broy 88b], which is suitable for a wide class of stream processing agents.

Example: Fair merge of two streams

We describe an agent that has two input channels and one output channel. It merges the streams on the input channels and writes the result on the output channel (cf. Fig. 2.3-6).

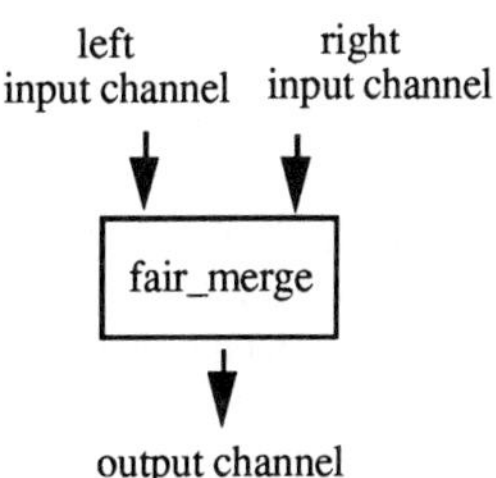

Fig. 2.3-6 Merge of input streams

"Fair" means that for infinite input streams in the end all data from both input channels are processed. This kind of agent is called *multiplexer* in communication systems.

We use a help function sched, which has three input streams: two action streams and one stream of boolean values. The boolean stream is a control stream. It successively determines from which of the action streams the next input must be taken: if the first item of the boolean stream is true, then the agent takes the next input action from the left stream, otherwise from the right one. This is repeated until one input stream stops.

fair_merge is a predicate that tells us whether a stream processing function (of correct arity) describes a particular behaviour of the fair-merge-agent. With sched, we get for every control stream z one stream processing function describing a behaviour. It is required that z contains both infinitely many true and false items, so infinitely many times an item is taken both from the left and the right input stream. Thus all items from both input streams are processed and fairness is guaranteed.

```
with ACTIONS, BOOLEANS, NAT_INF, STREAMS;
package FAIR_MERGER is
   package A is new STREAMS(ACTION);
   package B is new STREAMS(BOOLEAN);
   sched: (A.STREAM⊥;A.STREAM⊥;B.STREAM⊥) ==> A.STREAM⊥;
   predicate fair_merge: ((A.STREAM⊥;A.STREAM⊥) ==> A.STREAM⊥);
axiom for all x: A.STREAM⊥; y: A.STREAM⊥; z: B.STREAM⊥;
              f: (A.STREAM⊥;A.STREAM⊥) ==> A.STREAM⊥ ⇒
   sched(x,y,B.ap(true,z)) = A.ap(A.ft(x),sched(A.rt(x),y,z)),
   sched(x,y,B.ap(false,z)) = A.ap(A.ft(y),sched(x,A.rt(y),z)),
   fair_merge(f) ↔
      (for all x: A.STREAM⊥; y: A.STREAM⊥ ⇒
         exist z: B.STREAM⊥ ⇒
            (f(x,y) = sched(x,y,z) and
            B.length(B.filter(true,z)) = omega and
            B.length(B.filter(false,z)) = omega))
end FAIR_MERGER;
```

Note however that the agent is *strict:* this means that if at least one of the input streams is finite, then the output may be empty after all of the finite input stream has been processed. In particular, if one input stream is finite and the other is not, then an unexpected behaviour occurs. Everything works well if both input action streams are infinite. □

The case studies have shown that a wide range of agents can be described by sets of stream processing functions. However, the last example indicates that an agent like the *nonstrict fair merge* cannot be specified this way. We next touch on a solution to this problem (cf. [Broy 89], section 4.1 for more details).

The idea is to describe sets of functions with an *applicability condition*. Predicates then have the form C(f,x) which means that function f may be applied to input x (specifications of this kind are called *input choice specifications*). In [Broy 89] some further restrictions on such predicates for their sound application are given, e.g. to guarantee the existence of least fixpoints.

Example: Nonstrict fair merge

```
non_strict_fair_merge(f,x) ↔ fair_merge(f) and A.length(f(x,y)) = add(A.length(x),A.length(y));
```

By these examples the general method of specifying stream processing agents should have become clear. Examples for more complex functions can be found in the case studies. They can easily be transformed into the syntax of PA^{nn}dA-S.

2.3.5.4. Networks of Stream Processing Agents

Up to now we have described components that may occur in a network, not the network itself. We give two alternative description formalisms of networks: the first one is a set of equations defining the network; it works well in PA^{nn}dA-S. The second one is to regard a network as a composed agent; this approach causes difficulties in PA^{nn}dA-S, as is indicated below.

Describing networks by equations

We introduce stream variables for each channel and describe the interrelation of the processes in the network by equations using these variables.

For example the following network

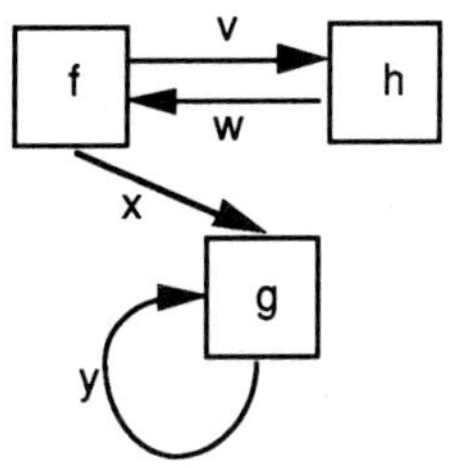

Fig. 2.3-7 A small network

is described by the equations

$$x = f_1(w),$$
$$v = f_2(w),$$
$$y = g(x,y),$$
$$w = h(v).$$

Note that we have one equation per output channel, therefore f is split into two function f_1 and f_2. Equivalently we could have written

$$(x,v) = f(w).$$

This idea goes back to [Kahn 74] and the intended meaning is the least fixpoint of this system of equations. Generalizing this to the case of nondeterminism, described by sets of stream processing functions, we get a least fixpoint for each choice of functions .

Describing networks as the composition of agents

Starting from agents as described in section 2.3.5.3., we can iteratively compose them to build new agents, which corresponds to iteratively constructing a network. Higher-order functions for parallel and sequential composition as well as feedback were needed, but PA^{nn}dA-S is not well-suited for formulating these composition principles. The reason is that not only *one* function for each kind of composition would have to be introduced, but for every combination of arities. This is because overloading in one package is not allowed: for a higher-order function parallel, parallel(f,parallel(g,h)) cannot be used in general, because f and g may have different arities.

Note however that we are able to introduce and axiomatize the least fixpoint operator for stream processing functions because the semantic ordering is uniquely determined and corresponds to the syntactic ordering is_prefix (cf. the appendix).

2.3.6. Program Notations: Abstract and Concrete Program

Abstract programs are also described using stream processing functions. The difference to the design specification is the *executability requirement.* We restrict ourselves to a subset of the stream processing formalism to fulfil this requirement.

First we note that our description of a distributed system includes both *environment components* and *implementable components*. We only give (abstract) programs ("implementations") of the implementable components. In particular, a design specification may offer a choice for the behaviour of an agent and in the phase of the abstract program we may choose just one behaviour and implement it.

In the case studies a mixture of *functional and logic programming techniques* (for infinite objects, i.e. streams) were used. A specification was given in the form

P_1 **and** ... **and** $P_n \Rightarrow f(s) = t$

for appropriate terms s and t (of type $\mathsf{STREAM}^{\perp}$) and *continuous* predicates P_1 ,..., P_n (w.r.t. the ordering "false is less than true"). Examples of executable specifications are the identity function and the summation of a stream (cf. above).

The *concrete program* is written in an imperative programming language for distributed systems. We may choose the language Ada, which is the target language for the transformation of PA^{nn}dA-S specifications.

2.3.7. Conclusion

We have shown that the formalism of streams and stream processing agents can be adapted to PA^{nn}dA-S. A comparison with previous papers on that formalism (e.g. [Broy 88a]) shows that the readability could be increased by introducing mixfix notation and a greater character set.

An open problem is to what extent the transformational approach of PROSPECTRA can be applied to these formalisms. Some effort is currently spent in transforming abstract programs (i.e. executable stream processing agents) into concrete, imperative parallel programs. We believe that this is a major target for transformations, because, roughly speaking, executable programs of one kind are translated into executable programs of another kind. As for the earlier phases, a lot of design decisions must be taken; therefore we consider (automatic) transformations to be less suitable for these phases. However, methodological guidelines for taking design decisions are urgently needed.

2.3.8. Appendix

2.3.8.1. Semantic Consistency of the Specification of Streams

We will show that we have uniquely characterized the stream domain by our specification. This implies that we can talk directly about the ordering of this domain. In particular, we can characterize *least* fixpoints of stream processing functions.

More precisely we will prove:

Proposition: For a flat domain ITEM, there is exactly one model of STREAMS(ITEM) (up to isomorphism).

Remark: In the semantics of PA^{nn}dA-S (cf. part II chapter 3), *model* means an algebra fulfilling the axioms of the specification STREAMS (this is the usual notion of model in logic) *and*

- the carrier sets are cpo's
- the carrier sets are "term-generated", i.e. the cpo consists of the denotations of finite terms and is closed under building least upper bounds (this is not exactly the notion common in algebraic specification), and
- the algebra does not contain a sub-cpo fulfilling these conditions.

Proof of the proposition:

Every (finite) term of type STREAM can be represented by a term of the form

$ap(d_1,ap(d_2,...,ap(d_n,es)...)$

where $n\geq 0$. For $n=0$ we get the empty stream es.
(We do not use exactly the PA^{nn}dA-S syntax here, PA^{nn}dA-S does not allow indices.)
First we will show that, whenever $(A,\leq)$ is a model of STREAMS, then

$s^A \leq t^A$ iff is_prefix$(s,t)^A$

where s^A means the denotation (value) of term s in A.
By the specification of is_prefix it follows that

is_prefix$(ap(d_1,ap(d_2,...,ap(d_n,es)...),ap(e_1,ap(e_2,...,ap(e_m,es)...))^A$

iff $n\leq m$ and "i: $1\leq i\leq n \Rightarrow d_i{}^A = e_i{}^A$.

a) We first show that

is_prefix$(s,t)^A$ implies $s^A \leq t^A$ (*)

If $s^A=t^A$ or $s^A= es^A$, then clearly (*) holds.
Otherwise we have $ft(s)^A = ft(t)^A$ and is_prefix$(rt(s),rt(t))^A$.
We can write s and t in the form

$s = ap(s_0,ap(s_1,...,ap(s_n,es))$ for some natural number n and
$t = ap(s_0,ap(s_1,...,ap(s_n,u))$ for some stream u.

We have

$es^A \leq u^A$
$ap(s_n,es)^A \leq ap(s_n,u)^A$ (by the monotonicity of ap)
...
$ap(s_0,ap(s_1,...,ap(s_n,es))^A \leq ap(s_0,ap(s_1,...,ap(s_n,u))^A$

and thus $s^A \leq t^A$.

b) We now show that

$s^A \leq t^A$ implies is_prefix(s,t)^A

Assume $s^A \leq t^A$ and **not** (is_prefix(s,t))^A.

By the monotonicity of ft and rt we have

ft(s)$^A \leq$ ft(t)^A and rt(s)$^A \leq$ rt(t)^A.

Let k be the smallest number such that

ft(rt^k(s))$^A = \perp$ and

ft(rt^i(s))^A = ft(rt^i(t))^A for all $i<k$.

Then rt^k(s)^A = es^A, because

defined (rt^k(s)$^A \leftrightarrow$ **defined** (ft(rt^k(s))^A (due to the specification of ap) and

not defined (rt^k(s)) $\leftrightarrow$ rt^k(s)^A = es^A.

Therefore s and t coincide on the first k items (for k=0, s=es and hence s≤t holds trivially) and then the suffix of s is es, which is smaller than or equal to the suffix of t. Therefore is_prefix(s,t)^A.

Now we consider least upper bounds of chains of the form

{ap(d_1,ap(d_2,...,ap(d_n,es)...)^A | n∈ Nat}

(W.l.o.g. we assume that the n-th element has length n.)

Let lub({ap(d_1,ap(d_2,...,ap(d_n,es)...)^A | n∈ Nat})

$\leq$ lub({ap(e_1,ap(e_2,...,ap(e_n,es)...)^A | n∈ Nat})

From the monotonicity of first and rest and the axioms of STREAMS it follows that $d_i \leq e_i$ for all $1 \leq i \leq n$ and hence $d_i = e_i$ because ITEM is flat. Hence both lub's coincide.

So a sub-cpo of A is given by the interpretation of (finite) terms and the least upper bounds of prefix-chains of the form {ap(d_1,ap(d_2,...,ap(d_n,es)...)^A | n∈ Nat}, which is a sub-cpo that is isomorphic to the stream domain. Due to the restriction to "term generated" models, this sub-cpo equals A. □

2.3.8.2. Definition of iterate

For a given (endo-)function f and a natural number i, iterate(f,i) results in f^i.

It is defined by:

```
with NAT;
generic
   type ITEM is private;
package ITERATE is
   subtype FCT is (ITEM⊥ ==> ITEM⊥);
   iterate: (FCT;NAT) ==> FCT;
   axiom for all f: FCT; x: ITEM⊥; i: NAT ⇒
   iterate(f,zero)(x) = x,
   iterate(f,succ(i))(x) = f(iterate(f,i)(x)),
end ITERATE;
```

Acknowledgements

I would like to thank Manfred Broy for his careful reading of the paper and helpful suggestions, Thomas Grünler for information concerning PAnndA-S, Friederike Nickl for the guidance with the semantics of PAnndA-S, and the referees for their remarks concerning the presentation of the paper.

3. Transformation

Junbo Liu, Bernd Krieg-Brückner, Universität Bremen

This chapter contains a Reference Manual for the Transformations that are presently available in the System, intended for the program developer. The individual transformations are described in a tutorial style using a semi-formal notation, with some examples. The catalogue will become more complete over time.

3.1. Introduction

3.1.1. Overview

This section is written for the program developer who will develop programs from an initial specification via correctness-preserving transformations that are in the system. The task of achieving a final (efficient) program would be, if not impossible, very difficult, if one had not well understood the transformations available in the system. So, for effective use of the transformations we shall in the following introduce transformations in such a way that, on the one hand, they are abstract and clear enough (like a requirement specification with some informal explanations), and on the other hand, details that are necessary to be able to interact with the system are added. As a whole, we hope the description will serve as a reference manual (cf. also some examples in section I.1).

3.1.2. Structure

Each section describing a transformation contains the following items:

The Format

contains the type information of a transformation function: its name that will appear in the menu of the system; the contextual type of the selected program fragment; the type of the selected program fragment; the type of the transformation's parameters (user input); and the type of resulting program fragment. The constraints that must be obeyed by all the transformation are: firstly, the type of the selected program fragment must be same as the type of resulting program fragment; secondly, the context type must be the selected program fragment's contextual type. The format of a transformation is as follows:

```
name: SP_CST ---> SP ---> USER_INPUT ---> SP
```

name is an identifier (as allowed in PA^{nn}dA-S). SP, USER_INPUT are arbitrary syntactic categories in the abstract syntax of PA^{nn}dA. The type of the context (suffix *_CST*) and user input are optional, since not every transformation has to be context sensitive or parameterised.

An Informal Description

conveys the underlying ideas, for example: the general purpose or strategic goal of the transformation in a development; the context in which it may be used; the relation to other transformation rules for possible combinations; and the references to the literature.

The Transformation Rule

is described in a variant of TrafoLa-S (extended with the higher-order matching and meta-functions). The extension serves to describe the pattern of the selected program fragment and its static constraints. In each description there are basically four parts: input pattern, output pattern, parameters and constraints. An *input pattern* is composed of the selected part (in italics) and its surrounding (i.e. the context of the selected program fragment). This context has, however, no influence on the selectivity of the transformation, it is only given to conveniently describe access to the context information. The *parameter* to be entered by the user is described by a pattern and static constraints. The constraints for the correctness of transformations are divided into *static constraints* and *verification conditions*. The static constraints can be automatically checked and are related directly to an input pattern or a parameter. The verification conditions can either be reduced automatically or by interactive proofs with the proof system. Finally, an *output pattern* is given using all information that has previously been provided, especially the substitutions derived from the matches. The above description is summarised below.

CONTEXT ⊕ *INPUT* ***Pattern*** *of program fragment*	= =>	CONTEXT ⊕ *OUTPUT* ***Pattern*** *of program fragment*
where *Static constraints on the input pattern*		
let *Parameters, with static constraints*		
where *Other constraints on pattern variables*		
such that *Verification Conditions*		

A transformation (described here by a rule as above) will only be available (included in the menu of available transformations) for a given selection, if its input pattern matches structurally and its static constraints are satisfied. Similarly, parameters entered by the user will only be accepted if they satisfy the given constraints. Whenever the verfication condition cannot be automatically deduced by the system, the user is explicitly prompted to verify it by a window to the verifier into which the resp. verfication condition has been generated.

Example

A small example to explain an application of the transformation.

3.1.3. The Meta-Environment

Basically, there are two families of meta-objects that should be explained: meta-type, meta-reasoning and meta-functions. The meta-type, in contrast to the actual type of an abstract term of a program fragment; is defined to represent all objects to be manipulated by meta-programs. For instance, every syntactic category of the abstract syntax of PA^{nn}dA is used in the transformation composition as a meta-type. It is assumed that the PA^{nn}dA abstract syntax is formalised as an abstract data type such that transformations can be defined over it. For instance, meta-types like: DECLARATION, EXPRESSION, PROGRAM etc. are all involved in the definitions of transformations. There are also two important meta-types: LOGICAL, the type for all logical formulae that define properties of models (programs), and LOCAL_THEORY, describing all kinds of semantic properties of a program fragment, in particular the visible axioms. We list some frequently used meta-types below:

```
PROGRAM,  STRING,  NATURAL,  LOGICAL,  LOCAL_THEORY,
EXPRESSION_LIST,  EXPRESSION_LIST_CST,   -- _CST denotes the context
DECLARATION_LIST,  DECLARATION_LIST_CST.
```

The sign /= denotes, that the logical formula to be proved is deduced in the context of the currently valid theory (using the attribute LOCAL_THEORY). This is done either automatically, or, if this fails, meta-reasoning is achieved via special meta-functions that connect the proof system and the transformation engine: the logical formula is sent to the proof system for interactive deduction by the user.

Other kinds of meta-functions are generally semantic functions. Various semantic properties are computed by these meta-functions to allow the composition of transformations. Actually, each function below stands for a family of overloaded meta-functions; this aspect is simply ignored for simplicity. They are only described informally.

occur: checks whether the first argument appears in the second one.

Freevars: computes the free variables of a program fragment at the object level.

Boundvars: computes the bound variables of a program fragment at the object level.

type_of: delivers the type of the parameter from the current meta-environment.

range_type_of: delivers the range type of a function symbol.

define: expresses the instantiated domain constraints of a function with respect to its parameters.

empty: expresses the sufficient conditions for the emptiness of a sort.

get_axiom: obtains the axiomatic definition of a function from the pre-condition and post-condition in the function declaration.

match: checks if the first parameter matches any element of the second parameter.

simplify: reduces the first parameter with respect to the rewrite rules given by the second.

Iter_Apply: reduces the first parameter with respect to the rewrite rules (given by the second parameter) iteratively until no more rules are applicable.

unfold: unfolds the function definitions (equations) given by the first parameter in the program fragment represented by the second parameter.

split: decomposes an axiom into a list of axioms such that both define the same set of functions but in the decomposed axiom list each contains only one function definition.

3.1.4. Pattern Matching

Some peculiar aspects of the description language are now explained: firstly, the use of higher-order matching, secondly, conditional pattern matching is defined; thirdly, some special pattern schemes are described.

Higher-Order Matching:

Pattern variables such as $\mathbb{E}$, $\mathbb{P}$ (initial upper case, shadow) denote a program phrase, i.e. a fragment (usually an expression) with variables, designating higher order matching. The use of these variables makes the description much more concise in the sense that substitution can be done explicitly. However, uniqueness of matching is lost. This is intentional: any selection of matchings will ensure that the transformation is correctness-preserving, but no specific one is preferred; thus the decision of matching selection can be left to the implementation. However, there is one assumption in the notation for higher-order matching: in a pattern of the form ***AX(E)***, ***AX*** denotes a phrase that does not contain any more occurrences of *E*.

Conditional Pattern Matching

We use the PAnndA-S syntax to denote conditional pattern matching. This pattern has the form:

Pattern:: Condition

where the condition can be described by any meta-function or other pattern constraint.

Some Special Pattern Schemes

- x: NAT — a pattern variable with the object type NAT.
- ⟦ S *op*⟧ — a list of patterns such that each element has the pattern S. The separator *op* will not appear in the last position of the list. By default, *op* is ","
- ⟦ S | T ⟧ — a list of patterns such that each element has either the pattern S or T.
- ⟦ S_i ⟧$_n$ — a list of patternsof length n such that each element has one of the patterns S_i.
- x:S — a list pattern, such that x, the list of variables, or S, the list of types, can be referred to separately.

Others

We will not give the type of all meta-variables used in the definition of transformations, but assume that a type inference mechanism exists.

We use the assignment sign := to define the binding of meta-variables.

$\oplus$, Θ, $\otimes$ denote arbitrary operators.

3.1.5. Meta-Sign

The signs between the left-hand side and the right-hand side of a rule have the following meaning:

=> denotes a *uni-directional* transformation rule preserving *robust* correctness (cf. section I.1.5.2): a choice between several possible models, or a restriction of this set, may be made. A program portion matching the left-hand side may be replaced by the right-hand side (after proper substitutions), provided that the applicability condition (given on the left-hand side in the ***such that*** section) is fulfilled;

= denotes a *bi-directional* transformation rule preserving *total* correctness : the left-hand side may be replaced by the right-hand side (after proper substitutions), provided that the applicability condition (given on the left-hand side) is fulfilled, and vice versa.

3.1.6. Further Notation

For operations of the type LOGICAL, the symbol $\wedge$ is used for the **and** operator, $\vee$ for **or** and $\neg$ for **not**.

3.2. Expressions

Some of the transformations in this section are used for simplification, others merely to overcome the different appearance of semantically equivalent (logical) expression lists or expressions in order to get a canonical form for further transformation.

3.2.1. Logical Expressions

In the following transformations of this section, the concrete type of the abstract term EXPRESSION must be LOGICAL. For simplicity, we will not explicitly write this type constraint but take it as an assumption. Another assumption is that there is no conditional expression with the condition **others**. All these constraints can be checked automatically.

3.2.1.1. Logical Equivalences

LogOpElim:	EXPRESSION —> EXPRESSION;
LogOpIntro:	EXPRESSION —> EXPRESSION;

$(E_1 \rightarrow E_2) \wedge (E_2 \rightarrow E_1)$	=	$E_1 \leftrightarrow E_2$
$(\neg E_1) \vee E_2$	=	$E_1 \rightarrow E_2$
$\neg(\neg E)$	=	E
$(E_1 \vee E_3) \wedge (E_2 \vee E_3)$	=	$(E_1 \wedge E_2) \vee E_3$
$(E_1 \wedge E_3) \vee (E_2 \wedge E_3)$	=	$(E_1 \vee E_2) \wedge E_3$

3.2.1.2. De Morgan's Laws

DeMorgan: EXPRESSION —> EXPRESSION;

$\neg(E_1 \wedge E_2)$	=	$(\neg E_1) \vee (\neg E_2)$
$\neg(E_1 \vee E_2)$	=	$(\neg E_1) \wedge (\neg E_2)$
$\neg$ (**exist** DL => $E_1, \dots, E_n$)	=	**for all** DL => $\neg(E_1 \wedge \dots \wedge E_n)$
$\neg$ (**for all** DL => $E_1, \dots, E_n$)	=	**exist** DL => $\neg(E_1 \wedge \dots \wedge E_n)$

3.2.1.3. Flatten Expression Lists

Flatten: EXPRESSION_LIST—> EXPRESSION_LIST;

$E_1, \dots, E_n, (F_1, \dots, F_m), G_1, \dots, G_k$	=	$E_1, \dots, E_n, F_1, \dots, F_m, G_1, \dots, G_k$

3.2.1.4. Logical Expression List to Conjunction

ListToAnd:	EXPRESSION_LIST —> EXPRESSION_LIST;
AndToList:	EXPRESSION_LIST —> EXPRESSION_LIST;

$E_1, \dots, E_n$	=	$E_1 \wedge \dots \wedge E_n$

3.2.1.5. List of Conditional Expressions to Conditional List

CondListElim:	EXPRESSION_LIST —> EXPRESSION_LIST;
CondListIntro:	EXPRESSION_LIST —> EXPRESSION_LIST;

$C \rightarrow E_1, \ldots, C \rightarrow E_n$ = $C \rightarrow (E_1, \ldots, E_n)$

3.2.1.6. Domain Constraint Elimination

ConstraintElim:	EXPRESSION —> EXPRESSION;
ConstraintIntro:	EXPRESSION —> EXPRESSION;

In PA^{nn}dA-S one can write type constraints either in a function declaration or the variable declarations of an axiom to express the constrained domains. In the case of the variable declaration of an axiom, this is semantically equivalent to a conditional axiom without these constraints. The following transformation explores the cases for universal quantification and existential quantification.

for all $[x_i\!: T_i :: C_i;]_n$ => $[E_i]_k$, = **for all** $[x_i\!: T_i;]_n$ => $[C_i \wedge]_n \rightarrow [E_i]_k$

exist $[x_i\!: T_i :: C_i;]_n$ => $[E_i]_k$, = **exist** $[x_i\!: T_i;]_n$ => $[C_i]_n$, $[E_i]_k$

3.2.2. Quantified Expressions

3.2.2.1. Combination of Quantified Expressions

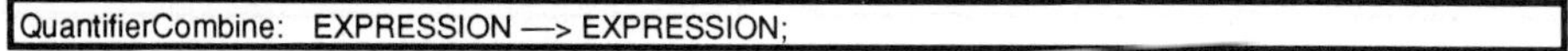

QuantifierCombine: EXPRESSION —> EXPRESSION;

The transformations in this section move the quantifiers to the outermost position for normalisation.

$[Q\ x_i\!:T_i :: C_i =>]_n$ => CEL = $Q\ [x_i\!:T_i :: C_i\ ;]_n$ => CEL

Example

for all x: NAT =>
for all y: NAT:: y = 0 => $x \geq y$ | **for all** x: NAT; y: NAT:: y = 0 => $x \geq y$

3.2.2.2. Elimination of Quantified Lists

QuantifierListElim:	EXPRESSION_LIST —> EXPRESSION_LIST;
QuantifierListIntro:	EXPRESSION_LIST —> EXPRESSION_LIST;

$[$ **for all** $x_i\!: S$ => $E_i(x_i)\,]_n$
where $x \notin$ Freevars $([E_i(x_i)]_n)$ = **for all** $x\!: S$ => $[E_i(x)]_n$

$[$ **exist** $x_i\!: S$ => $E_i(x_i) \vee]_n$
where $x \notin$ Freevars $([E_i(x_i)]_n)$ = **exist** $x\!: S$ => $[E_i(x) \vee]_n$

3.2.2.3. Moving Quantifiers inside Expressions

MoveInside: EXPRESSION —> EXPRESSION;

The transformation rules below are bi-directional even if the carrier of S is empty since then both expressions are equivalent to true. In the first rule, the result can be simplified by proving **exist** $x: S \Rightarrow E_1$ and then transforming to E_2 (or proving the opposite, i.e. **for all** $x: S \Rightarrow \neg E_1$, and replacing by true). The other three cases are similar.

for all $x: S \Rightarrow E_1 \rightarrow E_2$ **where** $x \notin Freevars(E_2)$	=	$($**exist** $x: S \Rightarrow E_1) \rightarrow E_2$
exist $x: S \Rightarrow E_1 \rightarrow E_2$ **where** $x \notin Freevars(E_2)$	=	$($**for all** $x: S \Rightarrow E_1) \rightarrow E_2$
for all $x: S \Rightarrow E_1 \rightarrow E_2$ **where** $x \notin Freevars(E_1)$	=	$E_1 \rightarrow ($**for all** $x: S \Rightarrow E_2)$
exist $x: S \Rightarrow E_1 \rightarrow E_2$ **where** $x \notin Freevars(E_1)$	=	$E_1 \rightarrow ($**exist** $x: S \Rightarrow E_2)$

3.2.2.4. Removal of "Unused" Variables

RemVars: EXPRESSION_LIST —> EXPRESSION_LIST;

for all $x: S \Rightarrow EL$ **where** $x \notin Freevars(EL)$, $\neg empty(S)$	=	EL

To satisfy the applicability condition "S is not empty", it is sufficient to have one 0-ary ("constant") function of type S. It could be weakened to "S is not empty or there is a superterm "**for all** y: S ..." of "**for all** x: S => E".

3.2.3. Tuples and Lists

TupleIntro: EXPRESSION_LIST —>	EXPRESSION_LIST;
TupleElim: EXPRESSION_LIST —>	EXPRESSION_LIST;

$(L_1, ..., L_n) = (R_1, ..., R_n)$	=	$L_1 = R_1, ..., L_n = R_n$
$B \rightarrow (L_1, ..., L_n) = (R_1, ..., R_n)$	=	$B \rightarrow L_1 = R_1, ..., B \rightarrow L_n = R_n$

Example

(head (cons e l), tail (cons e l)) = (e, l);	*head (cons e l) = e, tail (cons e l) = l;*

3.3. Requirement and Design Specifications

3.3.1. Creation of Design Specification

```
StartDesign:   PROGRAM —> PROGRAM;
```

This transformation is used to generate the private part of a requirement specification at the very beginning of the development of a design specification. The axioms in the requirement specification are copied to the private part and appropriate axioms derived from the (pre- and post-)conditions expressed by the predicates in the domain and range constraints of function declarations are added. This transformation is methodologically important as all subsequent development is carried out in the private part; every refinement in the private part will be correct with respect to the specification in the visible part.

```
with IL;
package PF is
   DL
end PF;
where
   the private part is empty,
   DL := [ fs:S ]; [ axiom LL => EL];
   ADL = [ get_axiom (fs: S )]; [ axiom LL => EL ]
```

=>

```
with IL;
package PF is
   DL;
private
   ADL;
end PF;
```

Example

```
with NAT_S;
package SQROOT is
   sqrt: (n: NAT) ->
            (k: NAT::  sqr k ≤ n ∧ sqr (succ k) > n);
end SQROOT;
```

```
with NAT_S;
package SQROOT is
   sqrt: (n: NAT) ->
            (k: NAT::  sqr k ≤ n ∧ sqr (succ k) > n);
private
   axiom for all n: NAT =>
      k = sqrt n → sqr k ≤ n ∧ sqr (succ k) > n;
end SQROOT;
```

Matches:

```
IL ≈     NAT_S
DL ≈     sqrt: (n: NAT) ->
                  (k: NAT:: sqr k ≤ n ∧ sqr (succ k) > n);
ADL ≈    axiom for all n: NAT; k: NAT =>
            k = sqrt n → sqr k ≤ n ∧ sqr (succ k) > n;
```

3.3.2. Enrichment and Extension

The transformations in this section are intended for the development of design specifications; however, semantically they are also applicable to requirement specifications to assist the revision activity.

3.3.2.1. Enrichment

```
Enrich:     DECLARATION_LIST_CST—> DECLARATION_LIST —>
            DECLARATION_LIST—> DECLARATION_LIST;
```

This transformation is used to *enrich* a specification during development, for example, by an axiom that *further restricts* the class of models; thus it may change the semantics of the given specification. Auxiliary types and functions may also be introduced.

```
   DL1;
let DL2 := [ type T is private | fs: S | axiom D ];
```

=>

```
   DL1; DL2;
```

Enrich:	*EXPRESSION_LIST_CST* —> EXPRESSION_LIST —> *EXPRESSION_LIST* —> EXPRESSION_LIST;

axiom for all X:D => *EL1;*	=>	**axiom for all** X:D => *EL1, EL2;*
let *EL2: LOGICAL:: X ⊇ Freevars (EL2)*		

3.3.2.2. *Extension*

Extend:	*DECLARATION_LIST_CST* —> DECLARATION_LIST —> *DECLARATION_LIST* —> DECLARATION_LIST;

This transformation is used to *extend* a specification during development, for example by an axiom that is in fact a *theorem* with respect to the existing axioms; thus it must not change the semantics of the given specification.

DL1;	=	*DL1; ADL;*
let *ADL: LOGICAL:: ADL=* **[axiom** *D***]**		
such that ⊨ *D*		

Extend:	*EXPRESSION_LIST_CST* —> EXPRESSION_LIST —> *EXPRESSION_LIST* —> EXPRESSION_LIST;

axiom for all X:D =>*EL1;*	=	**axiom for all** X:D => *EL1, EL2;*
let *EL2: LOGICAL :: X ⊇ Freevars (EL2) ;*		
such that ⊨ *EL2*		

3.3.2.3. *Deletion and Replacement*

Delete:	*EXPRESSION_LIST _CST* —>EXPRESSION_LIST —> EXPRESSION_LIST;

Deletion can be used for logical expressions in axioms that *extend* the specification, for example for a logical expression that is a theorem of the local theory.

axiom for all X: D =>EL1, *EL2;*	=>	**axiom for all** X: D => EL1;
such that ⊨ *EL2;*		

Replace:	*EXPRESSION_LIST _CST* —> EXPRESSION_LIST —> *EXPRESSION_LIST* —> EXPRESSION_LIST;

Replacement (a combination of extension and deletion) replaces an old logical expression by a new logical expression given as a parameter if the old one can be deduced from the local theory and the new logical expression.

axiom for all X: D => EL1, *EL2;*	=>	**axiom for all** X: D => EL1, *EL3;*
let *EL3: LOGICAL:: X ⊇ Freevars (EL3),*		
such that ⊨ *EL2 ↔ EL3*		

Example

The equation EL2 in the axiom on the left-hand side is replaced by the equation EL3 on right-hand side.

```
axiom for all m,n: NAT =>
      m + 0 = m,  m + n = n + m,
      m + succ(n) = succ(m + n);
```

```
axiom for all m,n: NAT =>
      m + 0 = m,  m + n = n + m,
      succ(n) + m = succ(n + m);
```

```
Matches:   EL2  ≈  m + succ(n) = succ(m + n)
           EL3  ≈  succ(n) + m = succ(n + m)
```

```
Applicability Condition
  m + succ(n) = succ(m + n)   ↔
  succ(n) + m = succ(n + m)
```

3.3.2.4. Extension with Abstract Data Types

```
ExtendWith:   PROGRAM_CST —> PROGRAM —> NAME_LIST —> PROGRAM;
```

This transformation is used to introduce additional visibility to packages (Abstract Data Types) for the purpose of algebraic implementation. The first methodological step or design decision is to decide which concrete types will be used to represent the specified abstract type; then one may proceed by further enrichments or extensions, e.g. introducing representation and abstraction functions (cf. chapter I.2.2). Note that this specialised extension guarantees the persistency automatically.

```
with IL;
package PF is
   DL
private with NL1;
   ADL;
end PF;
---
let   NL2 := list of visible package names
```

=>

```
with IL;
package PF is
   DL;
private with NL1, NL2;
   ADL;
end PF;
```

3.3.3. Robust Implementation

3.3.3.1. Weakening of Precondition, Strengthening of Postcondition

```
RobustImpl:   DECLARATION_CST —> DECLARATION —>
              (EXPRESSION × EXPRESSION) —> DECLARATION;
```

This is a transformation for "robust implementation" by refinement to a function that is "more" defined: on a wider domain (less partial) or for a smaller range, i.e. with "more precision" (less loosely, more design decisions).

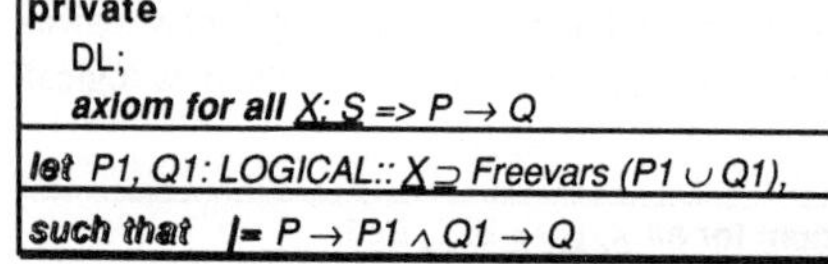

```
private
   DL;
   axiom for all X: S => P → Q
---
let P1, Q1: LOGICAL:: X ⊇ Freevars (P1 ∪ Q1),
---
such that   |= P → P1 ∧ Q1 → Q
```

=>

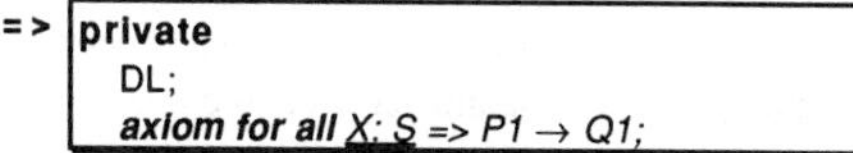

```
private
   DL;
   axiom for all X: S => P1 → Q1;
```

Example

```
private
  axiom for all x, y: NAT =>
    x > 0 ∧ y > 0 →
                    divides (comDiv(x, y), x) ∧
                    divides (comDiv(x, y), y);
```

```
private
  axiom for all m, x, y: NAT =>
  x ≥ 0 ∧ y ≥ 0 →
                (divides (comDiv (x, y), x) ∧
                comDiv (x, 0) = x ∧
                divides (comDiv (x, y), y) ∧
                comDiv (0, y) = y ∧
                (divides (m, x) ∧ divides (m, y) →
                                   comDiv (x, y) ≥ m));
```

Matches:

```
  P  ≈ x > 0 ∧ y > 0,
  P1 ≈ x ≥ 0 ∧ y ≥ 0,
  Q  ≈ divides (n, x) ∧ divides (n, y)
  Q1 ≈ (Q ∧ comDiv(x, 0) = x ∧
          comDiv (0, y) = y ∧
          (divides (m, x) ∧ divides (m, y)) →
                                comDiv (x, y) ≥ m))
```

comDiv is loosely specified as a common divisor at first; by the last axiom, it is made unique as the Greatest Common Divisor. Independently, its domain is widened to include 0 (to facilitate recursion later).

3.3.4. Design Methods

3.3.4.1. Split of Postcondition

```
SplitPost:  DECLARATION_LIST_CST —> DECLARATION_LIST —>
            (EXPRESSION × EXPRESSION) —> DECLARATION_LIST;
```

The goal is the synthesis of a first recursive version of a function from its predicative or axiomatic specification (note that predicative specifications are already translated to axiomatic specifications in the private part by the transformation for implementation, see above). The result is a functional specification. The applicability conditions include one for the proof of total correctness using a termination predicate *term*. See Dijkstra, Gries.

In the following, ***Inv*** denotes the invariant, and ***B*** the termination condition of the recursive function that is synthesised by the transformation. The starting value ***E*** and the recursion function ***H*** have to be provided as parameters.

```
private
axiom for all x: S; z: R =>
  z = f(x) → Inv(x,z) ∧ B(x,z);
--------------------------------------------
let  START: R :: START = E(x),
     REC: R :: REC = H(x,y)
--------------------------------------------
such that
  |= defined ( E(x)), defined ( H(x, y)),
  |= Inv(x,E(x)),
  |= Inv(x,y) ∧ ¬ B(x,y) → Inv(x,H(x,y)),
  |= exist i: NAT => B(x, term (x, E(x), i))
--------------------------------------------
where
  term: S × R × NAT —> R
axiom for all x: S; y: R; i: NAT =>
  i = 0 →   term (x, y, i) = y,
  i > 0 →   term (x, y, i) = H(x, term (x, y, i – 1));
```

=

```
private
  g: S × R —> R;
axiom for all x: S; y: R =>
                 f(x) = g(x, E(x)),
    B(x, y) →    g(x, y) = y,
¬ B(x, y) →      g(x, y) = g(x, H(x, y));
```

For an example see section I.1.3.1.

3.4. Operational Specifications

3.4.1. Algebra of Higher-Order Functions

3.4.1.1. (Un)Currying

UnCurry: *DECLARATION_LIST_CST* —> DECLARATION_LIST —> *EXPRESSION* —> DECLARATION_LIST;
Curry: *DECLARATION_LIST_CST* —> DECLARATION_LIST —> *EXPRESSION* —> DECLARATION_LIST;

Goal: (un)curry a function call in an axiom for a given function (whose name is entered as a parameter). A new function declaraton with the changed functionality will be produced. The name of the new function is still the "old" one, i.e. an overloaded name. However, an internal, unique name is automatically created.

f: $\underline{S}$ —> R;
axiom *Q DL* => ***EL*** *(f (x₁, ..., xₙ));*

let *g:* $\underline{S}$ *—> R :: g = f,*

where
$\underline{S}$:= $S_1 \times S_2 \times ... \times S_n$,
$\underline{S}'$:= S_1 —> S_2 —> ... —> S_n

=

f: $\underline{S}$ —> R;
f : $\underline{S}'$ *—> R;*
axiom *Q DL* => ***EL*** *(f* $x_1, ..., x_n$ *);*

Example

f: T × S —> R;
axiom for all *x: T => h(x) = f (a, b);*

Matches: *g* ≈ f,
EL ≈ h(x) = f (a, b),

f: T × S —> R;
f: T —> S —> R;
axiom for all *x: T => h(x) = f a b;*

3.4.2. Algebraic Simplification

3.4.2.1. Simple Rewrite

SimpleRewrite: *EXPRESSION_CST* —> EXPRESSION —> *EXPRESSION* —> EXPRESSION;

The goal is to rewrite a term by a (conditonal) equation. Note that ***B*** $E_1 ... E_n$ holds trivially if the equation is unconditional. In the conditional case, ***B*** $E_1 ... E_n$ holds if it can be simplified to true using the local theory.

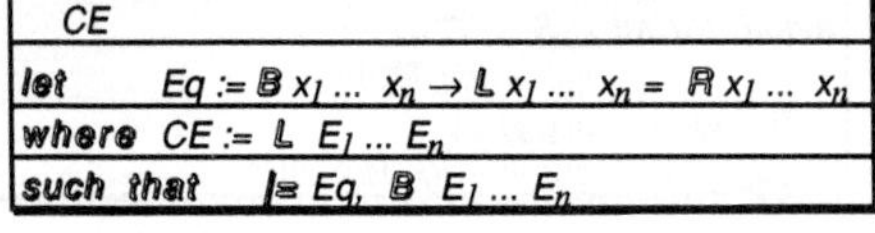

CE
let *Eq :=* ***B*** $x_1 ... x_n \rightarrow$ ***L*** $x_1 ... x_n$ = ***R*** $x_1 ... x_n$
where *CE :=* ***L*** $E_1 ... E_n$
such that |= *Eq,* ***B*** $E_1 ... E_n$

=> ***R*** $E_1 ... E_n$

Example

pred (succ zero)

Parameter:
Eq ≈ pred (succ x) = x;

zero

Matches:
L E_1 ≈ pred (succ zero),
E_1 ≈ zero

3.4.2.2. Rewrite with Equations and Patterns

Rewrite: *EXPRESSION_CST* —> EXPRESSION —> *(EXPRESSION_LIST* × *EXPRESSION_LIST)* —> EXPRESSION;

The rule has two parameters, one is an equation list used to rewrite a term, another is a pattern list used to control the pattern matching of the terms concerned. Goal: rewrite the term that occurs in the outermost leftmost position that also matches one of the patterns in the pattern list with the first applicable equation. If the pattern list is empty, then the outermost leftmost term that matches the left hand side of some equation will be rewritten. The equations are used as rewite rules from left to right, and from first to last. Notice that the position of the application is not specified below.

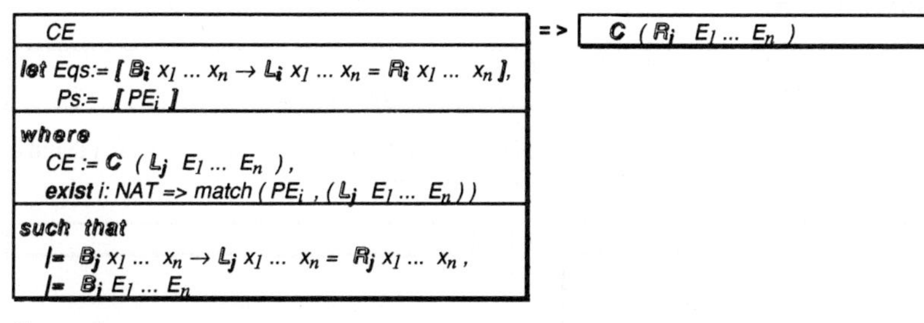

CE
let Eqs:= [B_i x_1 ... x_n → L_i x_1 ... x_n = R_i x_1 ... x_n],
Ps:= [PE_i]
where
CE := C (L_j E_1 ... E_n),
exist i: NAT => match (PE_i , (L_j E_1 ... E_n))
such that
|= B_j x_1 ... x_n → L_j x_1 ... x_n = R_j x_1 ... x_n ,
|= B_j E_1 ... E_n
=>
C (R_j E_1 ... E_n)

Example

h (pred (succ y)) (pred (succ zero)) → h (pred (succ y)) zero

Parameters:
Eqs ≈ pred (succ x) = x,
Ps ≈ pred (succ zero);

Matches:
L E_1 ≈ pred (succ zero),
E_1 ≈ zero

RewriteParallel: *EXPRESSION_CST* —> EXPRESSION —> *(EXPRESSION_LIST × EXPRESSION_LIST)* —> EXPRESSION;

CE
let
Eqs:= [$B_i\ x_{i1} \ldots x_{in} \rightarrow L_i\ x_{i1} \ldots x_{in} = R_i\ x_{i1} \ldots x_{in}$],
Ps:= [PE_i]
where
CE := **C** ($L_1\ E_{11} \ldots E_{1n}, \ldots, L_m\ E_{m1} \ldots E_{mn}$),
for all *j: NAT :: 1 ≤ j ≤ m =>* **exist** *i: NAT =>*
match (PE_i, ($L_j\ E_{j1} \ldots E_{jn}$))
such that
|= **for all** *j: NAT :: 1 ≤ j ≤ m =>*
$B_j\ x_{j1} \ldots x_{jn} \rightarrow L_j\ x_{j1} \ldots x_{jn} = R_j\ x_{j1} \ldots x_{jn}$,
$B_j\ E_{j1} \ldots E_{jn}$

=> **C** ($R_1\ E_{11} \ldots E_{1n}, \ldots, R_m\ E_{m1} \ldots E_{mn}$)

Example

h (pred (succ zero)) (pred (succ (pred y))) → h zero (pred y))

Matches:
Eqs ≈ succ (pred x) = x, pred (succ x) = x,
L_1 E_{11} ≈ succ (pred y), E_{11} ≈ y,
L_2 E_{21} ≈ pred (succ zero), E_{21} ≈ zero

Example: Expression Evaluation with Patterns

h (pred (succ zero)) (succ (pred (pred (succ y))))		h zero (succ (pred (pred (succ y))))

Matches:

Eqs ≈ succ (pred x) = x, pred (succ x) = x,
Ps ≈ pred (succ zero),
L_2 E_{11} ≈ pred (succ zero), E_{11} ≈ zero

3.4.2.3. *Iterative Rewrite*

IterateRewrite: *EXPRESSION_CST* —> EXPRESSION —> *(EXPRESSION_LIST × EXPRESSION_LIST)* —> EXPRESSION;

Goal: to simplify the expression as far as possible using the given list of rewrite rules, provided that the matched terms also appear in the pattern list given as a second parameter.

CE	=>	*CE'*
let *Eqs:=* [$B_i\ x_{i1} \ldots x_{in} \rightarrow L_i\ x_{i1} \ldots x_{in} = R_i\ x_{i1} \ldots x_{in}$], *Ps:=* [PE_i]		
where *CE' := Iter_Apply (CE, Eqs, Ps)*		
such that |= *Eqs*		

Notice that the auxiliary function *Iter_Apply* may not terminate (the termination depends on the properties of the given equations as rewrite rules). It also tries to deduce automatically the conditions involved by a matched conditional equation. A rule is only applied in case of successful deduction of the condition.

Example: Iterative Rewrite without Patterns

eq (succ zero) succ (pred (succ zero))		true

Parameters:

Eqs ≈ x > zero = true -> succ (pred x) = x,
succ x > zero = true,
eq x x = true

3.4.2.4. *(Un)Fold*

Unfold: *EXPRESSION_CST* —> EXPRESSION —> *EXPRESSION* —> EXPRESSION;
Fold: *EXPRESSION_CST* —> EXPRESSION —> *EXPRESSION* —> EXPRESSION;

Goal: produce recursive definitions / prepare further simplifications

$C\ (f\ E_1 \ldots E_n)$	=	$C\ (R\ E_1 \ldots E_n)$
let *f: S --> T*		
such that |= $B\ x_1 \ldots x_n \rightarrow f\ x_1 \ldots x_n = R\ x_1 \ldots x_n$, |= $B\ E_1 \ldots E_n$		

Example: Unfold

$g\ (x+2)\ (x+1)$

Matches:
$\mathcal{C}\ (f\ E_1\ E_2) \approx g\ (x+2)\ (x+1)$
Parameter:
$f \approx g$

$(x+2+x+1) * (x+2-x-1)$

Applicability Conditions:
$\mathcal{B}\ x_1\ x_2 \rightarrow f\ x_1\ x_2 = \mathcal{R}\ x_1\ x_2 \approx$
$y \le x \rightarrow g\ x\ y = (x+y) * (x-y),$
$\mathcal{B}\ E_1\ E_2 \approx (x+1) \le (x+2)$

Expand:	*EXPRESSION_CST* —> EXPRESSION —> *EXPRESSION_LIST* —> EXPRESSION;
Contract:	*EXPRESSION_CST* —> EXPRESSION —> *EXPRESSION_LIST* —> EXPRESSION;

In the expand version of unfold, a set of the definitions of a function (all defining equations) is substituted for expansion, provided the definitions are complete whenever the function application selected is defined on its domain. Note that the conditions are not deduced, but textually included in the result. The context $\mathcal{C}\ (...)$ must be a logical expression.

$\mathcal{C}\ (f\ E_1 \ldots E_n)$
let *Eqs*:= $[\ \mathcal{B}_i\ x_1 \ldots x_n \rightarrow f\ x_1 \ldots x_n = \mathcal{R}_i\ x_1 \ldots x_n\ ]_k$
such that $\models$ *Eqs*, $\models$ ***defined*** $(f\ E_1 \ldots E_n) \leftrightarrow (\ [\ \mathcal{B}_i\ E_1 \ldots E_n \vee]_k\ )$

=

$[\ \mathcal{B}_i\ E_1 \ldots E_n \rightarrow \mathcal{C}\ (\mathcal{R}_i\ E_1 \ldots E_n)\ ]_k$

Example: Expand

$h\ x = g\ (x+2)\ (2 * x)$

Matches:
$\mathcal{C}\ (f\ E_1\ E_2) \approx h\ x = g\ (x+2)\ (2 * x)$
Parameter:
$Eqs \approx y \le x \rightarrow g\ x\ y = (x+y) * (x-y),$
$x > 4 \rightarrow g\ x\ y = (x+2) * (x-2)$

$((2 * x) \le (x+2) \rightarrow h\ x = (x+2+2 * x) * (x+2-2 * x),$ $(x+2) > 4 \rightarrow h\ x = (x+2) * (x-2))$

Applicability Conditions:
defined $(f\ E_1\ E_2) \leftrightarrow (\ [\ \mathcal{B}_i\ E_1\ E_2 \vee]_2\ ) \approx$
defined $(g\ (x+2)\ (2 * x)) \leftrightarrow ((2 * x) \le (x+2) \vee x > 2)$

3.4.2.5. Partial Evaluation

Collaps:	DECLARATION_LIST —> DECLARATION_LIST;

An auxiliary functions that is (non-recursively) defined in just one equation can be deleted by unfold and deletion of the definition.

private *[f: S* ***| axiom*** *D]*
where *NS := Set of names of "deletable" functions* *DL' := Delete ([f: S* ***| axiom*** *unfold(D, NS)], NS)*

=

private *[DL'];*

Example

axiom for all *x: T => f(x) = g(x,* $\mathcal{C}$*(x));* ***axiom for all*** *x, y: T => g(x, y) = h(x, y,* $\mathcal{D}$*(x, y));*

axiom for all *x: T => f(x) = h(x,* $\mathcal{C}$*(x),* $\mathcal{D}$*(x,* $\mathcal{C}$*(x));*

3.4.3. Abstraction

3.4.3.1. *Variable Abstraction*

AbstrVar:	*DECLARATION_LIST_CST* —> DECLARATION_LIST —> *EXPRESSION* —> DECLARATION_LIST;

Goal: make a specification more compact, eliminate common subexpressions *E*.

axiom for all *DL => EL;*
let *E: T*
where *EL = K (E)* $x \notin$ *Freevars (EL),* *Freevars (E)* $\cap$ *Boundvars (EL)* = $\emptyset$
such that **|= defined** *(E),*

=

axiom for all *DL; x: T => x = E* $\rightarrow$ *K(x);*

Example

axiom for all *n: NAT =>* *sqr (sqrt n)* $\leq n \wedge$ *sqr (succ (sqrt n)) > n;*

Parameter:
E $\approx$ sqrt n

axiom for all *n, k: NAT =>* *k = sqrt n* $\rightarrow$ *sqr k* $\leq n \wedge$ *sqr (succ k) > n;*

Matches:
EL $\approx$ sqr (sqrt n) $\leq$ n $\wedge$ sqr (succ (sqrt n)) > n

3.4.3.2. *Functional Abstraction*

FunAbstr:	*DECLARATION_LIST_CST* —> DECLARATION_LIST —> *EXPRESSION* —> DECLARATION_LIST;

Goal: introduce a new function f to abstract from a certain expression in an axiom. The axiom is modified by folding the expression to the application of f.

axiom for all *DL => EL;*
let *FE: T :: FE =* **E** *(x₁, .., xₙ)*
where *EL :=* **C** *(* **[E** *(E_{i1}, .., E_{in})* **]** *_m),* *type_of (x_i) = T_i,* *{x_1,..,x_n } = Freevars (FE),* *Freevars (FE)* $\cap$ *Boundvars (EL)* = $\emptyset$;

=

f: $T_1 \times T_2 \times .. \times T_n$ *—>T;* **axiom for all** *DL;* **[** x_i*:* T_i **]**$_n$ *=>* **C** *(* **[** *f(* E_{i1}*, ..,* E_{in} *)* **]**$_m$*),* *f (* x_1*, ...,* x_n*) =* **E** *(* x_1*, ...,* x_n*);*

Example

axiom for all *x: NAT =>* *dist (x) =* *sqrt (sqr (x–1) + sqr (x–2)) + (sqr(x - 3) + sqr(x - 4));*

Parameters:
E *(y, z)* $\approx$ sqr (y) + sqr (z);

f: NAT × NAT —> NAT; **axiom for all** *x, y, z: NAT =>* *dist (x) = sqrt (f (x - 1, x -2)) + (f(x - 3, x - 4)),* *f (y, z) = sqr (y) + sqr (z);*

Matches:
C *(* **[E** *(* E_{i1}*, ..,* E_{in}*)* **]**$_m$*)* $\approx$ dist (x) =
sqrt (sqr (x–1) + sqr (x–2)) + (sqr(x - 3) + sqr(x - 4));

3.4.4. Embedding

3.4.4.1. General Embedding

```
GeneralEmbed:  DECLARATION_LIST_CST —> DECLARATION_LIST —>
               (EXPRESSION × DECLARATION) —> DECLARATION_LIST;
```

Embedding is a general principle known in mathematics for some time; if the original formulation of a problem does not lead to a solution directly, one tries to solve a "more general" problem that includes the original one as a special case.

Notice that finding a suitable embedding is due to the developer's ingenuity or experience; the rule only provides the formal framework to guide the developer's thoughts. The goal is to introduce the additional parameter that makes the decomposition possible, so that finally the definition can be more "deterministic".

```
  f: S —> R;
axiom for all x: S => f(x) EqOp H(x);
---
let  E: T:: x ⊇ FreeVars(E),
       D := axiom for all x: S; y: T =>
                                   g(y, x) EqOp K(x, y)
---
Where  EqOp := ↔ or EqOp := '='
---
such that
   |= for all x: S => K(x, E) EqOp H(x)
```

```
f:       S —> R;
g: T×S   —> R;
axiom for all x: S; y: T =>
f(x)       EqOp  g(E, x),
g(y, x)    EqOp  K(x, y);
```

3.4.4.2. Embedding of (Costly) Subexpression

```
EmbedExp:  DECLARATION_LIST_CST —> DECLARATION_LIST —>
           EXPRESSION —> DECLARATION_LIST;
```

Find "costly" subexpression *E* and embed it into a new function with *E* as an extra parameter (e.g. to prepare for finite differencing below). The rule is represented here only for recursion with one terminating case; it is generalised to an arbitray number of cases in the implementation.

```
  f: S —> R;

axiom for all x: S =>
       CB → f(x) = CH1,
     ¬ CB → f(x) = CH2;
---
let  CE: T :: CE = E(x)
---
where  CB :=    B(x, E(x)),
       CH1 :=   H1(x, E(x)),
       CH2 :=   H2(x, E(x), f(L(x, E(x))) );
   FreeVars(f(x)) ⊇ FreeVars(E(x)),
   y : T :: y ∉ Freevars (CH1, CH2),
   Freevars (CE) ∩ Boundvars (CH1, CH2) = ∅
---
such that    |= defined (CE)
```

=

```
  f: S —> R;
  g: S× T —> R;
axiom for all x: S; y: T :: y = E(x) =>
                   f(x) = g(x, E(x)),
    B(x, y) →      g(x, y) = H1(x, y),
  ¬ B(x, y) →      g(x, y) = H2(x, y, g(L(x, y), E(L(x, y)));
```

Example

```
 sqrt1:    NAT × NAT —> NAT;
axiom for all n, k: NAT =>
 sqr (succ k) > n → sqrt1 (n, k) = k,
 ¬ sqr (succ k) > n → sqrt1 (n, k) = sqrt1 (n, succ k);
```

Matches:

```
E(n, k)                          ≈ sqr (succ k)
B(n, k, E(n, k))                 ≈ E(n, k) > n,
H1(n, k, E(n, k))                ≈ k,
H2(n, k, E(n, k), f(L(n,k)))     ≈ f(L(n, k)),
L(n, k))                         ≈ (n, succ k),
E(L(n, k))   ≈  E(n, k+1)        ≈ sqr (succ (succ k))
```

```
 sqrt1:    NAT × NAT —> NAT;
 sqrt2:    NAT × NAT × NAT —> NAT;
axiom for all n, k: NAT;
             sq: NAT:: sq = sqr (succ k) =>
     sqrt1(n, k)  = sqrt2(n, k, sqr (succ k) ),
  sq > n → sqrt2 (n, k, sq)  = k,
 ¬ sq > n → sqrt2 (n, k, sq)  = sqrt2(n, succ k,
                                  sqr (succ (succ k)));
```

3.4.5. Finite Differencing

```
Differentiate:    EXPRESSION_CST —> EXPRESSION —>
                  (EXPRESSION × EXPRESSION_LIST) —> EXPRESSION;
```

The idea of Finite Differencing is to avoid that the "costly" subexpression of an embedding is computed over and over again in each recursion; instead, only the increment is computed each time (cf. also section I.1.3.2). This increment is supposedly an expression that is less "costly" to compute, for example using multiplication or addition instead of squaring; this corresponds to "strength reduction" in compiler optimisations.

After embedding (cf. above), we need to find an arbitrary operation $\oplus$ (this could be a binary numeric operation, or set union, for example) and an increment ΔE such that

$$E(L(x, y)) = E(x) \oplus \Delta E\,(x, y)$$

As a first strategy, this can be done by goal-oriented rewriting to find $E(x)$ and $\Delta E\,(x, y)$ (e. g. by applying equations). Then, $y \oplus \Delta E\,(x, y)$ is expected to be "cheaper" than $E(L(x, y))$.

The implemented transformation already includes the preparatory goal-oriented rewriting and the simplification using a set of equations as rewrite rules in a second parameter.

3.4.5.1. Goal-Oriented Finite Differencing

```
 E(L(x, y))                                       =    y ⊕ ΔE (x, y)
let   y: T,
      EQS :=  [B → E1 = E2]
where  E(x) ⊕ ΔE (x, y) := simplify (E(L(x, y)),EQS)
such that    |= y = E(x), EQS
```

Example: Integer Squareroot with Goal-Oriented Rewriting

```
 sqr (succ (succ k))                  sq + succ (succ k + succ k)
```

Matches:

```
E(L(n, k))   ≈  sqr (succ (succ k)),
ΔE (n, k)    ≈  succ (succ k + succ k)
```

Parameters:

```
y     ≈  sq,
EQS   ≈  sqr (succ a) = sqr a + 2*a + one,
         2*a = a + a,     a + one = succ a,
         (succ a) + (succ b) = succ (succ (a + b))
```

3.4.5.2. Partial Inverse

DifferentiateInv:	*EXPRESSION_CST* —> EXPRESSION —> *(EXPRESSION × EXPRESSION × EXPRESSION_LIST)* —> EXPRESSION;

As a second strategy, *ΔE (x)* can be achieved by simplifying *E(L(x, y)) Θ E(x)*, if an inverse operation Θ exists such that *E(x) ⊕ (E(L(x, y)) Θ E(x)) = E(L(x, y))* holds. Note that Θ may be a partial operation.

```
E(L(x, y))                                          =   y ⊕ ΔE (x, y)
let   y: T,
      INV :=   P (a, b) → a ⊕ (b Θ a) = b,
      EQS :=   [ B → E1 = E2 ],
where  ΔE (x, y) := simplify (E(L(x, y)) Θ E(x), EQS)
such that   |= P (E(L(x, y), E(x)),
            |= y = E(x),  INV,  EQS
```

Example: Integer Squareroot: Inverse Operation

```
sqr (succ (succ k))                                     sq + succ (succ (succ (k + k)))

Matches:   ⊕ ≈ +        Θ ≈ −        - - on NAT
  P (a, b)      ≈ a ≥ b
  E(L(n, k))    ≈ sqr (succ (succ k))
  ΔE (n, k)     ≈ E(L(n, k)) Θ E(n, k)
  ≈ sqr (succ (succ k)) − sqr (succ k)
  ≈ (sqr (succ k) + (2*succ k + one) ) − sqr (succ k)
  ≈ 2*succ k + one
  ≈ (succ k + succ k) + one
  ≈ succ (succ k + succ k)
  ≈ succ (succ (succ (k + k)))

Parameters:
  y     ≈  sq,
  INV   ≈  x ≥ y → y + (x - y) = x,
  EQS   ≈  sqr (succ a) = sqr a + 2*a + one,
           (a + b) − a = b,
           2*a = a + a,    a + one = succ a,
           (succ a) + (succ b) = succ (succ (a + b))
Applicability Conditions:
  x ≥ y → y + (x - y) = x,
  sqr (succ (succ k))≥ sqr(succ k)
```

3.4.5.3. Combination with Embedding

EmbedAndDiff:	*DECLARATION_LIST_CST* —> DECLARATION_LIST —> *(EXPRESSION × EXPRESSION × EXPRESSION_LIST)* —> DECLARATION_LIST;

Another implemented version combines embedding and finite differencing in one transformation (with suitable parameters).

```
f: S —> R;                                          =   f: S —> R;
axiom for all x: S =>                                   g: S × T —> R;
    CB → f(x) = CH1,                                    axiom for all x: S; y: T :: y = E(x) =>
  ¬ CB → f(x) = CH2;                                                 f(x) = g(x, E(x)),
let   CE :T:: CE = E(x);                                   B(x, y) →  g(x, y) = H1(x, y),
      INV :=   P (a, b) → a ⊕ (b Θ a) = b,               ¬ B(x, y) →  g(x, y) = H2(x, y, g(L(x, y),
      EQS :=   [ B → E1 = E2 ],                                                    y ⊕ ΔE (x, y) );
where CB :=    B(x, E(x)),
      CH1 :=   H1(x, E(x)),
      CH2 :=   H2(x, E(x), f(L(x, E(x))) );
      ΔE (x, y) := simplify (E(L(x, y)) Θ E(x), EQS),
  FreeVars(f(x)) ⊇ FreeVars(E(x)),
  y : T :: y ∉ Freevars (CH1, CH2),
  Freevars (CE) ∩ Boundvars (CH1, CH2) = ∅
such that   |= defined (CE),   INV,   EQS,
            |= P (E(L(x, y), E(x))
```

Status: The combination with embedding has not been implemented yet.

3.4.6. Linear Recursion to Tail-Recursion

Transformations to tail-recursion ("recursion removal") are classical examples of optimisations for conventional machines. The transformations described in [Bauer, Wössner 84] have been adapted here for operational specifications ("functional programs").

3.4.6.1. Linear Recursion with Associative Operation

```
MonoidRecRem: DECLARATION_LIST_CST —> DECLARATION_LIST —>
              EXPRESSION —> DECLARATION_LIST;
```

In this special, and perhaps most common, case, ⊕ and *n* form a Monoid, where ⊕ is an arbitrary associative operation.

```
f: S —> M;

axiom for all x: S =>
   B x →    f x = f (H x) ⊕ K x,
  ¬B x →    f x = T x;
let  n : M;
such that
  |= axiom for all x, y, z: M =>
       (x ⊕ y) ⊕ z = x ⊕ (y ⊕ z),   x ⊕ n = x;
```

=

```
f:    S —> M;
g:    S —> M —> M;
axiom for all x: S =>
                f x = g x n,
      B x →     g x y = g (H x) ((K x) ⊕ y),
     ¬B x →     g x y = (T x) ⊕ y;
```

Example: Factorial Function

```
fac:       NAT —> NAT;
axiom for all x: NAT =>
   x > 0 → fac x = fac (x–1) * x,
  ¬x > 0 → fac x = 1;
```

```
fac:       NAT —> NAT;
fac2:  NAT —> NAT —> NAT;
axiom for all x: NAT; y:NAT; z:NAT =>
              fac x = fac2 x 1,
   x > 0 →    fac2 x y = fac2 (x–1) (x * y),
  ¬x > 0 →    fac2 x y = 1 * y;
```

Matches:
  B x ≈ x > 0,   ⊕ ≈ * ,   H x ≈ x–1 ,
  K x ≈ x ,   T x ≈ 1
Parameter: n ≈ 1

Applicability Condition:
  (x * y) * z = x * (y * z),   x * 1 = x

```
AssocRecRem:  DECLARATION_LIST_CST —> DECLARATION_LIST —>
              EXPRESSION —> DECLARATION_LIST;
```

In the general case of associativity, ***D*** corresponds to the "dangling operation" and its counterpart ***U*** is entered by the user. Note the transformation is generalised by using higher-order matching for ***D*** .

```
f: T0 —> T1;
axiom for all x: T0 =>
   B x →    f x = D (f (H x)) (K x),
  ¬B x →    f x = T x;
let E : T2 :: E = U y z
where  T2 = type_of (K x ), y, z: T2 ,
       U: T2 —> T2 —> T2
such that
  |= axiom for all x: T1; y: T2; z: T2 =>
       D (D x y) z = D x (U y z);
```

=

```
f:  T0 —> T1;
g:  T0 —> T2 —> T1;
axiom for all x: T0; y: T2 =>
   B x →    f x = g (H x) (K x),
  ¬B x →    f x = T x,
   B x →    g x y = g (H x) (U (K x) y),
  ¬B x →    g x y = D (T x) y;
```

Example

```
fac:        NAT —> NAT;
axiom for all x: NAT =>
   x > 0 →   fac x = x * fac (x-1),
  ¬x > 0 →   fac x = 1;
```

Matches:

```
B x    ≈ x > 0
D x y  ≈ y * x      - - note the inversion
H x    ≈ x–1
T x    ≈ 1
K x    ≈ x
```

```
fac:        NAT —> NAT;
fac2:  NAT —> NAT —> NAT;
axiom for all x,y: NAT =>
   x > 0 →   fac x = fac2 (x–1) x,
  ¬x > 0 →   fac x = 1,
   x > 0 →   fac2 x y = fac2 (x–1) (y * x),
  ¬x > 0 →   fac2 x y = y * 1;
```

Parameters:

```
U y z  ≈ z * y
```

Applicability Condition:

```
D (D x y) z = D x (U y z) ≈
z * (y * x) = (z * y) * x
```

3.4.6.2. Linear Recursion with Commutative Operation

```
CommRecRem:  DECLARATION_LIST_CST —> DECLARATION_LIST —>
             EXPRESSION —> DECLARATION_LIST;
```

This is a generalisation (with higher-order matching) of the case where **D** and **U** correspond to a "right-commutative" operation.

```
f: T0 —> T1;
axiom for all x: T0 =>
   B x →   f x = D (f (H x)) (K x),
  ¬B x →   f x = T x;
let E: T1 :: E = U y z
where  T1 = type_of (K x ),
       y : T0, z: T1,
       U: T0 —> T1 —> T1
such that
  |= axiom for all x: T0; y: T1; z: T1 =>
     D (U x y) z    = U (D x z) y,
     D (T (g0 x)) z = U (T (g0 x)) z;
where
  g0:   T0 —> T0;
axiom for all x: T0 =>
   B x →   g0 x = g0 (H x),
  ¬B x →   g0 x = x;
```

=

```
f:     T0 —> T1;
g:     T0 —> T1 —> T1;
g0:    T0 —> T0;
axiom for all x: T0; y:T1 =>
              f x = g x (T (g0 x)),
   B x →    g x y = g (H x) (U y (K x)),
  ¬B x →    g x y = y,
   B x →    g0 x = g0 (H x),
  ¬B x →    g0 x = x;
```

Example: Factorial Function

```
fac:      NAT —> NAT;
axiom for all x: NAT =>
  x > 1 →  fac x = x * fac (x-1),
 ¬x > 1 →  fac x = x;
```

Matches:
```
  B x    ≈ x > 0
  D x y  ≈ y * x     - - note the inversion
  H x    ≈ x–1
  T x    ≈ x
  g0     ≈ fac3
  K x    ≈ x
```
Parameters:
```
  U y z ≈ y * z
```

```
fac:   NAT —> NAT;
fac2:  NAT —> NAT —> NAT;
fac3:  NAT —> NAT;
axiom for all x: NAT; y: NAT; z: NAT =>
              fac x = fac2 x (fac3 x),
  x > 1 →  fac2 x y = fac2 (x–1) (y * x),
 ¬x > 1 →  fac2 x y = y,
  x > 1 →  fac3 x = fac3 (x–1),
 ¬x > 1 →  fac3 x = x;
```

Applicability Condition:
```
  (D (U x y) z = U (D x z) y) ≈
     z * (y * x) = (z * y) * x
  (D (T (g0 x)) z = U (T (g0 x)) z) ≈
     z * (fac3 x) = (fac3 x) * z
```

```
constRecRem:   DECLARATION_LIST —> DECLARATION_LIST;
```

Special case: ***D*** is unary and trivially "right-commutative".

```
f: T0 —> T1;
axiom for all x: T0 =>
  B x →   f x = D (f (H x)),
 ¬B x →   f x = T;
```

=

```
f:    T0 —> T1;
g:    T0 —> T1 —> T1;
axiom for all x: T0; y: T1 =>
            f x = g x T,
  B x →   g x y = g (H x) (D y),
 ¬B x →   g x y = y;
```

Example: Length

```
length:   LIST —> NAT;
axiom for all x: LIST =>
 ¬ isEmpty x →   length x = length (tail x) + 1,
   isEmpty x →   length x = 0;
```

Matches:
```
B x ≈ ¬ isEmpty x
D x ≈ x + 1
H x ≈ tail x
T x ≈ 0
```

```
length:   LIST —> NAT;
length1:  LIST —> NAT —> NAT;
axiom for all x: LIST; y: NAT =>
    length x = length1 x 0,
 ¬ isEmpty x → length1 x y = length1 (tail x) (x +1),
   isEmpty x → length1 x y = y;
```

3.4.6.3. Function Inversion

```
InvRecRem:   DECLARATION_LIST_CST —> DECLARATION_LIST —>
             EXPRESSION —> DECLARATION_LIST;
```

```
f: T0 —> T1;
axiom for all x: T0 =>
  B x →   f x = D (f (H x)) (K x),
 ¬B x →   f x = T x;
let  E : T0 :: E = U y
where  U: T0 —> T0, y: T0
such that
  |= axiom for all x: T0 => U (H x) = x;
```

=

```
f:    T0 —> T1;
g:    T0 —> T0 —> T1 —> T1;
g0:   T0 —> T0;
axiom for all x,y: T0; z: T1 =>
    f x = g x (g0 x) (T (g0 x)),
   x = y →     g x y z = z,
 ¬ (x = y) →   g x y z = g x (U y) (D z (K (U y))),
   B x →       g0 x = g0 (H x),
  ¬ B x →      g0 x = x;
```

Example: Factorial Function

```
fac:  NAT —> NAT;
axiom for all x: NAT =>
  x > 0 →  fac x = x * fac (x–1),
 ¬x > 0 →  fac x = 1;
```

Matches:
- *B* x ≈ x > 0
- *D* x y ≈ y * x - - *note the inversion*
- *H* x ≈ x–1
- *T* x ≈ 1
- *K* x ≈ x

Parameters:
- *U* y ≈ y+ 1

```
fac:  NAT —> NAT;
fac2: NAT —> NAT —> NAT —> NAT;
fac3: NAT —> NAT;
axiom for all x, y, z: NAT =>
  fac x = fac2 x (fac3 x) 1,
  x = y → fac2 x y z = z,
¬(x = y) → fac2 x y z = fac2 x (y+1) ((y+1) * z),
  x > 0 → fac3 x = fac3 (x–1),
 ¬x > 0 → fac3 x = x;
```

Applicability Condition:
U (*H* x) = x ≈ (x–1) +1 = x

```
InvRecRem0:  DECLARATION_LIST_CST —> DECLARATION_LIST —>
             EXPRESSION —> DECLARATION_LIST;
```

This case has a special termination condition:

```
f: T0 —> T1;
axiom for all x: T0 =>
  (x = x0) →  f x = T x,
 ¬(x = x0) →  f x = D (f (H x)) (K x);
let   E : T0 :: E = U y
where  U: T0 —> T0, y: T0
such that
  |= axiom for all x: T0; i: NAT =>
     U (H x) = x,
     H^i x = x0 → x = U^i x0;
```

=

```
f:  T0 —> T1;
g:  T0 —> T0 —> T1 —> T1;
axiom for all x, y: T0; z: T1 =>
          f x = g x x0 (T x0),
  (x = y) → g x y z = z,
 ¬(x = y) → g x y z = g x (U y) (D z (K (U y));
```

Example: Factorial Function

```
fac:      NAT —> NAT;
axiom for all x: NAT =>
  x = 0 → fac x = 1,
 ¬(x = 0) → fac x = x * fac (x–1);
```

Matches:
- *B* x ≈ x = 0
- *D* x y ≈ y * x - - *note the inversion*
- *H* x ≈ x–1
- *T* x ≈ 1
- *K* x ≈ x

Parameters:
- *U* y ≈ y + 1

```
fac:      NAT —> NAT;
fac2:  NAT —> NAT —> NAT —> NAT;
axiom for all x, y, z:NAT =>
  fac x = fac2 x 0 1,
  x = y → fac2 x y z = z,
¬(x = y) → fac2 x y z = fac2 x (y+1) ((y+1) * z);
```

Applicability Condition:

U (*H* x) = x ≈ (x–1) +1 = x
H^i x = x0 → x = U^i x0 ≈
(x - n = 0) → (x = 0 + n)

3.4.6.4. Re-Computation with Counter

LinRecRemRecomputation: *DECLARATION_LIST_CST* —> DECLARATION_LIST —> DECLARATION_LIST;

The transformation computes the number of iterations as well as the terminating result of x. The calculation of f is then done with the auxilary function g that is a tail recursive function.

```
f: T0 —> T1;
axiom for all x: T0 =>
  B x →     f x = D (f (H x)) (K x),
  ¬B x →    f x = T x;
```

=>

```
f:    T0 —> T1;
g:    T0 —> T1 —> NAT —> T1;
g0:   T0 —> T0;
i0:   T0 —> NAT —> NAT;
it:   T0 —> NAT —> T0;
axiom for all x, y: T0; i: NAT =>
                f x = g x (T (g0 x)) (i0 x 0),
   i = 0 →      g x y i = y,
 ¬(i = 0) →     g x y i = g x (D y (K (it x (i - 1))) (i - 1),
     B x →      g0 x = g0 (H x),
    ¬B x →      g0 x = x,
     B x →      i0 x i = g0 (H x) (i+1),
    ¬B x →      i0 x i = i,
   i = 0 →      it x i = x,
 ¬(i = 0) →     it x i = it (H x) (i–1);
```

Example: Factorial Function

```
fac:      NAT —> NAT;
axiom for all x: NAT =>
  x > 1 →   fac x = x * fac (x-1),
 ¬x > 1 →   fac x = x;
```

Matches:

```
B x    ≈ x > 1
D x y  ≈ y * x     -- note the inversion
H x    ≈ x–1
T x    ≈ x
K x    ≈ x
```

```
fac:   NAT —> NAT;
fac2:  NAT —> NAT —> NAT —> NAT;
fac3:  NAT —> NAT;
fac4:  NAT —> NAT —> NAT;
fac5:  NAT —> NAT —> NAT;
axiom for all x,y, z: NAT =>
                fac x = fac2 x (fac3 x) (fac4 x 0),
   z = 0 →      fac2 x y z = y,
  ¬z = 0 →      fac2 x y z =
                    fac2 x (y * (fac5 x (z-1))) (z–1),
   x > 1 →      fac3 x = fac3 (x–1),
  ¬x > 1 →      fac3 x = x,
   x > 1 →      fac4 x z = fac4 (x–1) (z+1),
  ¬x > 1 →      fac4 x z = z,
   z = 0 →      fac5 x z = x,
  ¬z = 0 →      fac5 x z = fac5 (x–1) (z–1);
```

3.4.6.5. *Explicit Stack*

```
LinRecRemStack:   DECLARATION_LIST_CST —> DECLARATION_LIST —> DECLARATION_LIST;
```

```
  f: T0 —> T1;
axiom for all x: T0 =>
   B x →    f x = D (f (H x)) (K x),
 ¬ B x →    f x = T x;
```

=

```
 f:    T0 —> T1;
 package LT0 is new LISTS (T0);
 g:    LT0 .LIST —> T1 —> T1;
 g0:   T0 —> T0;
 it:   T0 —> LT0 .LIST —> LT0 .LIST ;
axiom for all x, y: T0; l: LT0 .LIST =>
               f x = g (it x empty) (T (g0 x)),
    B x →     g0 x = g0 (H x),
  ¬ B x →     g0 x = x,
    B x →     it x l = it (H x) ((single x) & l),
  ¬ B x →     it x l = l,
 isEmpty l → g l x = x,
¬ isEmpty l → g l x = g (tail l) (D x (K (head l)));
```

Example: Factorial Function

```
  fac:       NAT —> NAT;
axiom for all x: NAT =>
   x > 1 →   fac x = x * fac (x-1),
 ¬ x > 1 →   fac x = x;
```

Matches:

```
  B x    ≈ x > 1
  D x y  ≈ y * x     - - note the inversion
  H x    ≈ x–1
  T x    ≈ x
  K x    ≈ x
```

```
 package LNAT is new LISTS (NAT);
 fac:   NAT —> NAT;
 fac2:  LNAT.LIST —> NAT —> NAT;
 fac3:  NAT —> NAT;
 fac4:  NAT —> LNAT.LIST —> LNAT.LIST;
axiom for all x, y: NAT; l: LNAT.LIST =>
               fac x = fac2 (fac4 x empty) (fac3 x),
   x > 1 →   fac3 x = fac3 (x–1),
 ¬ x > 1 →   fac3 x = x,
   x > 1 →   fac4 x l = fac4 (x–1) ((single x) & l),
 ¬ x > 1 →   fac4 x l = l,
 isEmpty l → fac2 l x = x,
¬ isEmpty l → fac2 l x = fac2 (tail l) ((head l) * x);
```

3.4.7. Instantiation

3.4.7.1. *Case Introduction*

```
CaseIntro:  EXPRESSION_LIST_CST —> EXPRESSION_LIST —>
            EXPRESSION_LIST —> EXPRESSION_LIST;
```

Goal: introduce conditions which lead to a case distinction in the original definition. This may cause simplifications of right hand sides of equations, giving a chance for achieving a recursive definition.

```
axiom for all x: S => B → f(x) = H;
let B1,..., Bn: LOGICAL
where
  y ∈ (Frevar(B1) ∪ ... ∪ Frevar(Bn) ) ∧ type_of(y) = T
such that
  |= for all x: S; y: T=>B1 ∨ B2 ∨ ... ∨ Bn = true
```

=

```
axiom for all x: S; y: T=>
  B1 →     B →  f(x) = H,
  B2 →     B →  f(x) = H,
  ...,
  Bn →     B →  f(x) = H;
```

Example

axiom for all *n: NAT => sqr n = n * n;*

Matches:

$H \approx$ n * n

$f(x) \approx$ sqr n

Parameters:

$B_1 \approx$ n = zero,

$B_2 \approx$ ¬(n = zero),

axiom for all *n: NAT =>*
*n = zero → sqr n = n * n,*
*¬(n = zero) → sqr n = n * n;*

Applicability Condition

for all *n: NAT=> n = zero ∨ ¬(n = zero)*

3.4.7.2. Instantiation with Constructor Patterns

Instantiate: *DECLARATION_CST* —> DECLARATION—> *EXPRESSION_LIST* —> DECLARATION;

Goal: Introduce pattern-oriented notation (used in functional programming) by giving different constructor alternatives. The argument position where patterns should be introduced is indicated by the name of the respective argument variable. The transformation may be used to instantiate a variable to an expression; in general, the variable must be instantiated by a list of constructors that cover the whole domain of the variable.

axiom for all *x: S => B (x) → f (x) = H (x)*
let *CEL:= [c_1, , c_n]*
such that **|=** **for all** *x: S =>* **exist** *$\underline{y_1}$:$\underline{R_1}$; ...; $\underline{y_n}$:$\underline{R_n}$ =>* *$x = c_1(\underline{y_1}) \vee ... \vee x = c_n(\underline{y_n})$*
where *$\underline{R_i}$ = arg_type_of(c_i).*

=

axiom for all *$\underline{y_1}$:$\underline{R_1}$; ...; $\underline{y_n}$:$\underline{R_n}$ =>*
B ($c_1(\underline{y_1})$) → f ($c_1(\underline{y_1})$)) = H ($c_1(\underline{y_1})$),
...,
B ($c_n(\underline{y_n})$) → f ($c_n(\underline{y_n})$)) = H ($c_n(\underline{y_n})$),

Example

axiom for all *x: NAT = > sqr x = x * x;*

Matches: *H(x)* ≈ x * x;

Parameters: *CEL* ≈ [zero, succ]

axiom for all *y: NAT = >*
*sqr zero = zero * zero,*
*sqr (succ y) = succ y * succ y;*

3.4.8. Renaming

3.4.8.1. Linearisation of Argument Variables

Linearise: DECLARATION_LIST —> DECLARATION_LIST;

Goal: Abstract all argument variables occuring more than once on the left hand side of an equation, introducing fresh variables. This is one step towards the elimination of the pattern-oriented notation.

axiom for all *x:T; DL => B → f (x,x) = E;*
where *occur (y, DL) = false*

=

axiom for all *x,y:T; DL =>*
y = x ∧ B → f (x,y) = E;

Example

axiom for all *x:T => eq (x,x) = true;*

Matches: *E* ≈ true;

axiom for all *x,y:T => y = x → eq (x,y) = true;*

3.4.8.2. Consistent Renaming of Argument Variables

RenameArgs: DECLARATION_LIST —> DECLARATION_LIST;

Goal: RenamE argument variables consistently across function definitions such that, for a given function, the left hand sides of all equations have the same variables. This is one step towards the algorithmic form.

	=	
axiom for all x,y:T => $\mathcal{B}_1$ (x) → f(x) = $\mathcal{E}_1$ (x), $\mathcal{B}_2$ (y) → f(y) = $\mathcal{E}_2$ (y);	=	**axiom for all** x:T=> $\mathcal{B}_1$ (x) → f(x) = $\mathcal{E}_1$ (x), $\mathcal{B}_2$ (x) → f(x) = $\mathcal{E}_2$ (x),

Example

axiom for all x,y: NAT => x < 0 → f(x) = 0, y ≥ 0 → f(y) = y;	**axiom for all** x: NAT => x < 0 → f(x) = 0, x ≥ 0 → f(x) = x;

Matches:

$\mathcal{B}_1$ (x) ≈ (x < 0), $\mathcal{B}_2$ (y) ≈ (y ≥ 0),
$\mathcal{E}_1$ (x) ≈ 0, $\mathcal{E}_2$ (y) ≈ y

3.4.9. Collection of Rules

3.4.9.1. Combination of Axiomatic Parts

CollectAxioms: DECLARATION_LIST —> DECLARATION_LIST;

Goal: Compose the different declarations and axioms together, respectively.

	=	
[type S **is private** | f: S | **axiom** D **]**;	=	**[type** S **is private** | f: S**]**; **[axiom** D **]**;

3.4.9.2. Split of Axioms

Split: DECLARATION_LIST —> DECLARATION_LIST;

Goal: Decompose an axiom into axioms such that each axiom contains only one function definition.

	=	
[type S **is private** | f: S | **axiom** D **]**; **where [axiom** Di **]**$_n$:= split (**axiom** D)	=	**[type** S **is private** | f: S **]**; **[axiom** Di **]**$_n$;

3.5. Towards Imperative Programs

3.5.1. Introduction of Conditional Expression

IfIntro: EXPRESSION_LIST —> EXPRESSION_LIST;

Goal: combine all conditional equations defining a function into one equation witn a conditional expression. The transformation below just gives the special case of two symmetric equations.

	=	
axiom for all DL => $\mathcal{B}$ (x) → f (x) = $\mathcal{H}_1$(x), **not** $\mathcal{B}$ (x) → f (x) = $\mathcal{H}_2$(x)	=	**axiom for all** DL => f (x) = **if** $\mathcal{B}$(x) **then** $\mathcal{H}_1$(x) **else** $\mathcal{H}_2$(x)

3.5.2. Generation of Bodies

GenBody: PROGRAM —> PROGRAM;

Goal: introduce bodies for functions defined by a single equation. The transformation below just gives a special case for one function: there may be a sequence of variable abstractions and nested conditionals.

```
with IL;
package PF is
   f: S --> R;
   DL;
private with NL
   axiom for all x: S; y: T =>
      y = E(x) →
      f (x) = if B(x, y) then H1(x, y) else H2(x, y)
end PF;
```

=>

```
with IL;
package PF is
   f: S --> R;
   DL;
private with NL
   axiom for all x: S; y: T =>
      y = E(x) →
      f (x) = if B(x, y) then H1(x, y) else H2(x, y)
end PF;
package body PF is
   function F (X: S --> R) is
   y : T
   begin
      y:= E(x);
      if B(x, y) then
         return H1(x, y);
      else
         return H2(x, y);
      end if;
   end F;
end PF;
```

3.5.3. Introduction of Loops

```
WhileIntro: EXPRESSION —> EXPRESSION;
```

Goal: replace a tail recursive definition by a loop.

```
function F (X : S --> R) is
begin
   if B(X) then
      return T(X);
   else
      return F (H(X));
   end if;
end F;
```

=

```
function F (X : S --> R) is
begin
   while not B(X) loop
      X: = H(X);
   end loop;
   return T(X);
end F;
```

3.5.4. Translation to C

(analogously to ToAda)

```
ToC:    PROGRAM —> PROGRAM;
```

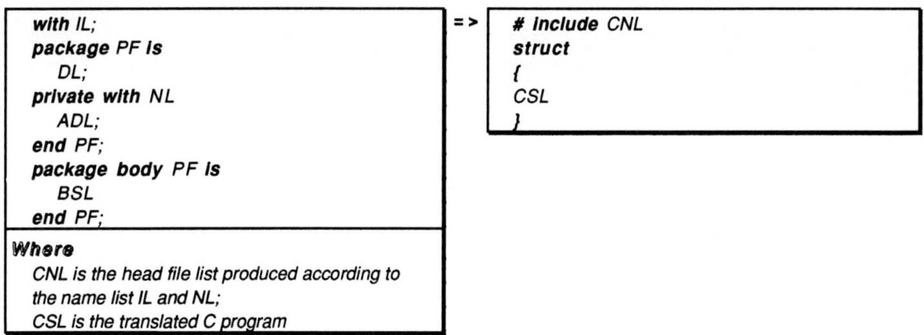

Acknowledgements

Many people were involved in developing and improving the transformations during the PROSPECTRA project including: D. Plump, F. Drewes, J. von Holten, O. Traynor, P. Flathmann, R. Seifert , Y. Wu, Z. Qian (Bremen), A. Lopez (Alcatel SESA). This document is based on a collection of transformations developed in the system.

4. Verification

Andrew D McGettrick, Owen Traynor[1]*, David Duffy,*
University of Strathclyde

Verification is an important facet of the PROSPECTRA methodology. In this chapter general verification issues are considered as well as the conceptual and the practical integration of proof into the methodology. The proof systems available within the PROSPECTRA system are described and their complementary roles in program development are presented.

The way in which the PROSPECTRA methodology and system are used to construct proof strategies and tactics is described. The principles underlying proof are closely related to the methodology for transformation and program development, and indeed a certain duality is apparent. This duality is exposed and shown to underpin many aspects of the design of the proof system.

4.1. Introduction

The main aim of this document is to illustrate the manner in which both proof development is carried out within the confines of the PROSPECTRA methodology. Associated with proof there is traditionally a set of tactics which serve to guide the process; thus meta proof development, as it is called, is a central concern in the discussion. A secondary aim is to give some insight, to those writing transformations, into the way in which the proof system deals with the correctness (applicability) conditions which are generally associated with a transformation. Composite transformations give rise to the need to combine applicability conditions and issues associated with this are discussed.

Prior to such a discussion it is important to capture some of the philosophy which underlies the development of the PROSPECTRA verification system.

4.1.1. Verification in a Transformational System

One of the claims of those involved in transformational programming is that this approach strikes at the very heart of the programming activity. In this paradigm programming steps are represented as transformations which can be invoked, recorded, replayed and so on. Typically the application of a transformation is accompanied by a verification requirement (such as the checking of an applicability condition or dealing with, in fact proving, lemmas associated with the working of a refinement mapping).

Within the verification activity associated with PROSPECTRA we have attempted to explore more fully the relationship between programming and logic, using transformational programming and transformations themselves as the essential vehicle on which to base the discussion. In the context of the PROSPECTRA project this analysis is intended to clarify issues associated with the design of the transformation system and its relationship to the verifier as well as related concepts which affect the human computer interface.

4.1.2. Duality between Program and Proof

The process of verification can be viewed as an activity which involves a mathematical argument whose aim is to establish the correctness of some formal statement. Viewed from another angle the statement has

[1]*Author's current address*: FB 3 - Informatik, Universität Bremen, Postfach 330 440, D-2800 Bremen 33

to be shown to be true - and one way of doing this is by means of a sequence of transformations (inference rules or proof rules) which processes the formal statement and gradually transforms this to true. In short verification can be seen as an activity which involves the application of transformations.

Within transformational programming itself there are sound reasons for recording transformations, replaying them, having the notion of transformation scripts, and so on; all these are an essential part of the PROSPECTRA project, influencing the design of the library manager, the user interface, and so on. The verification activity gives rise to a similar set of requirements for recording proofs, replaying these proofs and having the notion of tactics; tactics themselves just correspond to the notion of transformation script.

This discussion tends to suggest that there is a certain duality between transformational programming and the verification activity. The relationship allows a unified (and simplifying) approach to the design of

- the overall system architecture
- the basic transformations and rules of inference
- the transformation scripts and tactics
- the structure of the library manager
- the implementation.

In this connection see also Figure 1.

Duality between

program	*and*	proof
transformation script	*and*	tactic
recursion	*and*	induction
module	*and*	theory

Figure 1

The normal view of transformational programming suggests that verification conditions and applicability conditions are a by-product of the design process. An environment such as PROSPECTRA provides a very natural setting within which to embed program synthesis. This activity is normally viewed as a process whereby a program is a side effect of proof. In this context the proof is the essential ingredient with the program being the by-product. This compares with the more traditional view in which the by-product of transformational design is the set of conditions which need to be processed by a theorem prover.

Within the range of transformations present within PROSPECTRA is a set whose applicability covers both specification and proof. These include:

- moving quantifiers/declarations under appropriate conditions
- renaming of variables and instantiatons
- the concept of abstraction and the complementary activity of replacing an abstraction by an appropriate definition (embedding), i.e. folding and unfolding.

As far back as 1968 the designers of Algol 68 had identified in the formal definition of that language a formal correctness between syntactic issues and logic. For legal programs the Algol 68 predicates had to disappear, i.e. simplify by the application of simple rules or rewrites to the value true. Likewise, in the context of transformational programming the applicability rules and other such conditions have to simplify to true, again by the application of simple rules.

4.1.3. Role of the Verifier

Within PROSPECTRA there are several roles seen for the verifier:

- the simplification of logical expressions
- proving applicability conditions, including induction proofs
- ensuring that the predicates associated with such specification properties as hierarchy consistency, hold
- ensuring that certain specification language constructions are type-correct.

Other roles are also possible. For instance, establishing the correctness of transformations themselves, proving properties such as the completeness and consistency of specifications, etc. are all worthy and important activities. Program synthesis might also be included in this catalogue but this is linked rather intricately to (ii) above.

4.1.4. Design in the Context of Transformations and Verification

Within PROSPECTRA the notion of transformations and verification are intimately intertwined. However it is important to contemplate the nature of design in such an environment.

If, at each stage of development, the designer has to divert attention to establish the proof of a verification condition or applicability condition, the design process will become awkward, tedious and infuriatingly difficult. Design typically involves exploring several possible options and finally choosing one path which leads to a successful conclusion. Thus 'dead-ends' are likely to have been taken; proofs that have been performed may turn out to be unnecessary.

In the circumstances, the concept of delaying proof till a later stage, has at least two important attractions:

unnecessary proofs are avoided and the development process thus becomes more efficient

the process of design is not interrupted in a fashion that destroys creativity and frustrates development.

The design of the system must reflect these observations since they lie at the heart of making the system usable.

4.1.5. Outline of Document

A number of important topics are to be considered. Firstly the two proof systems available in PROSPECTRA are discussed. Their conceptual position in overall development and their complementary roles are placed in perspective. In section 4.3 the notion of delayed proof is discussed and there is a description of the way in which such a mechanism can be used effectively. section 4.4 discusses some issues associated with inductive reasoning in PROSPECTRA. In section 4.5 the development of composite proof rules, or tactics, is discussed; the development of these rules using the PROSPECTRA methodology is considered. Some examples are given. section 4.6 discusses the important issue of definition and composition of applicability conditions.

4.2. Background Illustrations

In the context of the present discussion it is assumed that verification of the transformation rules (and the resultant production of applicability conditions) has already been performed. These activities may be supported by the verification system but for the moment it is assumed that the verification of the transformations has been achieved outside the system. As described in [Krieg-Brückner 88, 89] and part I chapter 1, basic transformations are considered as axioms in the algebra of programs and all other transformations as theories in that algebra.

4.2.1. The Calculus

The inference rules used in proof are given below. All rules are presented in a top down manner with goal sequents on the bottom. Taking such an approach provides a closer correspondence with the transformation system; the goal directed application of a proof rule has a close correspondence with the application of a tactic. The rules are actually formulated as transformations within the PROSPECTRA system; this allows them to be composed in order to form proof strategies or tactics (as described in section 4.5.5).

In the following,

x' - denotes new free variable, not already used in the sequent.

z - denotes term, appropriately selected so as to allow a successful conclusion to the proof.

§ - denotes a possibly empty list of premisses.

Rules

Immediate Validity §, A |- A

Duplication

§, A |- C
----
§, A, A |- C

Rules for Logical Connectives

Connective	**Antecedent**	**Consequent**
& (and)	§, A & B |- C ------------------ §, A, B |- C	§ |- A & B ------------------ § |- A § |- B
v (or)	§, A v B |- C -------------------------- §, A |- C §, B |- C	§ |- A v B § |- A v B ------------- ------------ § |- A § |- B
⇒ (implication)	§, A⇒B |- C ----------------------- § |- A §, B |- C	§ |- A ⇒ B ---------------- §, A |- B
~ (not)	§, ~A |- C ---------------- § |- A	§ |- ~A ------------------------------ §, A |- contradiction

⇔ (iff)	$\frac{\S, A \Leftrightarrow B \vdash C}{\S, A \Rightarrow B, B \Rightarrow A \vdash C}$	$\frac{\S \vdash A \Leftrightarrow B}{\S, A \vdash B \quad \S, B \vdash A}$
∀ (for all)	$\frac{\S, \forall x\, A(x) \vdash C}{\S, A(z) \vdash C}$	$\frac{\S \vdash \forall x\, A(x)}{\S \vdash A(x')}$
∃ (exist)	$\frac{\S, \exists x\, A(x) \vdash C}{\S, A(x') \vdash C}$	$\frac{\S \vdash \exists x\, A(x)}{\S \vdash A(z)}$

The motivation behind the choice of a sequent calculus for the proof system may, at first, seem somewhat arbitrary. However, under closer examination there are a number of advantages. Firstly, proofs are constructive. The tautology from classical logic,

A or not A

does not hold. For such a conjecture to be proven a demonstration of A (or of **not A**) would have to be provided; of course the Excluded Middle axiom "**A or not A**" could be added as a premise which would allow such classical tautologies to be proven. Thus proofs performed in an intuitionistic calculus are much more useful in the context of program synthesis or transformation synthesis since the framework provided by a constructive system is closer to a logic which would be employed in a program development context. Secondly, the system has a natural feel about it; proofs can be read and abstracted and the sequent calculus provides a clean and elegant mechanism for interaction. Thirdly, the calculus is relatively efficient, providing a reasonable framework for automation.

4.2.2. Generating and Proving Applicability Conditions

Given that transformations have applicability conditions (preconditions on their application or post conditions on the correctness of objects produced by the transformation), these are derived by instantiation of the transformation in the context of the object being transformed. For the purposes of the ensuing discussion it is assumed that the applicability conditions on transformations are simple. That is, they are not the result of composition of a number of primitive transformations and their associated applicability conditions; the issues surrounding the composition of applicability conditions will be addressed later (see section 4.6.2).

For a rule to be applied the precondition part of its applicability conditions must be shown to be true *before* the transformation is carried out. Thus the part of the applicability condition, which cannot be shown to hold by means of syntactic or static semantic information, must be passed to the proof system for checking. Conceptually, this requires that the *focus* of development is shifted to some sort of proof system. The context in which this proof must be performed is the original context of the specification which existed when the transformation was applied. The postcondition part of the applicability condition is more complex. Here it may be necessary to show that some properties which were true in the original context are still true in the new context (resulting from the application of the transformation). In general, the construction of post-conditions on transformations is a difficult procedure. The conditions will generally be embedded in some inner context of the transformation rule. The associated problems are discussed in more detail in section 4.6.

Note, also, that the proof activity requires that there be some sort of focus change with respect to the development tool being used (i.e. changing from program development to proof development). Currently there are two options for performing proof; both systems are discussed in the following sections.

4.2.3. Proof: Transforming Logical Formulae

In the first proof system, the pure transformation system, proof is performed by the application of transformation rules (masquerading as proof rules) to the applicability condition. The process of rule application will continue until the condition has been proved (reduced to **true**). In this situation, the record of the rules being applied, together with any user interaction required to guide the application of the rules, is recorded in the development history. Any backtracking required must be done via manipulation of this development script.

As an aside, the transformations constituting the proof system do not have any applicability conditions other than syntactic ones. These are all computed by context preconditions which allow the rules to be applied in the first instance. Restrictions on any parameters to the proof rules are also defined in such a way. Both preconditions and parameter restrictions are evaluated automatically by the CSG. Any transformations which are visible in the system are *always* applicable.

The conjectures to be proven by the application of proof rules are represented as sequents. A sequent has two components: an antecedent and a conclusion.

Sequent: Antecedent ⊢ Conclusion

The antecedent contains a list of assumptions which may be used in attempting to show the conclusion (conjecture) holds (is true). The rules of the proof system determine the way in which formulae in both the antecedent and the conclusion may be manipulated (in a sound manner) with the objective of showing the conjecture to be true.

In the example below in Figure 2 the rule for 'for all elimination' is defined. This rule allows any well typed term to be substituted for a variable which is universally quantified in the antecedent of a sequent. The rule has the additional condition that variables in the terms introduced are not bound by quantifications in any inner context. Note that in the proof system, sequents are represented by formulae whose major connective is an implication; the implication corresponds to the normal turnstyle (⊢) in a sequent. The premise of the implication corresponds to the antecedent and the conclusion to the conjecture.

```
((A = [(for all V : B => X) → Y] and (Subst(V, P, X) = R) and not Captured(P, X)) →
                              For_All_Elim(A, P) = [R → Y])
```

Figure 2: For all elimination rule

To explain, the function For_All_Elim is being defined by way of a conditional equation. Variables are bound in the condition part; the definition must be left linear. Note then that For_All_Elim takes, as parameters, some sequent, A, together with some substitution, P, for the universally quantified variable, V, which may occur in the antecedent of A. On the first line the terms V, B, X and Y are pattern variables which match in the context in which the transformation is being applied.

The other text between the ⌊ ⌋ brackets corresponds to some pattern which will be matched in the context of some PAnndA-S expression. Given that the pattern variables correspond to the various components of the matched pattern, these are then further manipulated to determine the appropriate result of the rule for For_All _Elim:

- Subst (V, P, X) = R means that R is the result of replacing all occurrences of V by P in X.

- Captured(P, X) means that some variable in P is captured by a quantification somewhere in X.

Note that capturing is a concept applicable in the lambda calculus and in other such areas. In effect its presence is to prevent possible confusion between variables which are distinct but are represented by the same identifier.

Now assume that this rule is to be applied under the following conditions:

Context:

(**for all** X:BOOLEAN => **exists** Y:BOOLEAN => P(X, Y)) → P(a,a)

Rule:

For_All_Elim

Parameter:

A is a sequent and P a substitution which replaces all occurrences of V, a variable universally quantified in the antecedent of A

If it were possible to perform such an action then the result would be:

Result:

exists Y:BOOLEAN => P(Y,Y)) → P(a,a)

This would lead to a system that was unsound. The additional restriction in the original rule on the parameter, not Captured(P, X), avoids this problem.

Thus, in the transformation based proof system, it is never possible to apply an inappropriate rule (either in terms of contextual/syntactic aspects or in terms of the soundness of the inference system)[2]. This means that, for this version of the system, a very comfortable environment for the application of transformations is provided. Of course, the developer may still apply a rule which is 'wrong' in terms of a successful computation and completion of the proof. The developer must make the correct choice from the rules which are applicable and provide suitable parameters to allow a successful conclusion.

When treating the rules of the proof system as transformations over PA^{nn}dA-S expressions, the methodology employed is exactly analogous to that of program transformation. Even in terms of development histories there is no explicit distinction between transformation and proof. For the purposes of development, it should be noted that the development of proof in the transformational context is analogous (in a simplistic way) to the simplification or factorisation of terms during program development. As far as recording proof developments is concerned, they simply become part of the development history for the specification objects undergoing refinement; they become an explicit part of the same development.

4.2.4. Proof: Creating an Explicit Proof Term

The second possibility for performing proof is similar, in many respects, to that described above. The system is based on the same calculus and, in fact, exactly the same basic set of proof rules. Conceptually, however, there are some distinctions. From the point of view of the *focus change*, mentioned earlier, there are major conceptual differences. Essentially this is in the creation of the development history (or proof tree). The current state of the proof and its derivation (development history) can be explicitly

---

[2]This assumes that all conditions on the validity of the inference rule are specified as part of the transformation in such a way so as they may be evaluated automatically.

manipulated or modified by the user. There is a direct correspondence between the proof tree and the development history.

In proving a conjecture, the developer is required to construct the proof tree corresponding to the proof for the conjecture. Thus, instead of reducing a logical formula to true, the user must construct a proof tree, the evaluation of which deduces the validity of the associated conjecture.

In this system, the application of an inference rule adds a node to the proof tree. In the case where all subtrees result in valid leaf nodes and no intermediate node corresponds to an unsound inference, then a complete and correct proof for the conjecture has been constructed.

On returning from a proof 'call' the resultant proof tree is flattened (or may be) to give a development history. Thus the proof developed by the 'tree based' proof system has a corresponding equivalent proof in terms of the development history notion. In this sense the interactive proof system can be seen as an optimisation of the pure transformation approach. It can even be thought of, methodologically, as an elaborate browsing mechanism for proof development histories; essentially it is an instantaneous representation of development

Recording development in the case of the proof editor, where an explicit proof tree is produced rather than a development script, is rather simple. The proof tree, together which a reference to the appropriate context, is recorded as an explicit component of the development history. On replay of a development which required the use of the proof editor, resulting in a proof, the stored proof tree would be the basis for an attempted proof in the context of the re-developement. In any simple replay of a development the proof would, of course, be successful. However, in a situation where some modifications have been made to some previous part of the development history, the proof tree may not correspond exactly to a successful proof. Depending on the nature of the redevelopment, some minor (or major) redevelopment, with respect to the associated proofs, may be required.

4.3. Delayed Proof

From the point of view of the methodology it may be desirable to delay proof until after a sequence of developments has been performed; this avoids the proof of developments which were essentially 'dead ends' and saves on wasted effort.

In the cases where developers wish to 'delay' a proof, they will have the opportunity to call a function from the proof system called 'delay_proof'. The function terminates the current proof with ´success´ allowing the developer to continue program developments. The 'delay step' in a proof (of either proof system) will be recorded in the development history. Any development history which includes the 'delay_proof' development step will, of course, not constitute a correct or complete development.

To achieve a correct development, a development history would be replayed. At each point in the history where a delay is encountered, the proof development is resumed from that point. Once that development is finished, the replay would continue, allowing the user to finish any other delayed proofs. Proofs, of course, may be done in isolation from program developments. The same mechanism may be used to store incomplete proofs.

4.3.1. Milestones

From a practical point of view the replay of a whole development, in order to isolate one unfinished proof, is unreasonable. For this reason it should be possible to declare 'milestones' in developments. Thus, each development between milestones may be replayed in isolation to those preceding and possibly in isolation from subsequent developments; this is certainly the case for proof (assuming that developments are correct). There is always the possibility that the proof will uncover an error which was not detected when the transformation was originally applied. This is, after all, a possible consequence of undertaking proof within the transformational development system. In the current PROSPECTRA system, a milestone is implicitly declared after every refinement step. A refinement step is the primitive action recorded by the library manager. Each refinement step has an associated log-and-replay script. The log script contains a detailed account of the actions which were issued in order to derive the contents of the current refinement from the previous version.

4.3.2. Monolithic Proofs

It is neither possible, nor desirable, to collect all applicability conditions associated with a development at the end of that development as a monolithic object. Each of the individual applicability conditions has a particular context in which it must be proved; thus it requires that all independent contexts also be gathered at the end of the development. In practice, the context changes after each development step. It would therefore be cumbersome and inefficient to perform a monolithic proof of a whole development within the confines of the PROSPECTRA methodology. This is perhaps not a bad thing! In this way a framework is provided for reusing proofs.

Such restrictions on the methodology associated with the verification activity also reap other benefits. For example, proofs may be stored in such a way as to restrict the context of the proof to only the theories/specifications which are appropriate. Proofs can then be stored (and structured) in such a way as to reflext the context in which they were developed and the specification about whose properties they reason. This is a particularly important result from the point of view of re-use and abstraction. In fact, such structuring can be seen as the first step in some abstraction procedure.

4.4. Induction

Within the verification activity there is an important role for induction. This importance stems from a number of observations:

- induction underpins many important theories, e.g. the non-negative integers, strings, trees, finite sets, bags
- proof of properties such as commutativity, associativity, etc. depend on induction
- induction is intimately associated with program synthesis
- there is a duality between induction and recursion which is important; the link between recursion and strategies such as divide-and-conquer and stepwise refinement is an important source of induction.

In some of these cases multiple inductions are needed. At the time of writing, the induction functions take the form of schemas which are instantiated and then enacted. These schemas are generated for each type in a specification which may be a basis for an inductive proof. The schemas are generated by hand. Their correctness is, currently, not ensured by the system. Checking of such induction schemas will become possible when higher order rules are introduced into the system; such additions are planned for Release 5.0 of PROSPECTRA and are necessary since PA^{nn}dA-S is a higher order language allowing functionals and higher order variables. See however [Duffy 88] for some new ideas in this area.

Induction, as a concept, in the context of a language such as PA^{nn}dA-S, is important in its own right. The occasions where induction is appropriate, where it fits in with the methodology, etc. deserve some attention. The first problem is to determine which type definitions in a specification have some associated well founded ordering such that some rule of induction for that type exists (can be derived). The second issue is regarding the methodology and the persistence of inductive theorems through a specification. Given that an inductive conjecture is valid (true in all models) then there is no problem in using such a theorem in the context of some refinement of the initial specification or as a tool in some other package which imports the specification from which the relevant inductive theorem has been derived (in a **with** clause). The tools which currently exist within the methodology to support such activities associated with inductive reasoning/development are insufficient. Some additional work remains to be done.

4.5. Meta Proof Development (Tactics)

Given that two proof systems exists, it is important that the tactics developed in one system be applicable in the other. A mechanism for allowing such a situation is described in [Traynor 89]. The mechanism requires that tactics are written initially for the transformational proof system. Tactics exploit the basic proof functions which exists for the manipulation of sequents. The notion of a proof tree is not required. This is described towards the end of section 4.2. The fact that transformations for proof are written using only a small set of proof kernel functions is important. If tactics are written using only these kernel functions, and functions derived from them, then they are guaranteed to be correct, though not, of course, necessarily successful.

4.5.1. The Tactic Writers' Interface

All the primitive rules of the proof system are available for writing tactics. Together with this set of rules is a set of corresponding applicability functions. These functions are considered as predicates which determine the applicability of rules in context and the validity of those rules which require parameters. The signatures of these functions are given below. However they are available and can be used in writing TrafoLa-S specifications. The functions use only the basic types associated with the expression subset of the PA^{nn}dA language.

```
with Panndas, SomeTermExtras;
package Calculus is
   Exists_Elim, ForAll_Intro:                    (A: Exp × B: Exp:: Unique(B, A) and IsFreeVar B ) → Exp;
   Exist_Intro, ForAll_Elim:                                  (Exp × Exp) → Exp;
   And_Intro, Or_Intro, Implies_Intro, Not_Intro, Iff_Intro:  Exp → Exp;
   And_Elim, Or_Elim, Implies_Elim, Not_Elim, Iff_Elim:       Exp → Exp;
   Add, SInduct, Lemma:                                       (Exp × Exp) → Exp;
   Delete, Duplicate, Subst, Instantiate, PromiseToFront:     (Exp × Literal) → Exp;
   Immediate, Is_Sequent,
   Ante_Has_ForAll, Ante_Has_Exists,
   Ante_Has_AndLeft, Ante_Has_Or,
   Ante_Has_Not, Ante_Has_Equal, Ante_Has_Iff,
   Conc_Has_ForAll, Conc_Has_Exists,
   Conc_Has_AndLeft, Conc_Has_Or,
   Conc_Has_Not, Conc_Has_Equal, Conc_Has_Iff:                Exp → Boolean;
end Calculus;
```

4.5.2. Some Example Tactics

When performing proof interactively there are a number of tasks performed regularly which are prime candidates for encapsulation in tactics. Experience with the proof system has shown such rules to be for example:

- removal of quantifiers
- applying an explicitly quantified axiom directly to the conclusion.
- choosing a lemma, duplicating and applying it to the conclusion.
- repeated application of an axiom as a rewrite rule (till failure).

These are just a few of the more obvious, simple minded rules which are very useful, and which can very easily be specified. Some of these tactics are given below.

The function **Rem_Quant** removes a Quantifier from the sequent depending on the type and position of the quantification. Either a term allowing the quantified expression to match some other expression in the sequent, or a free, unused variable (or constant) is used to replace the quantified variable.

```
with Pr_basic, SomeTermExtras, Panndas
package SimpleQuantifierTactics is
   Rem_Quant:   Exp → Exp,
   Get_Quant:   (Exp× Exp) → Exp,

axiom for all E:Exp;E1:Exp; E2:Exp;E3:Exp; T: Type_Exp; X: Unique_Name =>
   Ante_Has_Exists(E) →  Rem_Quant(E) = Exists_Elim(E, GetUniqueVar(E)),
   Conc_Has_ForAll(E) →  Rem_Quant(E) =ForAll_Intro(E, GetUniqueVar(E)),
   ((E=[E1 -> E2]) = true and Ante_Has_ForAll(E)) →
                          Rem_Quant(E) = ForAll_Intro(E,Get_Quant(E1,E2)),

   -- The three cases below provide for the instances where the
   -- quantification may be anywhere in the antecedent.
   (E =[for all X : T => E1 ]) →             Get_Quant(E,E2) = GetVInst(X,E1,E2),
   (E= [(for all X : T => E1 ) and E3 ]) →   Get_Quant(E,E2) = GetVInst(X,E1,E2),
   (E = [E1 and E3]) →                       Get_Quant(E,E2) = Get_Quant(E3,E2),
end SimpleQuantifierTactics;
```

The tactic above assume the definitions for GetUniqueVar and GetVInst already exist. They are very general-purpose and relatively simple functions. GetUniqueVar generates a variable not already used in the formula provided as a parameter. GetVInst replaces the variable (first argument) in an expression (second argument) in order to match this expression with the third argument.

The PA^{nn}dA-S phrase, **[A and B]**, where A and B are pattern variables denoting operands matched in the context of the conjunction, is a concrete representation of the abstract syntax term:

> Mk_Call(Mk_Name(Mk_Unique_Name("and", mk_Logical_And_Key())),
>
> Mk_Tuple(Mk_Expression_List(A, Mk_Expr_List(B, Empty_Expr_List())))

Similarly for the other phrases in squared brackets in the specification.

It is important to note that the above tactic definition, when applied to a proof object, does not record the application of primitive component rules. An additional mechanism is defined which will lift the tactic specification from a transformation over expressions producing expressions to a transformation over expressions producing proof terms. This is illustrated below:

Transformation: EXPRESSION $\rightarrow$ EXPRESSION

$\Downarrow$ Lifting Transformations

Tactic: EXPRESSION $\rightarrow$ Proof

Thus instead of transforming the logical expression, a tactic will be created which will generate a proof tree which, when parameterised with the original logical expression, will perform an equivalent deduction.

It should be noted that, even though these tactics determine the instantiation of quantified variables, the proof tree produced allows the user to modify the instantiation using an appropriate parameter. Thus, if the automatic instantiation produces the wrong instance (or, as will happen in some cases, no instantiation at all), the user may then modify or determine the instance for the variable.

4.6. Specification and Composition of Applicability Conditions

In general there will be two kinds of applicability conditions on transformations - those which can be checked automatically by the transformer shell and those which require some sort of theorem proving activity in order to show they hold.

As well as considering the individual applicability conditions on transformations, there is a more general consideration. In composing transformations to produce transformals/strategies, the applicability conditions associated with the composed transformations must also be considered. This is discussed in section 4.6.2.

Static is to be used to refer to applicability conditions which can be proved without the help of the proof system. *Semantic* is be used for those terms which require such intervention.

4.6.1. Specification of Applicability Conditions

Applicability conditions can be thought of as being the combination of the pre- and post - conditions (*re* correctness) of transformation rules. When transformations are instantiated, enough information is provided for the condition also to be instantiated. A condition will be a logical expression or a predicate. Note, however, that the problem of context (i.e. in which context the proof should be carried out) is not as simple; the initial context of the transformation may not be sufficient (or correct) context in which to carry out the associated proofs.

Currently, preconditions on rules (the condition part of conditional axioms defining the transformation) are used to specify the static applicability of transformations. Applicability conditions, which require the use of a theorem proving tool, may also be specified in a similar way. The conditions are specified via an explicit interface function to the proof system. The function:

Verify(A, Context),

would be used to isolate the dynamic part of the applicability condition for a transformation. No work then has to be done in order to translate this to any target language in which the transformation is to be realised; it would be instantiated in context and its evaluation would automatically call the proof system. This is currently the case when transformations of this kind are written with SSL as the target language.

Alternatively, the applicability condition may be introduced into the text of the specification, acting as a barrier to further development until it has been reduced to insignificance. In many situations this is acceptable; however, when transformations have complex context requirements associated with their applicabilty conditions, this is insufficient since some part of the applicability condition requires some context which is different from that required by other parts of the `same´ condition.

4.6.1.1. The Context Problem

When reasoning about the applicability conditions associated with a transformation, the context in which the reasoning must be done is important. In particular, reasoning about the result of a transformation generally requires that the context used is that which is computed after the transformation is applied. The conceptual problem here is that context is computed after the application of the transformation has finished (by a different component of the transformation system). Therefore, any post condition part of the applicability condition that requires post context which is, as yet, still uncomputed.

One solution to this is to have rules within the transformation which, during the application of the transformation, generate the appropriate context information. This would require that the attribute grammar, used to compute context, is modelled in PA^{nn}dA-S and is realised in an operational way so as to be translatable to SSL. This type of activity becomes possible as more of the PROSPECTRA system is developed within the PROSPECTRA methodology. The specification of all system components in the system itself is currently underway.

4.6.2. Composition of Conditions

For the development of transformals and strategies to be sensible, there should be facilities provided which allow transformations and their associated applicability conditions to be combined in a sensible way. In the following section the mechanisms needed to perform such developments are outlined.

Consider the simple sequential development of a program fragment by the application of two transformation rules. Both rules have their associated applicability conditions. For the moment it is not important whether the verifier is required to process the conditions and ensure they hold in the current context. Let the two transformations appear as conditional rewrite rules of the form

condition → left side = right side

When the condition is true the left hand side is replaced by the right side. The rules are:

f(X,Y) → A(X,Y) = B(X,Y,0)   (i)

g(X,Z) → B(X,Y,Z) = C(X,H(Y,Z))   (ii)

Given that such a sequence could be considered a general strategy, it is desirable to combine the two rules into one. This is achieved, simply, by matching the tail of (i) with the head of (ii). This generates:

A(X,Y) = C(X,H(Y,0))

with the applicability condition:

f(X,Y) **and** g(X,0).

Given that the definition of g is available there is now perhaps scope for simplification of the applicability condition. For example, assuming the definition of g is:

```
g(X,Z) :: (X >= Z) and prime(X)
```

then such a definition could be simplified immediately since X >= 0 is true by definition. This, of course, assumes that the necessary typing information is available at analysis time. This may, in fact, not be the case.

What kind of rules are appropriate for performing this type of manipulation or simplification of applicability conditions? Many of the rules will be specific to the algebraic types being developed[3]. Such rules may be thought of as rewrite systems for these types (derived by analysis of the types by a completion procedure). The standard types and many commonly used types may have rewrite systems generated and stored in the library. The proof system could also be used at this point.

A transformation which is certainly applicable in this context is 'unfold'. Given the definition of the predicate, f, used above, the use of unfold together with transformations for simplication allow substantial simplification of the condition in the example:

```
f(X,Y) :: prime(X) and even(Y)
```

Together with the definition of g, we have:

```
prime(X) and even(Y) and (X >= 0) and prime(X)
```

which simplifies immediately to:

```
prime (X) and even(Y).
```

In this situation, sufficient information was provided by the composition process to allow verifiction of much of the condition prior to its application in any context. Essentially the composition has restricted the generality of the individual transformations to the intersection of their respective application contexts.

Such situations will not always arise. There will be many occasions when instantiation of a composite applicability condition will not be possible until after the composite transformation has been applied in context. Certainly, the context of the development will change after the application of the individual transformations. For the purposes of verification, if it is not possible to abstract this context to applicability condition on the correctness of the composite transformation, this context must somehow be preserved and used for the purposes of verifying the individual applicability conditions.

4.6.3. Abstraction over Composition

Careful consideration of such issues must be given by the developer of composite transformations. It may not be possible to construct post- (or pre-) conditions corresponding to the correctness of composite transformations. This is due to the fact that context, only visible from within the transformation, is required for the correctness proof of the transformation. This context, and therefore the ability to reason directly about the associated correctness issues, is lost when abstraction is carried over such a set of sequentially applied transformations. Composing transformations, without the associated property of abstraction over the composed rules, is not very useful; rules are composed together so as to avoid having to understand all the details of the individual rules. The 'internal' correctness of the transformation must

[3]Implying, of course, that the actual transformation rules are specific in this way.

be guaranteed if the abstraction process is to be appropriate. This means that any context or conditions, which cannot be fully abstracted to a pre- or post-condition, must be provable when the transformations are initially composed by the transformation developer.

The possibility exists of calling the verifier from within the composite transformation. This, however, contravenes the basic principle of abstraction (the basis for composition in the first place). It is also more likely that the developer will be unable to prove such conditions given that the context may be obscure and unfamilair with respect to the original context of the transformation.

This issue needs to be studied in detail, both from the point of view of transformational development and the associated verification issues. Hopefully, it is possible to determine some framework within the methodology which allows the development of transformations in a convienent way.

4.7. Using the Proof System for Program Development

Many workers, in the areas of both transformational development ([Manna, Waldinger 80], [Burstall, Darlington 77]) and in program synthesis ([Constable et al. 86], [Arsac, Kodratoff 82], [Dershowitz 83]), have advocated and extolled the virtues of proof systems, especially those with some induction mechanism, for aiding and performing the task of program transformation and program synthesis. In fact there are many instances where investigations of inductive theorem proving systems ([Boyer, Moore 79], [Aubin 79]) have been a major influence in the development of transformation systems and ideas ([Burstall, Darlington 77], [Duffy 88]). Also, given the results in the term rewrite field, it seems that the technologies are converging. Completion-based tools are both powerful in terms of program development and in their theorem-proving capabilities.

Given the context of the PROSPECTRA project, there is no doubt that the project is in a very good position to exploit completion-based transformers and results from inductive theorem proving, as aids directly in the development process. It remains to be seen how such facilities can be comfortably used within the development environment.

An important aspect of such an integration would be the identification of the class of problem to which such methods would be applicable. There is a wealth of examples in the literature, but many of these examples can be done more simply with the use of relatively primitive transformations (for example those for recursion removal). However, taking the case of recursion removal, there is no known complete set of rules for performing this task[4]. A general method, based on induction and described in [Arsac, Kodratoff 82], is generally applicable and certainly very useful in the cases where none of the standard rules apply.

What has been accomplished within the verification activity of PROSPECTRA can be seen as a (fairly substantial) start into a wider activity of exploring in more detail the link between programming and verification. Prior to the production of a prototype system which could be used to exploit and explore ideas in transformational programming, such developments were infeasible.

At the time of writing program synthesis is a topic of lively interest but at an early stage of development. The transformational environment provides a convenient setting in which to embed developments, these developments being captured in the form of tactics for the verification system.

The duality notion mentioned earlier in section 4.2.1 needs to be explored further in this context. In discussing design earlier (within the context of PROSPECTRA and the associated verification issue) the

[4]Huet and Lang in [Huet and Lang,78] describe a very general set of schema; however, these are not exhaustive.

remark was made that design should be completed, at least up to some level, before verification is undertaken; in this way unnecessary verification is avoided and verification does not detract from the design process. Likewise, within synthesis there are similar arguments which suggest that programs should be generated only when all aspects of a proof, at least up to some level, have been accomplished.

The ability to compose basic transformations to produce complex development strategies is fundamental to the success of a development system such as PROSPECTRA. The facility to abstract to a precondition the correctness obligations for composite transformations is also important. Some mechanisms which allow this to be done in simple cases have been outlined; this is an area for further work. The ability to perform/compose large development steps into simple strategies which don't result in large monolithic obligations would be useful.

4.8. Future Directions

Of vital importance here, and in the project generally, is the extension of the proof system with higher order rules. A mechanism for higher order matching and higher order inference rules is required before it is realistically possible to apply the proof system to program development.

Possible further uses of the proof system include:

- the synthesis of transformations from correctness/equivalence proofs of programs
- the development/testing of transformations by applying them as axioms in the proof system to conjectures which are essentially program fragments.
- the production of transformations from developments (synthesis) carried out by the proof system.

The integration of proof at levels of development other than the verification of applicability conditions and to support refinement is an exciting prospect.

PROgram Development by SPECification and TRAnsformation

Part II

Language Family

1. A Language Family for Programming and Meta-Programmming

Bernd Krieg-Brückner, Universität Bremen

This chapter contains a brief introduction to the PROSPECTRA language family. It gives a rationale for the relationship between the languages and relates this Part II to those on the Methodology and the System. The role of PA^{nn}dA-S as *the* central language of the family is explained and desired properties for it are defined in relation to the methodology. PA^{nn}dA is introduced as the "wide-spectrum language" extension to PA^{nn}dA-S in the direction of Ada (and similar imperative languages). The use of PA^{nn}dA-S for meta-programming (of transformation programs), i.e. its extension to TrafoLa-S, and its use for the formalisation of the development process and as a command language ControLa are described.

1.1. Uniform Approach

The uniform approach to program and meta-program development (cf. part I chapter 1, part III chapter 1) has had some major impact on the design of the languages within the methodology and the system. The approach leads to a uniform treatment of (specification and) programming language (PA^{nn}dA-S, PA^{nn}dA), transformation specification and program manipulation language (TrafoLa-S), and command language (ControLa).

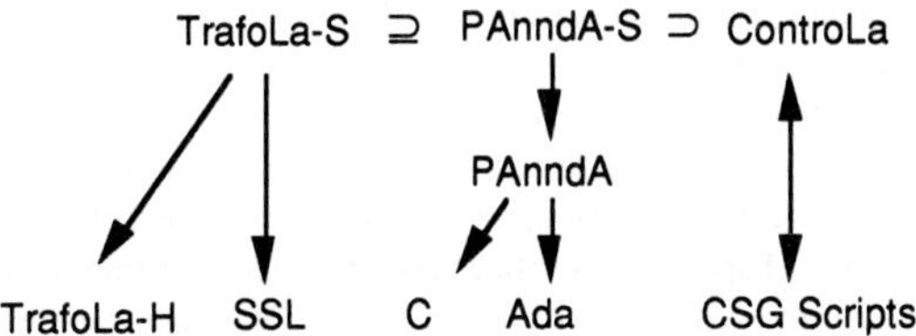

1.2. PA^{nn}dA-S

The *specification language PA^{nn}dA-S* (cf. chapters 2 and 3) is at the heart of the language family. It covers the "wide-spectrum language" levels for program development: formal requirement specification, design specification and applicative implementation (including higher-order functions). Some of its features have been derived from the originally intended target language Ada: the strong typing discipline, abstracted to the definition of Ada oriented, predefined PA^{nn}dA-S Standard Types and Type Schemata (see chapter 5), naming and visibility rules, hierarchical modularisation by packages (with visible interfaces and hidden bodies), parameterisation of (specification) modules as (nested) generics, etc. For the algebraic approach to specification, visible parts were inherited from Ada as signatures, augmented by logical formulae; the methodology (cf. part I section 1.2) required features such as looseness of requirement specifications, partial and non-strict functions, definedness premises etc.

In addition, PA^{nn}dA-S serves as a meta-language, cf. TrafoLa-S and ControLa below. Historically, the need, at the meta-level, for a definition of transformation, proof and development tactics induced the inclusion of higher-order functions. In the end, a notion of partial higher-order functions is now available (cf. chapter 3; for some remarks on limitations such as the notable lack of polymorphism see part I section 1.2.5).

1.3. PAnndA

PAnndA-S is a subset of *PAnndA* (cf. chapters 4 and 5) that also contains *imperative programming language* constructs towards Ada as a target (due to its rather general nature, transliteration to other imperative target languages such as C has turned out to be fairly easy). Note that specifications in PAnndA-S can be edited initially and then transformed, whereas programs in (the rest of) PAnndA are always generated by correctness-preserving transformation, no "active programming" in the imperative language constructs of PAnndA is allowed. Thus the "wide-spectrum language extension" of PAnndA-S towards PAnndA is implicitly defined by some transformations from the applicative subset of PAnndA-S (operational definitions of first-order functions).

1.4. TrafoLa-S

The (program) specification language PAnndA-S is also used, at the meta-level, as the *transformation specification language TrafoLa-S* (see chapter 6). TrafoLa-S additionally contains some syntactic abbreviations for phrases (program fragments with variables in concrete syntax, cf. part I section 1.5.1) and context-sensitive transformations that can be transformed into canonical PAnndA-S. Chapter 4 contains the abstract and concrete syntax, the static semantic attributes, etc. of PAnndA, for the description of transformations, proof strategies etc. in TrafoLa-S. The Abstract Syntax is described as a package (predefined abstract type schema) that corresponds to the underlying SSL description. The concrete syntax is described in terms of the syntax phrases associated with the Abstract Syntax of PAnndA.

It is quite important that abstract syntax trees are also decorated with semantic attributes, representing context-sensitive information, such as type information, but also e.g. the set of all applicable axioms (the "local theory", cf. part III section 1.2.5) to support efficient proofs, for checking semantic applicability of transformations and to allow the definition of some context-sensitive transformations that automatically gather information from this local theory (cf. part I chapter 3). The attribute domains, associated access functions etc. are described in chapter 4. Thus they serve as a basis for transformation development and proofs, and also as a basis for the system description in Volume III. Note that the proof tactics (meta-)language is also partially derived from TrafoLa-S / PAnndA-S (see part III section 4.4).

Translation to SSL, the applicative tree manipulation language of the Synthesizer Generator (see reference to [Reps, Teitelbaum 88] in part I), used both as an Editor and as a Transformer Generator in the system, is automatic. Alternatively, one can translate transformation scripts to a more powerful target language with higher order matching and functionals that is compiled into abstract machine code (presently context-free without attributes), the program manipulation and transformation language TrafoLa-H, see chapter 8 and Vol. III section 5.3.

1.5. ControLa

The use of PAnndA-S for the formalisation of the development process has been described in part I section 1.6. Thus *ControLa*, the command language of the system, is also a subset of TrafoLa: development histories can be abstracted as formal objects from concrete CSG scripts (the command language in the underlying implementation of the system), simplified or otherwise manipulated, translated back to CSG scripts, and replayed, see chapter 7 and Vol. III chapters 3 and 6. It should be noted, however, that although the basic technology is there, the process of abstraction from concrete developments to more generally applicable methods is still unsolved and remains a major challenge for future research.

2. PA^{nn}dA–S Reference Manual

Einar W. Karlsen[1] *and Jesper Jørgensen, Computer Resources International A/S*

2.1. Introduction

This manual describes the concrete syntax and the static semantics of PA^{nn}dA–S (PROSPECTRA Anna/Ada Specification Language). As PA^{nn}dA–S has been developed from the programming language Ada [Ada 1983] and the Ada-oriented specification and annotation language Anna [Anna 1987], the style of description is taken from the reference manuals for these two languages. For the Ada parts, the description model is a simplified version of that used in [Ada 1983].

2.1.1. Structure of the Reference Manual

Each language construct is described by its concrete syntax, the properties that instances of the construct possess and the set of static context conditions that a construct must fulfil. The context conditions are stated verbally, and are numbered consecutively within each subsection. A section termed *Notes* may contain further remarks concerning the construct.

In order to state the context conditions in a more readable way, a number of static semantic terms are defined. Their definitions are emphasized using *italics*. The definition of these terms are summarized in the index at the end of this document. The index also contains references to the syntactic definition of each language construct.

2.1.2. Syntax Notation

The concrete syntax of the language is given in the variant of Extended Backus-Naur-Form (EBNF) used in [Ada 1983]. In particular:

1. Lower case words (some with embedded underlines) denote syntactic categories, for example: function_-type_expression
2. Boldface words denote reserved words, for example: **package**
3. The symbol ::= defines the syntax of a syntactic category, for example:

   subtype_declaration ::= **subtype** identifier **is** type_expression ;

4. A vertical bar separates alternative items, for example:

   letter_or_digit ::= letter | digit

5. Square brackets enclose optional items. Thus the two following rules are equivalent.

   function_declaration ::= [--:] domain;

   function_declaration ::= domain; | --: domain;

6. Braces enclose a repeated item. The item may appear zero or more times. Thus the two following rules are equivalent.

   tuple_type_expression ::= extended_type_expression { # extended_type_expression}

   tuple_type_expression ::=
   extended_type_expression | tuple_type_expression # extended_type_expression

1. *Author's current address*: FB 3 - Informatik, Universität Bremen, Postfach 330 440, D- 2800 Bremen 33

7. If the name of any syntactic category starts with an italicized part, it is equivalent to the category name without the italicized part. The italicized part conveys some context property. For example *subtype_*-name and *generic_package_*name are both equivalent to the category name.

2.2. Lexical Elements

This section defines the lexical elements of the language.

2.2.1. Character Set

All language constructs may be represented with a graphic character set which is subdivided as follows:

- upper case letters: A B C D E F G H I J K L M N O P Q R S T U V W X Y Z
- lower case letters: a b c d e f g h i j k l m n o p q r s t u v w x y z
- digits: 0 1 2 3 4 5 6 7 8 9
- the space character
- special characters: " # & ' ( ) * + , – . / : ; < = > _ | ! $ % ? @ [\ ] ^ ‘ { } ~
- format effectors: the ISO (and ASCII) characters called *horizontal tabulation*, *vertical tabulation*, *carriage return*, *line feed*, and *form feed.*

Some non-ASCII characters are allowed for writing programs in "mathematical style" (e.g. in documents); rules for transliterating these characters into the graphic character set appear in section 2.2.8.

2.2.2. Lexical Elements, Separators, and Delimiters

The text of each compilation unit is a sequence of lexical elements. A lexical element is either a delimiter, a reserved word, an identifier, a numeric literal, a string literal, or a comment. The legality of a compilation unit depends only on the particular sequence of its lexical elements, excluding the comments, if any.

In some cases an explicit *separator* is required between adjacent lexical elements (namely, when without separation, interpretation as a single lexical element is possible). A separator is any of a space character, a format effector, or the end of a line. A space character is a separator except within a comment or a string literal. Format effectors other than horizontal tabulation are always separators. Horizontal tabulation is a separator except within a comment. The end of a line is always a separator.

One or more separators are allowed between any two adjacent lexical elements. At least one separator is required between an identifier and a numeric literal, or between two adjacent identifiers or numeric literals.

A *delimiter* is either one of the following special characters

```
& ' ( ) * + , - . / : ; < = > !
```

or one of the following *compound delimiters*

```
=>  **  /=  >=  <=  -->  ==>  ->  <->  --:  ::
```

Each of the special characters listed for single character delimiters is a single delimiter, except if this character is used as a character of a compound delimiter, or as a character of a comment or string literal.

Apart from the delimiters mentioned above, a given implementation may introduce more of the special characters as delimiters.

The other lexical elements are defined in the remainder of this section.

2.2.3. Identifiers

Identifiers are used as names (also as reserved words, see section 2.2.7).

```
identifier ::=
   letter {[ _ ] letter_or_digit}

letter_or_digit ::=
   letter | digit
```

All characters of an identifier are significant, including the underscore characters. Identifiers differing only in the use of corresponding upper and lower case letters are considered as the same.

2.2.4. Numeric Literals

Numerical literals denote constant functions of the predefined type INTEGER.

```
numeric_literal ::=
   digit {[ _ ] digit}
```

The conventional decimal notation is used. Underline characters are not significant in a numeric literal.

2.2.5. String Literals

String literals denote constant functions of the predefined type STRING.

```
string_literal::=
   "{graphic_character}"
```

A string literal denotes the sequence of characters enclosed by quotation characters. If a quotation character is to be represented in the sequence of characters, then a pair of adjacent quotation characters must be written at the corresponding place within the string literal.

Notes

A string literal must fit on one line since it is a lexical element. Longer sequences of graphic character values can be denoted by the predefined catenation operation & for string literals:

```
"FIRST PART OF A SEQUENCE OF CHARACTERS " &
"THAT CONTINUES ON THE NEXT LINE"
```

2.2.6. Comments

A comment starts with two adjacent hyphens and extends up to the end of the line. Its sole purpose is the enlightenment of the human reader. A comment can appear between any lexical elements.

2.2.6[1]: The first graphic character (if any) after the leading -- of a comment must not be ':' or '>' (the character sequences --: and --> are compound delimiters).

2.2.7. Reserved Words

The identifiers below are called *reserved words* and are reserved for special significance in the language:

abort	**case**	**entry**	**is**	**others**	**renames**	**type**
abs	**constant**	**exception**		**out**	**return**	
accept	**declare**	**exist**	**limited**		**reverse**	**undefined**
access	**defined**	**exit**	**loop**	**package**		**use**
all	**delay**	**for**		**predicate**	**select**	
and	**delta**	**function**	**mod**	**pragma**	**separate**	**when**
array	**digits**		**new**	**private**	**subtype**	**where**
at	**do**	**generic**	**not**	**procedure**		**while**
axiom		**goto**	**null**	**raise**	**task**	**with**
	else			**range**	**terminate**	
begin	**elsif**	**if**	**of**	**record**	**then**	**xor**
body	**end**	**in**	**or**	**rem**	**to**	

Reserved words differing only in the use of corresponding upper and lower case letters are considered as the same. For the presentation of programs in documents, the use of **bold** lower case letters (as above) is recommended.

Notes

Many of the reserved words have no special significance in PA^{nn}dA–S. They are only reserved in PA^{nn}dA–S because they are so in Ada.

2.2.8. Transliteration

The following table shows allowable replacements of delimiters and reserved words in type expressions, logical expressions, and expressions by mathematical symbols (for a "mathematical'' representation of programs, e.g. in documents):

type_expression		logical_expression		expression	
mathematical	*graphical*	*mathematical*	*graphical*	*mathematical*	*graphical*
$\rightarrow$	-->	$\neg$	**not**	$\leq$	<=
$\Rightarrow$	==>	$\wedge$	**and**	$\geq$	>=
$\times$	#	$\vee$	**or**	$\perp$	**undefined**
$\perp^{*}$	+	$\exists$	**exist**		
		$\forall$	**for all**		
		$\rightarrow$	->		
		$\leftrightarrow$	<->		
		$\neq$	/=		
* as a superscript		$\in$	**in**		

2.3. Declarations and Types

This section describes the types in the language, and the kinds of declarations.

2.3.1. Declarations

The language defines several kinds of entities that are declared, either explicitly or implicitly, by declarative items (see definition of this term in section 2.8.1). Such an entity can be a type, a subtype, a function, a predicate, a package, a generic unit, a quantified variable, a generic formal parameter, or a basic operation.

For each form of declarative item the language rules define a certain region of text called the scope of the declarative item (see section 2.8.2). A declarative item associates a designator with a declared entity. Within its scope, and only there, it is possible to use the designator to refer to the associated declared entity; these places are defined by the visibility rules (see section 2.8.3). At such places the designator is said to be a *name of the entity* (its simple name); the name is said to *denote* the associated entity.

```
declaration::=
      private_type_declaration |  subtype_declaration
    | function_declaration     |  predicate_declaration
    | package_declaration      |  generic_declaration
    | generic_instantiation    |  axiom
```

Subtype declarations are described in section 2.3.4. Private type declarations are described in section 2.7.2, function declarations in section 2.6.1, predicate declarations in section 2.6.2, package declarations in section 2.7.1, generic declarations in section 2.10.1, generic instantiations in section 2.10.2 and axioms in section 2.7.3.

2.3.2. Types and Subtypes

A type is characterized by a set of values and a set of operations. There exist several *classes of types*:

- a *private type* is declared by a private type declaration (including the predefined private types BOOLEAN, INTEGER and STRING),
- a *function type* is declared by a subtype declaration where the type expression denotes a function subtype,
- a *tuple type* is declared by a subtype declaration where the type expression denotes a tuple subtype,
- the *predefined meta type* LOGICAL.

The meta type LOGICAL is not accessible by the users, but appears only implicitly, as the result type of predicates and logical expressions.

A *subtype* is a type together with a constraint; a value is said to *belong to a subtype* of a given type if it belongs to the type and satisfies the constraint; the given type is called the *base type* of the subtype. A type is a subtype of itself; it corresponds to a condition that imposes no constraint. The base type of a type is the type itself.

A subtype declaration declares a subtype. In the case where the denoted subtype is a *function subtype* or a *tuple subtype*, the subtype declaration also declares the corresponding base type. The simple name declared by the subtype declaration then denotes the declared subtype, and the base type is anonymous. A type is said to be *anonymous* if it has no simple name.

The base type of a function subtype is defined recursively as the function type with the *formal parameter type* being the base type of the corresponding formal parameter subtype. Likewise the *result type* is the base type of the corresponding result subtype.

The base type of a tuple subtype is defined recursively as the tuple type with the same number of component types, each *component type* being the base type of the corresponding component subtype.

2.3.3. Operations of a Type

The set of *operations* of a type includes the explicitly declared functions that have the type as a constituent type (recursively); such functions are necessarily declared after the type declaration. The remaining operations are each implicitly declared for a given type. These implicitly declared operations comprise the *basic operations* and the *predefined operators* (see Appendix A). The operations implicitly declared for a given type declaration occur after the type declaration and before the next explicit declaration, if any.

A basic operation is an operation that is inherent in one of the following:

• a predicate for equality or inequality,

• a membership predicate,

• a definedness predicate,

• a qualification (in qualified expressions),

• a short-circuit control form,

• a numeric literal,

• a string literal or

• the literal **undefined**.

The set of basic operations for a private type is defined in section 2.7.2 and the set of basic operations of a subtype in section 2.3.4.

2.3.4. Subtype Declarations

A subtype declaration declares a subtype.

```
subtype_declaration ::=
  subtype identifier is type_expression;
```

The set of operations defined for a subtype of a given base type includes the operations that are defined for the base type. The only additional operations are membership predicates.

Notes

The definition of base type for a function and tuple subtype gives the language *structural equivalence* for function subtypes and tuple subtypes. For example MAP1 and MAP2 have the same base types:

```
MAP1: (ITEM --> ITEM) --> STACK --> STACK;

subtype ITEM_TRAFO is ITEM --> ITEM;
subtype STACK_TRAFO is STACK --> STACK;
MAP2: ITEM_TRAFO --> STACK_TRAFO;
```

2.3.5. Type Expressions

A type expression denotes a subtype.

```
type_expression ::=
  function_type_expression | tuple_type_expression

function_type_expression ::=
  tuple_type_expression function_arrow type_expression

function_arrow ::= --> | ==>

tuple_type_expression ::=
  extended_type_expression {# extended_type_expression}

extended_type_expression ::=
  subtype_expression [+]

subtype_expression::=
  type_or_subtype_name | (domain) | (type_expression)
```

The *function type constructors* --> and ==> are right associative. The arrow --> is called *weak function arrow*. The arrow ==> is called *strong function arrow*. The *tuple type constructor* # is not associative.

A function type expression denotes a function subtype. The *constituent type expression* at the left-hand side of the function arrow defines the *formal parameter subtype*. The constituent type expression on the right-hand side defines the *result subtype*.

A tuple type expression with more than one constituent extended type expression denotes a *tuple subtype*. Each constituent extended type expression of the tuple type expression defines the corresponding *component subtype*.

The only difference between a *subtype_*expression+ and the corresponding *subtype_*expression is that the *subtype_*expression+ has an extra value, namely the value **undefined** ($\perp$).

A domain appearing as a subtype expression denotes a subtype of the subtype denoted by the constituent type expression. It declares the designator to be a value name ranging over the values of the subtype as defined in section 2.3.6.

A subtype name denotes a type or a subtype. The base type of a subtype name is, by definition, the base type of the type or subtype denoted by the subtype name.

Notes

If the function type expression has named formal parameter types and/or result types:

```
(FP:FTt) --> (RP: RT);
```

then the identifier FP is called the *formal parameter* and RP is called the *result parameter*.

2.3.6. Domains

A domain declares an object.

```
domain ::=
  designator_list : type_expression [ :: constraint_logical_expression]

designator_list ::=
  designator {, designator}

designator ::=
  identifier | operator_symbol

operator_symbol ::=
  string_literal
```

A domain is called a *single object declaration* if its designator list has a single designator; it is called a *multiple object declaration* if its designator list has two or more designators. A multiple object declaration is equivalent to a sequence of the corresponding number of single object declarations. For each designator of the designator list, the equivalent sequence has a single object declaration formed by this designator, followed by a colon and the type expression and (optional) constraint; the equivalent sequence is in the same order as the designator list.

In the remainder of this reference manual, explanations are given for domains with a single designator; the corresponding explanations for domains with several designators follow from the equivalence stated here.

The simple name declared by a domain denotes an *object*. A domain declares the designator to be a name ranging over the values of the subtype denoted by the constituent type expression. Furthermore, the constraint logical expression is a predicate over this designator constraining the possible values of the subtype.

The *kind of object* declared by domain depends on the context of the domain. A domain appearing in the context of a function declaration declares a function; a domain appearing in the context of a predicate declaration declares a predicate; a domain appearing in the context of a domain list or a subtype expression declares a quantified variable.

The following context condition must be satisfied:

2.3.6[1]: The only operator symbols that can be used as designators in domains are those corresponding to the operators mentioned in section 2.4.4.

Notes

According to the equivalence rule stated, a multiple parameter declaration occurring in the context of a type expression (X1, X2: T :: P) is equivalent to (X1: T :: P) # (X2: T :: P).

Similarly, a multiple function or predicate declaration appearing in the context of a declaration F1,F2: T :: P; is equivalent to F1: T :: P; F2: T :: P;.

Likewise, a multiple parameter declaration appearing in the context of a domain (x1, x2: T :: P) is equivalent to (x1: T :: P; x2: T :: P).

2.4. Names and Expressions

2.4.1. Names

Names denote declared entities.

```
name ::=
  prefix  simple_name

prefix ::=
  { package_identifier . }

simple_name ::=
  designator
```

A simple name for an entity is the designator associated with the entity by its declaration. A name with non-empty prefix is called an *expanded name.*

2.4.1[1]: For an expanded name at least one of the following conditions must hold:

- the prefix denotes a package and the designator is the simple name of an entity declared immediately within its visible part.
- the prefix denotes an enclosing package and the designator is the simple name of an entity declared immediately within the package.

2.4.2. Literals

Literals denote basic operations of a given type.

```
literal ::=
  numeric_literal | string_literal | undefined
```

A numeric literal is of the predefined type INTEGER. A string literal is of the predefined type STRING. The literal **undefined** is a basic operation of any private type, and of any base type of a type expression of the form type_expression+.

2.4.3. Expressions

Expressions denote values.

```
expression::= relation
   |  relation and relation
   |  relation and then relation
   |  relation or relation
   |  relation or else relation
   |  relation xor relation
```

```
relation ::=
  simple_expression [relational_operator simple_expression ]

simple_expression ::=
  [unary_adding_operator] term { binary_adding_operator term }

term::=
  factor { multiplying_operator factor }

factor ::=
  secondary [** secondary] | abs secondary | not secondary

secondary ::=
  primary | function_call

primary ::=
  literal | name | qualified_expression | tuple_expression | (expression)
```

The type of an expression depends only on the type of its constituent expressions and on the operators applied; for an overloaded constituent or operator, the determination of the constituent type, or the identification of the appropriate operator, depends on the context. For each predefined operator, the operand and result types are given in appendix A.

A primary being a name denotes an object. The type of the primary is the same as the type of the object denoted.

The following context condition must be satisfied:

2.4.3[1]: The only names allowed as primaries are the names of quantified variables, functions and predicates.

2.4.4. Operators

The language defines the following six classes of operators.

```
logical_operator ::= and | or | xor

relational_operator ::= < | <= | > | >=

binary_adding_operator ::= + | – | &

unary_adding_operator ::= + | –

multiplying_operator ::= * | / | mod | rem

highest_precedence_operator ::= ** | abs | not
```

The operators above are given in the order of increasing *precedence*. The short-circuit control forms **and then** and **or else** have the same precedence as logical operators. For a term, simple expression, relation, or expression, operators of higher precedence are associated with their operands before operators of lower precedence.

2.4.5. Short-circuit Control Forms

The *short-circuit control forms* **and then** and **or else** are defined for two operands of the predefined type BOOLEAN and deliver a result of the predefined type BOOLEAN.

2.4.6. Qualified Expressions

A qualified expression is used to state explicitly the type of an operand that is the given expression.

```
qualified_expression ::=
  subtype_name ' (operand_expression)
```

2.4.6[1]: The operand expression must be of the base type of the subtype denoted by the subtype name.

Notes

A qualified expression is used to state which of a set of overloaded functions is meant. In contrast to Ada it cannot be used to constrain a value to a given subtype.

2.4.7. Tuple Expressions

A tuple expression denotes a tuple value.

```
tuple_expression ::=
  (expression , expression {, expression } )
```

The target type of a tuple expression is a tuple type, where the base type of each component is the base type of the corresponding constituent expression.

The type of a tuple expression $(e_1,...,e_n)$ is the tuple type $(t_1\#...\#t_n)$ where t_i is the base type of e_i, for $1 \le i \le n$.

2.5. Logical Expressions

2.5.1. Logical Expressions and Formulas

```
logical_expression ::=
   [ quantifier domain { ; domain } => ]
      implication {, implication}

quantifier ::= for all | exist

implication ::=
      [logical_formula implicator] logical_formula
   |  others implicator logical_formula

implicator ::= -> | <->

logical_formula::=
      logical_primary { and logical_primary }
   |  logical_primary { or logical_primary }
   |  not logical_primary

logical_primary ::=
      (logical_expression)
   |  boolean_expression
   |  simple_expression = simple_expression
   |  simple_expression /= simple_expression
   |  simple_expression in subtype_name
   |  defined expression
   |  predicate_call
```

The target type of a logical expression, implication, logical formula and logical primary is the predefined meta type LOGICAL.

The ',' appearing as separator between the implications of a logical expression corresponds to the logical connective **and** for the predefined type LOGICAL.

The membership predicate **in** has the same precedence as the equality predicates = and /=. The definedness predicate **defined** has the same precedence as the logical connective **not**.

A logical expression with a quantifier is called a *quantified expression*. The designators declared by the domains of a logical expression are called *quantified variables*.

The following context condition must be satisfied:

2.5.1[1]: An implication with **others** must be the last in a list of implications.

2.5.2. Logical Connectives

The following *logical connectives* are predefined for the type LOGICAL.

Logical Connective	Operation	Operand type	Result type
->	implication	LOGICAL	LOGICAL
<->	equivalence	LOGICAL	LOGICAL
and	conjunction	LOGICAL	LOGICAL
or	disjunction	LOGICAL	LOGICAL
not	negation	LOGICAL	LOGICAL

2.5.3. Implicit Conversion

A logical primary of the form *boolean*_expression is an abbreviation for *boolean*_expression = TRUE and defines an *implicit conversion* from the predefined type BOOLEAN to the predefined meta type LOGICAL.

2.5.4. Equality Predicate

The *equality predicates* = and /= are predefined for all types.

2.5.4[1]: The two operands of an equality predicate = or /= must be of the same type.

2.5.4[2]: The operand of an equality predicate = or /= must not be of the predefined meta type LOGICAL.

2.5.5. Membership Predicate

The *membership predicate* **in** is predefined for all types and subtypes.

2.5.5[1]: In a membership predicate **in** the type of the simple expression must be the base type of the subtype denoted by the subtype name.

2.5.6. Definedness Predicate

The *definedness predicate* **defined** is predefined for all types.

2.5.6[1]: The operand of the definedness predicate must not be of the predefined meta type LOGICAL.

2.6. Functions and Predicates

2.6.1. Function Declarations

A function declaration declares a function.

```
function_declaration ::=
   [ --: ] domain;
```

The function is defined by the domain: the simple name of the function is defined by the designator of the domain; the type of the function is defined by the type expression of the domain.

A function declaration with a preceding '--:' declares a so-called *auxiliary function*, or *virtual function* (see [Anna 87]). An auxiliary function may be used to define properties of a specification that are not necessary for its implementation. A function declaration where the type expression of the domain denotes a private type or a tuple type is called a *constant function.*

The same function identifier or operator symbol can be used in several function declarations. The identifier or operator symbol is then said to be *overloaded*; the functions that are denoted by this identifier or operator symbol are also said to be overloaded, and to overload each other. As explained in section 2.8.3, if two functions overload each other, one of them can hide the other only if both functions have the same type profile.

2.6.2. Predicate Declarations

A predicate declaration declares a *predicate*.

```
predicate_declaration ::=
  predicate domain;
```

The predicate is defined by the domain. The simple name of the predicate is given by the designator of the domain. The type of the predicate is a function type, where the formal parameter type is defined by the type expression of the domain, and the result type is the predefined meta type LOGICAL.

Apart from the fact that the predefined meta type LOGICAL is not accessible by the user, a predicate is equivalent to a function where the formal parameter subtype is defined by the type expression of the domain, and the result type is the predefined meta type LOGICAL. In the remainder of this reference manual (in particular in section 2.8 and 2.10), explanations are given for function declarations; the corresponding explanations for predicates follow from the equivalence stated here.

The following context condition must be satisfied:

2.6.2[1]: The type expression of the domain appearing in a predicate declaration must be a tuple type expression.

Notes

A predicate of the form is equivalent to a function declaration of the second form (which the user is not allowed to write):

```
predicate P: T :: Q;
P: T --> LOGICAL :: Q;
```

2.6.3. Function and Predicate Applications

A call denotes the application of a function or a predicate.

```
call ::=
  secondary [primary]
```

The secondary is called the *function part* and the primary is called the *actual parameter part.* The target type of a call is:

- if the function part denotes a predicate: the predefined type LOGICAL
- if the type of the function part is a function type: the corresponding result type of the function type,
- if the type of the function part is a tuple type or a private type: the type of the function part.

The following context conditions must be satisfied:

2.6.3[1]: The function part must denote a function value or a predicate if the primary is not missing.

2.6.3[2]: The actual parameter part must be absent if the type of the function part is a tuple type or a private type. Otherwise, the actual parameter part must have the same type as the formal parameter type of the function or predicate denoted by the function part.

2.6.3[3]: A call of an overloaded function is ambiguous (and therefore illegal) if the name of the function, the type of the actual parameter part, if any, and the result type are not sufficient to determine exactly one (overloaded) function declaration.

2.7. Packages

2.7.1. Package Declarations

Packages allow the specification of groups of logically related entities.

```
package_declaration ::=
      package_specification;

package_specification ::=
      package package_identifier is
         { declaration }
      end [package_identifier]
```

The list of declarative items of a package specification is called the *visible part* of the package. Entities declared in the visible part can be used inside as well as outside the package, except auxiliary functions which are only visible inside the package.

2.7.1[1]: If an identifier appears after the keyword **end** of a package specification it must be identical to the package identifier.

2.7.2. Private Type Declarations

A private type declaration declares a type.

```
private_type_declaration ::=
      type identifier is private;
```

The operations that are implicitly declared by a private type declaration are the following basic operations: equality and inequality predicates, membership predicate, definedness predicate, qualification and the literal **undefined**. Additional basic operations are implicitly declared for the predefined types BOOLEAN, INTEGER and STRING (see section 2.4.2 and appendix A).

The above basic operations, together with explicitly declared functions that have the private type as a constituent base type (recursively), are the only operations from the package that are available outside the package for the private type.

2.7.3. Axioms

Axioms defines the properties of declared entities.

```
axiom ::=
   axiom logical_expression;
```

Axioms in the visible part of a package are called *visible axioms*. Visible axioms express properties of the visible entities of the package. These properties can be assumed outside the package. For the properties of axioms in a generic formal part we refer to section 2.10.1.

2.8. Visibility Rules

2.8.1. Declarative Region

A *declarative item* is one of the following:

- a private type declaration,
- a subtype declaration,
- a function or predicate declaration,
- a (library) unit or

• a domain.

A *declarative region* is a portion of the program text. A single declarative region is formed by the text of each of the following:

• a subtype declaration,

• a package declaration,

• a generic declaration,

• a quantified expression,

• a function type expression,

• a tuple type expression,

• a domain.

In each of the above cases, the declarative region is said to be *associated* with the corresponding construct. A declarative item is said to *occur immediately within* a declarative region if this region is the innermost region that encloses the declarative item, not counting the declarative region (if any) associated with the declarative item itself.

A declarative item that occurs immediately within a declarative region is said to be *local* to the region. Declarations in outer (enclosing) regions are said to be *global* to an inner (enclosed) declarative region. A local entity is one declared by a local declarative item; a global entity is one declared by a global declarative item.

Notes

The package STANDARD forms a declarative region which encloses every library unit; the declaration of every library unit is assumed to occur immediately within this package. The implicit declarations of library units are assumed to be ordered in such a way that the scope of a given library unit includes any compilation unit that mentions the given library unit in a **with** clause. However, the only library units that are visible within a given compilation unit are those named by its with clauses.

2.8.2. Scope of Declarations

For each form of declarative item, the language rules define a certain portion of the program text called the *scope* of the declarative item. The scope of a declarative item is also called the scope of any entity declared by the declarative item. Furthermore, if the declarative item associates some notation with a declared entity, this portion of the text is also called the scope of this notation (either an identifier, an operator symbol, operator or the notation for a basic operation). Within the scope of an entity, and only there, are places where it is legal to use the associated notation in order to refer to the declared entity. These places are defined by the rules of visibility and overloading.

The scope of a declarative item that occurs immediately within a declarative region extends from the beginning of the declarative item to the end of the declarative region; this part of the scope of a declarative item is called the *immediate scope*. Furthermore, for any of the declarative items occurring immediately within the visible part of a package declaration, the scope of the declarative item extends to the end of the scope of the enclosing package declaration.

Notes

The above scope rules apply to all forms of declarative items defined in section 2.8.1; in particular, they apply also to implicit declarations. The rule extending the scope of a declarative item occurring immediately within the visible part of a package declaration does not apply to the package specification of a generic declaration. Note also, that for nested declarative items, this rule applies at each level.

2.8.3. Visibility

Visibility rules are stated for simple names, operator symbols, operators and basic operations. First visibility for simple names is defined. Visibility for the other constructs is defined at the end of this section.

The meaning of the occurrence of a simple name at a given place in the text is defined by the visibility rules and additionally, in the case of overloaded declarative items, by the overloading rules. The overloaded declarative items considered here are those for explicitly and implicitly declared functions.

For the applied occurrence of a simple name, the visibility rules determine a set of declarative items that define possible meanings of an occurrence of the simple name. A declarative item is said to be *visible* at a given place in the text when, according to the visibility rules, the declarative item defines a possible meaning of this occurrence. Two cases arise:

- The visibility rules determine at most one possible meaning. In such a case the visibility rules are sufficient to determine the declarative item defining the meaning of the occurrence of the simple name, or in the absence of such a declarative item, to determine that the occurrence is not legal at the given point.
- The visibility rules determine more than one possible meaning. In such a case the overloading rules are used to find a subset of the visible declarative items in the given context (see the next section).

A declarative item is only visible within a certain part of its scope; this part starts at the end of the declarative item with the following exceptions:

- For a package specification it starts at the reserved word **is** given after the identifier of the package specification.
- For a domain with a restriction it starts immediately before the restriction.

Visibility is either by selection or direct. A declarative item is *visible by selection* at places that are defined as follows.

- For a declarative item given in the visible part of a package declaration: at the place of the designator after the dot of an expanded name whose prefix denotes the package.
- Within the declarative region associated with a package specification, any declarative item that occurs immediately within the region is visible by selection at the place of the designator after the dot of an expanded name whose prefix denotes the package.

Where it is not visible by selection, a visible declarative item is said to be directly visible. A declarative item is *directly visible* within a certain part of its immediate scope; this part extends to the end of the immediate scope of the declarative item, but excludes places where the declarative item is hidden as explained below.

A declarative item is said to be *hidden* within (part of) an inner declarative region if the inner region contains a homograph of this declarative item; the outer declarative item is then hidden within the immediate scope of the inner homograph. Each of two declarative items is said to be a *homograph* of the other if both declarative items have the same designator and overloading is allowed for at most one of the two. If overloading is allowed for both declarative items, then each of the two is a homograph of the other if they have the same designator as well as the same type profile.

Declarative items, not being auxiliary functions, appearing in the visible part of a given package declaration are said to be *potentially visible* if and only if the package is visible. A potentially visible declarative item is directly visible except in the following two cases:

- A potentially visible declarative item is not made directly visible if the place considered is within the immediate scope of a homograph of the declarative item.
- Potentially visible declarative items that have the same designator are not made directly visible unless each of them is either a function declaration or an implicit declaration.

Whenever a declarative item with a certain designator is visible from a given point, the designator and the declared entity (if any) are also said to be visible from that point.

Direct visibility and visibility by selection are likewise defined for operator symbols. An operator is directly visible if and only if the corresponding operator declaration is directly visible. Finally, the notation associated with a basic operation is directly visible within the entire scope of this operation.

The following context conditions must be satisfied:

2.8.3[1]: For the applied occurrence of a given simple name, operator or basic operation the visibility rules must determine at least one possible meaning (see further the context condition of the next section on overloading rules).

2.8.3[2]: Two declarative items that occur immediately within the same declarative region must not be homographs.

Notes

The rules defining immediate scope, hiding, and visibility imply that the applied occurrence of a simple name within its own declarative item is illegal except for the simple name of a package or generic package (after **is**) and except for the simple name of a domain (in the restriction). The designator of the declarative item hides outer homographs within its immediate scope, that is, from the start of the declaration; on the other hand, the identifier is visible only after the end of the declarative item.

According to the properties of a generic package mentioned in section 2.10.1 and the context conditions for expanded names in section 2.4.1, the names GP.GT and GP.F are legal inside GP:

```
generic
  type GT is private;
package GP is
  F: GT--> GP.GT;
end GP;
```

2.8.4. Overloading Rules

Two functions are said to have *the same type profile* if and only if they have the same base type.

Overloading is defined for functions, operators and the operations that are inherent in several basic operations such as membership predicates.

For overloaded entities, overload resolution determines a subset of the possible meanings that an applied occurrence of a simple name can have, whenever the visibility rules have determined that more than one meaning is acceptable at the place of this occurrence; overload resolution likewise determines a subset of the possible meanings of an occurrence of an operator or some basic operation. For an applied occurrence to be legal the subset determined by the overload resolution rules must be a singleton set as expressed by the context condition below.

At the place of the occurrence all visible declarative items are considered. The overload resolution is performed in the innermost complete context, where a *complete context* is either a declarative item or an axiom.

When considering possible interpretations of the applied occurrences of simple names appearing in a given complete context, the only rules considered are the syntax rules, the scope and visibility rules, and the rules of the form described below.

1. Any context condition (see below) that requires a name or expression to have a certain type, or to have the same type as another name or expression.
2. Any rule (see below) that specifies a certain type as the result type of a basic operation, and any rule that specifies that this type is of a certain class.

3. The context condition, 2.6.3.[3], for the resolution of overloaded function calls.

The simple names given in **with** clauses (see section 2.9.2) follow different rules.

The following context condition must be satisfied:

2.8.4[1]: For the applied occurrence of a given simple name, operator or basic operation the overloading rules must determine exactly one meaning.

Notes

If there is only one possible interpretation, the simple name denotes the corresponding entity. However, this does not mean that the occurrence is necessarily legal since other requirements exist which are not considered for overload resolution.

Context conditions of the form (1): membership predicate: 2.5.5[1], function call: 2.6.3[2], type profile: 2.10.2[2], qualified expression: 2.4.6[1].

Rules of the form (2): logical expression: section 2.5.1, equality and inequality predicate: section 2.5.4, membership predicate: section 2.5.5, definedness predicate: section 2.5.6, short-circuit control form: section 2.4.5.

2.9. Program Structure

A PA^{nn}dA–S specification consists of one or more compilation units, each handled separately.

2.9.1. Compilation Units and Library Units

A specification is a collection of one or more compilation units.

```
compilation unit::=
      [ with_clause ] library_unit

library_unit ::=
      package_declaration
   |  generic_declaration
   |  generic_instantiation
```

The compilation units of a PA^{nn}dA–S specification are said to *belong to a program library*. The program library can be conceived of as an acyclic graph where the nodes are the library units belonging to the library, and the arcs are the dependencies (see section 2.9.2 below) between the library units.

A compilation unit containing errors cannot be stored in the program library, and thus has no effect whatsoever on the program library.

For the visibility rules, each library unit acts as an implicit declaration that occurs immediately within the package STANDARD.

The following context condition must be satisfied:

2.9.1[1]: Within a program library the simple names of all library units must be distinct.

2.9.2. With Clauses

A with clause specifies the library units whose names are needed within a compilation unit.

```
with_clause ::=
      with package_identifier {, package_identifier};
```

If a library unit is named by a with clause of a compilation unit, then the library unit is directly visible within the compilation unit, except where it is hidden. These library units are visible as if declared implicitly immediately within the package STANDARD.

With clauses define dependencies among library units; that is, a compilation unit that mentions other library units in its with clauses *depends* on those library units.

Unlike the Ada reference manual [Ada 1983] this manual does not define any ''order of compilation''. This is regarded as a matter of the program library.

The following context conditions must be satisfied:

2.9.2[1]: The identifiers appearing in a with clause must be the simple names of library units

2.9.2[2]: The identifiers appearing in a with clause must not introduce any circular dependencies between compilation units.

2.10. Generic Packages

A generic package is a *template* which may be parameterized, and from which corresponding (nongeneric) packages can be obtained. The resulting packages are said to be *instances* of the original generic package.

A generic package is declared by a generic declaration. This form of declaration has a generic formal part declaring any generic formal parameters. An instance of a generic package is obtained as the result of a generic instantiation with appropriate generic actual parameters for the generic formal parameters.

Generic packages are templates. As templates they do not have the properties that are specific to packages. For example, a generic package can be instantiated but none of the entities in its visible part are visible outside the generic package. In contrast, the instance of a generic package is a nongeneric package; hence, the entities in its visible part are (potentially) visible outside the instance.

2.10.1. Generic Package Declarations

A generic declaration declares a generic package.

```
generic_declaration ::=
      generic_formal_part package_specification;

generic_formal_part ::=
      generic {generic_formal_parameter | axiom}

generic_formal_parameter ::=
      private_type_declaration
   |  function_declaration
   |  predicate_declaration
```

A *generic formal parameter* is a private type declaration, a function declaration, or a predicate declaration. For an axiom appearing in a generic formal part, no corresponding actual parameter will appear in an instantiation of the generic package (see below).

The terms generic formal type (or simply, *formal type*), and generic formal function (or simply *formal function*) are used to refer to corresponding generic formal parameters.

Outside the declaration of a generic package, the name of this program unit denotes the generic package. In contrast, within the declarative region associated with a generic package the name of this program unit denotes the package obtained by the current instantiation.

Axioms in a generic formal part are called *formal axioms*, and constrain the actual generic parameters for each instantiation of the generic unit: they may be assumed to hold within the generic unit.

Notes

Within a generic package, the name of this program unit acts as the name of a package. Hence this name cannot appear after the reserved word **new** in a (recursive) generic instantiation.

2.10.2. Generic Instantiations

An instance of a generic package is declared by a generic instantiation.

```
generic_instantiation ::=
      package identifier is new generic_package_name [generic_actual_part];

generic_actual_part ::=
      (generic_actual_parameter {, generic_actual_parameter});

generic_actual_parameter ::=
      expression
   |  subtype_name
```

The instance is a copy of the generic package, apart from the generic formal part; thus the instance is a package. For each occurrence, within the generic package, of a name that denotes a given entity, the following list defines which entity is denoted by the corresponding occurrence within the instance.

1. For a name that denotes the generic package: The corresponding occurrence denotes the instance.
2. For a name that denotes a generic formal type: The corresponding name denotes the subtype named by the associated generic actual parameter (the actual subtype).
3. For a name that denotes a generic formal function: The corresponding name denotes the function named by the associated generic actual parameter (the actual function).
4. For a name that denotes a formal parameter or result parameter of a generic formal function: The corresponding name denotes the corresponding formal parameter or result parameter, if any, of the actual function associated with the formal function.
5. For a name that denotes a local entity declared within the generic package: The corresponding name denotes the entity declared by the corresponding local declaration within the instance.
6. For a name that denotes a global entity declared outside of the generic package: The corresponding name denotes the same global entity.

Similar rules apply to operators and basic operations: in particular, formal operators follow a rule similar to rule (3), local operations follow a rule similar to rule (5), and operations for global types follow a rule similar to rule (6). In addition, if within the generic package a predefined operator or basic operation of a formal type is used, then within the instance the corresponding occurrence refers to the corresponding predefined operation of the actual type associated with the formal type.

For the use in the context conditions below we define:

- a generic formal private type is *matched* by any type or subtype,
- a generic formal function is *matched* by an actual function if and only if they have the same type profile.

The following context conditions must be satisfied:

2.10.2[1]: An explicit generic actual parameter must be supplied for each generic formal parameter.

2.10.2[2]: Each generic actual parameter must match the corresponding generic formal parameter.

2.10.2[3]: A name denoting an auxiliary function is only allowed to appear in an expression being an actual generic parameter if the corresponding formal parameter is an auxiliary formal function.

Notes

If two overloaded functions declared in a generic package differ only by the (formal) type of their parameters and results, then there exist legal instantiations for which all calls of these functions from outside the instance are ambiguous. For example:

```
generic
  type A is private;
  type B is private;
package G is
  NEXT: A --> A;
  NEXT: B --> B;
end;

package P is new G(BOOLEAN,BOOLEAN);
-- calls of P.NEXT are ambiguous
```

2.A. Predefined Language Environment

The predefined types (for example the types BOOLEAN and INTEGER) are the types that are declared in a predefined package called STANDARD; this package also includes the declarations of their predefined operators. The signatures of the predefined operators in package STANDARD are given below. See chapter 5 for the definition of this package.

```
package STANDARD is

   type BOOLEAN is private;
   FALSE   : BOOLEAN;
   TRUE    : BOOLEAN;
   EQ      : BOOLEAN # BOOLEAN --> BOOLEAN;
   "<"     : BOOLEAN # BOOLEAN --> BOOLEAN;
   "<="    : BOOLEAN # BOOLEAN --> BOOLEAN;
   ">"     : BOOLEAN # BOOLEAN --> BOOLEAN;
   ">="    : BOOLEAN # BOOLEAN --> BOOLEAN;
   "and"   : BOOLEAN # BOOLEAN --> BOOLEAN;
   "or"    : BOOLEAN # BOOLEAN --> BOOLEAN;
   "xor"   : BOOLEAN # BOOLEAN --> BOOLEAN;
   "not"   : BOOLEAN --> BOOLEAN;
   FIRST   : BOOLEAN;
   LAST    : BOOLEAN;
   SUCC    : BOOLEAN --> BOOLEAN
   PRED    : BOOLEAN --> BOOLEAN;

   -- for the functions POS and VAL see after the subtype NATURAL below

   type INTEGER is private;

   -- additional operations: integer literals, see section 2.4

   EQ      : INTEGER # INTEGER --> BOOLEAN;
   "<"     : INTEGER # INTEGER --> BOOLEAN;
   "<="    : INTEGER # INTEGER --> BOOLEAN;
   ">"     : INTEGER # INTEGER --> BOOLEAN;
   ">="    : INTEGER # INTEGER --> BOOLEAN;
   "+"     : INTEGER --> INTEGER;
   "–"     : INTEGER --> INTEGER;
   "abs"   : INTEGER --> INTEGER;
```

```
    "+"     : INTEGER # INTEGER --> INTEGER;
    "-"     : INTEGER # INTEGER --> INTEGER;
    "*"     : INTEGER # INTEGER --> INTEGER;
    "/"     : INTEGER # INTEGER --> INTEGER;
    "rem"   : INTEGER # INTEGER --> INTEGER;
    "mod"   : INTEGER # INTEGER --> INTEGER;
    "**"    : INTEGER # INTEGER --> INTEGER;
    FIRST   : INTEGER;
    LAST    : INTEGER;
    SUCC    : INTEGER --> INTEGER;
    PRED    : INTEGER --> INTEGER;

    subtype NATURAL is X : INTEGER :: X >= 0;
    POS     : BOOLEAN --> NATURAL;
    VAL     : NATURAL --> BOOLEAN;

    subtype POSITIVE is X : NATURAL :: X > 0;

    type STRING is private;

    -- additional operations: string literals, see section 2.5

    EQ      : STRING # STRING --> BOOLEAN;
    "<"     : STRING # STRING --> BOOLEAN;
    "<="    : STRING # STRING --> BOOLEAN;
    ">"     : STRING # STRING --> BOOLEAN;
    ">="    : STRING # STRING --> BOOLEAN;
    "&"     : STRING # STRING --> STRING;
    FIRST   : STRING --> INTEGER;
    LAST    : STRING --> INTEGER;
    LENGTH  : STRING --> NATURAL;

end STANDARD;
```

3. Semantics of PA^{nn}dA-S

Michael Breu[1], *Manfred Broy*[2], *Thomas Grünler*[3], *Friederike Nickl*[4], *Universität Passau*

This document contains the definition of semantics of the PROSPECTRA specification language PA^{nn}dA-S that is used at the early stages of a PROSPECTRA program development.

3.1. Introduction

In this document the semantic specification of the language PA^{nn}dA-S is given. It is a combination of a denotational specification and an axiomatic (predicative) specification. PA^{nn}dA-S expressions are treated in a fully denotational style as mappings from environments to values. A family of declarations is considered as a predicate on environments, specifying the set of environments established by the definitions (the set of environments consistent with the declarations).

The reason for taking this approach is twofold: first, the language PA^{nn}dA-S provides a program notation for specifications of higher order functional objects. Since these specifications need not necessarily be constructive, it is impossible to use only classical techniques from denotational semantics as developed for pure (algorithmic) programming languages.

A particular problem in this respect is the treatment of specifications that are not complete, i.e. that for instance do not specify a function uniquely. Here a number of options are given, ranging from the considerations of nondeterministic ("set-valued") functions to the use of the concept of loose specifications (as developed in the field of algebraic specifications of abstract data types). The semantics of PA^{nn}dA-S is based on the latter approach, since it allows us to avoid a number of tricky questions occurring when dealing with nondeterministic functions and therefore will also make the transformation calculus more simple.

Second this way of semantic treatment is in particular well-suited for a program development by transformations, since the predicative semantics forms an appropriate basis for the verification of transformation rules. All what is needed is the calculus of predicate logics.

Before starting with the more technical treatment we shortly list the basic semantic concepts of (the semantics of) PA^{nn}dA-S.

- the language PA^{nn}dA-S encompasses the declaration of higher order functions. All declared functions are required to be monotonic and continuous, but they need not be strict.
- in addition to functions, PA^{nn}dA-S also includes the declaration of predicates. In contrast to functions, no monotonicity or continuity requirement is imposed on predicates.
- a two valued logic is used,
- the equality sign in formulas is interpreted by the strong equality.

---

[1] *Author's current address*: Siemens-Nixdorf AG, EMSC AP 432, Otto-Hahn-Ring 6, D-8000 München 83

[2] *Author's current address*: Institut für Informatik, Technische Universität München, Postfach 20 24 20, D-8000 München 2

[3] *Author's current address*: Philips Kommunikations Industrie AG, Thurn-und-Taxis-Straße 14, D-8500 Nürnberg

[4] *Author's current address*: Ludwig-Maximilians-Universität München, FORWISS, Leopoldstraße 11b, D-8000 München 22

A $PA^{nn}dA$-S program is given by a family of specifications of packages and generics. In this semantic description we consider generics only on the top-level, i.e. we do not consider nested generics. We give a semantic definition for $PA^{nn}dA$-S programs based on the concept of heterogeneous higher-order algebras.

We do not give a definition of syntactic context-correctness (sometimes also called "static semantics") here, but assume for all the program terms that we consider that they fulfil the context conditions (which are defined in the $PA^{nn}dA$-S Reference Manual, part II chapter 4)

The semantic definition for $PA^{nn}dA$-S is given in two steps: first we present the semantics of a sublanguage of $PA^{nn}dA$-S which we call the "kernel-language". The language constructs not contained in the kernel language are considered as notational variants, which, by suitable transformations can be reduced into the kernel language. Hence the semantics of the kernel-language together with the definition of the transformations for the remaining constructs of $PA^{nn}dA$-S provide a semantics of the entire language (comparable to the transformational semantics for CIP-L given in [Bauer et al. 85]).

The kernel-language is a higher order specification language which allows to specify arbitrary continuous function(al)s (including non-strict functions) between complete partially ordered sets (in short: cpo's). The kernel-language does not yet comprise the specification of subtypes and of function(al)s with domain predicates and result annotations. In order to define the transformations of these $PA^{nn}dA$-S constructs into the kernel language (denoted by L_0 in the sequel) we divide the language into three layers

$$L_0 \subseteq L_1 \subseteq L_2 = PA^{nn}dA\text{-S}$$

These language layers can be roughly described as follows:

- L_1 comprises the specification of function(al)s with domain predicates and result annotations,
- L_2 comprises subtypes.

We define transformations to reduce L_1 to the kernel-language and to reduce L_2 to L_1.

This document is organized as follows:

In section 3.2 we concentrate on basic formal definitions which are needed to give the semantics of the kernel language. In section 3.3 we present the semantic equations for the kernel language and in section 3.4 we define the transformations which are needed to reduce the remaining language constructs to the kernel language.

3.2. Basic Semantic Concepts

We base our approach on the concept of heterogeneous higher order algebras (for more details on higher order algebras see [Broy 87], [Möller 87], [Grünler 90]). For the special definitions on higher order algebras which are used in this document we refer to part I section 2.1.

In particular, we distinguish between atomic sorts (which are merely names) and sort expressions built from a function space constructor and a tupling constructor.

As carriers of algebras we admit *complete partially ordered sets* (*cpo's*).

3.2.1. Order-Theoretic Preliminaries

A partially ordered set D = (|D|,$\sqsubseteq$) is a *cpo* iff it has a least element (denoted by $\perp_D$ or more sloppily simply by $\perp$) and if every *directed* subset of D has a least upper bound. A subset of a partially ordered set is *directed* iff any two elements in this subset have an upper bound in the subset. Sometimes we will not make a notational distinction between a cpo and its underlying carrier set.

Particular cases of cpo's are the so-called *flat cpo's* with the *flat ordering* given by

$x \sqsubseteq y$ iff $x = \perp$ or $x = y$ (for all elements x, y)

Flat cpo's arise from discretely ordered sets by adjoining a least element $\perp$ which is used to totalize partial functions.

But notice that we do not require that the carriers of atomic sorts are flat cpo's. In particular, we also admit cpo's with infinitely ascending chains such as the cpo of finite and infinite streams, as described in part I, section 2.3. Here the approximation ordering $\sqsubseteq$ is of particular importance since it allows to reason about infinite elements via their finite approximations. For more details on infinite elements and Scott's approximation ordering we refer to [Scott 81], [Möller 85].

For cpo's $D_1,...,D_n$ we denote by

$$D_1 \times ... \times D_n$$

the cartesian product with the componentwise ordering. It is easily seen that $D_1 \times ... \times D_n$ again is a cpo with the least element $(\perp_1,..,\perp_n)$, where $\perp_i$ denotes the least element of D_i.

A function between cpo's is called *continuous* iff it preserves least upper bound of directed sets. In particular, every continuous function is *monotonic* (i.e. order-preserving). A function $f : D_1 \times ... \times D_n \rightarrow D$ is called *strict* iff for all $(d_1,...,d_n) \in D_1 \times ... \times D_n$ such that $d_i = \perp_i$ for some $1 \leq i \leq n$ the result $f(d_1,...,d_n)$ is $\perp_D$. It is easily seen that for flat cpo's $D_1,...,D_n$ every *strict* function $f : D_1 \times ... \times D_n \rightarrow D$ is continuous. The strict partial functions between flat cpo's are exactly the functions obtained by totalizing partial functions (between the sets without the $\perp$-elements). But notice that we do not require that all functions are strict: examples of non-strict functions are the predefined boolean operations "**and then**" and "**or else**".

For cpo's D and D' we denote by

$$[D \rightarrow D']$$

the set of continuous functions between D and D' ordered by the pointwise ordering ($f \sqsubseteq g$ iff for all $x \in D : f(x) \sqsubseteq g(x)$)

It is well known that $[D \rightarrow D']$ is a cpo with the least element being the function yielding $\perp_{D'}$ everywhere.

We restrict ourselves to such higher order algebras, where the carrier of a tuple sort is the cartesian product of the carriers of its constituents and the carrier of a functional sort is the cpo of all continuous functions over the carriers of its constituents. We call these algebras "function space algebras" (for the precise definition see part I chapter 2).

3.2.2. Function Space Algebras over DATA

With a $PA^{nn}dA$-S package-specification we associate the collection of all function space-algebras which are models of this specification (loose semantics). In order to stay in a set-theoretic framework we assume that all carriers of function space algebras are contained in a universe of functional objects. This universe is constructed as follows: starting from an (infinite) set DATA of data objects we inductively define a chain

$$FUN_0(DATA) \subseteq FUN_1(DATA) \subseteq \ldots \subseteq FUN_i(DATA) \subseteq FUN_{i+1}(DATA) \subseteq \ldots$$

of sets of higher order functional objects over DATA as follows:

$$FUN_0(DATA) := DATA$$

and

$$FUN_{i+1}(DATA) := FUN_i(DATA) \cup \{ f : M \to M' : M, M' \subseteq FUN_i(DATA)\} \\ \cup \{(d_1,\ldots,d_n) : n \geq 2 \text{ and } d_1,\ldots,d_n \in FUN_i(DATA) \}$$

Finally, we set

$$FUN(DATA) := \bigcup_{i \in \mathbf{N}} FUN_i(DATA).$$

Since every function between carriers of algebras should again be an element of FUN(DATA) we require that every carrier of an algebra is a subset of $FUN_i(DATA)$ for some $i \in \mathbf{N}$.

Hence we define the set DOM(DATA) of potential carriers of algebras as follows:

$$DOM(DATA) := \bigcup_{i \in \mathbf{N}} DOM_i(DATA)$$

where

$$DOM_i(DATA) := \{ D: D = (|D|, \sqsubseteq) \text{ is a cpo with } |D| \subseteq FUN_i(DATA) \}$$

We assume that all carriers of algebras are elements of DOM(DATA). It follows immediately that for elements $D, D', D_1,\ldots,D_n \in DOM(DATA)$ the cpo's $[D \to D']$ (of *continuous* functions) and $D_1 \times \ldots \times D_n$ again are elements of DOM(DATA).

We consider the following semantic entities for which identifiers may stand

- *elements of carrier sets* ("higher order functional objects")
  These are the elements of FUN(DATA) which by the definition above comprise elements of DATA as well as tuples and functions.

- *complete partially ordered carrier sets* (associated with "sorts")
  These are the elements of DOM(DATA) defined above.

- *relations on carrier sets* ("predicates")
  These are subsets of elements of DOM(DATA).

- *computation structures* ("packages")
  These are function space algebras with carriers in DOM(DATA).

- *generic computation structures* ("generics")
  These are sets of function space algebras with carriers in DOM(DATA).

We assume a set NAME of identifiers. Every identifier denotes objects from one of the above categories. According to the five semantic categories we introduce five semantic attributes that will be associated with semantic objects and also with identifiers that denote semantic entities. A semantic attribute is an element of the following set:

ATTRIBUTE := { **funct**, **sort**, **pred**, **pack**, **gen** }

With each semantic object with one of these attributes (except for **sort**) we associate some additional information of the appropriate form:

- with semantic objects and identifiers marked by the attribute **funct** or **pred** we associate a functionality which is a sort or a sort expression (a "higher order sort" - for a precise definition see below)
- with semantic objects and identifiers marked by the attribute **pack** we associate a generalized hierarchical signature sig (the definition is given below); sig indicates the signature of the respective package.
- with semantic objects and identifiers marked by the symbol **gen** we associate a pair (sig1, sig2) of generalized hierarchical signatures; sig1 is the signature of the generic formal part and sig2 is the signature declared in the generic package.

Here the set of *higher order sorts* is defined as follows:

Let SOR := { **sort** } × NAME be the set of identifiers standing for sorts.

The set H(SOR) of higher order sorts is defined to be the least set (w.r.t. inclusion) such that (i) - (iii) holds, where

(i) If s is an identifier (standing for a sort), then $s^{\perp}$ is a higher order sort.
(atomic sort)
The superscript $^{\perp}$ signals that every carrier contains a least element (also called bottom-element)#.

(ii) If $n \geq 2$ and $t_1, \ldots, t_n$ are higher order sorts, then $(t_1 \times \ldots \times t_n)$ is a higher order sort.
(tuple sort)

(iii) If t and t' are higher order sorts, then (t --> t') is a higher order sort.
(functional sort)

Notice that for a name s, s itself is not considered as a higher order sort. The higher order sorts defined here are those PA^{nn}dA-S type expressions which are considered in the kernel-language. The more general form of type expressions (where in particular sort names not marked by $^{\perp}$ may occur) is treated in section 3.4)

A *generalized hierarchical signature* is a sequence of sorts, of function names (or "operators") and predicate names together with higher order sorts (their functionalities) and of package names together with

---

In the concrete syntax of PA^{nn}dA-S instead of the notation $s^{\perp}$ for atomic sorts in (i) the notation s+ is required, similarly × for # in (ii). We will use $s^{\perp}$ and × throughout this document since we consider it to be more suggestive.

generalized hierarchical signatures. Hence the set SIG of generalized hierarchical signatures is defined recursively as follows:

$$\mathrm{SIG} = (\mathrm{SOR} \cup \mathrm{FUN} \cup \mathrm{PRD} \cup \mathrm{PAC})^*$$

where

$$\mathrm{SOR} = \{\mathbf{sort}\} \times \mathrm{NAME}$$

$$\mathrm{FUN} = \{\mathbf{funct}\} \times \mathrm{H(SOR)} \times \mathrm{NAME}$$

$$\mathrm{PRD} = \{\mathbf{pred}\} \times \mathrm{H(SOR)} \times \mathrm{NAME}$$

$$\mathrm{PAC} = \{\mathbf{pack}\} \times \mathrm{SIG} \times \mathrm{NAME}$$

The set SIG is defined to be the inclusion-least set fulfilling the above equations.

With names for generics we associate an attribute consisting of a pair of generalized hierarchical signatures: we define

$$\mathrm{GEN} = \{\mathbf{gen}\} \times (\mathrm{SIG} \times \mathrm{SIG}) \times \mathrm{NAME}$$

Every generalized hierarchical signature sig defines a higher order signature in the sense of part I, section 2.1, if we take the union of all sorts, function symbols and predicate symbols (including those in packages being a member of sig), where all sorts, function symbols and predicate symbols occurring in such packages are considered to be primitive (in the sense of part I, section 2.1.3.4)

More precisely, we define a function

$$\mathrm{FLATTEN}\colon\ \mathrm{SIG} \to \mathrm{P}(\mathrm{SOR} \cup \mathrm{FUN} \cup \mathrm{PRD} \cup \mathrm{PAC})$$

by the equations:

$$\mathrm{FLATTEN}(\varepsilon) = \varnothing$$

$$\mathrm{FLATTEN}(< (\mathbf{funct}, t, f) >) = \{ (\mathbf{funct}, t, f) \}$$

$$\mathrm{FLATTEN}(< (\mathbf{pred}, t, pr) >) = \{ (\mathbf{pred}, t, pr) \}$$

$$\mathrm{FLATTEN}(< (\mathbf{sort}, s) >) = \{ (\mathbf{sort}, s) \}$$

$$\mathrm{FLATTEN}(< (\mathbf{pack}, sig, p) >) = \{ (\mathbf{pack}, sig, p) \} \cup \mathrm{FLATTEN}(sig)$$

$$\mathrm{FLATTEN}(sig1 \circ sig2) = \mathrm{FLATTEN}(sig1) \cup \mathrm{FLATTEN}(sig2)$$

Here $sig1^\circ sig2$ means the concatenation of the two generalized hierarchical signatures sig1 and sig2.

The set USED_SORTS(sig) of sorts used in the signature sig is defined to be the set of all names s such that (**sort**, s) is an element of FLATTEN(sig) or such that there exists some (**funct**, t, f) or some (**pred**, t, pr) in FLATTEN(sig) with $s \in \mathrm{USED}(t)$, where

$$\mathrm{USED}:\ \mathrm{H(SOR)} \to \mathrm{P(NAME)}$$

is defined inductively as follows:

$$\mathrm{USED}(s^{\perp}) = \{ s \},$$

$$\mathrm{USED}(t_1 \times \ldots \times t_n) = \mathrm{USED}(t_1) \cup \ldots \cup \mathrm{USED}(t_n) \quad (\text{for } n \geq 2)$$

$$\mathrm{USED}\,(t \dashrightarrow t') = \mathrm{USED}(t) \cup \mathrm{USED}(t')$$

Hence

USED_ SORTS(sig) : SIG → P(NAME)

can be defined inductively as follows:

USED_SORTS(ε) = ∅

USED_SORTS(< (**funct**, t, f) >) = USED(t)

USED_SORTS(< (**pred**, t, pr) >) = USED(t)

USED_SORTS(< (**sort**, s) >) = {s}

USED_SORTS(< (**pack**, sig, p) >) = USED_SORTS(sig)

USED_SORTS(sig1 ∘ sig2) = USED_SORTS(sig1) ∪ USED_SORTS(sig2)

The definition of "function space algebra" in part I, section 2.1 is adapted to generalized hierarchical signatures and to the universe of higher order functional objects over DATA as follows:

Let sig be a generalized hierarchical signature. Let

S = USED_SORTS(sig) ,

F= { (f, t) : (**funct**, t, f) ∈ FLATTEN(sig) },

P = { (pr, t) : (**pred**, t, pr) } ∈ FLATTEN(sig) }.

A *sig-function space algebra over* DATA consists of

(i) a family $((s^\perp)^A)_{s \in S}$ of cpo's such that $(s^\perp)^A \in$ DOM(DATA) for all $s \in S$,

(ii) a family $((f_t)^A)_{(f,t) \in F}$ of elements of FUN(DATA) such that $(f_t)^A \in t^A$ for all $(f,t) \in F$,

(iii) a family $((pr_t)^A)_{(pr,t) \in P}$ of subsets of FUN(DATA) such that $(pr_t)^A \subseteq t^A$ for all $(pr,t) \in P$,

where for a higher order sort t built over the sorts in S the cpo t^A is inductively defined as follows:

for $t = s^\perp$,	$t^A := (s^\perp)^A$	as in (i)
for $t = (t_1 \times \ldots \times t_n)$ with $n \geq 2$,	$t^A := t_1{}^A \times \ldots \times t_n{}^A$	with the componentwise ordering
for $t = (t_1 \text{-->} t_2)$,	$t^A := [\, t_1{}^A \to t_2{}^A \,]$,	the set of continuous functions with the pointwise ordering.

Notice that by definition of DOM(DATA) it follows that t^A is an element of DOM(DATA) for all higher order sorts t built over S.

Let A be a sig-function space algebra and (**pack**, sig', p) ∈ FLATTEN(sig).

The sig'-*reduct* of A (written $A|_{sig'}$) is defined to be the sig'-function space algebra consisting of those cpo's $(s^\perp)^A$, functional elements $f_t{}^A$ and relations $pr_{t'}{}^A$ such that $s \in$ USED_SORTS(sig') and (**funct**, t, f) , (**pred**,t', pr) ∈ FLATTEN(sig').

By FUNALG(DATA) we denote the set of all function space algebras over DATA.

In the above definition of a sig-function space algebra, the indices in f_t and pr_t may be omitted, provided sig has the property that in FLATTEN(sig) a unique higher order sort t is associated to every function or predicate symbol (i.e. sig is a signature with non-overloaded function and predicate symbols). In this case we say that t is *the* functionality assigned to f (or pr respectively) in sig .

Since we do not want to overload our semantic specification by the rules for overloading function or predicate symbols (and since we see this rather as an issue of static semantics) we ignore the possibility of overloading and assume that originally overloaded function symbols, predicate symbols and operators are made distinct for instance by indexing them by their functionalities.

The universe of semantic objects is defined by

$$\begin{aligned} \mathbb{U} = \; & \mathrm{FUN(DATA)} \\ \cup \; & \{ D:\ D \text{ is a cpo with } D \in \mathrm{DOM(DATA)} \} \\ \cup \; & \{ M : \exists\ D = (|D|, \sqsubseteq) \in \mathrm{DOM(DATA)} : M \subseteq |D| \} \\ \cup \; & \mathrm{FUNALG(DATA)} \\ \cup \; & \{ G : \exists\ sig1, sig2 \in \mathrm{SIG}: G \text{ is a set of } sig1^{\circ}\, sig2\text{- function space algebras over DATA} \} \end{aligned}$$

If we add the attributes to this universe of semantic objects we obtain the set VAL of attributed semantic objects defined by

$$\begin{aligned} \mathrm{VAL} = \; & \{ (\textbf{funct}, t, f) : && t \in H(\mathrm{SOR}) \wedge f \in \mathrm{FUN(DATA)} \} \\ \cup \; & \{ (\textbf{sort}, (), D) : && D \text{ is a cpo with } D \in \mathrm{DOM(DATA)} \} \\ \cup \; & \{ (\textbf{pred}, t, M) : && t \in H(\mathrm{SOR}) \wedge \exists\ D = (|D|, \sqsubseteq) \in \mathrm{DOM(DATA)} : M \subseteq |D| \} \\ \cup \; & \{ (\textbf{pack}, sig, A) : && sig \in \mathrm{SIG} \wedge A \text{ is a sig-function space algebra over DATA} \} \\ \cup \; & \{ (\textbf{gen}, (sig1, sig2), G) : && sig1, sig2 \in \mathrm{SIG} \wedge \\ & && G \text{ is a set of } sig1^{\circ}\, sig2\text{- function space algebras over DATA} \} \end{aligned}$$

Recall that with sorts we do not associate further attributes. We here use the empty tuple () as a place-holder for the attribute part.

3.2.3. Environments

We base our semantic definition on a set of environments: An environment is a function that associates with every pair consisting of a semantic attribute and an identifier an attributed semantic object. The set of environments is defined by

$$\mathrm{ENV} \subseteq (\mathrm{AID} \rightarrow \mathrm{VAL})$$

where $\mathrm{AID} = \mathrm{ATTRIBUTE} \times \mathrm{NAME}$

and $(\mathrm{AID} \rightarrow \mathrm{VAL})$ denotes the set of all (total) functions from AID to VAL.

We assume that an environment $\sigma \in \mathrm{ENV}$ fulfils the following consistency conditions 0. - 4.:

0. For all **at** $\in$ ATTRIBUTE and all $x \in$ NAME we have

   $\sigma(\textbf{at}, x) = (\textbf{at}, z, a)$

   for some $(\textbf{at}, z, a) \in \mathrm{VAL}$. This means that we always get an attributed semantic object consistent with the resp. attribute used as the argument for the environment. Note that this introduces some redundancy which hopefully improves the readability of the semantic definitions.

In order to formulate the further conditions 1. - 4. on environments we introduce some notation:

For an environment σ (satisfying condition 0.) and an attribute **at** we write

val(σ, **at**, x) for a if σ(**at**, x) = (**at**, z, a),

att(σ, **at**, x) for z if σ(**at**, x) = (**at**, z, a).

Furthermore, with a higher order sort t and an environment σ we associate a cpo t^σ as follows:

(i) for $t = s^\perp$ with $s \in$ NAME, t^σ := val(σ, **sort**, s)

(ii) for $t = (t_1 \times \ldots \times t_n)$ with higher order sorts $t_1, \ldots, t_n$ $(n \geq 2)$, $t^\sigma := t_1^\sigma \times \ldots \times t_n^\sigma$

(iii) for $t = (t_1 \text{-->} t_2)$ with higher order sorts t_1, t_2, $t^\sigma := [\, t_1^\sigma \rightarrow t_2^\sigma \,]$

The remaining consistency conditions 1. - 4. now can be formulated as follows:

1. Every identifier f marked by **funct** is attributed in σ by a higher order sort (a functionality) t such that the value associated to f in σ is an element of the carrier t^σ :

   $\forall$ f $\in$ NAME : val(σ, **funct**, f) $\in$ att(σ, **funct**, f)$^\sigma$

2. Every identifier pr considered as a predicate is attributed in σ by a higher order sort t such that the value associated to pr in σ is a relation on the carrier t^σ :

   $\forall$ pr $\in$ NAME : val(σ, **pred**, pr) $\subseteq$ att(σ, **pred**, pr)$^\sigma$

   (Notice that the inclusion $\subseteq$ here is understood as mere set inclusion, i.e. we forget the order structure on the poset att(σ, **pred**, pr)$^\sigma$).

3. Every package identifier p is attributed in σ with a signature att(σ, **pack**, p), such that the value val(σ, **pack**, p) associated to p in σ is an att(σ, **pack**, p) - function space algebra over DATA. The identifiers mentioned in att(σ, **pack**, p) as being functions or predicates are related in σ to functions and predicates of the resp. functionalities, i.e. att(σ, **funct**, f) and att(σ, **pred**, pr) coincide with the functionalities assigned to f and pr in the signature att(σ, **pack**, p).

   For the identifiers pa mentioned in att(σ, **pack**, p) as being package names, the signature att(σ, **pack**, pa) coincides with the signature assigned to pa in att(σ, **pack**, p).

4. Every identifier g marked by **gen** is attributed in σ by a pair of signatures att(σ, **gen**, g) = (sig1, sig2) such that the value val(σ, **gen**, g) of g in σ is a set of sig1$\circ$ sig2 - algebras.

For a higher order sort t and an environment σ we denote as usual by

$\perp_{t\sigma}$

the least element of the cpo t^σ. Hence the following holds

(i) $\perp_{(s^\perp)\sigma} = \perp_{\text{val}(\sigma,\, \textbf{sort},\, s)}$, for s $\in$ NAME

(ii) $\perp_{(t_1 \times \ldots \times t_n)\sigma} = (\perp_{t_1\sigma}, \ldots, \perp_{t_n\sigma})$, for all higher order sorts $t_1, \ldots, t_n$

(iii) $\perp_{(t \text{-->} t')\sigma}$ is the function returning $\perp_{t'\sigma}$ everywhere, for all higher order sorts t,t'.

An environment is changed pointwise by the function

$.[./.] : \text{ENV} \times \text{VAL} \times \text{NAME} \rightarrow \text{ENV}$

which is defined by

$$\text{val}(\ \sigma[(\textbf{at2}, z, v)/y], \textbf{at1}, x\ ) = \begin{cases} v & \text{if } \textbf{at1} = \textbf{at2} \text{ and } x = y \\ \text{val}(\ \sigma, \textbf{at1}, x\ ) & \text{otherwise} \end{cases}$$

$$\text{att}(\ \sigma[(\textbf{at2}, z, v)/y], \textbf{at1}, x\ ) = \begin{cases} z & \text{if } \textbf{at1} = \textbf{at2} \text{ and } x = y \\ \text{att}(\ \sigma, \textbf{at1}, x\ ) & \text{otherwise} \end{cases}$$

For pairwise different elements $(\textbf{at}_1, y_1),\ldots,(\textbf{at}_k, y_k) \in$ AID we write:

$\sigma[(\textbf{at}_1, z_1, v_1)/y_1, \ldots, (\textbf{at}_k, z_k, v_k)/y_k]$ for $\sigma[(\textbf{at}_1, z_1, v_1)/y_1] \ldots [(\textbf{at}_k, z_k, v_k)/y_k]$

Strictly speaking, the function .[./.] is a partial function, since in changing an environment it must be guaranteed that the above consistency conditions are not violated.

For notational convenience we introduce the function COIN defined by:

$\text{COIN} : \text{ENV} \times \text{P(AID)} \rightarrow \text{P(ENV)}$

which gives for a given environment σ and a set $X \subseteq$ AID the set of all environments that coincide with σ for all identifiers in X:

$\text{COIN}(\sigma, X) = \{\ \sigma 1 \in \text{ENV}: \forall\, x \in X: \sigma(x) = \sigma 1(x)\ \}$

In analogy we define:

$\text{NOCOIN} : \text{ENV} \times \text{P(AID)} \rightarrow \text{P(ENV)}$

$\text{NOCOIN}(\sigma, X) := \text{COIN}\ (\sigma, \text{AID} \setminus X)$

which is the set of all environments that coincide with σ except for the identifiers in X.

In section 3.3 we will introduce a function DC which associates with every sequence of declarations the generalized hierarchical signature consisting of the identifiers (for sorts, function symbols and package names including their attributes) that are declared by it:

$\text{DC: declaration\_list} \rightarrow \text{SIG}$

Sometimes we are only interested in the set of declarations of sorts, and names for functions, predicates, packages and generics contained in a sequence of declarations. Therefore we define a function:

$\text{SET: SIG} \rightarrow \text{P(AID)}$

by :

$$\begin{aligned} \text{SET(sig)} = \ & \{\ (\textbf{sort}, s) : (\textbf{sort}, s) \in \text{FLATTEN(sig)}\ \} \\ \cup\ & \{\ (\textbf{funct}, f) : \exists\, t \in \text{H(SOR)} : (\textbf{funct}, t, f) \in \text{FLATTEN(sig)}\ \} \\ \cup\ & \{\ (\textbf{pred}, pr) : \exists\, t \in \text{H(SOR)} : (\textbf{pred}, t, f) \in \text{FLATTEN(sig)}\ \} \\ \cup\ & \{\ (\textbf{pack}, pa) : \exists\, sig' \in \text{SIG} : (\textbf{pack}, sig', pa) \in \text{FLATTEN(sig)}\ \} \end{aligned}$$

Let for a generalized hierarchical signature sig the sets SORTS(sig), FUNCTS(sig), PREDS(sig), and PACKS(sig) be defined by

$$\text{SORTS(sig)} = \{ s \in \text{NAME} : (\textbf{sort}, s) \in \text{SET(sig)} \}$$

$$\text{FUNCTS(sig)} = \{ f \in \text{NAME} : (\textbf{funct}, f) \in \text{SET(sig)} \}$$

$$\text{PREDS(sig)} = \{ pr \in \text{NAME} : (\textbf{pred}, pr) \in \text{SET(sig)} \}$$

$$\text{PACKS(sig)} = \{ p \in \text{NAME} : (\textbf{pack}, p) \in \text{SET(sig)} \}$$

The set SORTS(sig) consists of the sorts that are *declared* in the signature sig. But it may be the case that not every sort occurring in a functionality associated to a function or predicate symbol in sig is actually declared in sig. The sorts not declared in sig, but used in functionalities in sig are called *global* to sig. These global sorts are either predefined sorts, sorts declared in enclosing packages or sorts imported from other library-units. Hence we define

$$\text{GLOB\_SORTS(sig)} = \text{USED\_SORTS(sig)} \setminus \text{SORTS(sig)}$$

Every sequence of declarations of sorts, functions, predicates and packages defines some generalized hierarchical signature sig. If the attributed identifiers occurring in sig are interpreted w.r.t. an environment $\sigma \in$ ENV, then a sig-function space algebra is obtained. More precisely, we define a partial function

$$\text{ALG} : \text{ENV} \times \text{SIG} \rightarrow \text{FUNALG(DATA)}$$

as follows : Let $\sigma \in$ ENV and sig $\in$ SIG.

ALG(σ, sig) is defined iff for all f $\in$ FUNCTS(sig) the functionality associated to f in sig is att(σ, **funct**, f) and for all pr $\in$ PREDS(sig) the functionality assigned to pr in sig is att(σ, **pred**, pr).

In this case for each sort s $\in$ USED_SORTS(sig) we define

$$(s^{\perp})^{\text{ALG}(\sigma, \text{sig})} := \text{val}(\sigma, \textbf{sort}, s)$$

for each function symbol f with f $\in$ FUNCTS(sig) , we set

$$f^{\text{ALG}(\sigma, \text{sig})} := \text{val}(\sigma, \textbf{funct}, f)$$

and for each predicate symbol pr with pr $\in$ FUNCTS(sig) , we set

$$pr^{\text{ALG}(\sigma, \text{sig})} := \text{val}(\sigma, \textbf{pred}, pr).$$

Notice that by the consistency conditions imposed on environments it follows that ALG(σ,sig) thus defined indeed is a sig- function space algebra. It is easily seen that for every package symbol p $\in$ PACKS(sig) with the signature sig' associated to p in sig, the algebra ALG(σ,sig') is the sig'-reduct of the algebra ALG(σ,sig).

3.2.4. Term-Generated Algebras

We conclude this section by a remark concerning the generation principle we impose on algebras. For this purpose we need some further definitions.

We distinguish a subset $H_0(SOR) \subseteq H(SOR)$ of *zero order sorts* defined inductively as follows:

(i) if s is an identifier standing for a sort, then $s^{\perp} \in H_0(SOR)$ (*atomic sorts*)

(ii) if $n \geq 2$, $t_i \in H_0(SOR)$ for $1 \leq i \leq n$, then $(t_1 \times ... \times t_n) \in H_0(SOR)$

Hence H_0(SOR) consists of all tuple sorts formed from atomic sorts.

A function sort ft $\in$ H(SOR) is called *essentially first order* if

(i) ft = (t --> t') with t, t' $\in$ H_0(SOR) or

(ii) ft = (t --> ft'), where ft' is essentially first order and t $\in$ H_0(SOR).

Intuitively, the functionalities in (ii) can be seen as "curried" versions of the first order functionalities considered in (i). Therefore we call them *essentially* first order.

Consider for a generalized hierarchical signature sig (with non-overloaded function and predicate symbols) the "flattened" higher order signature

Σ := (S, F, P) with S := USED_SORTS(sig), F := FUNCTS(sig), P := PREDS(sig)

where the functionalities of the function and predicate symbols in F and P are those assigned to them in sig.

We write H(S) for the set of higher order sorts generated from the atomic sorts $s^{\perp}$, s $\in$ S and H_0(S) for the set of zero order sorts generated from the atomic sorts $s^{\perp}$, s $\in$ S.

For an H(S)-sorted family X of identifiers the family $(T_{\Sigma,t}(X))_{t \in H(S)}$ of (higher-order) terms of a higher order sort t $\in$ H(S) is defined inductively as follows (compare part I, section 2.1), where we write fct(f) for the functionality of a function symbol f in Σ

(i) $x \in T_{\Sigma,t}(X)$ for every $x \in X_t$

(ii) $f \in T_{\Sigma,fct(f)}(X)$ for every f $\in$ F

(iii) *tuples*
if n≥2 and ui $\in T_{\Sigma,ti}(X)$ for 1≤i≤n, then (u1,..., un) $\in T_{\Sigma,(t1 \times \ldots \times tn)}(X)$

(iv) *function application*
if u $\in T_{\Sigma,(t1 \dashrightarrow t2)}(X)$ and v $\in T_{\Sigma,t1}(X)$, then u(v) $\in T_{\Sigma,t2}(X)$
(if v is a tuple-term (built according to (iii)), then the parentheses around v may be omitted)

The interpretation $u^A[\beta]$ of a term u in a sig- function space algebra A w.r.t. a given valuation β: X$\rightarrow$A is defined as in part I section 2.1.

For s $\in$ S, we call a term u $\in T_{\Sigma,s^{\perp}}(X)$ a first order term iff

- all the variables occurring in u are of a zero order sort t $\in$ H_0(S), and
- all the function symbols occurring in u are of a zero order or an essential first order functionality.

Hence, by identifying function symbols of an essential first order functionality with the corresponding "uncurried" function symbols, the first order terms are exactly the terms considered in the "classical" first order algebraic framework.

We call a sig-function space algebra A "*first order term-generated*" provided every carrier of an atomic sort $s^{\perp}$ with $s \in$ SORTS(sig) $\subseteq$ USED_SORTS(sig) = S can be generated by the interpretations of first order terms of sort $s^{\perp}$. These first order terms may contain variables of global sorts, i.e. sorts in GLOB_SORTS(sig). That means that elements of predefined atomic sorts or atomic sorts defined in imported library units may be used to generate the carriers of atomic sorts $s \in$ SORTS(sig).

Hence in a first order term-generated algebra A the real higher order functions (i.e. functions that are not essentially first order) are not considered as constructors for the atomic sorts in A: first, the elements of atomic sorts are constructed using only essentially first order functions and then, in a second step the higher order functions are chosen as elements of the function spaces built over these domains.

The semantics of PA^{nn}dA-S will be based on first order term-generated function space algebras. A very similar approach has been taken in the semantic definition of the language CIP-L [Bauer et. al. 85], where the atomic sorts are given by term-generated models of first order specifications and the higher order sorts in the full applicative language are interpreted as the respective function domains built over the atomic domains.

To make the notion of first order term-generation more precise, we say that a cpo (C, $\sqsubseteq$) with least element $\perp$ is *generated by a subset* $U \subseteq C$ iff there is no proper subset C' of C such that

(i) $\{ \perp \} \cup U \subseteq C'$ and

(ii) C' is closed under least upper bounds of directed subsets.

Hence if C is a flat cpo, then C is generated by U iff $\{ \perp \} \cup U = C$.

Let sig be a generalized higher order signature (with associated flat signature Σ) and S' $\subseteq$ USED_SORTS(sig). Let S" := (S' $\cup$ GLOB_SORTS(sig)) and let Y be an H_0(S")-sorted family of variables. Then a sig-function space algebra A is called *relatively first order term-generated w.r.t. S'* iff for every $s \in$ SORTS(sig) the carrier $(s^{\perp})^A$ is generated by the set

$\{ u^A[\beta] : u \in T_{\Sigma,s^{\perp}}(Y)$ is a first order term and $\beta: Y \to A$ is a valuation of the variables in Y $\}$

Hence $(s^{\perp})^A$ is generated by the interpretation of all first order terms of sort $s^{\perp}$ with variables of such zero order sorts which are built from the sorts in S' and in GLOB_SORTS(sig).

In case S' = $\varnothing$ we call A *first order term-generated*.

We write

FUNALG$_{GEN}$(sig, S')

for the set of all sig-function space algebras over DATA which are relatively first order term-generated w.r.t. the set of sorts S' and

FUNALG$_{GEN}$(sig)

for the set of all first order term-generated sig-function space algebras over DATA.

3.3. Semantic Equations for the Kernel Language

In order to present the semantics of the kernel language we introduce the following semantic functions where **B** $=_{def}$ {tt, ff} denotes the set of truth values:

V: expression $\rightarrow$ ENV $\rightarrow$ FUN(DATA)

L : logical_expression $\rightarrow$ ENV $\rightarrow$ **B**

D: declaration_list $\rightarrow$ ENV $\rightarrow$ **B**

DL: library_unit_list $\rightarrow$ ENV $\rightarrow$ **B**

We use a very particular view of declarations here. Semantically each of them is understood as a predicate on the set of environments. Only expressions and formulas are treated in a classical denotational style.

Note that besides ordinary expressions there exists a syntactic category of "logical expressions" (or formulas). Logical expressions are considered to be of a meta-sort LOGICAL. The carrier-set associated to logical is the two-value set **B** = {tt, ff}. The value of a formula w.r.t. a given environment is either tt or ff, i.e. the logic is two-valued. The meta-sort LOGICAL is not available to the user in the sense that it must not occur in a higher order sort t (i.e. for all higher order sorts t it holds LOGICAL $\notin$ USED(t)). Hence LOGICAL must not occur in the functionalities of user-defined functions or predicates.

In the syntax of PA^{nn}dA-S the meta-sort LOGICAL is used to distinguish predicate declarations from function declarations: the declaration of a predicate pr of functionality t with a higher order sort t is written as pr : t --> LOGICAL. This has to be carefully distinguished from a function declaration f : t --> BOOLEAN$^{\perp}$. Recall from the previous section that the semantics of pr in a given environment σ is merely a subset of the cpo t^{σ} (thus ignoring the ordering on t^{σ}), whereas the semantics of f is a <u>continuous</u> function from the cpo t^{σ} to the cpo $(\text{BOOLEAN}^{\perp})^{\sigma}$.

We use the syntactic category "declaration_list" to stand for lists of declarations, where a declaration list is either the empty word (denoted by ε) or a declaration list followed by a single declaration. In part II chapter 4 this syntactic category is denoted by {declaration}. The elements of this syntactic category can be considered as sequences of declarations.

In the same way we consider the syntactic category "library_unit_list" to stand for the set of all sequences of library units, where a library unit is a package declaration, a generic package declaration or a generic instantiation. For the purpose of this semantic description we regard PA^{nn}dA-S-specifications as sequences of library units. Actually, a PA^{nn}dA-S specification consists of a set of compilation units which are said to belong to a program library (see part II section 4.9).

A compilation unit is a library unit preceded by a context clause (i.e. a "<u>with</u> clause"). This with-clause makes visible a number of other library units in the program library. Since circular dependencies are forbidden by the context condition (9.2) in part II chapter 4, program libraries can be seen as acyclic directed graphs, the nodes of which are library units and the arcs of which are the dependencies created by <u>with</u> clauses between the library units.

In our semantic description of PA^{nn}dA-S specifications, we consider sequentialisations of program libraries which respect the dependencies in the graph (i.e. if a library unit lu depends on a library unit lu´, then lu´ occurs in the sequence before lu)

We only consider such sequences of library units which are sequentialisations of context-correct program libraries. Since in every library unit all declarations of the predefined package STANDARD are visible we assume that every such sequence of library units contains the package STANDARD as its first element. Moreover we assume that unique names are provided for all the entities declared in the library units belonging to the program library by the static semantic analysis and that all applied occurrences of identifiers are replaced by these unique names. In particular this means that in the sequences of library units under consideration we assume that the context clauses have already been treated and overloading has been resolved. In the sequel, we will therefore ignore context clauses.

The semantic function DL is given in a such a way that it does not take into account the order of the library units in a sequence. Hence different sequentialisations of a PA^{nn}dA-S program library have the same semantics.

The syntax of the kernel language L_0 is obtained from the syntax of full PA^{nn}dA-S (see part II chapter 4) by cancelling subtype declarations (part II section 4.3.4) and membership predicates (part II section 4.5.5) and by restricting the syntax of type expressions in part II section 4.3.5 to type expressions given by the following syntax:

```
type_expression0:: =
      function_type_expression0
    | tuple_type_expression0
    | type_name⊥

function_type_expression0 :: =
    (type_expression0 --> type_expression0)

tuple_type_expression0 ::=
    (type_expression0 x type_expression0 {x type_expression0})
```

This defines a subset of the PA^{nn}dA-S type expressions defined in part II section 4.3.5.
The type expressions admitted in L_0 are exactly the elements of H(SOR) (higher order sorts) given in the previous section.

Since no subtype declarations are possible in L_0, the syntax for generic instantiations is changed in L_0 in such a way that higher order sorts (i.e. elements of the syntactic category type_expression$_0$) instead of actual (sub)type names are passed as actual types.

In section 3.4 the semantics of PA^{nn}dA-S with arbitrary type-expressions and subtype declarations is given via definitional transformations into L_0.

Notice that in the semantic description of PA^{nn}dA-S we only consider generic declarations at top-level. That means that in the syntax given in part II chapter 4 we ignore from 3.1 ("declaration") the alternative "generic declaration".

In the sequel we use the following conventions

- x, x_1, x_m, x_n stand for arbitrary identifiers
- f stands for names for higher order functional objects (i.e. for names for elements of FUN(DATA)),
- s, s_0, s_1, s_2, s_n stand for names for sorts,
- $t, t', t_1, \ldots, t_n, t_m$ stand for arbitrary higher order sorts

- p, pa stand for names for packages,
- pr stands for names for predicates
- e, e_0, e_1, e_2, e_n stand for arbitrary expressions of a sort different from LOGICAL
- l, l_0, l_1,l_2,l_n, q_1, q_2, q_n stand for expressions of sort LOGICAL (i.e. for logical formulas)
- d stands for an arbitrary (single) declaration
- ds, ds1, ds2 stand for arbitrary sequences of declarations,
- lu stands for an arbitrary (single) library unit
- lus stands for arbitrary sequences of library units
- sig, sig1, sig2 stand for arbitrary signatures.

We write $V_\sigma[e]$ for $V[e](\sigma)$, $L_\sigma[l]$ for $L[l](\sigma)$, and so on.

In the following sections we give the semantic definitions by structural induction on the syntactic structure.

3.3.1. Semantics of Expressions

As usual in denotational semantics an expression is interpreted as a mapping from environments to values. The meaning of expressions is defined by structural induction on the syntactic structure.

We assume that all expressions under consideration are well-typed, since the check for type-correctness is an issue of the static semantics (see the PA^{nn}dA-S Static Semantics in the PA^{nn}dA-S Reference Manual, part II chapter 4).

With every (well-typed) expression a type is associated, which is a higher order sort. The function V_σ is only applied to such expressions which are well-typed (w.r.t. σ). Therefore we define an auxiliary (partial) function

type: expression $\rightarrow$ ENV $\rightarrow$ H(SOR)

which associates with a given environment σ and an expression e a higher order sort $type_\sigma[e]$, provided the expression e is well-typed (w.r.t. σ).

3.3.1.1. Names

Let f be an identifier standing for a functional element (i.e. for a function, a tuple or an element of an atomic sort). Then we define

$type_\sigma[\, f\,] = att(\sigma, \textbf{funct}, f)$

$V_\sigma[f] = val(\sigma, \textbf{funct}, f)$

3.3.1.2. *Tuple Expressions*

Let e_i ($1 \le i \le n$ with $n \ge 1$) be expressions which are well-typed w.r.t. σ, then $(e_1,\ldots, e_n)$ is a well-typed expression with

$$\text{type}_\sigma[\,(e_1,\ldots, e_n)\,] = \begin{cases} (\,\text{type}_\sigma[e_1] \times \ldots \times \text{type}_\sigma[e_n]\,) & \text{if } n \ge 2 \\ \text{type}_\sigma[e_1] & \text{if } n=1 \end{cases}$$

$$V_\sigma[\,(e_1,\ldots, e_n)\,] = \begin{cases} (V_\sigma[e_1] \times \ldots \times V_\sigma[e_n]\,) & \text{if } n \ge 2 \\ V_\sigma[e_1] & \text{if } n=1 \end{cases}$$

3.3.1.3. *Function calls*

Let e be an expression with $\text{type}_\sigma[e] = (\,t_1 \dashrightarrow t_2\,)$ and e_1 be an expression with $\text{type}_\sigma[e_1] = t_1$, then $e\,(e_1)$ is well-typed w.r.t. σ with

$$\text{type}_\sigma[\,e\,(e_1)\,] = t_2$$
$$V_\sigma[\,e\,(e_1)\,] = V_\sigma[e]\,(V_\sigma[e_1]).$$

By the consistency conditions imposed on environments it is guaranteed that $V_\sigma[e]$ is a function between $t_1{}^\sigma$ and $t_2{}^\sigma$.

(In case e_1 is a tuple-expression, a name or a literal the paranthesis around e_1 can be omitted)

3.3.1.4. *Expressions built by predefined (overloadable) operators*

Let op stand for the unique name for a binary predefined operator (which was possibly originally overloaded).

Suppose att(σ, **funct**, op) = $(\,(t_1 \times t_2) \dashrightarrow t_3\,)$ and let e_1 and e_2 be expressions with $\text{type}_\sigma[e_1] = t_1$ and $\text{type}_\sigma[e_2] = t_2$. Then e_1 op e_2 is well typed with

$$\text{type}_\sigma[\,e_1 \text{ op } e_2\,] = t_3$$
$$V_\sigma[\,e_1 \text{ op } e_2\,] = \text{val}\,(\sigma, \textbf{funct}, \text{op})\,(\,V_\sigma[e_1], V_\sigma[e_2]\,)$$

The case of expressions built by predefined unary operators is treated analogouosly.

For the semantics of the predefined operators and functions on BOOLEAN, INTEGER and STRING we refer to the specification of the Standard Types in part II chapter 5, and to the semantics of declarations and formulas in this document. In particular it is assumed that the package STANDARD is already transformed into a library unit in the kernel language by the definitional transformations to be given in section 3.4.

3.3.1.5. *Undefined*

For every atomic sort s there is a predefined overloaded constant **undefined** of type $s^\perp$. Since we assume unique names , we consider a family of constants $\textbf{undefined}_s$ where s is a sort name and define

$$\text{type}_\sigma[\,\textbf{undefined}_s\,] = s^\perp$$
$$V_\sigma[\,\textbf{undefined}_s\,] = \perp_{\text{val}(\sigma,\, \textbf{sort},\, s)}$$

3.3.1.6. *Numeric Literals*

Let for $n \in \mathbf{N}$ the expression $\mathsf{SUCC}^n(\mathsf{ZERO})$ be inductively defined by

$$\mathsf{SUCC}^0(\mathsf{ZERO}) =_{def} \mathsf{ZERO}$$
$$\mathsf{SUCC}^{i+1}(\mathsf{ZERO}) =_{def} \mathsf{SUCC}(\ \mathsf{SUCC}^i(\mathsf{ZERO})\ ) \quad \text{for } i \in \mathbf{N}$$

Let num stand for a numeric literal representing a natural number nat(num). Then

$$\text{type}_\sigma[\text{num}] = \mathsf{INTEGER}^\perp$$
$$V_\sigma[\text{num}] = V_\sigma[\ \mathsf{SUCC}^{\text{nat(num)}}(\mathsf{ZERO})\ ]$$

3.3.1.7. *String Literals*

String literals can be considered as catenations of strings consisting of single characters.
Let str = "$c_1\, c_2 ... c_n$" be a string literal composed of the characters $c_1, c_2, ... c_n$. Then

$$\text{type}_\sigma[\text{str}] = \mathsf{STRING}^\perp$$
$$V_\sigma[\text{str}] = V_\sigma[\ (...(\ "c_1"\&"c_2")\&...\&"c_{n-1}")\ \&\ "c_n"\ ]$$

The interpretation of a string literal consisting of a single character is the interpretation of the corresponding constant of type $\mathsf{STRING}^\perp$ specified in the package STANDARD.

3.3.2. Semantics of Logical Expressions (Formulas)

Now we present the semantics of formulas (or logical expressions) in PA^{nn}dA-S. They are regarded as expressions of a meta-sort LOGICAL not available to the user (i.e. this sort must not occur in the functionalities of user-defined functions or predicates). The semantic function

$$L: \text{logical\_expression} \rightarrow \text{ENV} \rightarrow \mathbf{B}$$

is defined by induction on the structure of formulas.

We start by giving the semantics of predicate calls:

3.3.2.1. *Predicate Calls*

Let σ be an environment. For every predicate symbol pr and every well typed expression e with att(σ, **pred**, pr) = type$_\sigma$[e], pr(e) is a well-formed formula (w.r.t. σ) and we have

$$L_\sigma[\ \text{pr(e)}\ ] = \begin{cases} \text{tt} & \text{if } V_\sigma[e] \in \text{val}\ (\ \sigma, \mathbf{pred}, \text{pr}\ ) \\ \text{ff} & \text{otherwise.} \end{cases}$$

3.3.2.2. *Definedness Predicate*

There is a predefined "definedness predicate" **defined** which is defined for every higher order sort. Let as usual $\perp_{t\sigma}$ denote the least element of the cpo associated to a higher order sort t in the environment σ.

$$L_\sigma[\ \textbf{defined}\ e\ ] = \begin{cases} \text{tt} & \text{if } V_\sigma[e] \neq \perp_{\text{type}_\sigma[e]\sigma} \\ \text{ff} & \text{if } V_\sigma[e] = \perp_{\text{type}_\sigma[e]\sigma}\ . \end{cases}$$

Hence, if the type of e is of the form $s^{\perp}$ for a sort identifier s (an atomic sort) then the definedness predicate yields true iff the value of e is different from $\perp_{val(\sigma, \mathbf{sort}, s)}$.

3.3.2.3. *Equality and Inequality*

The predefined equality is the strong equality: Two expressions are equal iff their semantic interpretations are the same regardless of the fact whether they are undefined or not:

$$L_\sigma[\, e1 = e2 \,] = \begin{cases} tt & \text{if } V_\sigma[e_1] = V_\sigma[e_2] \\ ff & \text{if } V_\sigma[e_1] \neq V_\sigma[e_2] \end{cases}$$

Notice that e1 = e2 is a formula, whereas for boolean or integer or string expressions e1 and e2, e1 EQ e2 is an expression (built by the predefined equality operator of result type $BOOLEAN^{\perp}$) which is undefined as soon as the value of e1 or e2 is undefined.

The predefined inequality is interpreted as follows

$$L_\sigma[\, e_1 /= e_2 \,] = \begin{cases} tt & \text{if } V_\sigma[e_1] \neq V_\sigma[e_2] \\ ff & \text{if } V_\sigma[e_1] = V_\sigma[e_2] \end{cases}$$

3.3.2.4. *Semantics of Composite Formulas*

The predefined boolean operators "and", "or", "xor" and "not" are overloaded by logical combinators.The effect of the logical combinators is the same as of the corresponding boolean operators, but restricted to the two-valued case:

$$L_\sigma[\, l_1 \textbf{ and } l_2 \,] = \begin{cases} tt & \text{if } L_\sigma[\, l_1 \,] = tt \text{ and } L_s[\, l_2 \,] = tt \\ ff & \text{if } L_\sigma[\, l_1 \,] = ff \text{ or } L_s[\, l_2 \,] = ff \end{cases}$$

$$L_\sigma[\, l_1 \textbf{ or } l_2 \,] = \begin{cases} tt & \text{if } L_\sigma[\, l_1 \,] = tt \text{ or } L_s[\, l_2 \,] = tt \\ ff & \text{if } L_\sigma[\, l_1 \,] = ff \text{ and } L_s[\, l_2 \,] = ff \end{cases}$$

$$L_\sigma[\, l_1 \textbf{ xor } l_2 \,] = \begin{cases} tt & \text{if } L_\sigma[\, l_1 \,] \neq L_s[\, l_2 \,] \\ ff & \text{if } L_\sigma[\, l_1 \,] = L_s[\, l_2 \,] \end{cases}$$

$$L_\sigma[\, \textbf{not } l \,] = \begin{cases} tt & \text{if } L_\sigma[\, l \,] = ff \\ ff & \text{if } L_s[\, l \,] = tt \end{cases}$$

The logical operators "→" and "↔" are only defined on formulas :

$$L_\sigma[\, l_1 \rightarrow l_2 \,] = \begin{cases} tt & \text{if } L_\sigma[\, l_1 \,] = ff \text{ or } L_s[\, l_2 \,] = tt \\ ff & \text{if } L_\sigma[\, l_1 \,] = tt \text{ and } L_s[\, l_2 \,] = ff \end{cases}$$

$$L_\sigma[\, l_1 \leftrightarrow l_2 \,] = \begin{cases} tt & \text{if } L_\sigma[\, l_1 \,] = L_s[\, l_2 \,] \\ ff & \text{if } L_\sigma[\, l_1 \,] \,\pi\, L_s[\, l_2 \,] \end{cases}$$

A formula of the form

q_1 impl$_1$ l_1, q_2 impl$_2$ l_2, ... , q_n impl$_n$ l_n, **others** impl l

with {impl$_1$,..., impl$_n$, impl} $\subseteq$ {↔, →} and logical expressions q_1,..., q_n, l_1,..., l_n, l is considered as an abbreviation for the logical expression

q_1 impl$_1$ l_1 **and** q_2 impl$_2$ l_2 **and** ... **and** q_n impl$_n$ l_n **and not** (q_1 **or** q_2 **or** ... **or** q_n) impl l.

3.3.2.5. *Quantification*

Quantification over formulas is defined in the classical way: Consider formulas l_1,..., l_n with variables x_i ($1 \leq i \leq m$) of the higher order sorts t_i.

Let for $a = (a_1,..., a_m) \in (t_1 \times ... \times t_m)^\sigma$ the value C(a) be defined by

C(a) = $L_{\sigma 1}$[l_1 **and** ... **and** l_n]

where

$\sigma 1 = \sigma$[(**funct**, t_1, a_1)/x_1, ... , (**funct**, t_m, a_m)/x_m]

Then the semantics of the universal and existential quantification of l_1,...,l_n w.r.t. the variables x_1,..,x_m is given by

$$L_\sigma[\, \textbf{for all } x_1{:}t_1; \ldots; x_m{:}t_m \Rightarrow l_1,\ldots, l_n \,] = \begin{cases} tt & \text{if } \forall\, a \in (t_1 \times \ldots \times t_m)^\sigma\text{: } C(a) = tt \\ ff & \text{if } \exists\, a \in (t_1 \times \ldots \times t_m)^\sigma\text{: } C(a) = ff \end{cases}$$

$$L_\sigma[\, \textbf{exist } x_1{:}t_1; \ldots; x_m{:}t_m \Rightarrow l_1,\ldots, l_n \,] = \begin{cases} tt & \text{if } \exists\, a \in (t_1 \times \ldots \times t_m)^\sigma\text{: } C(a) = tt \\ ff & \text{if } \forall\, a \in (t_1 \times \ldots \times t_m)^\sigma\text{: } C(a) = ff \end{cases}$$

Notice that by this definition the quantification ranges over all elements of the cpo's tis- including their least elements ^tis .

3.3.3. Semantics of Declarations

Declarations are considered as predicates on environments. In order to define the semantic functions for declarations we first define auxiliary functions DC and DCL which indicate for which identifiers a sequence of declarations actually declares something.

3.3.3.1. Definition of the Functions DC and DCL

The function

DC : declaration_list → SIG

associates with every sequence of declarations a generalized signature containing all the globally defined identifiers. Here the declarations considered in the kernel-language are private type declarations, function declarations, predicate declarations, package declarations and axioms. Axioms do not introduce new bindings, but impose restrictions on the set of possible environments.
Notice that since we only consider generic declarations at top-level, we regard them as library units, but not as elements of the syntactic category "declaration".

The function

DCL : library_unit_list → (PAC ∪ GEN)*

associates with every sequence of package and generic specifications and generic instantiations the sequence of attributed package and generic symbols declared by it.

In order to cope with the declaration of auxiliary functions and predicates, we introduce an additional function

AUX-DC : declaration_list → SIG

which differs from DC only insofar as it includes also names and functionalities of auxiliary functions and predicates into the signature.

DC, AUX-DC and DCL are defined by the following equations:

DC[ε] = ε, AUX-DC[ε] = ε, DCL[ε] = ε

If we add a declaration d to a sequence ds of declarations this corresponds to the concatenation of the declared items:

DC[ds d] = DC[ds] ∘ DC[d]

and the same equation holds for AUX-DC.

In the same way we define for a sequence lus of library units and a single library unit lu

DCL[lus lu] = DCL[lus] ∘ DCL[lu]

Now we define DC and AUX-DC for single declarations:

A type declaration introduces a new sort name:

DC[**type** s **is private**;] = < (**sort**, s) >,

AUX-DC[**type** s **is private**;] = < (**sort**, s) >

A function declaration introduces a new function name together with its functionality:

DC[f : t;] = < (**funct**, t, f) >

AUX-DC[f : t;] = < (**funct**, t, f) >

Whereas the declaration of an auxiliary function is forgotten by the function DC, it is conserved by AUX-DC:

DC [--: f : t;] = ε

AUX-DC[--: f : t;] = < (**funct**, t, f) >

A predicate declaration introduces a new predicate name together with its functionality:

DC[pr : t --> LOGICAL;] = < (**pred**, t , pr) >

AUX-DC[pr : t --> LOGICAL;] = < (**pred**, t , pr) >

Whereas the declaration of an auxiliary predicate is forgotten by the function DC, it is conserved by AUX-DC:

DC[--: pr : t --> LOGICAL;] = ε

AUX-DC[--: pr : t --> LOGICAL;] = < (**pred**, t , pr) >

An axiom does not introduce any new bindings:

DC[**axiom** l;] = ε, AUX-DC[**axiom** l;] = ε

On package declarations and generic instantiations the functions DC and AUX-DC act in the same way as the function DCL which is defined below:

By a package declaration a new identifier for a package together with a signature is introduced. The signature that is declared by a package declaration indicates which of the identifiers in an environment are occurring on the left-handside of (non-auxiliary) declarations.

DCL[**package** p **is** ds **end**;] = < (**pack**, DC[ds], p) >

Notice that here we assume that the sequence ds of declarations does not contain the declaration of a generic package.

A generic specification introduces an identifier attributed with a pair of signatures:

DCL[**generic** ds1 **package** g **is** ds2 **end**;] = < (**gen**, (DC[ds1], DC[ds2]), g) >

Here DC[ds1] is the signature of the generic formal part and DC[ds2] is the signature of the package specification.

It remains to define the function DCL for a generic instantiation

package p **is new** g(act_pars);

with g ∈ NAME and where act_pars is a list of actual parameters, more precisely
act_pars ∈ (NAME ∪ H(SOR) ∪ expression)*

Suppose that the declaration of the generic g is given by

generic ds1 **package** g **is** ds2 **end**;

and let sig1 = DC[ds1] and sig2 = DC[ds2].

Here sig1 is the signature of the generic formal part. This signature may only consist of attributed sort, function and predicate symbols. In the above instantiation the list act_pars of actual parameters has to be a sequence of the same length as the signature sig1. In contrast to full $PA^{nn}dA$-S where in a generic instantiation the formal sorts have to be instantiated with identifiers standing for (sub)types, in the kernel language only instantiations with higher order sorts as actual sorts are considered. By matching the formal parameters in sig1 by the actual parameters occurring in the same position, every formal sort identifier has to be matched with a higher order sort, every formal predicate symbol with an actual predicate symbol and every formal function symbol with an expression denoting a function with a functionality matching the functionality of the formal function symbol. Hence the above instantiation defines a triple of mappings

$$\alpha_S : \mathrm{SORTS(sig1)} \rightarrow \mathrm{H(SOR)}$$

$$\alpha_F : \mathrm{FUNCTS(sig1)} \rightarrow \mathrm{expression}$$

$$\alpha_P : \mathrm{PREDS(sig1)} \rightarrow \mathrm{NAME}$$

The instantiation **package** p **is new** g(act_pars) yields a new package with a signature that is obtained from the signature sig2 of the package specification part of the generic package g by adapting the functionalities of all function and predicate symbols declared in sig2 according to the substitution which replaces every formal sort $s^{\perp}$ (with $s \in$ SORTS(sig1)) by the sort expression $\alpha_S(s) \in$ H(SOR).

More formally, we assume for every symbol in the signature sig2 a new symbol that is related to the package identifier p and is not declared in the context surrounding the instantiation:

We suppose that with all (**sort**, s), (**funct**, f), (**pack**, pa), (**pred**, pr) $\in$ SET(sig2) "new" attributed identifiers (**sort**, new(p,s)), (**funct**, new(p,f)), (**pack**, new(p,pa)), (**pred**, new(p,pr)) are provided such that new(p,s1) and new(p,s2) are different sorts for all s1, s2 $\in$ SORTS(sig2) with s1$\neq$ s2 and the same holds for the new function, predicate and package symbols.

In the concrete syntax of $PA^{nn}dA$-S the identifiers new(p, $\cdot$) are obtained by prefixing the respective identifiers by the symbol p.

We write

newsig(p, sig2) [act_pars / sig1]

for the signature obtained from the signature sig2 by replacing all symbols in SET(sig2) by the new symbols new(p, $\cdot$) and where the functionality of a function or predicate symbol new(p,f) (or new(p,pr)) is obtained from the functionality of f (or pr) by replacing every occurrence of a formal sort $s^{\perp}$ (with $s \in$ SORTS(sig1)) by the sort expression $\alpha_S(s)$ and every occurrence of a sort s' $\in$ SORTS(sig2) by the sort new(p,s').

The signature related to a "new" package symbol new(p,pa) is obtained from the signature sig' related to pa in sig2 by replacing all symbols in SET(sig') $\subseteq$ SET(sig2) by the new symbols (together with their new attributes).

Finally, we define

DCL[**package** p **is new** g(act_ pars);] = < (**pack**, newsig(p, sig2) [act_pars / sig1], p) >

3.3.3.2. *The Semantic Functions D and DL*

The semantics of a sequence ds of declarations is a predicate on the set of environments. This predicates yields true on an environment if the environment is consistent with respect to the declarations in ds. Notice that also axioms are considered as declarations.

Now we give the semantic equations for the semantic functions

$$D : \text{declaration\_list} \rightarrow \text{ENV} \rightarrow \mathbf{B}$$

$$DL: \text{library\_unit\_list} \rightarrow \text{ENV} \rightarrow \mathbf{B}$$

3.3.3.2.1. Semantics of Sequences of Declarations

The function D is defined on sequences of declarations of functions, predicates, types and packages (including generic instantiations), together with axioms which restrict the set of admissible environments. The function DL is defined on sequences of library units. The semantics of a sequence of declarations or library units is simply obtained by taking the conjunction of the predicates determined by the single declarations or library units from which the sequence is built :

$D_\sigma[\varepsilon] \;=\; tt, \; DL_\sigma[\varepsilon] \;=\; tt$

$D_\sigma[ds\ d] \;=\; D_\sigma[ds] \wedge D_\sigma[d],$

$DL_\sigma[lus\ lu] \;=\; DL_\sigma[lus] \wedge DL_\sigma[lu]$

Hence the particular ordering chosen in the sequentialisation of a program library does not influence the semantics.

Now we give the meaning of single declarations and of single library units.

3.3.3.2.2. Semantics of Axioms

Axioms define the same predicates as the corresponding logical formulas:

For a logical formula l we define

$D_\sigma[\,\textbf{axiom}\ l;] \;=\; L_\sigma[\,l\,]$

3.3.3.2.3. Semantics of Function Declarations

Declarations of functions are considered as predicates on environments. For a higher order sort t we define

$D_\sigma[\,f : t;] \;=\; (\,att(\,\sigma, \textbf{funct}, f\,) = t\,)$

$D_\sigma[\,\text{--}: f : t;] \;=\; (\,att(\,\sigma, \textbf{funct}, f\,) = t\,)$

Notice that by a function declaration in the kernel language just the functionality of the function is introduced. Properties of the function can be postulated by axioms.

In the kernel language, no restrictions occur in the functionalities of functions. Restrictions will be treated in section 3.4 by translating them into the kernel-language.

3.3.3.2.4. Semantics of Predicate Declarations

For a higher order sort t we define

D_σ[pr : t --> LOGICAL;] = (att(σ, **pred**, pr) = t)

D_σ[--: pr : t --> LOGICAL;] = (att(σ, **pred**, pr) = t)

3.3.3.2.5. Semantics of Type Declarations

A type declaration introduces a new sort name

D_σ[**type** s **is private**;] = tt

Note that this is only a rather trivial form of a type declaration. Declarations of subtypes will be treated in section 3.4 by replacing them by the specification of a characterizing predicate.

On package specifications and generic instantiations the semantic function D is defined in the same way as the function DL, which is defined in the following paragraph:

3.3.3.2.6. Semantics of Package Declarations

By a package declaration a new identifier for a package is introduced.

DL_σ[**package** p **is** ds **end**;] =

(att(σ, **pack**, p) = DC[ds]) ∧ (val(σ, **pack**, p) = ALG(σ, DC[ds]))

∧ ALG(σ, DC[ds]) ∈ $FUNALG_{GEN}$(DC[ds])

∧ ∃ σ1 ∈ NOCOIN(σ, {(**pack**, p)}∪(SET(AUX-DC[ds]) \ SET(DC[ds]))) : $D_{\sigma 1}$[ds]

Here ALG(σ, DC[ds]) denotes the DC[ds]- function space algebra that is formed by the posets, functions and relations that are associated to the sorts, function and predicate symbols of the signature DC[ds] in the environment σ. (as defined in section 3.2).

Recall from section 3.2 that $FUNALG_{GEN}$(DC[ds]) denotes the set of all first order term-generated DC[ds] -function space algebras (over DATA)).

In the last line of the above definition it is required that the algebra ALG(σ, DC[ds]) is the DC[ds]-reduct of an algebra ALG(σ1, AUX-DC[ds]) over the larger signature AUX-DC[ds] (comprising the auxiliary functions and predicates), where σ1 is an environment consistent with all the declarations in ds (including the axioms which are given in terms of the auxiliary functions and predicates). Hence the declaration of the auxiliary functions does not contribute to the signature associated to p, but the axioms in the package given in terms of the auxiliary functions and predicates restrict the set of possible environments (or models).

Notice that the above definition does not only imply that the algebra ALG(σ, DC[ds]) associated to p in σ is first order term-generated (as defined in section 3.2). It also implies that for all "primitive" package specifications declaring a package symbol (**pack**, sig, pa) in the signature DC[ds] the respective sig-reduct of the algebra ALG(σ, DC[ds]) is first order term-generated as well. That is, we only consider hierarchical models (see the definition in part I, section 2.1).

3.3.3.2.7. Semantics of Generic Package Declarations

The semantics of a generic package is a set of algebras:

DL_{σ}[**generic** ds1 **package** g **is** ds2 **end**;] =

(att(σ, **gen**, g) = (DC[ds1], DC[ds2])) ∧

(val(σ, **gen**, g) =

{ B ∈ $FUNALG_{GEN}$(DC[ds1] ∘ DC[ds2], SORTS(DC[ds1])) :

∃ σ1 ∈ NOCOIN(σ, SET(DC[ds1]) ∪ SET(AUX-DC[ds2]) ∪ {(**gen**, g)}) :

$D_{\sigma 1}$[ds1] ∧ $D_{\sigma 1}$[ds2] ∧ B = ALG(σ1, DC[ds1] ∘ DC[ds2]) })

Recall that $FUNALG_{GEN}$(DC[ds1] ∘ DC[ds2], SORTS(DC[ds1]) denotes the set of DC[ds1]∘DC[ds2]-function space algebras which are first order term-generated relative to the set of sorts in the formal signature DC[ds1].

In this way we associate with a generic declaration the set of all function space algebras over the signature given by the declarations in ds1 and ds2 which satisfy the axioms contained in ds1 and ds2 and are first order term-generated relative to the sorts in SORTS(DC[ds1]). Every such function space algebra is determined by an environment σ1 which coincides with the given environment σ except for all attributed identifiers declared by the declarations (and auxiliary declarations) in ds1 and ds2 and the attributed identifier (**gen**, g) itself. Moreover, σ1 has to be consistent with respect to all all declarations in the generic formal part and in the package part .

In other words, if we assume (not necessarily term-generated) algebras for the generic formal parameters, (i.e. algebras determined by environments consistent with the declarations in ds1) then the algebras belonging to the generic g are built around these according to the following demands:
they have to be consistent with all declarations in ds2 and the carriers of the new atomic sorts must be generated by the set of elements obtained by applying the first order operations of the algebra iteratively to the elements of the formal sorts.

3.3.3.2.8. Semantics of Generic Instantiations

If a generic is instantiated, then its parameter signature (which may only consist of sorts and function and predicate symbols together with their functionalities) is matched with a list of actual parameters of the same length as its parameter signature: every formal sort identifier is matched with a higher order sort, every formal predicate symbol with an actual predicate symbol and every formal function symbol with an expression denoting a function with a functionality "matching" the functionality of the formal function symbol. In order to make it more precise what we understand by a "matching" functionality, we need some definitions:

Let sig be a signature (standing for the formal signature of a generic) and

α_S: SORTS(sig) → H(SOR)

a substitution of the sorts declared in sig. α_S can be extended to a map $\underline{\alpha_S}$ defined on the set USED_SORTS(sig) of the sorts used in sig (for the definition see section 3.2) by leaving all the global sorts unchanged and marking them by the ⊥- symbol.

Hence

$\underline{\alpha}_S$: USED_SORTS(sig) $\rightarrow$ H(SOR)

is defined by setting

$\underline{\alpha}_S(s) = \alpha_S(s)$ for all $s \in$ SORTS(sig) and $\underline{\alpha}_S(s) = s^\perp$ for all $s \in$ GLOB_SORTS(sig).

Finally, α_S determines a (partial) map

$h(\alpha_S)$: H(SOR) $\rightarrow$ H(SOR)

which is defined on all higher order sorts built from sort identifiers contained in USED_SORTS(sig) in the following way:

$h(\alpha_S)(s^\perp) = \underline{\alpha}_S(s)$ for every $s \in$ SOR

$h(\alpha_S)(t_1 \times ... \times t_n) = h(\alpha_S)(t_1) \times ... \times h(\alpha_S)(t_n)$

$h(\alpha_S)(t \text{ --> } t') = h(\alpha_S)(t) \text{ --> } h(\alpha_S)(t')$.

In order to give the semantics of generic instantiations, we define a partial function

ALG_{der} : ENV $\times$ SIG $\times$ (H(SOR) $\cup$ expression $\cup$ NAME)* $\rightarrow$ FUNALG(DATA)

which associates with an environment σ, a (formal) signature sig and a sequence act_pars of actual parameters a sig-function space algebra which can be derived from the given environment by replacing the sorts and function symbols in sig by the corresponding actual parameters:

More precisely, the algebra $ALG_{der}(\sigma$, sig, act_pars) is well-defined iff

(i) sig $\in$ (FUN $\cup$ SOR $\cup$ PRD)* and

(ii) The sequences sig and act_pars have the same length and by matching the identifiers in sig with the corresponding actual parameters the pair (sig, act_pars) determines a triple of mappings

α_S : SORTS(sig) $\rightarrow$ H(SOR)

α_F : FUNCTS(sig) $\rightarrow$ expression

α_P : PREDS(sig) $\rightarrow$ NAME

(iii) the triple $(\alpha_S, \alpha_F, \alpha_P)$ is a signature morphism w.r.t. the functionalities of the function and predicate symbols in sig and the functionalities of the functional expressions α_F(FUNCTS(sig)) and the predicate symbols α_P(PREDS(sig)) in the environment σ, i.e. for every $f \in$ FUNCTS(sig) with the functionality t attributed to f in sig we have

$type_\sigma[\alpha_F(f)] = h(\alpha_S)(t)$

and for every pr $\in$ PREDS(sig) with functionality t' attributed to pr in sig we have

att(σ, **pred**, α_P(pr)) = $h(\alpha_S)(t')$.

Now suppose that the triple (σ, sig, act_pars) satisfies conditions (i) - (iii). Then we define the sig-function space algebra $ALG_{der}(\sigma$, sig, act_pars) - in the sequel abbreviated by A- as follows:

For a sort s in USED_SORTS(sig) we set

$(s^\perp)^A := \underline{\alpha}_S(s)^\sigma$,

where for a higher order sort $t \in$ H(SOR) and an environment σ, the carrier t^σ is defined as in section 3.2.

For a function symbol $f \in$ FUNCTS(sig) we set

$$f^A := V_\sigma[\ \alpha_F(f)\ ]$$

and for a predicate symbol $pr \in$ PREDS(sig) we set

$$pr^A := \text{val}(\ \sigma, \textbf{pred}, \alpha_P(pr)\ ).$$

By the consistency conditions imposed on environments and conditions (i) - (iii) it is guaranteed that A indeed is a sig- function space algebra.

Now we are ready to give the semantics of a generic instantiation:

The semantics of a generic instantiation is given by the set of all environments which determine models of the generic modulo the replacement of the formal parameter signature by the list of actual parameters. The attribute associated to a package symbol obtained by a generic instantiation is the signature chosen in the definition of the function DCL (see section 3.3.1).

D_σ[**package** p **is new** g(act_pars);] =

(∃ sig1, sig2 ∈ SIG:

att(σ, **gen**, g) = (sig1, sig2) ∧

att(σ, **pack**, p) = newsig(p, sig2) [act_ pars / sig1]

∧

(∃ B ∈ val(σ, **gen**, p) :

$B|_{sig1}$ = ALG_{der}(σ, sig1, act_pars) ∧

$(s^\perp)^B$ = val(σ, **sort**, new(p,s)) for all s ∈ SORTS(sig2) ∧

f^B = val(σ, **funct**, new(p,f)) for all f ∈ FUNCTS(sig2) ∧

pr^B = val(σ, **pred**, new(p,pr)) for all pr ∈ PREDS(sig2))

∧

val(σ, **pack**, p) = ALG(σ, att(σ, **pack**, p)) ∧

(val(σ, **pack**, new(p,pa)) = ALG(σ, att(σ, **pack**, new(p,pa))) for all pa ∈ PACKS(sig2))

The sorts, function and package symbols new(p,s), new(p,f) and new(p,pa) are the "new" symbols associated with the instantiation (compare the definition of the function DCL in section 3.3.3.1).

The signature newsig(p, sig2) [act_pars / sig1] is defined as in section 3.3.3.1. It is obtained from the signature sig2 by replacing the symbols in sig2 by the new symbols and changing the functionality of the function and predicate symbols according to the substitution of the sorts in sig1 (marked by ⊥) by the corresponding actual higher order sorts.

Recall that we defined in 3.3.3.1

DCL[**package** p **is new** g(act_pars);] = < (**pack**, newsig(p, sig2) [act_pars / sig1], p) >

By the consistency condition 3 imposed on environments (see section 3.2.3) it is guaranteed that for every environment σ with att(σ, **pack**, p) = newsig(p, sig2) [act_pars / sig1] the signature att(σ, **pack**, new(p,pa)) related in σ to the package name new(p,pa) (for pa ∈ PACKS(sig2)) coincides with the signature assigned to new(p,pa) in newsig(p,sig2) [act_pars / sig1].

Remark:

In many approaches to the semantics of generics, the semantics of a generic instantiation is defined by textual substitution, i.e. provided the actual parameters are specified in such a way that they satisfy the laws required in the formal part of the generic, the generic instantiation "yields" a package which is obtained from the package part of the generic by substituting the formal parameters by the corresponding actual parameters (see e.g. CIP-L [Bauer et al. 85]).

In PA^{nn}dA-S the "textual expansion" of a generic instantiation can be regarded as a transformation rule. This transformation is semantic-preserving (w.r.t. the above semantics for a generic instantiation), provided the formal sorts are replaced by zero order (actual) sorts. However, if a generic is instantiated with a higher order sort, then the semantics of the instantiation will in general not be the same as the semantics of the package obtained by textual substitution. This is due to the requirement of first-order term-generatedness:

If in the functionality of a function a formal sort $s^{\perp}$ is replaced by a zero order (actual) sort, then the property of being an "essential first order functionality" is not affected. However, if $s^{\perp}$ is replaced by a higher order sort which is not zero-order, a functionality that has been "essential first order" need not have this property after the replacement.

Therefore, it can happen that an instantiation **package** p **is new** g(..., t,...) where t is a functional type has a relatively first order term-generated model, whereas the package p' obtained from the package part of g by textual substitution has no first order term-generated model.

An example for this situation is the instantiation of a generic LISTS (yielding finite sequences over a formal sort ITEM). Let us assume that LISTS contains the specification of a function

make : ITEM$^{\perp}$ --> LIST$^{\perp}$ (turning items into one-element lists)

and of a concatenation operation on lists. Then a possible model for the instantiation

package LISTFUN **is new** LISTS(INTEGER$^{\perp}$ --> INTEGER$^{\perp}$)

will be finite sequences of functions, whereas the package obtained from LISTS by substituting ITEM$^{\perp}$ by INTEGER$^{\perp}$ --> INTEGER$^{\perp}$ will have no first order term-generated model, since the functionality of

make' : (INTEGER$^{\perp}$ --> INTEGER$^{\perp}$) --> LIST$^{\perp}$

is not essential first order.

Facit: If the rule of textual substitution is a desired transformation rule, then the following convention should be observed in the instantiation of generics: if inside a generic package a new (non formal) sort is introduced together with constructor functions from the formal sorts to the new sort, then this generic should only be instantiated with zero order sorts.

Let us now consider the case where all actual parameter sorts are zero order sorts. Moreover, we assume that we are given the set of all algebras which are relatively first order term-generated w.r.t. the formal parameter sorts. Informally, by a generic instantiation we choose first order term-generated carriers for all formal parameter sorts and thus obtain an algebra from that set which is first order term-generated on the whole.

3.4. Transformations of PA^{nn}dA-S into the Kernel-Language

In this section we define the semantics of entire PA^{nn}dA-S by presenting transformations for PA^{nn}dA-S programs containing language constructs not dealt with in the kernel-language (in particular subtypes and function declarations with domain and result restrictions) into the kernel-language.

In section 1 we consider the declaration of function(al)s and predicates with a more general functionality than admitted in the kernel-language: we consider functionalities with domain and result restrictions. In these functionalities we also consider a second function arrow (the "strong" arrow ==>) by which in particular strictness of functions can be expressed. In order to reduce such function and predicate declarations into the kernel-language, we associate with every such functionality with restrictions (also called "type expression") a characterizing formula and transform a function declaration with such a restricted functionality into a function declaration with a non-restricted functionality together with the axiom characterizing the restricted functionality.

In section 2 we consider PA^{nn}dA-S programs with subtypes. Subtypes can be seen as names for type expressions. Semantically, we regard them as predicates defined on the higher order sorts in the kernel-language: every subtype declaration is transformed into the declaration of a characterizing predicate, which is specified by the formula characterizing the type expression associated with the subtype.

Since subtypes can be used as actual parameters in generic instantiations, the instantiation mechanism for generics described in section 3.3 has to be slightly generalized: instead of the parameter sorts we have to consider pairs consisting of parameter ("base"-) sorts together with formal predicates (for the predicates characterizing the subtypes). We therefore distinguish between generics with a "normalized interface" which - as in the kernel language - may only be instantiated with unrestricted higher order sorts ($t \in H(SOR)$) and "PA^{nn}dA-S generics" which may be instantiated with names standing for arbitrary subtypes.

In section 2 we explain how every PA^{nn}dA-S program using PA^{nn}dA-S generics can be transformed into an equivalent program using generics with normalized interfaces.

In section 3 we give some methodological advice on the use of the two different function arrows.

3.4.1. On the Specification of Function(al)s and Predicates with Restrictions

In this section we treat the possibility of restrictions occurring in functionalities of functions and predicates and in quantifications used in formulas. These restrictions are formulas, restricting the domain and the range of functions.

Roughly speaking, function declarations with restrictions can be transformed into function declarations in the kernel-language in the following way:

Let t1 and t2 be higher order sorts in the kernel language (i.e. t1, t2 $\in$ H(SOR)) and P(x), Q(y) be formulas in the variables x and y. Then a function declaration of the form

```
f : (x:t1 :: P(x)) --> (y:t2 :: Q(y));
```

is considered as a notational variant for the declaration

```
f : ( t1 --> t2 );
axiom for all x:t1 fi P(x) ⇒ Q(f(x));
```

Hence if the precondition P holds for the argument x, the postcondition Q has to hold for the result f(x). Nothing is required for the case that P(x) does not hold. Therefore we call this interpretation of the restrictions in functionalities the "weak" interpretation.

Another variant to interprete the precondition P in the above function declaration is to say that additionally, as soon as P(x) is not valid, the result f(x) should be undefined. In order to support this interpretation (which we call the "strong" interpretation), a second ("strong") function arrow ==> is introduced, where

```
g : (x:t1 :: P(x) ) ==> (y:t2 :: Q(y));
```

is considered as a notational variant for

```
g : ( t1 --> t2 );
axiom for all x: t1 fi P(x) ⇒ Q(g(x)),
                        not P(x) ⇒ not defined g(x);
```

Caution is necessary in the use of the strong arrow, in order not to run into inconsistencies with respect to the requirement that all functions be monotonic and continuous. In particular, a necessary condition for the monotonicity of g above (in an algebra A) is, that if the formula P is not valid for an element a in the carrier t^A, then it is also not valid for all elements a' with a' $\sqsubseteq^A$ a (in the approximation ordering $\sqsubseteq^A$ of A). This condition obviously holds if t^A is a flat cpo and the formula P is not valid in A for the bottom element of t^A.

The use of the strong arrow does not cause inconsistencies to the requirement of monotonicity and continuity in such first order specifications where all functions are required to be strict: in models of such specifications the ordering on carriers (of atomic sort) can be chosen as the flat ordering, since every strict function between flat cpo's is continuous.

Strictness of first order functions can be specified using the strong arrow: Let $s_1,..., s_n$, s be sort names. Then

$$h : (x_1{:}s_1^{\perp} :: \textbf{defined}\ x_1) \times ... \times (x_n{:}s_n^{\perp} :: \textbf{defined}\ x_n) \ \texttt{==>}\ s^{\perp};$$

is considered as a notational variant for

$$h : (\ (s_1^{\perp}) \times ... \times (s_n^{\perp})\ \texttt{-->}\ s^{\perp}\ );$$
$$\textbf{axiom for all}\ x_1{:}s_1^{\perp};\ ...\ ;\ x_n{:}s_n^{\perp} \Rightarrow$$
$$\textbf{not (defined}\ x_1\ \textbf{and}\ ...\ \textbf{and defined}\ x_n) \rightarrow \textbf{not defined}\ h(x_1,..., x_n);$$

As a shorthand notation for the defined elements of an atomic sort, the bare sort name (not marked by the ⊥- sign) is used, i.e. h above might be also written in the form

$$h : s_1 \times ... \times s_n \ \texttt{==>}\ s^{\perp};$$

By using the bare sort name in connection with the *weak* arrow -->, totality of a function is required: for instance

```
f : INTEGER × INTEGER --> INTEGER;
```

is a notational variant for

```
f : ((INTEGER⊥ × INTEGER⊥) --> INTEGER⊥) ;
axiom for all x1: INTEGER⊥; x2 : INTEGER⊥ ⇒
   defined x1 and defined x2 → defined f(x1,x2);
```

If instead of the weak arrow the *strong* arrow is used, then in addition to totality also strictness is required:

```
g : INTEGER × INTEGER ==> INTEGER;
```

is a notational variant for

```
g : ((INTEGER⊥ × INTEGER⊥) --> INTEGER⊥) ;
axiom for all x1: INTEGER⊥; x2 : INTEGER⊥ ⇒
(defined x1 and defined x2 → defined g(x1,x2)) ,
( not (defined x1 and defined x2) → not defined g(x1,x2) );
```

We now proceed to give the formal definition of the set $H_{res}(SOR)$ of higher order sorts with restrictions (also called "type expressions"). Since the formulas used as restrictions may themselves contain quantifications over type expressions we simultaneously define the set of formulas with restricted quantifications.

The set $H_{res}(SOR)$ (with $H(SOR) \subseteq H_{res}(SOR)$) and the set of formulas with restricted quantifications are defined inductively as follows:

(i) if s is a name (standing for a predefined sort different from the meta-sort LOGICAL or a sort declared as **private**) then

$s^{\perp} \in H_{res}(SOR)$ (*atomic sort*)

$s \in H_{res}(SOR)$ (*bare atomic sort*)

If $n \geq 1$ and $x_1, \ldots, x_n$ are different identifiers, $t_1, \ldots, t_n, t \in H_{res}(SOR)$ are type expressions and $l_1, \ldots, l_n$ are formulas with restricted quantifications, then the following are type expressions:

(ii) $(x_1{:}t_1 :: l_1) \times \ldots \times (x_n{:}t_n :: l_n)$ (*tuple-type-expression*)

(iii a) $(x_1{:}t_1 :: l_1) \times \ldots \times (x_n{:}t_n :: l_n)$ --> t (*function-type-expression: weak arrow*)

(iii b) $(x_1{:}t_1 :: l_1) \times \ldots \times (x_n{:}t_n :: l_n)$ ==> t (*function-type-expression: strong arrow*)

In (ii) and (iii) above, several of the formulas l_i may be missing and in this case also the corresponding designators x_i may be missing. Furthermore, parentheses around sort names may be omitted (i.e. for s1, s2 ∈ NAME one usually writes s1 × s2 instead of (s1) × (s2)). Also parentheses around tuple types which are not nested inside another type expression may be omitted (for instance, if t_1 is a tuple type expression then instead of (t_1) --> t one usually writes t_1 --> t.)

iv) (*formulas with restricted quantifications*)

The formulas with restricted quantifications are essentially those considered in 3.3.2 with the only difference that in quantified formulas (see 3.3.2.5) the quantification may range over higher order sorts with restrictions:

if $n \geq 1$ and $x_1, \ldots, x_n$ are different identifiers, $t_1, \ldots, t_n \in H_{res}(SOR)$ are type expressions and $l_1, \ldots, l_n$, l are formulas with restricted quantifications and *quant* ∈ { **for all**, **exists** }, then

quant $x_1{:}t_1 :: l_1; \ldots ; x_n{:}t_n :: l_n \Rightarrow l$

is a formula with restricted quantification. Again several of the l_i may be missing.

Remark

a) Here we only regard "domains" (by referring to the syntactic categories used in the concrete syntax of $PA^{nn}dA$-S) of the form (x:t :: l) with a single designator x. The more general form with designator lists $(x_1,\ldots, x_n$:t :: l) can be reduced to a tuple of domains with single designators using the rules of the static semantics (see the $PA^{nn}dA$-S Reference Manual, part II chapter 4).

b) Notice that here we only allow to mark sort names by the ⊥-sign (or + -sign in the concrete syntax). We do neither consider "domains" marked by ⊥-sign nor tuple-type or function-type expressions (in parantheses) marked by the ⊥-sign. Such type expressions can be dealt with by introducing names for type expressions (i.e. subtype names as explained in the next section). ♦

In order to reduce function and predicate declarations having higher order sorts with restrictions as functionality into the kernel-language, we associate with every type expression $t \in H_{res}(SOR)$ a *base-type* $b[t] \in H(SOR)$ (which is a higher order sort in the kernel-language) and with every "domain" x:t[::l] where x is a designator, t a type expression and l a formula (which may be missing) we associate a *characterizing formula* $\Phi_{x:t\,::\,l}$ in the kernel-language with the free variable x (of sort b[t]). Then the $PA^{nn}dA$-S declaration

x:t :: l;

is considered as a notational variant for the sequence of declarations

x:b[t]; **axiom** $\Phi_{x:t\,::\,l}$;

in the kernel-language. Hereby we restrict ourselves in this section to declarations x:t :: l; which either do not contain generic formal sorts or which occur inside generics with *normalized interfaces*. Recall from the introduction to section 3.4 that those are the generics which, as in the kernel language, may only be instantiated with unrestricted higher order sorts $t \in H(SOR)$. The more general form of $PA^{nn}dA$-S generics which may be instantiated with names standing for arbitrary higher order sorts with restrictions is treated in the next section in connection with subtypes.

For $t \in H_{res}(SOR)$, the base-type b[t] is defined inductively as follows:

(i) for $s \in$ NAME, $b[s] = b[s^{\perp}] = s^{\perp}$

for $n \geq 1$, $t_1,\ldots, t_n, t \in H_{res}(SOR)$

(ii)

$$b[\,(x_1{:}t_1 :: l_1) \times \ldots \times (x_n{:}t_n :: l_n)\,] = \begin{cases} (\,b[t_1] \times \ldots \times b[t_n]\,) & \text{if } n \geq 2 \\ b[t_1] & \text{if } n=1 \end{cases}$$

(iii) $b[\,(x_1{:}t_1 :: l_1) \times \ldots \times (x_n{:}t_n :: l_n) \dashrightarrow t\,] =$

$$= b[\,(x_1{:}t_1 :: l_1) \times \ldots \times (x_n{:}t_n :: l_n) ==> t\,] = \begin{cases} (\,(b[t_1] \times \ldots \times b[t_n]) \dashrightarrow b[t]\,) & \text{if } n \geq 2 \\ (\,b[t_1] \dashrightarrow b[t]\,) & \text{if } n=1 \end{cases}$$

In the definition of the characterizing formulas we use a substitution operation on formulas given as follows: For a formula l, an identifier y and an expression e, l[e/y] denotes the formula obtained from l by replacing any free occurrence of y in l by e and renaming the bound variables in l in such a way that the free variables of e do not get bound by substitution.

The definition of the characterizing formulas $\Phi_{x:t::l}$ for domains of the form $x:t :: l$ goes simultaneously with the translation of every formula l with restricted quantifications into a formula Φ_l in the kernel language:

For a universally quantified formula we define (with the symbol ≡ standing for the syntactic equality of formulas):

$$\Phi_{\textbf{for all}\ x_1:t_1 :: l_1; \ldots ; x_n:t_n :: l_n \Rightarrow l} \equiv$$
$$\textbf{for all}\ x_1:b[t_1]; \ldots ; x_n:b[t_n] \Rightarrow (\Phi_{x_1:t_1 :: l_1})\ \textbf{and} \ldots \textbf{and}\ (\Phi_{x_n:t_n :: l_n}) \rightarrow (\Phi_l)$$

Here several of the restrictions l_i may be missing.

For an existentially quantified formula we define

$$\Phi_{\textbf{exists}\ x_1:t_1 :: l_1; \ldots ; x_n:t_n :: l_n \Rightarrow l} \equiv$$
$$\textbf{exists}\ x_1:b[t_1]; \ldots ; x_n:b[t_n] \Rightarrow (\Phi_{x_1:t_1 :: l_1})\ \textbf{and} \ldots \textbf{and}\ (\Phi_{x_n:t_n :: l_n})\ \textbf{and}\ (\Phi_l)$$

Again several of the l_i may be missing.

On all other forms of formulas the translation operator Φ is just applied inductively to all subcomponents which are formulas.

Now, we give the definition of the characteristic formulas for "domains":

(i) for $s \in$ NAME,

$\Phi_{x:s} \equiv$ **defined** x ,

$\Phi_{x:s\perp} \equiv$ **defined** x **or not defined** x (a tautology)

and for a formula l (usually containing the free identifier x)

$\Phi_{x:s :: l} \equiv$ **defined** x **and** (Φ_l) ,

$\Phi_{x:s\perp :: l} \equiv \Phi_l$

Recall that we do not yet consider specifications with subtype declarations (which will be treated in the next section) and therefore s here always stands for a sort which is one of the predefined sorts (excluding the meta-sort LOGICAL) or which is declared as **private**.

In order to define the characterizing formulas for tuple domains and function type domains we assume that in all tuple type expressions the component types are preceded by designators. The cases where some of the designators are missing are tackled by inserting "new" designators which are not yet used in the type expression under consideration .

Let $n \geq 1$, let f, x, $x_1, \ldots, x_n$ be distinct identifiers, $t_1, \ldots, t_n, t \in H_{res}(SOR)$ be type expressions and $l_1, \ldots, l_n, l$ be formulas with restricted quantifications.

(ii) *tuple type domain*

$\Phi_x : (x_1{:}t_1 :: l_1) \times \ldots \times (x_n{:}t_n :: l_n) :: l \equiv$

(**for all** $x_1{:}b[t_1]; \ldots ; x_n{:}b[t_n] \Rightarrow$

$x = (x_1,\ldots, x_n) \rightarrow (\Phi_{x_1:t_1} :: l_1)$ **and** ... **and** $(\Phi_{x_n:t_n} :: l_n)$)

and (Φ_l)

Here several of the l_i and the restriction l may be missing (in the latter case the conjunct "**and** (Φ_l)" is omitted). In case n = 1 the parentheses around x_1 may be omitted.

Notice that the scope of the universal quantification does not include the formula (Φ_l), since by the visibility rules for type expressions (see part II section 4.8), the designators $x_1,\ldots,x_n$ are not visible at the restriction l.

(iii) *function type domain*

(a) "weak" arrow

$\Phi_f : (x_1{:}t_1 :: l_1) \times \ldots \times (x_n{:}t_n :: l_n)$ --> t :: l $\equiv$

(**for all** $x_1{:}b[t_1]; \ldots ; x_n{:}b[t_n] \Rightarrow$

$(\Phi_{x_1:t_1} :: l_1)$ **and** ... **and** $(\Phi_{x_n:t_n} :: l_n) \rightarrow (\Phi_{y:t}\,[f(x_1,\ldots, x_n)/y])$)

and (Φ_l)

Here y is a "new" identifier not occurring in the type expression t and the restriction l. Again some of the l_i and the restriction l may be missing.

Intuitively, a function f satisfies the characteristic formula associated with the "weak" function domain $f : (x_1{:}t_1 :: l_1) \times \ldots \times (x_n{:}t_n :: l_n)$ --> t :: l if for all arguments $x_1,\ldots, x_n$ satisfying the characteristic formulas associated to $(x_i{:}t_i :: l_i)$, the result $f(x_1,\ldots, x_n)$ satisfies the characteristic formula associated with the type expression t and the formula Φ_l holds for f.

Notice that since a function type expression is a declarative region, the designators $x_1,\ldots,x_n$ are not visible at the restriction l. Hence in the characteristic formula above the scope of the universal quantification over $x_1,\ldots,x_n$ does not include the formula Φ_l.

b) "strong" arrow

$\Phi_f : (x_1{:}t_1 :: l_1) \times \ldots \times (x_n{:}t_n :: l_n)$ ==> t :: l $\equiv$

(**for all** $x_1{:}b[t_1]; \ldots ; x_n{:}b[t_n] \Rightarrow$

$(\Phi_{x_1:t_1} :: l_1)$ **and** ... **and** $(\Phi_{x_n:t_n} :: l_n) \rightarrow$ $(\Phi_{y:t}\,[f(x_1,\ldots, x_n)/y])$,

others $\rightarrow$ **not defined** $f(x_1,\ldots, x_n)$)

and (Φ_l)

This means that as soon as the arguments satisfy the associated characteristic formulas, the result satifies the characteristic formula associated with the type expression t, but if not all the arguments satisfy the associated formulas the result is undefined.

Now we are ready to define formally the transformation of function and predicate declarations using functionalities with restrictions and of axioms using restricted quantifications into the kernel-language. These transformations may only be applied according to the following conditions:

Transformation conditions:

(i) The transformations below may only be applied to declarations and axioms not containing type names declared by subtype declarations.

(ii) The transformations below may be applied outside generics. They may only be applied inside generics, provided

- these are generics with normalized interfaces (which as in the kernel language may only be instantiated with unrestricted higher order sorts $t \in H(SOR)$) or
- the type expressions under consideration do not contain generic formal sorts. ♦

Specifications with subtype declarations will be treated in section 3.4.2. For type expressions built over names declared by subtype declarations, the definition of their base-types and their characterizing formulas cannot be given as in this section: first, all names standing for subtypes have to be replaced by corresponding type expressions (as explained in 3.4.2.) In particular, for a subtype name s, the definition $\Phi_{x:s} \equiv$ **defined** x is not adequate.

The reason for not admitting generic formal sorts of $PA^{nn}dA$-S generics here is that those may be instantiated with arbitrary subtypes. The transformation of $PA^{nn}dA$-S generics into generics with normalized interfaces is given in section 3.4.2.

3.4.1.1. Axioms with Restricted Quantifications

Let l be a formula with restricted quantifications satisfying the above transformation conditions. Then

axiom l;

is considered as a notational variant for

axiom Φ_l;

3.4.1.2. Function Declarations with Restricted Functionalities

Let $t \in H_{res}(SOR)$ be a type expression, f an identifier and l a formula with restricted quantifications (usually containing the identifier f as a free variable) such that the declaration f : t :: l ; satisfies the transformation conditions above. Then

f:t :: l;

is considered as a notational variant for the sequence of declarations

f:b[t]; **axiom** $\Phi_{f:t}$ :: l;

Examples

(1) The declaration

```
g : (x:INTEGER :: (x > ZERO) = TRUE) --> (y:INTEGER :: (y > ZERO) = TRUE);
```

is considered as a notational variant for

```
    g : ( INTEGER⊥ --> INTEGER⊥ );
axiom for all x:INTEGER⊥ ⇒
    defined x  and  (x > ZERO) = TRUE →
        (for all y : INTEGER⊥ ⇒  g(x) = y →    defined y  and  (y > ZERO) = TRUE ) ;
```

which is semantically equivalent to

```
    g : ( INTEGER⊥ --> INTEGER⊥ );
  axiom for all x:INTEGER⊥ ⇒
    defined x and (x > ZERO) = TRUE →    defined g(x) and (g(x) > ZERO) = TRUE;
```

Hence, in case x is undefined or not greater ZERO, the result g(x) is unspecified.

In contrast, the "strong" specification

```
    g' : (x:INTEGER :: (x > ZERO) = TRUE) ==> (y:INTEGER :: (y >ZERO) = TRUE);
```

is considered as a notational variant for

```
    g' : ( INTEGER⊥ --> INTEGER⊥ );
  axiom for all x:INTEGER⊥ ⇒
    defined x and (x > ZERO) = TRUE →    defined g'(x) and (g'(x) > ZERO) = TRUE,
    others →                             not defined g'(x);
```

(2) The "higher order" specification

```
    F : ( INTEGER --> INTEGER ) --> INTEGER;
  axiom for all f: INTEGER --> INTEGER ⇒ F(f) = f(ZERO);
```

is a notational variant for

```
    F : ( ( INTEGER⊥ --> INTEGER⊥ ) --> INTEGER⊥ );
  axiom for all f: ( INTEGER⊥ --> INTEGER⊥ ) ⇒
    ( for all x:INTEGER⊥ ⇒ (defined x → defined f(x)) ) → defined F(f);
  axiom for all f: ( INTEGER⊥ --> INTEGER⊥ ) ⇒
    ( for all x:INTEGER⊥ ⇒ (defined x → defined f(x)) ) → F(f) = f(ZERO);
```

Hence in case f does not map defined integers to defined integers the result F(f) is unspecified.

3.4.1.3. Predicate Declarations with Restricted Functionalities

Let $n \geq 1$, let $x_1,\ldots, x_n, y$ be distinct identifiers, $t_1,\ldots, t_n \in H_{res}(SOR)$ be type expressions and let $l_1,\ldots, l_n$, lr , l be formulas with restricted quantifications.

A predicate declaration

pr : $(x_1{:}t_1 :: l_1) \times \ldots \times (x_n{:}t_n :: l_n)$ --> (y: LOGICAL:: lr) :: l;

is considered as a notational variant for

pr : $(b[t_1] \times \ldots \times b[t_n])$ --> LOGICAL;
axiom
(**for all** $x_1{:}b[t_1]$; ... ; $x_n{:}b[t_n]$ ⇒
$(\Phi_{x_1:t_1\,::\,l_1})$ **and** ... **and** $(\Phi_{x_n:t_n\,::\,l_n})$ → $(\Phi_{lr}\,[pr(x_1,\ldots,x_n)/y])$) **and** (Φ_l);

provided the predicate declaration satisfies the transformation conditions above.

Hence predicates are "weakly" specified. Only for those arguments satisfying the preconditions determined by the "domains" $(x_i{:}t_i :: l_i)$ the result restriction Φ_{lr} (with the formula $pr(x_1,\ldots,x_n)$ substituted for the "result parameter" y) is required.

Notice that in the above predicate declaration the scope rules for function type expressions are adopted. Hence the identifiers $x_1,...,x_n$ are not visible at the outer restriction l (but the identifier pr is visible at l). Therefore the scope of the universal quantification in the above axiom does not include the formula (Φ_l).

If the outer annotation l is missing, then the conjunct **and** (Φ_l) is omitted. If the result restriction lr is missing, then the domain restrictions $(x_i : t_i :: l_i)$ are irrelevant: the predicate declaration

pr : $(x_1{:}t_1 :: l_1) \times \ldots \times (x_n{:}t_n :: l_n)$ --> LOGICAL :: l;

is a notational variant for

pr : $(b[t_1] \times \ldots \times b[t_n])$ --> LOGICAL;
axiom Φ_l;

The possibility of specifying predicates by domain- and result restrictions is only considered for sake of uniformity with function declarations. The preferred way to specify predicates is by axioms.

To conclude this section, we remark that the above transformations 3.4.1.1 - 3.4.1.3 allow to transform every PA^{nn}dA-S program with function and predicate declarations and axioms using restricted functionalities into a program in the kernel-language, provided all generics in this program have a normalized interface. However, we did not treat yet the possibility of instantiating generics with restricted higher order sorts. This possibility will be tackled in the next section where we consider specifications with subtype declarations.

3.4.2. PA^{nn}dA-S Specifications with Subtypes

Subtypes are abbreviations for type expressions. A subtype declaration is of the form

subtype s **is** t;

where t is a type expression (not containing the identifier s). The sort names occurring in t (which are not predefined sorts) have to be previously declared by

- private type declarations
- subtype declarations

Here by "declarations" we also understand the implicit declaration via generic instantiations.

There are two predefined subtypes of the integers given by the declarations

```
subtype NATURAL is (x: INTEGER :: (x >= ZERO) = TRUE);
subtype POSITIVE is (x: NATURAL :: (x > ZERO) = TRUE);
```

The sets H(SOR) of higher order sorts and H_{res}(SOR) of higher order sorts with restrictions (or type-expressions) are defined as before with the only difference that in these type-expressions now also subtype names may occur. We call a type expression *subtype-free* if it does not contain names declared by subtype declarations.

We now also consider formulas of the form e **in** s , where e is an expression , s is a (sub)type name and **in** is the built-in membership predicate.

In order to reduce specifications with subtype declarations into specifications of the language layer described in the previous section, we roughly proceed as follows: (a precise formal description is given later).

(2) Let COPIES and COPIES_N be as above . Then the instantiation

```
package COPIESNAT is new COPIES ( NATURAL);
```

is considered as equivalent to the kernel-language instantiation

```
package COPIESNAT is new COPIES_N ( INTEGER⊥, is_in_NATURAL );
```

with is_in_NATURAL specified by

```
    is_in_NATURAL : INTEGER⊥ --> LOGICAL;
axiom for all x : INTEGER⊥⇒
    is_in_NATURAL(x) ↔ defined x and ( (x >=ZERO) = TRUE) );
```

In order to describe the transformation formally we introduce the notion of a *type-context* .

3.4.2.1 Type Contexts

A type context is a finite function mapping names (standing for types and subtypes) to pairs of higher order sorts (their base-types) and of names standing for characteristic predicates. Hence type contexts are elements of the set

$$SOR \rightarrow_{fin} (H(SOR) \times NAME)$$

where by $A \rightarrow_{fin} B$ we denote the set of partial functions f from A to B with a finite domain $dom(f) \subseteq A$.

For a finite function $f \in A \rightarrow_{fin} B$ and a subset $S \subseteq dom(f)$ we denote by $f|_S$ the restriction of f to S (with domain S.) By $\varnothing$ we denote the empty function with domain $\varnothing$.

For $f \in A \rightarrow_{fin} B$ and a pair $(a,b) \in A \times B$ we denote by $f[b/a]$ the updated function f' with $dom(f') = dom(f) \cup \{a\}$ and $f'(a) = b$ and $f'(x) = f(x)$ for $x \in dom(f) \setminus \{a\}$.

Moreover, for f_1, f_2 we denote by $f_1[f_2]$ the finite function f with $dom(f) = dom(f_1) \cup dom(f_2)$ and $f(x) = f_2(x)$ for all $x \in dom(f_2)$, $f(x) = f_1(x)$ for all $x \in dom(f_1) \setminus dom(f_2)$.

For an element $\tau \in SOR \rightarrow_{fin} (H(SOR) \times NAME)$ and a name s with $(\mathbf{sort}, s) \in dom(\tau)$ we write

$b_\tau[s]$ for the first component of $\tau(\mathbf{sort}, s)$ (the *base-type* of s) and

$cpred_\tau[s]$ for the second component (the name of the *characteristic predicate* associated to s)

By $SUB(\tau)$ we denote the set of all subtype names in the domain of τ. These are retrieved from τ as follows:

$$SUB(\tau) = \{ s \in NAME: (\mathbf{sort}, s) \in dom(\tau) \wedge b_\tau[s] \neq s^\perp \}$$

We say that $b_\tau[s]$ is *subtype-free w.r.t.* τ iff $b_\tau[s]$ is only built from type names which are not contained in $SUB(\tau)$. τ is called *subtype-free* iff $b_\tau[s]$ is *subtype-free w.r.t.* τ for all $(\mathbf{sort}, s) \in dom(\tau)$.
Since in sequences of PA^{nn}dA-S subtype declarations no circular dependencies are allowed, every sequence of declarations yields a subtype-free type context.

As types and subtypes can also be implicitly declared by generic instantiations we associate with every name standing for a generic its own type-context, or more precisely a pair, where the first component is the sequence of type names declared in the generic formal part and the second component is the type context determined by the package declaration.

Hence we define

$$\mathrm{TYCON}_0 =_{def} (\{\textbf{sort}\} \times \mathrm{NAME}) \rightarrow_{fin} (\mathrm{H(SOR)} \times \mathrm{NAME})$$

and

$$\mathrm{TYCON} \subseteq ((\{\textbf{sort}\} \times \mathrm{NAME}) \cup (\{\textbf{gen}\} \times \mathrm{NAME})) \rightarrow_{fin}$$
$$(\mathrm{H(SOR)} \times \mathrm{NAME}) \cup (\mathrm{NAME}^* \times \mathrm{TYCON}_0)$$

to be the set of those finite functions τ such that for all g, s $\in$ NAME

$$\tau(\textbf{sort}, s) \in \mathrm{H(SOR)} \times \mathrm{NAME} \quad \text{and} \quad \tau(\textbf{gen}, g) \in \mathrm{NAME}^* \times \mathrm{TYCON}_0$$

Since we do not consider nested declarations of generics it is sufficient to associate with names for generics type contexts defined on sorts only.

The definitions of $b_\tau[s]$, $cpred_\tau[s]$, $SUB_\tau[s]$ carry over immediately to the elements of TYCON (by considering their restrictions to sort names). We call a type context $\tau \in$ TYCON *subtype-free* iff $b_\tau[s]$ is *subtype-free w.r.t.* τ for all (**sort**, s) $\in$ dom(τ) and for all (**gen**, g) $\in$ dom(τ) the second component of τ(**gen**, g) is a subtype-free type context.

For a type expression t $\in H_{res}(SOR)$ and a type context $\tau \in$ TYCON we denote by

$$elim_\tau(t) \in H_{res}(SOR)$$

the type expression obtained from t by performing the following replacements simultaneously:

(i) for all s $\in$ SUB(τ) :
every occurrence of s (not marked by the $\perp$ - sign and not appearing in a membership fomula **e in** s)
is replaced by the restriction $(x{:}b_\tau[s] :: cpred_\tau[s](x))$
(with an appropriate choice of the identifier x as not to produce name clashes)

(ii) for all s $\in$ SUB(τ) :
every occurrence of $s^\perp$ is replaced by $(x{:}b_\tau[s] :: cpred_\tau[s](x)$ **or not defined** x)

(iii) for all s with (**sort**, s) $\in$ dom(τ): every formula (e **in** s) is replaced by the formula $cpred_\tau[s](e)$

If τ is subtype-free, then for every s $\in$ SUB(τ) there is no more applied occurrence of s in the type expression $elim_\tau(t)$, in other words : $elim_\tau(t)$ is subtype-free w.r.t. τ.

In the same way

$elim_\tau(l)$ is defined for every formula l and

$elim_\tau(d)$ is defined for a function or predicate declaration d.

In order to translate every PA^{nn}dA-S program with subtypes into a program in the language layer of the previous section we introduce the following functions:

$$T^{decl} : \text{declaration\_list} \rightarrow \mathrm{TYCON} \rightarrow \mathrm{TYCON}$$

Given a sequence of declarations and a type context τ, the function T^{decl} produces a new type context. As usual we write $T^{decl}_\tau[ds]$ for $T^{decl}[ds](\tau)$.

Additionally, for library units, we define a function

T^{lib} : library_unit_list → TYCON → TYCON

Using the above functions, we define transformation functions

Ψ^{decl} : declaration_list → TYCON → declaration_list

Ψ^{lib} : library_unit_list → TYCON → library_unit_list

which transform every sequence of declarations (or library units) into a sequence of declarations (or library units) in the language layer L_1 of the previous section. Recall that in L_1 no subtype declarations are possible, there is no built-in membership predicate **In** and the generics may only be instantiated with unrestricted higher order sorts $t \in H(SOR)$ (in other words: they are generics with normalized interfaces).

In order to define the above functions we need an auxiliary function

DECL_SORTS : declaration_list → TYCON → P(SOR)

which associates with a sequence of declarations the set of (sub)type names declared by it. Moreover, we need a further function

T^{gen} : generic_parameter_list → TYCON → TYCON

which enters for every formal parameter type a new base-type and a name for a characteristic predicate in into the type context. This is due to the fact that in the following transformation formal types of $PA^{nn}dA$-S generics are regarded as subtypes, since they may be instantiated with arbitrary subtypes. Using T^{gen}, we formulate a transformation function

Ψ^{gen} : generic_parameter_list → TYCON → generic_parameter_list

Moreover, we assume a function

norm : NAME → NAME

which provides for every name g of a $PA^{nn}dA$-S generic a name g_{norm} for the corresponding generic with a normalized interface.

In our transformation we will introduce characteristic predicates with names is_in_s (for type and subtype names s). We assume throughout that the introduction of these names does not cause name clashes, and hence that in the programs to be transformed there are no declarations of predicates with these names. Moreover, for every formal parameter type name fs we introduce a new name b_fs for a base-type of fs. Again we assume that the introduction of these new type names does not cause name clashes. In particular, we suppose that that these new names do not occur in the domains of type contexts.

Since we do not want to complicate the definition of the transformation functions by the scope rules of $PA^{nn}dA$-S (and since we rather regard this as an issue of the static semantics), we assume unique names for all the types and subtypes declared in a program library, i.e. we will restrict ourselves to such program libraries where in different (sub)type declarations different names are introduced.

3.4.2.2 *Definition of the Transformation Function* Ψ

Let $lu_1\, lu_2 ... lu_n$ be a sequentialisation of a context correct program library . Then we define

$$\Psi\ [lu_1\, lu_2 ... lu_n\ ] = \Psi^{lib}{}_{\varnothing}[lu_1\, lu_2 ... lu_n\ ]\ ,$$

where the definition of Ψ^{lib} is given below.

Before we present the effect of the transformations on single declarations and library units, we define them on sequences of declarations and library units:

For the empty sequence ε we define

$$\Psi^{decl}{}_{\tau}[\varepsilon] = \varepsilon,\ \Psi^{lib}{}_{\tau}[\varepsilon] = \varepsilon,\quad \Psi^{gen}{}_{\tau}[\varepsilon] = \varepsilon$$

$$T^{decl}{}_{\tau}[\varepsilon] = \tau\ ,\ T^{lib}{}_{\tau}[\varepsilon] = \tau\ ,\ \ T^{gen}{}_{\tau}[\varepsilon] = \tau$$

$$DECL\_SORTS_{\tau}\ [\varepsilon] = \varnothing.$$

For a sequence ds of declarations and a single declaration d we define

$$\Psi^{decl}{}_{\tau}[\ ds\ \ d\ ] = \Psi^{decl}{}_{\tau}[\ ds\ ]\ \Psi^{decl}{}_{\tau 1}[\ d\ ]\ ,\ \text{where}\quad \tau 1 = T^{decl}{}_{\tau}[\ ds]\ \ ,$$

$$T^{decl}[\ ds\ \ d\ ] = \quad T^{decl}[d] \circ T^{decl}[ds]\ \ (\text{ the function mapping } \tau \text{ to } T^{decl}[d](T^{decl}[ds](\tau))\ )\ ),$$

$$DECL\_SORTS_{\tau}\ [\ ds\ \ d] = DECL\_SORTS_{\tau}\ [\ ds\ ] \cup DECL\_SORTS_{\tau 1}\ [\ d]$$

If ds and d consist of generic parameters only (which are private type declarations, function or predicate declarations or axioms) we define analogously

$$\Psi^{gen}{}_{\tau}[\ ds\ \ d\ ] = \Psi^{gen}{}_{\tau}[\ ds\ ]\ \Psi^{gen}{}_{\tau 1}[\ d\ ]\ ,\ \text{where}\quad \tau 1 = T^{gen}{}_{\tau}[\ ds]\ \ \text{and}$$

$$T^{gen}[\ ds\ \ d\ ] = \ T^{gen}[d] \circ T^{gen}[ds]\ .$$

For a sequence lus of library units and a single library unit lu we define

$$\Psi^{lib}{}_{\tau}[\ lus\ \ lu\ ] = \Psi^{lib}{}_{\tau}[\ lus\ ]\ \Psi^{lib}{}_{\tau 1}[\ lu\ ]\ ,\ \text{where}\quad \tau 1 = T^{lib}{}_{\tau}[\ lu]\ \text{and}$$

$$T^{lib}[\ lus\ \ lu\ ] = \ T^{lib}[lu] \circ T^{lib}[lus]$$

Now we define the effect of the transformation functions on single declarations:

For a *function* or *predicate declaration* d we have

$$\Psi^{decl}{}_{\tau}[\ d] \ = \ \Psi^{gen}{}_{\tau}[\ d] \ = elim_{\tau}(d),$$

$$T^{decl}{}_{\tau}[d] \ = \ T^{gen}{}_{\tau}[d] \ = \ \tau\ ,$$

$$DECL\_SORTS_{\tau}[d] = \varnothing$$

Recall that in $elim_{\tau}(d)$ all applied occurrences of subtype identifiers in d are replaced by the respective restrictions built from the characteristic predicates. Hence if τ is subtype-free, then no name contained in $SUB(\tau)$ occurs in $elim_{\tau}(d)$.

In the same way we define for a logical formula l

$\Psi^{decl}{}_{\tau}$[**axiom** l ;] = $\Psi^{gen}{}_{\tau}$[**axiom** l ;] = **axiom** $elim_{\tau}$(l);

$T^{decl}{}_{\tau}$[**axiom** l ;] = $T^{gen}{}_{\tau}$[**axiom** l ;] = τ ,

$DECL\_SORTS_{\tau}$[**axiom** l ;] = ∅

On a *private type declaration* the functions Ψ^{decl} and Ψ^{gen} behave differently:

$\Psi^{decl}{}_{\tau}$[**type** s **is private** ;] = **type** s **is private**;
is_in_s : $s^{\perp}$ --> LOGICAL;
axiom for all x : $s^{\perp}$ ⇒ is_in_s(x) ↔ **defined** x;

$T^{decl}{}_{\tau}$[**type** s **is private** ;] = τ[($s^{\perp}$, is_in_s) / (**sort**, s)]

$DECL\_SORTS_{\tau}$[**type** s **is private**;] = { (**sort**, s) }.

For private types declared in a generic formal part, a new base-type is introduced:

$\Psi^{gen}{}_{\tau}$[**type** fs **is private** ;] = **type** b_fs **is private**;
is_in_fs : $b\_fs^{\perp}$ --> LOGICAL;

$T^{gen}{}_{\tau}$[**type** fs **is private**;] = τ[($b\_fs^{\perp}$, is_in_fs) / (**sort**, fs)]

On *subtype declarations* only T^{decl} and Ψ^{decl} are defined, since a subtype declaration is not a generic parameter:

Let t be a type expression, τ a type context and t' = $elim_{\tau}$(t). We define

$\Psi^{decl}{}_{\tau}$[**subtype** s **is** t;] = is_in_s : b[t'] --> LOGICAL;
axiom for all x : b[t'] ⇒ is_in_s(x) ↔ $\Phi_{x:t'}$;

where for the type expression t' ∈ H_{res}(SOR) its base-type b[t'] and the characteristic formula $\Phi_{x:t'}$ are defined as in the previous section.

$T^{decl}{}_{\tau}$[**subtype** s **is** t;] = τ[(b[$elim_{\tau}$(t)] , is_in_s) / (**sort**, s)]

If τ is subtype-free and the subtype name s does not occur in t and in b_{τ}[s'] for all (**sort**,s') ∈ dom(τ), then $T^{decl}{}_{\tau}$[**subtype** s **is** t;] is easily seen to be subtype-free. Finally, we define

$DECL\_SORTS_{\tau}$[**subtype** s **is** t;] = { (**sort**, s) }.

On *package declarations* the functions T^{decl} and T^{lib} (as well as Ψ^{decl} and Ψ^{lib}) coincide. We define

$\Psi^{lib}{}_{\tau}$[**package** p **is** ds **end**;] = **package** p **is** $\Psi^{decl}{}_{\tau}$[ds] **end**;

$T^{lib}{}_{\tau}$ [**package** p **is** ds **end**;] = $T^{decl}{}_{\tau}$[ds],

$DECL\_SORTS_{\tau}$[**package** p **is** ds **end**;] = $DECL\_SORTS_{\tau}$[ds]

Notice that this simple definition is possible due to the assumption of the distinctness of (sub)type names introduced by different (sub)type declarations in a program library.

In the case of *generic declarations* we define

$\Psi^{lib}{}_\tau$[**generic** ds1 **package** g **is** ds2 **end**;] =

generic $\Psi^{gen}{}_\tau$[ds1] **package** g_{norm} **is** $\Psi^{decl}{}_{\tau 1}$[ds2] **end**; with $\tau 1 = T^{gen}{}_\tau$[ds1]

Recall that by the transformation function Ψ^{gen} the formal types in the generic declaration are transformed into predicates on a newly introduced base-type. Moreover, by $\Psi^{decl}{}_{\tau 1}$ every occurrence of a formal type in ds2 is replaced by the corresponding restriction on the new base-type.

The new type context determined by the generic declaration is obtained by updating the old type context by an entry for the name g:

$T^{lib}{}_\tau$ [**generic** ds1 **package** g **is** ds2 **end**;] = τ [($pars_g$, τ_g) / (**gen**, g)], where

$pars_g$ = sort_seq(ds1)

with sort_seq(ds1) denoting the sequence of type names declared in the sequence ds1 of generic parameters, (i.e. the type names in sort_seq(ds1) are the names in the set DECL_SORTS(ds1) and they appear in the same order as in the sequence ds1) and

$\tau_g = T^{decl}{}_{\tau 1}[ds2]|_{DECL\_SORTS_{\tau 1}[ds2]}$

where $\tau 1 = T^{gen}{}_\tau$[ds1] (the type context determined by the generic formal part). Hence τ_g is the type context determined by the package specification.

Since the generic declaration itself does not introduce new type names, we define

$DECL\_SORTS_\tau$[**generic** ds1 **package** g **is** ds2 **end**;] = $\emptyset$

Finally, we present the transformation of *generic instantiations*. Also here T^{lib} and T^{decl} (as well as Ψ^{decl} and Ψ^{lib}) coincide. Let `inst` be an abbreviation for the instantiation

package p **is new** g(act_pars);

where act_pars is a sequence of (sub)type names, predicate names and expressions. In order to avoid too many technicalities we assume that it is known which of the actual parameters are (sub)type-names.

Let τ be a type context and suppose that (**gen**, g) is an element of dom(τ) with τ(**gen**,g) = ($pars_g$,τ_g), where $pars_g$= <fs_1,...,fs_n>. Suppose further that (**sort**, s) $\in$ dom(τ) for all actual (sub)type names s in the sequence act_pars. Furthermore let α_{inst}: $\{fs_1,...,fs_n\} \rightarrow$ NAME be the function which maps every formal parameter type to the corresponding actual subtype name in act_pars. We define

$\Psi^{lib}{}_\tau$[`inst`] = **package** p **is new** g_{norm}(act_pars_τ);

where act_pars_τ is obtained by replacing every (sub)type name s in act_pars by the pair (b_τ[s],$cpred_\tau$[s]).

To define the new type context $T^{lib}{}_\tau$[`inst`] determined by the generic instantiation let

β_{inst} : H(SOR) $\rightarrow$ H(SOR)

be the function on higher order sorts induced from α_{inst} as follows:

(i) for a name s we define

$$\beta_{inst}(s^{\perp}) = \begin{cases} b_{\tau}[\,\alpha_{inst}(fs_i)], & \text{if } s = b\_fs_i \text{ (the newly introduced base-type for } fs_i\text{) for some } 1 \le i \le n \\ p.s^{\perp}, & \text{if } (\textbf{sort}, s) \in dom(\tau_g) \\ s^{\perp}, & \text{if } s \notin \{b\_fs_1,\ldots,b\_fs_n\} \cup \{ s : (\textbf{sort}, s) \in dom(\tau_g) \} \end{cases}$$

(ii) $\beta_{inst}(t_1 \dashrightarrow t_2) = \beta_{inst}(t_1) \dashrightarrow \beta_{inst}(t_2)$

(iii) $\beta_{inst}(t_1 \times \ldots \times t_n) = \beta_{inst}(t_1) \times \ldots \times \beta_{inst}(t_n)$

Using these definitions we set

$DECL\_SORTS_{\tau}[\, \mathtt{inst}\,] = \{ (\textbf{sort}, p.s) : (\textbf{sort}, s) \in dom(\tau_g)\}$

$T^{lib}{}_{\tau}[\, \mathtt{inst}] = \tau\,[\,\tau_{inst}\,]$,

where τ_{inst} is given by

$dom(\tau_{inst}) = DECL\_SORTS_{\tau}[\, \mathtt{inst}\,]$, $\tau_{inst}(\textbf{sort}, p.s) = (\beta_{inst}(b_{\tau_g}[s]), p.cpred_{\tau_g}[s])$

In case (**gen**, g) is not contained in dom(τ) or (**sort**, s) is not contained in dom(τ) for some actual (sub)type name s we define

$T^{lib}{}_{\tau}[\mathtt{inst}] = \tau$, $\Psi^{lib}{}_{\tau}[\, \mathtt{inst}\,] = \varepsilon$, $DECL\_SORTS_{\tau}[\, \mathtt{inst}\,] = \varnothing$ (error-case)

Now, if $lu_1\ lu_2 \ldots lu_n$ is a sequentialisation of a context correct program library (including the package STANDARD), which respects the dependencies in the program library, and where distinct (sub)type names are chosen in different (sub)type declarations, then using the above definitions it is easily checked that all type contexts generated during the evaluation of $\Psi^{lib}{}_{\varnothing}[\, lu_1\ lu_2 \ldots lu_n]$ (starting from the empty context) are subtype-free. This is due to the fact that no cyclic dependencies are possible in the declaration of subtypes. Hence by the definition of the elim-function on type-expressions, formulas, functions and predicate declarations, all occurrences of subtype identifiers in function- and predicate declarations and axioms in the original program have been eliminated in the transformed program.

Since for every generic instantiation in some lu_i, the generic itself and all actual (sub)types must have been declared in some lu_j with $j \le i$ the above error case will not occur in this transformation and all generic instantiations with (sub)type names are replaced by generic instantiations of the corresponding generics with the normalized interface. Hence $\Psi^{lib}{}_{\varnothing}[\, lu_1\ lu_2 \ldots lu_n]$ is a context correct program of the previous language layer.

So far, we only presented the syntactic transformation of programs with subtypes into programs of the previous language layer. From a semantic point of view, however, the instantiation of generics with arbitrary subtypes has to be handled with care, since it may cause inconsistencies with respect to the requirement that all functions be continuous.

As an example consider the instantiation

```
subtype FT is UNIVERSAL.INTEGER --> UNIVERSAL.INTEGER ;
package P is new COPIES( FT );
```

where COPIES is the generic specified in the previous example and UNIVERSAL.INTEGER is specified in the predefined language environment STANDARD (see part II chapter 5) up to isomorphism as the infinite poset $\mathbf{Z} \cup \{\perp\}$ with the flat ordering (in contrast to INTEGER, which is specified as a finite set). The above instantiation is transformed into an instantiation of the normalized generic COPIES_N in the kernel-language :

```
package P is new
    new COPIES_N( (UNIVERSAL.INTEGER⊥ --> UNIVERSAL.INTEGER⊥), is_in_FT);
```

where the characterizing predicate is_in_FT yields true on all functions which map defined integers to defined integers (i.e. on all total functions):

```
    is_in_FT : (UNIVERSAL.INTEGER⊥ --> UNIVERSAL.INTEGER⊥) --> LOGICAL;
axiom for all f: (UNIVERSAL.INTEGER⊥ --> UNIVERSAL.INTEGER⊥) ⇒
    is_in_FT (f) ↔ ( for all x: UNIVERSAL.INTEGER⊥ ⇒ defined x → defined f(x) );
```

Then in every environment σ consistent with the above instantiation "P.make" is interpreted by a continuous function V_σ(P.make) of type

(UNIVERSAL.INTEGER$^\perp$ --> UNIVERSAL.INTEGER$^\perp$) --> P.COPY$^\perp$

which maps total functions to defined elements. Since the carrier of UNIVERSAL.INTEGER is infinite, and therefore every strict total function is the least upper bound of a set of proper partial functions, it follows by continuity that V_σ(P.make) does not map all partial functions to the undefined element of type P.COPY. As "back" is specified to map defined elements of sort COPY to elements satisfying the characteristic predicate of the parameter subtype, V_σ(P.back) maps defined elements of type P.COPY to total functions.

Hence the composed function V_σ(P.back) $\circ$ V_σ(P.make) maps some proper partial functions to total functions and is the identity on all total functions. Since every proper partial function approximates more than one total function and all total functions are incomparable with respect to the ordering on the function space, the function V_σ(P.back) $\circ$ V_σ(P.make) is not a monotonic function in contradiction to the requirement that both V_σ(P.back) and V_σ(P.make) be monotonic functions. Therefore there is no environment consistent with the above instantiation.

The same kind of inconsistency arises if the subtype consisting of all total functions over a type with infinite flat carrier is supplied as an actual parameter for a generic forming products or lists (with the respective constructor- and selector functions). The reason for these inconsistencies is that for types with an infinite flat carrier there exists no continuous projection function from the entire function space to the space of total functions (with the totally undefined function added as bottom element), which leaves the total functions fixed.

Therefore in the instantiation of such generics in which new (non-formal) sorts are introduced together with constructor and selector operations (specified by the weak arrow) the following rule should be observed: such generics should only be instantiated with such actual parameter subtypes for which there exists a continuous function on the entire actual base-type which has as its image the elements of the actual subtype (with the undefined element of the base-type added as bottom element) and is the identity on its image.

More precisely, such a function (for a subtype st with characterizing predicate is_in_st) is specified (not necessarily uniquely) by

```
pro : b[st] --> ( x : b[st] :: is_in_st(x) or not defined x )
axiom for all x: b[st] ⇒ is_in_st(x) or not defined x → pro(x) = x;
```

Hence all the elements satisfying the characteristic predicate of the subtype are fixed points of the projection function "pro". Since here we consider specifications with the weak arrow it is not required that elements x for which is_in_st(x) does not hold are mapped to the undefined element. The case of specifications using the strong arrow will be treated in the next section.

The continuity of "pro" together with the fact that $pro \circ pro = pro$ implies that its image is a cpo and that every continuous function defined on that cpo can be extended to a continuous function on the carrier of the base-type b[st] by first projecting every element of the base-type to the subtype.

Examples of subtypes for which such projection functions exist are subtypes of such atomic base-types which are specified by strict operations, since such base-types can be interpreted as flat cpo's and for every subset of a flat cpo a continuous projection function exists.

Moreover if st is a subtype with a continuous projection function pro : b[st] --> $st^{\perp}$, then there also exists a continuous projection function from the function type (b[st] -->b[st]) to the restricted function type (b[st] --> $st^{\perp}$). This projection function is defined by mapping a function f to the function $pro \circ f$.

3.4.3. Some Methodological Advice on the Use of the Strong Arrow

The use of the strong arrow has to be handled with care, since it may cause inconsistencies to the requirement of monotonicity and continuity imposed on functions.

However, it can be used throughout in first order specifications, with all argument sorts of functions not marked by the bottom sign and where all subtypes are declared by type expressions not involving the $\perp$-sign. In this case (strong arrow, sorts not marked by $\perp$) all functions are specified as strict. Due to the fact that every strict function between flat cpo's is continuous, in models for such specifications the ordering on the carriers of atomic sort can be chosen as the flat ordering.

In specifications with argument sorts marked by the $\perp$-sign and in higher order specifications the carriers of models in general are non-flat cpo's and therefore the use of the strong arrow has to be handled with more care (see examples 1 and 2 below). Moreover, if in functions specified by the strong arrow subtype names marked by $\perp$ appear as argument sorts, inconsistencies may arise (see example 3 below). No problems arise if the argument sorts are unrestricted higher order sorts ($t \in H(SOR)$) or if their characteristic predicate yields true on all defined elements of their base-type.
Hence, if $t_1, \ldots, t_n$, t are type expressions with base-types $b[t_i] = t_i$ or $b[t_i] = t_i^{\perp}$, then there always is a continuous function meeting the specification $f : t_1 \times \ldots \times t_n$ ==> t, provided the characteristic predicate associated to the type expression t yields true on at least one value.

We present some examples illustrating the effects of the use of the strong function arrow:

(1) In the specification

```
generic
   type ITEM is private;
package STREAMS is
   type STREAM is private;
   empty : STREAM⊥;
   app : ITEM × STREAM⊥ ==> STREAM; ...
```

"app" is specified as a function which is non-strict in the second argument. Therefore, STREAM is specified as a non-flat domain. In particular, in a specification

```
   f : (x:STREAM :: p(x)) ==> STREAM;
```

the predicate p(x) has to be chosen carefully : more precisely, in every model A of the generic, the set $p^A \subseteq (STREAM^{\perp})^A$ has to be upwards closed (monotonicity of f) and for every directed subset $I \subseteq (STREAM^{\perp})^A \backslash p^A$ the least upper bound of I also must not satisfy the predicate p (continuity of f).

(2) There is no continuous function g meeting the specification

```
g : ( UNIVERSAL.INTEGER --> UNIVERSAL.INTEGER ) ==> UNIVERSAL.INTEGER;
```

The argument type (UNIVERSAL.INTEGER --> UNIVERSAL.INTEGER) has the base-type (UNIVERSAL.INTEGER$^{\perp}$ --> UNIVERSAL.INTEGER$^{\perp}$) and the characteristic predicate associated to (UNIVERSAL.INTEGER --> UNIVERSAL.INTEGER) yields false on all proper partial function (i.e. on all functions yielding $\perp$ on some defined integer).

By the above specification g is specified as a function yielding undefined on all proper partial functions and a defined integer on all total functions. Since every strict total function is the least upper bound of a directed set of proper partial functions, g is not continuous.

However, there are continuous functions meeting the specification

```
h : ( UNIVERSAL.INTEGER --> UNIVERSAL.INTEGER ) --> UNIVERSAL.INTEGER;
```

where instead of the strong arrow the weak arrow is used.

(3) Consider the predefined subtype

```
subtype NATURAL is (x:INTEGER :: (x >= 0) = TRUE);
```

Then by the declaration

```
f : NATURAL ==> NATURAL;
```

f is specified as a strict, continuous function mapping natural numbers to natural numbers and negative integers to bottom. Since INTEGER is specified as a flat cpo, such functions obviously do exist.

However there is no monotonic (and hence also no continuous) function meeting the specification

```
g: NATURAL⊥ ==> NATURAL;
```

since such a function would have to map $\perp$ to a defined natural number, but all negative integers to $\perp$.

A final remark concerns the instantiation of such generics in which functions are specified by the strong arrow. Recall that generics may be instantiated with arbitrary subtypes, where in our semantic definition we consider a subtype as a pair consisting of its base-type and its characterizing predicate. Hence if fs is a formal sort of a PA^{nn}dA-S generic (and hence has to be regarded as a formal subtype parameter), t is a sort declared as private in the package part of the generic and g : fs ==> t; is a function specified by the strong arrow, then by the transformation rules in section 3.4.2, the above specification is transformed into g : (x:b_fs$^{\perp}$ :: is_in_fs(x)) ==> t; where b_fs$^{\perp}$ is the formal base-type and is_in_fs the formal characterizing predicate for the formal subtype fs.

Now, if the actual base-type is specified as a non-flat cpo, then it can happen that there is no continuous function on the base-type which is undefined exactly on all elements for which the characterizing predicate yields false. An example would be an instantiation with **subtype** NATURALBOT = NATURAL$^{\perp}$.

The instantiation of a PA^{nn}dA-S generic containing the declaration of functions specified by the strong arrow is unproblematic provided in such functions the argument sorts being formal (subtype) parameters are not marked by the ⊥-sign and the actual (subtype) parameters satisfy the conditions (1) or (2), where

(1) The actual subtypes correspond to zero order type expressions not containing the ⊥-sign and the atomic sorts from which their base-types are composed are specified by strict operations. (subtypes of smash-products of "flat" cpo's) or

(2) The actual subtypes correspond to unrestricted higher order sorts or their characteristic predicate yields true on all defined elements.

Examples for actual parameters satisfying (1) are

```
INTEGER, NATURAL,
subtype INT is UNIVERSAL.INTEGER;
subtype PROD is NATURAL × NATURAL;
subtype TRIANGLE is (pair: (x:NATURAL) × (y:NATURAL) :: (x >= y) = TRUE);
```

Examples for actual parameters satisfying (2) are

```
subtype T1 is INTEGER⊥;
subtype T2 is INT⊥ ;
subtype T3 is (p: INT⊥ × INT⊥ :: defined p);
subtype T4 is INT⊥ --> INT⊥;
```

More generally a PA^{nn}dA-S generic containing the specification of functions specified by the strong arrow (involving the parameter sorts) should only be instantiated with an actual subtype st (with base-type b[st]), and characteristic predicate is_in_st) if there is a continuous projection function "pro_strong" which meets the following specification

```
pro_strong  : b[st] --> ( x : b[st] :: is_in_st(x) or not defined x )
 axiom for all x: b[st] ⇒        is_in_st(x) →         pro_strong(x) = x,
                                 not is_in_st(x) →  not  defined pro_strong(x);
```

Notice that this is the "strong" version of the specification of a projection function given in the previous section to characterize appropriate actual subtypes for generics with weakly specified functions.

To sum up: *The use of the strong arrow is appropriate for strict, first order specifications and has to be handled with care in non-strict, higher order specifications. In such specifications there are cases where the use of the strong arrow leads to inconsistencies, whereas the weak arrow does not.*

3.A Appendix: Untreated Syntactic Categories

We regard the treatment of the following syntactic constructs of PA^{nn}dA-S as an issue of the static semantic analysis:
(The numbers refer to the concrete syntax summary given in the PA^{nn}dA-S Reference Manual, part II chapter 4)

4.6

```
qualified_expression ::= subtype_name'(expression)
```

9.2

```
context_clause ::= [with_clause]
with clause ::= with identifier {, identifier}
```

Furthermore, in this semantic description we do not consider nested generics, i.e. generic specifications are considered as library_units, but not as declarations. That means that we delete from 3.1 ("declaration") the alternative "generic_declaration".

4. PA^{nn}dA Reference Manual

Einar W. Karlsen[1], *Computer Resources International*

This chapter presents the rationale and syntax of the wide-spectrum language PA^{nn}dA.

4.1. Introduction

PA^{nn}dA (PROSPECTRA Ada/Anna) is the *imperative wide-spectrum language* of PROSPECTRA covering the specification, design and implementation phases of program development. PA^{nn}dA was designed to have an imperative language as simple as possible, yet useful for synthesizing efficient Ada programs. The language can therefore be viewed as a simplified subset of Ada which incorporates imperative Ada constructs that contribute to the expressive power at the implementation level: for example bodies, statements, exceptions, tasks and variables. PA^{nn}dA contains in extend a normalised form of PA^{nn}dA-S facilitating constructs that contribute to the expressive power at the applicative level, like axioms and higher order functions.

PA^{nn}dA can be considered a combination of Ada (see [Ichbiah et al. 79]) and PA^{nn}dA-S (see chapter 2,3). Familiarity with those two languages are therefore assumed in the rest of this manual. The rationale behind the design of the language is briefly described in section 4.2, the simplification with respect to Ada in section 4.3. A BNF definition of the syntax is given in the appendix.

4.2. Rationale

The fundamental design goal of PA^{nn}dA was to have an imperative language as simple as possible, yet useful for synthesizing efficient Ada programs. Simplicity was highly attractive from the viewpoint of the transformer developer, because the simpler the language the fewer and more compact the set of transformation rules. Simplicity was also important from the viewpoint of the tool implementors, in particular to avoid some of the subtle and complex constructs of Ada with insignificant contribution to the power of the language.

These design goals have been reflected by having three related PA^{nn}dA languages:

- *PA^{nn}dA–S* (S for *specification*) is the *applicative kernel specification language* in which requirement specifications are formulated. It mainly contains constructs for: modularisation of specifications in the form of packages and generic packages; declaration of types in the form of private types and subtypes; declaration of first and higher order functions; axiomatic annotations for the specification of properties.
- PA^{nn}dA–C (C for *canonical*) is the *imperative wide-spectrum language* containing a normalized form of PA^{nn}dA–S as a subset. Additionally it incorporates imperative Ada constructs that contribute to the expressive power at the imperative level: bodies, statements, exceptions, tasks and variables. It does not, however, incorporate Ada constructs that can be easily explained by or rewritten into other constructs.
- *PA^{nn}dA–E* (E for *extended* or *executable* as preferred) is an *executable subset* of Ada and incorporates all parts of Ada that we anticipate to be able to (and want to) generate at the end of the development. It includes all the constructs of PA^{nn}dA-C together with some constructs that can be viewed as notational extensions needed to generate executable code.

1. *Author's current address*: FB 3 - Informatik, Universität Bremen, Postfach 330 440, D-2800 Bremen 33

So $PA^{nn}dA$ basically has two imperative sublanguages: $PA^{nn}dA$-C on which the transformation rules are formulated, and $PA^{nn}dA$-E that includes constructs needed to generate legal and executable Ada programs in the end. In this chapter, when mentioning $PA^{nn}dA$ without qualification S, C, or E we refer to $PA^{nn}dA$–C.

4.3. Design of $PA^{nn}dA$-C

Design specifications, as well as applicative and imperative implementations are formulated at the level of $PA^{nn}dA$-C. The language is composed of a subset of Ada featuring constructs needed at the imperative level, plus a normalised form of $PA^{nn}dA$-S featuring constructs needed at the applicative level. One major task in the design of $PA^{nn}dA$ was to define a consistent and useful Ada subset, another to define the specification language. We refer to chapter 2 and 3 for a description of the specification language. The simplifications and deviations of $PA^{nn}dA$ with respect to Ada are briefly described in the following subsections, whereas a BNF definition is to be found in appendix 4.A.

4.3.1. Simplifications with Respect to Ada

$PA^{nn}dA$ does not incorporate Ada constructs that can be easily explained by or rewritten into other $PA^{nn}dA$ constructs. There are several places in the Ada Reference Manual where a condensed notation is considered to be equivalent to an expanded notation, and the rules are then given in terms of the expanded notation. In the case of $PA^{nn}dA$ only one of these alternatives is needed: the one that is most appropriate and simple with respect to static semantic checking and the definition of transformation rules (see figure 4.1).

For example, the Ada Reference Manual explicitly says that a sequence of multiple declarations is equivalent to a sequence of the corresponding number of single declarations, where the equivalent sequence is in the same order as the identifier list [Ada 83, 3.2(10)]. In $PA^{nn}dA$ there is no need for this abbreviation feature of Ada.

Another example is that in Ada pragmas may occur a lot of places with all the inherent complications on the formulation of transformation rules and implementation of tools. In $PA^{nn}dA$ some restrictions are put

Ada Representation	PAnndA Representation
multiple declarations	sequence of single declarations
membership test **not in**	negation of membership test **in**
else-if parts of an if statement	nested if statements
case statement	if statements
named associations for subprogram calls	positional associations
default expressions for subprograms	explicit parameter at call
exit statement with conditions	if statement with exit statement as consequence
named associations for generic parameters	positional associations
defaults for generic formal subprograms	explicit parameter at instantiation

Figure 4.1: Representation of Ada terms in PAnndA

on the allowed positions of pragmas: a pragma is allowed wherever a declaration is allowed.

The major simplification of PA^{nn}dA with respect to Ada is that PA^{nn}dA adopts a canonical view of Ada types. In programming languages like Ada, new data types can be defined by using type construction facilities like records, arrays, pointers etc. Types constructed this way can however be expressed by purely algebraic specifications, and this is the approach taken in PROSPECTRA. Figure 4.2 illustrates how a record type can be defined in an algebraic way without using the record type definition facilities of Ada. We refer to part II, chapter 5, for a detailed description of these so-called *type schemes* used for defining types in PA^{nn}dA.

The algebraic and encapsulated view of types has several advantages in terms of simplifying the syntax and static semantic rules. First, many of the Ada constructs for defining types like type definitions and discriminant parts can be ignored. Second, this implies a significant simplification to the syntax of names since there is no need for type specific names like indexing, selectors and attributes. As a result, both the syntax, the static semantics rules and the transformation rules of PA^{nn}dA are significantly simplified.

The following Ada constructs are not directly part of PA^{nn}dA:

- real literals,
- full type declarations,
- incomplete type declarations,
- discriminant parts,
- slices,
- indexed components,
- selected components,
- attributes,
- limited private types and
- scalar formal types.

The only types available in PA^{nn}dA are private types, subtypes and derived types. The syntax of derived

```
package rationals is
   type rational is private;
   EQ: (rational; rational) --> BOOLEAN;
   mk_rational: (num: integer; denom: positive) --> rational;
   num: rational --> integer;
   denom: rational --> positive;
   axiom for all A: rational; B: rational =>
      EQ( A, B) = (EQ( num(A), num(B)) and EQ( denom(A), denom(B)));
   axiom for all E1: integer; E2: positive =>
      num(mk_rational( E1, E2)) = E1,
      denom(mk_rational( E1, E2)) = E2;
end rationals;
```

Figure 4.2: Specification of Record Type in PAnndA-C

type declarations has in addition been simplified: a derived type is defined directly in terms of the parent type.

To have a simple language some further simplifications have been performed with respect to Ada. In PA^{nn}dA there is no notion of:

- renaming declarations,
- use clauses,
- body stubs and subunits,
- representation clauses.

Renaming declarations are used to resolve naming conflicts and to act as shorthands in Ada. They are therefore not covered by the language. Use clauses are not needed due to deviations in the static semantics rules. More on this in the next section.

4.3.2. Extensions and Deviations with Respect to Ada

The main place where PA^{nn}dA deviates from Ada is that PA^{nn}dA contains constructs needed at the specification level, namely axioms and higher order functions.

In PA^{nn}dA requirement specifications are formulated in the visible part of a package, design specifications in the private part and implementations finally in the body of the package (see figure 4.3). An optional with clause has been added to the syntax of packages immediately following the keyword **private**. This with clauses specifies the library units needed at the design level. The with clause before the package declaration then specifies the library units needed for the specification level, and the with clause associated to the package body the library units needed at the implementation level.

The rules defining the scope of declarations and the rules defining visibility of identifiers are basically the Ada rules. Each withed package is however implicitly used in order to achieve direct visibility of the declarations that appear in the visible part of the withed package. Use clauses are therefore not needed in the language. Consequently, to ensure that naming conflicts can be solved properly by using fully prefixed names, STANDARD cannot be used as the name of a user defined entity and loop and block statements must always include an identifier.

To have a more semantically clean language some further simplifications have been performed with respect to Ada:

- an exclamation mark has been added to the syntax of type conversions, to distinguish type conversions from function calls,
- all functions are purely applicative and are therefore not allowed to have side effects.

with R;
package P is
   requirement specification
private
   with D;
   design specification
end P;
	with I;
	package body P is
	   implementation
	end P;

Figure 4.3: Role of Visible Part, Private Part and Body

4.4. Design of PA^{nn}dA-E

PA^{nn}dA–C programs will not necessarily be legal and executable Ada programs due to the simplifications made in the design of the language. PA^{nn}dA-E incorporates however features needed to generate executable Ada, mainly constructs for representing Ada type declarations and type specific names and expressions. Renaming declarations, use clauses, else if statements and case statements are supported as well. A BNF definition is provided in appendix 4.B.

The example in figure 4.4 illustrates how the record type from figure 4.2 will be implemented by encapsulating the Ada type declarations in the private part of the package. The constuctor and selector functions are implemented in the package body, and the use of pragma INLINE ensures that the implementation is efficient.

```
package rationals is
   type rational is private;
   function EQ (X: rational; Y: rational) return BOOLEAN;
   function mk_rational (num: integer; denom: positive) return rational;
   function num (X: rational) return integer;
   function denom (X: rational) return positive;
private
   type rational is
      record
      num: integer;
      denom: positive;
      end record;
   pragma inline( EQ, mk_rational, num, denom);
end rationals;


package body rationals is
   function EQ (X: rational; Y: rational) return BOOLEAN is
   begin
      return X = Y;
   end EQ;

   function mk_rational (num: integer; denom: positive) return rational is
   begin
      return (num, denom);
   end mk_rational;

   function num (X: rational) return integer is
   begin
      return X.num;
   end num;

   function denom (X: rational) return positive is
   begin
      return X.denom;
   end denom;
end rationals;
```

Figure 4.4: Implementation of Record Type in PAnndA-E

Appendices

4.A. Syntax of PA^{nn}dA-C

lexical syntax

```
graphic_character ::= basic_graphic_character
  | lower_case_letter      | other_special_character

basic_graphic_character ::=
        upper_case_letter     | digit
  |     special_character     | space_character

basic_character ::=
        basic_graphic_character |   format_effector

identifier ::=
        letter {[underline] letter_or_digit}

letter_or_digit ::=
        letter  |   digit

letter ::=
        upper_case_letter  | lower_case_letter

numeric_literal ::= decimal_literal

decimal_literal ::= integer

integer ::=
        digit {[underline] digit}

string_literal ::=
        "{graphic_character}"
```

declarations and types

```
basic_declaration ::=
        private_type_declaration     |  derived_type_declaration
  |     object_declaration           |  subtype_declaration
  |     subprogram_declaration       |  predicate_declaration
  |     package_declaration          |  task_declaration
  |     generic_declaration          |  exception_declaration
  |     generic_instantiation        |  deferred_constant_declaration
  |     axiom

object_declaration ::=
        identifier : [constant] subtype_name [ := expression];

subtype_declaration ::=
        subtype identifier is type_expression;

type_expression ::=
        function_type_expression    |  tuple_type_expression

function_type_expression ::=
        tuple_type_expression  function_arrow  type_expression

function_arrow ::=  --> | ==>

tuple_type_expression ::=
        extended_type_expression {# extended_type_expresson}

extended_type_expression ::=
        subtype_expression [+]
```

subtype_expression ::=
*subtype*_name | (domain) | (type_expression)

derived_type_declaration ::=
type identifier **is new** *subtype*_name

discrete_range ::=
*subtype*_name | range

range ::=
simple_expression .. simple_expression

declarative_part ::=
{basic_declarative_item} {later_declarative_item}

basic_declarative_item ::= basic_declaration

later_declarative_item ::=
body | subprogram_declaration
| package_declaration | task_declaration
| generic_declaration | generic_instantiation

body ::= subprogram_body
| package_body | task_body

names and expressions

name ::=
designator | expanded_name

expanded_name ::=
name.designator

expression ::=
relation **and** relation
| relation **and then** relation
| relation **or** relation
| relation **or else** relation
| relation **xor** relation
| relation

relation ::=
simple_expression [relational_operator simple_expression]

simple_expression ::=
[unary_adding_operator] term {binary_adding_operator term}

term ::=
factor {multiplying_operator factor}

factor ::=
secondary [** secondary]
| **abs** secondary
| **not** secondary

secondary ::=
primary | *function*_call

primary ::=
numeric_literal | string_literal
| **undefined** | name
| type_conversion | qualified_expression
| (expression {, expression}) | conditional_expression

logical_operator ::= **and** | **or** | **xor**

relational_operator ::= < | <= | > | >=

binary_adding_operator ::= + | - | &

unary_adding_operator ::= + | -

multiplying_operator ::= * | / | **mod** | **rem**

highest_precedence_operator ::= ** | **abs** | **not**

type_conversion ::=
    *subtype*_name ! (expression)

qualified_expression ::=
    *subtype*_name'(expression)

conditional_expression ::=
    if condition **then**
        expression
    else
        expression
    end if

logical expressions

logical_expression ::=
    [quantifier domain { ; domain } =>]
        implication {, implication}

quantifier ::= **for all** | **exist**

implication ::=
    [logical_formula implicator] logical_formula
  | **others** implicator logical_formula

implicator ::= -> | <->

logical_formula ::=
    logical_primary {**and** logical_primary}
  | logical_primary {**or** logical_primary}
  | **not** logical_primary

logical_primary ::=
    (logical_expression)
  | condition
  | simple_expression = simple_expression
  | simple_expression /= simple_expression
  | simple_expression **in** *subtype*_name
  | **defined** expression
  | *predicate*_call

statements

sequence_of_statements ::=
    statement {statement}

statement ::=
    {label} simple_statement
  | {label} compound_statement

label ::= <<*label*_identifier>>

simple_statement ::=
    null_statement | assignment_statement
  | procedure_call_statement | exit_statement
  | return_statement | goto_statement
  | entry_call_statement | raise_statement

```
compound_statement ::= if_statement
  |  loop_statement           |  block_statement
  |  accept_statement         |  select_statement

null_statement ::= null;

assignment_statement ::=
      variable_name := expression;

if_statement ::=
      if condition then
         sequence_of_statements
      [else
         sequence_of_statements]
      end if;

condition ::= boolean_expression

loop_statement ::=
      loop_identifier:
         [iteration_scheme] loop
            sequence_of_statements
         end loop [loop_identifier];

iteration_scheme ::=
      while condition
  |   for loop_parameter_specification

loop_parameter_specification ::=
      identifier in [reverse] discrete_range

block_statement ::=
      block_identifier:
         [declare
            declarative_part]
         begin
            sequence_of_statements
         [exception
            exception_handler
            {exception_handler}]
         end [block_identifier];

exit_statement ::=
      exit [loop_name];

return_statement ::=
      return [expression];

goto_statement ::=
      goto label_name;
```

subprograms

```
subprogram_declaration ::=
      subprogram_specification;

subprogram_specification ::=
      [--:] domain;
  |   procedure identifier [formal_part]

predicate_declaration ::=
      predicate domain;

domain ::=
      designator : mode type_expression [:: constraint_logical_expression]
```

```
designator ::=
      identifier      | operator_symbol

operator_symbol ::= string_literal

formal_part ::=
      (domain {; domain})

mode ::= out    |  in out

subprogram_body ::=
      subprogram_specification is
         [declarative_part]
      begin
         sequence_of_statements
      [ exception
         exception_handler
         {exception_handler}]
      end [designator];

procedure_call_statement ::=
      procedure_name [(expression {, expression})]];

call ::=
      secondary primary
```

packages

```
package_declaration ::=
      package_specification;

package_specification ::=
      package identifier is
         {basic_declarative_item}
      [private
         private_context_clause
         {basic_declarative_item}]
      end [package_identifier]

package_body ::=
      package body package_identifier is
         [declarative_part]
      [begin
         sequence_of_statements
      [exception
         exception_handler
         {exception_handler}]]
      end [package_identifier];

private_type_declaration ::=
      type identifier is private;

deferred_constant_declaration ::=
      identifier : constant subtype_name;

axiom ::=
      axiom logical_expression ;
```

tasks

```
task_declaration ::=
      task_specification;
```

```
task_specification ::=
      task identifier is
         {entry_declaration}
      end [task_identifier]

task_body ::=
      task body task_identifier is
         [declarative_part]
      begin
         sequence_of_statements
      [exception
         exception_handler
         {exception_handler}]
      end [task_identifier];

entry_declaration ::=
      entry identifier [formal_part];

entry_call_statement ::=
      entry_name [actual_parameter_part];

accept_statement ::=
      accept entry_identifier [formal_part] do
         sequence_of_statements
      end [entry_identifier];

select_statement ::=
      select
         select_alternative
      {or
         select_alternative}
      [else
         sequence_of_statements]
      end select;

select_alternative ::=
      [when condition =>] selective_alternative

selective_alternative ::=
      accept_alternative
   |  terminate_alternative
   |  entry_call_statement sequence_of_statements

accept_alternative ::=
      accept_statement [sequence_of_statements]

terminate_alternative ::= terminate;
```

program structure

```
compilation ::=
      compilation_unit {compilation_unit}

compilation_unit ::=
      context_clause library_unit
   |  context_clause secondary_unit

library_unit ::= package_declaration
   |  subprogram_declaration          |  generic_declaration
   |  generic_instantiation           |  subprogram_body

secondary_unit ::=
      library_unit_body
```

library_unit_body ::=
    package_body | subprogram_body

context_clause ::=
    [with_clause]

with_clause ::=
    with *unit*_identifier {, *unit*_identifier};

exceptions

exception_declaration ::=
    identifier : **exception**;

exception_handler ::=
    when exception_choice {| exception_choice} =>
        sequence_of_statements

exception_choice ::=
    *exception*_name | **others**

raise_statement ::=
    raise [*exception*_name];

generic units

generic_declaration ::=
    generic_specification;

generic_specification ::=
    generic_formal_part package_specification
  | generic_formal_part subprogram_specification

generic_formal_part ::=
    generic {generic_formal_parameter | axiom}

generic_formal_parameter ::=
    private_type_declaration
  | identifier : [**in** [**out**]] *subtype*_name;
  | subprogram_declaration
  | predicate_declaration

generic_instantiation ::=
    package identifier **is new** *generic_package*_name [generic_actual_part];
  | **procedure** identifier **is new** *generic_procedure*_name [generic_actual_part];
  | **function** identifier **is new** *generic_function*_name [generic_actual_part];

generic_actual_part ::=
    (generic_actual_parameter {, generic_actual_parameter})

generic_actual_parameter ::=
    expression | *subtype*_name

4.B. Syntax of PA^{nn}dA-E

The syntax is presented in form of *extensions* to the canonical PA^{nn}dA syntax. The productions define the language constructs needed to generate executeable Ada. The numbers refer to the relevant sections of the Ada Reference Manual.

3.1

```
basic_declaration ::=
      type_declaration
   |  number_declaration
   |  use_declaration
   |  renaming_declaration
```

3.2

```
object_declaration ::=
      identifier : [constant] subtype_indication [:= expression];

number_declaration ::=
      identifier : constant := universal_static_expression;
```

3.3.1

```
type_declaration ::=
      private_type_declaration
   |  incomplete_type_declaration
   |  full_type_declaration

full_type_declaration ::=
      type identifier [discriminant_part] is type_definition;

type_definition ::=
      derived_type_definition
   |  enumeration_type_definition
   |  record_type_definition
   |  access_type_definition
```

3.3.2

```
subtype_declaration ::=
      subtype identifier is subtype_indication;

subtype_indication ::=
      type_mark [constraint]

type_mark ::=
      type_name  |  subtype_name

constraint ::=
      range_constraint      |  discriminant_constraint
```

3.4

```
derived_type_definition ::=
      new subtype_indication
```

3.5.1

```
enumeration_type_definition ::=
      (enumeration_literal_specification {,enumeration_literal_specification})

enumeration_literal_specification ::=
      enumeration_literal

enumeration_literal ::= identifier
```

3.7

```
record_type_definition ::=
      record
         component_list
      end record

component_list ::=
      component_declaration {component_declaration}
   |  {component_declaration} variant_part
   |  null;

component_declaration ::=
      identifier : component_subtype_definition;

component_subtype_definition ::=
      subtype_indication
```

3.7.1

```
discriminant_part ::=
      (discriminant_specification )

discriminant_specification ::=
      identifier : type_mark
```

3.7.2

```
discriminant_constraint ::=
      (discriminant_association)

discriminant_association ::=
      [discriminant_simple_name =>] expression
```

3.7.3

```
variant_part ::=
      case discriminant_simple_name is
         variant
         { variant }
      end case;

variant ::=
      when choice {| choice} =>
         component_list

choice ::=
      simple_expression
   |  discrete_range
   |  others
   |  component_simple_name
```

3.8

```
access_type_definition ::=
      access subtype_indication
```

3.8.1

```
incomplete_type_declaration ::=
      type identifier [discriminant_part];
```

4.1

```
name ::=
      selected_component  |  attribute
```

```
prefix ::=
      name      |  function_call
```

4.1.3

```
selected_component ::=
      prefix.selector

selector ::=
      simple_name  |      operator_symbol  |  all
```

4.1.4

```
attribute ::=
      prefix'attribute_designator

attribute_designator ::=
      simple_name [(universal_static_expression)]
```

4.3

```
aggregate ::=
      (component_association {, component_association})

component_association ::=
      [choice {| choice} => ] expression
```

4.4

```
relation ::=
      simple_expression  in range

primary ::=
      null      |  aggregate  |  allocator
```

4.6

```
type_conversion ::=
      type_mark(expression)
```

4.7

```
qualified_expression ::=
      type_mark'(expression)
   |  type_mark'aggregate
```

4.8

```
allocator ::=
      new subtype_indication  |  new qualified_expression
```

5.1

```
compound_statement ::=
      if_statement   |      case_statement
```

5.3

```
if_statement ::=
      if condition then
         sequence_of_statements
      {elsif condition then
         sequence_of_statements}
      [else
         sequence_of_statements]
      end if;
```

5.4

case_statement ::=
  case expression **is**
    case_statement_alternative
    {case_statement_alternative}
  end case;

case_statement_alternative ::=
  when choice {| choice} =>
    sequence_of_statements

6.1

subprogram_declaration ::=
  subprogram_specification;

subprogram_specification ::=
  function designator [formal_part] **return** type_expression
| **procedure** identifier [formal_part]

domain ::=
  designator : mode type_expression

formal_part ::=
  (domain_list)

7.1

package_declaration ::=
  package_specification;

package_specification ::=
  package identifier **is**
    {basic_declarative_item}
  [**private**
    {basic_declarative_item}]
  end [*package_*identifier]

7.4

private_type_declaration ::=
  type identifier [discriminant_part] **is private**;

8.4

use_clause ::=
  use *package_*name {, *package_*name};

8.5

renaming_declaration ::=
  subprogram_specification **renames** *subprogram_or_entry_*name;

10.1.1

compilation_unit ::=
  context_clause library_unit
| context_clause secondary_unit

context_clause ::= [with_clause [use_clause]]

5. PAnndA Standard Types and Predefined Type Schemata

Stefan Kahrs, Universität Bremen*

This section contains the description of the Ada-oriented Standard types and type schemata that are built-in to PAnndA or the PROSPECTRA system.

5. 1. Built-in Types

The predefined types of the package STANDARD are as follows:

5.1.1. BOOLEAN

The built-in type BOOLEAN is specified as below.

```
type BOOLEAN is private;
true, false: BOOLEAN;
axiom true /= false;
"not": BOOLEAN ==> BOOLEAN;
axiom not false = true, not true = false;
"and", "or", "xor", EQ: BOOLEAN × BOOLEAN ==> BOOLEAN;
axiom for all X: BOOLEAN =>
        (X and X) = X, (X and not X) = false,
        (X or X) = X, (X or not X) = true,
        (X xor X) = false, (X xor not X) = true,
        EQ(X,Y) = not (X xor Y);
-- "or else" : BOOLEAN × BOOLEAN+ ==> BOOLEAN+ ;
-- "and then" : BOOLEAN × BOOLEAN+ ==> BOOLEAN+ ;
axiom for all X: BOOLEAN+ =>
        true or else X = true,
        false or else X = X,
        true and then X = X,
        false and then X = false;
"<", ">", "<=", ">=": BOOLEAN × BOOLEAN ==> BOOLEAN;
axiom for all X, Y: BOOLEAN =>
        (X<Y) = (not X and Y), (X>Y) = (Y<X),
        (X<=Y) = (not X or Y), (X>=Y) = (Y<=X);
SUCC: (X: BOOLEAN::X=false) ==> BOOLEAN;
PRED: (X: BOOLEAN::X=true) ==> BOOLEAN;
axiom SUCC false = true, PRED true = false;
FIRST, LAST: BOOLEAN;
axiom FIRST = false, LAST = true;
POS: BOOLEAN ==> NATURAL;
axiom POS true = 1, POS false = 0;
VAL: (N: NATURAL :: (N <= 1) = true) ==> BOOLEAN;
axiom for all X: BOOLEAN => VAL (POS X) = X;
```

The status of this type is similar to an enumeration type (see below), but with one major exception: expressions of the type BOOLEAN can be used at places where LOGICAL is required - an implicit

* *Author's current address*: Department of Computer Science, University of Edinburgh, Edinburgh EH9 3JZ, Scotland

"=true" is added in this case, and ambiguities are solved by the rule: *convert to LOGICAL from the inside*. As a consequence, the BOOLEAN ⊥ works like the BOOLEAN **false** there. To avoid confusion, this abbreviation will not be used in the section about built-in types.

The definition of functions like POS or SUCC is motivated by Ada. In Ada, BOOLEAN is an enumeration type defined in the package STANDARD, any enumeration type is a discrete type and any discrete type has these operations available in Ada (in the form of attributes).

Note that the above specification is monomorphic and specifies the flat CPO {true, false, ⊥}. Note further that **and then** and **or else** are the only non-strict functions in the Standard types.

5.1.2. INTEGER

The built-in type INTEGER is specified beolow.

```
package UNIVERSAL is
    type INTEGER is private;
    ZERO: INTEGER;
    SUCC, PRED, "-": INTEGER ==> INTEGER;
    axiom for all X: INTEGER =>
        SUCC (PRED X) = X, PRED (SUCC X) = X,
        - ZERO = ZERO, - (- X) = X,
        - PRED X = SUCC (- X), - SUCC X = PRED (- X);
    "-", "+", "*" : INTEGER × INTEGER ==> INTEGER;
    axiom for all X, Y: INTEGER =>
        X - Y = X + (- Y), X + ZERO = X,
        X + SUCC Y = SUCC (X+Y), X + PRED Y = PRED (X+Y),
        X * ZERO = ZERO,
        X * SUCC Y = X*Y+X, X * PRED Y = X*Y-X;
    "<": INTEGER × INTEGER ==> BOOLEAN;
    axiom for all X, Y: INTEGER =>
        (X < SUCC X) = true, (X < X) = false,
        (X < Y) = true -> (X < SUCC Y) = true,
        (X < Y) = true -> (Y < X) = false;
    "/", "rem" : (L, R: INTEGER:: R≠ZERO) ==> INTEGER;
    axiom for all X, Y: INTEGER =>
        Y≠ZERO -> X = (X/Y)*Y + X rem Y,
        (ZERO < Y) = true -> (X rem Y < Y) = true,
        X rem Y = X rem (-Y), (-X) rem Y = - (X rem Y);
    "**": (I, N: INTEGER:: (ZERO<N)=true ∨ (ZERO=N ∧ I≠ZERO)) ==> INTEGER;
    axiom for all X, Y: INTEGER:: ZERO<Y =>
        X≠ZERO -> X**ZERO = SUCC ZERO,
        ZERO ** Y = ZERO,
        X≠ZERO -> X**Y = X * (X ** PRED Y);
end UNIVERSAL;
```

The definition of this type is given indirectly here, using an auxiliary type UNIVERSAL.INTEGER that is not part of STANDARD - but it is used to specify the constrained types in STANDARD.

The main role of UNIVERSAL.INTEGER is to avoid the technical problems involved by a constraint number type. For example, "+" is defined now for the unconstrained case (without any restrictions) and its definedness for the constrained case is derived from the definedness of the construction: map the arguments to UNIVERSAL.INTEGER, add there and try to come back - and the last step may fail, because the result is too large or too small. The advantage of this approach is the absence of rather specific definedness predicates for all the arithmetic operations.

All numeric literals are constants of type INTEGER, considering the usual conventions for decimal numbers. All literals representing bigger numbers than LAST are undefined constants. The set of numeric literals is infinite, and so the set of constants is. As a consequence, their behaviour cannot be fully specified on the level of specification, because the literals are unstructured objects here.

The BOOLEAN constant ONES would be better a LOGICAL constant, but just for syntactical restrictions we have no. ONES=true means that the implementation of numbers uses ones complement. The only distinction from the user's point of view concerns the (un-)definedness of expressions like "-FIRST".

Note that UNIVERSAL.INTEGER is specified as the flat CPO $\mathbb{Z}+\{\bot\}$.

```
type INTEGER is private;
--: ONES: BOOLEAN;
--: IU: INTEGER --> UNIVERSAL.INTEGER;
FIRST, LAST: INTEGER;
axiom
      ONES = true <-> IU FIRST = UNIVERSAL."-" (IU LAST)
      ONES ≠ true <-> IU FIRST = UNIVERSAL.PRED (UNIVERSAL."-" (IU LAST));
--: UI: (U: UNIVERSAL.INTEGER::
      false = UNIVERSAL."<" (IU LAST, U) or UNIVERSAL."<" (U, IU FIRST)) ==> INTEGER;
axiom for all X: INTEGER; Y: UNIVERSAL.INTEGER =>
      UI (IU X) = X,
      defined UI Y -> IU (UI Y) = Y;
ZERO: INTEGER;
axiom IU ZERO = UNIVERSAL.ZERO;
SUCC: (X: INTEGER:: X≠LAST) ==> INTEGER;
PRED: (X: INTEGER:: X≠FIRST) ==> INTEGER;
"-": (X: INTEGER:: ONES=true v X≠FIRST) ==> INTEGER;
axiom for all X: INTEGER =>
      SUCC X = UI (UNIVERSAL.SUCC (IU X)),
      PRED X = UI (UNIVERSAL.PRED (IU X)),
      - X = UI (UNIVERSAL."-" (IU X));
```

It is typical for specifications using strong equality that sometimes the definedness-requirements (necessary for existential equality) can be left out, because often the left-hand side of an equation is defined, if and only if the right-hand side is. Therefore, the last three equations do not need any premises.

```
EQ, "<", "<=", ">", ">=": (INTEGER x INTEGER) ==> BOOLEAN;
axiom for all X,Y: INTEGER =>
        (X < Y) = UNIVERSAL."<"(IU X, IU Y),
        (X <= Y) = not (X > Y), (X > Y) = (Y < X), (X >= Y) = (Y <= X),
        EQ (X,Y) = (X <= Y and X >= Y);
"-": (X,Y: INTEGER:: defined UI (UNIVERSAL."-" (IU X, IU Y))) ==> INTEGER;
axiom for all X,Y: INTEGER => X - Y = UI (UNIVERSAL."-"(IU X, IU Y));
subtype NATURAL is (X: INTEGER:: (X >= ZERO) = true));
subtype POSITIVE is (X: INTEGER:: (X > ZERO) = true));
"+": INTEGER ==> INTEGER; axiom for all X: INTEGER => +X = X;
"abs": (X: INTEGER:: defined -X) ==> INTEGER;
axiom for all X: INTEGER => abs X = abs (- X), (X>=ZERO) = true -> abs X = X;
"+": (X,Y: INTEGER:: defined UI (UNIVERSAL."+" (IU X, IU Y))) ==> INTEGER;
"*": (X,Y: INTEGER:: defined UI (UNIVERSAL."*" (IU X, IU Y))) ==> INTEGER;
axiom for all X, Y: INTEGER =>
        X + Y = UI (UNIVERSAL."+"(IU X, IU Y)),
        X * Y = UI (UNIVERSAL."*"(IU X, IU Y));
"/", "rem", "mod": (X,Y: INTEGER:: Y≠ZERO) ==> INTEGER;
axiom for all X, Y: INTEGER:: Y≠ZERO =>
        X / Y = UI (UNIVERSAL."/" (IU X, IU Y)),
        X rem Y = UI (UNIVERSAL."rem" (IU X, IU Y)),
        (exists M: INTEGER => X = Y * M + X mod Y),
        (abs (X mod Y) < abs Y) = true,
        (Y < ZERO) = true ->  (X mod Y <= ZERO) = true,
        (Y > ZERO) = true ->  (X mod Y >= ZERO) = true;
```

5.1.3. STRING

The definition of the type STRING does not strictly follow the conventions of Ada, it is - to some extent - a mixture of Ada and SSL. The most significant difference is the lack of a component type, i.e. there is no type CHARACTER in PAnndA. Consequently, STRING is *not* an array type and there are no selection operators.

Any string literal has the type STRING, furthermore we have the following:

```
type STRING is private;
length: STRING ==> NATURAL;
"&": (X,Y: STRING:: defined length X+length Y) ==> STRING;
axiom for all X,Y: STRING =>
        length (X&Y) = length X + length Y,
        length "" = 0;
axiom for all X,Y,Z: STRING => (X & Y) & Z = X & (Y & Z);
axiom for all X: STRING => X & "" = X, "" & X = X;
```

A full specification of the behaviour of "&" cannot be given. The reason is just that any string literal is a constant of type STRING, moreover, literals are objects without structure and hence there is a infinite number of constants. Reasoning about these constants is only possible at meta-level. For the same reasons, all the other predefined functions on strings can only be specified partially.

```
"<", "<=", ">", ">=", EQ: STRING x STRING ==> BOOLEAN;
axiom for all V, X,Y,Z: STRING =>
        ("" <= X) = true, ((X <= "") = true <-> X=""),
        length X = length Y and (defined X&Z) and (defined Y & V) ->
                (X & Z <= Y & V) = (X < Y or (EQ(X,Y) and Z<=Y))
        (X>Y) = (Y<X), (X<Y) = not (Y<=X),
        (X>=Y) = (Y<=X), EQ(X,Y) = ((X<=Y) and (X>=Y)),
        (X<=Y and Y<=Z)=true -> (X<=Z) = true
        (X<=X) = true,
        EQ(X,Y)=true <-> X=Y;
```

The last axiom is the anti-symmetry of "<=". Note that "<=" in Ada is *not* anti-symmetric, because Ada has different kinds of empty strings.

For historical reasons, the following operations are still defined. In fact, they are completely superfluous now because we cannot index an element of a string.

```
first, last: STRING ==> NATURAL;
axiom for all X: STRING =>
first X = 1, last X = length X;
```

5.2. Type Schemata

In programming languages like Ada, new data types can be defined using type construction facilities like records, arrays, pointer etc. Types constructed this way can be expressed by algebraic specifications defining isomorphic types. Partially, the definition of those algebraic types can be done automatically, e.g. for record types and this semi-automatism is supported by the PAnndA-S editor.

The textual representation of algebraic types that correspond to Ada types is often quite lengthy. The reason is that the most types defined in the ordinary way have a lot of implicit operations with implicit properties. So the type schemata supported by the PROSPECTRA system abbreviate the task of easily implementable types and avoid the user problems of making oversights in large texts of specifications.

Caution! These type-schemata should only be applied to such types which are not defined by type expressions in which functional types occur. This restriction is explained by the first-order generation principle imposed on the models of a specification (see part I, chapter 2). Moreover, due to the requirement of monotonicity and continuity for functions in the semantic definition (see part I, chapter 3) the instantiation of the type schemata with actual types declared as subtypes of base types specifiedby non-strict operations has to be handled with care (as explained in the note in 5.2.2 below). The type schemata can safely be instantiated with subtypes declared in strict, first order specifications.

Any type schema has the following form:

```
type_schema ::=
    package package_identifier is
    private
        type_declaration
    end package_identifier;
```

The Ada-like type schemata are: enumeration types, pure record types, i.e. records without variants (products), pure variant record types, i.e. record types with one variant and without other components (coproducts) and one special way to define recursive types.

```
type_declaration ::=
    Enumeration_Type |
    Pure_Record_Type |
    Variant_Record_Type |
    Recursive_Variant_Type
```

In the following, these forms of `type_declaration` will be taken for short for a `type_schema` containing them.

Some remarks to the notation of the type schemata: keywords are written boldface. The syntax is expressed using an extended BNF. As usual, curly braces denote iteration, indices at the closing brace bind the iteration, i.e. $\{w\}_1^n$ means "1 up to n occurrences of w". Inside of iterations "||" is used to specify delimiters, e.g. $\{w \parallel ,\}_1^n$ means "1 up to n occurrences of w, separated by ','". An index i at a non-terminal inside such an expression accesses the ith instance of that non-terminal. To make clear which index belongs to which iteration (in the presence of nested iterations) the notation $\{w \parallel ,\}_{i=1}^n$ is used sometimes, introducing i as the loop index of this iteration.

Another way to distinguish several occurrences of one non-terminal is the use of *italic* prefixes to a non-terminal, as for example *package*`_identifier` above.

5.2.1. Enumeration Types

An enumeration type has the following form:

```
Enumeration_Type ::=
    type type_identifier is ( { enum_identifier_i || , }_1^n );
```

A type schema containing an enumeration type corresponds to the following specification:

```
Enumeration_Type_Specification ::=
    package package_identifier is
        type type_identifier is private;
        enum_functions
        enum_axioms
    end package_identifier;
```

The *package*`_identifier` here is the identifier of the type schema (package) containing the enumeration type. The *type*`_identifier` of the `Enumeration_Type_Specification` is the same as the *type*`_identifier` of the `Enumeration_Type`; in the following such correspondences are assumed without explicit mention.

```
enum_functions ::=
    { enum_identifier_i : type_identifier; }_1^n
    FIRST, LAST: type_identifier;
    POS: type_identifier ==> NATURAL;
    VAL: (I: NATURAL:: I <= package_identifier.POS(LAST)) ==>
        type_identifier;
    SUCC: (E: type_identifier :: E/=LAST) ==> type_identifier;
    PRED: (E: type_identifier :: E/=FIRST) ==> type_identifier;
    EQ, "<", "<=", ">", ">=" : (L,R: type_identifier) ==> BOOLEAN;
```

The n at the closing curly brace is the same n as in the syntax rule for `enumeration_type`. Furthermore, the ith *enum_identifier* there is the same as the ith *enum_identifier* in the syntax rule for `enumeration_type`.

```
enum_axioms::=
    axiom for all e,f : type_identifier =>
        { POS enum_identifier_i = PRED({ SUCC( }_1^i ZERO) { ) }_1^i }_1^n ,
        FIRST = enum_identifier_1,
        LAST = enum_idenitifier_n,
        VAL (POS e) = e,
        EQ (e,f) = (e <= f and f <= e),
        (e < f) = (POS e < POS f),
        (e > f ) = (f < e), (e <= f) = not (f < e), (e >= f) = (f <= e),
        SUCC e = VAL (SUCC (POS e)),
        PRED e = VAL (PRED (POS e));
```

Again, the n corresponds to the n of the iteration of `Enumeration_Type`. Notice that a syntax expression like "`{ ) }`$_i^i$" stands for precisely i closing parentheses.

5.2.2. Pure Record Types

Semantically, the record types in Ada are a mixture of products and coproducts, because variant parts and components can be intermixed. On the level of specification, products and coproducts should be distinguished and so it has been done here. `Pure_Record_Type` stands for the products:

```
Pure_Record_Type ::=
    type type_identifier is
        record
            { selector_identifier_i: type_expression_i; }_1^n
        end record;
```

The corresponding specification is as follows:

```
Pure_Record_Type_Specification ::=
    package package_identifier is
        type type_identifier is private;
        record_functions
        record_axioms
    end package_identifier;
```

The functions for a product type are product construction, the projections and an equality function based on the equality of the components. For the product construction operation a new identifier is necessary - it is generated by adding the prefix "`Construct_`" to the name of the type.

```
record_functions ::=
    EQ: type_identifier × type_identifier ==> BOOLEAN;
    Construct_type_identifier: ( { type_expression_i || × }_1^n ) ==>
        type_identifier;
    { selector_identier_i: type_identifier ==> type_expression_i ; }_1^n
record_axioms ::=
    axiom for all A, B: type_identifier =>
        EQ(A,B) =
        { EQ(selector_identifier_i A, selector_identifier_i B) || and }_1^n ;
    axiom for all { E_i: type_expression_i || ; }_1^n =>
        { selector_identifier_i(
            Construct_type_identifier ({ E_j ||,}_1^n)) = E_i ||,}_1^n;
```

The first axiomatic part specifies the equality of a product as the conjunction of the equalities on each component. Not all component types do necessarily have `EQ` operations. If one of the components has not, the composed type has not either - so the parts of the declaration and the axioms belonging to `EQ` are optional. In the PAnndA-S editor this optionality is represented by a transformation "- EQ-function" to remove this optional part.

The second axiomatic part consists of the projection axioms, i.e. the ith selector selects the ith component. The identifiers E_i are new, so E_i is an identifier, whose string consists of an E and the string of decimal digits representing the number i.

It is assumed that the E_i identifiers and `A` and `B` are distinct from the selector identifiers - the former should not hide the latter. Similar assumptions are made for the other type schemata.

Note:

Notice the use of the strong function arrow (see part I, chapter 3.4) in the above type schema. It has been chosen to obtain a monomorphic specification. The constructor operation is specified as a function from the product of the base types of the "actual types" (standing for the type_expressions) to the new type, such that it maps tuples $(x_1,...,x_n)$ to the undefined element (also called "bottom"), if for some i, $1 \leq i \leq n$, the following holds:

(i) the "actual type" standing for type_expression_i is declared as private and the definedness predicate yields false on x_i,

or

(ii) the "actual type" standing for type_expression_i is declared as a subtype and the characteristic predicate of this subtype yields false on x_i.

Hence if some of the actual types is declared as a subtype of a base type with a non-strict constructor operation (in other words: if this actual type is specified as a subset of a non-flat poset), then the following has to be observed: before application of the record construct it has to be checked that there exists a monotonic and continuous function which maps all those elements in the base type to bottom which are not contained in the actual subtype and leaves all the elements of the actual type fixed.

The above type schema can be applied safely if all the actual types are declared by private type declarations or are declared as subtypes (consisting of defined elements) of types with elements constructed by strict operations only (i.e. subtypes of types which may be interpreted by flat posets). Notice also, that only on types specified as flat posets the (strict extension) of the usual equality on defined elements is a monotonic function.

All these comments also apply to the type schemata in 5.2.3 and 5.2.4.

5.2.3. Variant Record Types

Variant record types correspond to coproducts. To avoid too strongly nested records and to handle the problem of coproducts with the empty type, coproducts of products are directly supported (and not only indirectly using `Pure_Record_Type`).

```
Variant_Record_Type ::=
    type type_identifier ( discriminant_identifier: type_expression ) is
        record
            case discriminant_identifier is
            { when choice_i =>
                { selector_identifier_ik : type_expression_ik; }_{k=1}^{m}
            | when choice_i => null; }_{i=1}^{n}
            end case;
        end record;
```

The corresponding specification is as follows:

```
Variant_Record_Type_Specification ::=
    package package_identifier is
        type type_identifier is private;
        variant_functions
        EQ_axioms
        choice_axioms
    end package_identifier;
```

The remarks about the equality on pure record types apply on variant record types too.

```
variant_functions ::=
    discriminant_identifier: type_identifier ==> type_expression;
    EQ: type_identifier × type_identifier ==> BOOLEAN;
    constructors
    selectors
```

The non-terminals `constructors` and `selectors` have iterations corresponding to the iterations used for `Variant_Record_Type`. The structure of the iteration is the same, e.g. the outer iteration has an alternative. Note that a **`null`** component does not have any selectors.

```
constructors ::=
    { Construct_type_identifier_i: ( { type_expression_ik || × }_k=1^m ) ==>
        type_identifier;
    | Construct_type_identifier_i: type_identifier; }_i=1^n
```

The above syntax rule makes clear that **null** components of a coproduct are nothing else than new constants of the new type.

```
selectors ::=
    {   { selector_identifier_ik:
              (X: type_identifier :: discriminant_identifier X = choice_i)
                  ==> type_expression_ik ; }_k=1^m
    |   }_i=1^n
```

There are three kinds of axioms, the axioms for EQ, the axioms to describe the behaviour of the *discriminant*_identifier and the projections, the axioms for the selectors.

```
EQ_axioms ::=
    axiom for all A,B: type_identifier =>
    {   EQ(discriminant_identifier A, choice_i) and
        EQ(discriminant_identifier B, choice_i) -> EQ(A,B) =
        { EQ(selector_identifier_ik A, selector_identifier_ik B)
        || and }_k=1^m
    |   EQ(discriminant_identifier A, choice_i) and
        EQ(discriminant_identifier B, choice_i) ->
        EQ(A,B) = true
    || , }_i=1^n ,
        not EQ(discriminant_identifier A, discriminant_identifier B) ->
            EQ(A,B) = false ;
```

The axioms for the *discriminant*_identifier and the projections have been grouped - for each choice one block of axioms.

```
choice_axioms ::=
    {   axiom for all { E_ik: type_expression_ik || ; }_k=1^m =>
            discriminant_axiom_i , selector_axioms_i ; }_i=1^n
discriminant_axiom_i ::=
    discriminant_identifier(
        Construct_type_identifier_i ({ E_ik||,}_k=1^m )) = choice_i
    | discriminant_identifier Construct_type_identifier_i = choice_i
```

```
selector_axioms_i ::=
    { selector_identifier_ik(
          Construct_type_identifier_i ({ E_ip||,}^m_p=1 )) = E_ik
    ||,}^m_k=1
```

5.2.4. Recursive Variant Types

Imperative programming languages in general and Ada in particular do not provide features to solve recursive type equations. Recursive types can be only expressed through pointers (access types). Therefore, a restricted use of pointer types (allowing tree-like structures) is supported:

```
Recursive_Variant_Type ::=
    type record_identifier (discriminant_identifier : type_expression);
    type type_identifier is access record_identifier;
    type record_identifier
        (discriminant_identifier : type_expression) is
        record
            case discriminant_identifier is
            { when choice_i =>
                { selector_identifier_ik : type_expression_ik; }^m_k=1
            | when choice_i => null; }^n_i=1
            end case;
        end record;
```

There is one important difference between the above schema and the schema in section 5.2.3 for `Variant_Record_Type`: among the $\texttt{type\_expression}_{ik}$ there could be occurrences of *type*`_identifier` which make the type recursive.

The corresponding specification is now:

```
Recursive_Variant_Type_Specification ::=
    package package_identifier is
        type type_identifier is private;
        discriminant_identifier: type_identifier ==> type_expression;
        constructors
        selectors
        choice_axioms
    end package_identifier;
```

The non-terminals `constructors`, `selectors` and `choice_axioms` are the same as described above for variant record types.

Note that there is no predefined function `EQ` for a recursive type (equality on access types is not a congruence relation). Consequently, (variant) record types having a component of a recursive type have no predefined `EQ` either - at least their created `EQ`-function should be removed using the mentioned transformation "- EQ-function".

```
selector_axioms ::=
  (selector_identifier_i ( [illegible]
    constructor_type_constr [illegible] ) = R_i
  )
```


In [illegible] programming languages, in contrast [illegible] particular [illegible] features to [illegible] recursive type constructs [illegible] pointer [illegible] target type [illegible] Therefore, a restricted use of [illegible] the following recursive structure is suggested:

6. TrafoLa-S Reference Manual

Pedro de la Cruz, Alcatel Standard Eléctrica S.A.

6.1. Introduction

TrafoLa-S is the language for specifying transformations in PROSPECTRA. Based on ideas from [Krieg-Brückner 1988], [Krieg-Brückner 1989] [Gersdorf 1989], it is an extension to $\mathrm{PA}^{\mathrm{nn}}{}_{\mathrm{d}}\mathrm{A}$-S (as defined in chapters 2 and 3 of part II) made by considering the abstract syntax of $\mathrm{PA}^{\mathrm{nn}}{}_{\mathrm{d}}\mathrm{A}$ (as described in chapters 4 and 5 of part II) as a predefined abstract data type (ADT for short). Briefly, the basic idea is to use essentially the same language ($\mathrm{PA}^{\mathrm{nn}}{}_{\mathrm{d}}\mathrm{A}$-S) for specifying the objects under development (specifications, programs) and developments (transformations) on these objects.

The main idea behind TrafoLa-S is that abstract syntax trees (ASTs for short) representing $\mathrm{PA}^{\mathrm{nn}}{}_{\mathrm{d}}\mathrm{A}$ specifications or programs can be considered as values of an ADT. Nonterminal symbols in the abstract grammar of $\mathrm{PA}^{\mathrm{nn}}{}_{\mathrm{d}}\mathrm{A}$ (e.g. Name, Expression, Declaration) correspond to sorts in the ADT, and for each production rule in the abstract grammar there is a constructor function in the ADT.

Taking this point of view, transformations on $\mathrm{PA}^{\mathrm{nn}}{}_{\mathrm{d}}\mathrm{A}$ objects (specifications of programs) are nothing but functions on the ADT of $\mathrm{PA}^{\mathrm{nn}}{}_{\mathrm{d}}\mathrm{A}$ ASTs. Both the ADT and the transformations can be specified algebraically. Therefore, $\mathrm{PA}^{\mathrm{nn}}{}_{\mathrm{d}}\mathrm{A}$-S can be used as a transformation specification language as well.

But specifying transformations in terms of the constructors of the abstract grammar of a language is very cumbersome. Transformation specifications may become large and almost ununderstandable. For this reason, $\mathrm{PA}^{\mathrm{nn}}{}_{\mathrm{d}}\mathrm{A}$-S is extended to allow "$\mathrm{PA}^{\mathrm{nn}}{}_{\mathrm{d}}\mathrm{A}$ phrases" (i.e. subtrees representing parts of a $\mathrm{PA}^{\mathrm{nn}}{}_{\mathrm{d}}\mathrm{A}$ program or specification) to be written using their concrete syntax (that is, their textual representation) as a particular kind of $\mathrm{PA}^{\mathrm{nn}}{}_{\mathrm{d}}\mathrm{A}$-S expression. The result is the PROSPECTRA transformation specification language, TrafoLa-S .

6.2. Canonical and Concrete Form of $\mathrm{PA}^{\mathrm{nn}}{}_{\mathrm{d}}\mathrm{A}$ Phrases

The abstract syntax of any language can be seen as an abstract data type. For each nonterminal symbol in the grammar, there is a sort in the signature of the ADT. For each production rule, there is a corresponding constructor function in the signature. To each AST representing the derivation of a nonterminal, there corresponds an expression in terms of the constructors of the ADT.

As an example, consider the $\mathrm{PA}^{\mathrm{nn}}{}_{\mathrm{d}}\mathrm{A}$ expression "$3+2=5$". The corresponding AST is shown in figure 6.1, and the expression denoting the corresponding value of the ADT in figure 6.2. Notice that prefix notation is used for operators in $\mathrm{PA}^{\mathrm{nn}}{}_{\mathrm{d}}\mathrm{A}$ expressions.

We will call ASTs corresponding to "fragments" of $\mathrm{PA}^{\mathrm{nn}}{}_{\mathrm{d}}\mathrm{A}$ programs or specifications "$\mathrm{PA}^{\mathrm{nn}}{}_{\mathrm{d}}\mathrm{A}$ phrases" (or simply "phrases"); $\mathrm{PA}^{\mathrm{nn}}{}_{\mathrm{d}}\mathrm{A}$-S expressions denoting ADT values corresponding to phrases, the "canonical form" of these phrases; and strings representing phrases in its textual form, the "concrete form" of phrases. Very often, we will use the word "phrase" (or "$\mathrm{PA}^{\mathrm{nn}}{}_{\mathrm{d}}\mathrm{A}$ phrase") both for the AST and for the corresponding ADT value.

We will denote phrases by enclosing their concrete form in "phrase brackets" ("$\lceil$","$\rfloor$"), and consider this as a particular notation for $\mathrm{PA}^{\mathrm{nn}}{}_{\mathrm{d}}\mathrm{A}$-S expressions denoting phrases. So, the phrase corresponding to the example can be denoted by the long $\mathrm{PA}^{\mathrm{nn}}{}_{\mathrm{d}}\mathrm{A}$ expression in figure 6.2 or by the much shorter "$\lceil 3+2=5 \rfloor$".

In the sequel, we will use the name "concrete form" to refer to this notation for phrases, including the brackets.

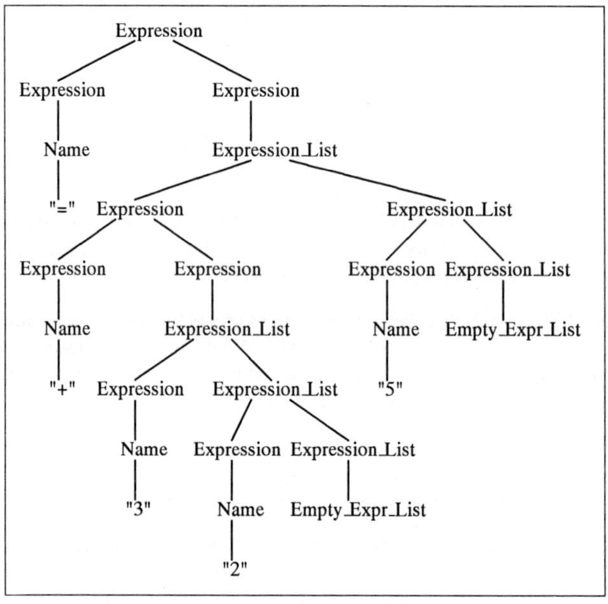

Figure 6.1: Abstract syntax tree for a simple PA$^{nn}{}_{d}$A expression: $3 + 2 = 5$

```
Mk_Call(
    Mk_Name(Mk_Unique_Name("=", "#L=", Mk_Polymorphic_Function_Nature)),
        Mk_Tuple(
            Mk_Expr_List(
                Mk_Call(
                    Mk_Name(Mk_Unique_Name("+", #Ib+", Mk_Predefined_Op_Nature)),
                        Mk_Tuple(
                            Mk_Expr_List(
                                Mk_Name(Mk_Unique_Name("3", #INT", Mk_Value_Nature)),
                            Mk_Expr_List(
                                Mk_Name(Mk_Unique_Name("2", #INT", Mk_Value_Nature)),
                            Empty_Expr_List)))),
            Mk_Expr_List( Mk_Name(Mk_Unique_Name("5", #INT", Mk_Value_Nature)),
            Empty_Expr_List)))
```

Figure 6.2: Expression denoting the ADT value for a simple PA$^{nn}{}_{d}$A expression: $3 + 2 = 5$

```
Mk_Call(
    Mk_Name(Mk_Unique_Name("=", "#L=", Mk_Polymorphic_Function_Nature)),
    Mk_Tuple(Mk_Expr_List(A, Mk_Expr_List(B, Empty_Expr_List))))
```

Figure 6.3: Canonical form of a simple phrase: $\lceil A = B \rfloor$

```
Mk_Call(
    Mk_Name (Mk_Unique_Name ("=", "#L=", Mk_Polymorphic_Function_Nature)),
    Mk_Tuple(
        Mk_Expr_List(
            Mk_Name (Mk_Unique_Name ("A", "17AB0@P", Mk_Declared_Function_Nature)),
        Mk_Expr_List(
            Mk_Name (Mk_Unique_Name ("B", "12CG4@P", Mk_Declared_Function_Nature)),
        Empty_Expr_List))))
```

Figure 6.4: Canonical form of a phrase with PA^nn^dA identifiers: $\lceil \underline{A} = \underline{B} \rfloor$

6.3. Embedded Identifiers and Expressions

Assume we are specifying a simple transformation applying the commutative law for the equality operator. We want to specify that, for any PA^nn^dA expressions A and B, the result of applying the transformation (let's call it "*Commute*") to an expression of the form "$A = B$", is another expression of the form "$B = A$". For this, we would write an axiom as

axiom for all A, B : *Expression* $\Rightarrow$ *Commute*$(\lceil A = B \rfloor) = \lceil B = A \rfloor$;

Consider the phrase in the left hand side of the axiom. Its canonical form is shown in figure 6.3.

The identifiers "A" and "B" stand for the quantified variables in the axiom, not for identifiers in the phrase. This is a general rule in TrafoLa-S : Identifiers inside phrases in concrete form always represent TrafoLa-S objects (variables or functions), and not identifiers in the phrase. We will call them "embedded identifiers".

Identifiers that are part of the phrase are denoted by underlining them (e.g. $\underline{A}$). So, if we want to specify that the precise PA^nn^dA identifiers "A" and "B" commute, we should write

axiom *Commute*$(\lceil \underline{A} = \underline{B} \rfloor) = \lceil \underline{B} = \underline{A} \rfloor$;

The canonical form of the phrase in the left hand side is shown in figure 6.4.

Assume now that we want to specify a transformation that recursively commutes all equalities in an expression (that is, it would transform an expression like "$A = B \rightarrow C = D$" into "$B = A \rightarrow D = C$". The specification will contain axioms like

axiom for all A, B : *Expression*; N : *Name* $\Rightarrow$
Commute$(\lceil A \rightarrow B \rfloor) = \lceil \{Commute(A)\} \rightarrow \{Commute(B)\} \rfloor$,
Commute$(\lceil A = B \rfloor) = \lceil \{Commute(B)\} = \{Commute(A)\} \rfloor$,
Commute$(\lceil N \rfloor) = \lceil N \rfloor$;

Consider the phrase in the right hand side of the first axiom. Of course, "*Commute*(B)" and "*Commute*(A)"

```
Mk_Call(
    Mk_Name(Mk_Unique_Name("-> ", "#L-> ", Mk_Predefined_Op_Nature)),
    Mk_Tuple(Mk_Expr_List(Commute(A), Mk_Expr_List(Commute(B), Empty_Expr_List))))
```

Figure 6.5: Canonical form of a phrase with embedded TrafoLa-S expressions

```
Mk_Call(Mk_Name(Mk_Unique_Name("-> ", "#L-> ", Mk_Predefined_Op_Nature)),
        Mk_Tuple(
            Mk_Expr_List(
                Mk_Call(Mk_Name(Mk_Unique_Name("Commute", "13BH9@P",
                                              Mk_Declared_Function_Nature)),
                        Mk_Name(Mk_Unique_Name("A", "17AB0@P",
                                              Mk_Declared_Function_Nature))),
            Mk_Expr_List(
                Mk_Call(Mk_Name(Mk_Unique_Name("Commute", "13BH9@P",
                                              Mk_Declared_Function_Nature)),
                        Mk_Name(Mk_Unique_Name("B", "12CG4@P",
                                              Mk_Declared_Function_Nature))),
            Empty_Expr_List))))
```

Figure 6.6: Canonical form of a phrase with many PA$^{nn}_{d}$A identifiers

are not part of the phrase, but TrafoLa-S expressions denoting values to be "inserted" at the given position in the phrase, much in the same way as embedded identifiers do. These expressions are called "embedded TrafoLa-S expressions", or simply "embedded expressions", and can be included in phrases in canonical form by enclosing them in curly braces. The canonical form of this phrase is shown in figure 6.5.

If we would like to specify that the particular identifiers "A" and "B" should be translated into the phrases "*Commute*(B)" and "*Commute*(A)", we should have written

$$\textbf{axiom}\ \mathit{Commute}(\lceil \underline{A} \rightarrow \underline{B} \rfloor) = \lceil \underline{\mathit{Commute}}(\underline{A}) \rightarrow \underline{\mathit{Commute}}(\underline{B}) \rfloor;$$

The canonical form of the phrase in the right hand side is shown in figure 6.6.

We will say that (the specification of) a transformation is in canonical (resp. concrete) form when all the phrases inside it are in canonical (resp. concrete) form. In appendix 6.A., both the canonical and concrete form of a simple transformation are given. By comparing their sizes, one can get a feeling of the compactness and expressive power of the concrete form of transformations, in comparison to the canonical form.

6.4. Context–Dependent Transformations and Context Notation

Assume we want to write a transformation that recursively commutes equalities among integer expressions, but only these. We could be tempted to write something like

Commute : *Expression* → *Expression*;
  axiom for all X, Y : *Expression* ⇒
    Type_Of(X) = ⌈*Predefined_Integer*⌋ **and** *Type_Of*(Y) = ⌈*Predefined_Integer*⌋ →

$$\mathit{Commute}(\lceil X = Y \rfloor) = \lceil \{\mathit{Commute}(Y)\} = \{\mathit{Commute}(X)\} \rfloor;$$

Consider the condition in the axiom, and in particular the function call "*Type_Of*(X)". The type of an expression can be determined very easily, if the expression involves some of the predefined operators, e.g.

$$\begin{array}{l} \textbf{axiom for all } X, Y : \mathit{Expression} \Rightarrow \\ \quad \mathit{Type\_Of}(\lceil X\ \{\mathit{Mk\_Unique\_Name}(" + ", "\#I + ", \mathit{Mk\_Predefined\_Op\_Nature})\}\ Y \rfloor) = \\ \qquad \lceil \mathit{Predefined\_Integer} \rfloor; \end{array}$$

But what about user-defined variable or function names?

$$\textbf{axiom for all } N : \mathit{Name} \Rightarrow \mathit{Type\_Of}(\lceil N \rfloor) = ???$$

The answer is that it is impossible in general to determine the type of an expression of such kind by simply inspecting it. The type of a variable or function name depends on its declaration. That is, the value of a function like "*Type_Of*" depends on the context in wich it is called, and so does a transformation like "*Commute*". We will call these functions and transformations "context–sensitive" or "context–dependent".

The problem can be overcome by providing such functions and transformations with an additional parameter carrying contextual information. Doing this, the specification of the transformation "*Commute*" would look like

$$\begin{array}{l} \mathit{Commute} : \mathit{Expression\_Context} \to \mathit{Expression} \to \mathit{Expression}; \\ \quad \textbf{axiom for all } C : \mathit{Expression\_Context}; X, Y : \mathit{Expression} \Rightarrow \\ \qquad \mathit{Type\_Of}(C)(X) = \lceil \mathit{Predefined\_Integer} \rfloor \textbf{ and } \mathit{Type\_Of}(C)(Y) = \lceil \mathit{Predefined\_Integer} \rfloor \to \\ \qquad\quad \mathit{Commute}(C)(\lceil X = Y \rfloor) = \lceil \{\mathit{Commute}(C)(Y)\} = \{\mathit{Commute}(C)(X)\} \rfloor; \end{array}$$

Notice that we have declared the context–dependent transformation as a curried function.

Analogously, "*Type_Of*" would be declared as

$$\mathit{Type\_Of} : \mathit{Expression\_Context} \to \mathit{Expression} \to \mathit{Name};$$

and the type of a variable or function name could be determined by searching the context.

Consider now the recursive calls to "*Commute*" in the left hand side of the axiom defining it. We have used the context of the original expression as the context for the subexpressions. This could work in this particular case, but not in general. Consider, for instance, a quantified expression. The context for the subexpressions in its kernel is clearly different from the context of the original expression. Or think on the context of the domain list in a quantified expression: it is even of a different type.

We could think of having a predefined set of functions deriving the context for the components of all constructors in the grammar, given the original context. Declarations for some of these functions are shown in figure 6.7. Using these functions, the transformation "*Commute*" can be specified with the right contexts, as shown in figure 6.8.

As it happened with transformations in canonical form, the notation is too cumbersome. Any useful transformation becomes tremendously long and almost unreadable. For this reason, a predefined, context-dependent operator representing the context of the phrase inmediately to its right is introduced. This operator is called "hat" and written "Λ". Using the "hat" operator, the specification of the transformation "*Commute*" would look like

$$\begin{array}{l} \mathit{Commute} : \mathit{Expression\_Context} \to \mathit{Expression} \to \mathit{Expression}; \\ \quad \textbf{axiom for all } X, Y : \mathit{Expression} \Rightarrow \\ \qquad \mathit{Type\_Of}\Lambda(X) = \lceil \mathit{Predefined\_Integer} \rfloor \textbf{ and } \mathit{Type\_Of}\Lambda(Y) = \lceil \mathit{Predefined\_Integer} \rfloor \to \end{array}$$

Select_Call_2: Expression_Context× (E:Expression:: Is_Mk_Call(E)) → Expression_Context;
Select_Tuple_1: Expression_Context× (E:Expression:: Is_Mk_Call(E))
→ Expression_List_Context;
Select_Expr_List_1: Expression_List_Context × (E:Expression_List :: Is_Mk_Expr_List(E))
→ Expression_Context;
Select_Expr_List_2: Expression_List_Context × (E:Expression_List :: Is_Mk_Expr_List(E))
→ Expression_List_Context;

Figure 6.7: Declarations of some context–dependent functions

axiom for all *C:Expression_Context; X,Y:Expression⇒*
Type_Of(C)(X)= ⌈ *Predefined_Integer*⌋ *and Type_Of(C)(Y)=* ⌈ *Predefined_Integer*⌋ →
Commute(C)(⌈ *X = Y* ⌋*) =*
⌈ {*Commute(Select_Expr_List_1(*
Select_Expr_List_2(Select_Tuple_1(Select_Call_2(C, ⌈ *X=Y* ⌋*),*
⌈ *(X,Y)* ⌋*),* ⌈ *X,Y* ⌋*),* ⌈ *Y* ⌋*)) (Y)* } =
{*Commute(Select_Expr_List_1(Select_Tuple_1(Select_Call_2(C,* ⌈ *X=Y* ⌋*),*
⌈ *(X,Y)* ⌋*),* ⌈ *X,Y* ⌋*)) (X)* } ⌋ ;

Figure 6.8: Specification of a context–dependent transformation with explicit context computation

$$Commute\Lambda(\lceil X = Y \rfloor) = \lceil\{Commute\Lambda(Y)\} = \{Commute\Lambda(X)\}\rfloor;$$

The "hat" operator can only appear in equations or conditional equations, and always in the context of a call to a context-dependent function. When it appears in the left hand side of an axiom, it represents the context of the phrase argument in the function call. When it appears in the condition or the right hand side, it represents the context of the (sub)phrase in the phrase argument in the left hand side that matches the phrase argument of the function call in the right hand side. Thus, the "Λ" in "$\Lambda(\lceil X = Y \rfloor$" represents the context of the expression with which the function "*Commute*" is called; the "Λ" in "$\Lambda(X)$" represents the context of the subexpression "X" in "$[X = Y]$".

A complete specification of a sample context-dependent transformation is given (in canonical form) in appendix 6.B..

6.5. The Abstract and Concrete Syntax of Phrases

The abstract syntax of phrases closely mirrors that of PA^{nn}dA, as described in chapters 4 and 5 of part II. For each nonterminal symbol in the abstract grammar of PA^{nn}dA, a corresponding nonterminal in the abstract grammar of phrases exists, and for each production in the grammar of PA^{nn}dA, a production for the corresponding symbol with corresponding components exists in the grammar of phrases.

In addition, a root symbol representing phrases is defined, with productions making a phrase from each of the symbols corresponding to symbols in the abstract grammar of PA^{nn}dA.

For each symbol in the grammar of phrases corresponding to a symbol in the abstract syntax of PA^{nn}dA, an additional production making the symbol in the phrase grammar from a PA^{nn}dA-S expression is included. These productions represent embedded TrafoLa-S expressions. Embedded identifiers are just a kind of embedded expressions.

Finally, two additional terminal symbols are included: PH_IDENTIFIER, representing PA$^{nn}_{d}$A identifiers in phrases (those denoted by underlining them), and HAT, representing the predefined "hat" operator ("Λ").

The full abstract syntax of phrases is given in [De la Cruz 1991] in the form of a PA$^{nn}_{d}$A-S package containing private types corresponding to symbols in the grammar and function declarations corresponding to the signatures of the constructors in the grammar.

The concrete syntax of phrases is a simplified version of the concrete syntax of PA$^{nn}_{d}$A-S as defined in chapter 3 of part II (PA$^{nn}_{d}$A-S Reference Manual), plus some extensions to handle the imperative part of PA$^{nn}_{d}$A and some symbols that do not exist in PA$^{nn}_{d}$A-S but are part of PA$^{nn}_{d}$A (object kinds, instantiation kinds, etc.). Also, for each nonterminal symbol corresponding to a symbol in the abstract grammar, two productions that allow parsing an identifier and an expression in curly braces as such nonterminal are added.

Lexical elements are basically the same as for PA$^{nn}_{d}$A-S. A few new reserved words (**aux**, **var** and **qvar**) have been introduced in order to make the concrete syntax for phrases corresponding to object kinds unambiguous.

The following symbols, that are part of the imperative part of PA$^{nn}_{d}$A but not of PA$^{nn}_{d}$A-S have been included as delimiters:

:= | .. << >>

Also, square brackets ("[" and "]") and curly braces ("{" and "}"), for enclosing phrases and embedded expressions respectively, and the circumphlex ("^"), to represent the "hat" operator ("Λ"), have been introduced.

All character and symbol replacements that are allowed in PA$^{nn}_{d}$A for publication purposes are allowed in phrases. Additionally, the following replacements are allowed:

<<	≪
>>	≫
[	⌈
]	⌋
^	Λ

PA$^{nn}_{d}$A identifiers embedded in phrases can be denoted by marking them with a leading underscore sign ("_"), instead of underlining them (e.g. "_foo" could be written instead of foo). A new lexical category (ph_identifier) has been defined to represent PA$^{nn}_{d}$A identifiers in phrases.

The full concrete syntax of phrases can be found in [De la Cruz 1991].

Appendixes.

6.A. Concrete and Canonical Form of a Sample Transformation

The following is the specification of a transformation that eliminates the "or" operation in a restricted subset of PA$^{nn}{}_{d}$A logical expressions: those composed only by names and the operators "and", "or" and "not". Fragments enclosed in square brackets are PA$^{nn}{}_{d}$A phrases inside TrafoLa-S text; fragments in curly braces are TrafoLa-S expressions inside PA$^{nn}{}_{d}$A phrases. All identifiers are TrafoLa-S identifiers. We ommit the applicability conditions of functions for simplicity.

```
with PAnndA;
package OR_TO_AND is
    Or_to_And: Expression ⟶ Expression;
    De_Morgan: Expression ⟶ Expression;
    Not_Elim: Expression ⟶ Expression;

axiom for all X:Expression; Y:Expression; V:Name ⇒

    De_Morgan (⌈X and Y⌋) = ⌈De_Morgan (X) and De_Morgan (Y)⌋,
    De_Morgan (⌈X or Y⌋)  = ⌈not (not De_Morgan (X) and not De_Morgan (Y))⌋,
    De_Morgan (⌈not X⌋)   = ⌈not De_Morgan (X)⌋,
    De_Morgan (⌈V⌋)       = ⌈V⌋,

                      Elim_Not (⌈not (not X)⌋) = Elim_Not (X),
                      Elim_Not (⌈X or Y⌋)      = ⌈Elim_Not (X) or Elim_Not (Y)⌋,
                      Elim_Not (⌈X and Y⌋)     = ⌈Elim_Not (X) and Elim_Not (Y)⌋,
    X ≠ ⌈not Y⌋ → Elim_Not (⌈not X⌋)         = ⌈not Elim_Not (X)⌋,
                      Elim_Not (⌈V⌋)           = ⌈V⌋,

    Or_to_And (X) = De_Morgan (Elim_Not (X));
end OR_TO_AND;
```

Note that, in the last axiom for De_Morgan, the brackets around V are not redundant. They are a way of "promoting" the Name "V" to the *Expression*⌈*V*⌋. The same is true for the last axiom for Elim_Not.

The following is the same specification in canonical form:

```
with PAnndA;
package OR_TO_AND is
  Or_to_And: Expression ⟶ Expression;
  De_Morgan: Expression ⟶ Expression;
  Not_Elim: Expression ⟶ Expression;

axiom for all X:Expression; Y:Expression; V:Name ⇒
  De_Morgan(Mk_Call(Mk_Name(Mk_Unique_Name("and", "#Land", Mk_Predefined_Op_Nature)),
              Mk_Tuple(Mk_Expr_List(X, Mk_Expr_List(Y, Empty_Expr_List))))) =
    Mk_Call(Mk_Name(Mk_Unique_Name("and", "#Land", Mk_Predefined_Op_Nature)),
              Mk_Tuple(Mk_Expr_List(De_Morgan(X), Mk_Expr_List(De_Morgan(Y), Empty_Expr_List)))),

  De_Morgan(Mk_Call(Mk_Name(Mk_Unique_Name("or", "#Lor", Mk_Predefined_Op_Nature)),
              Mk_Tuple(Mk_Expr_List(X, Mk_Expr_List(Y, Empty_Expr_List))))) =
    Mk_Call(Mk_Name(Mk_Unique_Name("not", "#Lnot", Mk_Predefined_Op_Nature)),
```

```
            Mk_Call(Mk_Name(Mk_Unique_Name("and", "#Land", Mk_Predefined_Op_Nature)),
              Mk_Tuple(Mk_Expr_List(
              Mk_Call(Mk_Name(Mk_Unique_Name("not", "#Lnot", Mk_Predefined_Op_Nature)),
                    De_Morgan(X)),
              Mk_Expr_List(Mk_Call(Mk_Name(Mk_Unique_Name("not", "#Lnot",
                                   Mk_Predefined_Op_Nature)),
                      De_Morgan(Y)), Empty_Expr_List)))),

  De_Morgan(Mk_Call(Mk_Name(Mk_Unique_Name("not", "#Lnot", Mk_Predefined_Op_Nature)), X)) =
     Mk_Call(Mk_Name(Mk_Unique_Name("not", "#Lnot", Mk_Predefined_Op_Nature)),
            De_Morgan(X)),

  De_Morgan(Mk_Name(V)) = Mk_Name(V),

  Elim_Not(Mk_Call(
        Mk_Name(Mk_Unique_Name("not", "#Lnot", Mk_Predefined_Op_Nature)),
        Mk_Call(Mk_Name(Mk_Unique_Name("not", "#Lnot", Mk_Predefined_Op_Nature)), X))) =
     Elim_Not(X),

  Elim_Not(Mk_Call(Mk_Name(Mk_Unique_Name("or", "#Lor", Mk_Predefined_Op_Nature)),
           Mk_Tuple(Mk_Expr_List(X, Mk_Expr_List(Y, Empty_Expr_List))))) =
     Mk_Call(Mk_Name(Mk_Unique_Name("or", "#Lor", Mk_Predefined_Op_Nature)),
           Mk_Tuple(Mk_Expr_List(Elim_Not(X), Mk_Expr_List(Elim_Not(Y), Empty_Expr_List)))),

  Elim_Not(Mk_Call(
        Mk_Name(Mk_Unique_Name("and", "#Land", Mk_Predefined_Op_Nature)),
        Mk_Tuple(Mk_Expr_List(X, Mk_Expr_List(Y, Empty_Expr_List))))) =
     Mk_Call(
        Mk_Name(Mk_Unique_Name("and", "#Land", Mk_Predefined_Op_Nature)),
        Mk_Tuple(Mk_Expr_List(Elim_Not(X), Mk_Expr_List(Elim_Not(Y), Empty_Expr_List)))),

X ≠ Mk_Call(Mk_Name(Mk_Unique_Name("not", "#Lnot", Mk_Predefined_Op_Nature)), Y) →
  Elim_Not(Mk_Call(Mk_Name(Mk_Unique_Name("not", "#Lnot", Mk_Predefined_Op_Nature)), X)) =
    Mk_Call(Mk_Name(Mk_Unique_Name("not", "#Lnot", Mk_Predefined_Op_Nature)), Elim_Not(X)),

  Elim_Not(Mk_Name(V)) = Mk_Name(V),

  Or_to_And(X) = De_Morgan(Elim_Not(X));
end OR_TO_AND;
```

6.B. A Context–Dependent Transformation

In this appendix, a full specification of a context–dependent transformation that recursively commutes equalities between integer expressions is given. First, a context–dependent function that computes the type of an expression is specified, assuming a predefined context–dependent function that returns the type of a Name in a given context is available.

For logical expressions (quantified expressions, membership tests) the empty type is returned. Tuple expressions with all components being logical expressions, that are a particular case of logical expressions, are correctly managed. For range expressions, as well as for the empty expression, the function remains unspecified.

Auxiliary functions for propagating "*Commute*" into declaration lists, etc., are not specified, in order to keep the example of a reasonable size.

```
with PAnndA,Context;
package TYPE_OF is
   Type_Of:  Expression_Context ⟶
             (X:Expression :: X≠⌈⌋,
             for all A,B:Expression; T:Type_Expression ⇒ X≠⌈range T⌋, X≠⌈A..B⌋)
             ⟶ Type_Expression
--: Type_Of: Expression_List_Context ⟶ X:Expression_List ⟶ Type_List;

axiom for all F,X,Y,Z: Expression; S, T: Type_Expression; L: Expression_List;
             D: Declaration_List; Q: Quantifier; N: Name ⇒

   Type_Of Λ(⌈N⌋) = Type_Of Λ(N),                       -- Basic Case (Name)
   Type_Of Λ(F)=⌈S⟶T⌋ → Type_Of Λ(⌈F(X)⌋) = T,         -- Function Call
   Type_Of Λ(⌈if X then Y else Z end if⌋) = Type_Of Λ(Y),-- Conditional
   Type_Of Λ(L)≠⌈⌋ → Type_Of Λ(⌈(L)⌋) = ⌈{Type_Of Λ(L)}⌋Tuple

-- Logical Expressions:
   Type_Of Λ(⌈Q D ⇒ L⌋) = ⌈⌋,                            -- Quantified Expression
   Type_Of Λ(⌈X ∈ N⌋) = ⌈⌋,                              -- Membership Test
   Type_Of Λ(F)=⌈⌋ → Type_Of Λ(⌈F(X)⌋) = ⌈⌋,             -- Predicate Call
   Type_Of Λ(L)=⌈⌋ → Type_Of Λ(⌈(L)⌋) = ⌈⌋,              -- Tuple
-- Axioms for expression lists
   Type_Of Λ(⌈⌋) = ⌈⌋,
   Type_Of Λ(X)=⌈⌋ → Type_Of Λ(X & L) = ⌈⌋,
   Type_Of Λ(X)≠⌈⌋ → Type_Of Λ(X & L) = Type_Of Λ(X) & Type_Of Λ(L);
end TYPE_OF;
```

with *PAnndA, Context, Type_Of;*
package *COMMUTE* **is**
Commute: Expression_Context ⟶ *Expression* ⟶ *Expression;*
Commute: Expression_List_Context ⟶ *Expression_List* ⟶ *Expression_List;*

axiom for all
F,X,Y,Z: Expression; L: Expression_List; D: Declaration_List; Q: Quantifier; N: Name ⇒

-- Basic Case
Type_Of Λ*(X)*=⌈*Predefined_Integer*⌋ **and** *Type_Of* Λ*(Y)*=⌈*Predefined_Integer*⌋ →
Commute Λ*(*⌈*X* = *Y*⌋*)* = ⌈{*Commute* Λ*(Y)*} = {*Commute* Λ*(X)*}⌋,

-- Termination Cases
Commute Λ*(*⌈⌋*)* = ⌈⌋,
Commute Λ*(*⌈*N*⌋*)* = ⌈*N*⌋,
Commute Λ*(*⌈**range** *N*⌋*)* = ⌈**range** *N*⌋,

-- Equality among non-integer expressions
Type_Of Λ*(X)*≠⌈*Predefined_Integer*⌋ **or** *Type_Of* Λ*(Y)*≠⌈*Predefined_Integer*⌋ →
Commute Λ*(*⌈*X* = *Y*⌋*)* = ⌈{*Commute* Λ*(X)*} = {*Commute* Λ*(Y)*}⌋,

-- Function/Predicate Call other than equality
F≠⌈=⌋ → *Commute* Λ*(*⌈*F(X)*⌋*)* = ⌈{*Commute* Λ*(F)*}({*Commute* Λ*(X)*})⌋,

-- Quantified Expression
Commute Λ*(*⌈*Q D* ⇒ *L*⌋*)* = ⌈*Q* {*Propagate* Λ*(D)*} ⇒ {*Commute* Λ*(L)*}⌋,

-- Membership Test
Commute Λ*(*⌈*X* ∈ *N*⌋*)* = ⌈{*Commute* Λ*(X)*} ∈ *N*⌋,

-- Conditional Expression
Commute Λ*(*⌈**if** *X* **then** *Y* **else** *Z* **end if** ⌋*)* =
⌈**if** {*Commute* Λ*(X)*} **then** {*Commute* Λ*(Y)*} **else** {*Commute* Λ*(Z*}*)* **end if** ⌋,

-- Tuple
Commute Λ*(*⌈*(L)*⌋*)* = ⌈({*Commute* Λ*(L)*})⌋,

-- Range with bounds
Commute Λ*(*⌈*X..Y*⌋*)* = ⌈{*Commute* Λ*(X)*} .. {*Commute* Λ*(Y)*}⌋,

-- Propagation into expression lists
Commute Λ*(*⌈⌋*)* = ⌈⌋,
Commute Λ*(X & L)* = *Commute* Λ*(X)* & *Commute* Λ*(L);*

end *COMMUTE;*

7. ControLa Reference Manual

Alain Marcuzzi, Syseca Logiciel
(revised by Berthold Hoffmann and Junbo Liu, Universität Bremen)

This chapter describes ControLa, the language for global user interaction with the PROSPECTRA System. For uniformity ControLa has been designed as an executable subset of the PAnndA-S language which is defined in part II, chapters 2 - 4.

7.1. Introduction

7.1.1. Scope

ControLa-C (where C stands for *Canonical*) is the language for global user interaction with the PROSPECTRA System. For uniformity ControLa has been designed as an executable subset of the PAnndA-S language (see part II, chapters 2-4) in every aspect:

- ControLa-C has a simplified *syntax*. The constructions of PAnndA-S that are not needed for system development are not included in the ControLa-C subset: ControLa-C packages have no private parts, and logical expressions have been specialized to conditional equations.

- Although ControLa-C programs satisfy the PAnndA-S *static semantics*, it has been designed to formulate developments on predefined system objects only; so the context conditions have been specialized for the semantics of those objects.

- As far as the *dynamic semantics* is concerned, ControLa-C is an applicative subset of PAnndA-S. All specification aspects have been excluded or adapted to provide an executable language. It describes developments in terms of system state transitions.

This chapter describes the syntactic and static semantic aspects of the subset.

7.1.2. Definition Method and Notation

The definition method follows that of the PAnndA-S Reference Manual (see part II, chap. 2). Since ControLa-C is a subset of PAnndA-S, the definitions given here restrict the syntactic and static semantics of PAnndA-S to formulate ControLa-C constructs. The following paragraphs formulate these aspects.

Syntactic Restrictions
The restrictions wrt. the full concrete syntax of PAnndA-S are given informally.

Concrete Syntax
The concrete syntax of ControLa-C is a specialisation of the PAnndA-S syntax.

Semantical Restrictions
This part expresses informally the static semantic restrictions of ControLa-C wrt. PAnndA-S.

Comments
These comments precise those given in the PAnndA-S Reference Manual.

7.2. Lexical Elements

Lexical elements are essentially the same as in PAnndA-S, to ensure bottom-up compatibility. Since not all operations of PAnndA-S are allowed in ControLa-C, some operators, and also some separators may not appear in the ControLa-C programs. These are:

```
delimiters           : ' !
compound delimiters  : <-> ** --:
graphic sequences    : .
```

See the PAnndA-S Manual for the definitions of identifier, literal, and comment.

7.3. Declarations and Types

7.3.1. Declarations

Syntactical Restrictions

ControLa-C has no type and subtype declarations. Only the types from the predefined packages STANDARD and STANDARDC are available. Only *functions* and *axioms* may be declared in a package.

Concrete Syntax

```
declaration ::= function_declaration
              | axiom
```

Semantical Restrictions

Generic units, and *generic formal parameters* are no entities of ControLa-C. The user-declared and standard entities of the language can be a type, a subtype, a function, a package, a domain or an operation. Among these entities only *packages*, *functions* and *axioms* can be declared explicitly.

7.3.2. Types and Subtypes

The types of ControLa-C include the predefined types of PAnndA-S, namely

```
standard_type ::= INTEGER | BOOLEAN | STRING
```

(see also part II, chap. 5). Two additional types are provided by the package STANDARDC:

- A type STATE representing the *system state*.
- A type TREE representing *untyped trees*.

Subtype declarations are not allowed in ControLa-C. Moreover, the standard subtypes POSITIVE and NATURAL are not legal in ControLa-C.

However, the standard package STANDARDC provides one functional subtype SCRIPT of *state transitions*:

```
subtype SCRIPT is STATE --> STATE;
```

Four classes of ControLa functions are distinguished:

- *Pure functions* have only standard types as arguments and results.

  standard_type { # standard_type } --> standard_type

- *Constructor functions* have results of type `TREE`, and standard types or the type `TREE` as arguments. Constructor functions cannot be explicitly declared within a ControLa-C package:

  (standard_type | `TREE`) { # (standard_type | `TREE`) } --> TREE

- *Selection functions* have an optional list of standard type arguments, and an argument of type `STATE`; their result is of a standard type or of the type `TREE`:

  standard_type { # standard_type } # `STATE` --> (standard_type | `TREE`)

- *Script functions* are state transition functions, with an optional list of further arguments of a standard type or of type `TREE`:

  (standard_type | `TREE`) { # (standard_type | `TREE`) } --> `SCRIPT`

7.3.3. Type Expressions

Syntactic Restrictions

Domains must be given without subtype restrictions, i.e. without where clauses. Instead, all restrictions have to be placed in the axioms. Only type expressions in the form of subtype names can be extended by a bottom element.

Concrete Syntax

```
type_expression::=
                  function_type_expression
              |   tuple_type_expression

function_type_expression ::=
                  tuple_type_expression '-->' type_expression

tuple_type_expression ::=
                  extended_type_expression { '#' extended_type_expression }

extended_type_expression ::=
              |   '(' subtype_name ')' '+'
              |   subtype_expression

subtype_expression ::=
                  subtype_name
              |   '(' domain ')'
              |   '(' type_expression ')'

domain     ::=  designator_list ':' type_expression

designator_list::=designator { , designator }
```

Semantic Restrictions

Function type expressions must denote pure function, selection function or script function subtypes. In particular, the result type of a function cannot be extended with the undefined element.

7.4. Names and Expressions

7.4.1. Names

Syntactic Restrictions

ControLa-C allows only identifiers to be declared, so the only operator symbols are predefined

Concrete Syntax

```
name        ::= designator
              | name . designator

designator  ::= identifier
              | operator_symbol
```

7.4.2. Expressions

Syntactic Restrictions

ControLa-C has no *type conversion*, *qualified expression* and *tuple expressions.*

Concrete Syntax

```
expression ::= relation
             | relation and relation
             | relation or  relation

relation   ::= simple_expression [ relational_operator simple_expression ]

simple_expression ::= [unary_adding_operator] term { binary_adding_operator term }

term       ::= factor { multiplying_operator factor }

factor     ::= { not } secondary

secondary  ::= primary
             | function_call
             | functional_expression

primary    ::= numeric_literal
             | string_literal
             | ( expression )
```

7.4.3. Operators

Syntactic Restrictions

The logical operator **xor**, the multiplying operators **mod** and **rem**, and the highest precedence operators ** and **abs** are not allowed.

Concrete Syntax

```
logical_operator         ::= and | or

relational_operator      ::= < | <= | > | >=

binary_adding_operator   ::= + | - | &
```

```
unary_adding_operator         ::=  + | -

multiplying_operator          ::=  * | /

highest_precedence_operator ::= not
```

Comments

The binary operators & and * have been overloaded in the package STANDARDC by the *reverse composition* operation, and the *conditional* operation on scripts, resp. (see section 7.9 for their semantics):

```
"&"  : SCRIPT+ # SCRIPT+ --> SCRIPT;
"/"  : SCRIPT+ # SCRIPT+ --> SCRIPT;
```

See section 7.9 for their semantics.

7.4.4. Logical Expressions or Equations

Logical expressions in ControLa-C differ a lot in their construction and in their meaning from those of PAnndA-S since they are be understood as *applicative*, not as predicative constructs. For that reason, we call them 'equations' in ControLa_C.

7.4.4.1. Equations

Syntactic Restrictions

There is no notion of existential quantification. Equations can be quantified only on the outermost level of axioms.

Concrete Syntax

```
equation  ::= for all domain { ; domain } => simple_equation { , simple_equation }
              | simple_equation
              | ( equation { , equation } )
```

7.4.4.2. Simple Equations

Syntactic Restrictions

Simple equations are conditional equations. There is no notion of equivalence. The definedness predicate can only be used as an atomic condition. Its operand is a designator.

Concrete Syntax

```
simple_equation ::= condition -> simple_equation
                  |condition -> ( simple_equation { ,simple_equation } )
                  |  pure_equation

condition ::=  logical_formula
             | defined_argument
             | others

defined_argument ::=
                defined ( argument_designator )
```

Semantic Restrictions

The designator subject to the definedness predicate must denote a quantified variable appearing as one of the formal parameters of the function being defined (i.e. the function on the left-hand side of a pure equation, see below).

No expression denoting a value of type `SCRIPT` can appear on the left-hand side of a conditional equation.

No expression denoting a value of type `STATE` can appear in an expression on the left-hand side of a conditional expression unless it is a simple name denoting a quantified variable. No expression or subexpression denoting a value of type `STATE` can appear in a pattern expression on the left-hand side of a conditional equation.

7.4.4.3. Pure Equations

Syntactic Restrictions

A pure equation associates a value to a function with particular parameters. These parameters must be pattern expressions.

Concrete Syntax

```
pure_equation ::= function_call_with_patterns = expression
```

Semantic Restrictions

The pattern expression associated to a formal parameter whose type is extended with the undefined value, must be a simple name.

7.4.4.4. Logical Formulas

Syntactic Restrictions

The operators **and then**, **or else**, **xor** are not allowed.

Concrete Syntax

```
logical_formula ::=
            logical_formula { and logical_formula }
          | logical_formula { or logical_formula }
          | not logical_formula
          | logical_primary
```

7.4.4.5. Logical Relations

Syntactic Restrictions

There is no inclusion expression.

Concrete Syntax

```
logical_primary ::= expression =  pattern_expression
                  | expression /= pattern_expression
                  | ( logical_formula )
```

Semantic Restrictions

Expressions denoting a value of type TREE can only appear:

- on the right-hand side (the pattern expression) of a relation,
- on the left-hand side of a relation, provided it is a simple name denoting a quantified variable on the result of an application of the predefined selection functions to a STATE argument.
- on the right-hand side of a pure equation, provided it is a simple name denoting a quantified variable.

7.4.4.6. Pattern Expressions

Concrete Syntax

```
pattern_expression ::=
            simple_name
          | literal
          | constructor_name ( pattern_expression { , pattern_expression } )
```

Semantic Restrictions

Literals in pattern expressions are of type INTEGER, STRING or BOOLEAN. Constructors are functions whose result type is TREE.

7.5. Functions and Functional Expressions

7.5.1. Function Declarations

Syntactic Restrictions

The designator part is an identifier, no operator. Predicates are not legal constructs of the language.

Concrete Syntax

```
function_declaration  ::= function_kind domain ;

function_kind         ::= [--:]

designator            ::= identifier
```

Semantic Restrictions

The same function identifier can be overloaded by several function specifications as in PAnndA-S, although not in the same package.

7.5.2. Function Calls

Syntactic Restrictions

The curried form of a function call is restricted to a depth of two curried arguments, the second one being a singleton. The function name cannot include operator symbols.

Concrete Syntax

```
function_call ::= function_name [ ( expression { , expression } ) [ ( expression ) ] ]
```

Semantic Restrictions

The base type of the second curried actual argument (if it exists) must be the type STATE. The base type of the function applied to the first curried actual argument (if the second exists) must be the function type SCRIPT.

Expressions appearing in actual parameters of a function call cannot be themselves function calls unless they denote a value of type SCRIPT. The application of an operator to its operands, or of a constructor pattern is not considered as a function call.

7.5.3. Functional Expressions

Concrete Syntax

```
functional_expression  ::= ( functional_term  script_operator functional_term ) ( expression )

functional_term        ::= functional_term script_operator functional_term
                         | function_call

script_operator        ::= & | /
```

Semantic Restrictions

The script operators are the predefined operators & and / acting on SCRIPT values. The base type of a functional term must be the functional type SCRIPT. The base type of the second curried argument of a functional expression must the type STATE.

7.6. Packages

7.6.1. Package Declarations

Syntactic Restrictions

A package declaration contains no private part. Moreover, it cannot be declared locally, in the declarative region of another package declaration.

Concrete Syntax

```
package_declaration ::= package_specification ;

package_specification ::=
        package identifier is
           { declaration }
        end [ package_identifier ]
```

7.6.2. Axioms

Syntactic Restrictions

The bodies of axioms must be equations.

Concrete Syntax

```
axiom  ::= axiom equation { , equation } ;
```

7.7. Visibility Rules

7.7.1. Declarative Items

Declarative items in ControLa-C are restricted to:

- function declarations
- package declarations
- axiom declarations
- domains without restriction of the form "designator: simple_type_expression".
- an implicit declaration of a predefined operator

7.7.2. Homographs

The definition of homographs in ControLa-C is a restriction of the PAnndA-S definition.

Each of two declarative items is said to be a homograph of the other if both declarative items have the same designator. No special case is made for overloadable items. The following context condition must hold:

> Two declarative items that occur immediately within the same declarative region must not be homographs.

7.8. Program Structure

7.8.1. Compilation Units and Library Units

Syntactic Restrictions
Generic declarations and instantiations are not allowed.

Concrete Syntax

```
compilation_unit ::= context_clause library_unit

library_unit     ::= package_declaration
```

7.8.2. Context Clauses - With Clauses

Concrete Syntax

```
context_clause   ::= [ with_clause ]

with_clause      ::= with unit_identifier [ , unit_identifier ] ;
```

7.9. Predefined Language Environment

The predefined entities in ControLa-C include those of PAnndA-S. In addition, a more system-oriented environment is specified in the predefined package `STANDARDC`.

The predefined package `STANDARDC` uses PAnndA-S to define the types and operators necessary to express system developments. `STANDARDC` is like any other package. Any program satisfying the syntactic and semantic restrictions of ControLa-C should reference it by a with clause. Below is a definition of STANDARDC. This definition is not complete. It would include all the definitions of the primitive commands of the CSG.

```
package STANDARDC is
    type TREE is private;          -- Untyped trees (No operations)
    type STATE is private;         -- Editor state

-- some predefined selection functions
    Context: STATE --> TREE;
    Selection: STATE --> TREE;
    ErrorFlag: STATE --> BOOLEAN;

   -- State transition
    subtype SCRIPT is STATE --> STATE;

   -- Reverse Composition
    "&" : SCRIPT+ # SCRIPT+ --> SCRIPT;

   -- Conditional evaluation
    "/" : SCRIPT+ # SCRIPT+ --> SCRIPT;

   axiom for all
         S: STATE; A: SCRIPT+; B: SCRIPT+ =>
        -- Extensional equalities
        -- Note that a state is always defined
         (A & B)(S) = B(A(S)),
         ErrorFlag(S) = TRUE -> (A/B)(S) = A(S),
         ErrorFlag(S) = FALSE -> (A/B)(S) = B(S);
    end STANDARDC;
```

7.10. The ControLa-C Concrete Syntax

```
compilation_unit ::=
    context_clause library_unit

library_unit ::=
    package_declaration

context_clause ::=
    [ with_clause ]

with_clause ::=
    with unit_identifier [ , unit_identifier ] ;

package_declaration ::=
    package_specification ;

package_specification ::=
    package identifier is
        { declaration }
    end [ package_identifier ]

declaration ::=
    function_declaration
  | axiom

axiom ::=
    axiom equation { , equation } ;

type_expression::=
    function_type_expression
  | tuple_type_expression

function_type_expression ::=
    tuple_type_expression '-->' type_expression

tuple_type_expression ::=
    extended_type_expression
        { '#' extended_type_expression }

extended_type_expression ::=
  | '(' subtype_name ')' '+'??????????????
  | subtype_expression

subtype_expression ::=
    subtype_name
  | '(' domain ')'
  | '(' type_expression ')'

domain ::=
    designator_list ':' type_expression

designator_list::=
    designator { , designator }

name ::=
    designator
  | name . designator

designator::=
    identifier
  | operator_symbol
```

```
expression ::=
    relation
  | relation and relation
  | relation or  relation

relation ::=
    simple_expression
        [ relational_operator simple_expression ]

simple_expression ::=
    [unary_adding_operator] term
        { binary_adding_operator term }

term ::=
    factor { multiplying_operator factor }

factor ::=
    { not } secondary

secondary ::=
    primary
  | function_call
  | functional_expression

primary ::=
    numeric_literal
  | string_literal
  | ( expression )

logical_operator::=and | or

relational_operator::=< | <= | > | >=

binary_adding_operator::=+ | - | &

unary_adding_operator::=+ | -

multiplying_operator::=* | /

highest_precedence_operator ::=not

equation ::=
    for all domain { ; domain }
        => simple_equation { , simple_equation }
  | simple_equation
  | ( equation { ,equation } )

simple_equation ::=
    condition -> simple_equation
  | condition
        -> ( simple_equation { ,simple_equation } )
  | pure_equation

condition ::=
    logical_formula
  | defined_argument
  | others
```

```
defined_argument ::=
    defined ( argument_designator )

pure_equation::=
    function_call_with_patterns = expression

logical_formula ::=
    logical_formula { and logical_formula }
  | logical_formula { or  logical_formula }
  | not logical_formula
  | logical_primary

logical_primary ::=
    expression =pattern_expression
  | expression /=pattern_expression
  | ( logical_formula )

pattern_expression ::=
    simple_name
  | literal
  | constructor_name
    ( pattern_expression { ,  pattern_expression } )

function_declaration ::=
    function_kind domain ;

function_kind ::= [--:]

designator ::=identifier

function_call ::=
    function_name [ ( expression { , expression } )
        [ ( expression ) ] ]

functional_expression ::=
    ( functional_term  script_operator
        functional_term ) ( expression )

functional_term ::=
    functional_term script_operator functional_term
  | function_call

script_operator ::= & | /
```

8. TrafoLa-H Reference Manual

Reinhold Heckmann, Georg Sander, Universität des Saarlandes

This chapter describes the transformation language TrafoLa-H of the PROSPECTRA system. It supports the definition of tree transformations as well as of transformation strategies. TrafoLa-H is mainly a functional language. Tree transformations are specified by first-order functions, whereas strategies may be defined by functions of higher order.
The first sections of this chapter define the constructs of TrafoLa-H by a simple denotational semantics, and illustrate them by many examples. The description is focused on the particularly powerful patterns of TrafoLa-H. The most advanced pattern operator allows to match and extract specific subtrees at arbitrary depth.
Then the type system of the language is described. It is derived from a conventional Hindley-Milner type system, but is more complex due to the operations of tree extraction and insertion. The chapter is concluded by a summary of the concrete syntax and the predefined system functions.

8.1. Introduction

In PROSPECTRA, a formal specification is gradually transformed into an optimized executable program by the stepwise application of individual transformation rules, or of transformation scripts systematically invoking such rules. The language TrafoLa-H for writing transformation scripts and rules is designed in a functional style since transformations are functions in some tree domain, and scripts may use higher order functions constructed from transformations and function composition.

The design of the transformation language TrafoLa-H has been based on the functional languages Hope [Burstall et al. 80], SML [Milner 85], and Miranda [Turner 85], which are quite similar with respect to their functional kernel. They all admit only very restricted forms of pattern matching. Patterns may be used to match some fixed region near the root of a term and to select subtrees adjacent to this region. Thus it is neither possible to specify the region for a match, nor to refer to a subtree whose root is far from the root of the whole tree, nor to bind the context of such a subtree to a variable.

In these languages, sequences are represented as trees, and thus their treatment is always biased toward their leftmost item. Patterns only allow to select a fixed number of items at the left end of the sequence. It is impossible to directly access items from the middle or the rear of a sequence. This restricted form of pattern matching seemed to be inappropriate for a language designed for specifying transformations at arbitrary subtrees.

Thus, TrafoLa-H has been developed by increasing the power of patterns compared to Hope, SML, and Miranda. Non-determinism is allowed to ease the description — the user need only specify the shape of the subtree he/she wants to select, not where or how such a subtree is to be found (although this is also possible). The resulting set of solutions is handled either by selecting one and discarding all others, or by considering all solutions in an arbitrary order.

TrafoLa-H is a statically typed language. There is a system to classify the objects on which the language operates. There are also language constructs to specify this classification. TrafoLa-H source code is compiled into code for an abstract machine. The compiler is described in part III, section 5.3. The compiler includes a static type checker that computes the classification so that no type error may occur at run-time. The advantages of a static type system are

- fewer programming errors because discipline is demanded of the programmer. He/she has to classify the programming objects with respect to types. This increases the information level of the program;

- detection of semantic errors at compile-time. No code is needed to test the applicability of an operation at run-time;
- improvement of the code. Types reflect the structure of the objects so that the compiler can generate more specific code.

The type discipline of TrafoLa-H is based on the Hindley/Milner theory of type polymorphism ([Hindley 69], [Milner 78]) and is extended with respect to the complex operations and patterns provided by TrafoLa-H. Type polymorphism allows to define functions that work uniformly for arguments of different types. Instead of a fully determined (monomorphic) type, we use a "type pattern" with type variables that describes the structure of the values permitted as arguments. The insertion/extraction operations of TrafoLa-H require that some monomorphic types occur in several versions, i.e., are treated similarly to type variables.

This chapter falls into two parts: the description of the language (how to program in TrafoLa-H, sections 8.2 through 8.5) and the description of the type discipline (the theoretical background: how the objects are classified, sections 8.6 and 8.7). After a short description of the lexical structure of TrafoLa-H in section 8.2, we consider the structure of the objects to be transformed (in section 8.3). In section 8.4, we define patterns and raise their power step by step. Ultimately, they will allow the partition of trees by arbitrary vertical and horizontal cuts. In section 8.5, we define the 'functional aspect' of the language with expressions, functions, and applications. In the second part, we illustrate the problem of classifying values in TrafoLa-H. The classification is difficult because of the powerful operations in the language. Thus, a sophisticated type system is needed that nevertheless allows static type inferencing. The chapter concludes by describing the context-free syntax of TrafoLa-H and its predefined operations.

8.2. Lexical Structure of the Transformation Language

8.2.1. Notational Conventions

When describing the syntax and semantics of TrafoLa-H, we use some notational conventions. Syntactic rules are specified in extended Backus Naur form, with keywords written in **boldface**. The symbol '|' separates alternative productions of a non-terminal. Square brackets '[...]' include optional parts. Braces '{...}' include parts that can be iterated zero or more times. Note the difference to the larger forms **|**, **[ ]**, and { }, which denote terminal symbols of the TrafoLa-H.

Semantic rules are given denotationally where we use abbreviations for syntactic and semantic objects that should be self explanatory. Examples of TrafoLa-H are written in Helvetica.

8.2.2. Basic Language Elements

The characters used to write a TrafoLa program are divided into three classes: The set of letters comprises **a** ... **z**, **A** ... **Z** and the underscore character _. The set of digits contains **0** ... **9**. All others are special characters. In general we distinguish between upper and lower case letters.

A basic language element is one of the following:

`number`	a sequence of digits,
`integer`	a `number`, perhaps preceded by '-',
`string`	a sequence of characters enclosed in double quotes ",

`hole`	`@` followed by a positive `number` (not 0),
`name`	a sequence of letters and digits starting with a letter,
`constructor`	a `name` preceded by a single quote ,
`identifier`	a `name` that is no keyword,
`typevariable`	a sequence of `?`'s, e.g. `?`, `??`, `???`, ...
`comment`	text enclosed between `/*` and `*/`.

8.2.3. Reserved Keywords

The following keywords are names that are an integral part of the language and cannot be redefined:

o	**all**	**and**	**bool**	**case**	**dec**
else	**false**	**forward**	**if**	**in**	**int**
let	**mod**	**of**	**rec**	**string**	**then**
true	**type**	**where**	**with**		

Except **o**, they may be written using upper and lower case letters in any combination, e.g., **DEC**, **Dec**, **dec**.

8.3. Objects of the Transformation Language

TrafoLa-H contains the following classes of values:

- basic values (Booleans, numbers, strings, and the empty tuple)
- structural values (sequences, tuples, and trees)
- abstract values (functions, constructors, and holes)
- the special value **fail**
- error values (exceptional values carrying a string as an error message; the '$\perp$'-value)

Structural values are subject of pattern matching, whereas abstract values cannot be partitioned by patterns.

These classes are described in the following sections. We also give examples and/or the concrete syntax for denoting the values, and the concrete syntax of the types assigned to the classes.

8.3.1. Basic Values

Basic values are stored and handled as atomic entities. Thus, they cannot be partitioned by patterns.

Booleans There are only two Booleans, **false** and **true**.
Their type is **bool**.

Numbers are integers ... **-2**, **-1**, **0**, **1**, **2** ...
The size of numbers is limited by the underlying run time system and is likely to depend directly on the hardware. On SUN work stations, the maximal number is $2^{31} - 1 = 2,147,483,647$, and the minimal number is $-2^{31} = -2,147,483,648$.
The type of numbers is **`int`**.

Strings are (almost) arbitrary sequences of characters enclosed by double quotes ":
"" "PROSPECTRA" "This is a string."
Their type is **string**. Unfortunately, it is impossible to include double quotes directly in a string. There are predefined operations to partition strings into subunits.

Unit is the empty tuple (). Its type is also denoted by ().

Among the predefined functions, there are some operations on basic values and conversions between strings and integers.

8.3.2. Structural Values

Structural values are the main subject of pattern matching. They may be decomposed into their constituents by patterns, and created by corresponding expressions.

Tuples are finite collections (v_1, ..., v_n) of values of arbitrary type. Here, the length n may be greater than 1, but not 1. The empty tuple () is considered a basic value. A formal one-tuple (v_1) cannot be distinguished from its only item.
($t_1, \ldots, t_n$) is the type of the above tuple if t_i is the type of v_i, for $1 \leq i \leq n$.
`(exp, exp { , exp })` is the concrete syntax of a tuple expression.
Examples: (1, "a", **true**) (1, 2, 3, 4, 5, 6, 7)

Sequences consist of an ordered finite collection [v_1, ..., v_n] of values. A sequence may be arbitrarily long, but all its items must share the same type.
The type of a list of items of type t is $t*$.
[ ] is the concrete syntax of the empty list, and `[ exp { , exp } ]` is the concrete syntax of other list expressions.
Examples: [] [1] [[]] [1, 2, 3, 4, 5, 6, 7]

Trees consist of a constructor denoting the root label of the tree, and an arbitrary value denoting the child. This value will mostly be a tuple.
The concrete syntax of a tree expression is `constructor exp`.
Trees are classified according to user defined data types. Only those constructors may be used that are introduced by such data type declarations. Examples of trees and data type definitions are given in section 8.3.6.

8.3.3. Abstract Values

Abstract values are meaningful only in connection with other values: *Holes* mark the places in values where subvalues are absent. *Constructors* are labels for tree nodes. *Functions* represent mappings from values to values.

Holes are objects @1, @2, @3, etc., i.e., there is a one-to-one correspondence between holes and positive integers. The first hole @1 can be abbreviated as @. Objects containing holes are called *fragments.* They result from the decomposition of values by pattern matching. The hole numbers indicate the order of extraction (@1 is produced last) and conversely the order of insertion (@1 is filled first). We thus distinguish between fragments and complete objects, i.e., nonfragments.
The types of holes are polymorphic *fragment types.* They describe what has to be inserted in a fragment value to result in a complete value. There is no language construct to denote a fixed fragment type. In type patterns and specifications, these types are included in the types of the

corresponding complete values, i.e., for instance the type **int** (as language construct) is used for integers 1,2,3, etc., and for holes @1,@2,@3 etc. that stand for integers in fragment values.

Constructors are declared by data type declarations at the top level and serve to label the nodes of a tree. Lexically, they are names starting by a single quote, e.g., 'op, 'add, 'node, etc.
t_1 ->> t_2 is the type of constructors producing trees of type t_2 from values of type t_1.

Functions are objects that may be applied to an argument value to produce a result value. They are considered as incomparable objects. Since TrafoLa-H is a 'call-by-value' language, function arguments are always evaluated completely before the function is applied.
The direct way to specify a function is by writing { `pat => exp {# pat => exp }`} .
t_1 -> t_2 is the type of functions with arguments of type t_1 and results of type t_2.

Every functional value is tagged by a unique label at the time of its creation. These labels are employed when functional values have to be compared because functions cannot be effectively compared directly. Thus, equality of functions is implementation dependent: functional values are equal iff they are shared instances of the same value.

8.3.4. The Special Value fail

If a function defined via pattern matching is applied to a value that does not match against the entry patterns of the function, then the function returns the special value **fail**. This value is similar to the exceptions of SML. Like these, it is propagated through ordinary function calls, i.e., a function applied to **fail** returns **fail**, but can be caught by special constructs. There is no direct syntax to specify the value **fail** and no special type for it. (In fact **fail** has every type.)

8.3.5. Error Values

Error values are not ordinary values. They result from erroneous evaluations and mostly correspond to run-time errors. There are no operations to process error values; once an error value results from the evaluation of a subexpression, it also becomes the result of the whole expression.

In the denotational semantics, we only distinguish between two error values: the value **error** results from ill-typed use of operand values, whereas the value '$\perp$' is the result of undefined or infinite calculations. For instance, integer addition of lists results in **error** and division by zero in '$\perp$'. This difference is important from the view point of type theory.

In practice, the value **error** cannot occur since language constructs containing type errors are refuted by the compiler. In contrast, the value '$\perp$' is differentiated according to whether it results from a runtime error or denotes an infinite calculation. Runtime errors produce error messages indicating the kind of error that occurred. Many predefined operations issue fixed error messages. The user may create his/her own error messages by means of the predefined function Error.

If an expression contains more than one erroneous part, it nevertheless results in only one error value. The particular error value result depends on the temporal order of the evaluation of subexpressions.

In the following examples, the error messages tagged by Error: are issued by the runtime system, whereas the messages tagged by Typeerror: are generated by the type checking component of the compiler. In this case, only a prefix of the real message is shown.

Examples:

```
1 / 0                              →  Error: division by 0
1 2                                →  Typeerror: no applicable function/constructor type ...
if 1 then 1 / 0 else 1 2           →  Typeerror: no boolean found after if ...
dec pred = { x => if x == 0 then Error "pred 0" else x - 1 };
pred 2                             →  1
pred 0                             →  Error: pred 0
pred "a"                           →  Typeerror: no applicable function/constructor type ...
```

8.3.6. Declaration of Data Types

In typed TrafoLa-H, all occurring tree values are classified by declarations of structured data types. These are rules for constructing trees with constructors and values of appropriate types. All constructors have to be introduced by a type declaration, and all legal tree values have to obey the given rules. Data types may be polymorphic. Alternatives are separated by #.

Examples:

```
type inttree   = 'ileaf int # 'inode (inttree, inttree);
type Tree ?    = 'leaf ? # 'node (Tree ?, Tree ?);
type Pair ? ?? = 'tup (?,??);

type program   = 'Prog stm*               /* program stm1; ... end */
and stm        = 'Pcall(var,exp*)         /* procedure call */
               # 'Assign(var,exp)         /* assignment: var := exp */
               # 'Ifs(exp, stm*, stm*)    /* if-then-else statement */
               # 'While(exp,stm*)         /* while statement */
               # 'Noop                    /* no operation */
and exp        = 'Fcall(var,exp*)         /* function call */
               # 'Ife(exp, exp, exp)      /* if-then-else expression */
               # 'Add (exp, exp)          /* addition: exp1 + exp2 */
               # 'Eq (exp, exp)           /* equality: exp1 = exp2 */
               # 'true # 'false # 'Num int # 'Id var
and var        = string;
```

These examples introduce the new types inttree, Tree ? (also Tree **int**, Tree **bool**, Tree inttree, ...), Pair ? ?? (also Pair **int bool**, Pair **string** (Tree **int**), ...), program, stm, exp, and var. The type var is only a synonym for the type **string**. The constructors 'ileaf, 'inode, 'leaf, 'node, 'tup, ... are also introduced. A value of type inttree is a tree consisting either of a node with constructor 'ileaf and an integer value as leaf, or a node with constructor 'inode and a tuple with two inttree values as subtree. The declarations of Tree and Pair are polymorphic. Here, the type variables are placeholders for types: each variable denotes the same type at all occurrences. Thus, the branches of 'node must have the same type, but the branches of 'tup may have different types. Tree and Pair are called *type-forming operators*. Together with the instances of the *schematic type variables*, they represent types.

The last example is a combined type declaration. It defines a representation of the abstract syntax of a tiny language and introduces four new types in one declaration. The user-defined types in such declarations may be mutually recursive.

Examples: of type inttree:

```
'ileaf 255
'inode ('ileaf 1, 'inode ('ileaf 2, 'ileaf 3))
```

of type Tree **int**:	'leaf 255 (is different from 'ileaf 255 because of the constructor)
of type Tree **bool**:	'leaf **true**
	'node ('leaf **true**, 'leaf **false**)
of type Pair **int bool**:	'tup (1,**true**)
of type Pair **bool int**:	'tup (**true**,1)
of type stm:	'While('Eq('Id "a",'Num 1),['Assign("a",'Id "b")])
	(represents the statement: **while** a = 1 **do** a := b **od**)

8.4. Patterns

8.4.1. Informal Semantics of Patterns

The following transformations of the above data types seem to be useful:

```
dec  Iftrue     =  { 'Ife ('true, T, E)    =>  T }
dec  Iffalse    =  { 'Ife ('false, T, E)   =>  E }
dec  Whilefalse =  { 'While ('false, S)    =>  'Noop }
```

These are declarations binding functional values — denoted by the construct { `pat => exp`} — to the variables Iftrue, etc.

What is the semantics of the function { `p => e`} applied to some value v?

If p does not match v, the rule fails, i.e., returns **fail**. Otherwise, the variable names occurring in p are bound to values (subterms of v). Thus p matched against v returns an environment r. Then the expression e is evaluated to a new value v' in this environment. The transformation {`p => e`} thus describes a partial mapping of values. Iftrue, for instance, is undefined for 'while' statements, even when a matching 'if' expression occurs in its condition or body.

Later, we shall consider non-deterministic patterns that may match in different ways, thus returning several environments when matched against a value v. The failure case fits well with this view: the pattern then returns no environment at all.

From a more abstract point of view, a pattern returns a set of environments since order and number of environments are considered immaterial. In practice however, these 'sets' are implemented as lists. Eventual repetitions of the same environment are not suppressed. The order of the environments in the list is not specified by the language definition of TrafoLa-H. In the present implementation, the order depends on the temporal order of matching operations. This order is chosen by the compiler according to efficiency considerations.

In TrafoLa-H, the lists of environments produced by a pattern match can be used in two ways:

- The expression e can be evaluated for each environment in the list, giving a list of result values, or
- e is evaluated only for the first environment in the list.

These two techniques will be presented in more detail below.

8.4.2. Formal Semantics of Patterns

For specifying the denotational semantics of TrafoLa-H, we use several domains of objects that are considered as complete partial orders (for mathematical reasons). The elements of syntactic domains are obvious from the rules of the syntax:

- Identifier: contains all identifiers.
- Pattern: contains all terminal words that may be derived from the nonterminal `pat`.
- Expression: contains all terminal words that may be derived from the nonterminal `exp`.
- Definition: contains all terminal words that may be derived from the nonterminals `ndeclist` and `rdeclist`.

Value is the only semantic domain. It contains all values described in section 8.3. There are several domains combining syntactic and semantic elements:

- Type: contains all types. As a first approximation, consider a type as a property of values, or as the set of all values with this property. Types will be explained more thouroughly in sections 8.5 and 8.6.
- Env: contains environments, i.e., mappings from identifiers to values or types or **unbound**: Env = Identifier $\rightarrow$ (Value $\cup$ Type $\cup$ {**unbound** }). We shall denote environments by

  $$\langle A_1 \rightarrow v_1; \ldots ; A_n \rightarrow v_n \rangle$$

  where A_i are distinct variables and v_i are values or types (not **unbound**).
- Env*: the set of all finite lists of environments.

The meta language used for the denotational semantics originated in λ–calculus. It has been enriched with if–then–else and special operators that are introduced when needed.

The formal semantics of patterns is described by means of a semantic function

$$\mathbf{P}\text{: Pattern} \rightarrow \text{Env} \rightarrow \text{Value} \rightarrow \text{Env}^*$$

that matches a pattern against a value in some environment, producing a list of environments.

Note that we abstract from error cases when we present parts of the definition of **P**. Matching the values **error** and '$\perp$' results in **error** and '$\perp$'. Matching **fail** returns [] (the empty list), which leads again to **fail** when the evaluation proceeds.

8.4.3. Atomic Patterns

Atomic patterns are constructors, constants, and the wild card. The concrete syntax of atomic patterns is

```
pat     ::= integer
          | boolean
          | string
          | constructor
          | hole
          | _
          | ()
```

A constructor or constant (number, character, hole, etc.) c matches just itself:

$$\mathbf{P}[\![c]\!]\ r\ v \ = \ \text{if}\ \ v = c\ \ \text{then}\ \ [\langle\rangle]\ \ \text{else}\ \ [\,]$$

If the value equals c, the match succeeds. It returns just one environment, namely the empty environment $\langle\rangle$, mapping all variables to **unbound**. Otherwise, the match fails, returning the empty list [ ] of environments.

The wild card '_' matches any value except **error**, **fail**, and '$\perp$':

$$\mathbf{P}[\![\_]\!]\ r\ v \ = \ [\langle\rangle]$$

Examples:

1	matches 1
"ABC"	matches "ABC"
'node	matches 'node

8.4.4. Type Patterns

Type patterns are similar to wild cards. The concrete syntax is:

```
pat     ::= type
          | >type
type    ::= int
          | bool
          | string
          | type *
          | ()
          | ( type , type { , type } )
          | type -> type
          | type ->> type
          | identifier { type }
          | typevariable
          | ( type )
```

The pattern 't' (where t is a type expression) matches complete values of type t. The pattern '> t' matches fragment values of type t. When a type (which may contain user-defined types or type-forming operators such as inttree, Tree, Pair, stm, etc.) is encountered in a pattern, its meaning is looked up in the environment of the match. The meaning will be a predicate characterizing the values belonging to the type.

$$\mathbf{P}[\![t]\!]\ r\ v \ = \ \text{if}\ \ (r\ (t))\ v = \mathbf{true}\ \ \text{and}\ \ v\ \text{is complete}\ \ \text{then}\ \ [\langle\rangle]\ \ \text{else}\ \ [\,]$$
$$\mathbf{P}[\![{>}t]\!]\ r\ v \ = \ \text{if}\ \ (r\ (t))\ v = \mathbf{true}\ \ \text{then}\ \ [\langle\rangle]\ \ \text{else}\ \ [\,]$$

Examples:

int	matches 1, 2, 3, etc.
int *	matches [ ], [1], [1,2,3], etc.
>(**int** *)	matches [ ], [1], [1,2,@1], [1,@5,@7,@9], etc.
Tree **int**	matches 'leaf 5, 'node ('leaf 1, 'leaf 3), etc.

Notice that different occurrences of the same type in a pattern may match different values.

8.4.5. Variables in Patterns

Variables are all those identifiers that are not used as user-declared type names. They may be used in two ways: either to bind subvalues, or to import values into a match. Binding variables match any value and create a new environment in which they are bound to this value:

$$\mathbf{P}[\![A]\!]\; r\; v \;=\; [\langle\, A \rightarrow v \,\rangle]$$

Importing variables are preceded by `%`. They match just the value of the variables in the environment of the match:

$$\mathbf{P}[\![\texttt{\%}A]\!]\; r\; v \;=\; \text{if } v = r\,(A) \text{ then } [\langle\rangle] \text{ else } [\,]$$

If we do not want to bind a subvalue to a variable, we may use '_' or the name of a syntactic sort such as **int**, inttree, stm, etc. Constructors, binding variables, and the wild card also occur in Hope, SML, and Miranda, but importing variables and types do not.

Examples: X matches 1 binding X to 1
%X matches 1 if X is bound to 1, but does not match 2 if X is bound to 1

8.4.6. Structural Patterns

Structural patterns specify the structure of the matched value. They consist of subpatterns to match designated subvalues. The resulting lists of environments are combined into one. The syntax of structural patterns is:

```
pat      ::= [ pat { , pat } ]
           | [ ]
           | ( pat , pat {, pat } )
           | pat*
           | pat+
           | pat pat
```

8.4.6.1. Sequence and Tuple Enumeration

The pattern '$[p_1, \ldots, p_n]$' matches values of shape $[v_1, \ldots, v_n]$:

$$\mathbf{P}[\![\,\texttt{[}p_1, \ldots, p_n\texttt{]}\,]\!]\; r\; v \;=\; \text{if } v = [v_1, \ldots, v_n] \text{ then } \mathbf{P}[\![p_1]\!]\; r\; v_1 \oplus \ldots \oplus \mathbf{P}[\![p_n]\!]\; r\; v_n \text{ else } [\,]$$

If $n = 0$, this degenerates to $\mathbf{P}[\![\texttt{[]}]\!]\; r\; v \;=\; \text{if } v = [\,] \text{ then } [\langle\rangle] \text{ else } [\,]$

The tuple pattern '$(p_1, \ldots, p_n)$' behaves completely analogously.

The associative combination '$\oplus$' will be defined in section 8.4.8. As a first approximation, assume that it superposes all environments in its first argument with all in its second one.

8.4.6.2. Uniform Sequence

The pattern '$p*$' matches sequences of arbitrary length whose items are all matched by p, and '$p+$' matches the same sequences except the empty one [ ]. The pattern '$p*$' should not contain binding variables since no values are bound to the variables if it matches [ ].

$$\mathbf{P}[\![p\star]\!]\; r\; v \;=\; \text{if } v = [v_1, \ldots, v_n], n > 0 \text{ then } \mathbf{P}[\![p]\!]\; r\; v_1 \oplus \ldots \oplus \mathbf{P}[\![p]\!]\; r\; v_n \text{ else}$$
$$\text{if } v = [\,] \text{ then } [\langle\rangle] \text{ else } [\,]$$

$$\mathbf{P}[\![p+]\!]\; r\; v \;=\; \text{if } v = [v_1, \ldots, v_n], n > 0 \text{ then } \mathbf{P}[\![p]\!]\; r\; v_1 \oplus \ldots \oplus \mathbf{P}[\![p]\!]\; r\; v_n \text{ else } [\,]$$

8.4.6.3. Tree Pattern

A pattern '$p\; q$' matches trees whose operator is matched by p and whose child is matched by q. Here, p has to be a constructor.

$$\mathbf{P}[\![p\; q]\!]\; r\; v \;=\; \text{if } v = \text{op } w \text{ then } \mathbf{P}[\![p]\!] \text{ r op} \oplus \mathbf{P}[\![q]\!] \text{ r } w \text{ else } [\,]$$

Examples:

(1, **bool**) matches (1, **true**) and (1, **false**).

(**int**, **bool**) matches integer-boolean tuples. It makes no difference whether the pattern is considered one type pattern or a tuple enumeration of type patterns.

int∗ matches integer lists like [1, 2, 3] (as type pattern and also as star pattern).

> (**int**∗) matches @1, [@2], [1, @3], etc. This is a type pattern.

(> **int**)∗ matches [@2], [1, @3], etc., but not @1. This is a star pattern containing a type pattern.

1∗ matches [ ], [1], [1,1], [1,1,1], etc.

1+ matches [1], [1,1], [1,1,1], etc. but not [ ].

'Ife ('true, T, E) matches 'if' expressions with condition 'true' and binds T and E to the 'then' and 'else' parts.

'Ife A matches any 'if' expression and binds A to its child, i.e., A is bound to a value of type (exp, exp, exp).

'Ifs (C, stm∗, stm∗) is equivalent to 'Ifs (C, _, _) because of the structure of the object language. Both patterns match 'if' statements and bind the condition to C.

8.4.7. Nonlinear Patterns

A pattern is nonlinear if a binding variable occurs more than once in it, or occurs at least once inside a subpattern p+. In subpatterns $p\star$, no binding variables may occur.

For example, the nonlinear pattern 'Add (E, E) matches the value 'Add (a, b) iff the subvalues a and b are equal. E is then bound to a.

Examples:

Pattern	Value	Result
'Add (E, E)	'Add (1, 1)	$[\langle \mathsf{E} \rightarrow 1\rangle]$
'Add (E, E)	'Add (1, 2)	$[]$
A+	[1, 1, 2]	$[]$
A+	[1, 1, 1]	$[\langle \mathsf{A} \rightarrow 1\rangle]$

Nonlinear patterns are allowed in Miranda and Prolog, but forbidden in Hope and SML.

8.4.8. Combination of Lists of Environments

Now, we shall define the combination $s \oplus t$ of two lists of environments s and t. The result is a list of all pairwise superpositions of environments where the case of inconsistent bindings of variables must be excluded in order to achieve the desired semantics of nonlinear patterns. As mentioned above, we do not specify the order of the items in the result list. This is indicated notationally by using a list comprehension in the definition.

Definition 1

$s \oplus t \;=\; [\, a + b \mid a \; in \; s, \; b \; in \; t, \; a \text{ and } b \text{ are consistent} \,]$

$a + b \;=\; \lambda N.\ \text{if } b(N) = \textbf{unbound} \text{ then } a(N) \text{ else } b(N)$

a and b are consistent iff

for all variables N,

$a(N) = \textbf{unbound} \text{ or } b(N) = \textbf{unbound} \text{ or } a(N) = b(N)$

Examples: Remember that $\mathbf{P}[\![[p, q]]\!]\ r\ [u, v] \;=\; \mathbf{P}[\![p]\!]\ r\ u \oplus \mathbf{P}[\![q]\!]\ r\ v$

Pattern	Value	Result
[A, B]	[1, 2]	$[\langle \mathsf{A} \rightarrow 1\rangle] \oplus [\langle \mathsf{B} \rightarrow 2\rangle] \;=\; [\langle \mathsf{A} \rightarrow 1; \mathsf{B} \rightarrow 2\rangle]$
[A, 2]	[1, 2]	$[\langle \mathsf{A} \rightarrow 1\rangle] \oplus [\langle\rangle] \;=\; [\langle \mathsf{A} \rightarrow 1\rangle]$
[A, 1]	[1, 2]	$[\langle \mathsf{A} \rightarrow 1\rangle] \oplus [] \;=\; []$
[A, A]	[1, 1]	$[\langle \mathsf{A} \rightarrow 1\rangle] \oplus [\langle \mathsf{A} \rightarrow 1\rangle] \;=\; [\langle \mathsf{A} \rightarrow 1\rangle]$
[A, A]	[1, 2]	$[\langle \mathsf{A} \rightarrow 1\rangle] \oplus [\langle \mathsf{A} \rightarrow 2\rangle] \;=\; []$

The superposition of environments '+' is not commutative — the second operand dominates the first one — but associative, and has a neutral element, namely the empty environment $\langle\rangle$. Hence, the combination '$\oplus$' is associative, has neutral element $[\langle\rangle]$, and satisfies $s \oplus [] = []$. If the order of list items is not taken into consideration, i.e., the lists are considered as multisets, then combination becomes commutative since for environments, $a + b = b + a$ holds iff a and b are consistent.

8.4.9. Correspondence between Patterns and Expressions

In TrafoLa-H, some syntactic forms may occur in patterns as well as in expressions, e.g., constants, variables, tuples, sequences, and trees. The meaning of a syntactic form in a pattern is inverse to the meaning of the corresponding form in an expression.

For instance, a variable in a pattern is bound to a value, whereas a variable in an expression denotes the value to which it is bound. A pair pattern (A, B) decomposes pairs, binding A and B to their components, whereas the expression (A, B) composes a pair from the values bound to A and B. The operators denoting concatenation and insertion — introduced below — will behave analogously.

8.4.10. Concatenation and Splitting

Assume we want to delete superfluous 'noop' statements in statement lists. Then we need a rule

```
{ (L1 . ['Noop] . L2) => (L1 . L2) }
```

where the dot denotes concatenation of sequences in expressions and splitting in patterns. The pattern L1 . ['Noop] . L2 matches sequence values consisting of three subsequences such that the second one equals ['Noop], binding L1 and L2 to the first and third subsequence. The expression L1 . L2 concatenates the sequences bound to L1 and L2 to a new sequence. Thus, dot patterns split sequences, whereas dot expressions concatenate sequences.

By abstracting from 'Noop, we obtain an example for importing variables:

```
{ X => { L1 . [% X] . L2 => L1 . L2 } }
```

This is a function of second order. Given an argument x, it returns a function that removes an occurrence of x from a sequence.

Examples for splitting patterns:

L1 . ['While (C, B)] . L3	matches lists of arbitrary length containing a 'while' statement.
[S, 'Noop] . L	matches lists whose second element is 'Noop.

The dot operator is a potential source of nondeterminism:

L1 . ['Noop] . L2 matched against $[a_1, \text{'Noop}, a_2, \text{'Noop}]$

where the subvalues a_i are statements other than 'Noop, yields a list of two environments:

$\langle$ L1 $\rightarrow [a_1]$; L2 $\rightarrow [a_2, \text{'Noop}]\rangle$ and $\langle$ L1 $\rightarrow [a_1, \text{'Noop}, a_2]$; L2 $\rightarrow [\,]\rangle$

Formally, the semantics of the dot operator is defined by a union over all possible partitions:

$$\mathbf{P}[\![p \,.\, q]\!]\; r\; v \;=\; \sum_{u.w=v} \mathbf{P}[\![p]\!]\; r\; u \oplus \mathbf{P}[\![q]\!]\; r\; w$$

where '$\sum$' denotes concatenation of lists of environments. This operator allows the selection of arbitrary subsequences, and is not contained in Hope, SML, or Miranda. These languages only provide a less powerful version of the pattern, splitting a list into head and tail. This pattern is also available in TrafoLa-H:

$$\mathbf{P}[\![p :: q]\!]\; r\; v \;=\; \mathbf{P}[\![[p] \,.\, q]\!]\; r\; v$$

8.4.11. Fragments, Insertion, and Extraction

The dot operator for patterns allows the partition of values by vertical cuts into a left and a right hand side, since it inverts concatenation. Now we want to introduce an operation — also not contained in Hope, SML, or Miranda — that performs horizontal cuts to decompose values into a subvalue and its context. The context is not a complete value; it contains a hole '@1' denoting the place where the subvalue was cut out.

In TrafoLa-H expressions, the operator ^ denotes insertion of a value into the hole of a fragment: This is done by replacing all occurrences of '@1' in the left operand by the right operand, and changing all occurrences of '@n' where $n > 1$ into '@$(n-1)$'. Insertion into a complete value, i.e., a value without holes, leaves this value unchanged.

'Ife (c, @1, e) ^ t	=	'Ife (c, t, e)
'Add @1 ^ (a, b)	=	'Add (a, b)
'Ifs (c, @1, @2) ^ [s_1, s_2]	=	'Ifs (c, [s_1, s_2], @1)
[s_1, @1, @1, @3, @4] ^ s_2	=	[s_1, s_2, s_2, @2, @3]
(@3, **true**) ^ t	=	(@2, **true**)
(1, **true**) ^ t	=	(1, **true**)

The pattern operator ^ inverts insertion as the dot operator inverts concatenation. When a pattern 'p ^ q' is matched against a value v, v is cut in all possible ways into two values u and w such that $v = u$ ^ w where u contains exactly one hole @1. Then p is matched against u and q against w:

$$\mathbf{P}[\![p \,\hat{}\, q]\!]\; r\; v \;=\; \sum_{u \,\hat{}\, w = v \text{ and } noho(u)=1} \mathbf{P}[\![p]\!]\; r\; u \oplus \mathbf{P}[\![q]\!]\; r\; w$$

Here $noho(u)$ is the number of holes '@1' in u. In fact, it is not the full inverse of insertion since extraction generates left results containing exactly one occurrence of '@1', whereas insertion is possible for any left operand without '@1', or with many occurrences of '@1'.

For the examples, remember that U:>exp denotes a variable U that must be bound to a (perhaps incomplete) value of type exp.

Examples:
Let v = 'Eq ('Add (a, b), 'Add (c, d)) and w = 'Eq (@1, 'Add(c, d)).

'Add (A, B)	does not match v or w.
U:>exp ^ 'Add (A, B)	matches v in two ways: ⟨U → 'Eq (@1, 'Add (c, d)); A → a; B → b⟩ and ⟨U → 'Eq ('Add (a, b), @1); A → c; B → d⟩.
U:>exp ^ 'Add (A, B)	matches w in one way: ⟨U → 'Eq (@2, @1); A → c; B → d⟩
(U:>exp ^ 'Eq (@1, A)) ^ B	matched against v also gives one solution only: ⟨U → @1; A → 'Add (c, d); B → 'Add (a, b)⟩.
(U:>exp ^ 'Eq (@1, A)) ^ B	matched against w gives the solution: ⟨U → @1; A → 'Add (c, d); B → @1⟩.

8.4.12. Boolean Pattern Operators

The following pattern operators have no direct correspondents in the world of expressions. They serve to extend or restrict the set of environments produced by pattern matches.

```
pat      ::= pat & pat
           | pat : pat
           | pat | pat
           | ! pat
           | { pat }
           | pat where exp
```

8.4.12.1. Intersection

The pattern 'p & q' is used to specify that a value to be matched must satisfy both the requirements imposed by pattern p and by pattern q. If the pattern p is simply a variable — this is an important special case — we write 'V: q' instead of 'V & q' for aesthetic reasons. Hope and SML contain only this special case whereas Miranda does not contain the feature at all.

Example: S : (L1 . [W: 'While _] . L2) & stm* matches any sequence of statements containing a 'while' statement. The 'while' statement is bound to W, its left context to L1, and its right context to L2, whereas the whole sequence is bound to S. The test of stm* is not necessary since the type system ensures that a list containing a statement is a list of type stm*. Thus, the compiler/optimizer will not generate code for the test of stm*.

The formal semantics of intersection is the superposition of the environments of the both matches:

$$\mathbf{P}[\![p \mathbin{\&} q]\!]\ r\ v \;=\; \mathbf{P}[\![p]\!]\ r\ v \oplus \mathbf{P}[\![q]\!]\ r\ v$$

8.4.12.2. Union

The pattern 'p | q' matches all values matched by p or q or by both p and q. Here, p and q should contain the same set of variables such that all variables are bound if p matches and also if q matches. The lists of environments produced by p and by q are simply joined together:

$$\mathbf{P}[\![p \mid q]\!]\ r\ v \;=\; \mathbf{P}[\![p]\!]\ r\ v + \mathbf{P}[\![q]\!]\ r\ v$$

where '+' denotes merging or concatenation of two lists of environments.

Example: ('Add (exp, exp) | 'Eq (exp, exp)) matches 'sum' or 'equal' expressions.

The '|' operator is also a potential source of nondeterminism.

8.4.12.3. Complement

If p is a pattern matching some values, then $!p$ is a pattern matching all but these values.

$$\mathbf{P}[\![\,!p]\!]\ r\ v \;=\; \text{if } \mathbf{P}[\![p]\!]\ r\ v = [\,] \text{ then } [\langle\rangle] \text{ else } [\,]$$

Note that the pattern **!** p does not bind variables since there are no subvalues to which they could be bound when **!** p matches, i.e., p does not match. Thus, the pattern **! !** p is not equivalent to p — it matches the same values but does not bind variables. This is equivalent to the unbind pattern $\{p\}$ introduced as syntactic sugar:

$$\mathbf{P}[\![\{\, p \,\}]\!]\; r\; v \;\; = \;\; \mathbf{P}[\![!!p]\!]\; r\; v \;\; = \;\; \text{if } \mathbf{P}[\![p]\!]\; r\; v = [\,] \text{ then } [\,] \text{ else } [\langle\rangle]$$

The complementary pattern is similar to Prolog's *not* predicate (see [Clocksin, Mellish 81]).

Examples: Pattern	Value	Result
'Add (A, B) & ! 'Add (E, E)	'Add (1, 2)	[⟨ A → 1; B → 2⟩]
'Add (A, B) & ! 'Add (E, E)	'Add (1, 1)	[]

A deterministic 'Noop' elimination rule can thus be specified as follows:

{ (L1: (stm & !'Noop)*) . ['Noop] . (L2: Stm*) => L1 . L2 }

The sequence bound to L1 must not contain 'noop' statements so that the rule eliminates the first occurrence of 'Noop.

8.4.12.4. Restriction by a Boolean Expression

The pattern 'p **where** e' first lets p match and then filters the resulting environments with the boolean expression e. The pattern matches if p matches and e results in **true**.

$$\mathbf{P}[\![p \;\mathbf{where}\; e]\!]\; r\; v \;\; = \;\; [\, r' \in \mathbf{P}[\![p]\!]\; r\; v \;\mid\; \mathbf{E}[\![e]\!]\; (r + r') = \mathbf{true}\,]$$

Example: (A, B) **where** A = B corresponds to (A, A & B)

8.5. Expressions and Definitions

Besides patterns, TrafoLa-H contains two other basic syntactic sorts: expressions and definitions. Patterns serve to analyze values, whereas expressions are used to synthesize values. Definitions occur at the top level of TrafoLa-H and in 'let' constructs, and declare variables bound to values.

The potential nondeterminism in the world of patterns introduced by the pattern operators **.**, **^**, and **|** does not affect the world of expressions and definitions. They are completely deterministic, since the non-determinism is removed at the borderline between patterns and expressions. Thus, the semantic functions for definitions and expressions have the types

D: Definition → Env → Env

R: Definition → Env → Env (for recursive definitions)

E: Expression → Env → Value

8.5.1. Definitions

Definitions take two different forms. There are non-recursive definitions and (mutually) recursive ones. The syntax of non-recursive definitions is:

```
declaration ::= dec pat = exp { and pat = exp }
```

Here, the expressions are evaluated in the environment of the definition, and the resulting values are matched against the patterns. The outcoming lists of environments are combined by means of the '$\div$' operator. From the resulting list of environments, the first environment is extracted. This is the ultimate result of the definition.

A recursive definition is introduced by the keyword **rec** instead of **dec**. The patterns p_i are restricted in this case to just variable names. The expressions e_i are evaluated in the recursive environment where all the names A_i are assumed to be already bound. Since TrafoLa-H is a call-by-value language, all recursive occurrences of the defined names should be hidden inside a functional abstraction to prevent their immediate evaluation, which would cause non-termination.

Semantics:

$$\mathbf{D}[\![p_1 = e_1 \textbf{ and} \ldots \textbf{ and } p_n = e_n]\!]\, r \;=\; \mathbf{D}[\![(p_1, \ldots, p_n) = (e_1, \ldots, e_n)]\!]\, r$$

$$\mathbf{D}[\![p = e]\!]\, r \;=\; \text{if } s = [\,] \text{ then } \textbf{fail} \text{ else } \textbf{hd}\, s \qquad \text{where } s = \mathbf{P}[\![p]\!]\, r\, (\mathbf{E}[\![e]\!]\, r)$$

$$\mathbf{R}[\![d]\!]\, r \;=\; \mathbf{Y}\,(\,\lambda r'.\, \mathbf{D}[\![d]\!]\,(r + r'))$$

Here, **Y** is the fixed point operator and **hd** returns the first item of the argument list. Because the order of the items in this list is not completely specified, the actual outcome is implementation dependent and cannot be predicted by programmers.

A type specification may precede a definition. This is optional because the type checker is able to determine the type from the context. Type specifications may restrict a polymorphic type. They have the syntax

```
spec ::= forward var :=: type
```

Examples:

```
forward odd :=: int -> bool;
forward even :=: int -> bool;
rec odd = { 0 => false # n => even (n-1) }
and even = { 0 => true # n => odd (n-1) };
```

8.5.2. Expressions: an Overview

In contrast to patterns, most TrafoLa-H expressions are similar to those in other functional languages. We thus refrain from a thorough description of their meaning. Only abstraction is a bit sophisticated and is therefore introduced in greater detail in the next section.

```
exp ::= integer
      | boolean
      | string
```

```
    | constructor
    | hole
    | ()
    | variable
    | [ exp { , exp } ]
    | []
    | ( exp , exp { , exp } )
    | exp exp
    | let declaration in exp
    | { pat { , pat } [ with exp ] =>[ all ] exp
        { # pat { , pat } [ with exp ] =>[ all ] exp }}
    | ( exp )
```

Application exp_1 exp_2 also comprises tree construction, e.g., 'Add (1, 2), and the application of predefined infix operators such as concatenation '$e_1 . e_2$', insertion 'e_1 ^ e_2', comparison '$e_1 == e_2$', addition '$e_1 + e_2$', and some syntactic forms such as '**if** e_1 **then** e_2 **else** e_3' and '**case** e_1 **of** e_2' (see section 8.5.5). Application associates to the left, i.e., $e_1\,e_2\,e_3$ means $(e_1\,e_2)\,e_3$.

The present evaluation strategy is call-by-value since the complex patterns — especially ^ — make lazy evaluation difficult, and abstract syntax trees to be transformed are usually finite.

8.5.3. Functional Abstraction

The simplest form of abstraction has the syntax { p **=>** e } where p is a pattern and e an expression. It contains an implicit cut operator as known from Prolog: The function **hd**: Env* → Env returns one environment from a list of environments. With this environment, the expression is evaluated deterministically.

$$\mathbf{E}[\![\{\ p \ \texttt{=>}\ e\ \}]\!]\, r \;=\; \lambda x.\ \text{if } s = [\,]\ \text{then } \textbf{fail} \text{ else } \mathbf{E}[\![e]\!]\,(r + \textbf{hd}\ s)$$
$$\text{where } s = \mathbf{P}[\![p]\!]\ r\ x$$

fail is a special value indicating that the pattern p failed to match the argument value v. All expressions except the '|' construct of the next section are assumed to be strict with respect to **fail**, i.e., if one operand evaluates to **fail**, then the whole expression will do as well.

The most general form of an abstraction with environment selection looks like

$$\begin{array}{l} \{\ p_{11}, p_{12}, \ldots, p_{1n}\ \texttt{with}\ g_1\ \texttt{=>}\ e_1 \\ \#\ p_{21}, p_{22}, \ldots, p_{2n}\ \texttt{with}\ g_2\ \texttt{=>}\ e_2 \\ \qquad\vdots \\ \#\ p_{k1}, p_{k2}, \ldots, p_{kn}\ \texttt{with}\ g_k\ \texttt{=>}\ e_k\ \} \end{array}$$

where p_{ij} are patterns, g_i are Boolean expressions (guards), and e_i are expressions. The guards are optional and may be omitted together with their introducing keyword **with**. In this case, they are assumed to be **true**.

The whole construct describes a curried function with n parameters. If the function is called with n arguments, the evaluated arguments are matched against the patterns p_{11} through p_{1n}. The resulting set of environments is filtered through the guard g_1, i.e., only the environments making the guard evaluate to **true** are retained. If environments are left over, one of them is selected, and e_1 is evaluated in it for the final result. Otherwise, the second case is tried. If even the last (kth) case fails to match, the special value **fail** is returned.

Let A be the abstraction as defined above. Then

$$
\begin{aligned}
\mathbf{E}[\![A]\!]\, r \;=\; & \lambda x_1.\, \lambda x_2.\, \ldots \lambda x_n. \\
& \quad \text{if } S_1 \neq [\,] \text{ then } \mathbf{E}[\![e_1]\!]\,(r + \mathbf{hd}\; S_1) \text{ else} \\
& \quad \text{if } S_2 \neq [\,] \text{ then } \mathbf{E}[\![e_2]\!]\,(r + \mathbf{hd}\; S_2) \text{ else} \\
& \quad \ldots \\
& \quad \text{if } S_k \neq [\,] \text{ then } \mathbf{E}[\![e_k]\!]\,(r + \mathbf{hd}\; S_k) \text{ else} \\
& \quad \textsf{fail} \\
& \text{where } S_i = [\; r' \in \mathbf{P}[\![p_{i1}]\!]\, r\, x_1 \oplus \cdots \oplus \mathbf{P}[\![p_{in}]\!]\, r\, x_n \;\mid\; \mathbf{E}[\![g_i]\!]\,(r + r') = \mathbf{true}\;]
\end{aligned}
$$

Example: the Ackermann function, which works only with positive numbers (rule 1) and not with very large numbers (rule 2) because of time complexity. The operator || is Boolean *or*.

```
rec acker = { n,m with (n < 0 || m < 0)  => Error "too small args for the acker function !"
            # n,m with (n > 5 || m > 70) => Error "too large args for the acker function !"
            # 0,m                        => m+1
            # n,0                        => acker (n-1) 1
            # n,m                        => acker (n-1) (acker n (m-1))              };
```

Besides the abstraction with ‘=>’ that selects one match from the list of all matches, there is a second abstraction mechanism that delivers the list of all solutions.

The simplest form of the ‘all’-abstraction is ‘{ p **=> all** e }’ where p is a pattern and e an expression. The most general form of this kind of abstraction is

$$
\begin{aligned}
\{\;& p_{11}, p_{12}, \ldots, p_{1n}\; \texttt{with}\; g_1\; \texttt{=> all}\; e_1 \\
\#\;& p_{21}, p_{22}, \ldots, p_{2n}\; \texttt{with}\; g_2\; \texttt{=> all}\; e_2 \\
& \vdots \\
\#\;& p_{k1}, p_{k2}, \ldots, p_{kn}\; \texttt{with}\; g_k\; \texttt{=> all}\; e_k\; \}
\end{aligned}
$$

The semantics of this abstraction A is

$$
\begin{aligned}
\mathbf{E}[\![A]\!]\, r \;=\; & \lambda x_1.\, \lambda x_2.\, \ldots \lambda x_n. \\
& \quad \text{if } S_1 \neq [\,] \text{ then } [\; \mathbf{E}[\![e_1]\!]\,(r + r') \mid r' \in S_1\;] \text{ else} \\
& \quad \text{if } S_2 \neq [\,] \text{ then } [\; \mathbf{E}[\![e_2]\!]\,(r + r') \mid r' \in S_2\;] \text{ else} \\
& \quad \ldots \\
& \quad \text{if } S_k \neq [\,] \text{ then } [\; \mathbf{E}[\![e_k]\!]\,(r + r') \mid r' \in S_k\;] \text{ else} \\
& \quad \textsf{fail} \\
& \text{where } S_i = [\; r' \in \mathbf{P}[\![p_{i1}]\!]\, r\, x_1 \oplus \cdots \oplus \mathbf{P}[\![p_{in}]\!]\, r\, x_n \mid \mathbf{E}[\![g_i]\!]\,(r + r') = \mathbf{true}\;]
\end{aligned}
$$

Example: We may also mix both kinds of abstraction. Let Length be the ‘length of a list’ function and Hd the ‘first element on a list’ function:

```
dec f = { N, [1]                              =>    [[N]]
        # N, A.[1].B with (Length B = Hd B)   =>all A.[N].B };
```

This is a peculiar function for demonstration only. f replaces the item '1' in a list by N, if the length of the tail after the '1' equals its first element. It returns the list of all possible results of such replacements. If '1' is the last, but not the only, element of the list, the function call results in **error**:

f 9 [1]	returns	[[9]]	
f 9 [1, 5, 1, 1, 2, 3]	returns	[[9, 5, 1, 1, 2, 3], [1, 5, 1, 9, 2, 3]]	
f 9 [1, 2]	returns	**fail**	
f 9 []	returns	**fail**	
f 9 [1, 1]	returns	**error**	since **Hd** is applied to [ ]

8.5.4. Superposition of Functions

The superposition of (partial) functions is denoted by ' | '. This operator is only applicable to functions and produces a new function. When '$f \mid g$' is applied to some value v, then f is applied to v first. The result is the final result unless it is **fail**. In this case, the final result is $g\ v$.

$$\mathbf{E}[\![f \mid g]\!]\ r \;=\; \lambda x.\ \text{if}\ \mathbf{E}[\![f]\!]\ r\ x = \textbf{fail}\ \text{then}\ \mathbf{E}[\![g]\!]\ r\ x\ \text{else}\ \mathbf{E}[\![f]\!]\ r\ x$$

Example: Let g be { _ => [] } and f as above. Now:

((f 9)| g) [1]	returns	[[9]]
((f 9)| g) [1, 5, 1, 1, 2, 3]	returns	[[9, 5, 1, 1, 2, 3], [1, 5, 1, 9, 2, 3]]
((f 9)| g) [1, 2]	returns	[ ]
((f 9)| g) []	returns	[ ]
((f 9)| g) [1, 1]	returns	**error**

8.5.5. Some Syntactic Sugar

For aesthetic reasons, there are several forms of alternative syntax:

Original form:	Alternative syntax:
$\{p_1$ **=>** e_1 **#** ... **#** p_n **=>** $e_n\}\ e$	**case** e **of** $\{p_1$ **=>** e_1 **#** ... **#** p_n **=>** $e_n\}$
$\{$**true =>** e_1 **# false =>** $e_2\}\ e$	**if** e **then** e_1 **else** e_2
let dec d **in** e	**let** d **in** e
let d_1 **in let** d_2 **in** ... **let** d_n **in** e	**let** d_1**;** d_2**;** ... d_n **in** e

8.5.6. Examples

Some of the examples in the following section are predefined system functions that need not be redefined. To introduce their semantics, we show how to simulate them in TrafoLa-H.

8.5.6.1. General Functions

Identity:	**dec** I	=	{ X => X };
Totalization by identity:	**dec** Total	=	{ F => (F | I) };
Repetition:	**rec** Rep	=	{ F, x => (((Rep F) o F) | I) x };
Fixpoint:	**rec** Repeat	=	{ F, x => **if** x == F x **else** x **else** Repeat F (F x) };

where 'o' denotes the predefined operator of functional composition: (f o g) x = f (g x)

Total f v computes f v. If it is defined, i.e., not **fail**, it is the result. Otherwise, the result is the original argument v. Rep f repeatedly applies f until it is no longer possible, i.e., until f returns **fail.** Note that the call by value mechanism requires the additional abstraction in the body of Rep. Repeat f repeatedly applies f until the fixed point is reached. This is different from Rep f.

8.5.6.2. Functions for Sequences

Head of list:	**dec** Hd	=	{ H::T => H };
Tail of list:	**dec** Tl	=	{ H::T => T };
Length of list:	**rec** Length	=	{ [] => 0 # H::T => 1 + (Length T) };
Nth of list:	**dec** Nth	=	{ N, A.[X].B **with** Length A == (N-1) => X };
Nth_Tl of list:	**dec** Nth_Tl	=	{ N, A.B **with** Length A == N => B };
Member of list:	**dec** Member	=	{ X, A.[X].B => **true** # _ => **false** };
Duplicate:	**dec** Double	=	{ X => [X, X] };

8.5.6.3. Functionals for Sequences

rec Map = { F, [] => [] # F, H :: T => (F H) :: Map F T };

rec Extend = { F, [] => [] # F, H :: T => (F H) . Extend F T };

Note that Map applies a function item by item to a list, whereas Extend performs a homomorphic extension of its argument function from items to lists:

Map Double [1, 2, 3] = [[1, 1], [2, 2], [3, 3]]

Extend Double [1, 2, 3] = [1, 1, 2, 2, 3, 3]

Other classical functionals are

rec Foldr = { F, X0, [ ] => X0 # F, X0, H :: T => (F H (Foldr F X0 T))};
rec Foldl = { F, X0, [ ] => X0 # F, X0, H :: T => (F (Foldl F X0 T) H)};
dec Fold = Foldr;

Here F is a binary function and X0 is typically its neutral element, for example:

Fold (*) 1 [1, 2, 3, 4, 5] = 120.

rec Filter = { P, [] => [] # P, H :: T => (**if** P H **then** [H] **else** []). Filter P T };

Filter removes all list items not satisfying the predicate P.

The following three functions delete all 'noop' statements from statement sequences:

```
Rep      {S1 . ['Noop] . S2 => S1 . S2}
Extend   {'Noop => [] # X => [X]}
Filter   {X => X != 'Noop}
```

8.6. Illustration of TrafoLa-H Types

In section 8.3, we discussed the classes of values of TrafoLa-H and the concrete syntax to write down types in patterns and type specifications. Now, we explain in detail the conditions under which values have a type, i.e., we give the semantics of types. However, we need first a more detailed syntax of types to explain the semantics, because the concrete syntax of the language does not specify all information necessary for the type semantics. This difference between concrete syntax and semantic syntax originated in the handling of fragment values. For example, we write $\text{int}_1 \rightarrow \text{bool}_2$ and $\text{int}_1 \twoheadrightarrow \text{bool}_2$ for the semantical types that describe the meaning of **int** – > **bool** and **int** – >> **bool**. Only the latter types may be TrafoLa-H input.

8.6.1. Monomorphic and Polymorphic Types

TrafoLa values are classified as the monomorphic types (monotypes): "int", "bool", "string", "unit", $(t_1, \ldots, t_n)$, $t*$, $t_1 \rightarrow t_n$, $t_1 \twoheadrightarrow t_n$ (the type of constructors; they are considered as special "functions" producing tree values of type t_n) and the monomorphic user types "*name*" or "*name* $t_1 \ldots t_n$" where t, $t_1, \ldots t_n$ are monomorphic types and *name* is a tree type or a typeforming operator declared by the user. However, some values have many monomorphic types according to this classification: For instance, the empty list [ ] has every type $t*$, the identity function *I* has every type $t \rightarrow t$, and the function *Hd* has every type $t* \rightarrow t$, etc. All types of such a value are constructed according to a fixed pattern that is sufficient to classify the value. We describe such patterns with type variables $\alpha, \beta, \gamma \ldots$ that denote the parts of the type that are not fixed. So [ ] has the type $\alpha*$, *I* has the type $\alpha \rightarrow \alpha$, etc. Different occurrences of the same type variable denote dependencies: *I* has the type int $\rightarrow$ int by substituting int for α, but not int $\rightarrow$ bool, because in that case, different types would be substituted for α.

Definition 2 *If a type contains no type variable, it is* **monomorphic** *(a monotype), else it is* **polymorphic** *(a polytype).*
Let t be a polytype containing the type variable α and let $t_\alpha^{t'}$ be the type resulting from substituting t' for α in t. A value possesses the type t if it possesses the type $t_\alpha^{t'}$ for all monomorphic types t'.

We use the word polytype when we wish to imply that a type contains, or may contain, a type variable. We use $\mu_1, \mu_2, \mu_3, \ldots$ to range over monotypes and $\sigma_1, \sigma_2, \sigma_3, \ldots$ to range over polytypes.

8.6.2. Fragment Types

Fragment values are values that are *not complete*. If they are structured, then some subvalues are absent. If they are basic, then they are missing completely. The places of absent subvalues are marked by holes @1, @2, @3, ..., into which we may insert values to get complete values. Holes may occur in every structured value and hold place for all values except functions and constructors. Functions are considered as indivisible objects, and the constructor names are needed to distinguish between user-defined types and the types of subtrees.

We need new types for values that are not complete. We wish to guarantee that only suitable values are inserted into holes in order to produce legal values. The underlying idea is that fragment values are similar to functions: e.g., @1 is a value into which we may insert a value of type τ resulting in the same value of type τ; analogously, the identity function $\lambda x.x$ takes an argument of type τ resulting in the same value of type τ. A value with several holes of different numbers is like a function with several arguments. Function application is similar to insertion. It is not exactly the same, because we can insert values into complete values, whereas there are no functions without formal parameters. We can insert holes into holes that hold place for integers, but we cannot apply integer functions to arguments that are functions. We also have no functional analogy to the extraction of values.

Even so, we use a type for fragment values that is similar to the type of functions. We use the fragment operator $\mathrel{+\!\!+\!\!\!\rightarrow}$ instead of the functional operator $\rightarrow$ (both associate to the right) and specify:

Rule 1 *A value v possesses the type $\tau_1 \mathrel{+\!\!+\!\!\!\rightarrow} \tau_2$ (where τ_1 and τ_2 are types) if every value of type τ_1 can be inserted into v, resulting in a value of type τ_2.*

Such types are called *fragment types*. Some examples:

@1	has the type $\alpha \mathrel{+\!\!+\!\!\!\rightarrow} \alpha$
@2	has the type $\beta \mathrel{+\!\!+\!\!\!\rightarrow} \alpha \mathrel{+\!\!+\!\!\!\rightarrow} \alpha$ (i.e., $\beta \mathrel{+\!\!+\!\!\!\rightarrow} (\alpha \mathrel{+\!\!+\!\!\!\rightarrow} \alpha)$)
@3	has the type $\gamma \mathrel{+\!\!+\!\!\!\rightarrow} \beta \mathrel{+\!\!+\!\!\!\rightarrow} \alpha \mathrel{+\!\!+\!\!\!\rightarrow} \alpha$
[1, 2, @1]	has the type int $\mathrel{+\!\!+\!\!\!\rightarrow}$ (int$*$)
the ^-operator	has the type $(\alpha \mathrel{+\!\!+\!\!\!\rightarrow} \beta) \rightarrow \alpha \rightarrow \beta$

A complete value has several types since it has a nonfragment type. One also can insert values, so, for instance, by rule 1 every integer number (with type int) also has the type $\alpha \mathrel{+\!\!+\!\!\!\rightarrow}$int, because we are allowed to insert something into the number resulting in the same number again. We need a mechanism to handle these cases.

Structured values with holes are a second source of type diversity. The integers 1 and 2 have the type int and also the type int $\mathrel{+\!\!+\!\!\!\rightarrow}$ int and, since @1 also has this type, all elements of the list [1, 2, @1] have the same type int $\mathrel{+\!\!+\!\!\!\rightarrow}$ int. Therefore, the list has the second type (int $\mathrel{+\!\!+\!\!\!\rightarrow}$ int)$*$ as well as int $\mathrel{+\!\!+\!\!\!\rightarrow}$ (int$*$). More examples:

[@1, @1] has the types $(\alpha \mathrel{+\!\!+\!\!\!\rightarrow} \alpha)*$ and $\alpha \mathrel{+\!\!+\!\!\!\rightarrow} (\alpha*)$
(@1, @1) has the type $(\alpha \mathrel{+\!\!+\!\!\!\rightarrow} \alpha) \times (\beta \mathrel{+\!\!+\!\!\!\rightarrow} \beta)$
and the type $\alpha \mathrel{+\!\!+\!\!\!\rightarrow} (\alpha \times \alpha)$
(@2, 5) has the types $(\beta \mathrel{+\!\!+\!\!\!\rightarrow} \alpha \mathrel{+\!\!+\!\!\!\rightarrow} \alpha) \times$ int,
$\beta \mathrel{+\!\!+\!\!\!\rightarrow} ((\alpha \mathrel{+\!\!+\!\!\!\rightarrow} \alpha) \times$ int$)$ and $\beta \mathrel{+\!\!+\!\!\!\rightarrow} \alpha \mathrel{+\!\!+\!\!\!\rightarrow} (\alpha \times$ int$)$

8.6.3. Type Versions

In connection with the meaning of fragment types, we now analyze the rôle of the basic types “int”, “bool”, “string”, and “unit”. There is the following problem:

To produce a legal list, we can insert a hole @1 into [1, 2, @1], resulting in the same list. This list has the type int $\mapsto\!\!\!\!\!+\!\!+$(int*), thus the type $\alpha \mapsto\!\!\!\!\!+\!\!+ \alpha$ of @1 has to unify with int. The type after insertion is int*, but this is not a correct type of the result [1, 2, @1] since it is the type of a complete value, into which we may insert anything producing the same complete value. But the insertion of 'true' into the result will not produce a legal value.

The idea for solving this problem originates from the handling of type variables: it is necessary to note the dependencies between the types of values that may be inserted and the type of the result. We notify different types int_1, int_2, int_3, ... called *type versions*, which all are types of integer values. Analogously, there are bool_1, bool_2, string_1, string_2, unit_1, unit_2, ... For instance, if int_1 occurs in several types and has to unify with $\tau_1 \mapsto\!\!\!\!\!+\!\!+ \text{int}_2$, this is done by replacing all occurrences of int_1 by $\tau_1 \mapsto\!\!\!\!\!+\!\!+ \text{int}_2$. This mechanism of replacement is the same as for type variables: we bind $\tau_1 \mapsto\!\!\!\!\!+\!\!+ \text{int}_2$ to int_1.
In the example:

[1, 2, @1] has the types $\text{int}_1 \mapsto\!\!\!\!\!+\!\!+ (\text{int}_1*)$ and $(\text{int}_1 \mapsto\!\!\!\!\!+\!\!+ \text{int}_1)*$. int_1 unifies with $\alpha \mapsto\!\!\!\!\!+\!\!+ \alpha$ giving $\text{int}_2 \mapsto\!\!\!\!\!+\!\!+ \text{int}_2$, which is a type of @1. Thus we may insert @1 into the list resulting in the same list with the calculated type $(\text{int}_2 \mapsto\!\!\!\!\!+\!\!+ \text{int}_2)*$ by replacing $\text{int}_2 \mapsto\!\!\!\!\!+\!\!+ \text{int}_2$ for int_1. We see that this type is in fact a type of the result.

The problem is how to realize the dependencies, i.e., how to recognize that a value has the type $\text{int}_1 \mapsto\!\!\!\!\!+\!\!+ (\text{int}_1*)$ and not $\text{int}_1 \mapsto\!\!\!\!\!+\!\!+ (\text{int}_2*)$. Dependencies have to be calculated if holes are produced, i.e., if extraction is done, or if a hole explicitly occurs in the program.
Let us consider the expression [1, 2, @1]. We require that all elements of a list have the same type: the number 1 has the type int_1, the number 2 has the type int_2 (because initially there is no dependence on the number 1) and the hole @1 has the type $\alpha \mapsto\!\!\!\!\!+\!\!+ \alpha$ with the unbound type variable α. Now we have to unify these types, i.e., we are looking for a substitution (bindings of type variables/versions) with the result that all element types to be equal:

int_2 is bound to int_1, thus the number 2 has the type int_1.
α is bound to int_3, thus the hole @1 has type $\text{int}_3 \mapsto\!\!\!\!\!+\!\!+ \text{int}_3$.
int_1 unifies with $\text{int}_3 \mapsto\!\!\!\!\!+\!\!+ \text{int}_3$ by binding $\text{int}_3 \mapsto\!\!\!\!\!+\!\!+ \text{int}_3$ to int_1.
Now unification is successful and all elements of the list have the type $\text{int}_3 \mapsto\!\!\!\!\!+\!\!+ \text{int}_3$. The list has the type $(\text{int}_3 \mapsto\!\!\!\!\!+\!\!+ \text{int}_3)*$ with the necessary dependencies.

The extraction pattern ^ is more difficult. It seems to have the same type as the insertion expression but this leads to errors in dependencies. In this case, we have to use a special analysis that searches all places in a type where the extracted value could be cut out and unifies its type with the type of the hole.

To sum up, we give the substitution rules for type variables and type versions:

Rule 2 *For a type variable α_i one may substitute every type not containing α_i.*

Rule 3 *For a type version int_i one may substitute every type version int_j and every type $\tau \mapsto\!\!\!\!\!+\!\!+ int_j$ that does not contain int_i.*
Analogously for $bool_i$, $string_i$, and $unit_i$.

Type versions int_i are used as initial types of the basic values "integer numbers". τ cannot be substituted for a type int_1 if τ contains int_1, because substitution means that all occurrences of int_1 (the occurrence in τ, too) would be replaced. This would lead to infinite sequences of replacements: insert τ for int_1 into τ, insert τ into the inserted τ, insert τ into the inserted τ of the inserted τ, etc.

8.6.4. (Inverse) Fragment Type Normal Form

There is another problem: How does one unify types of different structure? For example: The value [1, 2, @1] has the type $int_1 \mathrel{+\!\!\!+\!\!\!\to} (int_1 *)$ and the type $(int_1 \mathrel{+\!\!\!+\!\!\!\to} int_1)*$. During type checking, there are many calculations to test equality or compatibility of types. We need a mechanism to unify the types $int_1 \mathrel{+\!\!\!+\!\!\!\to} (int_1 *)$ and $(int_1 \mathrel{+\!\!\!+\!\!\!\to} int_1)*$. They must be unifiable because they are types of the same value. The solution is to transform the types into a normal form so that the structures are comparable.
Thus, we first define the *inverse fragment type normal form* (IFNF):

Definition 3 *A type is an* **IFNF** *iff it has the form* $\tau_1 \mathrel{+\!\!\!+\!\!\!\to} \tau_2 \mathrel{+\!\!\!+\!\!\!\to} \ldots \mathrel{+\!\!\!+\!\!\!\to} \tau_n$ *where* τ_n *contains no fragment type and* $\tau_1, \ldots, \tau_{n-1}$ *are IFNF's.*

Examples: $int_1 \mathrel{+\!\!\!+\!\!\!\to} (int_1 *)$ is an IFNF but $(int_1 \mathrel{+\!\!\!+\!\!\!\to} int_1)*$ is not.
$\alpha_1 \mathrel{+\!\!\!+\!\!\!\to} (int_1 \times \alpha_1)$ is an IFNF but $int_1 \times (\alpha_1 \mathrel{+\!\!\!+\!\!\!\to} \alpha_1)$ is not.

Types transformed into IFNF are easily unified by the normal structural unification. The transformation rules necessary to obtain IFNF's are obvious from the examples:

Rule 4 (a) $(\tau_1 \mathrel{+\!\!\!+\!\!\!\to} \tau_2)*$ *transforms into* $\tau_1 \mathrel{+\!\!\!+\!\!\!\to} (\tau_2 *)$.

Rule 5 (a) $(\tau_1 \mathrel{+\!\!\!+\!\!\!\to} \tau_2) \times (\tau_1 \mathrel{+\!\!\!+\!\!\!\to} \tau_3)$ *transforms into* $\tau_1 \mathrel{+\!\!\!+\!\!\!\to} (\tau_2 \times \tau_3)$.

Repeated use of these rules leads to an IFNF if one exists. However, not all types have an IFNF, e.g. there is no possibility of transforming the type $(int_1 \mathrel{+\!\!\!+\!\!\!\to} int_2) \times (bool_1 \mathrel{+\!\!\!+\!\!\!\to} bool_2)$ into IFNF, but there are values that may have such types. We cannot insert a value into such a value since we have to look for a value that is integer and boolean at the same time, but this is no reason to forbid such types. So we need another normal form.

The rules 4(a) and 5(a) take the fragment operator $\mathrel{+\!\!\!+\!\!\!\to}$ out of the parentheses. The converse may be done, too. In fact, if we use the rules 4(a) and 5(a) in the opposite direction, this leads to another normal form, where the fragment operator is inside the parentheses. We call this *fragment type normal form* (FNF) and use it in unification. The transformation rules now are:

Rule 4 $\tau_1 \mathrel{+\!\!\!+\!\!\!\to} (\tau_2 *)$ *transforms into* $(\tau_1 \mathrel{+\!\!\!+\!\!\!\to} \tau_2)*$.

Rule 5 $\tau \mathrel{+\!\!\!+\!\!\!\to} (\tau_1 \times \ldots \times \tau_n)$ *transforms into* $(\tau \mathrel{+\!\!\!+\!\!\!\to} \tau_1) \times \ldots \times (\tau \mathrel{+\!\!\!+\!\!\!\to} \tau_n)$.

A type is a FNF if no transformation rule is applicable to a subtype of the type. Now the types $(int_1 \mathrel{+\!\!\!+\!\!\!\to} int_2) \times (bool_1 \mathrel{+\!\!\!+\!\!\!\to} bool_2)$, $(int_1 \mathrel{+\!\!\!+\!\!\!\to} int_2)*$ and $int_1 \times (\alpha \mathrel{+\!\!\!+\!\!\!\to} \alpha)$ are FNF's. There are types that are neither IFNF nor FNF, but all types can be transformed into FNF.

8.6.5. User Declared Types and Short Types

In patterns, type specifications, and type declarations, it is sufficient to specify user-defined types by their names (perhaps followed by the instances of the type variables). In type theory, we need a more detailed syntax: we have to describe the dependencies between the types of values that may be inserted and the type of the result. For instance, the value 'Pair (@1, true) must have a type $int_1 \mathrel{+\!\!\!+\!\!\!\to} \ldots$ where the type int_1 must occur on the right side of the fragment operator. If we insert @1 into the value, the result is not complete such that it has a fragment type. So the type $\text{int}_1 \mathrel{+\!\!\!+\!\!\!\!\rightarrow} \text{inttree}$ is insufficient in type theory, because the result after insertion would be inttree.

We use $N\{\kappa_1, \ldots, \kappa_n\}$ for monomorphically declared user types and $N(\tau_1, \ldots, \tau_m)\{\kappa_1, \ldots, \kappa_n\}$ for polymorphically declared user types, where N is the name of the tree type or the typeforming operator, τ_1, $\ldots$, τ_m are the instances of the type variables and $\kappa_1, \ldots, \kappa_n$ are shortened versions of the types that may occur in subtrees. So the value 'ileaf @1 has the type $\text{int}_1 \mathrel{+\!\!\!+\!\!\!\!\rightarrow} \text{inttree}\{\text{int}_1, \text{inttree}_1\}$. The dependencies between the insertable values and the result are reflected by the multiple use of int_1. If we insert a hole @1, the substitution of int_1 by $\text{int}_2 \mathrel{+\!\!\!+\!\!\!\!\rightarrow} \text{int}_2$ leads to the type $\text{inttree}\{\text{int}_2 \mathrel{+\!\!\!+\!\!\!\!\rightarrow} \text{int}_2, \text{inttree}_1\}$. This is in fact a fragment type. Now we need a rule to transform such types into fragment type normal form:

Rule 6 *$\tau \mathrel{+\!\!\!+\!\!\!\!\rightarrow} N\{\kappa_1, \ldots, \kappa_n\}$ transforms into $N\{\tau \mathrel{+\!\!\!+\!\!\!\!\rightarrow} \kappa_1, \ldots, \tau \mathrel{+\!\!\!+\!\!\!\!\rightarrow} \kappa_n\}$.
$\tau \mathrel{+\!\!\!+\!\!\!\!\rightarrow} N(\tau_1, \ldots, \tau_m)\{\kappa_1, \ldots, \kappa_n\}$ transforms into
$N(\tau \mathrel{+\!\!\!+\!\!\!\!\rightarrow} \tau_1, \ldots, \tau \mathrel{+\!\!\!+\!\!\!\!\rightarrow} \tau_m)\ \{\tau \mathrel{+\!\!\!+\!\!\!\!\rightarrow} \kappa_1, \ldots, \tau \mathrel{+\!\!\!+\!\!\!\!\rightarrow} \kappa_n\}$.*

Some examples (compare with the type declaration in section 8.3.6):

'ileaf 5	has the type $\text{inttree}\{\text{int}_1, \text{inttree}_1\}$
'ileaf @1	has the types $\text{int}_1 \mathrel{+\!\!\!+\!\!\!\!\rightarrow} \text{inttree}\{\text{int}_1, \text{inttree}_1\}$
	and $\text{inttree}\{\text{int}_1 \mathrel{+\!\!\!+\!\!\!\!\rightarrow} \text{int}_1, \text{int}_1 \mathrel{+\!\!\!+\!\!\!\!\rightarrow} \text{inttree}_1\}$
	and $\text{inttree}\{\text{int}_1 \mathrel{+\!\!\!+\!\!\!\!\rightarrow} \text{int}_1, \text{inttree}_1\}$
'inode('ileaf 5, @1)	has the type $\text{inttree}\{\text{int}_1, \text{inttree}_1\} \mathrel{+\!\!\!+\!\!\!\!\rightarrow} \text{inttree}\{\text{int}_2, \text{inttree}_1\}$
	and $\text{inttree}\{\text{int}_2, \text{inttree}\{\text{int}_1, \text{inttree}_1\} \mathrel{+\!\!\!+\!\!\!\!\rightarrow} \text{inttree}_1\}$
'inode @1	has the type $(\text{inttree}\{\text{int}_1, \text{inttree}_1\} \times \text{inttree}\{\text{int}_1, \text{inttree}_1\}$
	$\mathrel{+\!\!\!+\!\!\!\!\rightarrow} \text{inttree}\{\text{int}_1, \text{inttree}_1\}$
'leaf true	has the type $\text{Tree}(\text{bool}_1)\{\text{Tree}_1\}$
'leaf @1	has the type $\alpha \mathrel{+\!\!\!+\!\!\!\!\rightarrow} \text{Tree}(\alpha)\{\text{Tree}_1\}$
	and $\text{Tree}(\alpha \mathrel{+\!\!\!+\!\!\!\!\rightarrow} \alpha)\{\alpha \mathrel{+\!\!\!+\!\!\!\!\rightarrow} \text{Tree}_1\}$
	and $\text{Tree}(\alpha \mathrel{+\!\!\!+\!\!\!\!\rightarrow} \alpha)\{\text{Tree}_1\}$

The types $\kappa_1, \ldots, \kappa_n$ of the subtrees are *short types*. A tree with type "inttree" may contain a subtree of type "inttree", but in type $\text{inttree}\{\ldots\}$ it is impossible to denote the full type of the subtree, because this would contain a full type "inttree" again. This leads to an infinite type $\text{inttree}\{\ldots,\text{inttree}\{\ldots,\text{inttree}\{\ldots,\text{inttree}\{\ldots$ Hence, we use short types instead. These are the type versions of user-declared types, e.g., inttree_1, inttree_1, Tree_1, Tree_1, etc. Versions are needed to denote the dependencies. We have a substitution rule for short type versions that is analogous to the rule for basic type versions:

Rule 7 *For a short type version N_i of a user type N, one may substitute every short type version N_j and every short type $\tau \mathrel{+\!\!\!+\!\!\!\!\rightarrow} N_j$ that does not contain N_i.*

The aim of short types is to denote the instances and dependencies of type versions. Thus, we need only the basic type versions and user type versions contained in a type of a subtree, and the fragment types that are bound to them, but we do not need to classify tuple types, list types, etc., as short types. During type calculation, we also use type variables as auxiliary short types.

8.6.6. Generic Instances of Types

The type checker labels each subexpression and subpattern of a program with a type. It starts at the leaves of the syntax tree of the program and works bottom-up towards the root. Let us consider a type calculation for an expression:

```
let f = { x => (x,x) }
in ( f true, f 5 );
```

When a new formal parameter such as f or x is introduced, we do not know its real type. Thus, we assume the most general type α, where α is a new type variable. Later, we may substitute a more specialized type for α. Now let α_1 be the initial type of f and α_2 the initial type of x. Then the tuple (x,x) has the type $\alpha_2 \times \alpha_2$ and the function { x => (x,x) } has the type $\alpha_2 \rightarrow (\alpha_2 \times \alpha_2)$. The types on the left and right hand side of '=' in a let expression must be the same: we unify the types by binding $\alpha_2 \rightarrow (\alpha_2 \times \alpha_2)$ to α_1.

The analysis of the in-part of the let expression reveals a problem: when we calculate the type of f **true**, we have to bind α_2 to bool_1, whereas we have to bind α_2 to int_1 when the type of f 5 is calculated. However, this is not possible at the same time. The solution is obvious: both occurrences of f are *applicative*. In applicative occurrences, we refresh the type of a variable, by renaming all type variables and type versions with new variables/versions that were not used before. So, we produce a *generic instance* of the type: for f, we use the type instance $\alpha_3 \rightarrow (\alpha_3 \times \alpha_3)$ in f 5, and $\alpha_4 \rightarrow (\alpha_4 \times \alpha_4)$ in f **true**. Now calculation succeeds, binding int_1 to α_3 and bool_1 to α_4.

Notice that all occurrences of x in the function { x => (x,x) } are *defining*. Thus we must not refresh the type of x. Otherwise, the function would obtain the type $\alpha_2 \rightarrow (\alpha_3 \times \alpha_4)$ which is obviously wrong: If we apply f to an integer (substituting int_1 for α_2), the result does not have the type $(\alpha_3 \times \alpha_4)$. The defining occurrences of a variable are all occurrences in the defining part of the variable in the construct. The defining part of $\{ p => e \}$ is the whole function, i.e., all binding variables of p are defining in p and e. The defining part of **let** $p = e$ **in** e' (and also **dec** $p = e$ or **rec** $p = e$) is the pattern p and the expression e, but not the body e'.

Definition 4 *A type variable or type version is called* **ungeneric** *iff it is part of a type of a variable and occurs in the defining part of the variable. Otherwise it is called* **generic**.

Definition 5 *A* **generic instance** *of a type is an instance of the type where only the generic type variables and versions are instantiated.*

In the type system, we assume that we can easily determine whether a type variable or version is generic or not. Practically, this can be solved by a count assigned to every defining part and a count assigned to every type variable/version indicating that the variable/version occurs in a type of a syntactic variable of a defining part with this count. We need a *count* instead of a *flag* since defining scopes may be nested. Thus, if the type calculation terminates a defining part, all type variables/versions with the same count as the part will be generic.

8.7. Type System

8.7.1. Types and their Semantics

Calculation with types is a syntactic process. We transform types by expansion, substitution, and renaming. Therefore we need the syntax of types as introduced above, but distinguish this from the TrafoLa syntax to write down types as language constructs. We give a formal summary of the syntax and semantics of types.

8.7.1.1. Syntax of Types

First, we define **full types:**

1. There are enumerable sets of basic type versions:
   { int_1, int_2, int_3, ... }
   { bool_1, bool_2, bool_3, ... }
   { string_1, string_2, string_3, ... }
   { unit_1, unit_2, unit_3, ... }

2. There is an enumerable set of type variables: $\{ \alpha_1, \alpha_2, \alpha_3, \ldots \}$

3. τ_1*, $\tau_1 \times \ldots \times \tau_n$, $\tau_1 \rightarrow \tau_n$, $\tau_1 \twoheadrightarrow \tau_n$, $\tau_1 \mathrel{+\!\!\!+\!\!\!\rightarrow} \tau_n$ are full types if $\tau_1, \ldots, \tau_n$ are full types.

4. $N\{ \kappa_1, \ldots, \kappa_m\}$ for monomorphically declared user types named N and $N(\tau_1, \ldots, \tau_n)\{ \kappa_1, \ldots, \kappa_m\}$ for polymorphically declared user types N (with n type variables) are full types if $\tau_1, \ldots, \tau_n$ are full types and $\kappa_1, \ldots, \kappa_m$ are short types.

Short types are:

1. all basic type versions int_i, bool_i, string_i, unit_i.

2. type versions N_i of user declared types N.

3. fragment types $\tau \mathrel{+\!\!\!+\!\!\!\rightarrow} \kappa$, where τ is a full type and κ is a short type.

8.7.1.2. Semantics of Initial Monomorphic Types

The semantics of types is the conditions under which a value v possesses a type τ. We denote this by $v{:}\tau$. Since the type may be ambiguous (e.g., integers have the types int_i and $\tau \mathrel{+\!\!\!+\!\!\!\rightarrow}\text{int}_i$), we first define the *initial monomorphic type* of a value and then the *derived types*.

(M1)	$v{:}\text{int}_i$	$\Leftrightarrow$ v is integer, $\perp$, or fail
	$v{:}\text{bool}_i$	$\Leftrightarrow$ v is boolean, $\perp$, or fail
	$v{:}\text{string}_i$	$\Leftrightarrow$ v is string, $\perp$, or fail
	$v{:}\text{unit}_i$	$\Leftrightarrow$ v is (), $\perp$, or fail
(M2)	$v{:}\mu*$	$\Leftrightarrow$ v is [$v_1, \ldots, v_n$] and $v_1{:}\mu, \ldots, v_n{:}\mu$ or v is [ ], $\perp$, or fail
(M3)	$v{:}\mu_1 \times \ldots \times \mu_n$	$\Leftrightarrow$ v is ($v_1, \ldots, v_n$) and $v_1{:}\mu_1, \ldots, v_n{:}\mu_n$ or v is $\perp$ or fail
(M4)	$v{:}\mu_1 \rightarrow \mu_2$	$\Leftrightarrow$ v is a function and $(v\ w){:}\mu_2$ holds for all $w{:}\mu_1$ or v is $\perp$ or fail
(M5)	$v{:}\mu_1 \twoheadrightarrow \mu_2$	$\Leftrightarrow$ v is a constructor and $(v\ w){:}\mu_2$ holds for all $w{:}\mu_1$ or v is $\perp$ or fail
(M6)	$v{:}\mu_1 \mathrel{+\!\!\!+\!\!\!\rightarrow} \mu_2$	$\Leftrightarrow$ v is a structured value and $(v\,\hat{}\,w){:}\mu_2$ holds for all $w{:}\mu_1$ or v is $\perp$ or fail
(M7)	$v{:}N\{\kappa_1, \ldots, \kappa_m\}$ or $v{:}N(\mu_1, \ldots, \mu_n)\{\kappa_1, \ldots, \kappa_m\}$	$\Leftrightarrow$ v is value of a tree domain defined by a type declaration of N, without, or with n type variables and m type versions in the subtrees. $\mu_1, \ldots, \mu_n$ are the monomorphic instances of type variables and $\kappa_1, \ldots, \kappa_m$ are the instances of (short) type versions that may occur in types of subtrees or v is $\perp$ or fail

Note that 'fail' and '$\perp$' have every monomorphic type, but a value containing 'error' has no type. If it is possible to assign a type to every part of the program, then 'error' cannot occur at runtime. The type system is able to detect semantic errors resulting in 'error', but is not able to detect 'fail' or '$\perp$'. The value 'error' denotes the static errors while 'fail' and '$\perp$' denote dynamic errors. The 'error' value in denotational semantics was not really needed to explain the runtime errors but to explain the cases that we wish to avoid by using a type checker. Thus, we consider the result of undefined calculations (like division by zero) as '$\perp$' and not as 'error'.

8.7.1.3. Semantics of Derived Types

To define the semantics of derived types including polytypes, we give the **substitution rules**: We permit the following substitutions (with i $\neq$ j and τ not containing the type that is replaced):

int_j	for int_i
$\tau \mathrel{+\!\!\!+\!\!\!\!\rightarrow} \text{int}_j$	for int_i
bool_j	for bool_i
$\tau \mathrel{+\!\!\!+\!\!\!\!\rightarrow} \text{bool}_j$	for bool_i
string_j	for string_i
$\tau \mathrel{+\!\!\!+\!\!\!\!\rightarrow} \text{string}_j$	for string_i
unit_j	for unit_i
$\tau \mathrel{+\!\!\!+\!\!\!\!\rightarrow} \text{unit}_j$	for unit_i
N_j	for N_i
$\tau \mathrel{+\!\!\!+\!\!\!\!\rightarrow} N_j$	for N_i
τ	for α_i

Now we lift the substitutions to all types. We use $\tau_1 \leq \tau_2$ to express that τ_1 may be obtained from τ_2 by substitutions. Clearly $\leq$ is reflexive and transitive. If $\tau_1 \leq \tau_2$, then $\tau_1 = \tau_2$ or there are type variables/versions in τ_2 that we can substitute resulting in τ_1.

Examples: $\mu_1 \rightarrow \mu_1 \leq \alpha_1 \rightarrow \alpha_1 \leq \alpha_2 \rightarrow \alpha_3$.
$\text{bool}_1 \mathrel{+\!\!\!+\!\!\!\!\rightarrow} \text{int}_1 \leq \text{int}_2 \leq \text{int}_3 \leq \alpha_1$.
However: $\alpha_1 \rightarrow \alpha_2 \not\leq \alpha_3 \rightarrow \alpha_3$.
$\text{int}_1 \not\leq \text{bool}_1 \mathrel{+\!\!\!+\!\!\!\!\rightarrow} \text{int}_2$.

Semantics: **derived types**

(P) $v{:}\sigma \Leftrightarrow \forall\, \mu{\leq}\sigma\;\; v{:}\mu$

For instance, by rule (M6) the hole @1 has the initial type $\mu_1 \mathrel{+\!\!\!+\!\!\!\!\rightarrow} \mu_1$ for every monotype μ_1, because we may insert any value resulting in the same value. So it has the type $\alpha_i \mathrel{+\!\!\!+\!\!\!\!\rightarrow} \alpha_i$ by rule (P). A hole on place for an integer has the type $\text{int}_i \mathrel{+\!\!\!+\!\!\!\!\rightarrow} \text{int}_i$, but not the type int_j, since $\text{int}_j \not\leq \text{int}_i \mathrel{+\!\!\!+\!\!\!\!\rightarrow} \text{int}_i$. On the other hand, an integer function of type $\text{int}_1 \rightarrow \tau$ has the type $(\text{int}_2 \mathrel{+\!\!\!+\!\!\!\!\rightarrow} \text{int}_2) \rightarrow \tau$, too. Thus, the function also has to work with holes. In fact, the type checker is not able to distinguish between holes and basic values. But this is not surprising, because holes are often nondeterministically produced by the '^'-pattern, and the type checker cannot detect whether a hole is produced or not. Errors in calculations such as addition of holes (addition works only with numbers, not with holes) are considered as unforeseeable, similar to division by zero, etc. They result in '$\perp$'. Surely, the type checker *is able* to detect real transformation errors like the insertion of noncompatible values into holes.

With the semantics of types, we can prove the rules 4, 5, and 6 for transformation into FNF, so we expand the operator $\leq$ to transformations of types: $\tau_1 \leq \tau_2$ iff τ_1 is derivable from τ_2 by substitutions and transformations. (In fact, we need a more detailed semantics of user-defined types to prove rule 6, but this would blow up this chapter.) The proofs are left to the reader. Instead, we describe the more practical part of the type checker: the way to find the types.

8.7.2. Fragment Type Normal Form

We give the function that returns a FNF from a type in a TrafoLa-like syntax. It is not exactly a TrafoLa function since we use the syntax for types introduced above, which is not part of TrafoLa-H, and an ellipsis "..." instead of applications of 'Map'. All this is done for improving readability. The function 'MakeFNF' uses the type transformation rules:

rec MakeFNF =
{ int_i => int_i
bool_i => bool_i
string_i => string_i
unit_i => unit_i
N_i => N_i
α_i => α_i
$\tau*$ => (MakeFNF τ)*
$\tau_1 \times \ldots \times \tau_n$ => (MakeFNF τ_1) $\times \ldots \times$(MakeFNF τ_n)
$\tau_1 \rightarrow \tau_2$ => (MakeFNF τ_1) $\rightarrow$ (MakeFNF τ_2)
$\tau_1 \twoheadrightarrow \tau_2$ => (MakeFNF τ_1) $\twoheadrightarrow$ (MakeFNF τ_2)
$N\{\kappa_1, \ldots, \kappa_m\}$ => N\{ MakeFNF $\kappa_1, \ldots,$ MakeFNF κ_m\}
$N(\tau_1, \ldots, \tau_n)\{\kappa_1, \ldots, \kappa_m\}$
=> N(MakeFNF $\tau_1, \ldots,$ MakeFNF τ_n) \{MakeFNF $\kappa_1, \ldots,$ MakeFNF κ_m\}
$\tau_1 +\!\!\!+\!\!\!\rightarrow \tau_2$ =>
let t1 = MakeFNF τ_1 **and** t2 = MakeFNF τ_2 **in**
case t2 **of**
{ $\tau*$ => (MakeFNF (t1 $+\!\!\!+\!\!\!\rightarrow \tau$))*
$\tau_1 \times \ldots \times \tau_n$ => MakeFNF (t1 $+\!\!\!+\!\!\!\rightarrow \tau_1$) $\times \ldots \times$MakeFNF (t1 $+\!\!\!+\!\!\!\rightarrow \tau_n$)
$N\{\kappa_1, \ldots, \kappa_m\}$ => N\{ MakeFNF (t1 $+\!\!\!+\!\!\!\rightarrow \kappa_1$), $\ldots,$ MakeFNF (t1 $+\!\!\!+\!\!\!\rightarrow \kappa_m$)\}
$N(\tau_1, \ldots, \tau_n)\{\kappa_1, \ldots, \kappa_m\}$ => N(MakeFNF (t1 $+\!\!\!+\!\!\!\rightarrow \tau_1$), $\ldots,$ MakeFNF (t1 $+\!\!\!+\!\!\!\rightarrow \tau_n$))
\{ MakeFNF (t1 $+\!\!\!+\!\!\!\rightarrow \kappa_1$), $\ldots,$ MakeFNF (t1 $+\!\!\!+\!\!\!\rightarrow \kappa_m$)\}
# _ => t1 $+\!\!\!+\!\!\!\rightarrow$ t2 }
};

8.7.3. Unification

Most calculations with types are unifications. Consider the application 'Length [1, 2, @1]'. The type checker calculates types bottom-up, so it knows *Length* : $\alpha_1* \rightarrow \text{int}_1$ and [1, 2,@1] : $\text{int}_2 +\!\!\!+\!\!\!\rightarrow (\text{int}_2*)$ and tries to check the type of the application. Corresponding to rule (M4), it looks for a type τ with $\tau \leq \alpha_1$ $*$ and $\tau \leq \text{int}_2 +\!\!\!+\!\!\!\rightarrow (\text{int}_2*)$. The method to find it is called unification: trying to make both types equal by binding type variable/versions and by transforming into FNF.

We give the unification function 'Uf' in a TrafoLa-like syntax. It returns a substitution $< \alpha_i \rightarrow \tau_i, \ldots >$ such that both types τ_1 and τ_2 are equalized or 'not unifiable'. We use a test function 'occurs', indicating that a type variable/version occurs in a type. '+' denotes the superposition of substitutions. We assume that we may get a new type variable/version never previously used whenever needed.

rec Uf =

Pattern	Result
$\{\ \tau, \tau$	$=> < >$
$\#\ \tau, \alpha$	$=>$ **if** occurs $\alpha\ \tau$ **then** 'not unifiable' **else** $< \alpha \rightarrow \tau >$
$\#\ \alpha, \tau$	$=>$ **if** occurs $\alpha\ \tau$ **then** 'not unifiable' **else** $< \alpha \rightarrow \tau >$
$\#\ \mathrm{int}_i, \mathrm{int}_j$	$=> < \mathrm{int}_i \rightarrow \mathrm{int}_j >$
$\#\ \mathrm{int}_i, \tau \mathrel{+\!\!+\!\!\!\rightarrow} \mathrm{int}_j$	$=>$ **if** occurs $\mathrm{int}_i\ (\tau \mathrel{+\!\!+\!\!\!\rightarrow} \mathrm{int}_j)$ **then** 'not unifiable' **else** $< \mathrm{int}_i \rightarrow (\tau \mathrel{+\!\!+\!\!\!\rightarrow} \mathrm{int}_j) >$
$\#\ \mathrm{bool}_i, \mathrm{bool}_j$	$=> < \mathrm{bool}_i \rightarrow \mathrm{bool}_j >$
$\#\ \mathrm{bool}_i, \tau \mathrel{+\!\!+\!\!\!\rightarrow} \mathrm{bool}_j$	$=>$ **if** occurs $\mathrm{bool}_i\ (\tau \mathrel{+\!\!+\!\!\!\rightarrow} \mathrm{bool}_j)$ **then** 'not unifiable' **else** $< \mathrm{bool}_i \rightarrow (\tau \mathrel{+\!\!+\!\!\!\rightarrow} \mathrm{bool}_j) >$
$\#\ \mathrm{string}_i, \mathrm{string}_j$	$=> < \mathrm{string}_i \rightarrow \mathrm{string}_j >$
$\#\ \mathrm{string}_i, \tau \mathrel{+\!\!+\!\!\!\rightarrow} \mathrm{string}_j$	$=>$ **if** occurs $\mathrm{string}_i\ (\tau \mathrel{+\!\!+\!\!\!\rightarrow} \mathrm{string}_j)$ **then** 'not unifiable' **else** $< \mathrm{string}_i \rightarrow (\tau \mathrel{+\!\!+\!\!\!\rightarrow} \mathrm{string}_j) >$
$\#\ \mathrm{unit}_i, \mathrm{unit}_j$	$=> < \mathrm{unit}_i \rightarrow \mathrm{unit}_j >$
$\#\ \mathrm{unit}_i, \tau \mathrel{+\!\!+\!\!\!\rightarrow} \mathrm{unit}_j$	$=>$ **if** occurs $\mathrm{unit}_i\ (\tau \mathrel{+\!\!+\!\!\!\rightarrow} \mathrm{unit}_j)$ **then** 'not unifiable' **else** $< \mathrm{unit}_i \rightarrow (\tau \mathrel{+\!\!+\!\!\!\rightarrow} \mathrm{unit}_j) >$
$\#\ N_i, N_j$	$=> < N_i \rightarrow N_j >$
$\#\ N_i, \tau \mathrel{+\!\!+\!\!\!\rightarrow} N_j$	$=>$ **if** occurs $N_i\ (\tau \mathrel{+\!\!+\!\!\!\rightarrow} N_j)$ **then** 'not unifiable' **else** $< N_i \rightarrow (\tau \mathrel{+\!\!+\!\!\!\rightarrow} N_j) >$
$\#\ \tau_1*, \tau_2*$	$=>$ Uf $\tau_1\ \tau_2$
$\#\ \tau_1*, \tau_2 \mathrel{+\!\!+\!\!\!\rightarrow} \alpha$	$=>$ **let** α' be a new type variable **in** $< \alpha \rightarrow \alpha'* > +$ Uf $\tau_1\ (\tau_2 \mathrel{+\!\!+\!\!\!\rightarrow} \alpha')$
$\#\ \tau_1*, \tau_2 \mathrel{+\!\!+\!\!\!\rightarrow} \tau_3$	$=>$ **let** t = MakeFNF $(\tau_2 \mathrel{+\!\!+\!\!\!\rightarrow} \tau_3)$ **in** **if** t is list **then** Uf (τ_1*) t **else** 'not unifiable'
$\#\ \tau_1 \times \ldots \times \tau_n, \tau_1' \times \ldots \times \tau_n'$	$=>$ Uf $\tau_1\ \tau_1' + \ldots +$ Uf $\tau_n\ \tau_n'$
$\#\ \tau_1 \times \ldots \times \tau_n, \tau' \mathrel{+\!\!+\!\!\!\rightarrow} \alpha$	$=>$ **let** $\alpha_1, \ldots, \alpha_n$ be new type variables **in** $< \alpha \rightarrow \alpha_1 \times \ldots \times \alpha_n > +$ Uf $\tau_1\ (\tau' \mathrel{+\!\!+\!\!\!\rightarrow} \alpha_1) + \ldots +$ Uf $\tau_n\ (\tau' \mathrel{+\!\!+\!\!\!\rightarrow} \alpha_n)$
$\#\ \tau_1 \times \ldots \times \tau_n, \tau' \mathrel{+\!\!+\!\!\!\rightarrow} \tau$	$=>$ **let** t = MakeFNF $(\tau' \mathrel{+\!\!+\!\!\!\rightarrow} \tau)$ **in** **if** t is n-tuple **then** Uf $(\tau_1 \times \ldots \times \tau_n)$ t **else** 'not unifiable'
$\#\ N\{\kappa_1, \ldots, \kappa_n\}, N\{\kappa_1', \ldots, \kappa_n'\}$	$=>$ Uf $\kappa_1\ \kappa_1' + \ldots +$ Uf $\kappa_n\ \kappa_n'$
$\#\ N\{\kappa_1, \ldots, \kappa_n\}, \tau' \mathrel{+\!\!+\!\!\!\rightarrow} \alpha$	$=>$ **let** $\alpha_1, \ldots, \alpha_n$ be new type variables **in** $< \alpha \rightarrow N\{\alpha_1, \ldots, \alpha_n\} > +$ Uf $\kappa_1\ (\tau' \mathrel{+\!\!+\!\!\!\rightarrow} \alpha_1) + \ldots +$ Uf $\kappa_n\ (\tau' \mathrel{+\!\!+\!\!\!\rightarrow} \alpha_n)$
$\#\ N\{\kappa_1, \ldots, \kappa_n\}, \tau' \mathrel{+\!\!+\!\!\!\rightarrow} \tau$	$=>$ **let** t = MakeFNF $(\tau' \mathrel{+\!\!+\!\!\!\rightarrow} \tau)$ **in** **if** t is user-defined type N **then** Uf $N\{\kappa_1, \ldots, \kappa_n\}$ t **else** 'not unifiable'
$\#\ N(\tau_1, \ldots, \tau_m)\{\kappa_1, \ldots, \kappa_n\}, N(\tau_1', \ldots, \tau_n')\{\kappa_1', \ldots, \kappa_n'\}$	$=>$ Uf $\tau_1\ \tau_1' + \ldots +$ Uf $\tau_m\ \tau_m' +$ Uf $\kappa_1\ \kappa_1' + \ldots +$ Uf $\kappa_n\ \kappa_n'$
$\#\ N(\tau_1, \ldots, \tau_m)\{\kappa_1, \ldots, \kappa_n\}, \tau' \mathrel{+\!\!+\!\!\!\rightarrow} \alpha$	$=>$ **let** $\alpha_1, \ldots, \alpha_n, \beta_1, \ldots, \beta_m$ be new type variables **in** $< \alpha \rightarrow N(\beta_1, \ldots, \beta_m)\{\alpha_1, \ldots, \alpha_n\} > +$ Uf $\tau_1\ (\tau' \mathrel{+\!\!+\!\!\!\rightarrow} \beta_1) + \ldots +$ Uf $\tau_m\ (\tau' \mathrel{+\!\!+\!\!\!\rightarrow} \beta_m) +$ Uf $\kappa_1\ (\tau' \mathrel{+\!\!+\!\!\!\rightarrow} \alpha_1) + \ldots +$ Uf $\kappa_n\ (\tau' \mathrel{+\!\!+\!\!\!\rightarrow} \alpha_n)$
$\#\ N(\tau_1, \ldots, \tau_m)\{\kappa_1, \ldots, \kappa_n\}, \tau' \mathrel{+\!\!+\!\!\!\rightarrow} \tau$	$=>$ **let** t = MakeFNF $(\tau' \mathrel{+\!\!+\!\!\!\rightarrow} \tau)$ **in** **if** t is user-defined type N **then** Uf $(N(\tau_1, \ldots, \tau_m)\{\kappa_1, \ldots, \kappa_n\})$ t **else** 'not unifiable'
$\#\ \tau_1 \rightarrow \tau_2, \tau_3 \rightarrow \tau_4$	$=>$ Uf $\tau_1\ \tau_3 +$ Uf $\tau_2\ \tau_4$
$\#\ \tau_1 \twoheadrightarrow \tau_2, \tau_3 \twoheadrightarrow \tau_4$	$=>$ Uf $\tau_1\ \tau_3 +$ Uf $\tau_2\ \tau_4$
$\#\ \tau_1 \mathrel{+\!\!+\!\!\!\rightarrow} \tau_2, \tau_3 \mathrel{+\!\!+\!\!\!\rightarrow} \tau_4$	$=>$ Uf $\tau_1\ \tau_3 +$ Uf $\tau_2\ \tau_4$
$\#\ \tau_1 \mathrel{+\!\!+\!\!\!\rightarrow} \tau_2, \tau$	$=>$ Uf $\tau\ (\tau_1 \mathrel{+\!\!+\!\!\!\rightarrow} \tau_2)$
# _, _	$=>$ 'not unifiable' };

8.7.4. Typing Rules

Finally, an extract of the type checker is given: the function 'TC' labels a TrafoLa program part with types and returns the type of that part. We use a unification function 'Unify' that is based on 'Uf', returns the equalized type, and applies the substitution to every existing type as a side effect. (This side effect cannot be expressed in TrafoLa-H.)

dec Unify = { t1,t2 => **let** s = Uf t1 t2 **in**
        if s = 'not unifiable' **then** 'typeerror' **else** s t1 };

Further, we assume that 'TC' stops with a message if 'typeerror' occurs. We do not explain the scoping of the syntactic variables, but the function 'Fresh', which returns a generic instance of a type, should know which types are generic, i.e. about the scoping and defining parts of variables.

rec TC =

{ 'dec p=e' | 'rec p=e'	=> Unify (TC p) (TC e)
# *integer*	=> **let** int_i be new **in** int_i
# *boolean*	=> **let** $bool_i$ be new **in** $bool_i$
# *string*	=> **let** $string_i$ be new **in** $string_i$
# '()'	=> **let** $unit_i$ be new **in** $unit_i$
# '@1'	=> **let** α be new **in** $\alpha \mathrel{+\!\!+\!\!\to} \alpha$
# '@2'	=> **let** α_1,α_2 be new **in** $\alpha_2 \mathrel{+\!\!+\!\!\to} \alpha_1 \mathrel{+\!\!+\!\!\to} \alpha_1$
	⋮
# '*A*'	=> **if** *A* is a pattern variable **then**
	if *A* is its first occurrence **then let** α be new **in** α
	else let t = (type of *A* in current scope) **in** t
	else let t = (type of *A* in current scope) **in** Fresh t
# '(x1,...,xn)'	=> (TC x1) $\times \ldots \times$(TC xn)
# '[ ]'	=> **let** α be new **in** $\alpha*$
# '[x1,...,xn]'	=> (Unify (Unify (... (Unify (TC x1) (TC x2)) ...)) (TC xn)) *
# 'e1 e2'	=> **let** t1 = (TC e1); t2 = (TC e2);
	α be new; subst = (Uf t1 (t2 $\to \alpha$))
	in (subst α)
# 'e1 op e2'	=> TC ('((op) e1) e2')
# 'let p = e1 in e2'	=> **let** t1 = Unify (TC p) (TC e1) **in** (TC e2)
# '+' | '-' | '*' | '/' | 'mod'	=> **let** int_1,int_2,int_3 be new **in** $int_1 \to int_2 \to int_3$
# '==' | '<>'	=> **let** α,$bool_i$ be new **in** $\alpha \to \alpha \to bool_i$
# '^'	=> **let** α_1,α_2 be new **in** $(\alpha_1 \mathrel{+\!\!+\!\!\to} \alpha_2) \to \alpha_1 \to \alpha_2$
# '|'	=> **let** α_1,α_2 be new **in** $(\alpha_1 \to \alpha_2) \to (\alpha_1$ func $\alpha_2) \to (\alpha_1 \to \alpha_2)$
	⋮
# '{ p => e }'	=> **let** t1 = (TC p) **and** t2 = (TC e) **in** t1 $\to$ t2
# '{ p =>all e }'	=> **let** t1 = (TC p) **and** t2 = (TC e) **in** t1 $\to$ (t2$*$)
# '{ p1=>e1#... pn=>en }'	=> TC ('{p1=>e1} | ... | {pn=>en}')
# '{ p1=>all e1#... pn=>all en }'	=> TC ('{p1=>all e1} | ... | {pn=>all en}')
	⋮
# 'p*' | 'p+'	=> (TC p)$*$
# 'p1.p2'	=> **let** α be new **in** Unify ($\alpha*$) (Unify (TC p1) (TC p2))
# 'p1&p2' | 'p1|p2'	=> Unify (TC p1) (TC p2)
	⋮

};

Most other rules are analogous or can be derived because of syntactical sugar (if-then-else, case-of, ::, etc.). Note that the nested use of unification often forces the types to be equal: e.g., the types of all elements on a list have to be equal. The introduced type variables help checking, e.g., on 'p1.p2': instead of testing that type(p1) = type(p2) = list-type, we calculate 'Unify ($\alpha*$) (Unify type(p1) type(p2))' with the same meaning.

8.7.5. Example

Finally, let us consider the expression **let** f = { x => (x,x) } **in** f (f 5);

The type checker calculates the type for this expression as follows:

TC (**let** f = { x => (x,x) } **in** f (f 5)) :
  TC (f)   (first occurrence of pattern variable f)
  $\leftarrow \alpha_1$
  TC ({ x => (x,x) }) :
    t1 = TC (x)   (first occurrence of pattern variable x)
      $\leftarrow \alpha_2$
    t2 = TC ((x,x)) :
        TC (x)   (exp.variable: Fresh (α_2) = α_2 since α_2 is nongeneric)
        $\leftarrow \alpha_2$
        TC (x)   (same)
        $\leftarrow \alpha_2$
      $\leftarrow (\alpha_2 \times \alpha_2)$
  $\leftarrow (\alpha_2 \rightarrow (\alpha_2 \times \alpha_2))$
  t1 = Unify α_1 $(\alpha_2 \rightarrow (\alpha_2 \times \alpha_2))$:
      Uf α_1 $(\alpha_2 \rightarrow (\alpha_2 \times \alpha_2))$:
      $\leftarrow < \alpha_1 \rightarrow$ '$(\alpha_2 \rightarrow (\alpha_2 \times \alpha_2))$' >   (subst.is appl.to all types)
    $\leftarrow (\alpha_2 \rightarrow (\alpha_2 \times \alpha_2))$ (now: f has this type in current scope)
  TC (f (f 5)) :
    t1 = TC (f)   (exp. variable: α_2 is now generic)
      $\leftarrow (\alpha_3 \rightarrow (\alpha_3 \times \alpha_3))$
    t2 = TC (f 5) :
      t1 = TC (f)   (same)
        $\leftarrow (\alpha_4 \rightarrow (\alpha_4 \times \alpha_4))$
      t2 = TC (5)
        $\leftarrow int_1$
      subst= (Uf t1 (t2 $\rightarrow \alpha$))
        $\leftarrow < \alpha \rightarrow$ '$(int_1 \times int_1)$' >
      in (subst α)
      $\leftarrow (int_1 \times int_1)$
    subst= (Uf t1 (t2 $\rightarrow \alpha'$))
      $\leftarrow < \alpha' \rightarrow$ '$(int_1 \times int_1) \times (int_1 \times int_1)$' >
    in (subst α')
  $\leftarrow (int_1 \times int_1) \times (int_1 \times int_1)$
$\leftarrow (int_1 \times int_1) \times (int_1 \times int_1)$

8.8. Concrete Syntax

This section contains a summary of the concrete syntax of TrafoLa-H.

```
Trafola      ::= inputlist
               | exp ;

inputlist    ::= input ; { input ; }

input        ::= dec ndeclist                    (non-recursive declaration)
               | rec rdeclist                    (recursive declaration)
               | type typelist                   (type declaraton)
               | forward variable :=: type       (type specification)

ndeclist     ::= ndec { and ndec }

rdeclist     ::= rdec { and rdec }

typelist     ::= datatype { and datatype }

datatype     ::= identifier { typevariable } = typespec

typespec     ::= constructor [ type ] { # constructor [ type ] }
               | type

type         ::= int
               | bool
               | string
               | type *                          (list type)
               | ()
               | ( type , type { , type } )      (tuple type)
               | type -> type                    (function type)
               | type ->> type                   (constructor type)
               | identifier { type }             (user declared type)
               | typevariable
               | ( type )

ndec         ::= pat = exp

rdec         ::= identifier = function

pat     ::= integer
          | boolean
          | string
          | constructor
          | hole
          | _                                    (wildcard)
          | type
          | > type
          | variable                             (variable to be bound)
          | % variable                           (imported variable)
```

```
             |  ()
             |  ( pat , pat { , pat } )        (tuple pattern)
             |  [ ]                            (empty list pattern)
             |  [ pat { , pat } ]              (list pattern)
             |  pat *                          (uniform sequence)
             |  pat +                          (uniform not-empty sequence)
             |  pat pat                        (tree pattern)
             |  pat . pat                      (list partitioning)
             |  pat :: pat                     (head and tail of list)
             |  pat ^ pat                      (extraction of parts)
             |  pat & pat                      ('and' pattern)
             |  pat : pat                      ('and' pattern)
             |  pat | pat                      ('or' pattern)
             |  ! pat                          ('not' pattern)
             |  { pat }                        ('unbind' pattern)
             |  pat where exp                  (restriction)
             |  ( pat )

exp         ::= integer
             |  boolean
             |  string
             |  constructor
             |  hole
             |  variable
             |  function
             |  ()
             |  ( exp , exp { , exp } )        (tuple)
             |  [ ]                            (empty list)
             |  [ exp { , exp } ]              (list)
             |  exp operator exp               (infix operator)
             |  exp exp                        (application)
             |  - exp                          (unary minus)
             |  ~ exp                          (not)
             |  if exp then exp else exp       (condition)
             |  case exp of exp                (selection)
             |  let letlist in exp
             |  ( operator )
             |  ( exp )

operator    ::= +                              (addition)
             |  -                              (subtraction)
             |  *                              (multiplication)
             |  /                              (division)
             |  mod                            (modulo)
             |  &&                             (and)
             |  ||                             (or)
             |  .                              (list append)
             |  ::                             (list construction)
             |  ^                              (insertion)
             |  ++                             (string concat)
             |  o                              (function composition)
```

```
              |  |                                    (function alternation)
              |  ==                                   (equal)
              |  <>                                   (unequal)
              |  <                                    (less)
              |  >                                    (greater)
              |  <=                                   (less or equal)
              |  >=                                   (greater or equal)

letlist      ::= letpart { ; letpart }

letpart      ::= dec ndeclist
              |  ndeclist                             (alternative syntax)
              |  rec rdeclist

function     ::= {  funpart { #  funpart } }           (abstraction)

funpart      ::= patlist => exp
              |  patlist => all exp

patlist      ::= pat { ,  pat }
              |  pat { ,  pat } with exp
```

8.9. System Functions

Finally, here is an overview of all build in functions of TrafoLa-H with examples and types. These functions should not be redefined. They are implemented directly. Thus, their simulation in TrafoLa-H given in section 8.5.6. should not be used, due to lower efficiency.

Abs returns the absolute value of a number.
  Examples: Abs (-5) → 5, Abs 5 → 5
  Type: int → int

Reverse produces the reverse of a list.
  Example: Reverse [1, 2, 3] → [3, 2, 1]
  Type: $\alpha* \rightarrow \alpha*$

Hd returns the first element of a list. Hd [] is undefined, i.e., returns an error message.
  Example: Hd [1, 2, 3] → 1
  Type: $\alpha* \rightarrow \alpha$

Last returns the last element of a list. Last [] is undefined.
  Example: Last [1, 2, 3] → 3
  Type: $\alpha* \rightarrow \alpha$

Tl returns the tail of a list. Tl [] is undefined.
  Example: Tl [1, 2, 3] → [2, 3]
  Type: $\alpha* \rightarrow \alpha*$

Nth returns the nth element of a list. If there are not enough elements or if the number is negative or 0, the result is undefined.
  Example: Nth 3 [1, 2, 3, 4] → 3
  Type: int → $\alpha* \rightarrow \alpha$

Nth_Tl returns the rest of a list after the nth element.
Example: Nth_Tl 3 [1, 2, 3, 4] → [4]
Type: int → $\alpha*$ → $\alpha*$

Empty is a predicate indicating empty lists.
Examples: Empty [] → true, Empty [1, 2] → false
Type: $\alpha*$ → bool

Length returns the length of a list.
Example: Length ["a", "b", "c"] → 3
Type: $\alpha*$ → int

Iota builds up a list of numbers from 1 to n. If the number n is less than 0, the result is undefined.
Example: Iota 5 → [1, 2, 3, 4, 5], Iota 0 → [ ]
Type: int → int*

Sum sums up all elements of an integer list.
Example: Sum [1, 2, 3, 4, 5] → 15
Type: int* → int

Mkset eliminates repetitions of list items.
Example: Mkset [1, 2, 1, 2, 3, 2] → [1, 2, 3]
Type: $\alpha*$ → $\alpha*$

Member tests for the occurrence of an element in a list.
Examples: Member 2 [2, 5] → true, Member 4 [2, 5] → false
Type: $\alpha \rightarrow \alpha* \rightarrow$ bool

Filter filters a list through a predicate.
Example: Filter Empty [[1], [2,3], [], []] → [[], []]
Type: $(\alpha \rightarrow \text{bool}) \rightarrow \alpha* \rightarrow \alpha*$

Map applies a function to all items of a list.
Example: Map Empty [[1], [2,3], [], []] → [false, false, true, true]
Type: $(\alpha \rightarrow \beta) \rightarrow \alpha* \rightarrow \beta*$

Foldl, Foldr, Fold reduce a list by means of a binary function and a starting element to one element. Fold is similar to Foldr.
Examples: Foldl (-) 1 [2, 3, 4] → ((1-2)-3)-4 = -8, Foldr (-) 1 [2, 3, 4] → 2-(3-(4-1)) = 2.
Type of Foldl: $(\alpha \rightarrow \beta \rightarrow \alpha) \rightarrow \alpha \rightarrow \beta* \rightarrow \alpha$
Type of Foldr: $(\alpha \rightarrow \beta \rightarrow \beta) \rightarrow \beta \rightarrow \alpha* \rightarrow \beta$
Type of Fold: $(\alpha \rightarrow \alpha \rightarrow \alpha) \rightarrow \alpha \rightarrow \alpha* \rightarrow \alpha$

Implode concatenates all elements of a string list to one string.
Example: Implode ["a","b","c"] → "abc", Implode [ ] → ""
Type: string* → string

Explode breaks a string down into a list of strings of length 1.
Example: Explode "abc" → ["a","b","c"], Explode "" → [ ]
Type: string → string*

Substr returns the substring of a string from a position n to a position m (n,m from 0 to Strlen-1, otherwise the result is undefined).
Example: Substr "abcdef" 2 4 → "cde"
Type: string → int → int → string

Strlen returns the length of a string.
Example: Strlen "aaa" → 3
Type: string → int

NtoS produces a string from a number.
Example: NtoS 123 → "123"
Type: int → string

StoN produces a number from a string. The result is undefined if the string argument cannot be translated into a number.
Example: StoN "123" → 123
Type: string → int

Ascii produces a string consisting of a single character from its ASCII code. It is undefined if the argument is not in the range from 0 to 127.
Example: Ascii 65 → "A"
Type: int → string

Repeat, Rep repeatedly apply a function to a start value. They differ in the stop condition.
Rep f n computes f(...(f(f(f n)))...) until the result is 'fail'. Then the last result ≠ 'fail' is returned.
Repeat f n computes f(...(f(f(f n)))...) until two consecutive results are equal, i.e., a fixed point is reached that is the result of the whole computation.
Example: Rep { 1::R => R } [1, 1, 1, 2, 3] → [2, 3]
Repeat { 1::R => R } [1, 1, 1, 2, 3] → fail
Rep { n => n / 2 } 10 → infinite calculation
Repeat { n => n / 2 } 10 → 0
Type: $(\alpha \rightarrow \alpha) \rightarrow \alpha \rightarrow \alpha$

The next four functions are used for input/output. Files are specified by their name as string argument. The special name "term" is used for standard input/output, i.e., keyboard and terminal if not redirected.

Consume always returns true. The function has the side effect that the list elements are evaluated from left to right. This is important in input/output programming. Normally, the evaluation order of lists is not specified.
Example: Consume [Write 1 "term", Write 2 "term"] → true. On the terminal, 1 occurs first, 2 occurs later as side effect.
Type: $\alpha* \rightarrow$ bool

Readstring reads a string from a file.
Example: Readstring "FILE" → the contents of the file named "FILE" as a string.
Type: string → string

Print writes a string to a file.
Example: Print "AAA" "FILE" → true if successful.
Type: string → string → bool

Read reads a structural value from a file.
Example: Read "FILE" → whatever "FILE" contains.
Type: string → T. The type T has to be monomorphic and depends on the context (perhaps use 'forward').

Write writes a structural value to a file.
Example: Write [1, 2, 3] "FILE" → true if successful.
Type: $\alpha \rightarrow$ string → bool

Error generates an exception with an error message. This exception is considered as '$\perp$' in denotational semantics, because the type checker should not reject programs containing occurrences of the function 'Error'.
Example: Error "Something is wrong!" $\rightarrow$ the evaluation stops with this message.
Type: string $\rightarrow \alpha$

8.10. Conclusion

In this chapter, we have presented the syntax and semantics of TrafoLa-H together with the type system. Some properties of the denotational semantics are proven in [Heckmann 87]. The type discipline is made safe by the theoretical discussion in [Sander 90]. Here, we explained the practical part: How to program in TrafoLa-H and how to classify data objects in the type system.

We did not illustrate all possibilities for writing *fast* programs in TrafoLa-H. In fact, there are four versions of the system according to whether or not there is a type checker, and whether or not the tree parser is included. Each version leads to its own characteristic style of programming, because some features are more or less supported. The details are explained in part III, section 5.3.

PROgram Development by SPECification and TRAnsformation

Part III

System

1. Uniform Transformational Development

Bernd Krieg-Brückner, Einar W. Karlsen, Junbo Liu, Owen Traynor, Universität Bremen

This chapter relates the uniformity of the methodological approach to program and meta-program development (for transformation, proof and development tactics, command language, even library access and system configuration, cf. part I chapter 1) to the generic structure of the PROSPECTRA system. See also chapter 2 for an introduction to the system as a Guided Tour.

1.1. The Generic Development System

The actual development system for the PROSPECTRA methodology is a rather large and complex set of inter-related tools. The various components are brought together, in a unified way, by structuring the system to reflect the methodology it supports. The methodology itself has also been employed to develop and structure many of the constituent system components.

The PROSPECTRA system structure is notable for a number of reasons:

(i) The orthogonality achieved by treating all system's activities as transformations

(ii) The uniform interface to all system components

(iii) The preservation of the "simple" transformation paradigm even in the Meta Development Systems

(iv) The uniform management of *all* system objects in the library (even parts of the system itself)

(v) The description of the interface to all system components in the specification language PA^{nn}dA-S

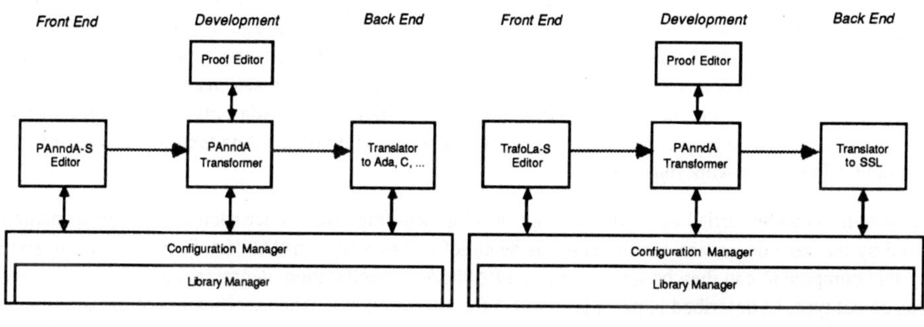

(1-1) The Program Development Subsystem

(1-2) The Meta Program Development Subsystem

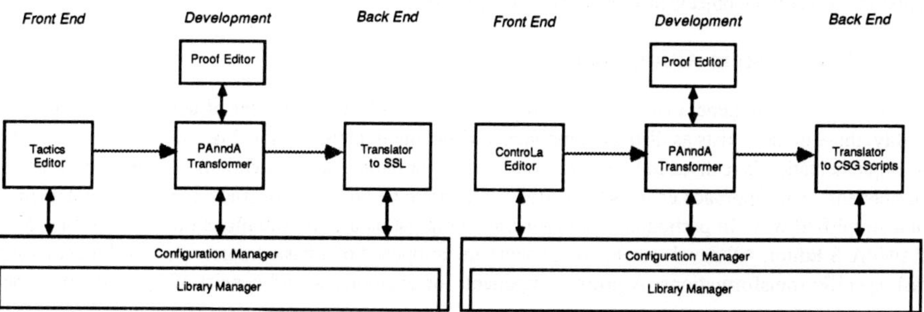

(1-3) The Proof Tactics Development Subsystem

(1-4) The System Development Subsystem

The sub-systems shown in (1-1) to (1-4) are instances of the generic development system. Generation of a particular system component requires some instantiation of the various generic components, in particular an *Editor* in the Front End and some *Translator* in the Back End. For almost all kinds of developments, the required instantiation or specialisation of specific components can be done within the system; exceptions are, of course, translators to the target languages. Note that the *PAnndA Transformer* is the same generic component, but instantiated with a possibly different set of transformations.

The relationship between the generic development system and the (generic) transformational development model is rather straight-forward. We start the development with an initial requirements specification (using an *Editor*). The specification is then passed to a *Transformer* for further development and refinement. Correctness conditions are ensured by the *Proof System*. Finally, a *Translator* will generate an executable version of the objects produced by the Transformer and configure some environment for compilation/execution of these objects. All activities are recorded and carried out under the supervision of a controller in the context of some library. The *Library and Configuration Managers* coordinate and organise the various objects passed between and processed by the other system components.

Activity	***Component***
Initial Formulation of Requirements	PAnndA-S Editor
Development to Constructive (and Optimised) Design	PAnndA Transformer
Verification of some Correctness Conditions	Proof Editor
Translation to Target Language (Ada, C or other)	Translator to Ada, C

(1-5) Activities and Components for Program Development

As an example take the instantiation of the generic development system to the components used for program development in (1-1). The table in (1-5) illustrates the activities and the different components employed. This example shows the manner in which development proceeds in a typical subsystem. Each of the individual steps described varies in complexity. Some are completely automatic while others require a high degree of user guidance. In this particular case, the translator to Ada only unfolds abstract type definitions (introduced by pre-defined type definiton schemata) into proper Ada text; in the case of C, for example, a little more work must be done.

All activities can be carried out within a single development framework since each of the objects manipulated by the various system components has been defined as a type in PAnndA-S. An activity in some system component can then be formulated as a PAnndA-S specification, denoting a transformation over this object type, as described in part I section 1.5 for meta programs. The specification of the activity can then be developed in a transformational manner and ultimately installed in the appropriate component as a transformation on the objects processed by that component.

1.2. The System Components

Associated with the generalised presentation of (1-1) to (1-4) are a number of actual (sub)systems. In reality, these do not exists as distinct components within the implementation. For each conceptual system, its implementation is realised in terms of a combination (or particular instantiation) of some generic system components. This approach enables the system structure to be presented (learned, used, and implemented) in a simplified way. In particular, the Front End components are instantiations (and extensions) of the PAnndA-S Editor. All development components are composed of a basic transformer shell together with task specific transformations. A proof component, for example, would consist of a transformer shell, transformations for proofs, and an additional mechanism for proof representation. The following, actual, development subsystems can be identified:

• Program • Meta Program • Proof • Proof Tactics • Command and Control

1.2.1. The Controller

All development steps and movements within and throughout the various system components are controlled by a general purpose manager called the *Controller*, in accordance with the methodology. It also provides a uniform interface to the user, as well as supplying a means of interfacing the various system components that must communicate. Each system command is formulated as a transformation in the Controller subsystem; the command language Controla is a sublanguage of the (meta) specification language PAnndA-S.

The Controller interprets actions upon the various objects stored in the library and starts up the appropriate component for manipulation of an object in a way consistent with the requested action. For example, a revision request on a PAnndA-S object causes the controller to retrieve the contents of the appropriate specification from the library and to start up the PAnndA-S Editor on this specification. Given that general commands are issued in the context of library objects, the controller determines the component and object combinations appropriate for the context and associated request.

Every system activity is viewed as a tranformation from an initial state to some final state of the system. The controller is based on the concept of a *local state* of a component, and regards a specific component as a function with the following signature:

Component: (User_Interaction × Library) —> Local_State —> Local_State

The local state contains the minimal set of information that a given component needs to carry out the associated transformation. The library manager, the configuration manager, the specification editor, the transformer, the proof system etc. all have associated local states. For example, the local state for a specification would consist of the specification itself together with the configuration of the library defining specific versions of modules used by that specification. Roughly speaking, a global state is a local state of some component embedded in a configuration of the library.

Each user interaction is then seen as a transformation from one (local) state to a new (local) state. When a development subsystem is invoked, the initial (local) state is constructed from the current content of the library that represents the global state of the system. The global state of the system can be changed in two ways: either by invoking simple library commands that do not require the facilities provided by other components, or by invoking a specific system component. Since all components are considered as functions on the local state, a component can be called from another in a *call-return relationship*, with an initial local state as a parameter. The component then returns either the changed local state resulting from the call of the component (confirmed development) or the initial local state (cancelled development). The change is then incorporated into the current library structure by turning the local into a global state.

The Controller is responsible for recording the actual development steps in the development history: a *log and replay script* (a step by step account of the activities carried out by the developer resulting in the refined/revised object) is stored and associated with the development. Scripts are written in the CSG script language that has been designed to express every possible action carried out using a system (this is a PROSPECTRA extension of the Synthesizer Generator ([Reps, Teitelbaum 88], abbreviated CSG here), see chapter 6). The replay of actual developments is facilitated by the CSG script interpreter. The replay of a development script can either be fully automatic or involve the user in a step by step replay.

There are several ways to generate a script for further (re)play. One is to record the development history of an object, another to specify it using the ControLa development subsystem. In general, the ControLa development subsystem allows to abstract from concrete developments (in the form of log scripts) to a representation on the level of the ControLa specification language, i.e. a subset of PAnndA-S. This means that developments themselves are formal objects that can be manipulated (cf. sections 3 and 5.2) and provide the basis for abstraction from particular developments to general methods that can be re-used.

1.2.2. The Library and Configuration Managers

The current *Library Manager* is based on the prototype design and implementation described in [Houdier 90]. The Library Manager supports concurrency in the sense that several users can develop new objects simultaneously. Essentially it consist of two components: an underlying object base and a user interface.The Object Base stores *all* the objects that are manipulated or referenced from within the system, together with all the relationships defined between the stored objects. The object base is incremental in the sense that nothing is deleted or changed during development; new versions are added as derivations of existing versions. Mechanisms to purge/delete objects are supplied for maintenance purposes (although these functions are not considered to be part of the development framework, but rather functions that would be used by a project/system administrator, in connection with archiving activities).

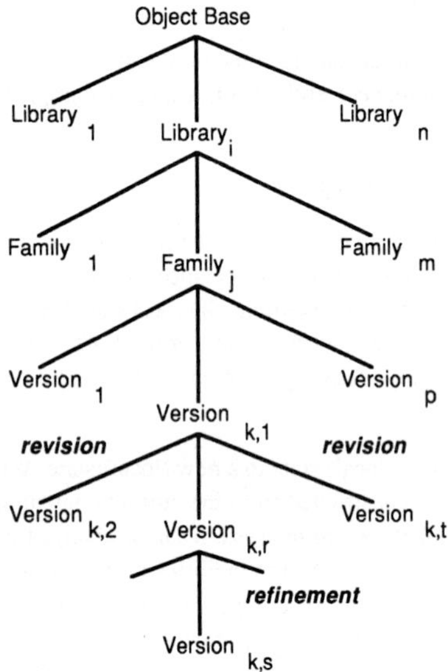

(2-1) Structure of the Library

The *LibLa editor* constitutes the interface between the user and the object base and allows the user to display and modify the information contained in the underlying object base. The editor manipulates partial but consistent views of objects. Such views are defined in terms of so-called LibLa trees. LibLa is aimed at representing the hierarchical structure of libraries (such structure being used to reflect the development activities in PROSPECTRA). Version Management, as every other operation in the system, is understood as a set of transformations on a language, in this case LibLa. The LibLa transformers are particular in the sense that they have side effects on the underlying object base. The Libary Manager adopts an object-oriented approach to object management since the various non-terminals of the LibLa language correspond to object types of the underlying object base.

The conceptual model of the object base, as it is embodied in the definition of the LibLa grammar, is as follows. Each *object base* consist of a set of libraries, and *libraries* in turn of a set of families.

Each *family* contains a set of related versions of an object with a particular name (for example the name of a specification module in PAnndA-S), organised into a version tree showing the development relations among the versions. A *version* is either a refinement or a revision of an (initial) version, depending on whether the development was correctness preserving or not, respectively. Moreover, additional information such as the development history (represented as a CSG script), textual documentation, status information, and so on, is stored in the library with each object. In particular, the total development history of a version is the concatenation of the particular development histories of its ancestors along a path to the original root version. A schema for a LibLa structure is given in (2-1).

Besides development relations between versions within one family, the library also records the relations between versions of *different* families (as depicted by the with-clauses of a specification or program in PAnndA). Such with-relations form a directed acyclic graph. The versions belonging to such a graph are called a *configuration*. Configurations are defined and manipulated using the *Configuration Manager*. With-dependencies are generally handled by calling the Configuration Manager from one of the development components in a call-return relationship. The Configuration Manager may also be called directly from the LibLa Editor since configurations are first class objects: they can be created, revised and refined as any other object on the level of the library. This utility is vital when refining the definition of (PROSPECTRA) system configurations using the system itself, see section 1.3.3.

1.2.3. The Editors

The Specification Editor is a language based editor for PAnndA-S, the specification language of PROSPECTRA, and serves as a basis for all other (sub)language editors derived from it, such as for TrafoLa (section 5.1 and part III chapter 6), ControLa, etc. Its main purpose is to allow the user to enter requirement specifications and then check such specifications for syntactic and static semantic correctness. The Specification Editor(s) have been generated using the Synthesizer Generator [Reps, Teitelbaum 88], extended in the PROSPECTRA project, and make heavy use of its facilities for attribute grammars and incremental attribute (re-)evaluation.

Knowledge of the language syntax and context conditions have been built into the editor. This knowledge is used to assess whether a specification contains errors and where such errors occur. The static analysis is performed interactively and incrementally during editing rather than by compilation. Two editing paradigms are supported: text editing and structure editing. In the text editing mode, phrases are entered on a character by character basis. Structure editing guarantees the syntactic correctness; specifications are created top-down by inserting new well-formed templates in the skeleton of previously entered templates.

Context errors are detected by the static semantic analyser, a function of the editor that may be enabled or disabled during an editing session as appropriate. The static semantics of the specification language has been inspired and partially derived from the static semantics of Ada, with all the inherent complications for the static semantic analyser in performing overload resolution of names and expressions, modelling scope and visibility rules and instantiating generic packages. Consequently, the static semantic editor incorporates the notion of separate development ("separate compilation") of modules as a means of improving the general performance of the editor. In addition, it is possible to change fragments of a specification in isolation from the rest of the specification and thus momentarily avoiding change propagation.

The specification editor for PAnndA-S has an associated utility that supports the definition of a limited set of (Ada) types. A type declaration is entered by the user in its conventional (Ada) syntactic form. The equivalent Abstract Data Type form (a signature of constructor, selector and other operations with appropriate algebraic axioms) is then generated by transformation upon user request. This facility is referred to as a (pre-defined) *type definition scheme*. Type definition schemes are currently provided for the Ada enumeration, (recursive variant) record types, etc., and for the definition of the abstract syntax of languages, i.e. for the definition of tree types. The type definition schemes form the basis for type development towards a particular target language, such as Ada, within the program development system. A translation to C is complete; corresponding type schemes for other target languages are being incorporated. The type definition scheme for tree types provides a basis for generating the term algebra of an object language.

This term algebra is later used in developing transformers within the meta development system. Translations to SSL and TrafoLa-H (see section 5.3) are available.

1.2.4. The Transformer Shell

The central component concerned with program development by transformation is the *PAnndA Transformer Shell*, a language based component (used to apply transformations) for the complete wide-spectrum language PAnndA. The Transformer Shell is invoked from the LibLa Editor in a call-return relationship and is used during all transformational development phases, instantiated to a particular Transformer.

There is one fundamental distinction between the Specification Editor and the Transformer Shell: the Specification Editor is used for developing revisions of specifications and allows non-correctness-preserving operations in the form of text and structure editing commands. In contrast, neither structure nor text editing is allowed within the Transformer Shell. Only the application of correctness preserving transformations is admissible to change or refine the object being developed.

The Transformer Shell displays the program being developed as well as the set of applicable transformations in a given context (for example the transformations applicable to a selected subexpression). The reduction of the list of applicable transformations to a minimum is an important consideration for the user interface. In the extension of the facilities of the Synthesizer Generator made during the PROSPECTRA project, applicability (and therefore suppression of in-applicable transformations) can also be checked w.r.t. static semantic conditions. The Transformer Shell is a shell (or frame) in the sense that the required set of transformations must be developed, using the PROSPECTRA system, and then included in the generation of a new and extended version of a PAnndA Transformer.

Context information, needed for checking applicability conditions of transformations, has been provided by means of various attributes. Attributes have been defined for static semantic analysis of PAnndA programs, for example, attributes for reasoning about the type of expressions, properties of named entities, and the scope and visibility of names. Additional attributes are provided for reasoning about the semantics of specifications in terms of functions and their defining axioms. These attributes, termed the *local theory* (cf. section 1.2.5), contain all signatures and axioms accessible from the current context. The local theory forms the basis for efficient proof development and for the checking of semantic applicability conditions, i.e. for context-sensitive transformations.

Parameterised transformations, another extension of the Synthesizer Generator, may require information from the user at application time. Such parameters can be supplied using the parameter editor, either following the copy/paste paradigm, in which a suitable fragment is copied from the program proper, or by providing the parameter by editing. In the latter case the fragment will be analysed for static semantic errors in the context of the application and the transformation for which it is a parameter.

One notable component of the Transformer Shell is the unparser. The built-in attributes for static semantic analysis are used by the unparser to perform visibility and scope analysis of names. An unambigous unparsing of the program is provided, on the basis of this analysis, by automatic insertion of expanded names and qualified expressions when needed. Transformation rules are generally relieved from taking into account most of the visibility rules of Ada since names are represented in a unique way in the Transformer Shell.

1.2.5. The Proof Subsystem

The Proof Subsystem is based on the Transformer Shell. The basic Shell is augmented with facilities for representing proof derivations. All refinements and developments in the Proof Subsystem are formulated as transformations of logical formulae, i.e. terms of the specification language. An instantaneous representation of developments is provided that allows interactive replay and re-development of proofs. The Proof Subsystem is fully integrated with the Transformation Subsystem. The transformation writer is provided with a set of functions defining the interface to the Proof Subsystem. The justification required for the correctness of a transformation rule, not normally known until the transformation is applied in some context, may be included, via these functions, in the definition of the transformation itself. When the transformation is then applied in some context, the Proof Subsystem will be called to justify the instantiated applicability conditions. Details and example proofs may be found in part II section 4.4. Proofs have associated theorems, these may be used directly in subsequent development (of both proofs and programs) by including a reference to the proof in the configuration of the development. A complete integration of the Proof Subsystem with the PAnndA Transformer Shell requires not only that the logical formulae (generated, for example, by a transformation and corresponding to some applicabilty condition) be passed from the Transformer to the Proof Subsystem, but also context information is required, in particular, the local theory.

The Local Theory

The local theory has been defined to serve two purposes: firstly, to allow context-sensitive transformations to perform developments using axioms and definitions visible in the current context, secondly, to aid in proving proof obligations resulting from applicablity conditions (and in deducing properties of specifications), by providing the definitions needed for such deductions.

Context-sensitive transformations are seen as a major advance in transformation technology: transformations can be more automated and need less interaction with the user. One way to do this is by using the static semantic information in the context, for example to check type or visibility information. In addition, however, axioms from the local theory can be used to try to derive semantic context conditions automatically (for example the property of associativity) or as rewrite rules to provide automatic simplification.

The local theory is a normalised representation of all axioms and definitions that are accessible from the current context. All specialised specification language constructs are removed from the normalised representation. This normalised representation is in the spirit of the kernel language used to define the formal semantics of the language, cf. part II chapter 3.

The normalisation, while flat, still retains structure. This is done by requiring that the local theory is accessed and filtered using the syntax of the original specification. For example, all objects relating to subtypes are represented with respect to their base types (plus appropriate restrictions). However, they may be accessed via a reference to their original subtype. Interface functions (available when defining transformations, tactics, and when browsing interactively) are also defined to allow filtered views of the local theory to be generated dependent upon context. Such mechanisms are necessary since, even for small specifications, the local theory is rather large.

In addition to the Proof Subsystem and the basic *Transformer Shell* described in section 1.2.4, there is another component in the system that can be used for proofs and as a transformer: the Conditional Equational Completion subsystem (see [Ganzinger 87] and part III section 4.3).

1.2.6. The Translators

The Translators at the back end of the system define projections from efficient PA^{nn}dA formulations of problem solutions to a target language for implementation and execution, cf. also the type definition schemes in section 1.2.3. The system currently supports a number of target languages (TrafoLa-H is a powerful, higher order language, with associated compiler and interpreter, for pattern matching and transformation, not discussed here; see [Heckmann 88a], part II chapter 8, part III section 5.3):

Language	***Purpose***
Ada, C	General program development
SSL	Definition of transformers to be incorporated into the Transformer Shell, and re-development of the system in itself
CSG Script	Formulation of executable development scripts and recording of histories
TrafoLa-H	Definition of transformers to be executed by a separate transformation engine

1.3. Meta Development and System Development

1.3.1. Meta Development in the System

Meta Program Development

Transformation development is done using the Meta Program Development Subsystem following the methodology for meta program development (cf. part I section 1.5, 1.6). Transformation rules are specified in TrafoLa-S, the transformation specification sublanguage of PA^{nn}dA-S. In addition to the PA^{nn}dA-S constructs, it contains some syntactic abbreviations for phrases (PA^{nn}dA program fragments in their concrete syntax form) and context-sensitive transformations to translate into canonical PA^{nn}dA-S.

Activity	***Component***
Specification of Transformations	TrafoLa-S Editor
Development of Meta Programs for Transformation	Transformer (General + TrafoLa)
Translating Transformations to SSL	Translator to SSL
Incorporation of Transformations into a Transformer	Configuration Manager, Synthesizer Generator

(3-1) Activities and Components for Meta Program Development

The subsystem for meta program development in (1-2) is another example for an instantiation of the generic development system; cf. also (3-1). The editor for TrafoLa-S is derived from that for PA^{nn}dA-S; the requirement specification is frozen; a PA^{nn}dA transformer with general transformations (and possibly special ones for meta development) is then applied to develop meta programs in the framework, and finally a particular kind of specification is compiled into an applicative tree manipulation program in SSL, the input language of the Synthesizer Generator. Note that in this case, objects produced by a particular target generator are subsequently incorporated into the system itself by the configuration manager. For example, a meta program for transformation may have been developed within the system; it is then compiled, integrated into a revision of the configuration of the transformer, and may then be executed with that version of the transformer in subsequent sessions.

Proof Tactics Development

The proof system also has an associated meta development component. Proof tactics development is carried out in exactly the same way as meta program development. The same components and languages are employed. The resulting transformations for proofs are then analogous to the tactics used in the LCF system [Gordon et al. 78]. An additional set of transformations is provided to allow the basic tactics for logical expressions to be developed into *true tactics*. Instead of merely transforming logical formulae, these *true tactics* generate proofs when applied to a logical formula (rather than just the result true or false). The proof trees correspond to the construction of a proof for a given logical formula. A typical scenario for meta proof development is given in (1-3), (3-2) .

Activity	*Component*
Specification of Tactics	Tactics (TrafoLa-S) Editor
Development of Transformations	Transformer (General Trafos)
Lifting Transformation (Expressions -> Proofs)	Transformer (Proof Generator Trafo)
Translating Tactics to SSL	Translator to SSL
Incorporation of Tactics into a Proof Editor	Configuration Manager, Synthesizer Generator

(3-2) Activities and Components for Proof Tactics Development

1.3.2. System Development

The System Development Subsystem (cf. (1-4), (3-3)) for the command language ControLa provides the facilities for enriching the development environment with new commands and scripts. Commands are formulated on the level of ControLa, an applicative subset of PAnndA-S. ControLa specifications are entered using the ControLa Editor, a restricted PAnndA-S editor, which checks that the specifications are within the ControLa subset of PAnndA-S. A translator is provided from ControLa specifications to executable implementations in terms of CSG scripts. In addition, a translation is provided from abstract CSG scripts (the form in which concrete developments are recorded, cf. chapter 6) to basic ControLa expressions. Concrete developments can therefore be manipulated and abstracted on the level of ControLa using the PROSPECTRA methodology; this provides the basis for abstraction from particular developments to general methods that can be re-used. Thus the ControLa subsystem is both a System Development and a "Development Development" Subsystem.

Activity	*Component*
Specification of (System) Developments	ControLa Editor
Development of Developments	Transformer (General Trafos)
Translating Developments to CSG Scripts	Translator to CSG Scripts

(3-3) Activities and Components for System Development

ControLa is restricted to the formulation of developments on pre-defined system objects. The system environment is specified in a pre-defined package that defines the types and the basic operations necessary to express system developments. It defines the basic notions of control such as (local) states, state transitions and composition of commands. The model of the system is in terms of state transitions and reflects the methodology by considering every activity as a transformation.

Due to the unified approach to the system model and implementation, the user interacts by means of transformations on local states. The functions for formulating system development can be grouped into four categories: pure functions to compute values on predefined types such as integers, strings and booleans; constructor functions to manipulate abstract syntax trees (they are basically imported from the packages defining the abstract syntax trees of the various languages of the system), selection functions to extract information from a given state, and finally state transition functions that are the only ControLa functions capable of expressing side effects. User interactions have been modelled as non-strict (or lazy) state transition functions with user inputs defined in terms of non-strict parameters to functions.

1.3.3. Developing the System in Itself

All the various components of PROSPECTRA should, ultimately, be described as configurations of objects under the control of the library. Currently, most of these objects have been written by hand in SSL, the specification language of the Synthesizer Generator. As the system evolves, such a representation of the system components then allows the re-development of these components within the sytem itself. Small pieces of a component can be replaced by an equivalent piece that has been completely developed within the PROSPECTRA system.

Re-generation of components should also be done from within the system. The transformations for re-generation of components take a revised configuration in the system part of the library for that component and generate commands that, when interpreted, result in a new version of the component being produced. If, for any reason, such a re-generation is not successful, then the old version of the component is obtained by backtracking in the development history for the component.

Such incremental re-development of the PROSPECTRA system, using the system and the PROSPECTRA methodology, imposes a number of restrictions upon the way in which the original system was developed. To re-develop the system in an incremental manner requires that sensible increments be defined. Also, these increments should have minimal couplings with other components within the current re-development. The original developer of the component has already chosen the, hopefully, cohesive increments for such re-development (defined by the structure of the source code and the inter-dependencies between source modules). This requires that the abstract and actual structure of the original component take into account the possibility of subsequent, transformational, re-development. The re-development of system components within the system may be seen as a kind on maintenance activity. Hopefully, components of the system have been structured in such a way so as not to hinder maintenance.

The re-development restriction arises from the nature of the re-development process; it is incremental. If the system was completely re-developed and re-implemented as a whole, such problems would not arise.

Re-development of Framework Components

The central constituents of the PROSPECTRA system, transformations, are already completely developed within the system as described above. However, the way in which re-development of one of the framework components, such as the proof subsystem, is undertaken, may illustrate how general system re-development is carried out.

Given a module, which has been developed within the system and is to be used to replace some existing system object, a configuration for the system component being developed must be identified. The configuration is then revised. The revision replaces the reference to the original, hand coded module with a reference to the new, transformationally developed module. For example, the propositional rules for the manipulation of sequents within the proof subsystem will be formulated in PAnndA-S and developed to an efficient implementation in SSL. The resultant SSL module replaces the existing module in the configuration of the proof subsystem.

From the configuration, a projection is defined that produces the dependency information required to generate a configuration control file. The configuration control file is subsequently used to control re-compilation of the component. A generate command is then issued that starts the re-generation process. The resultant component is finally added to the actual system configuration, a library object defining the structure of the whole PROSPECTRA development system.

1.4. Conclusion

An overview of the PROSPECTRA system and its structure was given, relating the uniformity of the methodological approach to program and meta-program development (cf. part I chapter 1) to the generic structure of the PROSPECTRA system (this chapter updates [Karlsen, Krieg-Brückner, Traynor 91] and [Krieg-Brückner et al. 91]).

Meta-Development and Formalisation of Program Development

An important aspect of the PROSPECTRA approach is its use for *meta-development* and formalisation of developments (see part I sections 1.5, 1.6). The methodology and transformation technology for program development is carried over to the development of *transformation programs*. Moreover, an automatically generated transscript of a development "history" allows re-play upon re-development when requirements have changed, containing goals of the development, design decisions taken, and alternatives discarded but relevant for re-development. A *development script* is thus a formal object that does not only represent a documentation of the past but is also a plan for future developments. It can be used to abstract from a particular development to a class of similar developments, a *development method*, incorporating a certain strategy. The correspondence between the system architecture and the methodology in this instance is very clear and direct. In this sense, the system architecture is a very accurate reflection of the transformational methodology of PROSPECTRA.

Uniformity of the Approach

Since any system interaction can be formalised as a transformation of some "program" (term), the PROSPECTRA approach leads to a uniform treatment of programming language, program manipulation and transformation language, proof and proof development language, also command language and even library access. This uniformity is one of the main results of the PROSPECTRA project and its exploitation is manifest in the structure of the PROSPECTRA system.

The essence of the uniform approach is the use of the specification language PAnndA-S as the transformation specification language TrafoLa-S. In this case, an abstract type schema to define Abstract Syntax is predefined, and translation to the applicative tree manipulation language of the Synthesizer Generator [Reps, Teitelbaum 88] (used both as an Editor and as a Transformer Generator in the system) is automatic (cf. part I section 1.5). ControLa, the command language of the system, is also a subset of PAnndA-S: development histories can be treated as formal objects, developed, translated to executable scripts, and replayed.

There is a close analogy to the development of efficient proof tactics for a given proof or inference system (transformation rules in the algebra of proofs). Again, the Proof (sub)system uses the PAnndA-S language as the vehicle for specifying proof tactics (as well using PAnndA-S to specify all the basic inference rules). In re-using the methodology and languages to achieve the uniform approach, many of the actual system components are re-used in a similar fashion.

Context-Sensitive Transformation, Filtering of Proof Obligations

Experience with the transformational approach and the implementation of non-trivial transformations has shown, that context-sensitivity of transformations is essential. Transformations need complex applicability conditions; thus the first requirement is that such conditions can be specified. As has been demonstrated in the examples of part I section 1.3, the combination of algebraic specification and restrictions on parameters (such as the monoid property) is quite powerful in this sense. Objects (and terms) can be "lifted" to meta-objects (and terms) and thus can become subject to manipulation during transformation and proof.

Furthermore, complex applicability conditions give rise to complex proof obligations. It is crucial to discard as many of them as possible automatically. The use of static semantic attributes, representing, for example, type information, allows the automatic check of static semantic conditions. A special context attribute, the "local theory" (cf. section 1.2.5), contains the set of all applicable axioms and theorems, accessible during proof. It also permits a search, during transformation, for some implicit parameters with certain restrictions (e.g. an associative operation and the corresponding neutral element), or some limited automatic theorem proving, leaving those conditions that need user interaction during proof as a residue. Thus a combination of compiler technology, theorem proving and a knowledge-based approach achieve the required filtering of proof obligations and need for interaction. This is one reason why the integration of construction and verification in the transformational approach of PROSPECTRA becomes practical.

Another use of attributes is the filtering of available transformations in the menue. It is quite important that those transformations that cannot be applied to a given term do not clutter the menue; they should be suppressed and not shown. Structural applicability is checked by the built-in pattern matching; (static) semantic applicability conditions can be defined to be checked automatically before the transformation is shown to be (potentially) applicable in the menue; others are only checked when the user has selected a transformation or are filtered out as residual proof obligations.

The Synthesizer Generator [Reps, Teitelbaum 88], the major tool used in implementing the system, provides trees with attributes and incremetal re-evaluation. However, parameters with interaction from the user, static applicability conditions, interaction with the Proof Editor, re-computation of the context when moving about in trees, recording and replay of the development history, etc. all had to be added to the Synthesizer Generator to adapt it to the needs of PROSPECTRA (cf. chapter 6).

A Retrospective

In order to put the final state of the PROSPECTRA system into some sort of perspective, an outline of the state of the PROSPECTRA system as of March 1990 may be useful. Here the main components of the PROSPECTRA development system and their relative levels of integration are outlined.

The main aim of the PROSPECTRA project was to provide a prototype system that would allow the effectiveness of the transformational paradigm for program development to be demonstrated. However, in the construction of the prototype system a number of fundamental problems had to be solved. These problems ranged from the development of a language which provided a suitable basis for transformation and the identification of a paradigm suitable for expressing the application of transformations to the theoretical problems of practically integrating the processes of construction and verification.

A significant portion of the project resources should have been devoted to developing examples which actually demonstrated the effectiveness of the transformational development paradigm, but because of various problems this goal was never really achieved. Only small examples, with minimal verification requirements, were produced using the PROSPECTRA system.

In addition, none of the transformations themselves were formally proved correct within the system; the verification conditions associated with transformations were derived by pencil and paper analysis of the transformations. The system did, however, provide substantial support for the construction and analysis of formal requirements specifications. A transformation harness, which allowed for the development and integration of transformations within the system itself, was provided. This transformation harness incorporated an integrated proof system and proof theory generation components.

Various target languages were also supported: SSL, the language of the Synthesizer Generator (see [Reps, Teitelbaum 88]), the C language, the Trafola-H language (a language for higher order pattern matching and rewriting, see part II chapter 8), and a subset of the Ada language are generated by the system.

Furthermore, a comprehensive library and configuration management system is provided. All objects within the PROSPECTRA system are stored in the library. All developments are considered as operations on library objects. The library manager also maintains development histories of objects; included are any proofs required to ensure the correctness of a development.

Throughout the lifetime of the project, language design was an on-going activity (not unreasonable since language design is a complex and iterative activity). There were six major language revisions and numerous minor revisions. In fact, just eighteen months before the end of the project a completely separate transformation language (as far as abstract syntax is concerned) was defined into which all requirement specifications were translated (frozen) prior to undergoing transformational development. The last revision came only six months before the (official) end of the project.

These revisions had a number of implications. Firstly, the concrete and underlying abstract syntaxes of the language changed. This meant that any language oriented tools required substantial maintenance in order to be usable with the new language version. Virtually all the tools in the system relied to some degree on the syntax of the specification language.

Another implication for those working on the formal definition of the language was that any change in syntax usually implied a change in (at least) the static semantics of the language. In turn, such changes imply revisions of the dynamic semantics. Inevitably, there is a latency period between the language modifications and the production of a revised static and then a revised dynamic semantics. These frequent language revisions resulted in a large amount of effort being invested in maintaining system tools. Since many of the system components are closely linked with the syntax, static semantics, and dynamic semantics of the PROSPECTRA language, these are particularly sensitive to language changes. The numerous revisions of the language also made version control a problem. Eight of the nine partners in the PROSPECTRA project were constructing components that contributed to the transformational development environment. Ensuring that each component conformed to the correct language version was a difficult task.

Additionally, since the transformations developed within the system are themselves language specific, any modifications to the PROSPECTRA language implied that all existing transformations would require some sort of revision. As a result of the numerous language revisions much of the effort of those involved with the project at a technical level was spent maintaining and revising software tools and updating transformation definitions.

The choice of the environment used to develop the PROSPECTRA system also had a substantial impact on the productivity of those technically involved with the construction of the development system. The main factor here was the choice of the Synthesizer Generator as the means of providing the basic development harness.

Using the Synthesizer Generator had a number of implications. The largest of these resulted from the fact that the Synthesizer Generator did not support separate compilation for its language SSL. This meant that the development cycle for both the production of the PROSPECTRA system and for the transformations used within the system was painfully long. After modifying any part of the system (or any transformation within the system) recompilation required around two hours (This assumed that a reasonably powerful SUN 3/60 machine with sufficient memory resources was available to compile the system.). Even the identification of syntax or type errors could a long time.

Even though separate compilation is not supported by the Synthesizer Generator, a degree of configuration control was required due to the size of the PROSPECTRA system. The result was a configuration control file that was around four thousand lines long. The file itself was rather complex, but it turned out to be the only feasible means of controlling the integration of the various system components.

A final problem that was met (due to the nature of the Synthesizer Generator) was that the executables being produced were so large that various limitations (of the UNIX environment used as the basic platform to develop the system) were encountered. Currently the full PROSPECTRA system, including all transformations, is too large to compile on a standard SUN workstation with eight megabytes of RAM and forty megabytes of swap space.

Using the Synthesizer Generator also dictated the interface that would be provided for the whole PROSPECTRA development system. Fortunately, it provided a consistent and flexible mechanism for interaction over the whole system which ultimately turned out to be a major benefit.

As a final summary, the PROSPECTRA system is a sophisticated operational prototype. However, the system is very large and (an unforeseen result of) the choice of the implementation technology (the Synthesizer Generator) means that maintenance is troublesome. This, in combination with the fact that the system components were developed in a distributed fashion at various (isolated) sites, means that the level of integration of some components is not as high as would be expected. Nevertheless, substantial achievements, in terms of overall architecture and structure of the system, were made. Effective developments of non-trivial examples were undertaken and, subsequent to the official end of the project, the system has been used as the basis of conducting research in a number of areas of formal program development (cf. [Liu, Traynor, Krieg-Brückner 92] and [Maher, Traynor 92].

Research Perspectives

Considerably more work is needed in the areas of automating the transformational process, development of efficient, compact context-sensitive transformations (using, e.g., incremental attribute evaluation), of a classification and categorisation of transformations in the system to allow specific sets of transformations to be used more effectively in a goal directed development situation, and of goal-orientation during transformation, driven by efficiency considerations and target systems, trying to assist the user in the choice of transformations and methods. The abstraction from concrete developments to development methods, incorporating formalised development tactics and strategies, and the formalisation of programming knowledge as *transformation rules + development methods*, will be a challenge for the future.

Acknowledgements

We wish to thank the other members of the PROSPECTRA project, in particular Pedro de la Cruz, Bernd Gersdorf and Alain Marcuzzi, for their contributions.

2. Guided Tour of the PROSPECTRA System

Junbo Liu, Owen Traynor, Universität Bremen,
Steen Lynenskjold, Computer Resources International

This chapter gives an introduction to the PROSPECTRA System in the form of a "guided tour" to its functionality and philosophy. The guided tour is based on concrete examples that show how the different components of the system can be used. The examples illustrate the development of programs and transformations based on the PROSPECTRA methodology.

2.1. Introduction

The purpose of this chapter is to give the reader a first impression of the PROSPECTRA methodology and support system. After a brief description of the individual components of the system, the reader is taken on a guided tour of PROSPECTRA. The tour presents example developments of programs and transformation rules and gives an illustration of the various system commands.

2.1.1. System Components

The different components have all been implemented using the Cornell Synthesizer Generator (CSG) [Reps and Teitelbaum 88]. This provides a homogenous user interface to all parts of the system. The main system components are summarised below.

Editors: All CSG based editors have two parts - a *common*, language-independent, kernel offering basic editing and navigation commands, and a *specific*, language-dependent part offering syntax-directed editing and static semantic checking. The editors are used when constructing initial requirements specification - and on subsequent revisions of these specifications.

Transformer: The transformers are used during the refinement by transformation phase. In this way the user interface is identical to the editors, except that *text-editing* has been disabled - the contents of an editor buffer may only be modified by the application of transformation rules. Transformers are parameterised by transformation rules where the transformations of any specific transformer will be oriented towards a specific task or development method.

Proof Subsystem: The proof subsystem serves two purposes: first to verify the correctness of stated properties in e.g. a design specification, and second to verify the applicability conditions associated with the use of a conditional transformation rule. The proof subsystem can automatically construct e.g. an induction proof given the base case and the induction case.

Translators: The translators are used in the last step of a development to generate, for example, C source code.

Controller: The controller defines how the different components are used in accordance with the PROSPECTRA methodology.

Library & Configuration Managers: The library manager enables and controls the access to a project database during development. The database is incremental. The configuration manager makes it possible to define and control compositions of versions within a particular project library.

CEC: The Conditional Equational Completion component is a specialised transformer which, given a set of axioms, generates all additional axioms that can be derived from the initial axioms and removes redundant axioms (see section 2.5 and part III, section 4.3). The CEC transformer can be invoked from a CSG based transformer.

2.1.2. Languages

In the PROSPECTRA system there are three related languages which are used in development: $PA^{nn}dA$-S, used for the development of programs, TrafoLa-S used for the development of transformation rules, and ControLa used for constructing development methods or control strategies. All three languages may be considered as subsets of the base language $PA^{nn}dA$.

$PA^{nn}dA$-S: Requirements specifications for the development of programs are written in the PA^{nn}-dA-S specification language using an editor incorporating static semantic checking. Before refinement by transformation begins, the requirements specification is translated to $PA^{nn}dA$, essentially the same language as $PA^{nn}dA$-S, but where text-editing is disabled and the abstract syntax is oriented towards transformation.

TrafoLa: Transformation rules are specified in TrafoLa-S, which is identical to $PA^{nn}dA$-S except that a few specialised constructs for specifying $PA^{nn}dA$-S program fragments have been added. This means that the development of transformation rules follows the same methodology as the development of programs. In the final implementation step TrafoLa-S is translated to SSL (the source code language used by CSG).

ControLa: Development methods are specified in ControLa, an applicative subset of $PA^{nn}dA$-S. In refining ControLa specifications, the same methodology as for development of programs may be used. In the final implementation step ControLa is translated into executable CSG scripts.

2.1.3. A Working Example

The example used to illustrate program development is the pattern matching problem (see [Partsch and Stomp 90] and [Liu et al 91]). The informal description of this is:

"*Given two strings p and s, find the first occurrence of p in s, provided it exists.*"

This example is chosen for two reasons. Firstly, it is relatively simple and secondly, it is sufficiently rich to enable all interesting aspects of development to be illustrated. In subsequent sections, the problem is formally specified and then refined to an executable program.

2.2. Getting Started: Requirements Specification

2.2.1. Starting the PROSPECTRA System

To start the PROSPECTRA system, one needs just to type the command "**spannda**". Afterwards a window is created as shown in figure 2.2.1. The examples in this chapter are all based on the Sun-View and/or X interfaces provided by CSG

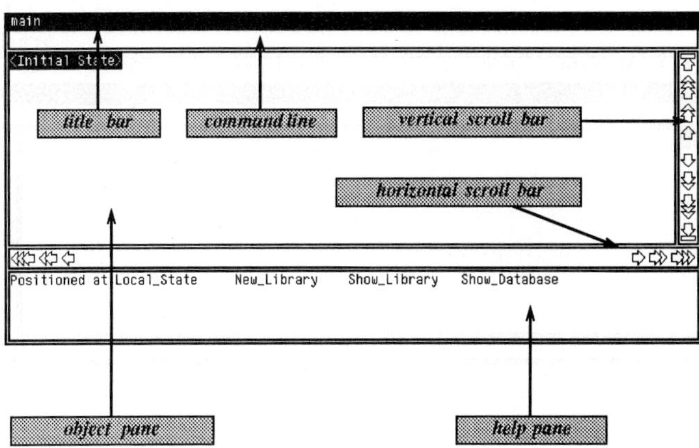

Figure 2.2.1: Having entered the PROSPECTRA system.

Figure 2.2.1 shows the SunView interface of the CSG generated PA^{nn}dA system. The window is split into six sub-windows. The central sub-window, the *object pane*, contains the current package being edited. Below and to the right of this are two sub-windows, the *horizontal* and *vertical scroll bars* containing 'buttons' which when clicked cause the main sub-window to scroll horizontally and vertically, respectively. The top sub-window, the *title bar*, shows the name of the buffer. Immediately below this is the command line containing 'general' error messages from the editor, like "syntax error" and "Cannot open file ...". It is also a sub-window in which the user can enter and invoke CSG system commands, for e.g. reading and writing files. The bottom sub-window, the *help pane*, contains an indication of the current syntactic category and 'buttons' that activate the *transformations* available for this category.

2.2.2. Working at the Library Level

In the "*help pane*" of figure 2.2.1, there are three commands available (in general these kinds of commands are called syntax-directed transformations); namely, "**New_Library**", "**Show_Library**" and "**Show_Database**". The result of the command "**Show_Database**" is to list of all library names in the PROSPECTRA database. The commands "**New_Library**" and "**Show_Library**" are so-called parameterized transformations, that is, the developer is required to supply some parameters via a parameter window which will appear when the transformation is invoked. Each library consists of a set of families of related components. "**New_Library**" allows the user to create a new library. "**Show_Library**" allows the user to extend an existing library. For instance, figure 2.2.2 shows the invocation of "**Show_Library**" with the library "*guided_tour*".

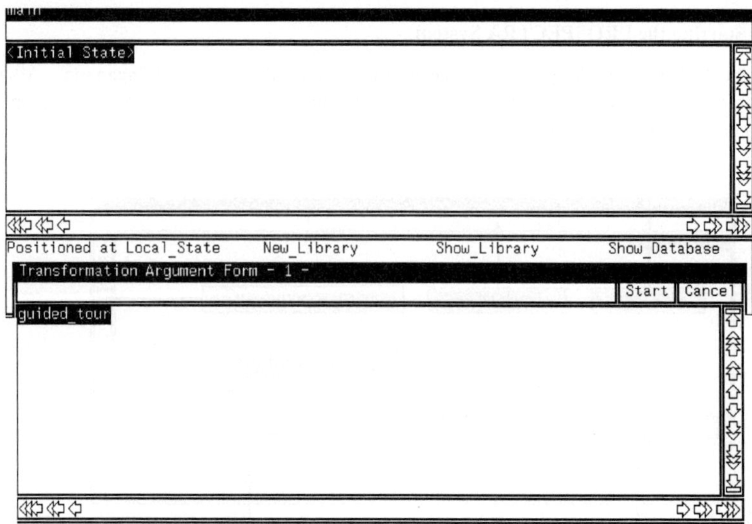

Figure 2.2.2: Extending an existing library.

A library is made up of a set of families, where each family represents a requirements specification of some problem together with its refinements and revisions. The structure of the library reflects the development of a software product. In the system, a family is represented by versions, where a base version represents the requirement specification and is created by a user through commands "**New_Family**" and "**New_Origin**". The other versions form a tree structure with the base version as the root (cf part III, chapter 1). The nodes of a tree (except the root) are created by the transformations "**New_Refinement**", "**--> PAnndA**" or "**Revision**".

Another important aspect of the library structure is the relationship between the various versions of families. This relation reflects the dependency between different specifications and programs. Dependencies are established by referring to one specification from another via a *with-clause*. The with-relations between versions of different families form a number of acyclic, directed graphs. The set of versions belonging to such a graph (starting from a given root) is called a *configuration*. Within a configuration it is illegal to have two versions belonging to the same family. Configurations are defined using the "**Revise_Configuration**" command. For instance, in the library "brick" there exist two families: "sequence" and "match_domain", where "match_domain" is based on "sequence". Now, based on "match_domain", a new family is created whose base requirements specification defines the pattern matching problem, the new family is named "pattern_match". Figure 2.2.3 shows the library "brick".

```
main

project library brick is
families
  family match_domain is
    origin match_domain$0 is
      ...
      contents: PAnndA_S;
      status: Validated;
      phase: Requirement Specifications;
      dependencies: sequence$0;
      generic instantiations: none;
    end origin match_domain$0;
  end family match_domain;
  family sequence is
    origin sequence$0;
  end family sequence;
end library brick;
```

Figure 2.2.3: The library brick.

Figure 2.2.4 shows the creation of a new family in an existing library. Notice that this command can also be used in a new library created by the "**New_Library**" command.

Figure 2.2.4: Creating a new family.

After having selected the "**New_Family**" command, a form command window is opened. The name of the family, "pattern_match", is entered and the start button is selected. After a new family is created, the command "**New_Origin**" can be chosen. This starts up an editor to allow the construction of a requirements specification (Figure 2.2.5).

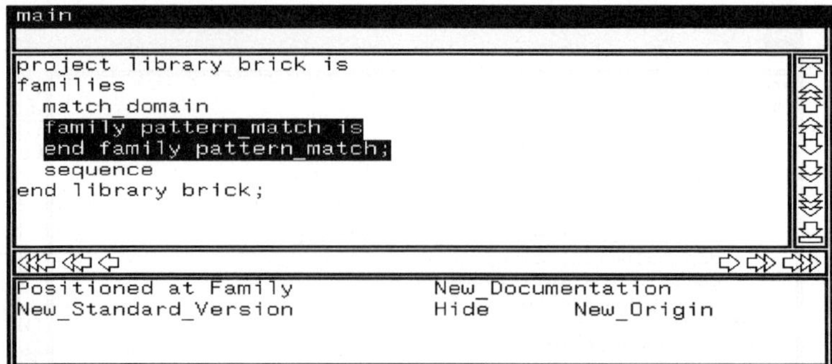

Figure 2.2.5: A new family has been created.

In this case the PA^{nn}dA-S editor is called. Figure 2.2.6 shows the initial state of the editor resulting from the transformation "**New_Origin**".

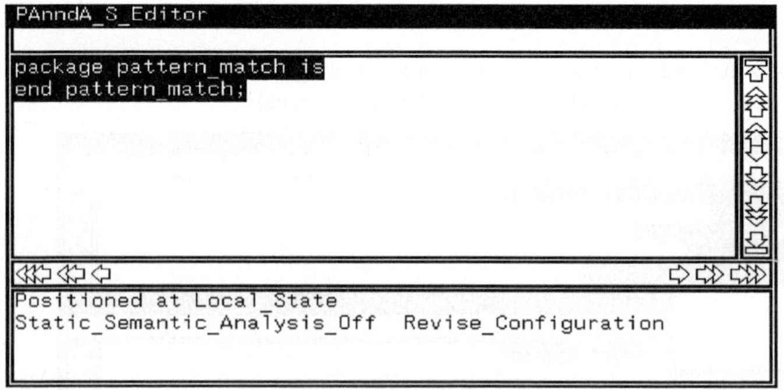

Figure 2.2.6: Initial state of the PA^{nn}dA-S editor.

Before beginning to construct a specification, the mode of editing must be chosen. There are two possibilities here: to check the static semantic correctness incrementally, or turn off the static semantic checking until some later time. By default, the editor always enables static semantic checking. The command "**Static_Semantic_Analysis_Off**", shown in figure 2.2.6, allows static semantic checking to be disabled. If it had already been turned off, the command "**Static_Semantic_Analysis_On**" would be available instead.

It may also be necessary to revise the configuration, for example, if the current specification is based on some other specifications. For instance, the package "pattern_match" depends on the package "match_domain"; so the command "**Revise_Configuration**" is selected. This command switches control from the PA^{nn}dA-S editor to the configuration manager as depicted in figure 2.2.7. Transformations such as "**Add_Dependency**" are used to revise the dependencies between versions of different families in the library. Constraints, such as no cyclic dependencies and no more than one dependency on the different versions of a particular family, will be checked automatically.

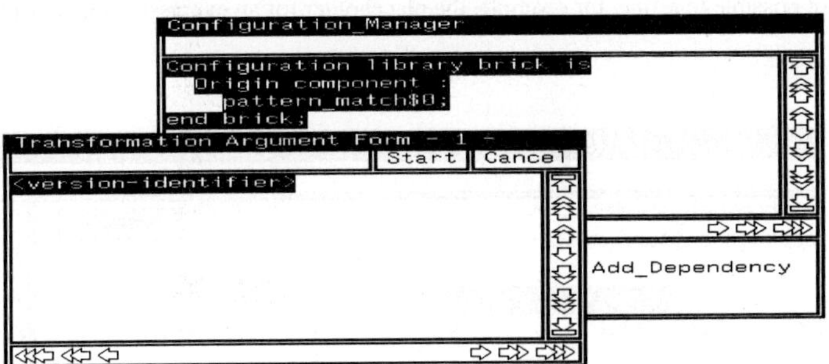

Figure 2.2.7: The configuration manager.

Invoking the command "**Add_Dependency**" allows the addition of a new dependency, for example the base version of "match_domain" is taken as the dependent version of the base version of "pattern_match". This is illustrated in figure 2.2.8.

```
Configuration_Manager

Configuration library brick is
  Origin component :
    pattern_match$0 with (match_domain$0);

  dependencies :
    match_domain$0 with (sequence$0);
    sequence$0
end brick;
```

Figure 2.2.8: Defining the configuration for "pattern_match".

To transfer control back to the PA^{nn}dA-S editor, the main menu must be called by pressing the middle mouse button within the window of the configuration manager. The command "**Confirm_Development**" is selected to commit the revision of the dependencies of "pattern_match". After the revision, all the visible objects in "match_domain" are now also visible within "pattern_match".

2.2.3. Using the PA^{nn}dA-S Editor

Each specification is constructed within the editor either by structure editing or text editing. In structure editing mode operations directly manipulate abstract syntax trees. In text editing mode phrases are constructed on a character by character basis. While structure editing always guarantees well-formed fragments, text editing provides more flexibility. With structure editing, a template can be introduced at the current selection by a *template inserting transformation.* Text editing is only permitted at the placeholders. Figure 2.2.9 shows the editing of "pattern_match" after introducing a *with-clause* and invoking several *template inserting transformations* for defining a function declaration. As stated beforehand, *template inserting transformations* guarantee the structural well-formedness of the program at every step: only applicable transformations are presented in the help pane. These transformations are enabled/disabled dynamically depending on the current selection. It is therefore not possible to refine, for example, the placeholder for an expression into a declaration.

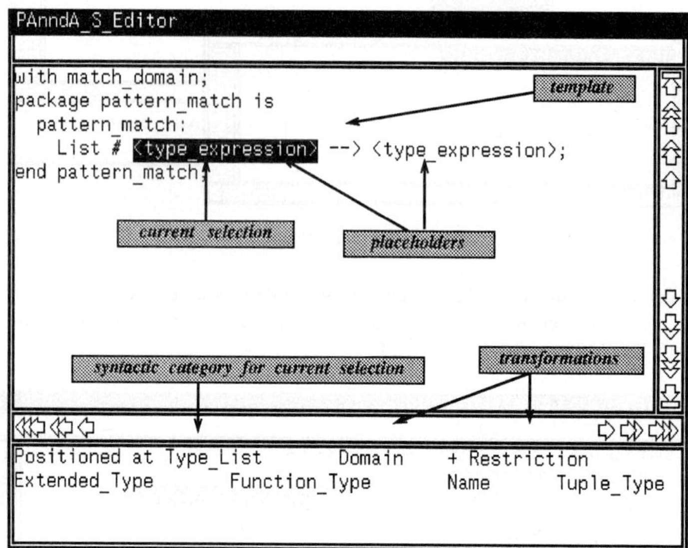

Figure 2.2.9: Editing a PAnndA-S package.

In figure 2.2.9 the inverted text represents the current selection. A template is a predefined formatted pattern for a specific syntactic category. A placeholder identifies areas where insertions are permitted. The help pane shows the name of the syntactic category of the current selection, and the currently available transformations.

The editor accepts *text input* for all syntactic categories – in a sense, it is a violation of the principles of structure editing to insert text directly instead of using the appropriate template. However, for an experienced user, directly inserting text can be much faster. The user is allowed to type in a phrase of text when positioned at a placeholder. Upon typing in the phrase of text, the text is parsed and the subtree constructed. Errors in user-typed text are detected immediately. Figure 2.2.10 shows an example.

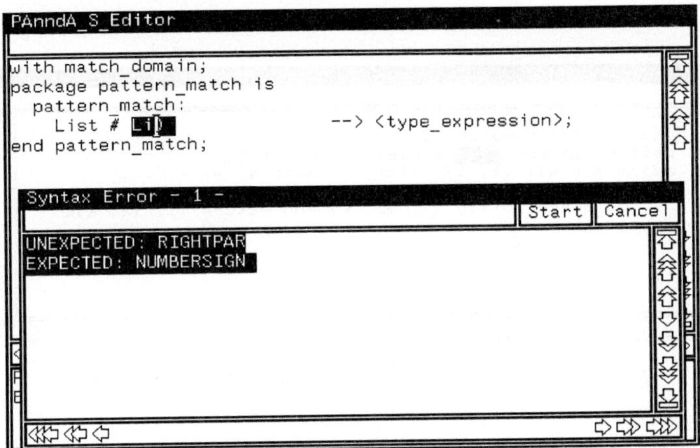

Figure 2.2.10: An example of a syntax error.

The syntax error window indicates that an unexpected right parenthesis was found. It is not possible to continue editing, before the syntax error has been corrected. As a direct result, only syntactically well formed specifications can be stored in the library. Besides syntax errors, editing may introduce static semantic errors. According to the static semantic definition of PA^{nn}dA-S (cf part II chapter 2), every variable used within an axiom must be declared beforehand. Figure 2.2.11 shows such an error.

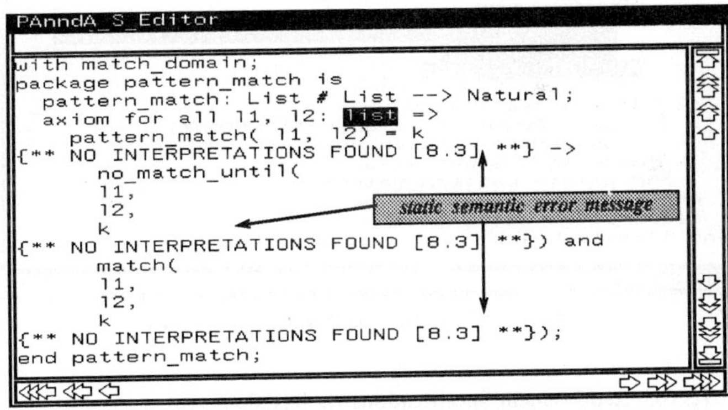

Figure 2.2.11: A static semantic error.

The specification contains a static semantic error, which is reported immediately inside the '{**' '**}' symbols. The reason for the error in the example is that an undeclared name ("k") is used. The specification is checked for static semantic correctness incrementally. In this way, it is easy to resolve such errors before a development is committed to the library. Figure 2.2.12 shows the specification after the static semantic error has been corrected. This completes the requirements specification of "pattern_match".

```
PAnndA_S_Editor

with match_domain;
package pattern_match is
  pattern_match: List # List --> Natural;
  axiom for all l1, l2: list; k: Natural =>
    pattern_match( l1, l2) = k ->
      no_match_until( l1, l2, k) and match( l1, l2, k);
end pattern_match;
```

Figure 2.2.12: The requirements specification for 'pattern_match'.

The specification in figure 2.2.12 represents the initial requirements specification for the package "pattern_match". The package is added into the library by selecting the system command "**Confirm_Development**" from the menu. This results in the updated library structure shown in figure 2.2.13.

```
main
Log file closed.
project library brick is
families
  match_domain
  family pattern_match is
    origin pattern_match$0 is
      information:
        creation_date: Wed May 20 10:10:18 1992;
        owner: prost;
      end information;
      contents: PAnndA_S;
      status: Validated;
      phase: Requirement Specifications;
      dependencies: match_domain$0;
      generic instantiations: none;
    end origin pattern_match$0;
  end family pattern_match;
  sequence
end library brick;
```

Figure 2.2.13: The updated library structure.

2.2.4. Constructing Requirement Specifications via Revision

In the PROSPECTRA system, every program development starts from an initial requirement specification. We have seen in previous sections how to construct an initial specification by invoking "**New_Family**" and "**New_Origin**" etc. However, this is not the only means of creating an initial requirements specification. Requirements specifications may also be obtained by the revision of an existing specification (i.e. with no formal relation of correctness with the original; this is in contrast to transformational refinement). Such revisions are also supported by the methodology since reuse of existing development scripts (associated with the specifications being revised) can also be made. Here, we initiate the construction of a new, initial specification by invoking the transformation

"**New_Revision**". This command causes the specification under revision to appear in the PA^{nn}dA-S editor. After the necessary modifications the command "**Confirm_Development**" is issued to confirm the revision and commit the result to the library. A revision of "pattern_match" is shown in figure 2.2.14.

```
main
Log file closed.
project library brick is
families
  match_domain
  family pattern_match is
    origin pattern_match$0 is
      ...
      contents: PAnndA_S;
      status: Validated;
      phase: Requirement Specifications;
      dependencies: match_domain$0;
      generic instantiations: none;

      revision pattern_match$1 is
        information:
          creation_date: Wed May 20 10:30:24 1992;
          owner: prost;
        end information;
        contents: PAnndA_S;
        status: Validated;
        phase: Requirement Specifications;
        dependencies: match_domain$0;
        generic instantiations: none;
      end revision pattern_match$1;
    end origin pattern_match$0;
  end family pattern_match;
  sequence
end library brick;
```

Figure 2.2.14: Revising "match_domain".

2.2.5. Summary

We have briefly introduced how to create an initial requirements specification within the PROSPECTRA system. Our working example is used to illustrate the construction in a concrete way. Notice, however, that there are many issues pertinent to the construction of requirements specifications which have not been addressed. For example, the issues associated with the use of generic packages, auxiliary functions, and so on, have not been considered. These issues are considered in detail in the corresponding sections of this text (cf part II, chapter 2 and part III, section 4.1).

2.3. Refinement by Transformation

2.3.1. Translation to PA^{nn}dA-C

A base version of an initial requirement specification written in PA^{nn}dA-S must be translated into PA^{nn}dA before refinement by transformation can start. The translation can be carried out by invoking the transformation "**--> PAnndA**". Figure 2.3.1 shows the translation of "pattern_match".

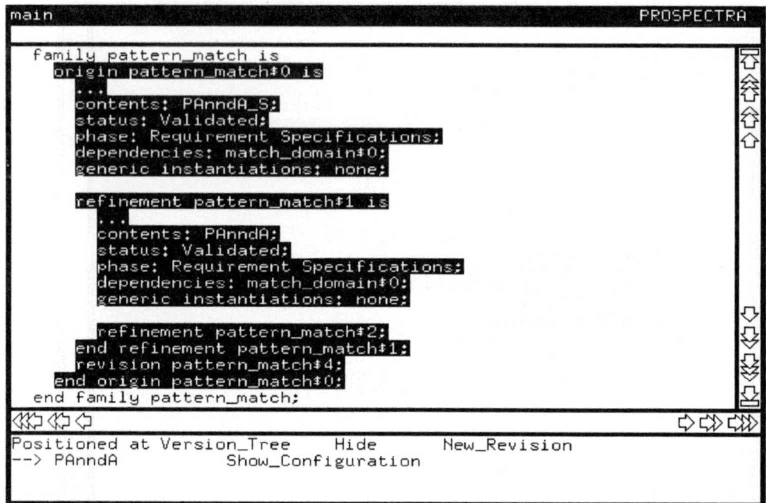

Figure 2.3.1: The translation to 'PA^{nn}dA'.

In the PROSPECTRA system, all activities that involve correctness-preserving transformations are carried out within the PA^{nn}dA transformer. The transformer is based on the PA^{nn}dA language and is interfaced to the Proof subsystem. To enter into the transformer, a PA^{nn}dA version is chosen to be refined. Then the command "**New_Refinement**" is issued which has the effect of starting the transformer on the chosen version. Within the transformer, either the command "**Confirm_Development**" or "**Cancel_Development**" can be selected to add the development as a refinement to the current family or to abandon the refinement respectively.

2.3.2. Starting the Design

In the PA^{nn}dA transformer, normal text editing is forbidden. The specification (program) fragment can only be modified by application of the available transformations. Three constraints restrict the transformations that are applicable in any context. Firstly, type constraints are specified that bind the transformation to a particular syntactic category. Secondly, some decidable semantic properties can be given: for instance, pattern constraints can be specified by using the constructors of the PA^{nn}-dA abstract syntax, and static semantic properties (also relating to context) may be specified (cf part III section 5.2). Finally, a grouping mechanism provided by the system can be used to control the set of transformations available within the transformer at any time. As a consequence, whenever the transformer is invoked, the command "**Trafo_Modules_Info**" must be used to enable the particular transformation module appropriate for the current development. Figure 2.3.2 shows an example.

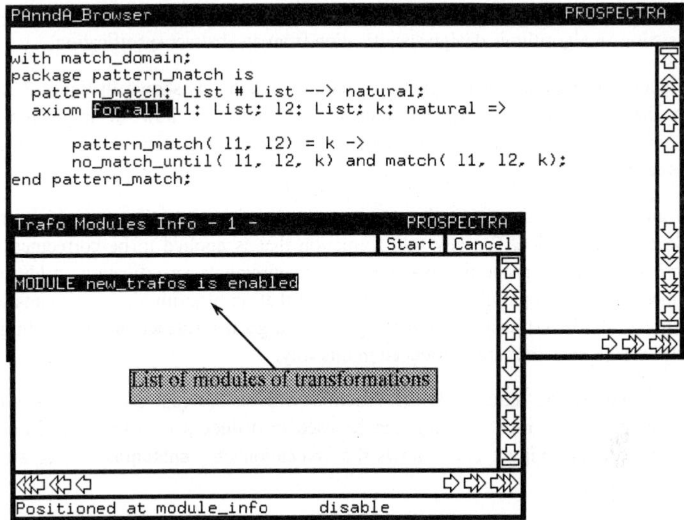

Figure 2.3.2: Selecting transformation modules.

After selecting a transformation module for development, refinement can start. Each time a specification/program fragment is selected, the applicable transformations will appear in the *help pane* (and under the mouse button as a menu) According to the methodology of PROSPECTRA, a design specification is represented in the private part of a package. In this way the visible part, that serves as the interface to other packages, remains unchanged throughout development. As a consequence of this, a decision must be made to fix the interface before beginning the development of the design specification. The transformation "**start_design**" achieves this goal. The result is shown in figure 2.3.3.

```
PAnndA_Browser                                        PROSPECTRA

package pattern_match is
  pattern_match: List # List --> natural;
  axiom for all l1: List; l2: List; k: natural =>

      pattern_match( l1, l2) = k ->
      no_match_until( l1, l2, k) and match( l1, l2, k);
private
  axiom for all l1: List; l2: List; k: natural =>

      pattern_match( l1, l2) = k ->
      no_match_until( l1, l2, k) and match( l1, l2, k);
end pattern_match;
```

Figure 2.3.3: The result of applying 'start_design'.

In the private part, only axioms that are used for the definition of functions are taken into consideration. Only properties of the visible functions are preserved.

2.3.3. Refining Design Specifications

Generally, the functions in the requirements specification are only loosely specified. There is a significant gap between abstract specifications and algorithmic specifications. The initial goal of refinement is to develop an algorithmic design specification from an abstract specification.

The requirements specification of the package "**pattern_match**", as shown in figure 2.3.3, is *non-constructive* in the sense that it does not contain any hints on how to implement the function "pattern_match". In fact, any function that satisfies the given properties will be a valid implementation of the specification.

To develop an implementation from the requirements specification, the appropriate transformations must be selected and applied. For any transformation that is applied to be correctness preserving, it must preserve the original properties given by the requirements specification. Additional properties may be defined and will hopefully be *constructive* so that an algorithmic implementation can be derived. The choice of which transformation to apply has a great influence on the resulting implementation. Actually, *design decisions* are introduced in this way.

For instance, selecting the axioms of the function will enable (amongst others) a transformation called "**splitofpostv**". This transformation can be used to deduce a recursive definition of a function given certain constraints. Figure 2.3.4 shows the invocation of "**splitofpostv**" (see also part I chapters 1 and 3).

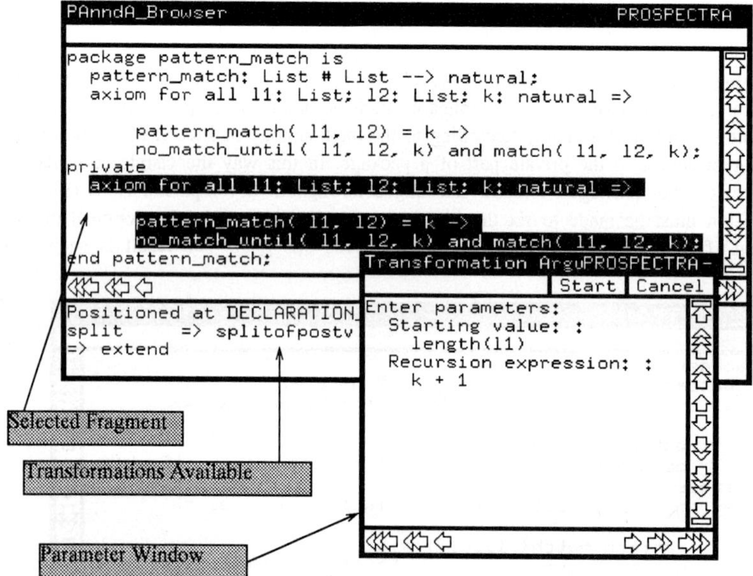

Figure 2.3.4: Applying 'splitofpostv'.

As depicted in figure 2.3.4, it is required that the developer supply two parameters to aid in the construction of a recursive definition. The parameter window is used for input. The functionality of the parameter window is equivalent to that of the PAnndA-S editor, so any parameters supplied by the user are guaranteed to be syntactically and static semantically correct. Moreover, additional constraints on the parameters can also be specified and are automatically checked by the system. Such interaction will generally lead to the construction of a proof obligation (to be established by the Proof system). If the "**start**" button of the parameter window is pressed, then the proof obligation is constructed automatically, according the developer's input, and transferred to the Proof system.

2.3.4. Verification: Invoking the Proof System

Figure 2.3.5 shows the proof obligation generated for the transformation "**splitofpostv**" and transferred to the Proof system.

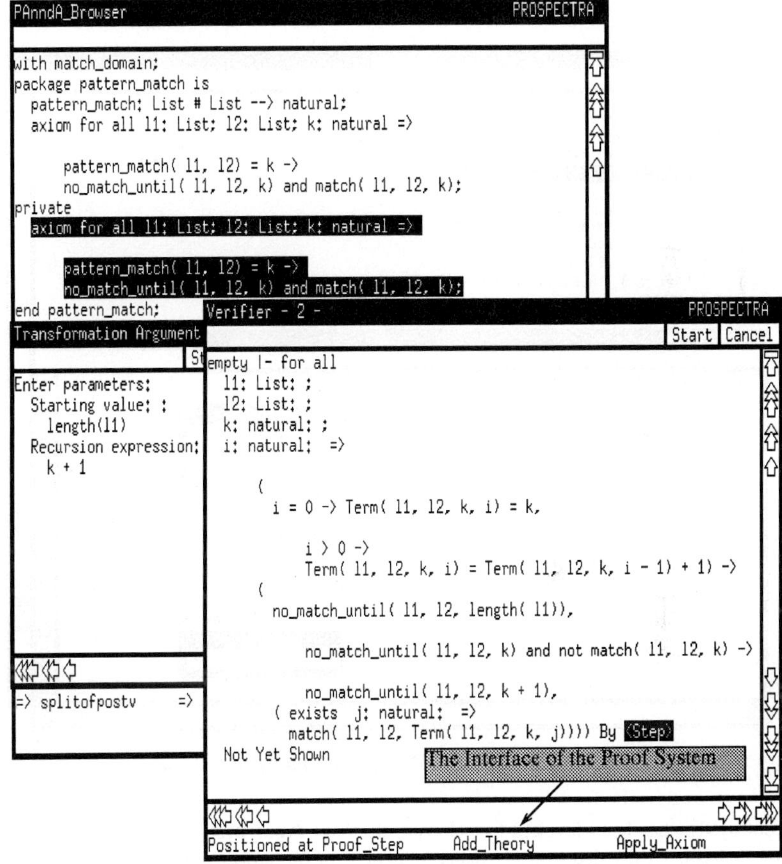

Figure 2.3.5: The Proof obligation for 'splitofpostv'.

There are several ways in which interaction with the proof system can proceed. In the case where the proof obligation has been shown to hold, the proof is recorded in the development history and the transformation is applied. Where the proof obligation cannot be established (or can be shown not to hold), the invocation of the transformation is cancelled. Alternatively, and from a practical point of view a very pragmatic option, the proof may be delayed. Here it is assumed that the proof obligation can somehow be established, allowing the development to proceed. The correctness of the development is then modulo the generated proof obligation. Later, in replay for example, the recorded proof obligation is presented again for verification. This *delay of proof obligation* can be very useful in cases where the developer is experimenting with possible refinement strategies. For the application of "**splitofpostv**" the delay of proof obligation is chosen. Instead of the lengthy proof associated with this development, the reduction of a simpler proof obligation is illustrated.

The proof system may also be invoked by selecting a logical formula from the axiom part of a specification and applying the transformation rule "**==> Proof_System2**". The result of invoking this rule is shown in figure 2.3.6.

Figure 2.3.6: Choosing schema induction.

The proof system has been invoked by selecting the "**==> Proof_System2**" command for the current selection. It has been decided to use schema induction for the proof, which is chosen from the transformations menu.

Various strategies can be employed for proof (cf part III section 4.4). The actual choice will depend on the users experience. In this example the proof can be established using the principle of induction.

The argument that should be provided for schema induction describes the base and induction cases for all predicates (F) of the type Natural. The result of pressing **"Start"** is shown in figure 2.3.7.

Figure 2.3.7: Using a schema induction proof.

The proof system is also based on the *transformational* paradigm used in all other parts of the system. Developing a proof is, in this sense, similar to developing a specification: a proof tree is transformed into a more detailed one by the application of transformation rules. *Backtracking* is easy, it simply implies the deletion of a sub-proof.

The proof system includes a semi-automatic proof mechanism that can be used to handle some of the more tedious tasks. For instance, after pressing the "**start**" button on the window of the argument form, all kinds of proof rules can be employed to deduce the base case and induction step of the above proof schema. For details of the use of the Proof system see part III section 4.4.

2.3.5. Program Construction

In refining a design specification, the goal is to restrict the set of possible models (standing for the implementations) by various design decisions introduced through the application of transformations. The application of transformation rules continues until a unique solution is obtained (or can easily be extracted by some *projection* transformations). From this stage onwards, the transformations applied aim to either optimize the solution further or to meet certain syntactic preconditions of the transformations for program generation. For instance, although the last version of "pattern_match" already defines a unique solution, the axiom part does not satisfies the syntactic constraints of the transformation "**Pannda-body**" (explained later); that is, each axiom part should contain only the axioms needed to define a single function. For that reason, the transformation "**split**" is applied here (the result is shown in figure 2.3.8).

```
PAnndA_Browser                                                    PROSPECTRA

private
  pattern_match_h: List # List # natural --> natural;
  axiom for all l1: List; l2: List =>
    pattern_match( l1, l2) = pattern_match_h( l1, l2, length(l1));
  axiom for all l1: List;
     l2: List;
     k: natural :: no_match_until( l1, l2, k) =>
    match( l1, l2, k) -> pattern_match_h( l1, l2, k) = k,

      not match( l1, l2, k) ->

        pattern_match_h( l1, l2, k) =
        pattern_match_h( l1, l2, k + 1);
end pattern_match;
```

Figure 2.3.8: The result of applying 'split'.

A very important step towards code generation in the development process is the decision of the language paradigm (e.g. imperative, functional programming language, etc.). This can be supported by the various transformations designed to generate bodies. For example, if an imperative program is the goal, then a transformation for that paradigm can be constructed. If a functional language is preferred, then a transformation for functional code generation can be defined. We can further specialise this generation for different concrete languages by adding more syntactic constraints to the applicability conditions of body generation transformations. Currently, there is only one such transformation available in the system: "**Pannda_body**", this is oriented more towards the imperative programming paradigm. There are some syntactic constraints which must be satisfied before this transformation is applied. For example, the transformation "**split**" (described above) must be applied before body generation. Such syntactic constraints make the body easier to synthesise. As mentioned, the transformation "**Pannda_body**" is oriented to the imperative language paradigm. For this reason transformations like "**if_intro**" can be applied to normalize the code to be generated after the "**split**". Figure 2.3.9 shows the application of "**if_intro**" and figure 2.3.10 shows the generated body.

```
PAnndA_Browser                                                    PROSPECTRA

private
  pattern_match_h: List # List # natural --> natural;
  axiom for all l1: List; l2: List =>
    pattern_match( l1, l2) = pattern_match_h( l1, l2, length(l1));
  axiom for all l1: List;
     l2: List;
     k: natural :: no_match_until( l1, l2, k) =>

      pattern_match_h( l1, l2, k) =
      if match( l1, l2, k) then k else pattern_match_h( l1, l2, k + 1) end if;
end pattern_match;
```

Figure 2.3.9: The result of applying 'if_intro'.

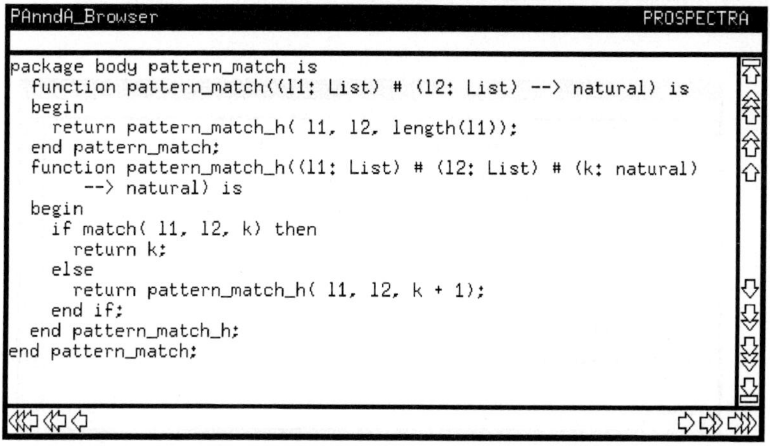

```
PAnndA_Browser                                              PROSPECTRA

package body pattern_match is
  function pattern_match((l1: List) # (l2: List) --> natural) is
  begin
    return pattern_match_h( l1, l2, length(l1));
  end pattern_match;
  function pattern_match_h((l1: List) # (l2: List) # (k: natural)
       --> natural) is
  begin
    if match( l1, l2, k) then
      return k;
    else
      return pattern_match_h( l1, l2, k + 1);
    end if;
  end pattern_match_h;
end pattern_match;
```

Figure 2.3.10: Result of applying 'Pannda_body'.

Within the imperative paradigm, there are still some transformations that can be applied with a view to optimising the resultant code. One of theses transformation is introduced below.

The transformation rule **"TailRec => Loop"** transforms a tail-recursive function into an imperative procedure containing a while-loop. The base case of the transformation rule is specified in figure 2.3.11. It takes three arguments: *B* which is the loop condition, *T* which ends the recursion, and *H* the expression changing the arguments in the recursive call.

```
function F(X:S --> R) is                    function F(X:S --> R) is
begin                                       begin
   if B(X) then                                while not B(X) loop
      return T(X);          ------>               X := H(X);
   else                                        end loop;
      return F(H(X));                          return T(X);
   end if;                                  end F;
end F;
```

Figure 2.3.11: Specification of the transformation "TailRec => Loop".

For the general case, there are additional syntactic constraints for the variable occurrences in the recursion. The function to be considered ("pattern_match_h") satisfies all applicability conditions. The result of the transformations is shown in figure 2.3.12.

```
PAnndA_Browser                                          PROSPECTRA

package body pattern_match is
  function pattern_match((l1: List) # (l2: List) --> natural) is
  begin
    return pattern_match_h( l1, l2, length(l1));
  end pattern_match;
  function pattern_match_h((l1: List) # (l2: List) # (k: natural)
       --> natural) is
  begin
    while
      not match( l1, l2, k)  loop
        k := k + 1;
      end loop ;
    return k;
  end pattern_match_h;
end pattern_match;
```

Figure 2.3.12: Result of applying 'Tailrec => loop'.

2.3.6. Source to Source Translation

The above program can be translated to pure Ada, as an alternative, a translation to the C programming language is provided. The translation takes the whole program (which must include a body). If the body is an imperative body, then it is translated to a C program (figure 2.3.13). The translator only works for a subset of PA^{nn}dA-C (imperative subset of PA^{nn}dA). Generic packages, for example, are not yet considered by the transformation which produces C code (see [Wu 91]).

```
PAnndA_Browser                                PROSPECTRA

#include "match_domain.h"
extern natural pattern_match();

natural pattern_match(l1, l2)
  List l1;
  List l2;
{
  return pattern_match_h(l1, l2, length(l1));
}

natural pattern_match_h(l1, l2, k)
  List l1;
  List l2;
  natural k;
{
  while (!(match(l1, l2, k))) k = k + 1;
  return k;
}
```

Figure 2.3.13: Result of applying '-->C'.

It should be pointed out that this translation (to C) enables complete development within a purely formal development framework. The C abstract syntax is specified separately from the abstract syntax of the PA^{nn}dA language. The translation is based on the consistency of the operational semantics of subsets of PA^{nn}dA-C and C.

2.3.7. Re-Development

In the library manager of the PROSPECTRA system, the development of a program is represented as a tree structure. This has been designed to reflect the real development history, since rarely are developments achieved without considering alternative development strategies or performing some redesign activity. Also, an initial development may well be very naive, but will make the crucial steps in the refinement process clear. In this situation, the crucial design steps may be reused in subsequent, more sophisticated developments. The PROSPECTRA methodology provides moderate support for re-development in this sense. For example, when considering the construction of a requirement specification, it was mentioned that the transformation "**New_Revision**" can be used to construct a new (but related version) of the original problem specification.

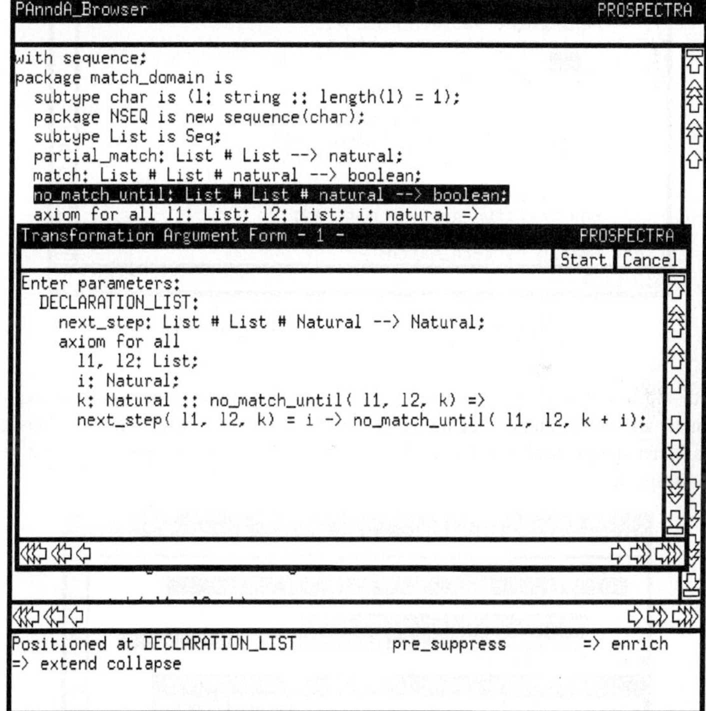

Figure 2.3.14: Applying 'enrich'.

In the development of "pattern_match", a very important design decision is introduced by the transformation "**splitofpostv**". This transformation requires two parameters for constructing the recursive version of "pattern_match", one of two parameters being the expression controlling the recursion. In the first development, a conservative decision (but obviously correct) has been taken, namely, to move the matching position by one character on each iteration. A much more efficient decision would be to move the match position as far as possible if there are no positions in-between that can result in a match. For this purpose, the visible part of "match_domain" is enriched with the function "next_step" with the desired properties (figure 2.3.14).

Now "pattern_match" can be revised through "**New_Revision**" with the modified dependency on the refined version of "match_domain". In the new environment, the function "next_step" is available in the package "pattern_match". The revision is also translated to a PA^{nn}dA version for further refinement (figure 2.3.15).

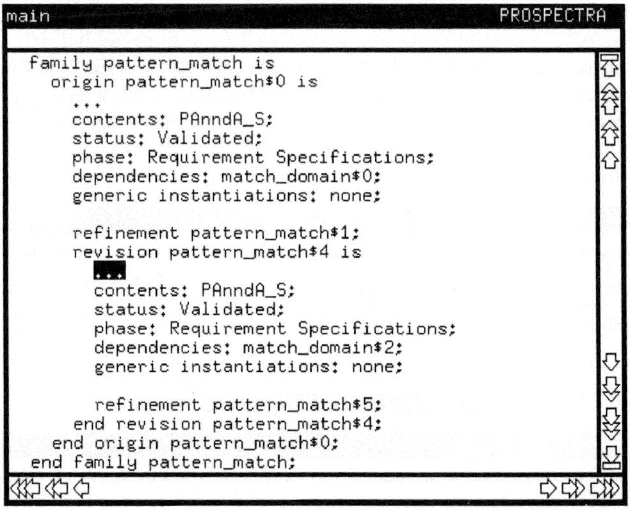

```
main                                                    PROSPECTRA

 family pattern_match is
   origin pattern_match$0 is
     ...
     contents: PAnndA_S;
     status: Validated;
     phase: Requirement Specifications;
     dependencies: match_domain$0;
     generic instantiations: none;

     refinement pattern_match$1;
     revision pattern_match$4 is
       ...
       contents: PAnndA_S;
       status: Validated;
       phase: Requirement Specifications;
       dependencies: match_domain$2;
       generic instantiations: none;

       refinement pattern_match$5;
     end revision pattern_match$4;
   end origin pattern_match$0;
 end family pattern_match;
```

Figure 2.3.15: Revision of "pattern_match".

Equipped with the new knowledge from the package "match_domain", the recursive expression (the second parameter of transformation "**splitofpostv**") will be the "next_step" function. This choice corresponds to a better design decision. Figure 2.3.16 and 2.3.17 show the application and result of the transformation respectively.

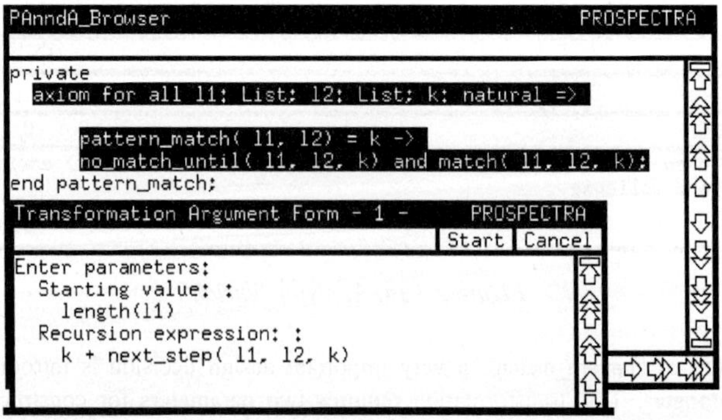

```
PAnndA_Browser                                          PROSPECTRA

private
  axiom for all l1: List; l2: List; k: natural =>

     pattern_match( l1, l2) = k ->
     no_match_until( l1, l2, k) and match( l1, l2, k);
end pattern_match;

Transformation Argument Form - 1 -          PROSPECTRA
                                        Start | Cancel
Enter parameters:
  Starting value: :
    length(l1)
  Recursion expression: :
    k + next_step( l1, l2, k)
```

Figure 2.3.16: Applying 'splitofpostv'.

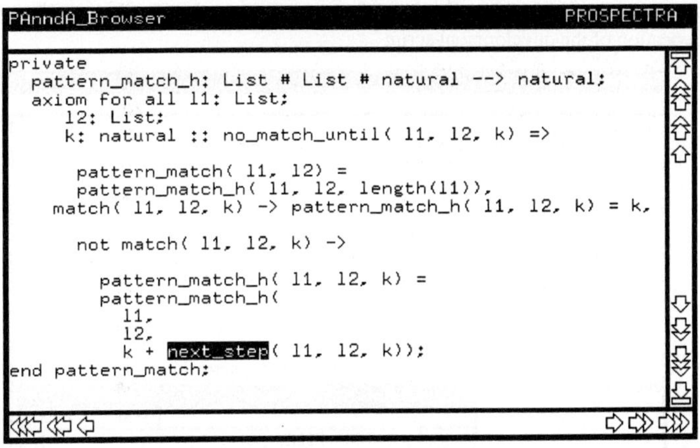

```
PAnndA_Browser                                        PROSPECTRA

private
  pattern_match_h: List # List # natural --> natural;
  axiom for all l1: List;
     l2: List;
     k: natural :: no_match_until( l1, l2, k) =>

       pattern_match( l1, l2) =
       pattern_match_h( l1, l2, length(l1)),
    match( l1, l2, k) -> pattern_match_h( l1, l2, k) = k,

       not match( l1, l2, k) ->

         pattern_match_h( l1, l2, k) =
         pattern_match_h(
           l1,
           l2,
           k + next_step( l1, l2, k));
end pattern_match;
```

Figure 2.3.17: After the application of 'splitofpostv'.

The modular approach taken here in the re-development makes not only the problem easier to understand and manipulate, but also promotes a certain degree of automation in the re-development process.

In the PROSPECTRA system, a "*log & replay*" facility is provided. It is used to store development scripts in the form of commands issued in a CSG based editor. This allows for the definition of milestones during development. If, for instance, the application of some transformation rules turns out to be unsuccessful, it is possible to backtrack to a milestone and replay the development as far as is necessary (or in re-development, it can be reused for a similar refinement process). The figure 2.3.18 shows the development script "*pattern_c.log*" of the first development of "pattern_match" after the application of the transformation "**splitofpostv**".

```
move-to-buffer("PAnndA_Browser"),
'trafo-modules-info'(enable'),
navigate("1/2/4/2/1"),
'split',
navigate("../../../../2/1/1/1/3/1/2/1/1/1/1"),
navigate("../../../../../2/1/2/1/1/1/1\\"),
'intro_if',
navigate("../../../../../../../.."),
'Pannda_body',
navigate("../../../../../../../../2/3/2/1"),
'Tail_Rec => Loop',
navigate("../../../1"),
'-->C'
```

Figure 2.3.18: A development script.

Since there is no interaction in the development script, it can be used in the development of the revised "pattern_match" (after the application of the transformation "**splitofpostv**"). Figure 2.3.19 shows the invocation of the development script

Figure 2.3.19: Applying 'pattern_c.log'.

The final C program is shown in figure 2.3.20.

```
PAnndA_Browser                                              PROSPECTRA

#include "match_domain.h"
extern natural pattern_match();

natural pattern_match(l1, l2)
  List l1;
  List l2;
{
  return pattern_match_h(l1, l2, length(l1));
}

natural pattern_match_h(l1, l2, k)
  List l1;
  List l2;
  natural k;
{
  while (!(match(l1, l2, k))) k = k + next_step(l1, l2, k);
  return k;
}
```

Figure 2.3.20: The result of applying " --> C".

Development histories are all stored in the PROSPECTRA library. The figure 2.3.21 shows the development trees of "match_domain" and "pattern_match".

```
main                                                    PROSPECTRA
project library guided_tour is
families
  family match_domain is
    origin match_domain#0 is
      refinement match_domain#1 is
        refinement match_domain#2 is
          refinement match_domain#3;
        end refinement match_domain#2;
        refinement match_domain#4;
      end refinement match_domain#1;
    end origin match_domain#0;
  end family match_domain;
  family pattern_match is
    origin pattern_match#0 is
      refinement pattern_match#1 is
        refinement pattern_match#2 is
          refinement pattern_match#3;
        end refinement pattern_match#2;
      end refinement pattern_match#1;
      revision pattern_match#4 is
        refinement pattern_match#5 is
          refinement pattern_match#6 is
            refinement pattern_match#7;
          end refinement pattern_match#6;
        end refinement pattern_match#5;
      end revision pattern_match#4;
    end origin pattern_match#0;
  end family pattern_match;
  sequence
end library guided_tour;
```

Figure 2.3.21: The development tree.

2.3.8. Summary

The use of PA^{nn}dA transformer was introduced with a working example. The transformer is a very important part of the PROSPECTRA system. All transformational development of (meta-) programs takes place within the transformer. Although only the simple development of a problem solution is demonstrated, it has already reflected the PROSPECTRA methodology. Note also, that the transformer is not only used for program development, but can also be used for meta-program development. Indeed, this is an essential property of the system: extensibility. Meta-program development is the subject of the next section.

2.4. Meta Programming

2.4.1. Extending System Knowledge

The usability of the PROSPECTRA system depends on the available transformals (i.e. transformation rules, development scripts, and methods). Once a transformal has been specified, developed, and shown to be correct it will be present for (re)use in all subsequent developments. As such, the development of transformals can be seen as a way to extend the amount of knowledge built into the system. The PROSPECTRA system provides only a set of basic transformals, but during the use of the system, users will inevitably write their own transformals depending on their requirements and application areas.

Transformation rules are developed using the TrafoLa system (cf part III chapter 5). There are basically two differences between the TrafoLa system and the PA^{nn}dA system:

- The specification language, TrafoLa-S, is a conservative extension of PA^{nn}dA-S offering a more convenient syntax for specifying transformation rules.
- Translators from TrafoLa-S to SSL (the language used to specify CSG editors) are included, this allows transformation rules developed with the TrafoLa system to be incorporated into the development environment.

Since the TrafoLa-S specification language is to a large extent identical to PA^{nn}dA-S - in fact it can be translated into PA^{nn}dA-S - the development of transformation rules follows the same methodology as 'ordinary' program development.

Development scripts are obtained by recording the development of programs using the "log & replay" mechanism provided by the PROSPECTRA system. These development scripts are reusable in similar developments. Essentially, the development scripts define the composition of transformations required to achieve a particular development. They also record interaction and proofs.

Development methods are constructed using the command development system, ControLa. A development method is made up of system commands and of transformation rule applications.

ControLa is very similar to the program development system, PAnndA. There are basically three differences:

- The specification language, ControLa-C, is a conservative extension of PA^{nn}dA-S, that offers a more convenient environment and syntax for specifying development methods.
- A translator from PA^{nn}dA-C to CSG scripts is included.
- A translator from CSG scripts to ControLa-C is included.

A *CSG script* is written in a command language which allows the user to specify the invocation and execution of commands within a CSG generated tool. It can be used to execute CSG generated tools in batch mode or, alternatively, the scripts may be considered as commands and executed within a CSG generated tool.

2.4.2. Development of Transformation Rules

In the same way that the development of a program starts with a requirements specification and ends with some target language implementation, the development of a transformation rule starts with a requirements specification, written using TrafoLa-S, and ends with a SSL program. The objects (specifications or programs) to be manipulated by meta-programs are all specified within the system as abstract data types. For example, the '`pandas`' package contains type definitions of all constructor functions that exist in the abstract syntax of PA^{nn}dA-S. These objects are represented in TrafoLa-S as PA^{nn}dA-S phrases (a concrete syntax paraphrasing of the abstract data types). These phrases are delimited by the symbols '`[`' and '`]`'. The specification and development of a very simple transformation rule is given here. Figure 2.4.1 shows the specification of the "demorgan" transformation. After completing the requirements specification, further developments will be all carried out in the PA^{nn}dA transformer. Before translation to PA^{nn}dA, the package must be translated into a canonical form (i.e. pure PA^{nn}dA-S). This means that, instead of having concrete syntax phrases in the specification, the constructors of PA^{nn}dA abstract syntax are used.

The result of this translation is shown in figure 2.4.2.

```
TrafoLa_S_Editor

with p_ssl, p_nature, panndas;
package demorgan is
  is_demorgan: EXPRESSION --> BOOL;
  demorgan: (e: EXPRESSION :: is_demorgan(e) = true) --> EXPRESSION;
  axiom for all x, y: EXPRESSION =>
    demorgan([not x and not y]) = [not (x or y)];
end demorgan;
```

Figure 2.4.1: Specification of the transformation rule 'demorgan'.

```
TrafoLa_S_Editor

with p_ssl, p_nature, panndas;
package demorgan is
  is_demorgan: EXPRESSION --> BOOL;
  demorgan: (e: EXPRESSION :: is_demorgan(e) = true) --> EXPRESSION;
  axiom for all x, y: EXPRESSION =>
    demorgan(
      Mk_Call(
        Mk_Name(Mk_Unique_Name( "and", "@Land", mk_Predefined_Op_Nature)),
        Mk_Tuple(
          Mk_Expr_List(
            Mk_Call(
              Mk_Name(
                Mk_Unique_Name( "not", "@Lnot", mk_Predefined_Op_Nature)),
              x),
            Mk_Expr_List(
              Mk_Call(
                Mk_Name(
                  Mk_Unique_Name( "not", "@Lnot", mk_Predefined_Op_Nature)),
                y),
              Empty_Expr_List))))) =
      Mk_Call(
      Mk_Name(Mk_Unique_Name( "not", "@Lnot", mk_Predefined_Op_Nature)),
      Mk_Call(
        Mk_Name(Mk_Unique_Name( "or", "@Lor", mk_Predefined_Op_Nature)),
        Mk_Tuple(Mk_Expr_List( x, Mk_Expr_List( y, Empty_Expr_List)))));
end demorgan;

Positioned at Identifier
```

Figure 2.4.2: Translation to canonical form.

The development of the specification is now complete, and the resulting version is translated to PA^{nn}dA. The updated library structure is shown in figure 2.4.3.

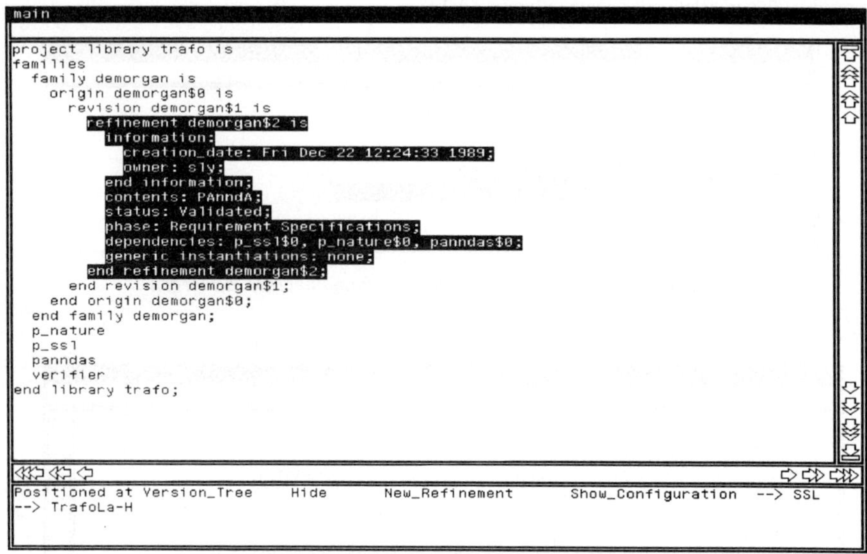

Figure 2.4.3: Changed library structure.

After the translation to PA^{nn}dA, the specification of the transformation rule can either be further refined, using the transformer as described earlier, or translated directly into the target languages SSL. SSL is the meta-language used in the CSG system. .The translations are invoked by selecting

Figure 2.4.4: Translation to SSL.

the PA^{nn}dA version in the library, and then applying the transformation rule **"--> SSL"**. The result is shown in figure 2.4.4

The example shown is actually a very simple transformation rule. A classification of the various kinds of transformation rules can be given as follows: context-free transformations; context-sensitive transformations; parameterised transformations; and conditional transformations. The simple transformation rule illustrated previously is context-free. A context-sensitive transformation rule requires some information from the surrounding context to construct the output or generate applicability conditions. For convenience in obtaining context information, TrafoLa-S is extended with the *hat notation.* With this facility the explicit specification and computation of context can be avoided. Instead, a meta-transformation can be invoked to "unfold" all hat operators to the correct context representation (see part III section 5.2.9).

A parameterised transformation is used to indicate that user interaction may be required, this is the only instance where the user may, in any sense, "edit" a program. The static semantic correctness of a user supplied parameter is, however, dynamically checked by the system. Finally, there are the conditional transformations. These are used when the universal correctness of a transformation cannot be established and the proof system is needed to ensure the applicability conditions which are generated when the transformation is applied to a concrete program fragment.

2.4.3. Producing Development Scripts

The log & replay facility that is provided by the PROSPECTRA system makes it possible to store system activities in the form of commands issued in a CSG based editor. With this facility, development activities can be recorded and named as development scripts. A development script begins with any system activity and ends with another one. The logging mechanism is invoked by selecting the "**start-log**" command. A form command buffer is created which will request the name of a logfile, see figure 2.4.5. Notice that since the log *"pattern_c.log"* already exists in the library, the sys-

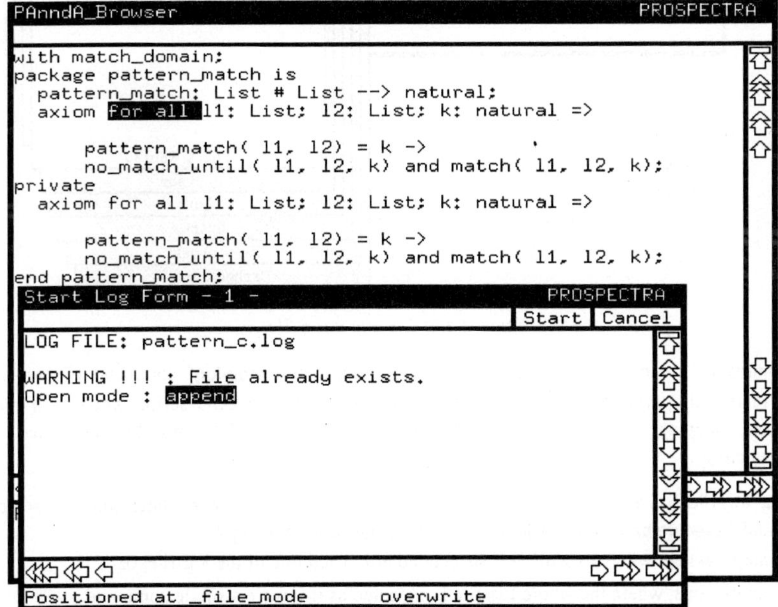

Figure 2.4.5: Starting the log facility.

tem requests that the user indicate whether the current development should replace the existing log file, or be appending to the existing log.

In the example, after the log file is opened, any number of development activities can take place. When a C program is finally produced, then the log file can be closed. Only after a log file is closed by the corresponding command "**stop-log**", is it available as a development script (figure 2.4.6).

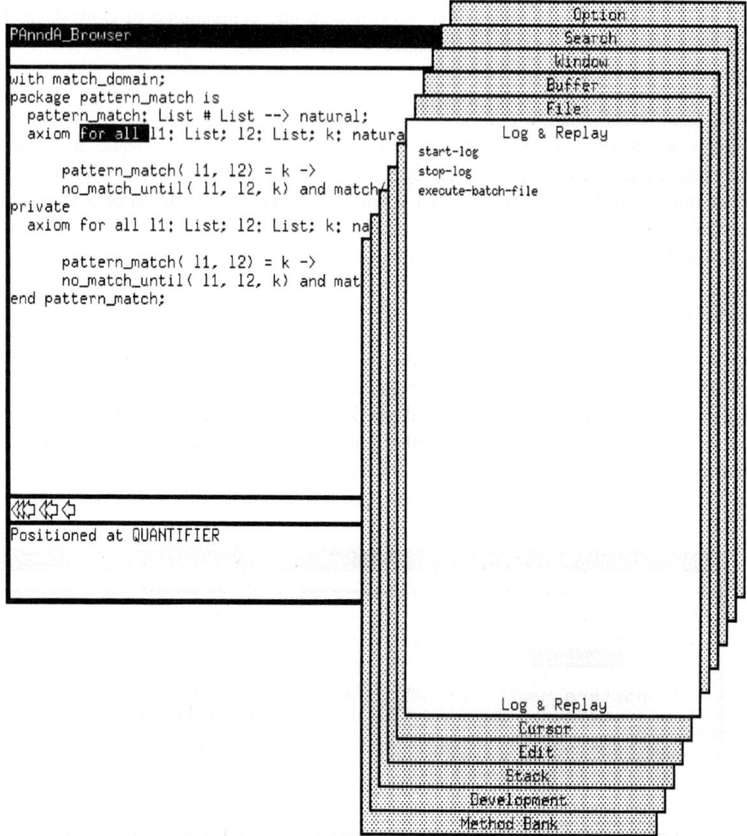

Figure 2.4.6: Closing a log file.

All commands given from the point of "**start-log**" until the "**stop-log**" command is issued, will be saved in the file *"pattern_c.log"*. The log-file has the form of a CSG script, which is a specialized command language developed for CSG editors. Figure 2.4.7 shows the generated log file *"pattern_c.log"*.

After a log-file has been generated, it is possible to replay it at some later time by selecting the command "**execute-batch-file**". A log-file can be replayed in two ways:

- step-by-step, where execution is suspended after each line of the log-file, or
- continuous, where the whole log-file is executed as if it were a single command.

The log-file implicitly assumes that the editor is in a state where it makes sense to replay the log-file. If, for instance, the editor is not in a such state (for example if the initial selection prior to the invocation of the log file is incompatible with that assumed by the log file) then the execution of the log-file will fail. The log-file contains different kinds of commands: for example, navigate changes the current selection in the abstract syntax tree. "**split**", "**Pannda_body**" and "**Tail_Rec => Loop**" are all transformations.

```
move-to-buffer("PAnndA_Browser"),
'trafo-modules-info'(enable'),
navigate("1/2/4/2/1"),
'split',
navigate("../../../../2/1/1/1/3/1/2/1/1/1/1"),
navigate("../../../../../2/1/2/1/1/1/1\\"),
'intro_if',
navigate("../../../../../../../.."),
'Pannda_body',
navigate("../../../../../../../../2/3/2/1"),
'Tail_Rec => Loop',
navigate("../../../1"),
'-->C'
```

Figure 2.4.7: Example of development script.

Figure 2.4.8 shows the form command buffer opened by the "**execute-batch-file**" command.

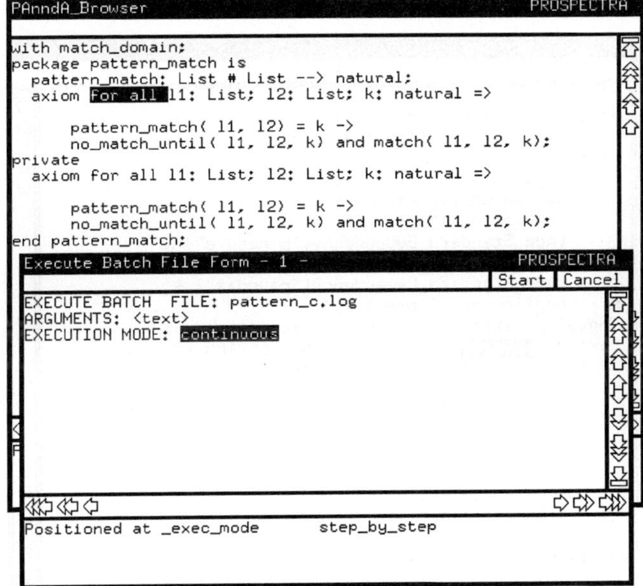

Figure 2.4.8: Replaying a log-file.

2.4.4. Constructing Development Methods

The process of constructing a development method involves first of all creating a requirement specification in ControLa. There are two possible ways to do this. Firstly, the construction can begin from scratch, as with normal requirements specifications for programs. Secondly, an existing development script can be "imported" into the library and the necessary modifications made to the existing script.

Two important points to consider when constructing a development method are the available basic transformations together with the specification of the system commands used in developing programs. The following package (figure 2.4.9) is an example of such a specification. Only with these interface definitions can the construction of a development method be completed.

```
ControLa_Browser

package aux_funcs is
  Revise_Configuration: script;
  navigate: string --> script;
  Add_Standard_Dependency: string --> script;
  confirm_development, cancel_development: script;
  Find_Family, New_Family, insert_file: string --> script;
  New_Origin, beginning_of_file, delete_selection: script;
end aux_funcs;
```

Figure 2.4.9: System Interface Functions.

```
ControLa_Browser

with aux_functions;
package sample_development is
  Make_Standard_Configuration: script;
  axiom
    Make_Standard_Configuration =
      Revise_Configuration &
      (navigate("1") &
      (Add_Standard_Dependency("p_nature") &
      (Add_Standard_Dependency("verifier") &
      (Add_Standard_Dependency("panndas") &
      confirm_development))));
  develop: string # string --> script;
  axiom for all family, filename: string =>
    family /= "" and filename /= "" ->
      develop( family, filename) =
      New_Family(family) &
      (New_Origin &
      (Make_Standard_Configuration &
      (beginning_of_file &
      (delete_selection &
      (insert_file(filename) &
      confirm_development)))));
end sample_development;
```

Figure 2.4.10: A development method.

Based on the previous package, a sample development method can be specified. This is illustrated in figure 2.4.11. The result of this development method is the addition of a new family in the library.

The next step should be the translation of the ControLa specification into the PA^{nn}dA version with subsequent development of the requirements specification towards the CSG scripts language. At present this facility is not fully supported.

2.5. Specialised Transformer: CEC

2.5.1. Why is a Specialised Transformer Needed ?

The previous sections described the kernel parts of the PROSPECTRA system. It has been shown how programs, transformation rules, and system command scripts can be developed using the same basic methodology.

This section describes a specialised transformer which extends the functionality of the CSG based tools described earlier. The CEC transformer allows the use of completion algorithms during development of specifications.

2.5.2. Conditional Equational Completion

The Conditional Equational Completion (CEC) transformer allows for the development of specifications using the principles of *completion.* Completion can be considered as the transformation of an initial (non-executable) specification into an (executable) canonical term rewrite system.

The CEC transformer accepts a specification written in a subset of PA^{nn}dA-S, and translates this into a conditional equational specification. This specification can then be completed using an extended version of the Knuth-Bendix completion algorithm, (cf part III section 4.3).

Figure 2.5.1 shows the specification of a generic list package. Connection to the CEC transformer is established by selecting the **"connect"** command from the **"CEC commands"** menu. The **"connect"** command opens a window in which the communication with the CEC transformer is displayed. The specification (currently in the PA^{nn}dA-S editor) is transferred to the CEC transformer by selecting the **"transfer"** command.

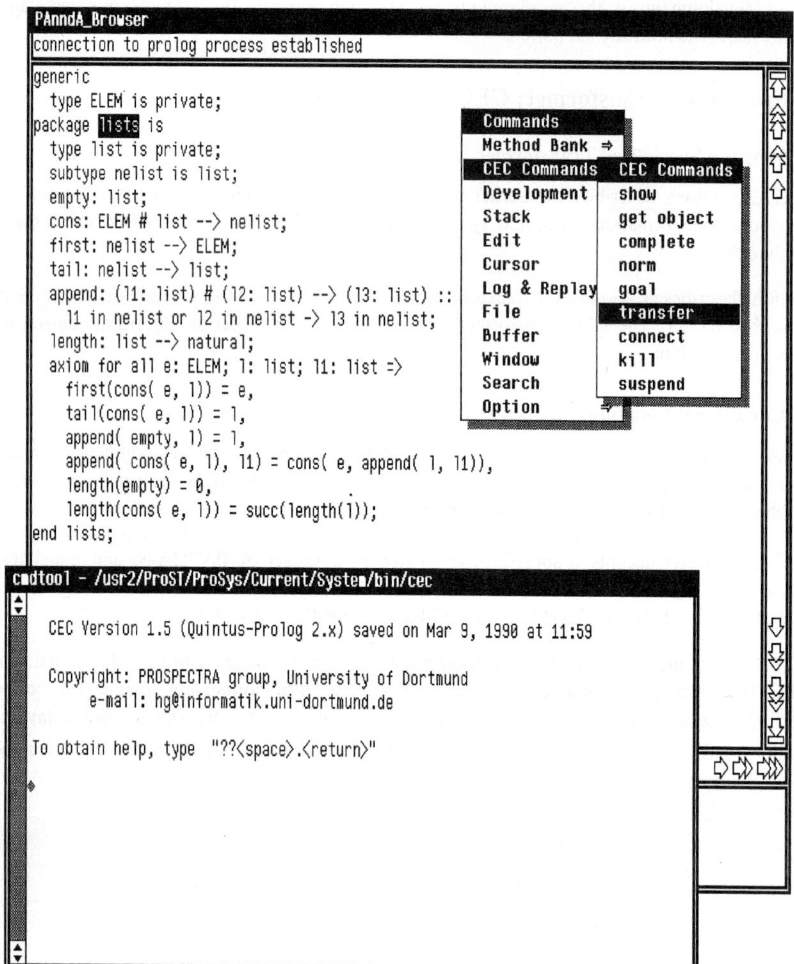

Figure 2.5.1: Connecting to the CEC transformer.

Choosing the **"transfer"** command brings up a form command window asking for the *orderings* to be used by the CEC transformer when attempting to complete the specification. The ordering concept is described in detail in the corresponding parts of part III, section 4.3. The result of the **"transfer"** command is displayed in the commandtool as shown in figure 2.5.2.

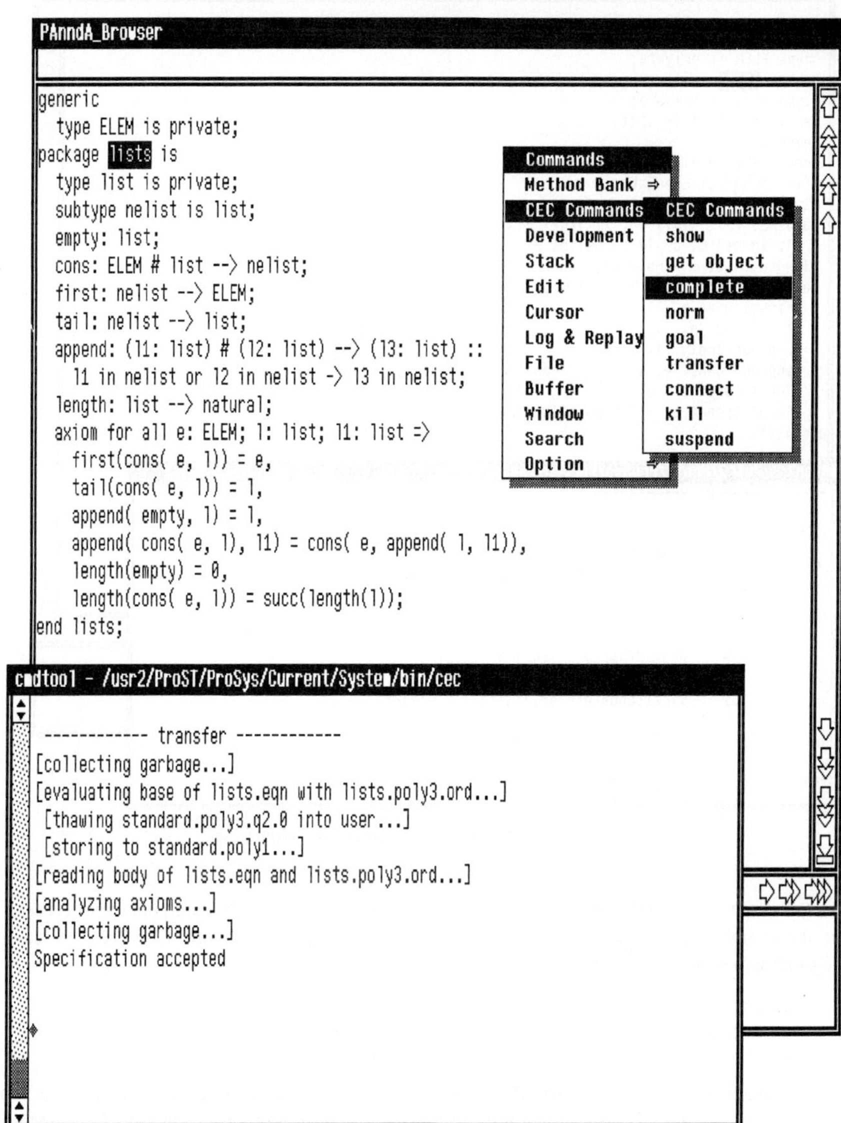

Figure 2.5.2: Results of the 'transfer' command.

After having selected the **"complete"** command, the completion algorithm will be executed for the transferred specification. The result is shown in figure 2.5.3.

PAnndA_Browser

```
generic
  type ELEM is private;
package lists is
  type list is private;
  subtype nelist is list;
  empty: list;
  cons: ELEM # list --> nelist;
  first: nelist --> ELEM;
  tail: nelist --> list;
  append: (l1: list) # (l2: list) --> (l3: list) ::
    l1 in nelist or l2 in nelist -> l3 in nelist;
  length: list --> natural;
  axiom for all e: ELEM; l: list; l1: list =>
    first(cons( e, l)) = e,
    tail(cons( e, l)) = l,
    append( empty, l) = l,
    append( cons( e, l), l1) = cons( e, append( l, l1)),
    length(empty) = 0,
    length(cons( e, l)) = succ(length(l));
end lists;
```

cmdtool - /usr2/ProST/ProSys/Current/System/bin/cec

```
------------ c ------------

rule deleted:
        145     append(X2:nelist,list(X1:nelist)) =
                        append(list(X2:nelist),X1:nelist)

new rule 149    length(empty) = natural(0) .

new rule 150    append(empty,l:list) = l:list .

new rule 151    first(cons(e:elem,l:list)) = e:elem .

new rule 152    tail(cons(e:elem,l:list)) = l:list .

new rule 153    length(list(cons(e:elem,l:list))) =
```

Figure 2.5.3: Results from the 'completion' algorithm.

The output from the completion algorithm is rather long (it describes the computations necessary to derive the completed specification) and cannot be shown in the same figure. However, the completion algorithm generates two additional axioms:

```
axiom for all e: ELEM; l: list; nel: nelist =>
  append(empty, nelist) = nelist,
  append(cons(e, l), nelist) = cons(e, append(l, nelist));
```

In the user manual of CEC (see part III section 4.3), a more detailed description of the CEC transformer is given. There, it is also shown how to transfer the results produced by the CEC transformer back to the CSG editor.

2.6. Concluding Remarks

The purpose of this chapter was to give the reader a first impression and brief overview of the PROSPECTRA methodology and support system. Further details of the more advanced components of the PROSPECTRA system can be found in the corresponding chapters of part III.

3. Control

3.1. Controller

Alain Marcuzzi, Syseca Logiciel
(revised by Berthold Hoffmann and Junbo Liu, Universiät Bremen)

This document constitutes a reference manual for the transformations supported by the Controller (release 2.6 of the PROSPECTRA system), as transitions on local states. It also presents additional features on development histories.

3.1.1. Introduction

The PROSPECTRA system includes various tools that are related dynamically through strict call-return relationships. The model of this system is integrated in a framework set up by the local state and transformation notions. Four different local states exist in the Controller, corresponding to four distinct languages:

- Configuration Editor Language for configuration management,
- Library Editor Language for version management,
- PAnndA-S for editing requirements specifications, and
- PAnndA for developing design specifications and programs.

The last two languages are not disjoint (PAnndA-S is a subset of PAnndA), however they involve different actions (see part II, chapters 2 and 4). Thus, we distinguish three specific kinds of development activities in the controller:

- The transformations for Library management and Configuration management.
- The transformations for editing requirement specifications and developing design specifications and implementations.
- The development scripts that are composed by aforementioned transformations through Controla constructs.

These activities form the basis of tools for the development of programs, basic transformations and development scripts. All transformations that represent the activities concerning first two kinds in the above can be referred in the corresponding sections. We present below the development of composed transformations, i.e. development scripts.

3.1.2. Development Histories

Developments are recorded in two ways by CSG scripts in the Controller:

- The developments at the library level are represented by means of transformations of the Library such as revision, refinement etc.
- At the unit level (that is, editing PAnndA-S specifications or developing PAnndA specifications and programs), every action is either recorded as a text insertion or represented by a basic transformations attached to a specific version.

The composition of these two records gives the global development history of a particular version from its origin. A recorded development can be replayed by the Controller automatically or stepwise.

3.1.3. The Development of Development Scripts

The uniformity of PROSPECTRA framework, namely, to adopt the same algebraic approach in the formalization of the specification, transformation, verification, development activities and meta-development, motivates the use of Controla, a subset of PAnndA-S, for expressing system actions, or transformations on system objects. Consequently, the development of development scripts is just a special case of program development.

3.1.4. Using ControLa to Specify Development Scripts

ControLa is the PROSPECTRA language for expressing system developments (see part II, chapter 7). It has been defined as a subset of the PAnndA-S language. ControLa programs satisfy the PAnndA-S static semantics, but the language scope has been restricted to formulate developments only on predefined system objects.

Its semantics is *operational.* More precisely, ControLa is an applicative subset of PAnndA-S. Conditional equations are used with basic system primitives to build more complex developments. It describes developments in terms of system state transitions.

3.1.4.1. ControLa Types

Since it concerns system developments, the language ControLa does not have an expressive type system, in particular, it does not possess any notion of type declarations. All the needed types are predefined in standard packages. Only two entities may be declared, functions for grouping a set of actions under a header, and axioms to describe them.

The predefined types that may be used in ControLa closely correspond to the various notions used to model and implement the system (section 3.1 above). The type STATE is a private type which is aimed at representing an anonymous type for the several local states of the system. In the same way, the type TREE represents the type of all the (untyped) trees that may be manipulated.

Every action in the system is seen as a transformation. In the terminology of the model used, this amounts to consider it as a state transition. The associated type in ControLa is the subtype SCRIPT which can be defined (without strictness/partialness consideration) as the functional subtype
(STATE-> STATE).

3.1.4.2. ControLa Functions

ControLa has been designed to express state transition actions into an applicative framework. Applicative programs may be formulated in PAnndA with conditional recursion equations. To keep the main property of functional programming, referential transparency, as well as to keep a sequential aspect to the state transitions, special kinds of equations and functions have been designed. They are restrictions from the existing possibilities of PAnndA-S.

The main strategy has been to separate clearly features involving state transitions from those which do not (side-effect free), both in the functions declarations and in the equations. This has resulted in a definition of several categories of functions, as well as of predefined operators for combining them:

- *Pure functions* do not involve any state transition action. They are free of side-effects on states, and are generally used to compute values on predefined types such as integers, strings and booleans which are PAnndA-S standard types.

- *Constructor functions* are untyped tree constructors. They are used to manipulate the abstract data types (e.g. abstract syntax trees) defined in the editors. They compose elements of type TREE and of PAnndA-S standard types. Constructor functions cannot be explicitly declared in a ControLa package. Rather, they are imported from the packages defining (e.g.) the abstract syntax trees of the various languages of the system. Since these latter constructors are typed, an appropriate subtyping to the type TREE is needed.

- *Selection functions* involve a state, but are free of side-effects since they only extract, from a state, values of standard types and also untyped trees. They act as selectors in the abstract data types terminology.

- Script functions are state transition functions. They are the only functions that may express side-effects in ControLa.

The function profiles of the four categories is shown below:

Pure functions:	**(STANDARD_TYPE)* --> (STANDARD_TYPE)**
Constructor functions:	**((STANDARD_TYPE) | (TREE))* --> (TREE)**
Selection functions:	**((STANDARD TYPE) -->)* (STATE) --> ((STANDARD TYPE)|(TREE))**
Script functions:	**((STANDARD TYPE) | TREE | (SCRIPT))* --> (SCRIPT)**

3.1.4.3. Basic expressions

The language allows the formulation of high level features of PAnndA-S. However, it may also be used to express basic developments, such as direct user actions, during a session with the system. The result of all these actions may be understood as the composition of all the transformations that have been performed.

More clearly, sequences of actions may be expressed in ControLa by a composition of primitive actions on local states which is called *reverse composition.* A reverse composition operator has been defined in ControLa to express sequences of actions on the system. The binary adding operator '&' has been overloaded in the ControLa package STANDARDC to work on operands of type SCRIPT.

```
"&" : SCRIPT+ # SCRIPT+ --> SCRIPT;
axiom for all
  S: STATE;
  A: SCRIPT+;
  B: SCRIPT+ =>
  (A & B)(S) = B(A(S)),
```

In this context, basic expressions in ControLa are sequences of actions just like in the script below, used as a shorthand for importing standard versions of standard packages from an editor. Note that the curried state argument does not appear; thus the expression is functional. The form of this expression is very similar to that of the corresponding CSG script (see part III, in the appendix of chapter 6).

```
Revise_Configuration &
navigate("1") &
Add_Standard_Dependency ("p_nature") &
Add_Standard_Dependency ("verifier") &
Add_Standard_Dependency ("panndas") &
confirm_development
```

3.1.4.4. Equations on State-Transition Functions

Since they manipulate states by means of state transition functions, these expressions will be said to produce side-effects. A decision in the design of ControLa has been to confine all side effect operations to these expressions and keep all other constructs free of them. This has the nice effect to preserve the PAnndA-S semantics and to make the language model the system adequately.

Additional constructs are provided in the language to help with expressing *control* during system development. As the operational paradigm used is the applicative, control is expressed in terms of conditional recursion equations, with pattern matching used for case analysis. A sample development is presented below.

```
with STANDARDC;
package sample_development is
Make_Standard_Configuration: SCRIPT;
axiom
        Make_Standard_Configuration =
        Revise_Configuration &
        navigate("1") &
        Add_Standard_Dependency ("p_nature") &
        Add_Standard_Dependency ("verifier") &
        Add_Standard_Dependency ("panndas") &
        confirm_development
Find_Family: STRING --> SCRIPT;
axiom for all family_name : STRING; S : STATE; d,s,v : TREE =>
   Selection(S)/= mk_Family(mk_Id(family_name), d,s,v) ->
        Find_Family (family_name)(S) =
              search_forward ("",family_name,"")(S),
   others -> Find_Family = Void;
develop : (STRING # STRING) --> SCRIPT;
axiom for all family:STRING; filename:STRING =>
   family /= "" and filename /= "" ->
        develop(family,filename) = New_Family(family) &
                    Find_Family(family) &
                    New_Origin &
                    Make_Standard_Configuration &
                    beginning_of_file &
                    delete_selection &
                    insert_file (filename) &
                    confirm-development
end sample_development;
```

3.1.4.5. User Interactions

Modelling a system that may interact with users obliges to include them in the model. This amounts to consider user actions and input. Such interactions can be modelled in an applicative style where non-strict/partial functions can be expressed and used. Due to the unified approach to the system model and implementation, the user interacts by means of transformations on local states. Thus user interactions are nothing else than *non-strict* (or lazy) state transition functions, and user inputs are non-strict objects (strings, numbers).

In the example given above, the function 'develop' may be redefined to include user interactions instead of importing a file from outside. The non-strict object that is introduced is intending to model the sequence of actions the user has performed to enter its package contents.

```
develop : (STRING # SCRIPT+) --> SCRIPT;
axiom forall family:STRING, C:SCRIPT+ =>
family /= "" ->
develop(family) = New_Family(family) &
                  Find_Family(family) &
                  New_Origin &
                  Make_Standard_Configuration &
                  beginning_of_file &
                  delete_selection &
                  C &
                  confirm-development
```

3.1.5. Translating ControLa to CSG Scripts

3.1.5.1. Introduction

The ControLa to CSG scripts translation is a set of transformations aimed at obtaining executable CSG script code for the Cornell Synthesizer Generator, from a high level specification of a development in ControLa.

The translation is not straightforward due to the totally different philosophies, the two languages adopt. On one hand, we may use all the advanced features of functional programming such as higher order functions, case analysis by pattern matching, algebraic data types, while the other language adopts an imperative approach that is necessary to handle internal editor states.

So the translation may be roughly divided in three main parts, which consist first in reducing the language strength by expanding the high-level features into elementary pieces of code, then in passing from a functional specification of the ControLa code to an imperative implementation, and finally, to translate this last result into CSG scripts in a quite straightforward manner.

It may be noted that this development follows the PROSPECTRA approach in going from the specification to the implementation. In fact, the first two steps may be embedded in the traditional development of PAnndA-S specifications with only little variations, concerning the particular data types ControLa handles.

3.1.5.2. Translating Expressions

Expressions, as they appear in ControLa-C are not directly expressible in CSG scripts which do support only flat expressions formed of basic values, predefined operators, argument names, a local variable name ($msg). No function calls appear in CSG scripts. The way function calls are included in the computation of expressions is by sequencing the evaluation and using the $msg variable to store and retrieve the result of the last script call. This reduction of expressions to the process of evaluation is shown informally below.

We have to abstract a subexpression into a new condition. Below is an example of the successive transformations performed on an expression Exp(u,v). It is presented as the transformation of a set of recursive equations without type information.

```
Exp(u,v) = f(u) + v * g(u,h(u,v),k(u))
```

This expression contains two function calls at the outermost level. The second one has to be abstracted.

```
g(u,h(u,v),k(u)) = a0 -> Exp(u,v) = f(u) + v * a0
```

The parameter list of the call to the function 'g' has two parameters which are function calls. They have to be abstracted into matching operations.

```
h(u,v) = a2 and
k(u) = a1 and
g(u,a2,,a1) = a0 -> Exp(u,v) = f(u) + v * a0
```

This sequence may be sequentialised to bring imperative code. The CSG script below gives an idea of the result (the form used is not the precise syntax of CSG scripts to make things appear clearer.

```
SCRIPT EXP (int u; int v)
h(u,v),
let (a2 = $msg),
k(u),
let (a1 = $msg),
g(u, a2, a1),
let (a0 = $msg)
f(u),
$msg + v * a0
```

3.1.5.3. *Reducing Types*

CSG scripts do not include pure functions but rather use procedures. Functions are handled by keeping the result of the last evaluation in a location denoted by $msg. As a consequence, all functions have to be translated into procedures by replacing the result type by the script type.

3.1.5.4. *Reducing States and Composition*

As the functions are reduced to procedures, the program may be transformed in a imperative form by suppressing the higher-order state argument and by replacing reverse composition by sequences of instructions.

3.1.5.5. *Transforming Lazy Parameters into Explicit I/O Operations*

The paradigm of lazy evaluation has been used to model user interaction in ControLa. This has to be translated to explicit I/O operations, by means of a static analysis using the denotation of the current theory of the program fragments. This lazy evaluation is simulated at the level of the CSG scripts by using a primitive 'read' that should test whether the value to be read has already been read or not.

3.1.5.6. *From the Imperative Level to Scripts*

This is the more straightforward part of the translation. It takes package bodies resulting from the previous operations, and yields an equivalent CSG script.

3.1.6. Abstracting from Concrete Developments

This activity, coupled with the recording of development histories, is aimed at enhancing the system functionality by allowing the *reuse* of global developments and the synthesis of *design strategies* from particular developments. It is regarded as one of the promising features to be supported by the

PROSPECTRA system. For the moment, a translation is provided to abstract CSG scripts, which are the form in which developments are recorded, to basic ControLa expressions.

3.1.7. Conclusion

The Controller has been designed for managing the various tools of the system according to the methodology, and for providing a uniform interface between the user and its components. This is guaranteed by the present implementation which fully supports a model of the system that is integrated in the methodology of development by transformations.

It is now ready to support system development as a forward or reverse activity and to replay developments. In this respect, it will provide the basis for more conceptual tasks such as design activities or the development of strategies, by automating major parts of developments steps, and thus abstracting from low-level parts of developments.

3.2. Library Manager

Dominique Houdier, Syseca Logiciel
(revised by Berthold Hoffmann and Junbo Liu, Universität Bremen)

This document presents the functions of the Library Manager in the context of development with the PROSPECTRA methodology and constitutes the User Manual of the Library and Configuration editors.

3.2.1. Introduction

This section describes the functions of the Library Manager. The Library Manager is made of two modules: The *Version Manager* controls access to the database of program versions. The *Configuration Manager* defines and controls dependency relationships between versions.

According to the PROSPECTRA methodology (see below), operations on the database are *persistent* by default: Whenever an object is changed, its new version is added to the database, and the old version is stored, as part of the object's development history. Operations for explicit deletion also exist.

The Library Manager supports *concurrency*, e.g. several users can develop new versions from the same object.

The first part of the document gives some hints about development context using the PROSPECTRA methodology. It explains in particular the attributes defining the component properties and the management of relationships between components. The second part describes the database architecture. The third one deals with the editor interfaces (Library & Configuration tools). The Appendix gives a demonstration of these tools.

3.2.2. Requirements for the Library

The Library Manager deals with storage and retrieval of the different versions of a program during its development. The term *component* is used to denote any version of a program handled by the Library Manager.

3.2.2.1. The Program Development Model and its Impact on the Library Structure

The structure of the library is tailored to the PROSPECTRA methodology of program development by transformation.

- According to this methodology, programs are developed in a *modular* way, so programs consist of *families* of packages.

- For each package, the user starts program development by editing a *requirements specification.* The activity of composing and changing requirements specifications is called *revision* because it changes the meaning of the specification.

- Once a requirements specification is deemed to be complete, it is gradually derived to an executable program package by applying interactive transformations which produce new *refinements* of packages; these steps preserve correctness.

It is important to keep not only the latest or *standard versions* of a package in the library because each intermediate version may be the starting point of *alternative developments.* Thus a *family of versions* is stored for each package; the versions are structured as a tree where each node is linked to its immediate revisions and refinements.

This program development model and library structure is used on several levels, in different languages:

- Specifications (in PAnndA-S) are developed to programs (in PAnndA) on the *program level.*
- Transformation specifications (in TrafoLa-S) are developed to transformation programs (in TrafoLa-H or SSL) on the *meta level.*
- Commands (in ControLa-S) are developed to command scripts (in the CSG Scripts language) on the *control level.*

3.2.2.2. The Dependency Graph

In addition to the physical links between components, logical dependencies are created when a component uses another one, by a **with** clause. Such relations are defined and managed by the Configuration Manager. Each time a component is created, the Configuration Manager unit associates packages names that occur in **with** clauses to specific versions of the package.

Logical dependencies between components impose constraints on them. Imported components must not be changed without using functions of the Library Manager. Versions used in composed components can no longer be revised (their interface is frozen), but they can be refined by transformation, and can be used by other components.

The *dependency graph* has components as nodes and **with** dependencies as arcs. It must satisfy the following constraints:

- Only one version of a package may be used within a component.
- The dependency graph must be acyclic.

Another aspect is the evolution of the dependency graph while components are developed. If a component is revised, there is no reason to suppose that the component imports the same units. If it is refined, the same included units have to be accessible.

3.2.2.3. Storage and Retrieval

Direct access to database components must be forbidden because they may destroy the integrity of the database. A component is stored by creating a new version of the program, or by updating its attributes. Consistency with the dependencies must be checked before storage. Components are retrieved by returning a *copy* of the attributes which have been stored before. This way components can be handled without destroying the integrity of the database.

3.2.3. Database Structure

The PROSPECTRA database consists of objects such as Libraries, Families and Components and their attributes. These objects are organized in an hierarchical way and may depend on each other (see figure 3.1 below).

The PROSPECTRA database is a set of libraries, and each library is a set of families. A family contains a development (in one of the languages PAnndA_S, TrafoLa_S or ControLa_C). A family may have an *origin*, which is the first version created within this family, and a *standard version*, which is

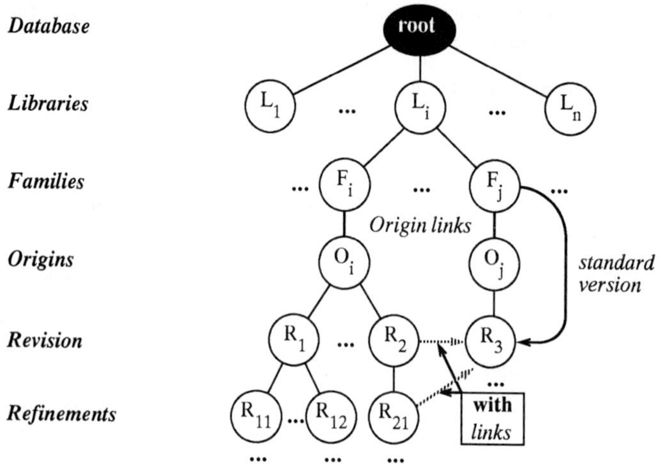

Figure 3.1: Library Structure

the version intended for external use. Except for the origin version, each version is either a revision or a refinement of a parent version in the same family, and each version can be the root of a tree of (alternative) derivations.

The import relations between PAnndA units (expressed by **with** clauses) create logical dependencies between components which are drawn as dashed edges in the figure.

3.2.4. Library Editor Interface

The editor has been generated with the Synthesizer Generator form Cornell University ([Reps Teitelbaum 88). It displays views of the database and manipulates it by direct interaction with the Library Manager. The interactions are performed by transformations on library trees. In this section, we describe, for each type of node in the database, its attributes, and the transformations on the node.

As the Library Manager controls concurrency, partial views of the database do not necessarily reflect the exact database knowledge because several users can update it in parallel. In the case where an operation fails, the user has to verify by the "Show" facilities that the database corresponds to the view he has on screen.

3.2.4.1. The Database (Local State)

On its top level called the *local state*, the database consists of a set of libraries, one for each project.

Show_Database displays a the list of libraries within the database, in a Transformation Argument Form buffer (see figure 3.2 below).

Show_Library replaces the current library by a view of the library given as argument.

New_Library creates a new library and replaces the current view by the empty library given as argument.

Delete_Library deletes the current library if it is empty, and replaces the current view by the initial Local State.

New_Standard_Library creates a new library containing a copy a the standard library..

3.2.4.2. Library

A library defines the set of developments related to a project, or a set of related entities such as transformation rules or scripts.

A library is characterized by a *name*, a *documentation*, and a *set of families*.

New_Family creates a new family given as argument and places it in alphabetic order in the family list.

Delete_Family deletes the family given as argument from the library if it is without development.

New_Documentation updates the library documentation.

3.2.4.3. Family

A family defines the development of a package. It represents a set of versions of the package, structured as a derivation tree. The root of the tree is called the *origin*; several derivations (refinements and revisions) of a package are possible. Each family may have a standard version, which is the version intended for external use.

A family is characterized by a *name*, a *documentation*, a *standard version*, and a *derivation tree* whose origin version is the root. A family can be displayed partially, (the family name appearing in the family list), or fully, (the internal information is then displayed).

Show_Family displays the full view of the family.

Hide displays the partial view of the family.

New_Origin creates the first version of the family. The operation calls either the PAnndA_S, Trafo-La_S or ControLa_C editors. A new component is created, containing the program developed with the editor.

Delete_Origin deletes the origin version if its derivation tree is empty.

New_Documentation updates the family documentation.

New_Standard_Version designates a program version as the standard version.

3.2.4.4. Version_Tree

Version trees are trees whose nodes are the various versions of the same unit and whose edges are revisions or refinements. Version trees may be displayed partially or fully.

Show_Version displays the full view of a version.

Show_Revisions displays the partial version tree of all immediate revisions of the selected version.

Show_Refinements displays the partial version tree of all immediate refinements of the selected version.

Show_Version_Tree displays the full version tree of the selected version.

Show_Configuration calls the Configuration Editor to show the dependencies of the selected version.

Hide displays the top of the version tree.

Delete_Version deletes the version given as argument located in the immediate derivation list if it has no revision and refinement.

Several transformations depending on the content field of a version are available to create new components.

--> *PAnndA* transforms either a PAnndA_S, TrafoLa_S or ControLa_C program into its equivalent PAnndA program which may be refined. This command creates the first refinement of a program.

--> *Ax_To_Tr* transforms the axioms contained in a PAnndA_S unit into TrafoLa_S phrases. This operation creates a new revision of the current version without calling any editor.

--> *SSL* transforms a PAnndA program refined from a TrafoLa_S unit into a SSL program without calling any editor.

--> *Trafola-H* transforms a PAnndA program refined from a TrafoLa_S unit into a TrafoLa-H program without calling any editor.

3.2.4.5. Components

A component defines the version of a package with its attributes. Each component has a unique name in the family (a number given by the system, prefixed by the name of the family). Two types of contents are associated to a component: the program and its denotation. Each component can have a *composition* representing the versions of those unit it depends on.

A component is characterized by a *name*, a *contents*, a *denotation*, a *composition*, a *documentation*, a *phase*, a *status*, and an *information*.

The *contents* defines the language family employed:

PAnndA_S, *PAnndA* and *Ada* languages for programs.
TrafoLa_S, *PAnndA*, *SSL* and *Trafola_H* languages for transformation rules.
ControLa_C language and *CSG scripts* for scripts and development histories.

The *phase* defines the development phase the component belongs to. Three levels are distinguished according to the development model (see 3.2.2.1 above):

Requirement specification
Design specification
Implementation

The *status* indicates how far the component is developed, and whether it can be used by other components:

Planned	if the program is empty.
Incomplete	if the program contains placeholders.
Incorrect	if the program contains semantic errors.
Validated	if the program is validated by the user.
Verified	if the program is validated by proof tools.
Public	if the program is usable by other programs.
Released	if the program is frozen for development.

A last attribute *information* contains information about the owner and the creation date of the component.

3.2.4.6. Version

A version node contains management information, the contents and references to the immediate derivations of the version.

Hide replaces the full view of the version by it partial view.

New_Revision creates a new revision of the selected version. This operation calls the language editor specified in the content field.

New_Refinement creates a new refinement of the version. This operation calls the PAnndA Transformer with a set of transformation rules given as argument.

Show_Configuration shows the configuration of the selected version. This operation calls the Configuration editor.

3.2.4.7. Info

Show_Info displays the full view of the information field.

Hide displays the partial view of the information field.

3.2.4.8. Contents

Display calls the appropriate editor to show the content of the program.

3.2.4.9. Documentation

Show_Documentation displays the full view of the documentation.

Hide displays the partial view of the documentation

3.2.5. Configuration Editor Interface

The Configuration Manager is used to define the composition of versions of a component. The Configuration editor manipulates the full dependency graph of a component and directly interacts with the Library Manager to display and modify the composition of a component. The composition of a version defines which versions will be used by the units contained in the with clauses field of a program. The aim of this editor is to construct this composition and to check the laws described in section [3.2.2.2].

The Configuration editor is called by two commands: *Show_Configuration* which is available in the Library editor, or by *Revise_Configuration* which is available in languages editors (PAnndA_S, TrafoLa_S, ...).

3.2.5.1. Project_Config

Show_Dependency_Graph displays the whole dependency graph.

Hide_Dependency_Graph replaces the graph view by the initial configuration view.

Add_Dependency add a specific version given as argument to the composition.

Add_Standard_Dependency add the fmily's standard version given as argument to the composition.

Delete_Dependency deletes the version given as argument in the composition.

APPENDICES

3.2.A. Interaction with the Library and Configuration Editor

This section presents a demonstration of the Library and Configuration tools. Figures representing tool screens show the effect of each operation presented in section 3.2.4.

Figure 3.2: *View of the database*

The list of libraries contained in the PROSPECTRA database is displayed in the parameter form buffer by clicking *Show_Database*.

Show_Library and *New_Library* give a view of a library.

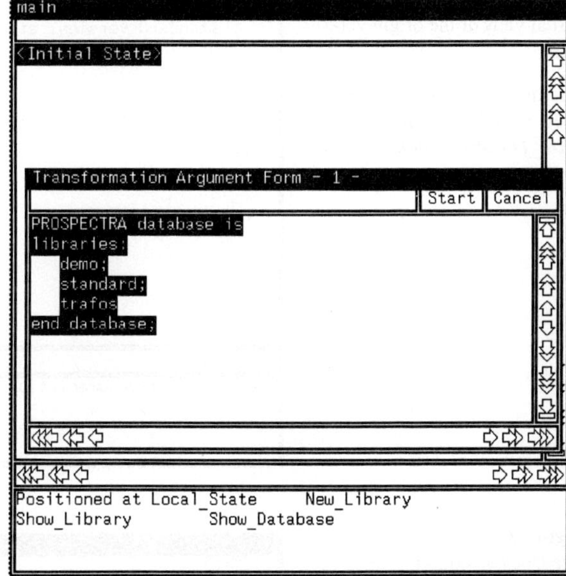

Figure 3.3: *View of a library*

The partial view of a library consists of a folder of partial or full views of a set of families, classified in alphabetical order, and a documentation shown by "..." if it exists.

Each family stands for a derivation tree starting from an origin. The family "stack" is displayed after selecting it and applying the transformation *Show_Family*.

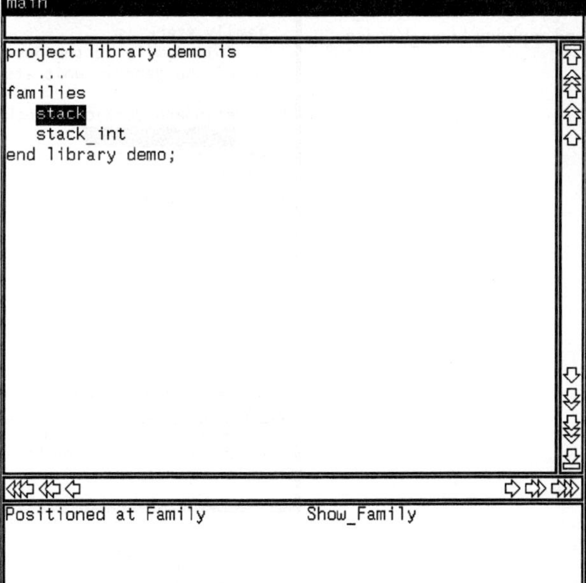

Figure 3.4: *View of a Family*

A family contains general information on the whole derivation tree, such as a documentation, the standard version, and the partial view of the origin version.

The documentation is displayed after selecting it and applying *Show_Documentation.*

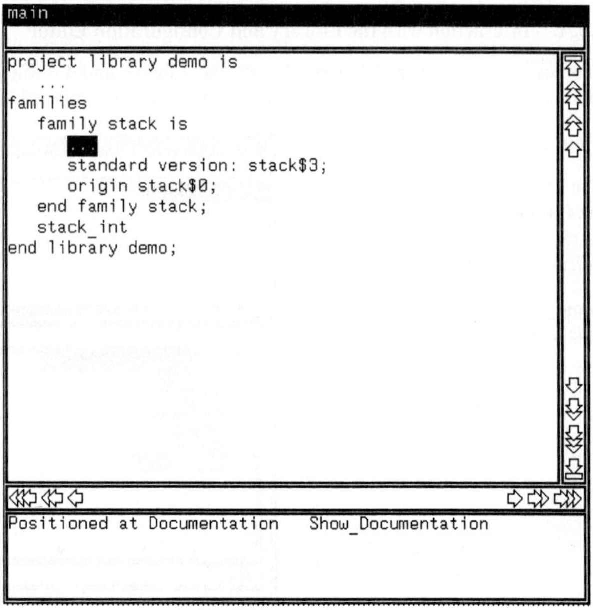

```
main

project library demo is
   ...
families
   family stack is
      ...
      standard version: stack$3;
      origin stack$0;
   end family stack;
   stack_int
end library demo;

Positioned at Documentation    Show_Documentation
```

Figure 3.5:
The Documentation

The origin version of the family is displayed after selecting it and applying *Show_Version.*

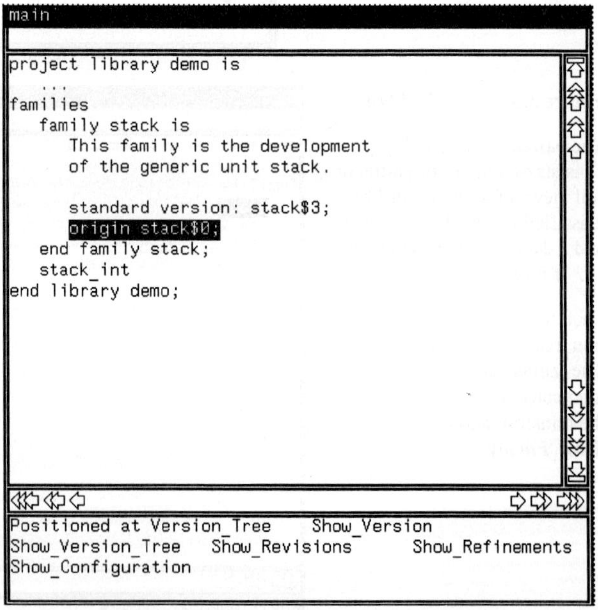

```
main

project library demo is
   ...
families
   family stack is
      This family is the development
      of the generic unit stack.

      standard version: stack$3;
      origin stack$0;
   end family stack;
   stack_int
end library demo;

Positioned at Version_Tree    Show_Version
Show_Version_Tree   Show_Revisions     Show_Refinements
Show_Configuration
```

Figure 3.6:
The Origin Version

A partial view of the development of "stack" is displayed. Only the origin version is visible. It contains the information about the version and the immediate derivations (i.e. revision "stack$1"). The info field is displayed as "...". It is fully displayed by applying *Show_Info*.

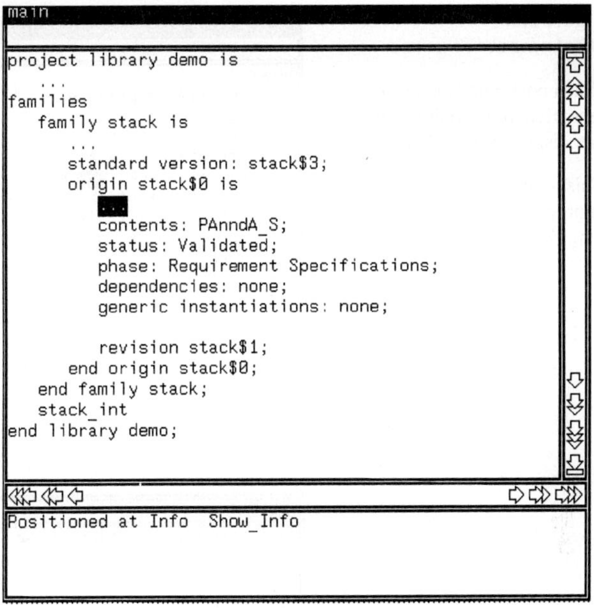

```
main
project library demo is
   ...
families
   family stack is
      ...
      standard version: stack$3;
      origin stack$0 is
         ...
         contents: PAnndA_S;
         status: Validated;
         phase: Requirement Specifications;
         dependencies: none;
         generic instantiations: none;

         revision stack$1;
      end origin stack$0;
   end family stack;
   stack_int
end library demo;

Positioned at Info  Show_Info
```

Figure 3.7: *The Info Field*

This field contains the documentation of the version represented by "..." if it exists, and information about the owner and the creation date.

The component content is displayed after applying *Display*.

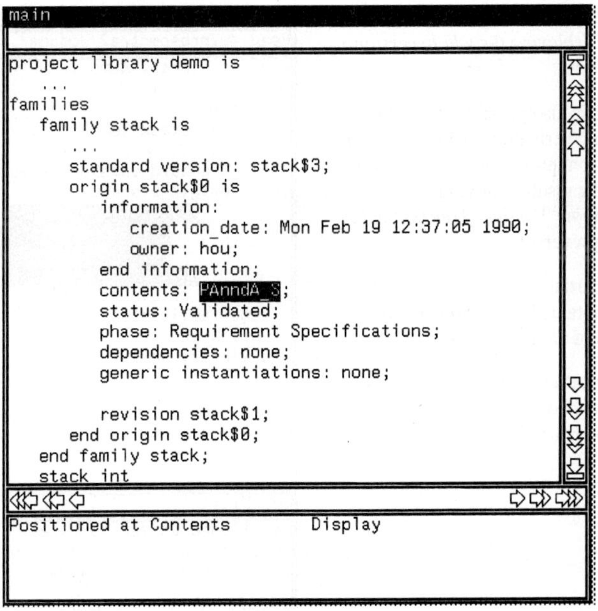

```
main
project library demo is
   ...
families
   family stack is
      ...
      standard version: stack$3;
      origin stack$0 is
         information:
            creation_date: Mon Feb 19 12:37:05 1990;
            owner: hou;
         end information;
         contents: PAnndA_S;
         status: Validated;
         phase: Requirement Specifications;
         dependencies: none;
         generic instantiations: none;

         revision stack$1;
      end origin stack$0;
   end family stack;
   stack_int

Positioned at Contents        Display
```

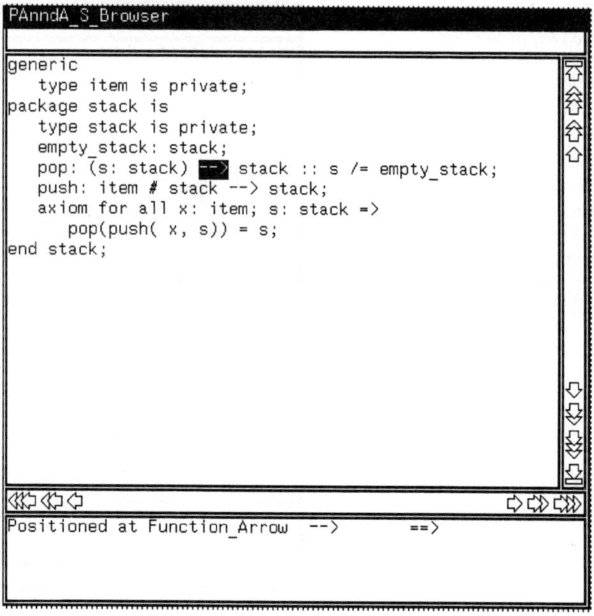

Figure 3.8:
Displaying the contents

When positioned on the contents field of a version, one can display it with *Display*.

This transformation calls the appropriate browser for the language of the version.

```
PAnndA_S_Browser

generic
   type item is private;
package stack is
   type stack is private;
   empty_stack: stack;
   pop: (s: stack) --> stack :: s /= empty_stack;
   push: item # stack --> stack;
   axiom for all x: item; s: stack =>
      pop(push( x, s)) = s;
end stack;

Positioned at Function_Arrow  -->       ==>
```

Figure 3.9:
Displaying the whole version tree.

It is also possible to display the derivation tree without version information. This view is the result of allying *Show_Version_Tree* on the origin version.

Partial views of this tree can be obtained with *Show_Revisions* and *Show_Refinements.*

The refinement "stack$2" is displayed by applying *Delete_-Version*.

```
main
Read /u/prospectra2/domdom/.syn_profile
project library demo is
   ...
families
   family stack is
      ...
      standard version: stack$3;
      origin stack$0 is
         revision stack$1 is
            refinement stack$2;
            revision stack$3;
         end revision stack$1;
      end origin stack$0;
   end family stack;
   stack_int
end library demo;

Positioned at Version_Tree    Show_Version
Show_Version_Tree    Show_Revisions     Show_Refinements
Delete_Version       Hide       Show_Configuration
```

Figure 3.10: *Delete a version*

This figure shows the way to delete a component from the derivation of another one by applying *Delete_Version.*

The Transformation Argument window appears to ask the version to be deleted. The result is shown too.

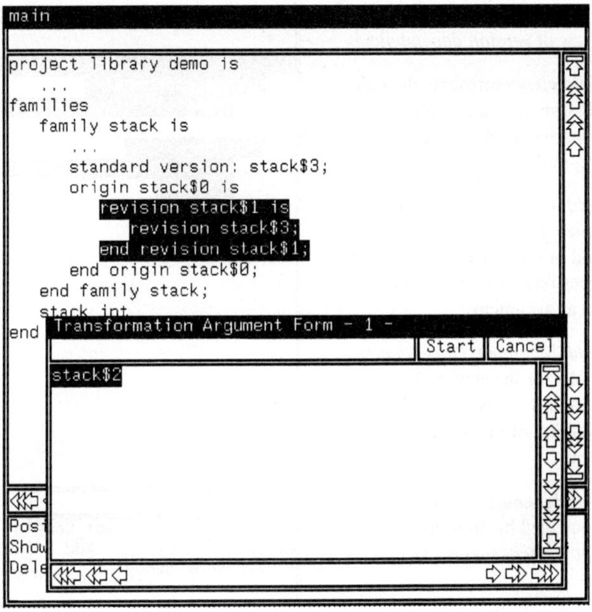

```
main
project library demo is
   ...
families
   family stack is
      ...
      standard version: stack$3;
      origin stack$0 is
         revision stack$1 is
            revision stack$3;
         end revision stack$1;
      end origin stack$0;
   end family stack;
   stack_int
end
Transformation Argument Form - 1 -
Start  Cancel
stack$2
Pos
Show
Dele
```

Figure 3.11: *View of dependencies*

The figure shows a library of transformation development. The "commute" unit depends on the "panndas" and "p_nature" units.

The configuration of the version "commute$0" is displayed by applying *Show_Configuration.*

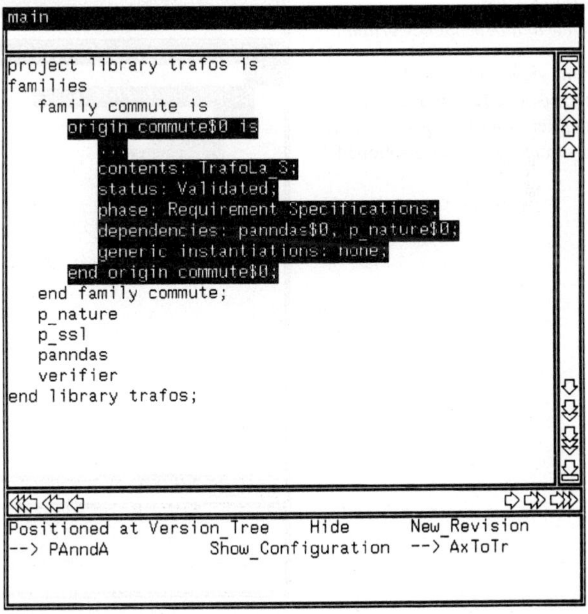

```
main
project library trafos is
families
   family commute is
      origin commute$0 is
         ...
         contents: TrafoLa_S;
         status: Validated;
         phase: Requirement Specifications;
         dependencies: panndas$0, p_nature$0;
         generic instantiations: none;
      end origin commute$0;
   end family commute;
   p_nature
   p_ssl
   panndas
   verifier
end library trafos;
Positioned at Version_Tree     Hide                 New_Revision
--> PAnndA                     Show_Configuration   --> AxToTr
```

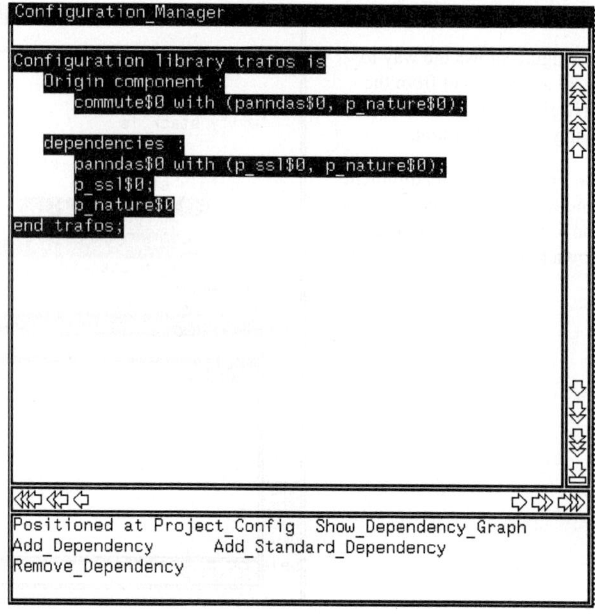

Figure 3.12:
View of version dependencies

This view represents the configuration of a component which consists of all versions appearing in the dependency graph.

Add_Dependency and *Remove_Dependency* allow to add or remove dependency subtrees related to the version given as argument.

Add_Standard_Dependency looks for the standard version of a unit to insert it in the composition of the origin component.

The dependency graph is then displayed by applying *Show_Dependency_Graph*.

```
Configuration_Manager

Origin component commute$0 is
with
   component panndas$0 is
   with
      p_ssl$0;
      p_nature$0
   end panndas$0;
   p_nature$0
end commute$0;

Positioned at Project_Config   Hide_Dependency_Graph
```

Figure 3.13:
View of a dependency graph

This view represents the directed acyclic graph. If "..." markers appear, this mean that a subtree is not yet developed.

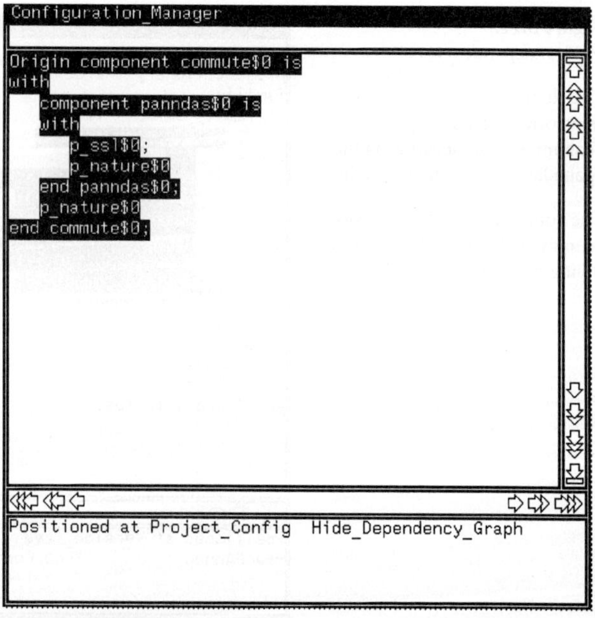

3.2.B. Integrity Control

This appendix introduces the integrity control concepts and mechanisms which are supported in the PCTE and UNIX versions of the Library Manager.

3.2.B.1. Objectives

There are two concepts of database integrity control:

- control program behaviour
- prevent the user from doing dangerous actions.

When a user executes a command, the database goes from a consistent state to another. A command is a sequence of atomic operations. If one of these operations fails, the database must recover its initial state instead of leaving objects in an undefined or inconsistent state.

For this purpose, access mechanisms must be provided for keeping the database in a consistent state. The access rights to objects have to be defined, and locking mechanisms have to be provided in order to avoid damages of the database.

3.2.B.2. Integrity Mechanisms

Object Access Rights

Object access rights control *who* can perform *which* operations on the database. The access rights available are those common to the UNIX file system (*read - write - execute*), but their signification is slightly modified, as explained below.

Library access

read: All families of a library node can be read as well as the documentation

write: New families can be created and the documentation can be modified

execute: The attributes related to the families can be read.

Family access

read: All information related to the family node can be read as well as the documentation.

write: An origin component can be created, the documentation can be modified and the standard version can be referenced

execute: The attributes related to the components can be read.

Component access

read: The component content can be read as well as the documentation, and all information related to the component.

write: New revisions and refinements can be created and the documentation can be modified. However, to create new version of a component, the user must have read rights too.

execute: The program version represented by the component can be imported by another unit.

Furthermore, similar to UNIX, each user belongs to one of the three categories *owner, group, others*.

Locking Services

The database can be accessed by several users at the same time. If a read operation is performed, there is no problem: all file systems allow concurrent read actions. This is not the case as soon as write and read requests shall be performed concurrently, on the same object.

To solve this problem, blocking and non-blocking lock services have been implemented for all nodes in the tree. The locking facilities are applied locally, only to the objects requested, thus still allowing several accesses to different nodes of the database. Once the operation is performed, the resource is released. Before performing a write or read request to an object, the node itself and its parent node are locked with appropriate requirements. This means that the lock can be shared or exclusive, and blocking or non-blocking.

Shared locks allow concurrent reading but forbid writing requests. *Exclusive* locks forbid other reading and writing requests. For a *blocking* lock, a process will wait for the release of the resource, and then perform the operation; for a *non-blocking* lock, it will return with a failure.

In the Library Manager, three kinds of commands are available at each node: SHOW displays the existing links, NEW adds a link, and DELETE removes a link (see next section).

During a SHOW operation the system places a shared read lock on the node containing the set of links.

During the NEW command, the system places an exclusive write lock on the node containing the links to be updated. These locks are in general blocking, each request to an object will wait the resource unlocking.

To avoid too long wait or deadlock problems, the non blocking locks are implemented for critical point in the database where a unique link relies two objects.

Three critical operations have been identified:

• the origin version creation

• the modification of any documentation

• the modification of the standard version.

Indeed, before creating an origin version or modifying a documentation, the parent node is locked until the end of the command. These two operations can be very long. So it would not be efficient to create a waiting situation for processes.

Deletion

A deletion facility has been integrated in the Library Manager tool, although it is not supported by the PROSPECTRA methodology. The DELETE command can only be performed if a node has no child links, and has no **with** links to another node..

The locking mechanisms are used but in an enforced mode. On one hand, the parent node of the object to be deleted is locked to remove the chosen link. On the other hand, the object itself gets a non-blocking lock to prevent access for further derivation (by revision or refinement) and for importation.

Now the NEW object commands have to take into account that a parent object can disappear before the end of the operation. This implies that if a root objects has no child links, it must be locked against deletion, in a non blocking mode. An analogous problem arises if a version is imported during a development. Each used unit must be locked against deletion too.

4. Program Development

4.1. PA^{nn}dA–S Editor

Einar W. Karlsen[1], Jesper Jørgensen, Computer Resources International

This document constitutes the user guide for the language-based PA^{nn}dA–S editor implemented using the Cornell Synthesizer Generator.

4.1.1. Introduction

The PA^{nn}dA–S editor is a'full-screen' language-based editor for the PA^{nn}dA-S language (the PA^{nn}dA–S specification language described in volume II, chapters 2,3 and 5).

The editor is *hybrid* editor: it supports conventional text editing of specifications as well as structure editing. In text editing mode phrases are constructed character by character, almost as in any other editor. In structure editing mode, specifications are created top-down by inserting templates in the skeleton of previously entered templates. The insertion of new templates is done by invoking built in transformations. This mode of operation guarantees the context-free well-formedness of the specification at every editing step.

Templates corresponds to typographical, predefined units where keywords, delimiters, indentation and line breaks are provided automatically. Formatting of the specification is performed interactively, and the screen always shows the final layout (What You See Is What You Get).

The editor applies knowledge of the PA^{nn}dA–S language to ensure that specifications are always well-formed. Knowledge of the language syntax is built into the editor in order to assess whether a specification contains syntax errors and to determine where such errors occur. This syntactic analysis is performed *interactively* during editing rather than by compilation. Both context-free errors, like simple syntax errors, and context-sensitive errors, like the violation of type checking rules, can be immediately detected and displayed on the screen to provide feedback to the user.

The PA^{nn}dA–S editor is an integrated part of the PROSPECTRA Program Development System. It contains facilities for interfacing the Library Manager, in particular the version and configuration manager, and for editing specifications. Additionally it provides schemes for defining types in a canonical way: a type can be entered according to Ada syntax in the private part of a package, and its canonical representation in terms of private type declarations and constructor functions in pure PA^{nn}dA–S can then be generated automatically.

A short description of the basic concepts is given in section 4.1.2. The invocation of the editor, in particular its interfaces to the library manager, is described in section 4.1.3. Section 4.1.4 contains a description of facilities for controlling the static semantic analysis. The type definition schemes for declaring Ada types are described in section 4.1.5. The appendices contain a command summary, an error message summary, and definitions of keyboard bindings.

Implementation

The *PA^{nn}dA–S editor* has been generated using the *Cornell Synthesizer Generator* (*CSG* for short). It is implemented on a Sun Workstation running revision 3.2 of Unix BSD 4.2. for SunView and X-Windows (release 10.4).

1. *Author's current address*: FB 3 - Informatik, Universität Bremen, Postfach 330 440, D-2800 Bremen 33

4.1.2. Basic Concepts

All editors generated by CSG share a common, language-independent user interface and a set of language-independent features which are extended with language-specific commands and features (the reader is referred to the Synthesizer Generator Manual [Teitelbaum & Reps 1988] for a complete description of the language-independent commands and how they are invoked). Basically the editor provides language independent services for:

- navigating through a specification,
- modifying a specification,
- managing buffers of specifications,
- saving and restoring a specification in the file system,
- interfacing to the window system, keyboard and mouse.

What distinguishes editors generated by CSG from conventional text editors is that each buffer contains an abstract syntax tree representing the specification. Essentially, an abstract syntax records the structure of a specification without the syntactic marks like reserved words, delimiters etc. which are required for parsing and prettyprinting (see figure 4.1.1). Text phrases are translated to the abstract syntax form by *parsing* the input text and constructing the corresponding abstract syntax tree. Vice versa, *unparsing* displays the abstract syntax tree as a text in a window on the screen. The editor provides facilities for saving and restoring a specification as a file. Files can be either saved in structure form, or in conventional textual form.

The user controls the editor using the keyboard and the mouse. In a buffer (a window on the screen), a specification is represented as a text while its internal representation is an abstract syntax tree. The specification is modified by changing subtrees of the underlying abstract syntax tree. The unparsing is then updated accordingly.

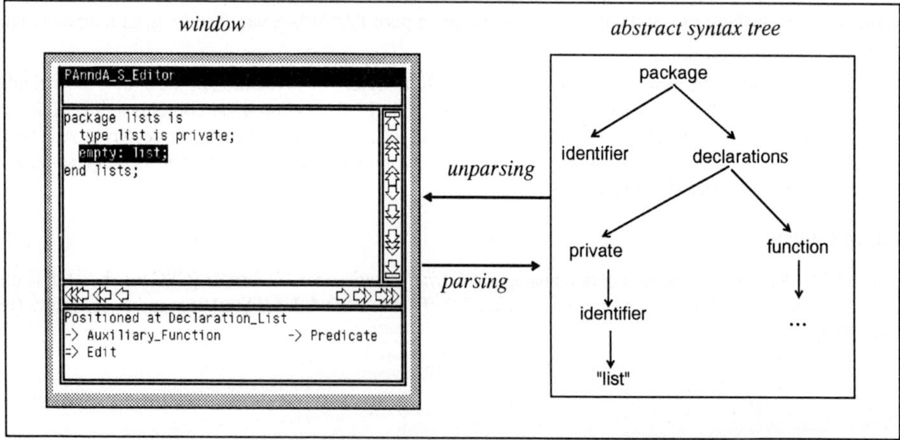

Figure 4.1.1: External and Internal Representation of PA^{nn}dA–S Specifications

4.1.2.1. Windows

Figure 4.1.2 shows an example window of the PA^{nn}dA–S editor. The window is split into six subwindows as follows.

The *object pane* contains the specification text, and error messages generated from the static semantic analysis. The specification is displayed in the object pane in the way it is usually displayed by a text editor, with some crucial differences. It is automatically formatted with indentations, keywords in lower case and identifiers as typed in by the user. Error messages (enclosed in braces) are given at the point where an error is discovered; they appear immediately after the error has been made, and disappear as soon as the error has been corrected.

Below and to the right of the object pane are a *horizontal* and a *vertical scroll bar s* with buttons which, when clicked by the mouse, cause the contents on the object pane to scroll horizontally and vertically, respectively.

The *title bar* on top of the object pane shows the name of the buffer. Immediately below is the *command line* containing general error messages, like “syntax error” and “cannot open file ...”. This is also the place where the user can enter and invoke CSG system commands, e.g. for reading and writing files. These commands can also be invoked from a pop-up menu using the mouse (see figure 4.1.2).

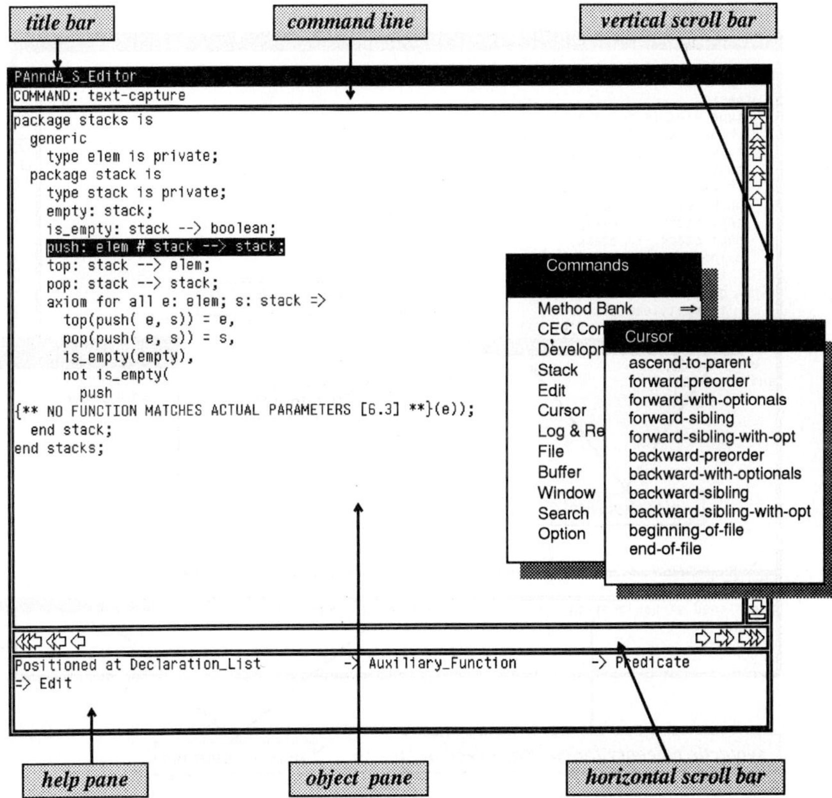

Figure 4.1.2: An Editor Window and its Subwindows

The *help pane* below the object pane indicates the syntactic category (e.g. Declaration_List) currently selected in the object pane, and buttons to initiate transformations on specification fragments. In figure 4.1.2, **-> Auxiliary_Function** transforms the function declaration selected into an auxiliary function declaration.

4.1.2.2. Structure Editing

The editor supports two modes of operation: *structure editing* and *text editing*. The specification is constructed character by character in text editing mode, whereas structure editing mode enforces an editing paradigm where commands operate directly on the abstract syntax tree by modifying or inserting whole subtrees.

In structure editing mode the specifications are created top-down by inserting new *fragments* (subtrees) within the skeleton of previously entered fragments. A fragment is one of the terminals or nonterminals defined by the grammar of the language, i.e. either an expression, a declaration, an identifier etc. One fragment, called the *current selection*, is highlighted and represents the subtree which can be modified by commands. A *template* is a predefined formatted pattern, e.g. the template for the function declaration in figure 4.1.3. In general, the current selection is advanced from one template to another and from one template to it constituents, or from a constituent to an embodying template. It is only possible to position the cursor where insertions and deletions are allowed. The editor views a partially developed specification as a hierarchical composition of nested templates and phrases rather than as successive lines of text.

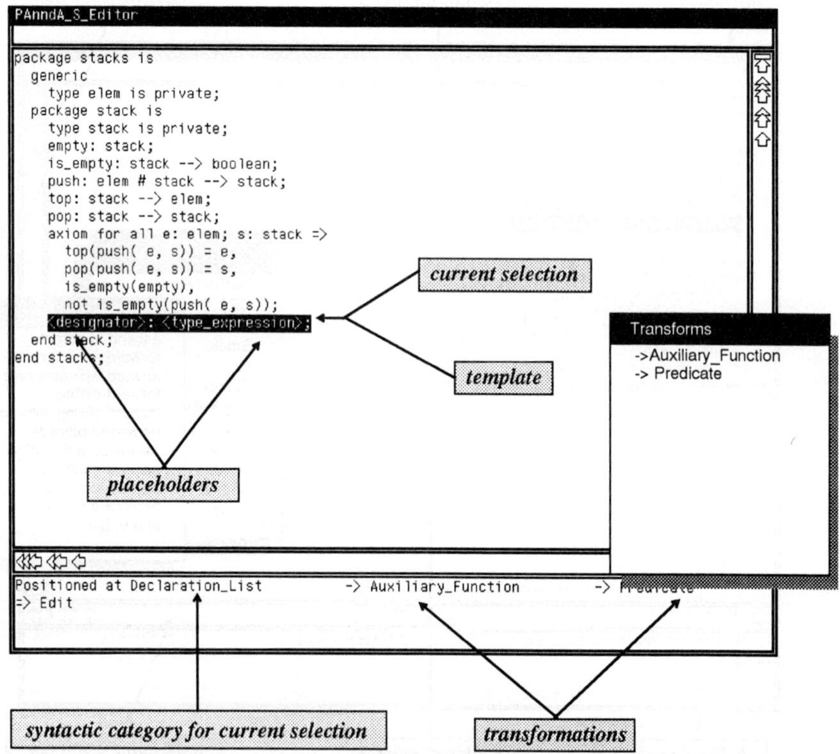

Figure 4.1.3: Basic Editing Concepts

Within templates, *placeholders* (e.g. <designator>) identify the locations where insertions can be made. Placeholders for specification fragments are displayed by the name of their syntactic category, enclosed in angular brackets.

Placeholders represent unexpanded nonterminals. Refinement of the specification, i.e. expansion of a placeholder into a template of the designated syntactic category, is achieved by invoking a transformation, either by clicking the buttons in the help pane or by selecting menu items from a pop-up menu (see figure 4.1.3). Transformations which expand a placeholder to a template are called *template-inserting transformations*. One such example is the transformation that inserted the template for the function declaration when positioned at the placeholder for a declaration. Other transformations replace a given construct by another construct of the same syntactic category, as for example **-> Auxiliary_Function** which transforms a function declaration into an auxiliary function declaration. Transformations guarantee the structural well-formedness of the specification at every step: only enabled transformations are presented in the help pane. Transformations are enabled dynamically depending on the success of a pattern match at the current selection.

One of the inherent advantages of structure oriented editors is that the editor incorporates knowledge of the language. When the editor is used in structure-editing mode, changes to the specification are accomplished by removal and insertion of entire, well-formed language fragments. However, the editor only operates with a subset of the non-terminals defined in the language reference manual. The concrete syntax of the PA^{nn}dA–S language defines the syntax of the language in a way that is appropriate from a conceptual and semantic point of view. For example, the structure of expressions and type expressions is defined in a hierarchical way that reflects the precedence and associativity of operators.

Using structure-oriented editors, parsing issues are of minor concern since the abstract syntax tree is constructed by manipulating it directly. The abstract syntax has been flattened into a single level for expressions, called Expression, in order not to burden a user with to many commands when editing an expression fragment. There is for example no distinction between simple expressions and terms in the internal, abstract representation of expressions. When positioned at the placeholder for an expression several template-inserting transformations are enabled. The template inserting commands **Binary_Operator** and **Unary_Operator**, provide the templates for binary and unary expressions, respectively. Thus, operators are split into the classes of binary and unary operators. The placeholder term for an operator can be refined by application of transformations (see figure 4.1.3). An operator can also be changed into another one belonging to the same class by application of transformations.

For enlightenment of the human reader, the PA^{nn}dA–S editor supports the insertion of *comments* and *empty lines* into the specification text. A comment or an empty line can be inserted at places where a declaration, an expression (in an expression list) or a generic formal parameter is allowed. A comment starts with two adjacent hyphens and extends up to the end of the line (see figure 4.1.3).

4.1.2.3. Unparsing of Specifications

Templates corresponds to typographical, predefined units where the syntactical marks like keywords and delimiters are provided automatically. Indentation of specification fragments is also automatic, both when a template is introduced and when it is modified. Formatting is performed interactively, and the screen always shows the final layout (What You See Is What You Get).

<expression> <binary_operator> <expression> <unary_operator> <expression>	**package** <identifier> **is new** <generic_package_name>;
package <identifier> **is** **end** <identifier>;	**package** <identifier> **is** **new** <generic_package_name> (<expression>);

Figure 4.1.4: Templates

When the editor is set in word-wrapping mode, the display is forced into a column of text no wider than the window. The editor breaks lines that are too long to fit in the window, and formats the text nicely in most cases. However, the editor does not work perfectly in all circumstances, mainly because CSG offers only a limited formatting functionality.

Placeholder terms are defined as the name of their syntactic category, enclosed in angular brackets. For the category name, however, the definition is intended to be more suggestive for the user. Depending on the context, the placeholder is displayed as <subtype_name>, <generic_package_name>, or simply <name>, as e.g. shown in figure 4.1.4. In order to distinguish identifiers from reserved words, the editor represents reserved words in lower case and identifiers in the style typed in by the user (the used version of CSG does not support prettyprinting of various fonts and styles).

Abbreviating the unparsing of parts of a document is known as *holophrasting*. Using the alternate unparsing scheme command **alternate-unparsing-toggle** of CSG, only some parts of a text may be displayed while the rest is abbreviated to '...'. Currently, such abbreviations are provided for all list items of the language, e.g. lists of declarations, formal parameters and expressions in an axiomatic annotation. It should be noted that the holophrasting information is kept when the specification is saved using the PROSPECTRA Library Manager, and thus has effect when the specification is read into the editor again.

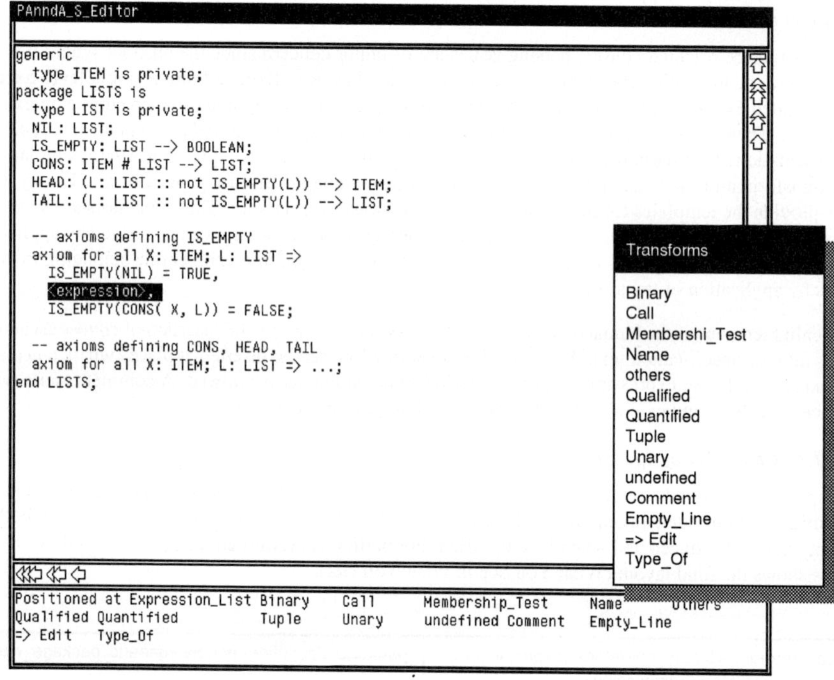

Figure 4.1.5: Holophrasting

The command **alternate-unparsing-toggle** has been applied to the expression list of the last axiom. The expression list is therefore abbreviated to '...'.

The editor automatically inserts parentheses when needed. Figure 4.1.6 shows two different abstract syntax trees together with their canonical unparsing.The unparsed text properly reflects the PA^{nn}dA–S semantics of the underlying abstract syntax tree.

A similar flattening of the abstract syntax, in combination with automatic unparsing of parenthesis on the basis of precedence rules, has been adopted for the representation of type expressions.

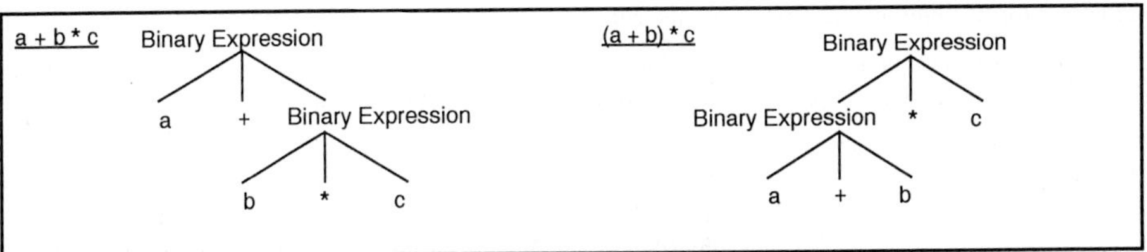

Figure 4.1.6: Internal and External Representation of Expressions

4.1.2.4. Text Editing

The editor accepts text input for all syntactic categories – in a sense, this is a violation of the principles for structure editors to insert text directly instead of using the appropriate template, but in some cases and/or for some users, it is more convenient. The user is allowed to type in a phrase of text when positioned at a placeholder. Upon typing in the phrase of text, and pressing return, the text is parsed and the subtree constructed. Errors in user-typed text are detected immediately because the parser is invoked by the editor on a phrase-by-phrase basis. By invoking the **text-capture** command of CSG, the user is also allowed to edit existing specification fragments and templates in text-editing mode.

When typing in text directly, care should be taken to ensure that the cursor is positioned at the appropriate point in the syntax tree. For example, when positioned at the placeholder for a name, the phrase entered must be a legal phrase for a name. The name of the syntactic category is displayed in the help pane (e.g. "Positioned at Name"). This information refers to the name of the abstract syntax category, and is of very little use if the abstract syntax definition does not conform to the concrete syntax of the language. The editor usually keeps a straightforward relation between abstract and concrete syntax. One deviation from this principle is the abstract syntax of expressions. Another deviation is that the user is not able to select all nonterminals of the grammar.

The editor accepts complete specifications, fragments of specifications as well as error messages, placeholder terms and comments. When a specification containing errors is written to a text file, this file will include the error messages, and consequently, the syntax for error messages has been included in the syntax of the language, in order to be able to read the file later. Existing error messages are ignored but regenerated when the specification is read.

The editor also allows incomplete specifications to be entered as text. The syntax for placeholders has been included in the syntax of the language and it is therefore possible to leave specification fragments unspecified simply by entering the corresponding placeholder term.

It should be noted that empty lines will disappear since they are recognized as whitespace when reading in specifications as text. The empty line indicator "$$" should be used instead.

4.1.2.5. Commands

The editor provides several classes of language dependent transformations:

• *template-inserting transformations* for the expansion of placeholders into templates,

• *construct-to-construct transformations* which transform a language construct into another,

• *optional construct-inserting transformations* which provide an optional part of a given construct,

• *auxiliary transformations* for controlling the editor.

A command summary of all the transformations accompanied with the editor is given in Appendix 4.1.B. For a detailed description of the auxiliary transformations, we refer to section 4.1.4.

Names of a construct-to-construct transformations are generally prefixed with "**->**". Among these are transformations for changing a function declaration to an auxiliary function or a predicate and vice versa. For language constructs containing optional parts (like e.g. the with clause of a compilation unit) facilities are provided for inserting optional parts explicitly. For example, invoking the transformation named **Package** inserts the template for a package with no placeholder for the optional with clause and the optional declaration list, whereas the transformation **+ With_Clause** inserts the templates for a package together with the template for a with clause. Generally, the prefix '+' is used to indicate that the transformation additionally inserts the placeholder for an optional part.

Figure 4.1.2 shows the main menu of language-independent *system commands* leading to a number of submenus:

Development commands for controlling developments, exit the editor, start, cancel and repeat a command.

Stack commands for pushing and popping fragments to parameterized transformations.

Edit commands for structural editing following the cut-copy-paste paradigm.

Cursor cursor commands for navigating through the abstract syntax tree.

Log & Replay commands for controlling the log and replay of sessions.

File commands for reading specifications from, and writing them to the file system.

Buffer commands for handling buffers of specifications.

Window commands for creating and deleting windows.

Search commands.

Option commands for setting various global parameters of the editor.

Most of the system commands are available in the pop-up menu. This may be sufficient for the novice user, but for more experienced user, menu-based systems tend to be inappropriate. Consequently, the editor has a *keyboard definition* with the most commonly used commands for the SUN keyboard, as described in Appendix 4.1.D. Other commands can be invoked using keyboard accelerators. We refer to [Teitelbaum & Reps 1988] for a complete description of system commands.

The language independent system commands can be invoked either by using the keyboard or by using the mouse. The mouse can be used to:

• change the current selection by clicking the mouse on a character or placeholder, or dragging the mouse between two characters,

• invoke a transformation by clicking on the transformation name in the help pane,

• scrolling the object pane by clicking on one of the arrows in the scroll bars,

• selecting language-independent system commands from a pop-up menu.

• invoking one of the currently enabled language-dependent transformations from another pop-up menu.

4.1.3. Invoking the Editor

The PA^{nn}dA–S editor is invoked from the LibLa editor. This editor provides partial views to the underlying library of specifications. It also provides means for interacting with the this library by invoking transformations. This editor is described in detail in section 3.2 of part III. We refer to that document for a detailed description of the library manager interface, whereas a short introduction will be given below.

4.1.3.1. Starting a Development

The LibLa editor provides three commands for invoking the PA^{nn}dA–S editor (see figure 4.1.7 below). The command **New_Origin** is enabled when positioned on a family tree. It invokes the editor with a specification that is an empty package named by the family. The command **Revision** is enabled when positioned at a version tree. It creates a new revision of an existing specification. The buffer of the PA^{nn}dA–S editor will contain the version to be revised. Apart from these two commands, another command called **Display** is provided for opening the editor in *read-only mode*, as a browser of PA^{nn}dA–S specifications.

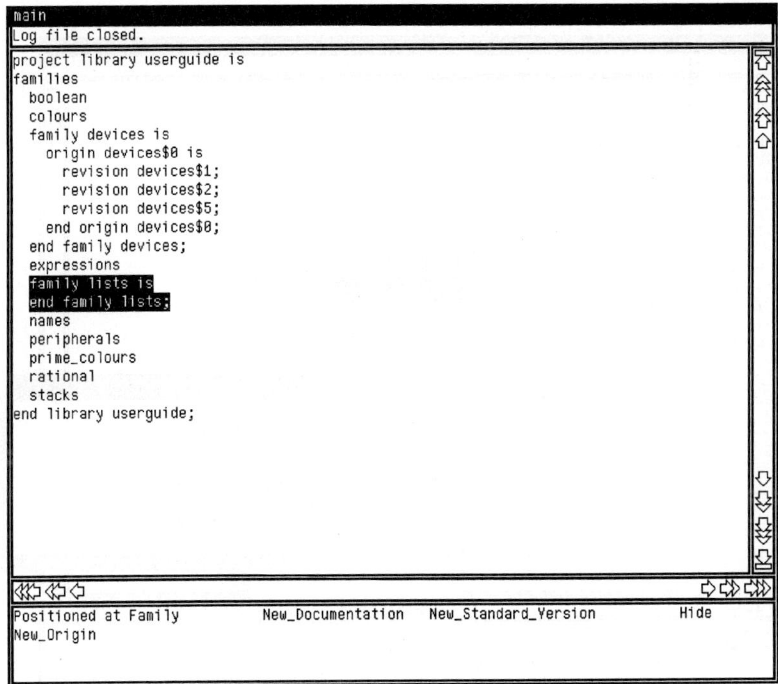

Figure 4.1.7: Invoking the PA^{nn}dA–S Editor

A project library consists of a set of families. Each family contains a set of versions. The family devices contains three developments (revisions) of the original version. The family lists is currently empty. The transformation **New_Origin** invokes the PA^{nn}dA–S editor, and the user may provide an initial specification of package lists.

4.1.3.2. Calling the Library Editor from the PA^{nn}dA–S Editor

The library is needed during a development to import existing versions of imported units using the configuration manager, e.g.:

```
with lists;
package integer_list is new lists(integer);
```

Since several versions of the package list may exist in the library, the configuration manager must be used to select a specific one to be used in the instantiation (see section 3.2. of part III for a detailed description of the version and configuration manager of the LibLa editor).

4.1.3.3. Ending a Development

Returning to the LibLa editor is achieved by invoking one of two system commands: **confirm-development** which saves the resulting version and returns to the LibLa editor or **cancel-development** which returns to the LibLa editor and quits the development. Global effect on the library is only achieved by committing the development.

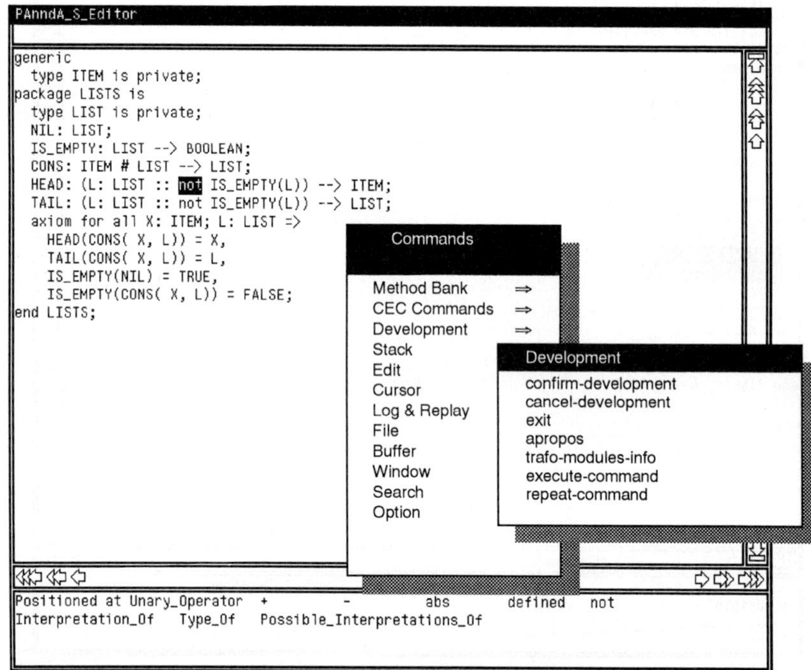

Figure 4.1.8: Confirming a Development

The figure shows an initial specification of package LISTS. There are two system commands to return to the LibLa editor: **confirm-development** and **cancel-development**, corresponding to save and quit respectively in conventional texteditors.

4.1.4. Static Semantic Analysis

The editor reports context-sensitive errors during the editing session. Each modification to the specification causes all affected analysis and error messages to be (re)done immediately. The error messages are determined by means of a *static semantic analyser* that has been built into the editor. Consider the simple example in figure 4.1.9.

A particular error message will appear on a new line immediately after the error is discovered. It is enclosed by "{**" and "**}". All error messages include a reference (in square brackets) to a section of the PA^{nn}dA–S language reference manual. In the above example the reference is to the chapter describing visibility and scope rules. The error message indicates that no entity named i is visible in the applied context. Obviously a typing error has been made. The error message disappears when the axiom is changed as showed in the second example of figure 4.1.9.

Error recovery has been built into the static semantic analyser, in order to avoid spurious and meaningless avalance errors. For example, no legal interpretation can be found for the equality in the example, since the type of i is unknown, but the editor recognises that an error has been detected in one of the subexpressions, and stops reporting avalance errors.

The static semantics of PA^{nn}dA–S has been inspired by the static semantics of Ada, with all the inherent complications for the static semantic analyser. Since updates of a fragment must, in general, be propagated to the entire rest of the specification, such updates are rather time-consuming and unnecessary re-analysis must be avoided if possible. Suppose for example that the name of the generic formal parameter is changed from elem to item. This change is then automatically propagated to the complete generic package, resulting in error messages for all applied occurrences of the name elem.

The part of specification affected by a change depends on the kind of fragment being changed. E.g. if an expression is modified, then the change is propagated to the uppermost enclosing logical expression. In the example this means that changing the name of the quantified variable from i to e only affects the equation for pop, but leaves that for top unaffected.

Changes to declarations have more serious effect in terms of the amount of re-analysis to be done. Generally the change must be propagated to all fragments (declarations and expressions) within the scope of the declaration being changed. This means that adding a function is_empty after the function empty, will require a re-analysis of all declarations from push to the end of the package.

For medium-sized to large specifications re-analysis will in general be rather time-consuming. The editor has therefore been equipped with several options to avoid or restrict static semantic analysis in order to speed up editing. These facilities are described in the following subsections.

```
generic
   type elem is private;
package stack is
   type stack is private;
   empty: stack;
   push: elem # stack --> stack;
   top: stack --> elem;
   pop: stack --> stack;
   axiom for all e:elem; s:stack =>
      top(push(e,s)) = e,
      pop(push(e,s)) = i
{** NO INTERPRETATION FOUND [8.3] **};
end stack;
```

```
generic
   type elem is private;
package stack is
   type stack is private;
   empty: stack;
   push: elem # stack --> stack;
   top: stack --> elem;
   pop: stack --> stack;
   axiom for all e:elem; s:stack =>
      top(push(e,s)) = e,
      pop(push(e,s)) = e;
end stack;
```

Figure 4.1.9: Static Semantic Analysis of Specifications

4.1.4.1. Enabling and Disabling Static Semantic Checking

When performing major rearrangement to a specification, e.g. changing the name of a type, it is often of no use to have incremental, immediate checking. Error messages keep appearing because not all necessary changes have yet been made. To prevent such error messages, and to speed up the editing process, the editor therefore supports two modes of operation: *local syntactic analysis* to detect context-free syntax errors, and *global syntactic analysis* to detect context-free as well as context-sensitive errors.

To enable the user to toggle between the local and global mode of analysis, two commands have been provided can be invoked when positioned at the Local_State: **Static_Semantic_Analysis_On** enables global static semantic analysis, **Static_Semantic_Analysis_Off** disables static semantic analysis.

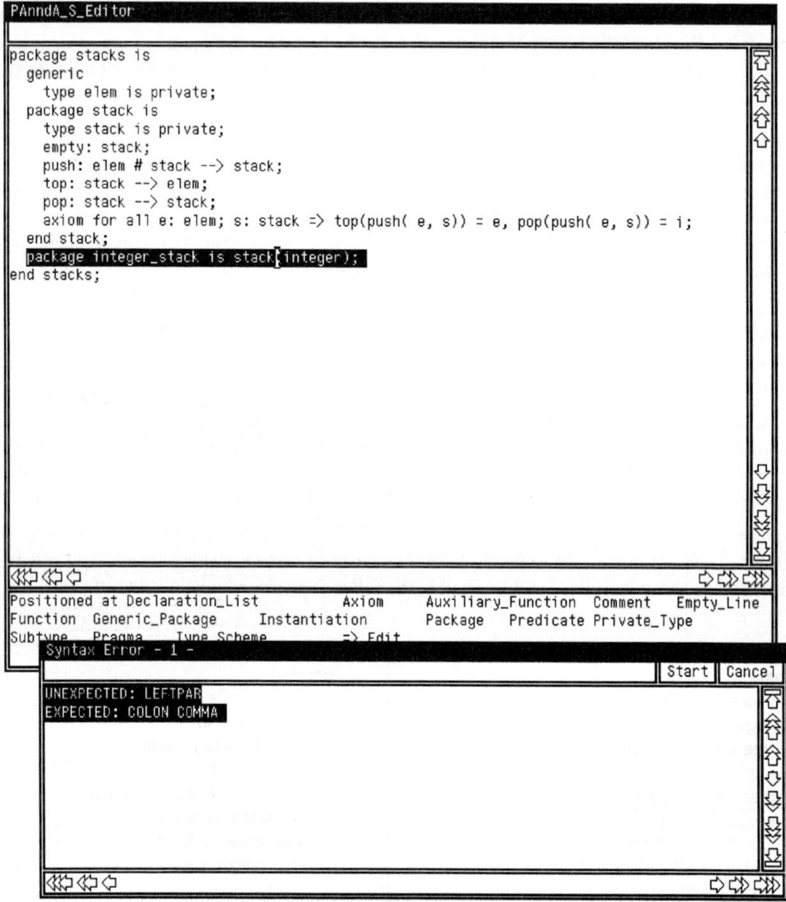

Figure 4.1.10: Disabled Static Semantic Analysis

Only context free errors are reported during local syntactic analysis, whereas context sensitive errors like the use of undeclared names (i in the last axiom) remains undetected..

4.1.4.2. Local Editing of Fragments.

When performing major rearrangement in an existing specification it is often of no use to have the changes immediately propagated to the rest of the specification. On the other hand it could still be useful to have incremental, immediate checking, in particular if the changes concern only a few successive declarations. To enable the global mode of syntax checking, and at the same time speeding up the editing process, the editor can be called recursively. The transformation **=> Edit** takes the current selection of the main buffer and passes it to the parameter editor where it can be edited in isolation. The content in the parameter form

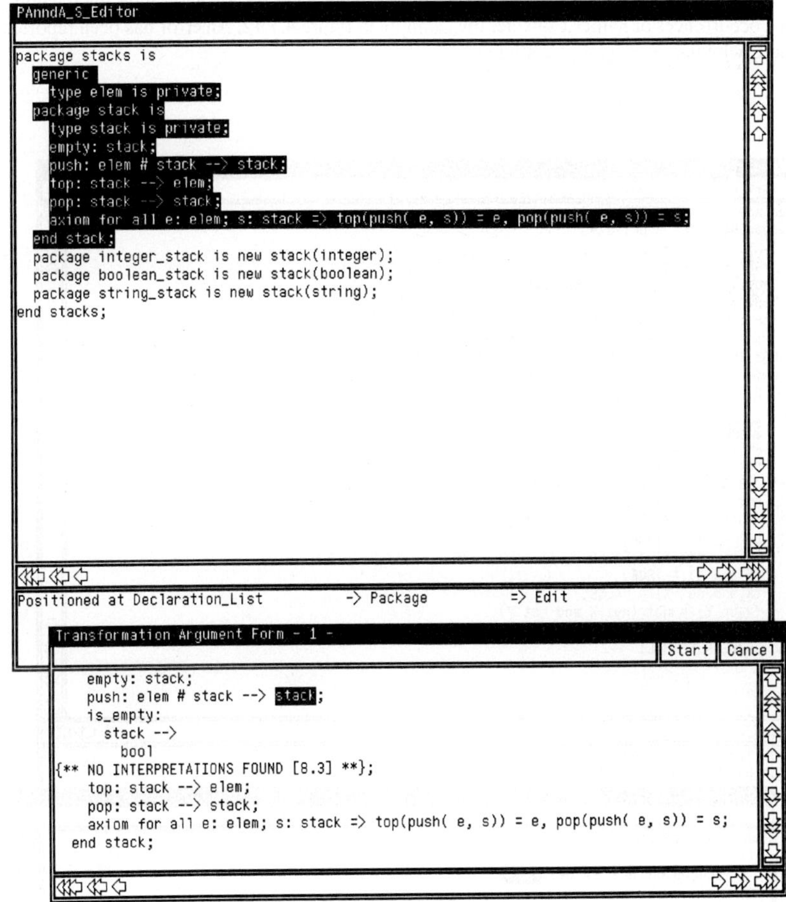

Figure 4.1.11: Local Editing of Fragments

The transformation **=> Edit** has been invoked. The current selection of the main buffer is put into the parameter form. The function is_empty has then been added by the user. The content in the parameter form replaces the selection in the main buffer when the **Start** button is clikked. The changes to the generic package are then propagated to the generic instantiations.

replaces the selection in the main buffer when the **Start** button is clicked and cancelled by clicking the **Cancel** button (see figure 4.1.11).

During the *local editing* in the parameter form, any analysis is performed in isolation from the rest of the specification. No changes are propagated to the main buffer. Nevertheless static semantic analysis is enabled in the parameter form although the context (e.g. the set of visible declarations) is the same as the one for the fragment initially put into the parameter form.

4.1.4.3. Interpretation of Names and Expressions

PA^{nn}dA–S contains facilities for *overloading* identifiers. For the static semantic checker, as well as the human reader, overloading sometimes results in inherent complications in determining the meaning (if any) of applied occurrences of names.Consider the example in figure 4.1.12. An error has been reported but it is not obvious why the expression is ambiguous.

```
PAnndA_S_Editor
Placed answer in Help
package BOOLEAN_KERNEL is
  type BOOLEAN is private;
  FALSE: BOOLEAN;
  TRUE: BOOLEAN;
  "not": (R: BOOLEAN) --> BOOLEAN;
  "and": (L: BOOLEAN) # (R: BOOLEAN) --> BOOLEAN;
  "or": (L: BOOLEAN) # (R: BOOLEAN) --> BOOLEAN;
  "xor": (L: BOOLEAN) # (R: BOOLEAN) --> BOOLEAN;
  EQ: (L: BOOLEAN) # (R: BOOLEAN) --> BOOLEAN;
  axiom for all
    X: BOOLEAN;
    Y: BOOLEAN =>
    FALSE /= TRUE
{** AMBIGUOUS EXPRESSION [8.4] **},
    not FALSE = TRUE
{** AMBIGUOUS EXPRESSION [8.4] **},
    not TRUE = FALSE
{** AMBIGUOUS EXPRESSION [8.4] **},
    EQ( X, X) = TRUE,
    EQ( X, not X) = FALSE,
    (X and X) = TRUE,
    (X and not X) = FALSE,
    (X or Y) = not (not X and not Y),
    (X xor Y) = not EQ( X, Y);
end BOOLEAN_KERNEL;

Positioned at Expression      => Edit   Interpretation_Of   Type_Of
Possible_Interpretations_Of

Help
Possible Interpretations:
  1:
    standard.boolean_kernel.false
  2:
    standard.false
```

Figure 4.1.12: Help Facilities

The editor is equipped with three transformations that helps the user in analysing the meaning of names and expressions: the transformation **Interpretation_Of** determines the unique interpretation (if any) of a given construct; **Type_Of** determines the type of a name, an expression or an operator; **Possible_Interpretations_Of** determines the possible (visible) interpretations of a name or an operator.The result of these transformations will be put into the buffer named Help. To open this buffer invoke the system commands **split-current-window** and **switch-to-buffer**(Help).

4.1.4.4. Analysis of Incomplete Fragments

Generally it is unnecessary to redo the static semantics checking when a template for a declaration is inserted since such a template contains placeholders. Thus, the editor is speeded up considerably when it, in the case of *incomplete fragments* (fragments that contain placeholder terms), does not propagate changes and trigger re-analysis. A declaration is therefore not visible as long as it contains placeholder terms. Similarly, there is generally no way to perform context-sensitive analysis of an expression as long as it contains placeholders. Consequently, the editor does not perform overload resolution and type checking as long as the expression contains placeholders that make overload resolution and type checking meaningless.

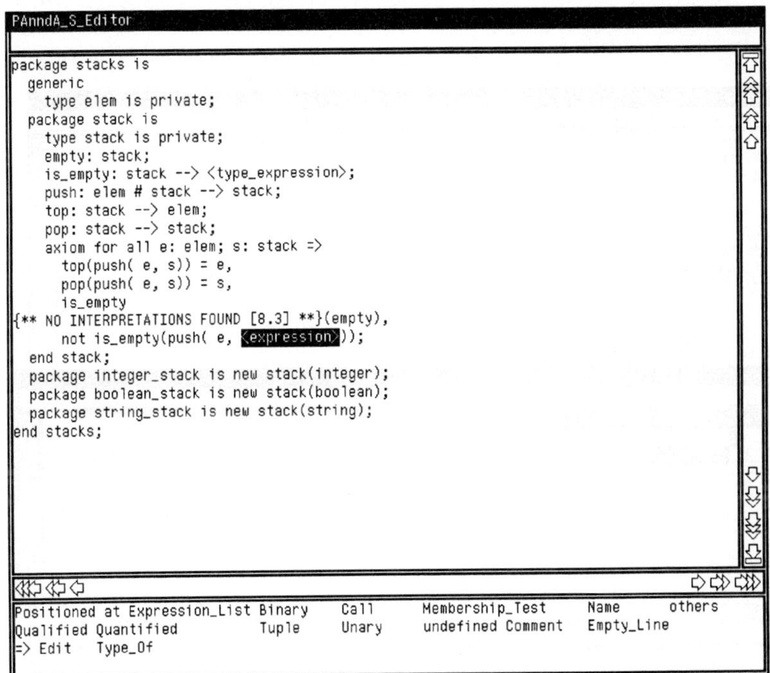

Figure 4.1.13: Analysis of Incomplete Fragments

The declaration of the function is_empty contains a placeholder term and it has therefore no effect on the rest of the specification. Thus, an error is reported on the first logical expression defining empty. However, since the second logical expression defining empty is incomplete, no analysis is performed on that expression, thus resulting in the absence of error messages.

4.1.5. Type Definition Schemes

The editor supports the definition of a selected set of Ada types that is entered by the user in the private part of a package. The equivalent canonical representation in the algebraic form in the visible part is generated by transformation upon user request. This facility is called a *type definition scheme* and is provided for:

- *enumeration types,*
- *pure record types* without discriminants and variant parts,
- *variant record types* with exactly one discriminant and variant part,
- *recursive variant types* which are as variant types except that they may be recursive.

In addition to these Ada types there is a type scheme for the definition abstract syntax trees. This scheme takes as input the definition of the abstract syntax of a language, and generates the equivalent term algebra.

4.1.5.1. Declaration of Types

The type definition scheme is defined as an alternative of a package declaration. Syntactically, it looks like any other package, just the private part of the package will contain one or more type declarations representing the Ada type declarations corresponding to the type scheme. The transformation named **Type_Scheme**

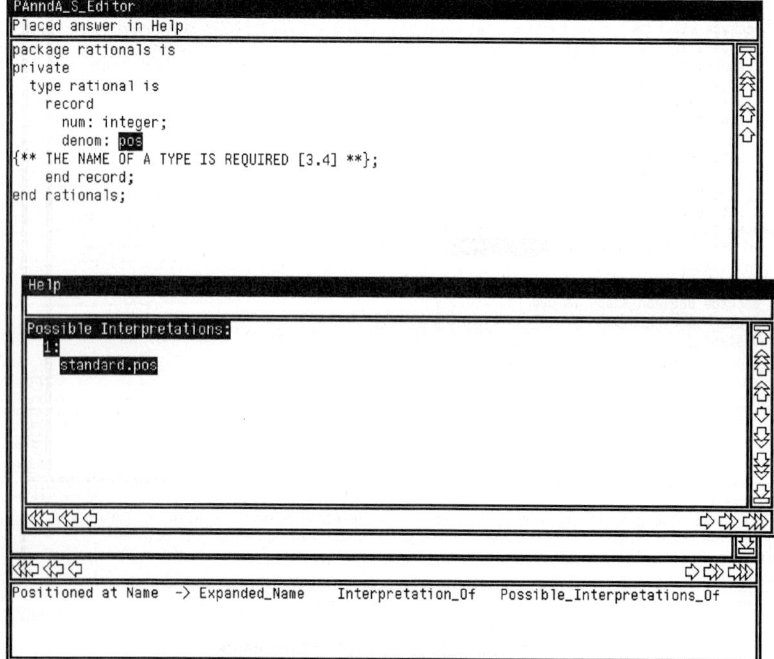

Figure 4.1.14: Entering Type Declarations

During specification of the type declaration in the private part any errors according to the Ada rules will immediately be reported.

provides a template which can be further specified. Commands are provided for inserting templates for the type declarations mentioned above. We refer to the appendix 4.1.A for a BNF definition of the type schemes and to appendix 4.1.B.1 for a complete summary of the template inserting commands.

The type declarations are analysed to provide the user with feed-back upon e.g. type errors. Some of these errors are related to the rules of the Ada language, e.g. that the type of a discriminant must be discrete. Such error messages refer explicitly to the corresponding paragraph in the Ada Reference Manual.

4.1.5.2. Generating the Canonical Representation

When the type declaration has been completely specified in the private part, the corresponding canonical representation in the visible part is generated by a transformation **-> Canonical_Representation.** This command is parameterized. The user must specify whether *equality functions* shall be generated or not. One type for which the equality function will not make sense is the record type for rational numbers, with components denoting the nominator and denominator. The equality function generated by the type definition scheme would not be correct since it would test the equality of the single components.

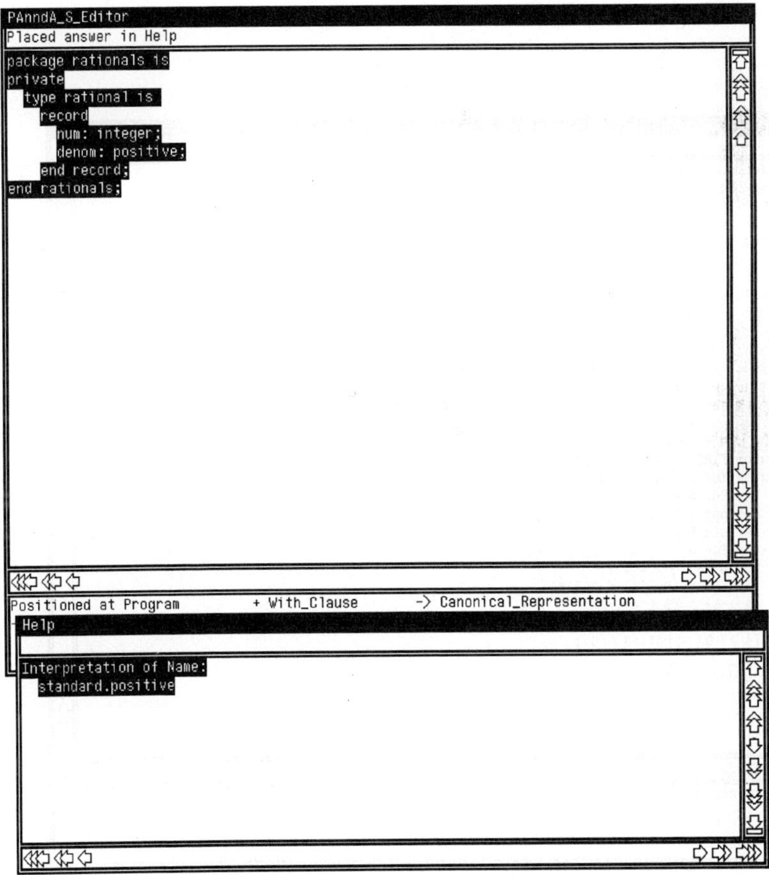

Figure 4.1.15: Generating Canonical Representations

More generally, the equality function of a record type will be defined as a conjunction of the equality of its components. If such equality functions have not been defined for the component types, then static semantic errors will be introduced.

It should be noted that inconsistencies may occur between the content of the private part of a type scheme and the content of the visible part. It is the responsibility of the user to generate the canonical part upon changes to the private part, thus propagating the changes to the rest of the specification.

4.1.5.3. Enumeration Types

For enumeration type schemes, the user specifies the type name and the enumeration literals. The visible part of the package is generated by the transformation **->Canonical_Representation** and contains:

- a private type declaration,
- a zero-adic function for each enumeration literal,
- an equality function,
- a function for each of the relevant Ada attributes,
- a function for each of the predefined operators.

```
PAnndA_S_Editor

package devices is
  type device is private;
  printer: device;
  disk: device;
  drum: device;
  EQ: device # device --> BOOLEAN;
  FIRST: device;
  LAST: device;
  POS: device --> NATURAL;
  VAL: (X: NATURAL :: X <= POS(device'(LAST))) --> device;
  SUCC: (X: device :: not (X = LAST)) --> device;
  PRED: (X: device :: not (X = FIRST)) --> device;
  "<": device # device --> BOOLEAN;
  "<=": device # device --> BOOLEAN;
  ">": device # device --> BOOLEAN;
  ">=": device # device --> BOOLEAN;
  axiom FIRST = printer, LAST = drum, POS(printer) = 0, POS(disk) = 1, POS(drum) = 2;
  axiom for all A: device =>
    VAL(POS(A)) = A,
    defined SUCC(A) -> SUCC(A) = VAL(SUCC(POS(A))),
    defined PRED(A) -> PRED(A) = VAL(PRED(POS(A)));
  axiom for all A: device; B: device =>
    EQ( A, B) <-> A = B,
    (A < B) = (POS(A) < POS(B)),
    (A > B) = (B < A),
    (A <= B) = not (A > B),
    (A >= B) = not (A < B);
private
  type device is (printer, disk, drum);
end devices;

Positioned at Function_Arrow  -->        ==>
```

Figure 4.1.16: Enumeration Types

4.1.5.4. Pure Record Types

Pure record types are in nature cartesian products. The user specifies the type name and the record component list. Type marks in the component list must obey the usual visibility rules. The generated canonical representation consists of:

- a private type declaration,
- an equality function,
- a constructor function,
- and a selector function for each component of the record.

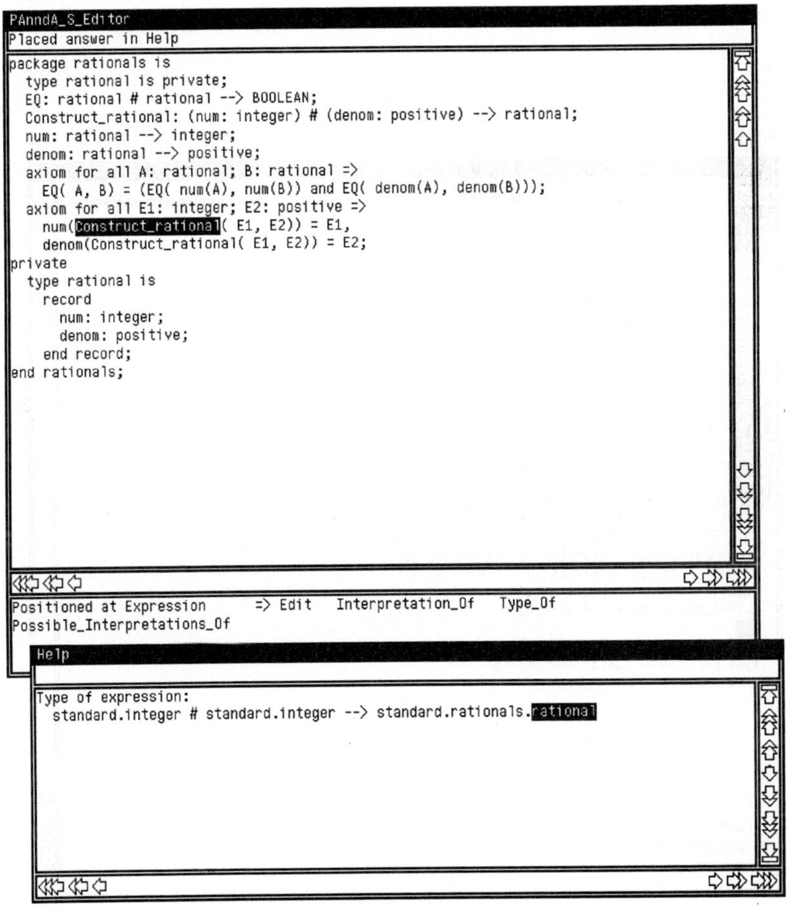

```
PAnndA_S_Editor
Placed answer in Help
package rationals is
  type rational is private;
  EQ: rational # rational --> BOOLEAN;
  Construct_rational: (num: integer) # (denom: positive) --> rational;
  num: rational --> integer;
  denom: rational --> positive;
  axiom for all A: rational; B: rational =>
    EQ( A, B) = (EQ( num(A), num(B)) and EQ( denom(A), denom(B)));
  axiom for all E1: integer; E2: positive =>
    num(Construct_rational( E1, E2)) = E1,
    denom(Construct_rational( E1, E2)) = E2;
private
  type rational is
    record
      num: integer;
      denom: positive;
    end record;
end rationals;

Positioned at Expression      => Edit   Interpretation_Of   Type_Of
Possible_Interpretations_Of

Help
Type of expression:
  standard.integer # standard.integer --> standard.rationals.rational
```

Figure 4.1.17: Pure Record Types

4.1.5.5. Variant Record Types

Variant record types correspond to non-recursive unions. The type name, the discriminant declaration and the variant part is entered by the user. The generated visible part consists of:

- a private type declaration,
- an equality function,
- a function for accessing the discriminant value.

In extend, for each alternative in the variant part including the others-part, the following is generated:

- a constructor function,
- a selector function for each component.

The constructor function for the others choice takes a parameter of the discriminant type in order to initialize the discriminant of the variant record. This is not the case for the remaining constructor functions, because the fact that there is always one choice ensures a one to one correspondence between the constructor function and the discriminant value.

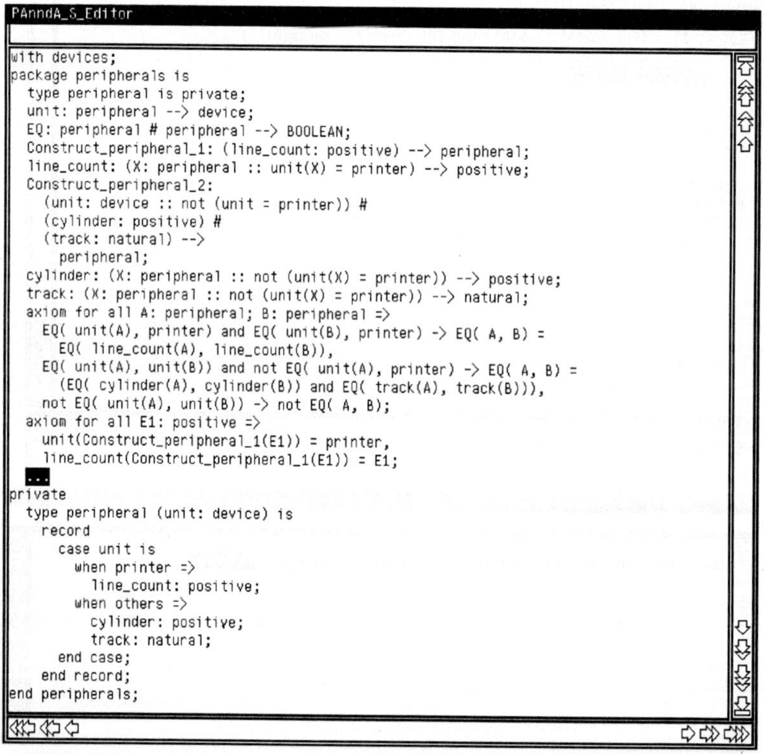

```
PAnndA_S_Editor
with devices;
package peripherals is
  type peripheral is private;
  unit: peripheral --> device;
  EQ: peripheral # peripheral --> BOOLEAN;
  Construct_peripheral_1: (line_count: positive) --> peripheral;
  line_count: (X: peripheral :: unit(X) = printer) --> positive;
  Construct_peripheral_2:
    (unit: device :: not (unit = printer)) #
    (cylinder: positive) #
    (track: natural) -->
      peripheral;
  cylinder: (X: peripheral :: not (unit(X) = printer)) --> positive;
  track: (X: peripheral :: not (unit(X) = printer)) --> natural;
  axiom for all A: peripheral; B: peripheral =>
    EQ( unit(A), printer) and EQ( unit(B), printer) -> EQ( A, B) =
      EQ( line_count(A), line_count(B)),
    EQ( unit(A), unit(B)) and not EQ( unit(A), printer) -> EQ( A, B) =
      (EQ( cylinder(A), cylinder(B)) and EQ( track(A), track(B))),
    not EQ( unit(A), unit(B)) -> not EQ( A, B);
  axiom for all E1: positive =>
    unit(Construct_peripheral_1(E1)) = printer,
    line_count(Construct_peripheral_1(E1)) = E1;
  ...
private
  type peripheral (unit: device) is
    record
      case unit is
        when printer =>
          line_count: positive;
        when others =>
          cylinder: positive;
          track: natural;
      end case;
    end record;
end peripherals;
```

Figure 4.1.18: Variant Record Types

4.1.5.6. Recursive Variant Types

Recursive variant types specifies recursive unions. If there is only one alternative they are recursive cartesian products. The user specifies the name of the recursive type in an access type declaration whereas a variant record type declaration with its incomplete type declaration contains the definition of the components.

The generated visible part consists of:

- a private type declaration,
- a function for accessing the discriminant value.

In extend, for each alternative in the variant part including the others part, the following is generated for each component:

- a constructor function,
- a selector function.

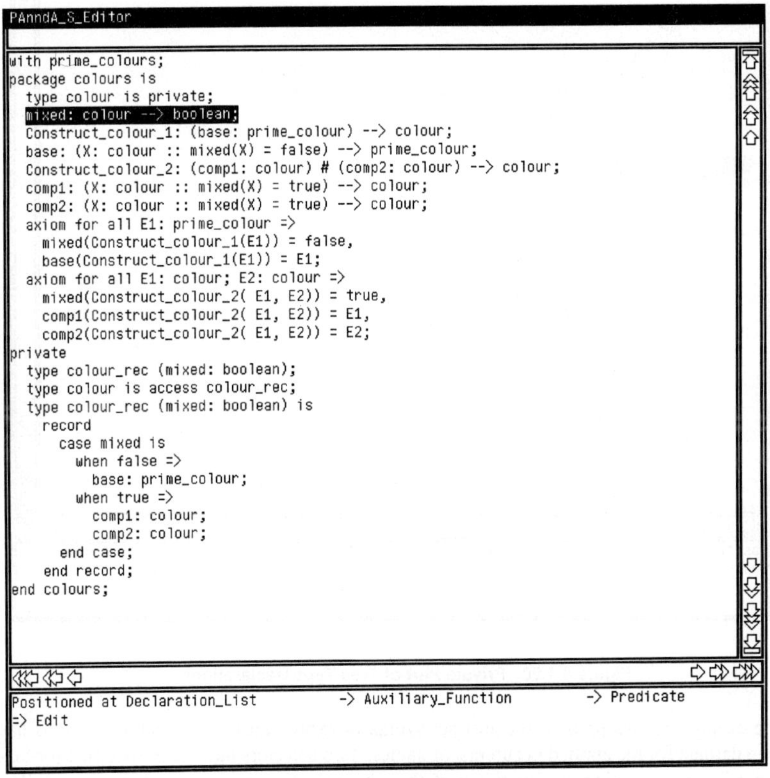

```
PAnndA_S_Editor

with prime_colours;
package colours is
  type colour is private;
  mixed: colour --> boolean;
  Construct_colour_1: (base: prime_colour) --> colour;
  base: (X: colour :: mixed(X) = false) --> prime_colour;
  Construct_colour_2: (comp1: colour) # (comp2: colour) --> colour;
  comp1: (X: colour :: mixed(X) = true) --> colour;
  comp2: (X: colour :: mixed(X) = true) --> colour;
  axiom for all E1: prime_colour =>
    mixed(Construct_colour_1(E1)) = false,
    base(Construct_colour_1(E1)) = E1;
  axiom for all E1: colour; E2: colour =>
    mixed(Construct_colour_2( E1, E2)) = true,
    comp1(Construct_colour_2( E1, E2)) = E1,
    comp2(Construct_colour_2( E1, E2)) = E2;
private
  type colour_rec (mixed: boolean);
  type colour is access colour_rec;
  type colour_rec (mixed: boolean) is
    record
      case mixed is
        when false =>
          base: prime_colour;
        when true =>
          comp1: colour;
          comp2: colour;
      end case;
    end record;
end colours;

Positioned at Declaration_List        -> Auxiliary_Function        -> Predicate
=> Edit
```

Figure 4.1.19: Recursive Variant Types

4.1.5.7. Tree Types

In addition to the Ada types there is a type scheme for the definition of the *abstract syntax of languages*, i.e. for the definition of 'tree types'. This scheme takes as input the definition of the abstract syntax of a language, and generates the equivalent term algebra. This term algebra then forms the basis for specifying transformations over language terms.

The type scheme supports the specification of union types, cartesian products and type synonyms: the user specifies types, constructor functions, selector functions, subtypes and pragmas. A BNF definition of the syntax is provided in appendix 4.1.A.

This type scheme is different from the others: visibility is non-linear in the private part of the type scheme in order to support the specification of recursive types and errors concerning e.g. use of undeclared names or constructor functions being homographs will not appear until the canonical representation is generated..

```
PAnndA_S_Editor

with names;
package expressions is
private
  declare
  pragma ON( selector_functions);

  pragma ON( predicate_functions);

  type Expression is
      mk_Name: Name
    | mk_Binary: Expression # Binary_Operator # Expression
    | mk_Unary: Unary_Operator # Expression
    | mk_Call: ( function_part: Expression) # ( actual_part: Expression);

  <type_declaration>
end expressions;

Positioned at Tree_Type_Declaration_List          Pragma    Tree_Type Subtype    Comment
Empty_Line
```

Figure 4.1.20: Private Part of Tree Type Declarations

The example shows parts of the abstract syntax of expressions. Constructor functions have been defined for the applied occurence of names. Two selectors have been specified for function calls: one selecting the function part, the other selecting the actual parameter part. Pragmas have been supplied such that the generation to the canonical form will provide selector and predicate functions in the visible part of the type definition scheme (see figure 4.1.21).

The following pragmas control the generation of the canonical part:

pragma ON (equality_functions);	generates equality functions.
pragma ON (selector_functions);	generates selector functions.
pragma ON (predicate_functions);	generates predicate functions.
pragma LIST(<type_name>);	generates a concatenation operator "&" for the type.
pragma OPTIONAL_LIST(<type_name>);	generates a concatenation operator "&" for the type.

The order in which pragmas are provided is insignificant. The region of text over which the pragma has effect is the type definition scheme in which it occurs.

```
PAnndA_S_Editor
with names;
package expressions is

  -- TYPE DECLARATIONS
  type Expression is private;

  -- FUNCTION DECLARATIONS

  -- Expression
  mk_Name: Name --> Expression;
  is_mk_Name: Expression --> BOOLEAN;
  axiom for all A: Expression; E1: Name =>
    A = mk_Name(E1) -> is_mk_Name(A) = TRUE,
    others -> is_mk_Name(A) = FALSE;
  mk_Binary: Expression # Binary_Operator # Expression --> Expression;
  is_mk_Binary: Expression --> BOOLEAN;
  axiom for all A: Expression; E1: Expression; E2: Binary_Operator; E3: Expression =>
    A = mk_Binary( E1, E2, E3) -> is_mk_Binary(A) = TRUE,
    others -> is_mk_Binary(A) = FALSE;
  mk_Unary: Unary_Operator # Expression --> Expression;
  is_mk_Unary: Expression --> BOOLEAN;
  axiom for all A: Expression; E1: Unary_Operator; E2: Expression =>
    A = mk_Unary( E1, E2) -> is_mk_Unary(A) = TRUE,
    others -> is_mk_Unary(A) = FALSE;
  mk_Call: Expression # Expression --> Expression;
  is_mk_Call: Expression --> BOOLEAN;
  axiom for all A: Expression; E1: Expression; E2: Expression =>
    A = mk_Call( E1, E2) -> is_mk_Call(A) = TRUE,
    others -> is_mk_Call(A) = FALSE;
  function_part: Expression --> Expression;
  axiom for all A: Expression; E1: Expression; E2: Expression =>
    A = mk_Call( E1, E2) -> function_part(A) = E1;
  actual_part: Expression --> Expression;
  axiom for all A: Expression; E1: Expression; E2: Expression =>
    A = mk_Call( E1, E2) -> actual_part(A) = E2;
private
  declare
  pragma ON( selector_functions);
```

Figure 4.1.21: Canonical Representation of Tree Type Declarations

The canonical representation generated after having invoked the transformation **-> Canonical_Representation** includes: a private type for each type declared in the private part, the constructor functions given in the private part, selector functions and predicate functions according to the provided pragmas.

Appendices

4.1.A. Syntax of Type Definition Schemes

The current implementation is defined in accordance with the PAnndA-S standard types (see part II, chapter 5) with the following exceptions:

• tree-trees have been added,

• **others** is allowed as choice for variant records and recursive variant records,

• null records are allowed.

type scheme

```
package_specification ::=
        ...
    |   package identifier is
            declarative_item_list
        private
            type_declaration
        end [identifier];

type_declaration ::=
        type identifier type_definition;
    |   recursive_variant_type_declaration
    |   declare tree_type_declaration {tree_type_declaration}

type_definition ::=
        enumeration_type_definition
    |   pure_record_type_definition
    |   variant_record_type_definition
```

enumeration type

```
enumeration_type_declaration ::=
        is (enumeration_literal_list)

enumeration_literal_list ::=
        identifier {, identifier}
```

pure record type definition

```
pure_record_type_definition ::=
        is record
            component_part
        end record

component_part ::=
        component_declaration {component_declaration}
    |   null;

component_declaration ::=
        identifier: subtype_indication;
```

variant record type definition

```
variant_record_type_definition ::=
        record
            case identifier is
                {variant}
                [others_part]
```

recursive variant record type declaration

recursive_variant_type_declaration ::=
    type identifier (identifier: name);
    type identifier **is access** identifier;
    type identifier (identifier: name) **is** variant_record_type_definition;

tree type declaration

tree_type_declaration ::=
    type identifier **is** type_constructor {| type_constructor};
  | **subtype** identifier **is** type_expression;
  | comment
  | pragma

type_constructor ::=
    *constructor_*identifier
  | *constructor_*identifier : component_type {# component_type}

component_type ::=
    *subtype_*name
  | (*selector_*identifier: *subtype_*name)

4.1.B. Command Summary

In this appendix the transformations available in the editor are given. Together with the command names there is a short summary of their purpose, the syntactic category to which they apply, and the parameters they require, if any. Transformations are generally conditional, they only become active when it is sensible to apply them.

4.1.B.1. Template Inserting Transformations

These transformations apply if the current selection is a placeholder term of the indicated syntactic category.

Axiom (Declaration_List, Generic_Parameter_List): inserts template for axiomatic annotation.

Auxiliary_Function (Declaration_List, Generic Parameter List): inserts template for auxiliary function.

Binary (Expression): inserts template for binary expression.

Call (Expression): inserts template for function call.

Comment (Declaration_List, Expression_List, Generic_Parameter_List): inserts template for comment.

Domain (Type_Expression): inserts template for domain.

Empty_Line (Declaration_List, Expression_List, Generic_Parameter_List): inserts empty line.

Enumeration_Type (Type_Declaration): inserts template for an enumeration type declaration.

Expanded_Name (Name): inserts template for expanded name.

Extended_Type (Type_Expression): inserts template for an extended type.

Function (Declaration_List, Generic_Parameter_List): inserts template for a function.

Function_Type (Type_Expression): inserts template for a function type.

Generic_Package (Declaration_List, Program): inserts template for a generic package declaration.

Instantiation (Declaration_List, Program): inserts template for a generic instantiation.

Membership_Test (Expression): inserts template for a membership test.

Name (Type_Expression, Expression): inserts template for a name.

Package (Declaration_List, Program): inserts template for a package declaration.

Pragma (Declaration_List, Tree_Type_Declaration_List): inserts template for a pragma.

Predicate (Declaration_List, Generic_Parameter_List): inserts template for a predicate.

Private_Type (Declaration_List, Generic_Parameter_List): inserts template for a private type.

Pure_Record_Type (Type_Declaration): inserts template for a pure record type declaration.

Qualified (Expression): inserts template for a qualified expression.

Quantified (Expression): inserts template for a quantified expression.

Recursive_Variant_Type (Type_Declaration): inserts template for a recursive variant type declaration.

Selector_Argument (Type_Argument): inserts template for a type name and name for a selector function.

Subtype (Declaration_List, Tree_Type_Declaration): inserts template for a subtype declaration.

Tree_Type (Tree_Type_Declaration): inserts template for a tree type type declaration.

Tree_Type_Declarations (Type_Declaration): inserts template for a list of tree type type declaration.

Tuple (Expression): inserts template for a tuple expression.

Tuple_Type (Type_Expression): inserts template for a tuple type.

Type_Name (Type_Argument): inserts template for a type name.

Type_Scheme (Declaration_List, Program): inserts template for a type scheme.

Unary (Expression): inserts template for a unary expression.

Variant_Type (Type_Declaration): inserts template for a variant type declaration.

Component_List (Component_Part): inserts template for a list of record components.

Null_Component_List (Component_List): inserts the literal **null** (null record).

and, or, xor, <, <=, >, >=, &, *, /, mod, rem, **, abs (Name, Binary_Operator, Designator): inserts operator.

=, /= (Binary_Operator): inserts the corresponding equivalence operator.

+, - (Name, Unary_Operator, Binary_Operator): inserts the corresponding operator.

->, <-> (Binary_Operator): inserts the corresponding implicator.

--> (Function_Arrow): inserts symbol for a weak function arrow.

==> (Function_Arrow): inserts symbol for a strong function arrow.

4.1.B.2. Construct to Construct Transformations

-> **Auxiliary_Function** (Declaration_List, Generic_Parameter_List): transforms a function or predicate declaration into an auxiliary function declaration.

-> **Canonical_Representation** (Declaration_List, Program): provides the canonical representation in the visible part of a type definition scheme. It must be specified whether the canonical part shall include equality (EQ) functions or not.

-> **Component_List** (Component_Part): transforms a null record into a record with components.

-> **Designator** (Name): transforms an expanded name into a simple name by dropping the prefix.

-> **Domain** (Type_Expression): transforms a type expression into a domain with placeholders for the designator list and the restriction.

-> **Expended_Name** (Name): transforms a name into an expanded name with a placeholder for the prefix.

-> **Function** (Declaration_List, Generic_Parameter_List): transforms an auxiliary function or predicate declaration into a function declaration with the same domain.

-> **Generic_Package** (Declaration_List): transforms a generic package into a non-generic package. The generic formal parameters are added to the declarations of the package.

-> **Predicate** (Declaration_List, Generic_Parameter_List): transforms a (auxiliary) function declaration into a predicate declaration.

-> **Private_Type** (Declaration_List): transforms a subtype declaration into a private type declaration.

-> **Quantified** (Expression): transforms a tuple expression into a quantified expression with placeholders for the domain list.

-> **Subtype** (Declaration_List): transforms a private type declaration into a subtype declaration.

-> **Type_Expression** (Type_Expression): transforms a domain into a type expression by dropping the designator list and the restriction (if any).

-> **Type_Scheme** (Declaration_List, Program): removes the canonical representation (visible) of a type scheme.

-> **Tuple** (Expression): transforms a quantified expresion into a tuple expression keeping the expression list.

+ **With_Clause** (Program): adds a template for an empty with clause to a progam.

+ **Restriction** (Type_Expression): adds an empty restriction to a domain.

4.1.B.3. Transformations for Static Semantic Analysis

=> **Edit** (Declaration_List, Domain_List, Expression_List, Generic_Parameter_List): copies the content of the current selection into a parameter form where it can be edited. Static semantic analysis is performed in isolation from the rest of the program, without any propagation. The changes are commited by clicking the **Start** button of the parameter form, cancelled by clicking the **Cancel** button.

Static_Semantic_Analysis_On (Local_State): enables static semantic analysis of specifications.

Static_Semantic_Analysis_Off (Local_State): disables static semantic analysis of specifications.

Interpretation_Of (Name, Expression, Binary_Operator, Unary_Operator): determines the unique interpretation (if any) of a given construct, and places the result in the Help buffer.

Type_Of (Name, Expression, Binary_Operator, Unary_Operator): determines the type of a name, an expression or an operator and places the result in the Help buffer.

Possible_Interpretations_Of (Type_Expression, Name, Expression, Binary_Operator, Unary_Operator): determines the possible interpretations of a name or operator and places the result in the Help buffer.

Visible_Declarations_Of (Name): determines the visible declarations with the given designator and places the result in the Help buffer.

4.1.C. Error Message Summary

The error messages available in the editor are explained.

the name of a type is required [3.4] (Type_Expression): indicates that the name occuring in a type expression is not the name of a type or a subtype. *Example*: **subtype** st **is** standard;

name is not declared in the visible part of the package [4.1] (Name): indicates that the selector is not the simple name of an entity declared immediatly within the visible part of the package denoted by the prefix.

prefix does not denote the name of a package [4.1] (Name): indicates that the prefix of an expanded name does not denote a package. *Example*: "+".integer

selector is not declared in enclosing unit [4.1] (Name): indicates that the selector is not the simple name of an entity declared immediatly within the visible part of the enclosing package (denoted by the prefix) .

illegal context for a logical expression [4,5] (Expression): indicates that a logical expression is illegal in the current context. *Example*: **defined (true in** boolean)

expression of incompatible type [4,5] (Expression): indicates that the expression is of an incompatible type in the current context. *Example*: 1 **in** boolean;

arguments must have same base type [4,5] (Expression): indicates that the two arguments of a short circuit form or equality test do not have the same base type. *Example*: 1 = "1"

wrong context for others [5.0] (Expression): indicates that the literal **others** is only allowed as the condition of the last implication in a list of implications.*Example*: **axiom others** -> P(f), P(g);

an expression of type logical is expected [5] (Expression): indicates that the expression is not of the predefined logical type. *Example*: **axiom** 1;

no operator or function matches actual parameters [6.3] (Expression): indicates that none of the possible interpretations of the function part can be matched with any of the possible interpretations of the actual part.

Example: standard."**not**"(1)

name is not yet useable [8.3] (Name): indicates that the name of an entity has been used illegally within its own declaration. *Example*: **subtype** integer **is** integer;

ambigious name of enclosing unit [8.3] (Name): indicates that the prefix of an expanded name is ambigous (several possible interpretations have been found using the overloading rules).

no interpretations found [8.3] (Name): indicates that no declaration with the given name is visible in the current context.

illegal homograph [8.3] (Declaration): indicates that two declarative items occuring immediatly within the same declarativepart are homographs.*Example*: **axiom for all** x,x: integer => x = x;

ambigous expression [8.4] (Expression): indicates that several possible interpretations of an expression have been found using the overloading rules.

ambigous name [8.4] (Name): indicates that several possible interpretations of a name have been found using the overloading rules.

the name of a library unit is required [9.1] (With_Clause): indicates that no dependency to a version of the given family has been specified using the configuration manager (see the command **Add_Dependency** of the configuration manager).
Example: **with** stck; **package** integer_stack **is new** stack(integer);

too few generic actual parameters [10.2] (Expresion_List): indicates that too few generic actual parameters have been provided in an instantiation.*Example*: **package** my_stack **is new** stack;

too many generic actual parameters [10.2] (Expression_List): indicates that too many generic actual parameters have been provided for an instantiation. *Example*: **package** my_stack **is new** stack(integer,integer);

the name of a generic package is required [10.2] (Declaration): indicates that the name of a generic instantiation does not denote a generic package. *Example*: **package** my_standard **is new** standard;

no function matches formal parameter [10.2] (Expression_List): indicates that the actual function in a generic instantiation does not have the same profile as the corresponding formal function.

ambigous matching function [10.2] (Expression_List): indicates that more than one actual generic parameter matches the corresponding generic formal function.

4.1.D. Keyboard Definitions

The editor is accompanied by a keyboard definition with the most commonly used commands for the sun terminal type:

F1 – F5:

caps	text capture	delete selection	cut to clipped	copy from clipped
		delete next character	copy to clipped	copy text from clipped

F6 – F10:

	write current file	read file	read unit	**back space**
	write named file	insert file	write unit	

R1 – R15:

gold	undo	repeat command
		execute command
switch buffer	list buffer	split window
new buffer		delete window
search forward	backward sibling	
search reverse	... with optionals	
backward preorder	ascend to parent	forward preorder
... with optionals	selection to top	... with optionals
alternate unparsing on	forward sibling	alternative unparsing toggle
alternate unparsing off	... with optionals	

4.2. PA^{nn}dA Transformer Shell

Einar W. Karlsen[1], *Computer Resources International*

4.2.1. Introduction

The PROSPECTRA methodology integrates program construction and verification during the development process of software systems. The development process starts with the formalization of a requirement specification in the specification language PA^{nn}dA–S (see part II, chapter 2), using the PA^{nn}dA–S editor (se part III, chapter 2) described in the last section. The requirement specification is then gradually transformed into an optimized executable Ada program by stepwise application of correctness-preserving transformation rules. These transformations are carried out by the *PA^{nn}dA transformer shell* with interactive guidance by the implementor.

The PA^{nn}dA transformer shell is a language based tool for the widespectrum language PA^{nn}dA (see part II, chapter 4). It is not an editor in the traditional sense since it does not support editing of PA^{nn}dA program phrases, rather it is a tool that presents the program being developed to the user and provides the user interface for developing PA^{nn}dA programs.

The PA^{nn}dA transformer is a *shell* in the sense that only a few transformations are predefined. These built-in transformations control the overall behavior of the PA^{nn}dA transformer. "Proper" transformations for developing and refining PA^{nn}dA programs are to be developed using the PROSPECTRA system. These transformations are presented to the user in a transformation menu. The user may then invoke one of the enabled transformations from the menu upon which the program is transformed.

Transformations are *context-sensitive* in general, i.e. they are applicable only if an *application condition* is satisfied. Applicability conditions ensure that the application of the transformations preserves correctness. These conditions are defined in terms of predicates and retrieval functions on the context of the place where the transformation is applied. Context information is provided in the PA^{nn}dA transformer by various built-in *attributes*. Some of these attributes have been built in for the static semantic analysis of PA^{nn}dA programs, e.g. attributes for the *type* of expressions, *binding* and *scope* of names. Further attributes have been provided for reasoning about the *semantics* of specifications, e.g. the properties of functions in terms of their defining axioms.

The built-in attributes for static semantic analysis are used by the PA^{nn}dA unparser (prettyprinter) which performs visibility and scope analysis of names. On the basis of this analysis, an unambiguous unparsing of the program is provided, by automatic insertion of expanded names and qualified expression into the prettyprinted text when needed. Transformation rules are therefore relieved from taking into account most of the complex scope and visibility rules of Ada.

Transformations may also require information from the user at application time. A parameter editor has been built into the PA^{nn}dA transformer so that the user can provide such parameters.

A survey of the PA^{nn}dA transformer, its architecture and basic facilities are given in section 4.2.2.-4.2.8. The appendices contains a command summary in (4.2.A), a syntax summary for constructs accepted by the parameter editor (4.2.B), a definition of the abstract syntax of programs (4.2.C), a brief introduction to the static semantic attributes (4.2.D) and a description of the attributes needed for e.g. proof (4.2.E).

---

1. *Author's current address*: FB 3 - Informatik, Universität Bremen, Postfach 330 440, D-2800 Bremen 33

Implementation

The transformer shell has been generated using the *Cornell Synthesizer Generator* (*CSG* for short) running revision 3.2 of Unix BSD 4.2. for SunView and X-Windows (release 10.4). All tools generated by CSG share a common, language-independent user interface and a set of language-independent features which are extended with language-specific commands and features. The reader is referred to the Synthesizer Generator Manual [Teitelbaum & Reps 1988] for a detailed description of the interface, or to the introduction given as part of the chapter on the PA^{nn}dA-S Editor (part II, section 4.1). Familiarity with that chapter is assumed in the rest of this chapter.

The status of the tool is that of a first version prototype. Care should therefore be taken in its use.

4.2.2. Basic Architecture

The main tool concerned with program development by transformation is the transformer shell. The *proof system* (see part III, section 4.4), for proving e.g. the correctness of certain transformations, and the *CEC system* (see part III, section 4.3), for rewriting and completion, is closely integrated with the transformer shell. Control is a decentralized activity where the tools interact in a "call and return" relationship. The *controller* (see part III, chapter 3) is therefore considered as a set of commands more or less equally integrated within each tool. Interaction with the library for retrieving program components and transformation rules is done using the *LibLa Editor* (see part III, section 3.2) which serves as an interface to the underlying *library manager* (see part III, section 3.2). Objects, whether they are programs or transformation rules, reside in this object repository.

There are three related PA^{nn}dA languages:

- *PA^{nn}dA–S* (S for *specification*) is the *applicative kernel specification language* in which requirement specifications are formulated.
- PA^{nn}dA–C (C for *canonical*) is the *imperative wide-spectrum language* containing a normalized form of PA^{nn}dA–S and Ada as a subset.
- *PA^{nn}dA–E* (E for *extended* or *executable* as preferred) is an *executable subset* of Ada and incorporates all parts of Ada that we anticipate to be able to (and want to) generate at the end of the development.

Editing of PA^{nn}dA-S specifications takes place using the PA^{nn}dA-S editor. Implementations are created by applying correctness preserving transformation using the PA^{nn}dA transformer shell. The *PA^{nn}dA-S to PA^{nn}dA-C transformation* is used initially to bring PA^{nn}dA-S requirement specifications into a canonical form that can be accepted by the transformer shell. The *PA^{nn}dA-C* to *PA^{nn}dA-E transformation* is used finally to bring PA^{nn}dA-C programs into a form that is executable Ada. During transformation of a program, the *parameter editor* is used to enter transformation parameters. This editor in turn interfaces to the PA^{nn}dA-S editor when parameters are edited, or to the transformer shell, for parameters that are transformed.

The architecture of the transformer shell, and its integration with e.g. the PA^{nn}dA-S editor and the proof system reflects the PROSPECTRA methodology that integrates program construction and verification. The development process starts with the formalization of a requirement specification in the specification language PA^{nn}dA–S using the PA^{nn}dA–S editor. Design specifications, as well as applicative and imperative implementations are developed by stepwise application of correctness-preserving transformation rules at the level of the widespectrum language PA^{nn}dA. This further development towards executable code is performed using the transformer shell.

There is a fundamental distinction between the editor and the transformer shell. The editor is used for *revising* specifications. In general, editing operations do not preserve the semantics of a specification and the editor therefore performs interactive and immediate static semantic analysis of programs in order to report on the violation of the static semantic rules. In contrast, the transformer shell is used for *refining* PA^{nn}dA programs, covering the full spectrum of PA^{nn}dA–C. All operations at the level of the transformer shell are deemed to be correctness-preserving transformations. Thus no form of editing is allowed in this tool.

What distinguishes editors generated by CSG from conventional text editors is that each buffer contains an abstract syntax tree representing the program. Essentially, an abstract syntax records the structure of a specification without the syntactic marks like reserved words, delimiters etc. which are required for parsing and prettyprinting. Unparsing displays the abstract syntax tree as a text in a window on the screen. Externally, to the user, a program is represented as a text while its internal representation is an abstract syntax tree. The program is modified by changing subtrees of the underlying abstract syntax tree. The unparsing is then updated accordingly.

The transformer shell provides the following main functionalities:

- a user interface for controlling the tool and invoking transformations,
- an unparser that provides the external representation on the screen as text,
- a static and dynamic analyser featuring attributes needed for e.g. type checking and proof,
- a parameter editor for support of parametrized transformations.

These features will be described in more detail in the following sections.

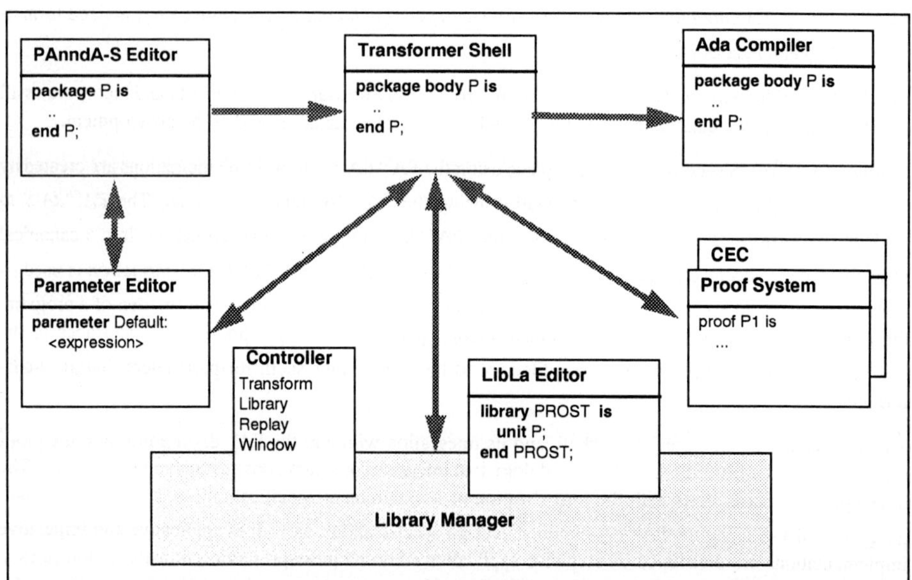

Figure 4.2.1: The Transformer Shell and its Interfaces.

4.2.3. Invoking the Transformer Shell

The transformer shell is invoked from the LibLa editor which provides views to the underlying library of specifications and programs in terms of version trees. Each version tree represents a requirement specification together with its refinements and revisions.

There is an initial, one pass transformation called **--> PAnndA**, that converts a requirement specification developed by the editor into a form accepted by the transformer shell. To invoke this command, the user have to select the version tree denoting a checked and validated PA^{nn}dA-S specification. The effect of the command will be to create an initial refinement.

Further development of the initial refinement is then performed by invoking the command **New_Refinement** which starts up the transformer shell. The buffer of the transformer shell will contain the program version to be refined. The development may finally be committed by invoking the command **Confirm_Development** or cancelled by invoking the command **Cancel_Development.** The LibLa editor provides a third command, called **Display**, that invokes the transformer shell as a browser of PA^{nn}dA programs.

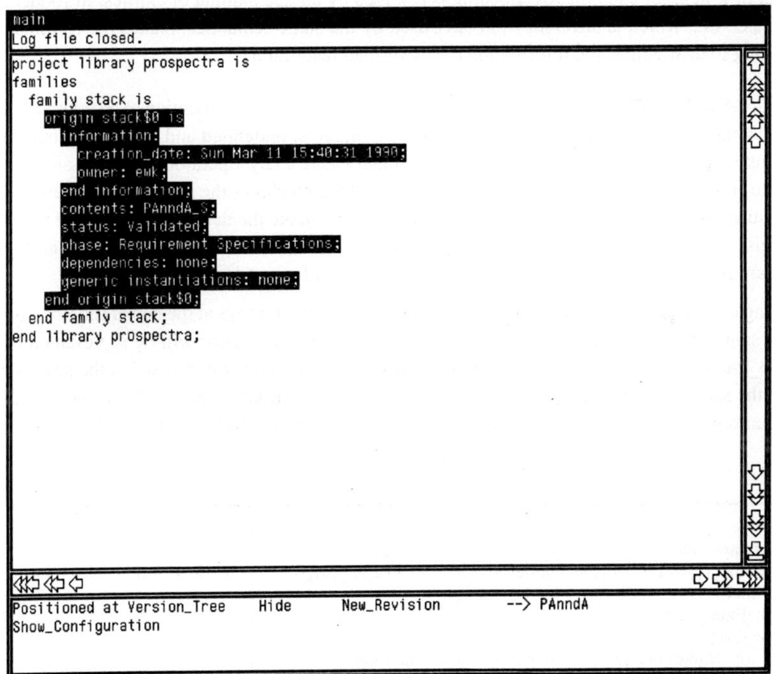

Figure 4.2.2: Invoking the Transformer Shell

The command **-> PAnndA** is enabled by the Libla editor when positioned at the version tree for a validated requirement specification. The command creates an initial refinement for the transformer shell by calling the PA^{nn}dA–S to PA^{nn}dA–C transformation.

4.2.4. PA^{nn}dA-S to PA^{nn}dA-C Transformation

As mentioned earlier, each program is represented as an abstract syntax tree that records the structure of the program without the syntactic tokens like reserved words, delimiters etc. which are required for parsing and prettyprinting. Given the fundamental difference between *revision* of programs with the PA^{nn}dA–S editor, and *refinement* of programs with the transformer shell, two different internal representations have been defined. An abstract syntax has been defined for the PA^{nn}dA–S editor which is appropriate for the structural editing of requirement specifications and for performing static semantic analysis of PA^{nn}dA–S specifications using CSG generated editors. Conversely, an abstract syntax has been defined for the transformer shell which is appropriate for program development by applying correctness preserving transformations (see appendix 4.2.A for the definition). The translation from the representation of the editor to the representation of the transformer shell is done by invoking the command **-> PAnndA** mentioned in the previous section. This solution has been inspired from the VDM methodology, where the static semantics of some language is defined on the basis of some abstract syntax called AS1 whereas the dynamic semantics is defined on the basis of an abstract syntax called AS2. The AS2 form of a program is obtained from its AS1 form used in the static semantics by means of an AS1 –> AS2 transformation. This transformation, and hence the AS2, is only defined for correct programs. Since the dynamic semantics deals with legal programs on which the static semantics analysis has been performed, it can benefit from this knowledge by letting the AS2 conform to a syntax in which, for example, overloading is resolved by unique naming of entities. Introducing an abstract syntax, AS2, which is different from AS1 used by the static semantics, makes the formulas simpler by not having to deal with static information (e.g. overload resolution)

The PA^{nn}dA–S to PA^{nn}dA–C transformation assumes the PA^{nn}dA–S specification to be complete, and correct w.r.t. syntax and static semantics. Literals (strings, integers, **undefined** and **others**) are translated into applications of parameterless functions. Similarly, binary and unary operators in expressions are transformed into (prefix) function applications (see figure 4.2.3 which shows the internal and external representation of a declaration and one of its applied occurrences). To make the description of transformation rules more concise, expanded names are replaced by unique simple names resolving overloading, and type qualifications are removed from expressions since they are needed for overload resolution only.

Overloading of names is resolved by inserting unique symbols called *keys* at the declaration of a designator x, and the same *unique key* at all applied occurrences of x. Any designator will be represented by a tuple Mk_Unique_Name(id, key) where first component is the designator which will be used in the unparsing of the name and the second component is the key, uniquely identifying the entity within the program.This simplified internal representation of names is projected onto the screen in a form where overloaded entities may

<table>
<tr>
<td><pre>mk_Object(
   mk_Unique_Name("zero", kzero),
   mk_Name_Type(mk_Unique_Name("integer",mk_Integer_Key)),
   mk_Func(
      mk_Expr_List(
      mk_Call(
         mk_Name(mk_Unique_Name("=",mk_Equal_Key),
         mk_Tuple(
            mk_Expr_List(mk_Name(mk_Unique_Name("zero", kz)),
            mk_Expr_List(mk_Name(mk_Unique_Name("0", kzlit)),
            empty_Expr_List))
      ))))</pre></td>
<td>zero : integer :: zero = 0;</td>
</tr>
</table>

Figure 4.2.3: Internal and External Representation of Program Phrases

occur. The problem to provide an unambiguous unparsing of the program is solved by automatic insertion of expanded names and qualified expressions into the text whenever needed. The built-in static semantic attributes, which models e.g. the scope and visibility rules of the language, is used by the transformer shell for this purpose. The unparsing will be described in more detail in section 4.2.7.

4.2.5. Invoking Transformations

The transformer shell provides the user interface for the transformation of PA^{nn}dA programs. It presents the program being transformed to the user, as well as the set of transformations applicable in a given context. The user may invoke one of the enabled transformations upon which the program is transformed.

The transformer shell is a shell in the sense that only a few transformations are predefined. These *built-in commands*, like **Type_Of** that determines the type of an expression, control the overall behavior of the tool. Similar commands have been provided to interface other tools of the system, like the command **==> Proof_-System** that calls the proof system. *Proper transformations*, like **substitute** and **curry**, for developing and refining PA^{nn}dA programs are to be developed using the TrafoLa editor (see section 5.1 of part III), translated into the target language of CSG for transformations (see section 5.2 of part III), and included to generate a new version of the transformer shell.

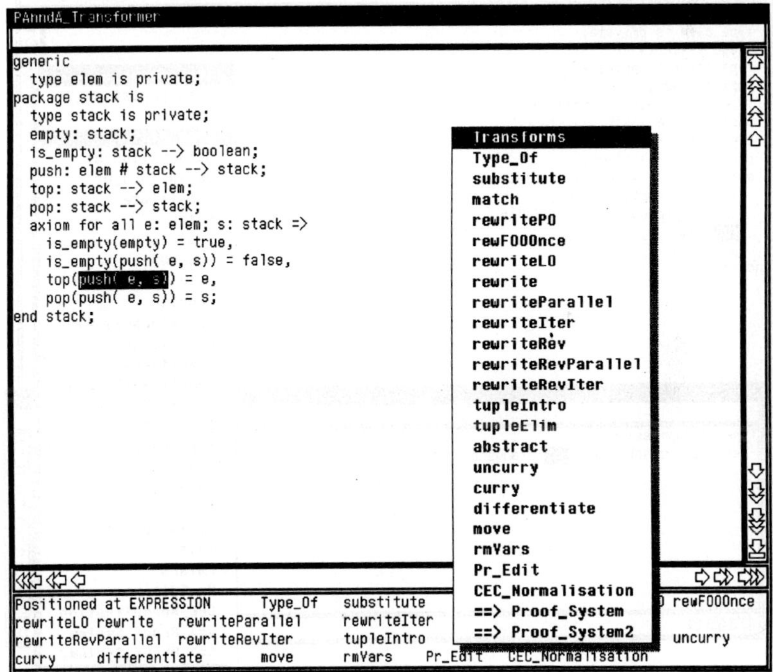

Figure 4.2.4: The PA^{nn}dA Transformer

The figure shows the requirement specification of a package stack. The transformations enabled at the current selection are shown in the transformation command menu as well as in the help pane.

4.2.6. Context Sensitive Analysis of Programs

To carry out program transformations, certain preconditions must generally be fulfilled. These conditions ensure that the application of the transformation preserves some relation mainly with respect to'correctness' (e.g. equivalence). The correctness preserving transformations carried out by the transformer shell are generally *context-sensitive*, i.e. they are applicable only if certain *applicability condition* s are satisfied - conditions like for example *"F is associative"*, *"the variable V does not occur in the Expression E"*, or *"the fragment F is side-effect-free"*. Applicability conditions can be defined in terms of predicates and retrieval functions on the *context* provided in form of various built-in *attributes*. Some of these attributes have been built into the transformer shell for the static semantic analysis of PA^{nn}dA programs, e.g. attributes for the *type* of expressions, *binding* and *scope* of names etc. Further attributes have been provided for reasoning about the *semantics* of specifications, e.g. the properties of functions in terms of their defining axioms.

The context information is provided by means of various attributes implemented in SSL - the specification language of CSG. The underlying attribute grammar for static semantic analysis is briefly explained in appendix 4.2.D, whereas attributes needed for transformation and proof are described in appendix 4.2.E.

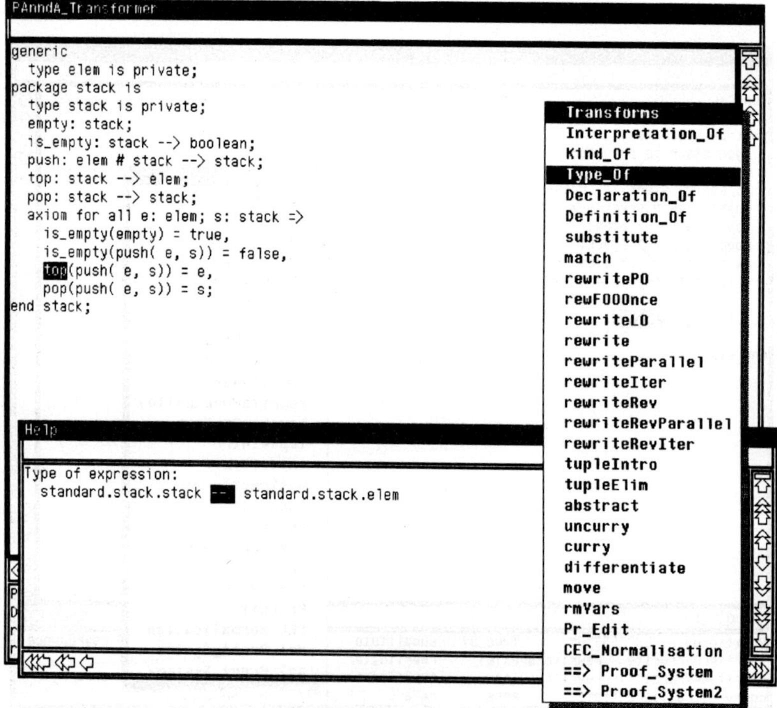

Figure 4.2.5: Static Semantic Attributes

The transformer shell is accompanied with a few commands that shows the interpretation and type of expressions and names. These commands have been implemented on top of the static semantic attributes used for analysis of programs.

The transformer shell is accompanied with a few commands that can be used by a developer in analyzing the meaning of names and expressions. For example, the command **Interpretation_Of** determines the unique interpretation of a name. The result of this command will be put into the buffer named Help. To open this buffer invoke the system commands **split-current-window** and **switch-to-buffer**("Help"). A similar command called **Kind_Of** determines the kind of entity denoted by a name. Likewise, the command **Type_Of** determines the type of a type expression, name or an expression.

Syntactic conditions will be checked automatically by the transformer shell when applying a transformation. The check of semantic conditions will require a proof in general. Thus the application of transformation rules involving semantic applicability conditions will lead to the generation of *proof obligations* as a side effect. As programs are developed, these proof obligations will be collected as the result of applying transformations. Attributes providing the basis for reasoning about the semantics of specifications have been built into the transformer shell, as described in chapter 4 of part II.The commands **Declaration_Of** and **Definition_Of** accesses context information that has been built into the transformer shell for transformation and proof. They retrieve the declaration of an entity and the definition of a given function, respectively.

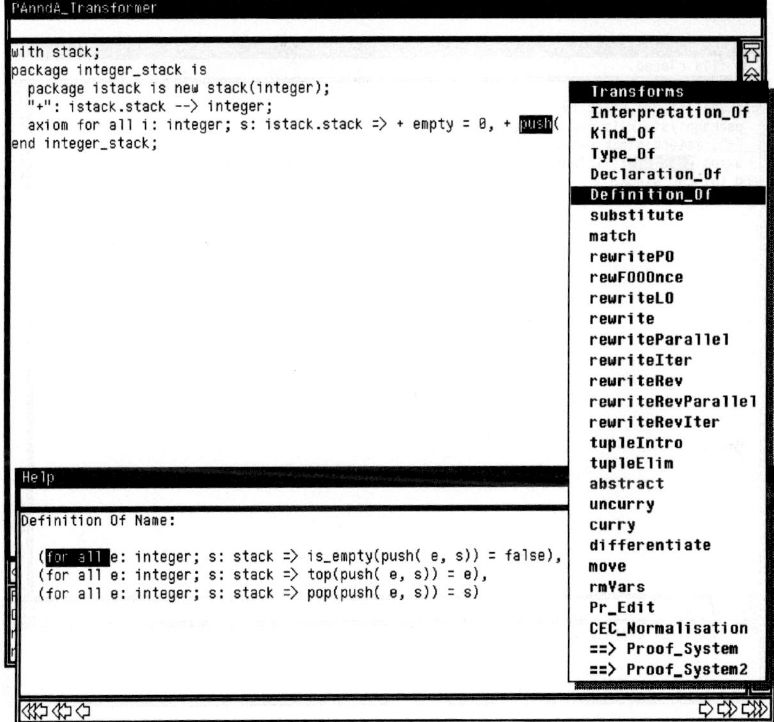

Figure 4.2.6: Semantics of Functions

The command called **Definition_Of** retrieves all relevant axioms giving the semantics of a given function. The axioms are placed in the Help buffer. This command has been implemented on top of the attributes holding information about the semantics of entities.

4.2.7. Unparsing of PA^{nn}dA Programs

One task of the transformer shell is to provide the projection from the extremely simplified and normalized internal representation of programs as abstract syntax trees onto the screen in an appropriate readable form as text. Every time the user invokes a transformation, and hence changes the program, a static semantic analyses is performed by the transformer shell to determine the new unparsing of the program. The context dependent unparsing of PA^{nn}dA programs is determined on the basis of static semantic attributes which is also used to carry out transformations. Unparsing of PA^{nn}dA programs may therefore be rather time consuming and the transformer shell consequently supports two modes of operation: disabled and enabled context dependent unparsing. The tool works considerably faster in the first mode.

The transformer shell is equipped with two commands that allows the user to toggle between context free and context sensitive unparsing: the command **Context_Dependent_Unparsing_On** enables context dependent unparsing of programs, whereas **Context_Dependent_Unparsing_Off** disables it. Both commands are enabled when positioned at the root of the buffer (Local_State).

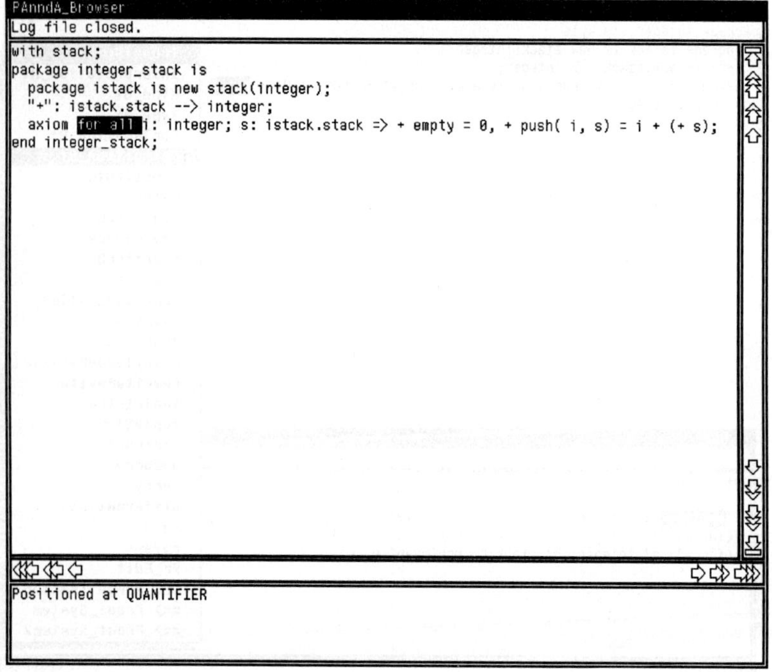

Figure 4.2.7: Enabled Context Dependent Unparsing

The command **Context_Dependent_Unparsing_On** enables context dependent unparsing of names and expressions. Expanded names (and qualified expressions if needed) will therefore appear in the unparsing of the program.

The unparsing of PA^{nn}dA programs involves the following subtasks:

- unambiguous unparsing of the program by automatic insertion of expanded names and qualified expressions.
- automatic unparsing of function calls as infix expressions whenever possible.
- automatic insertion of parenthesis in expressions whenever needed.
- automatic insertion of parenthesis in type expressions whenever needed.
- automatic insertion of linebreaks and tabs whenever needed for the appropriate unparsing of fragments.

The algorithm for disambiguating names and expressions in the presence of overloaded entities is based on the static semantic rules of Ada, basically the scope and visibility rules, and makes extensive use of context information (see appendix 4.2.D).

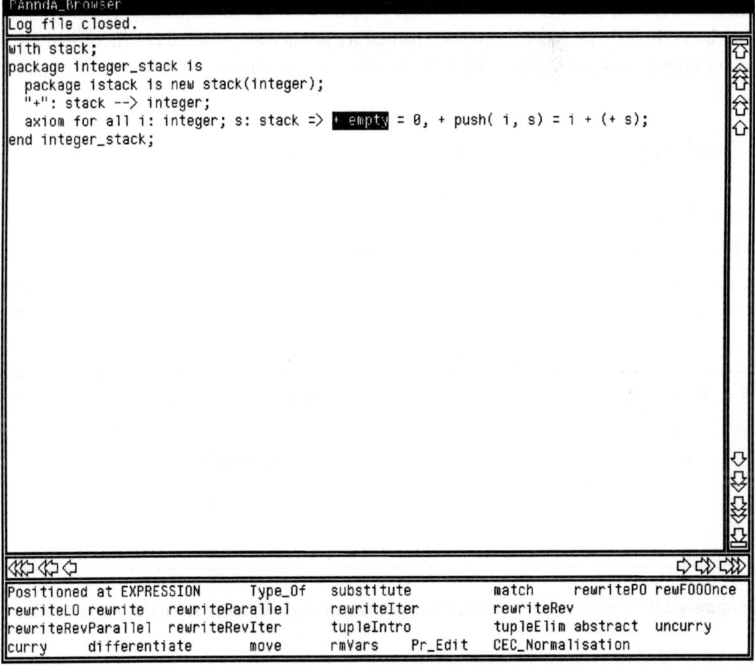

Figure 4.2.8: Disabled Context Dependent Unparsing

The command **Context_Dependent_Unparsing_Off** disables context dependent unparsing of names and expressions. Neither expanded names, nor qualified expressions will therefore appear in the unparsing of the program text. Consequently, the program may look as if it is ambiguous or illegal.

4.2.7.1. Unparsing of Templates

The projection from abstract syntax trees onto readable text is defined by *templates* - typographical, predefined units where the syntactical marks like keywords and delimiters are provided automatically. Indentation of a program fragments is also automatic, both when a template is introduced and when it is modified. Formatting is performed interactively, and the screen always shows the final layout (What You See Is What You Get).

When the transformer shell is set in word-wrapping mode, the display is forced into a column of text no wider than the window. The transformer shell breaks lines that are too long to fit in the window, and formats the text nicely in most cases. However, the transformer shell does not work perfectly in all circumstances, mainly because CSG offers only a limited formatting functionality.

4.2.7.2. Unparsing of Function Calls

The infix and prefix notation of function calls are syntactically equivalent. To relieve the transformer developers from the tedious task of specifying the same transformation rule for syntactic equivalents, the transformation from PA^{nn}dA–S to PA^{nn}dA–C normalizes the representation by choosing the prefix notation as the only and canonical representation. At the level of the concrete syntax, however, the PA^{nn}dA transformer will shift between the infix notation as binary expressions on one hand, and the function call notation on the other hand. In the case where expanded names are not needed to solve conflicts, and the designator is an unary or binary operator symbol, the infix notation will be chosen since it is more readable (see e.g. figure 4.2.8).

4.2.7.3. Unparsing of Expressions and Type Expressions

The transformer shell automatically inserts parentheses for expressions when needed. Figure 4.2.9 shows two different abstract syntax trees together with their canonical unparsing.The unparsed text properly reflects the PA^{nn}dA semantics of the underlying abstract syntax tree.

A similar flattening of the abstract syntax, in combination with automatic unparsing of parenthesis on the basis of precedence rules, has been adopted for the representation of type expressions.

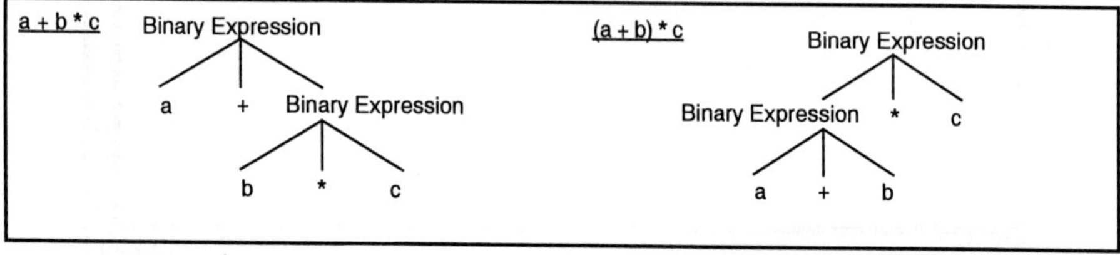

Figure 4.2.9: Internal and External Representation of Expressionstransformations are

4.2.7.4. Unparsing of Overloaded Entities

The simplified internal representation of names (as being unique) is projected onto the screen in a form where overloaded entities may occur. The problem to provide an unambiguous unparsing of the program is solved by automatic insertion of expanded names and qualified expressions into the text whenever needed. The built-in static semantic attributes, which models e.g. the scope and visibility rules of the language, is used by the transformer shell for this purpose.

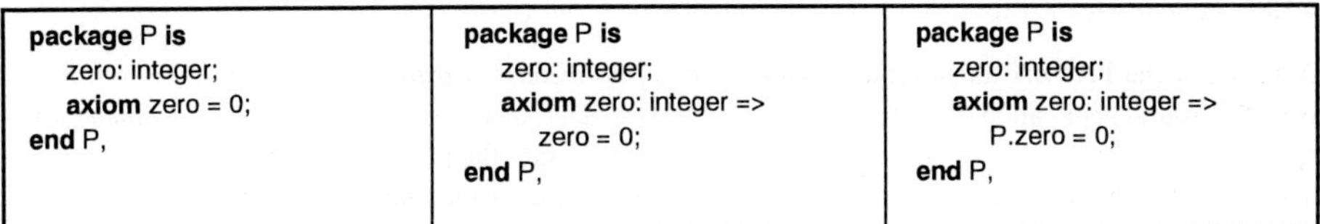

Figure 4.2.10: Context Dependent Unparsing of Programs

To show the implications of the approach, consider the simple example in Figure 4.2.10. The first package is the starting point. A specific class of transformations may introduce new declarations needed in the refinement process. Suppose, that a quantified variable zero was introduced at the beginning of the axiom. If the unparsing of the equation had been kept as in the second package P, the meaning of the specification would change since the equation would refer to the quantified variable and not the function P.zero. However, since all names have a unique representation at the level of the abstract syntax, the transformer shell knows what entities are really denoted. On the basis of this knowledge, and by using the context information modelling the PA^{nn}dA visibility and scope rules, the transformer shell will be able to determine that expanded names are needed to solve the conflict. The program is therefore correctly unparsed as shown in the third package P of Figure 4.2.10.

The main attribute needed for the context dependent unparsing is the *static semantic environment* (env) - a *symbol table* that is synthesized at the level of the declarations and inherited to e.g. expressions and names. This attribute contain sufficient information to model the scope and visibility rules. Synthesized attributes like type_of, that holds the type of the name, and prefix, that holds the prefix needed for unparsing expanded names, can be derived from the environment. This derivation is defined in terms of auxiliary functions like Type_Of, Hidden and Expand that needs the context Name.env and the key component.

The current approach to representing and unparsing PA^{nn}dA programs has the unquestionable advantage that transformations do not have to consider the complex visibility rules of the PA^{nn}dA language - such mundane issues are handled automatically by the transformer shell. Neither will the transformation rules have to consider syntactic issues such as unparsing expressions in infix style, providing parenthesis for type expressions and expressions etc.

attribute name	**kind**	**type**	**corresponding function**
env	inherited	ENV	
type_of	synthesized	TYPE	Type_Of: KEY -> ENV -> TYPE;
prefix	synthesized	NAME_LIST	Hidden,Unique_Intrp : KEY -> ENV -> BOOLEAN; Expand: KEY -> ENV -> NAME_LIST;

attribute equations

```
Name.type_of = Type_Of(Name.key, Name.env);

Name.prefix =
    if Hidden(Name.key, Name.env) or not Unique_Intrpr(Name.key, Name.env) then
            Expand(Name.key, Name.env)
    else
            Empty_Name_List
```

Figure 4.2.11: Attributes for Static Semantic Analysis and Unparsing

4.2.8. Parameter Editor

A subset of the PA^{nn}dA transformation rules, called *parameterized transformations*, require information from the user at application time. When such a parameterized transformation is invoked, a *parameter editor* appears and becomes the current editor. The user may then enter the parameter, and continue the transformation by clicking the **Start** button, or cancel the transformation by clicking the **Cancel** button.

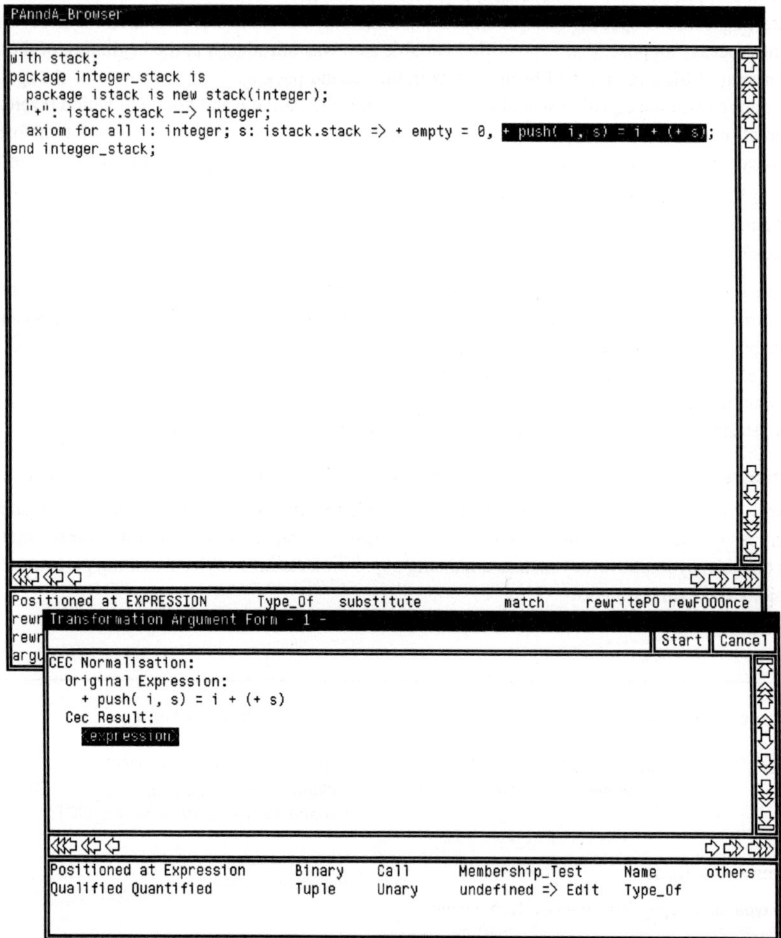

Figure 4.2.12: The Parameter Editor

The parametrized transformation **CEC_Normalisation** has been invoked on the selected input fragment. The result of the transformation is another parameter titled "CEC Result".

The parameter editor accepts either a *single parameter*, or a *parameter sequence* consisting of two or more parameters. Each single parameter is accompanied with an explanatory and informative text which serves as a prompt. Immediately after the explanatory text follows the fragment, which is to be provided by the user.

The structure of the parameter is specified when defining the transformation rule. This means that the following properties are fixed at application time: the number of parameters, the explanatory text, the syntactic category of the fragment and the initial value of the fragment (if any).

Fragments occur in two different forms, either according to the abstract syntax of the PA^{nn}dA–S editor or according to the abstract syntax of the transformer shell. Fragments on the form of the PA^{nn}dA–S editor must be provided by textual or structural editing. During editing, the parameter editor performs static semantic analysis of each fragment to report on violation of context conditions. Fragments on the form of the transformer shell must be provided by using a copy mechanism following the cut/copy/paste paradigm, in which a suitable fragment is copied from the program text prober, stored in the parameter stack, and pasted into the parameter editor. System commands under the menu item Parameter_Stack have been provided for that purpose. It should be noted that fragments on the form of the transformer shell may be further developed using transformations.

Whether fragments are to be edited or copied can be determined by the name of the fragment. The help pane of the parameter editor contains an indication of the current syntactic category. The syntactic category name of a fragment to be edited starts with an upper case letter followed by lower case letters (e.g. Expression), in contrast to the syntactic category name of a fragment to be copied which is given in upper case letters solely (EXPRESSION).

The parameter editor is accompanied with two commands that allows a user to switch between editing of parameters, and transformational development of parameters. The command **-> Edit** converts a parameter such that it has to be developed by editing. The command **-> Transform** converts a parameter such that it has to be developed by transformation.

Appendices

4.2.A. Command Summary

The transformer shell is equipped with the following built in commands:

Context_Dependent_Unparsing_On (Local_State) enables context dependent unparsing of programs

Context_Dependent_Unparsing_Off (Local_State) disables context dependent unparsing of programs

Interpretation_Of (TYPE_EXPRESSION, UNIQUE_NAME, EXPRESSION) determines the unique interpretation of a name and places the result in the Help buffer.

Kind_Of (TYPE_EXPRESSION, UNIQUE_NAME, EXPRESSION) determines the kind of entity denoted by a name and places the result in the Help buffer.

Type_Of (TYPE_EXPRESSION, UNIQUE_NAME, EXPRESSION) determines the type of a type expression, name or an expression and places the result in the Help buffer.

Declaration_Of (TYPE_EXPRESSION, UNIQUE_NAME, EXPRESSION) retrieves the declaration of an entity, and places the result in the Help buffer.

Definition_Of (EXPRESSION) determines the definition of a given function, and places the result in the Help buffer.

-> Edit (Parameter) converts a parameter such that it has to be developed by editing

-> Transform (Parameter) converts a parameter such that it has to be developed by transformation.

4.2.B. Syntax of Parameters

Transformation parameters must be in accordance with the following BNF definition:

```
transformation_parameter :=
      single_parameter  |parameter_sequence

single_parameter ::=
      prompt  fragment

parameter_sequence ::=
      prompt single_parameter {single_parameter}

promptt ::=
      {graphic_character}

fragment ::=
      identifier                    |    designator
    | numeric_literal               |    string_literal
    |  declaration                  |    declaration {declaration}
    | type_expression               |    domain
    | domain {; domain}             |    name
    | expression                    |    expression {, expression}
    | logical_expression            |    implication {, implication}
    | with_clause                   |    generic_parameter
    | generic_parameter {generic_parameter}
```

4.2.C. Abstract Syntax

The abstract syntax is the basic data structure on which transformation rules are formulated: all transformation rules can be viewed as partial functions from one syntactic category to a term of the same syntactic category. The abstract syntax also defines the way in which programs are stored by the PA^{nn}dA transformer shell. The major goal behind the design of the current abstract syntax was therefore to simplify the formulation of the transformation rules as much as possible, and secondary to simplify the functionality of the PA^{nn}dA transformer shell.

The abstract syntax definition has been generated using a so-called type scheme for defining tree types (see section 4.1 of part III). This scheme takes as input the definition of the abstract syntax of the language, and generates the equivalent term algebra. This term algebra then forms the basis for specifying transformations over language terms. The user specifies types, constructor functions, selector functions, subtypes and pragmas in the private part of the package. The corresponding term algebra is generated in the visible part of the package.

An almost complete definition of the abstract syntax of PA^{nn}dA is given in appendix 4.2.C.2. The structure of the definition is briefly sketched in Figure 4.2.13. The package pannda is defined in terms of the package basic_types which, as the name indicates, contain definition of basic types like strings and designators needed for the definition of the abstract syntax. The package basic_types defines in a sense the lexemes needed for the definition of the abstract syntax. The abstract syntax itself is defined in the private part of the package pannda. The equivalent term algebra, in terms of basic types, subtypes and constructors, is presented in the visible part of the package pannda.

with basic_types;
package PANNDA **is**
  type declarations
  subtype declarations
  constructor declarations
private
  abstract syntax definition
end PANNDA;
	package basic_types **is**
	  type STR
	  type INT
	  type BOOL
	  type DESIGNATOR
	  type KEY
	  type NATURE
	end basic_types;

Figure 4.2.13: Structure of the Abstract Syntax Definition

4.2.C.1. Design of the Abstract Syntax

When defining an abstract syntax, one can follow some general principles that address the scope for which such an abstract syntax is defined. A major principle behind the design of the abstract syntax is that it should be as simple, flat and *compact* as possible. This is very beneficial for the transformation rules since there is a simple relationship between the complexity of the abstract syntax and the complexity of transformation rules for the same language. A second major principle behind the design is that there should be a natural and simple correspondence between the concrete syntax and the abstract syntax. The types and the constructors of the abstract syntax must therefore have intuitive and meaningful names that relates to corresponding concepts of the concrete syntax.

These two principles are to some sense contradicting and we have therefore described the main deviations between the abstract and concrete syntax in the following subsections. These subsections also presents a discussion on the techniques that have been applied in order to achieve the design goals.

Removing Intermediate Levels

The abstract syntax has been designed such that there are as few intermediate levels as possible. Intermediate syntactic categories are not represented in the abstract syntax if the syntactic category occurs in a single context only, or if it for other reasons makes sense to avoid an extra, and hence superfluous, level of abstract syntax (see Figure 4.2.14).

Concrete syntax	Abstract syntax

package_declaration ::= package_specification;
 	
package_specification ::=
    package identifier **is**
        {basic_declarative_item}
    [**private**
        *private*_context_clause
        {basic_declarative_item}]
    end [*package*_identifier]
	Mk_Package:
	    IDENTIFIER #
	    DECLARATION_LIST #
	    WITH_CLAUSE #
	    DECLARATION_LIST --> DECLARATION;

Figure 4.2.14: Concrete and Abstract Syntax of Package Declarations

Ignoring Syntactic Aspects

The abstract syntax has been simplified by ignoring purely syntactic aspects. For e.g. package specifications a simple name may appear after the reserved word **end**. It is then required that this simple name repeat the package identifier. Such syntactic constructs only affects the legality of the program, and are therefore ignored in the definition of the abstract syntax (see Figure 4.2.14).

Moving Things Around

An attempt has been made to let the abstract syntax reflect the underlying semantics in a better way than the concrete syntax in order to simplify the formulation of transformation rules.

A package body, task body or subprogram body consists for example of the same components: a unique identification of the entity, a sequence of declarations, a sequence of statements and a sequence of exception handlers. This uniformity has been reflected in the abstract syntax by having all kind of bodies represented by a single constructor Mk_Body. The abstract syntax type BODY_KIND then serves as a discriminator between the different kind of bodies (see Figure 4.2.15). The type expression of a function or procedure body kind defines the parameter and result type profile of the subprogram.

Concrete syntax	Abstract syntax

package_body ::=
    package body *package*_identifier **is**
        [declarative_part]
    [**begin**
        sequence_of_statements
    [**exception**
        exception_handler
        {exception_handler}]]
    end [*package*_identifier];
	Mk_Body:
	    DESIGNATOR #
	    BODY_KIND #
	    DECLARATION_LIST #
	    STATEMENT_LIST #
	    HANDLER_LIST --> DECLARATION;
	
	Mk_Package_Body, Mk_Task_Body: BODY_KIND;
	Mk_Function_Body, Mk_Procedure_Body:
	    TYPE_EXPRESSION -->BODY_KIND;

Figure 4.2.15: Concrete and Abstract Syntax of Package Bodies

Merging Syntactic Categories

The abstract syntax has been significantly simplified by merging syntactic categories. There is a trade-off between having restrictions reflected by the context free grammar or putting such restrictions into context conditions. Ada adopts the first approach. Many simplification to the abstract syntax have been done by adopting the second approach and not having context conditions represented on the level of the syntax. Knowledge on the syntax has therefore been moved from the context free syntax to the transformation rules that generates PA^{nn}dA programs.

One such example is that the data type DECLARATION_LIST has been used uniformly to represent all kind of declarations, whether basic declarative items, later declarative items etc. It is then up to the transformation rules to ensure that generated programs are legal, e.g. that later declarative items does not appear in the specification of a package (see Figure 4.2.15).

The abstract syntax has in extend been simplified at the expense of complicating the unparsing rules. The type NAME_LIST has for example been used to represent with clauses and a sequence of exception choices disregarding the fact that the keyword and the delimiter is different at the level of the concrete syntax. The unparsing then depends on the context in which the name list occurs (see Figure 4.2.16). Observe that subtypes have been defined and used in the definition of the various constructor functions in order to make the abstract syntax definition more self-explanatory.

A major simplification is that the abstract syntax of expressions (and type expressions) have been flattened, and for expressions parentheses must be provided automatically using the knowledge of operator precedence and the Ada concrete syntax rules for expressions. Function calls are represented using the constructor Mk_Call. The corresponding infix notation is viewed as syntactic sugar to be provided by the unparser.

```
exception_handler ::=
   when exception_choice {| exception_choice} =>
      sequence_of_statements

exception_choice ::=
   exception_name | others
```

```
type NAME_LIST is private;
subtype EXCEPTION_CHOICE_LIST is NAME_LIST;

Mk_Handler:
   EXCEPTION_CHOICE_LIST #
   STATEMENT_LIST --> HANDLER;
```

Figure 4.2.16: Concrete and Abstract Syntax of With Clauses and Exception Choices

The abstract syntax of e.g. subprogram declarations deserves a detailed explanation. PA^{nn}dA is a higher order language which means that functions are values. This property has been reflected in the abstract syntax by having the following entities represented as objects: functions, procedures, entries, predicates, (quantified) variables, constants, formal parameters and generic formal parameters. The abstract syntax type OBJECT_KIND then serves as a discriminator between the different kind of objects. For functions, predicates and quantified variables the logical expression list represents the annotation. The expression part of a variable or constant kind represents the initialization expression.

It should be noted that the abstract syntax of procedure and entry declarations is defined in terms of the constructor Mk_Function_Type where the result type is given by the constructor Empty_Type. A similar trick, using an "empty constructor" has been used for raise statements and exit statements where the name is optional: the constructor Empty_Name is then used to represent the absence of a name. Similar, the constructor Empty_Expr represents the absence of an expression in the initialization expression of variable declarations, deferred constant declarations and in return statements.

```
-- DECLARATION
Mk_Object: DESIGNATOR # TYPE_EXPRESSION # OBJECT_KIND --> DECLARATION;

-- OBJECT_KIND
  Mk_Func: LOGICAL_EXPRESSION_LIST --> OBJECT_KIND;
  Mk_Aux_Func: LOGICAL_EXPRESSION_LIST --> OBJECT_KIND;
  Mk_Pred: LOGICAL_EXPRESSION_LIST --> OBJECT_KIND;
  Mk_Quantified_Var: LOGICAL_EXPRESSION_LIST --> OBJECT_KIND;
  Mk_Var: EXPRESSION --> OBJECT_KIND;
  Mk_Const: EXPRESSION --> OBJECT_KIND;
  Mk_In: OBJECT_KIND;
  Mk_Out: OBJECT_KIND;
  Mk_Entry: OBJECT_KIND;
  Mk_Proc: OBJECT_KIND;

-- TYPE_EXPRESSION
Empty_Type: TYPE_EXPRESSION;
Mk_Name_Type: UNIQUE_NAME --> TYPE_EXPRESSION;
Mk_Extended_Type: TYPE_EXPRESSION --> TYPE_EXPRESSION;
Mk_Function_Type:
    TYPE_EXPRESSION #
    FUNCTION_ARROW #
    TYPE_EXPRESSION -->TYPE_EXPRESSION;
  Mk_Tuple_Type: TYPE_LIST --> TYPE_EXPRESSION;
  Mk_Domain_Type: DOMAIN --> TYPE_EXPRESSION;
```

Figure 4.2.17: Abstract Syntax of Objects and Type Expressions

Ignoring Static Semantic Issues

To make the description of transformation rules more concise, expanded names are replaced by unique simple names resolving overloading, and type qualifications are removed from expressions since they are needed for overload resolution only. Overloading of names is resolved by inserting unique symbols called *keys* at the declaration of a designator x, and the same *unique key* at all applied occurrences of x. Any designator will be represented by a tuple Mk_Unique_Name(id, key,nature) where first component is the string representation which will be used in the unparsing of the name and the second component is the key, uniquely identifying the entity within the program. The third component specifies the nature of the denoted entity, i.e. whether the name refers to a variable, a function, a generic package etc. This information has been requested by the transformation developers in order to make a specific class of transformation rules context free. This simplified internal representation of names must then be projected onto a concrete form where overloaded entities occur.

x	Mk_Unique_Name("x", k, mk_Logical_Var_Nature)
STANDARD	Mk_Unique_Name(mk_Standard_Des, mk_Standard_Key, mk_Package_Nature)
others	Mk_Unique_Name("others", mk_Others_Lit_Key, mk_Value_Nature)
"<"	Mk_Unique_Name(mk_Less_Des, mk_Bool_Less_Key, mk_Predefined_Op_Nature) Mk_Unique_Name(mk_Less_Des, mk_String_Less_Key, mk_Predefined_Op_Nature)

Figure 4.2.18: Syntax of Names and Literals

Syntactic Category	Type Name	Constructor Name
literals (incl. undefined, others, defined)	UNIQUE_NAME	Mk_Unique_Name
identifier, operator, designator	UNIQUE_NAME	Mk_Unique_Name
basic declaration, basic declarative item, later declarative item	DECLARATION	
range, discrete range	EXPRESSION	Mk_Subtype_Range Mk_Range_With_Bounds
name, expanded name	UNIQUE_NAME	Mk_Unique_Name
expression, relation, simple expression, term, factor	EXPRESSION	Mk_Call
numeric literal, undefined, string literal, name	UNIQUE_NAME	Mk_Unique_Name
logical expression	EXPRESSION	Mk_Quantified, Mk_Tuple
implication, logical formula, equality test, definedness test	EXPRESSION	Mk_Call
membership test	EXPRESSION	Mk_Membership
logical implicator	UNIQUE_NAME	Mk_Unique_Name
statement, simple statement, compound statement	STATEMENT	
subprogram declaration	DECLARATION	Mk_Object
predicate declaration	DECLARATION	Mk_Object
sequence of domains	DECLARATION_LIST	
domain	DECLARATION	Mk_Object
formal part	TYPE_EXPRESSION	Mk_Tuple_Type
deferred constant declaration	DECLARATION	Mk_Object
entry call statement	STATEMENT	Mk_Procedure_Call
compilation unit	DECLARATION	Mk_Compilation
library unit	DECLARATION	
body, secondary unit, library unit body	DECLARATION	Mk_Body
with clause	NAME_LIST	
exception choices	NAME_LIST	
exception choice	UNIQUE_NAME	Mk_Unique_Name
generic formal part	DECLARATION_LIST	
generic formal parameter	DECLARATION	Mk_Object Mk_Type
generic instantiation	DECLARATION	Mk_Instantiation
generic actual part	EXPRESSION_LIST	
generic actual parameter	EXPRESSION	

Figure 4.2.19: Representation of PAnndA Program Fragments

4.2.C.2. Abstract Syntax Definition

This appendix contains the specification of the abstract syntax of PA^{nn}dA-C, in form of two packages: the package basic_types contains, as the name suggest, specifications of basic types needed, whereas the package pannda contains the types and constructors defining the abstract syntax.

```
with basic_types;
package pannda is

   -- TYPE DECLARATIONS
   type DECLARATION is private;
   type OBJECT_KIND is private;
   type BODY_KIND is private;
   type INSTANTIATION_KIND is private;
   type TYPE_EXPRESSION is private;
   type FUNCTION_ARROW is private;
   type TYPE_LIST is private;
   type DECLARATION_LIST is private;
   type UNIQUE_NAME is private;
   type NAME_LIST is private;
   type EXPRESSION_LIST is private;
   type EXPRESSION is private;
   type QUANTIFIER is private;
   type STATEMENT_LIST is private;
   type STATEMENT is private;
   type ITERATION_SCHEME is private;
   type SELECT_ALTERNATIVE_LIST is private;
   type SELECT_ALTERNATIVE is private;
   type PROGRAM is private;
   type HANDLER_LIST is private;
   type HANDLER is private;
   type PRAGMA_DECLARATION is private;
   type ARGUMENT_ASSOCIATION_LIST is private;
   type ARGUMENT_ASSOCIATION is private;

   -- SUBTYPE DECLARATIONS
   subtype Name is UNIQUE_NAME;
   subtype LITERAL is UNIQUE_NAME;
   subtype NUMERIC_LITERAL is LITERAL;
   subtype STRING_LITERAL is LITERAL;
   subtype OTHERS_LITERAL is LITERAL;
   subtype UNDEFINED_LITERAL is LITERAL;
   subtype DESIGNATOR is UNIQUE_NAME;
   subtype DESIGNATOR_LIST is NAME_LIST;
   subtype IDENTIFIER is DESIGNATOR;
   subtype WITH_CLAUSE is NAME_LIST;
   subtype DISCRETE_RANGE is EXPRESSION;
   subtype ENTRY_DECLARATION_LIST is DECLARATION_LIST;
   subtype ENTRY_DECLARATION is DECLARATION;
   subtype GENERIC_PARAMETER is DECLARATION;
   subtype GENERIC_PARAMETER_LIST is DECLARATION_LIST;
   subtype GENERIC_ACTUAL_PART is EXPRESSION_LIST;
   subtype GENERIC_ACTUAL_PARAMETER is EXPRESSION;
   subtype EXCEPTION_CHOICE_LIST is NAME_LIST;
   subtype EXCEPTION_CHOICE is UNIQUE_NAME;
   subtype DOMAIN is DECLARATION;
```

```
subtype DOMAIN_LIST is DECLARATION_LIST;
subtype LOGICAL_EXPRESSION_LIST is EXPRESSION_LIST;
subtype LOGICAL_EXPRESSION is EXPRESSION;
subtype COMPILATION_UNIT is DECLARATION;
subtype UNIT is DECLARATION;

-- DECLARATION_LIST
Empty_Decl_List: DECLARATION_LIST;
Mk_Decl_List: DECLARATION # DECLARATION_LIST --> DECLARATION_LIST;

-- DECLARATION
Null_Decl: DECLARATION;
Empty_Decl: DECLARATION;
Mk_Private_Type: IDENTIFIER --> DECLARATION;
Mk_Derived_Type: IDENTIFIER # UNIQUE_NAME --> DECLARATION;
Mk_Subtype: IDENTIFIER # TYPE_EXPRESSION --> DECLARATION;
Mk_Object: DESIGNATOR # TYPE_EXPRESSION # OBJECT_KIND --> DECLARATION;
Mk_Body:
  DESIGNATOR # BODY_KIND # DECLARATION_LIST # STATEMENT_LIST # HANDLER_LIST -->
     DECLARATION;
Mk_Package:
  IDENTIFIER # DECLARATION_LIST # WITH_CLAUSE # DECLARATION_LIST --> DECLARATION;
Mk_Axiom: LOGICAL_EXPRESSION_LIST --> DECLARATION;
Mk_Task: UNIQUE_NAME # ENTRY_DECLARATION_LIST --> DECLARATION;
Mk_Compilation_Unit: WITH_CLAUSE # UNIT --> DECLARATION;
Mk_Exception: IDENTIFIER --> DECLARATION;
Mk_Generic: GENERIC_PARAMETER_LIST # DECLARATION --> DECLARATION;
Mk_Instantiation:
  INSTANTIATION_KIND # DESIGNATOR # UNIQUE_NAME # GENERIC_ACTUAL_PART -->
     DECLARATION;
Mk_Pragma_Decl: PRAGMA_DECLARATION --> DECLARATION;
Mk_Type_Scheme:  UNIQUE_NAME # DECLARATION_LIST # TYPE_DECLARATION --> DECLARA-
TION;

-- OBJECT_KIND
Mk_Func: LOGICAL_EXPRESSION_LIST --> OBJECT_KIND;
Mk_Aux_Func: LOGICAL_EXPRESSION_LIST --> OBJECT_KIND;
Mk_Pred: LOGICAL_EXPRESSION_LIST --> OBJECT_KIND;
Mk_Quantified_Var: LOGICAL_EXPRESSION_LIST --> OBJECT_KIND;
Mk_Var: EXPRESSION --> OBJECT_KIND;
Mk_Const: EXPRESSION --> OBJECT_KIND;
Mk_In: OBJECT_KIND;
Mk_Out: OBJECT_KIND;
Mk_Entry: OBJECT_KIND;
Mk_Proc: OBJECT_KIND;

-- TYPE_EXPRESSION
Null_Type: TYPE_EXPRESSION;
Empty_Type: TYPE_EXPRESSION;
Mk_Name_Type: UNIQUE_NAME --> TYPE_EXPRESSION;
Mk_Extended_Type: TYPE_EXPRESSION --> TYPE_EXPRESSION;
Mk_Function_Type:
     TYPE_EXPRESSION # FUNCTION_ARROW # TYPE_EXPRESSION -->TYPE_EXPRESSION;
Mk_Tuple_Type: TYPE_LIST --> TYPE_EXPRESSION;
Mk_Domain_Type: DOMAIN --> TYPE_EXPRESSION;
```

```
-- FUNCTION ARROW
 Mk_Weak_Arrow: FUNCTION_ARROW;
 Mk_Strong_Arrow: FUNCTION_ARROW;

 -- TYPE_LIST
 Empty_Type_List: TYPE_LIST;
 Mk_Type_List: TYPE_EXPRESSION # TYPE_LIST --> TYPE_LIST;

-- UNIQUE_NAME
 Null_Name: UNIQUE_NAME;
 Empty_Name: UNIQUE_NAME;
 Mk_Unique_Name: STR # STR # TP_NATURE --> UNIQUE_NAME;

 -- NAME_LIST
 Empty_Name_List: NAME_LIST;
 Mk_Name_List: UNIQUE_NAME # NAME_LIST --> NAME_LIST;

 -- EXPRESSION_LIST
 Empty_Expr_List: EXPRESSION_LIST;
 Mk_Expr_List: EXPRESSION # EXPRESSION_LIST --> EXPRESSION_LIST;

 -- EXPRESSION
 Null_Expr: EXPRESSION;
 Empty_Expr: EXPRESSION;
 Mk_Name: UNIQUE_NAME --> EXPRESSION;
 Mk_Membership: EXPRESSION # UNIQUE_NAME --> EXPRESSION;
 Mk_Quantified: QUANTIFIER # DOMAIN_LIST # LOGICAL_EXPRESSION_LIST --> EXPRESSION;
 Mk_Tuple: EXPRESSION_LIST --> EXPRESSION;
 Mk_Call: EXPRESSION # EXPRESSION --> EXPRESSION;
 Mk_Conversion: UNIQUE_NAME # EXPRESSION --> EXPRESSION;
 Mk_Conditional: EXPRESSION # EXPRESSION # EXPRESSION --> EXPRESSION;
 Mk_Subtype_Range: UNIQUE_NAME --> EXPRESSION;
 Mk_Range_With_Bounds: EXPRESSION # EXPRESSION --> EXPRESSION;

 -- QUANTIFIER
 Mk_For_All: QUANTIFIER;
 Mk_Exist: QUANTIFIER;

-- STATEMENT_LIST
 Empty_Stat_List: STATEMENT_LIST;
 Mk_Stat_List: STATEMENT # STATEMENT_LIST --> STATEMENT_LIST;
 EQ: STATEMENT_LIST # STATEMENT_LIST --> BOOLEAN;


 -- STATEMENT
 Mk_Null: STATEMENT;
 Mk_Labelled: IDENTIFIER # STATEMENT --> STATEMENT;
 Mk_Assignment: UNIQUE_NAME # EXPRESSION --> STATEMENT;
 Mk_Return: EXPRESSION --> STATEMENT;
 Mk_Goto: UNIQUE_NAME --> STATEMENT;
 Mk_If: EXPRESSION # STATEMENT_LIST # STATEMENT_LIST --> STATEMENT;
 Mk_Loop: IDENTIFIER # ITERATION_SCHEME # STATEMENT_LIST --> STATEMENT;
 Mk_Block:  IDENTIFIER # DECLARATION_LIST # STATEMENT_LIST #  HANDLER_LIST -->
            STATEMENT;
 Mk_Procedure_Call: UNIQUE_NAME # EXPRESSION --> STATEMENT;
 Mk_Accept: IDENTIFIER # TYPE_EXPRESSION # STATEMENT_LIST --> STATEMENT;
 Mk_Select: SELECT_ALTERNATIVE_LIST # STATEMENT_LIST --> STATEMENT;
 Mk_Raise: UNIQUE_NAME --> STATEMENT;
```

```
  -- ITERATION_SCHEME
  Empty_Iteration_Scheme: ITERATION_SCHEME;
  Mk_While_Scheme: EXPRESSION --> ITERATION_SCHEME;
  Mk_For_Scheme: IDENTIFIER # DISCRETE_RANGE --> ITERATION_SCHEME;
  Mk_Reverse_For_Scheme: IDENTIFIER # DISCRETE_RANGE --> ITERATION_SCHEME;

 -- SELECT_ALTERNATIVE_LIST
  Empty_Select_Alternative_List: SELECT_ALTERNATIVE_LIST;
  Mk_Select_Alternative_List:
      SELECT_ALTERNATIVE #  SELECT_ALTERNATIVE_LIST --> SELECT_ALTERNATIVE_LIST;

  -- SELECT_ALTERNATIVE
  Mk_Select_Alternative: EXPRESSION # STATEMENT #  STATEMENT_LIST -->
        SELECT_ALTERNATIVE;
  Mk_Terminate_Alternative: EXPRESSION --> SELECT_ALTERNATIVE;

  -- PROGRAM
  Mk_Program: COMPILATION_UNIT # COMPILATION_UNIT --> PROGRAM;

  -- BODY_KIND
  Mk_Function_Body: TYPE_EXPRESSION --> BODY_KIND;
  Mk_Procedure_Body: TYPE_EXPRESSION --> BODY_KIND;
  Mk_Package_Body: BODY_KIND;
  Mk_Task_Body: BODY_KIND;

  - HANDLER_LIST
  Empty_Handler_List: HANDLER_LIST;
  Mk_Handler_List: HANDLER # HANDLER_LIST --> HANDLER_LIST;


  -- HANDLER
  Mk_Handler: EXCEPTION_CHOICE_LIST # STATEMENT_LIST --> HANDLER;


  -- INSTANTIATION_KIND
  Mk_Package_Inst: INSTANTIATION_KIND;
  Mk_Function_Inst: INSTANTIATION_KIND;
  Mk_Procedure_Inst: INSTANTIATION_KIND;

end pannda;


package basic_types is
   subtype INT is INTEGER;
   subtype BOOL is BOOLEAN;
   subtype STR is STRING;

   CONC: STR # STR --> STR;
   STR_TO_LOWER, STR_TO_UPPER: STR --> STR;
   INT_TO_STR: INTEGER --> STR;
   STR_TO_INT: STR --> INTEGER;
   SUBSTRING: INT # INT # STR --> STR;
   LENGTH: STR --> INTEGER;
   QUOTED: STR --> STR;

   subtype TP_DESIGNATOR is STR;

   mk_Des: STR --> TP_DESIGNATOR;
```

```
mk_Anonymous_Des, mk_Error_Des, mk_Void_Des, Dummy_Des, mk_Standard_Des,
mk_Boolean_Des, mk_Integer_Des, mk_Positive_Des, mk_Natural_Des, mk_String_Des,
mk_False_Des, mk_True_Des, mk_First_Des, mk_Last_Des, mk_Pos_Des, mk_Val_Des, mk_Succ_Des,
mk_Pred_Des, mk_Eq_Des, mk_Length_Des, mk_And_Then_Des, mk_Or_Else_Des,
mk_Implication_Des, mk_Equivalence_Des, mk_Conjunction_Des, mk_Disjunction_Des,
mk_Non_Equivalence_Des, mk_Equal_Des, mk_Not_Equal_Des, mk_Less_Des, mk_Less_Equal_Des,
mk_Greater_Des, mk_Greater_Equal_Des, mk_Plus_Des, mk_Minus_Des, mk_Catenation_Des,
mk_Multiplication_Des, mk_Division_Des, mk_Modulus_Des, mk_Remainder_Des,
mk_Exponentiation_Des, mk_Absolution_Des, mk_Negation_Des, mk_Defined_Des:
   TP_DESIGNATOR;

subtype TP_KEY is STR;

mk_Key: STR --> TP_KEY;

mk_Any_Discrete_Key, mk_Any_Integer_Key, mk_Any_String_Key, mk_Logical_Key,
mk_Any_Type_Key, mk_Others_Lit_Key, mk_Undefined_Lit_Key, mk_Empty_Lit_Key,
mk_Contradiction_Lit_Key, mk_Immediate_Lit_Key, mk_Logical_Defined_Key,
mk_Logical_Implication_Key, mk_Logical_Equivalence_Key, mk_Logical_Equal_Key,
mk_Logical_Not_Equal_Key, mk_Logical_And_Key, mk_Logical_Or_Key, mk_Logical_Not_Key,
mk_And_Then_Key, mk_Or_Else_Key, mk_Boolean_Key, mk_Boolean_And_Key,
mk_Boolean_EQ_Key, mk_Boolean_False_Key, mk_Boolean_Greater_Equal_Key,
mk_Boolean_Greater_Key, mk_Boolean_Less_Equal_Key, mk_Boolean_Less_Key,
mk_Boolean_Not_Key, mk_Boolean_Or_Key, mk_Boolean_True_Key, mk_Boolean_Xor_Key,
mk_Boolean_First_Key, mk_Boolean_Last_Key, mk_Boolean_Pos_Key, mk_Boolean_Val_Key,
mk_Boolean_Succ_Key, mk_Boolean_Pred_Key, mk_Integer_Key, mk_Integer_EQ_Key,
mk_Integer_Greater_Equal_Key, mk_Integer_Greater_Key, mk_Integer_Less_Equal_Key,
mk_Integer_Less_Key, mk_Integer_Unary_Plus_Key, mk_Integer_Unary_Minus_Key,
mk_Integer_Absolution_Key, mk_Integer_Binary_Minus_Key, mk_Integer_Binary_Plus_Key,
mk_Integer_Multiplication_Key, mk_Integer_Division_Key, mk_Integer_Remainder_Key,
mk_Integer_Modulus_Key, mk_Integer_Exponentiation_Key, mk_Integer_First_Key,
mk_Integer_Last_Key, mk_Integer_Succ_Key, mk_Integer_Pred_Key, mk_Natural_Key,
mk_Positive_Key, mk_String_Key, mk_String_EQ_Key, mk_String_Greater_Equal_Key,
mk_String_Greater_Key, mk_String_Less_Equal_Key, mk_String_Less_Key,
mk_String_Catenation_Key, mk_String_First_Key, mk_String_Last_Key, mk_String_Length_Key,
mk_Standard_Key:
   TP_KEY;

type TP_NATURE is private;

mk_Value_Nature, mk_Void_Nature, mk_Error_Nature, mk_Base_Type_Nature,
mk_Formal_Type_Nature, mk_Subtype_Nature, mk_Type_Nature, mk_Declared_Function_Nature,
mk_Aux_Function_Nature, mk_Predefined_Op_Nature, mk_Predicate_Nature,
mk_Formal_Predicate_Nature, mk_Formal_Function_Nature, mk_Formal_Aux_Function_Nature,
mk_Generic_Package_Spec_Nature, mk_Logical_Var_Nature, mk_Package_Nature,
mk_Polymorphic_Function_Nature, mk_Declared_Constant_Nature, mk_Declared_Variable_Nature,
mk_Deferred_Constant_Nature, mk_Label_Nature, mk_Loop_Nature, mk_Loop_Parameter_Nature,
mk_Block_Nature, mk_Procedure_Nature, mk_In_Parameter_Nature, mk_Out_Parameter_Nature,
mk_Inout_Parameter_Nature, mk_Task_Nature, mk_Entry_Nature, mk_Exception_Nature,
mk_Formal_In_Object_Nature, mk_Formal_Inout_Object_Nature, mk_Formal_Procedure_Nature:
   TP_NATURE;

end basic_types;
```

4.2.D. Static Semantic Attributes

Within the transformation and verification systems of PROSPECTRA there is a requirement for context dependant information. In the following discussion the attributes required to allow static semantic analysis to be carried out within PA^{nn}dA are discussed. An outline of the modelling and realization of these attributes, termed the static semantic environment, is given. Additionally, some interface functions for accessing the environment are presented.

4.2.D.1. Basic Requirements

The basic attribute for static semantic analysis is the static semantic environment of type TP_ENV. This environment mainly contains information on entities in scope and information for modelling the visibility. It contains in extend information that can be used for ensuring the main bulk of static semantic conditions, e.g. all the type rules of the language.

In order to describe more closely what are the entities represented in the environment at a given point consider the example in Figure 4.2.20. The environments at the individual points contain information on:

- Point 1: the predefined package STANDARD as well as its local entities BOOLEAN, INTEGER, "<", "+", ...
- Point 2: the information from point 1 and additionally the package P. P is here known to be an enclosing package but it is without any local entities.
- Point 3: the environment is changed in comparison to the one at the previous point in that P now has one local entity, namely T, which is known to be a private type.
- Point 4: Here F is known as a local entity of P and the type T is known to be a type derived from INTEGER. Furthermore we have as local entities of P the 19 predefined operators of T (EQ, "<", "<=", "+", SUCC...).

Now consider a slightly extended example in the second part of Figure 4.2.20, where we have added an inner package IP to P. The environment reflects the visibility structure and can be thought of as a stack. On the top level the local entities are represented; at the next-to-top level the entities local to the immediately surrounding scope is represented, a.s.o. At point 5 we have three levels:

- Level 1: the local declarations of IP: ST.
- Level 2: the local declarations of P: T, F, operators for T, IP.
- Level 3: the local declarations of STANDARD (including P).

The static semantic environment contains in addition detailed information on each entity in scope. One of the basic interface functions is the function Select (see Figure 4.2.21) that takes a unique identification of

```
-- point 1
package P is
   -- point 2
   type T is private;
   -- point 3
   F: (T;T) --> T;
private
   type T is new INTEGER;
   -- point 4
   axiom for all X: T; Y: T => F(X,Y) > X + Y;
end P;
```

```
package P is
   type T is private;
   F: (T;T) --> T;
private
   type T is new INTEGER;
   package IP is
      subtype ST is ...;
      -- point 5
   end IP;
   axiom for all X: T; Y: T => F(X,Y) > X + Y;
end P;
```

Figure 4.2.20: Entities in Scope

an entity and the static semantic environment as arguments and returns as result a descriptor of the entity. Another basic function is the function Lookup that takes a designator and a static semantic environment as parameters, and return as result the set of possible interpretations.

The descriptor TP_DESCR contains sufficient information on the entity to model the static semantic conditions, i.e:

- the nature of the entity, i.e. wether the entity is a function, a package or a generic etc.
- the properties of the entity, i.e. for a package information on the entities of the visible part, for an object the type profile, for a generic package the formal entities and the description of the package itself etc.

All interface functions have been defined in terms of the type ENTITY_ID - the unique identification of an entity. An entity is uniquely identified by the unique key or by the unique name. In the kernel model of the environment it will be more appropriate to use keys for denoting the individual entities. In the interface to applicability conditions for transformations, however, names will be more appropriate. Note that there is a one-to-one correspondence between keys and names as explained in the former appendix.

A number of predicates and auxiliary functions can be built on top of the environment. In the following we will present a few of these functions to be used both for static semantics and for transformations.

Enclosing Constructs

For the current scope the local declarations, the immediately enclosing unit and all the enclosing units can be extracted by the functions Enclosing_Unit and Enclosing_Units. The function Get_Enclosing extracts the name of the construct in which the given entity is immediately declared (see Figure 4.2.22).

Furthermore, for checking the legal placement of various constructs functions are available that extract information on the enclosing constructs on the basis of the three functions above. First, for checking exit statements, the functions In_Loop and In_Named_Loop test whether the current point is within a loop excluding within an inner body or accept statement. Second, for checking return statements, the functions In_Procedure_Or_Accept and In_Function test whether the current point is within a subprogram or accept statement excluding within inner tasks or packages. Third, for checking accept statements, the function In_Entry_Task testa whether the current point is within a task with the entry given by the name, excluding within inner bodies or accept statements for the same entry. Fourth, for checking the correct placement of deferred constant with respect to the private type, the function In_Visible_Part_Of test whether the current point is in the visible part of the given package.

```
with pannda, env, basic_types, descr;
package env_interface is

    type ENTITY_ID is private;
    type ENTITY_ID_LIST is private;

    Name_Id: UNIQUE_NAME -->ENTITY_ID;
    Key_Id: TP_KEY -->ENTITY_ID;

    Lokup: TP_DESIGNATOR  --> TP_ENV --> ENTITY_ID_LIST;
    Select: ENTITY_ID --> TP_ENV --> TP_DESCR;
    ...
end env_interface;
```

Figure 4.2.21: Basic Interface Functions

Nature of Entities

For entities in scope, we are able to determine the nature of the entity by applying the functions given in Figure 4.2.22. First of all we have a function Nature_Of returning the nature of the entity. A number of derived predicates and auxiliary functions have been defined on the basis of this function.

```
-- Enclosing Constructs

Local_Declarations: TP_ENV --> NAME_LIST;
Enclosing_Unit: TP_ENV --> NAME_LIST;
Enclosing_Units: TP_ENV --> NAME_LIST;
Get_Enclosing: ENTITY_ID --> ENV --> ENTITY_ID;

In_Loop: TP_ENV --> BOOLEAN;
In_Named_Loop: ENTITY_ID --> TP_ENV --> BOOLEAN;

In_Procedure_Or_Accept:: TP_ENV --> BOOLEAN;
In_Function: TP_ENV --> BOOLEAN;
In_Entry_Task: ENTITY_ID --> TP_ENV --> BOOLEAN;

In_Visible_Part_Of: (n: ENTITY_ID) --> (e: TP_ENV :: Is_Package(n)(e)) --> BOOLEAN;
In_Private_Part_Of: (n: ENTITY_ID) --> (e: TP_ENV :: Is_Package(n)(e)) --> BOOLEAN;
In_Body_Of: (n: ENTITY_ID) --> (e: TP_ENV) --> BOOLEAN;
In_Formal_Part_Of: (n: ENTITY_ID) --> (e: TP_ENV) --> BOOLEAN;

-- Nature of Entity

Nature_Of: ENTITY_ID --> TP_ENV --> NATURE

Is_Base_Type, Is_Subtype, Is_Declared_Constant, Is_Declared_Variable, Is_Deferred_Constant,
Is_Universally_Quantified, Is_Existentialy_Quantified, Is_Label, Is_Loop, Is_Loop_Parameter,
Is_Block, Is_Declared_Function, Is_Aux_Function, Is_Predef_Operator, Is_Procedure, Is_Predi-
cate, Is_In_Parameter, Is_Out_Parameter, Is_Inout_Parameter, Is_Package, Is_Task, Is_Entry,
Is_Exception, Is_Generic_Function, Is_Generic_Procedure, Is_Generic_Package,
Is_Formal_Type, Is_Formal_In_Object, Is_Formal_Inout_Object, Is_Formal_Function,
Is_Formal_Predicate, Is_Aux_Formal_Function, Is_Formal_Procedure:
   ENTITY_ID --> TP_ENV --> BOOLEAN;

Is_Function, Is_Constant, Is_Variable, Is_Ada_Object, Is_Generic, Is_Type, Is_Overloadable:
   ENTITY_ID --> TP_ENV --> BOOLEAN;

-- Type Information

Type_Of: ENTITY_ID --> TP_ENV --> ENTITY_ID;
Same_Base_Type: ENTITY_ID # ENTITY_ID --> TP_ENV --> BOOLEAN;

Is_Predef_Logical_Type, Is_Predef_Boolean_Type, Is_Predef_Integer_Type,
Is_Predef_String_Type, Is_Universal_Integer_Type, Is_Any_String_Type,
Is_Private_Type, Is_Derived_Type, Is_Function_Type, Is_Tuple_Type:
   ENTITY_ID --> TP_ENV --> BOOLEAN;

Is_Boolean_Type, Is_Integer_Type, Is_String_Type, Is_Discrete_Type:
   ENTITY_ID --> TP_ENV --> BOOLEAN;

Get_Parent_Type, Get_Ancestor_Type: ENTITY_ID --> TP_ENV --> ENTITY_ID;
Is_Convertable: ENTITY_ID # ENTITY_ID --> TP_ENV --> BOOLEAN;
```

Figure 4.2.22: Basic Interface Functions for the Static Semantic Environment

Type Information

For the modelling of the static semantic conditions it is in general not required that domain restrictions on types are held in the environment. Static semantic rules are defined in terms of base type relationships whereas subtype constraints are taken into account by the dynamic semantics (and hence the transformer and proof system)

For a name denoting a (sub)type or an object we can extract the base type using the function Type_Of. For two subtypes we can check whether they have the same base type using the function Same_Base_Type. A type can be tested for its kind, e.g. the functions Is_Predef_Logical_Type and Is_Predef_Boolean_Type. Some derived predicates can be defined on top of those basic ones. For a given derived type we can extract the parent type using the function Get_Parent_Type, and the ancestor type using the function Get_Ancestor_Type. For two types we can in addition determine whether they are convertible using the function Is_Convertable.

For a given function type we can extract the parameter types and the result type using the functions Argument_Types and Result_Type. A part of checking for equivalence involves for function types checking for having the same profile using the function Same_Profile.

4.2.D.2. Structure of the Static Semantic Environment

The static semantic environment contains a description of all entities which have been declared so far and whose scope encloses a specific position in the program text. It also contains the necessary information to support the identification of a designator according to the visibility rules.

The static semantic environment consists of the following components (see Figure 4.2.23):

- the component local_explicit_entities describes all local entities explicitly declared in the current declarative region.
- the component local_implicit_entities describes all local entities implicitly declared (i.e. derived subprograms) in the current declarative region.
- the component enclosing_regions describes all declarative regions that enclose the current declarative region.
- the component local_implicit_used describes all entities declared in the declarative regions enclosed by the current region, and potentially visible by implicit use clause.
- the component global_implicit_used describes all entities declared in packages named by context clauses, and potentially visible by implicit use clauses.
- the component current_declarative_region describes the key of the current declarative region.

The type TP_ENCL_LIST describes the levels and content of the enclosing declarative regions. Each element TP_ENCL contains the key of the associated declarative region, and the descriptions of all entities declared within that declarative region.

The structure of the environment reflects the visibility rules of the language. Ignoring the details for a moment, we may say that a search is generally performed starting from the top components to the bottom components of the environment. The distinction between explicitly and implicitly declared local entities is needed to model that explicit declarations hide implicit homographs.

```
with basic_types, descr;
package env is

        type TP_ENV is private;
        type TP_ENCL_LIST is private;
        type TP_ENCL is private;

        mk_Env:
            (local_explicit_entities: TP_DESCR_LIST) #
            (local_implicit_entities: TP_DESCR_LIST) #
            (enclosing_regions: TP_ENCL_LIST) #
            (local_implicit_used: TP_DESCR_LIST) #
            (global_implicit_used: TP_DESCR_LIST) #
            (current_declarative_region: TP_KEY) #
            TP_KEY --> TP_ENV;

        empty_Encl_List: TP_ENCL_LIST;
        mk_Encl_List: TP_ENCL # TP_ENCL_LIST --> TP_ENCL_LIST;
        mk_Encl: TP_KEY # TP_DESCR_LIST  --> TP_ENCL;

end env;
```

Figure 4.2.23: Structure of the Static Semantic Environment

4.2.D.3. Entity Descriptors

An entity descriptor of type TP_DESCR holds information about the properties of an entity in scope. A descriptor has the following components (see Figure 4.2.24):

- the designator of the entity,
- the unique key of the entity,
- the nature of the entity,
- the static semantic denotation, and
- the key of the immediately enclosing unit.

The type TP_NATURE represents information about the nature of the entity (see appendix 4.2.C.2). There is one value of this type for every kind of entity in the language.

The type TP_DEN represents the main information on each entity:

- for a base type the denotation contains information on the type kind (boolean, string, derived, integer or private). For a derived type the type kind contains the key of the parent type.
- for an object the subtype is recorded (to be enriched in the future to record information about the mode of formal parameters).
- for a package the list of descriptors representing the visible part and a list of descriptors representing locally declared entities. The first list is used for modeling the visibility outside the package, the last is used for establishing the initial visibility within the package body.
- for a task the list of descriptors of the entries is recorded.
- for a generic, the formal parameters and the denotation of the constituent package, function or procedure is recorded.

The type TP_SUBTYPE is of significant importance: it establish the basis for type checking of e.g. expressions and type expressions. For a non-functional subtype the key of the base type is recorded, for a function subtype the parameter and result subtypes and for or a tuple type the component types number.

```
with basic_types;
package descr is

   type TP_DESCR is private;
   type TP_DESCR_LIST is private;
   type TP_STATE is private;
   type TP_DEN is private;
   type TP_TYPE_KIND is private;
   type TP_SUBTYPE is private;

   mk_Descr: (designator:TP_DESIGNATOR) #
           (key:TP_KEY) #
           (state:TP_STATE) #
           (nature:TP_NATURE) #
           (denotation:TP_DEN) #
           TP_ORIGIN #
           (enclosing:TP_KEY) -->TP_DESCR;
   empty_Descr_List: TP_DESCR_LIST;
   mk_Descr_List: TP_DESCR # TP_DESCR_LIST --> TP_DESCR_LIST;

   mk_Complete: TP_STATE;
   mk_Id_Established: TP_STATE;
   mk_Implicitly_Declared: TP_STATE;
   mk_Incomplete_Private: TP_STATE;
   mk_In_Formal: TP_STATE;
   mk_In_Generic: TP_STATE;
   mk_In_Private: TP_STATE;
   mk_In_Visible: TP_STATE;

   mk_Object_Den: (object_type:TP_SUBTYPE)  --> TP_DEN;
   mk_Generic_Den: (formal_part:TP_DESCR_LIST) # TP_DEN --> TP_DEN;
   mk_Package_Den: TP_DESCR_LIST # TP_DESCR_LIST --> TP_DEN;
   mk_Subtype_Den: (base_type: TP_SUBTYPE) --> TP_DEN;
   mk_Type_Den: TP_TYPE_KIND #  TP_TYPE_OP_CLASS --> TP_DEN;
   mk_Task_Den: (entries: TP_DESCR_LIST) -> TP_DEN;
   mk_Label_Den, mk_Loop_Den, mk_Block_Den, mk_Exception_Den: TP_DEN;

   mk_Boolean_Type_Kind: TP_TYPE_KIND;
   mk_String_Type_Kind: TP_TYPE_KIND;
   mk_Derived_Type_Kind: (parent_type: TP_KEY) # (declared_in_visible_part: BOOL) -->
      TP_TYPE_KIND;
   mk_Discrete_Type_Kind: TP_TYPE_KIND;
   mk_Private_Type_Kind: (discrete:BOOL) # (declared_in_visible: BOOL) --> TP_TYPE_KIND;

   mk_Simple_Subtype: (base_type:TP_KEY)  --> TP_SUBTYPE;
   mk_Function_Subtype: ( param_type:TP_SUBTYPE) # ( result_type:TP_SUBTYPE) -->
      TP_SUBTYPE;
   mk_Tuple_Subtype: ( component_types: TP_SUBTYPE_LIST) # (card: INT) --> TP_SUBTYPE;

end descr;
```

Figure 4.2.24: Structure of Entity Descriptors

The type TP_STATE contains information regarding the state of an entity. The state of a private type is mk_-Incomplete_Private until it is completed by a derived type declaration in the private part of the package. The state is then changed to mk_Complete. The state mk_Id_Established is used within the declaration of the entity itself: the visibility rules can then determine that the simple name of the entity is hidden.

4.2.D.4. Design of the Attribute Grammar

The attribute grammar has been designed in accordance with the main requirement concerned: to provide the basis for static semantic analysis of programs.

The most important attribute in this context is the static semantic environment which holds information about declared entities and facilitates the imposing of the visibility rules and other static semantic rules. The static semantic environment is basically synthesized by two attributes associated with e.g. declarations and list of declarations: env_in and env_out. The attribute env_in contains the static semantic environment for declarations in scope immediately before the declaration itself; the attribute env_out is defined as env_in enriched with a descriptor for the current declaration. All other nodes in a PA^{nn}dA tree have the attribute env_in holding information about declared entities in scope. This attribute is in particular used to perform static semantic analysis of names and expressions.

The relationship between the two attributes for e.g. function declarations and names are illustrated in Figure 4.2.25. The function Add_Descriptor enriches the current static semantic environment with the relevant descriptors. The function Get_Descriptor retrieves the descriptor of an entity in scope given the name and the static semantic environment as parameters.

The static semantic environment establish the basis for determine the following attributes:

- the attribute descr_of holding information about the entity denoted by a name.
- the attribute type_of holding information about the base type of an expression.

attribute name	**kind**	**type**	**nodes**
env_in	inherited	TP_ENV	all
env_out	synthesized	TP_ENV	DECLARATION DECLARATION_LIST
descr_of	synthesized	TP_DESCR	UNIQUE_NAME
type_of	synthesized	TP_TYPE	TYPE_EXPRESSION EXPRESSION

attribute equations

```
Mk_Object.env_out = Add_Descriptor(Mk_Object.descr, Mk_Object.env_in);
Mk_Unique_Name.descr = Get_Descriptor( Mk_Unique_Name.key, Mk_Unique_Name.env_in);
Mk_Name.type_of = Type_Of(Mk_Unique_Name.descr);
```

Figure 4.2.25: Basic Static Semantic Attributes

4.2.E. Attributes for Transformation and Proof

Einar W. Karlsen, Computer Resources International,
Owen Traynor, University of Strathclyde[1]

4.2.E.1. Introduction

Within the transformation and verification systems of PROSPECTRA there is a requirement for context dependant information. Such information is used when reasoning about the properties of specifications, in particular about the properties of types and functions. In the following discussion the attributes required to allow such activities to be carried out within PA^{nn}dA(-S) are discussed. An outline of the modelling and realization of these attributes, termed the local theory, is given. Additionally, some interface functions for accessing the local theory are presented. The framework is classified with respect to the class of specification which it is able to model; some examples are given.

The basic attribute for static semantic analysis is the static semantic environment (TP_ENV), described in detail in the former appendix. This environment mainly contains information on entities in scope and information for modelling the visibility rules and context conditions of PA^{nn}dA. For the modelling of the static semantic conditions it is in general not required that domain restrictions on types are held in the environment. Static semantic rules are defined in terms of base type relationships whereas subtype constraints are taken into account by the dynamic semantics (and hence the transformer and proof system). For the abstract design of attributes it is therefore natural to distinguish between attributes and attribute types needed for the static semantic analysis on one hand, and attributes needed for the proof and transformation system on the other hand. We have therefore decided to distinguish between the static semantic environment and the denotation of the local theory. The latter could be thought of as a'dynamic semantic' environment.

In modeling the local theory a number of considerations were taken into account. Efficiency and simplicity were paramount objectives. Some compromises were made with respect to the position from which efficiency is viewed; efficiency from the view point of generation of the local theory or from the view of accessing the local theory. Since some information is implicit in the context information, some work must be done for its retrieval. Conversely, an elegant and compact (relatively) set of attributes have been defined which will provide the basis for implementation and experimentation.

Both the proof system and the transformation system will use information from the local theory in order to manipulate PA^{nn}dA(-S) specifications, fragments, and terms. Equations from the local theory is used as rewrite rules by the proof system, in performing deduction, as well as in transformer system, for simplification. Such equations may be viewed as rewrite rules. For example, considering the proof system, axioms will be selected from the local theory in order to help prove the current goal.

In order to determine context sensitive information, of any sort, there is a requirement to define attributes which will represent the appropriate information for this computation. In the following sections a definition of the (local theory) attribute requirements for verification and transformation is outlined. The discussion continues with a detailed analysis of the requirements of the verification system with respect to interface functions needed for verification. Next a definition of a set of attributes and attribute dependencies representing the model is given together with a discussion of some implementation considerations.

---

1. *Authors' current address*: FB 3 - Informatik, Universität Bremen, Postfach 330 440, D-2800 Bremen 33

4.2.E.2. Basic Requirements

The attributes required for reasoning about the semantics of specifications correspond to what is called the local theory. That is, a denotation of all types, functions and related axioms. The following information is included in the denotation of the local theory:

- for each package the set of visible axioms defined in this package,
- all axioms defined in the current package, including any axioms in the private part of the package,
- all axioms of package STANDARD,
- all visible axioms of packages mentioned in with clauses (transitively),
- all axioms of inner (nested) package declarations,
- for each generic instantiation, the axioms of the instantiated package together with any axioms of the generic formal part with appropriate substitution of references to formal functions by references to the corresponding actual ones,
- for derived types, the axioms defining the derived functions.

For the proof system the local theory provides, what can be considered, the proof theory of a specification at a particular context. The proof theory determines, in a normalized representation, the meaning of the specification. This normalization will be described in detail in the next subsection.

Bearing in mind that the local theory contains axioms from the current package, as well as those from package STANDARD and any package mentioned in with clauses (transitively[1]), it is obvious that even for small specifications the size of the local theory exceeds the limit where it will be reasonable to expect a user to choose from such a large number of axioms, even to solve a well defined task. To allow such a denotation of the local theory to be usable, in the context of the proof and transformer system, it has been of paramount importance that appropriate access and filtering functions are provided so as to restrict the functions presented as appropriate for use in a given context.

Basically three access functions are needed:

- a function that, given the name of a function and the local theory, returns the axioms defining the function,
- a function that, given the name of a type and the local theory, returns the axioms defining the type and its functions,
- a function that, given the name of a package and the local theory, returns axioms defined in that package.

The functions provided must initially include the basic and derived interface functions given in Figure 4.2.26. The requirement for additional restriction and filtering functions may arise when specific transformation rules are developed for the proof and transformer system. Such application oriented filtering functions must be developed on the level of TrafoLa-S in parallel with the development of the transformation rules.

For example, additionally filtering functions will be defined by the proof system which will provide a finer degree of tuning with respect to the way in which context of current proofs (transformations) can be used to determine the axioms which are deemed appropriate for a specific task.

Additional browsing facilities will be provided by the proof system which will allow the user to select the context which will be useful for a session.

The tactic system will require exactly the same interface in terms of attribute access as the transformation system in order for tactics to be considered context sensitive. Tactics, in general, will perform the same tasks as are carried out interactively by the developer. Since this is the case, the tactic may appeal to context sensitive information in order to carry out the task at hand. This requires an interface to the local theory.

```
with PAnndA, predefined_names, theory ....;
package Local_Theory_Interface is
   -- basic access functions
   Get_Type_Theory: UNIQUE_NAME --> TP_THEORY --> TP_PROPERTY_DESCR_LIST:
   Get_Function_Theory: UNIQUE_NAME --> TP_THEORY --> TP_PROPERTY_DESCR_LIST;
   Get_Package_Theory: UNIQUE_NAME --> TP_THEORY --> TP_PROPERTY_DESCR_LIST;

   -- derived interface functions
   Get_Standard_Unit: TP_THEORY --> TP_PROPERTY_DESCR_LIST:
   Get_Predefined_Boolean: TP_THEORY --> TP_PROPERTY_DESCR_LIST:
   Get_Predefined_Integer: TP_THEORY --> TP_PROPERTY_DESCR_LIST:
   Get_Predefined_String: TP_THEORY --> TP_PROPERTY_DESCR_LIST:
   Get_Current_Unit: TP_THEORY --> TP_PROPERTY_DESCR_LIST:

   axiom for all I: TP_THEORY =>
         Get_Standard_Unit(I) = Get_Package_Theory( Predefined_Standard, I),
         Get_Predefined_Boolean = Get_Type_Theory( Predefined_Boolean, I),
         Get_Predefined_Integer(I) = Get_Type_Theory( Predefined_Integer, I),
         Get_Predefined_String(I) = Get_Type_Theory( Predefined_String, I);

end Local_Theory_Interface;
```

Figure 4.2.26: Basic Interface Functions

Consider the simple example of stacks in Figure 4.2.27. Inside the generic package STACK the denotation of the local theory must provide sufficient information for reasoning about the functions empty, top and pop. It is therefore required that the local theory provides means for accessing the relevant axioms defining the semantics of a given function, i.e. a function like:

```
Get_Function_Theory: UNIQUE_NAME --> TP_THEORY --> TP_PROPERTY_DESCR_LIST;
```

where UNIQUE_NAME denotes the unique name of a function, THEORY the local theory, and TP_PROPERTY_DESCR_LIST the descriptor used to hold a normalised list of logical expressions.

For example, the semantics of the function top is given by the logical expression:

```
axiom for all s: stack; e: elem => top( push( e, s)) = e;
```

Notice that, according to the principle of hierarchy consistency of specifications, it is sufficient that the function Get_Function_Theory returns relevant axioms from the visible part of the package enclosing the function.

In general, a function must be provided that returns the set of logical expressions giving the semantics of a package, whether this is a non-generic package, generic package, generic instantiation, inner package or even a compilation unit. This is achieved by the function Get_Package_Theory. For the package STACK this function would return all the axioms of the visible (and formal) part of the generic package.

As a continuation of the stack example, consider now the generic instantiation giving a stack of integers. The instance of a generic unit is a copy of the generic unit, apart from the generic formal part. The generic instantiation may be obtained by appropriate substitutions (renamings) as described in the Ada Reference Manual [Ada 83, paragraphs 12.3(6-14)]. We refer to [Ada 83] for a detailed description of the substitution rules. Note that it is still possible to determine the original context of elements from the local theory when they are used. This is important since it allows developments (proofs) which use of axioms from some small, restricted context, to have such a restricted context recorded. For example, the proof of a lemma, requiring

```
generic                                       with STACK;
    type elem is private;                     package P is
package STACK is                                  package ISTACK is new STACK( integer);
    type stack is private;                        subtype integer_stack is ISTACK.stack;
    empty: stack;                                 sum: integer_stack --> INTEGER;
    isestack: stack --> boolean;                  axiom for all s: integer_stack; i: integer =>
    top: s:stack --> elem:: not(isestack(s));         sum( empty) = 0,
    pop: s:stack --> stack:: not(isestack(s));        sum( push( i, s)) = i + sum(s);
    push: elem x stack --> stack;             end p:
    axiom for all s: stack; e: elem =>
        isestack(empty) = true,
        isestck(push(e,s) = false,
        top( push( e, s)) = e,
        pop( push( e, s)) = s;
end STACK;
```

Figure 4.2.27: Definition and Instantiation of Package STACK

on some small part of the available context information, need only have this restricted context recorded when the proof is stored. Recording such minimal amounts of information is important in having an effective basis for reuse.

One additional function must be provided which returns the set of axioms associated with a given type, namely the function Get_Type_Theory. Consider for example the type stack defined in package STACK. The result of applying Get_Type_Theory with STACK.stack as parameter would be all the axioms defined in package STACK.

A derived type declaration declares a new type and a set of implicitly declared subprograms [Ada 83, section 3.4]. To get the definition of the derived type one may textually repeat the definitions for the parent type with appropriate substitutions. The function Get_Type_Theory must in the case of derived type declarations return a list of expression descriptors similar to the ones for the parent type, but where references to the parent type and derivable subprograms are substituted by the corresponding references to the derived type and the derivable subprograms. The similarity between derived type declarations and generic instantiations means that the framework for modelling generic instantiations can directly be used to obtain the denotation of derived types.

In all, only a few general purpose access functions are provided. These provide a coarse level of filtering on the local theory. Such coarseness allows the information contained in the local theory to be useful for both the transformation and proof components of the system.

4.2.E.3. Normalisation of Expressions

The transformations described as part of the definition of the (dynamic) semantics of PA^{nn}dA-S (see chapter 2 of part II), are used as a basis for the normalisation of expressions. The semantic description of PA^{nn}dA-S introduces three levels, the lowest of these being the kernel language which includes base sorts, functions, packages and axioms; specifications using the various structuring and abstraction features of PA^{nn}dA must be reduced to an equivalent representation in the kernel language.

The second level includes functionals, domain restrictions and result annotations. The third subtypes. Transformations are defined to take specifications from the third level into the second level and from the second to the kernel language. It is therefore possible to describe all PA^{nn}dA-S specifications in the kernel language.

Normalisation of a specification then means that the denotation of the local theory represents the specification in terms of kernel language constructs. In particular:

- All axioms and restrictions are described in terms of their base sorts with appropriate conditions (left hand side of implications) added to the definition of the appropriate functions in the axiom part.
- Restrictions on subtypes represent the composite restriction with respect to the base type of that subtype.
- All domain restrictions on functions are moved to the appropriate axiom part for the package where those functions are defined.
- Membership tests are substituted by an explicit predicate checking whether the value of the expression is within the domain of the subtype.

Due to the limitations of the representation described in section 2.2, the actual representation is in the spirit of the kernel language. The transformation (or normalisation) does not follow exactly those described by the PA^{nn}dA-S semantics. Certainly, it is a reasonable approximation which is essential for both proof and transformation.

The basic normalisation functions are given in Figure 4.2.28. The function Normalise_Subtype, given a local theory and a subtype descriptor, will return the normalised subtype descriptor, containing the composed subtype restriction, with respect to the theory. Normalise_Expression, given an expression descriptor and a local theory, will return the expression normalised with respect to the given theory (domain restrictions, etc. incorporated as conditions on the axioms). The function named with the prefix Extract are provided as access functions for the local theory. They serve to extract the appropriate component of the local theory attribute. Additional constructors for TP_PROPERTY_DESCR_LIST etc. are defined in PA^{nn}dA-S to allow manipulation and extraction of the various components and list constituting the local theory.

The proof system will among other tasks be used to show that the restriction of a subtype declaration is compatible (e.g. in the sense of Ada 83, paragraph 3.3.2(8)) with the type or subtype denoted by the type expression, i.e. that the set of values denoted by the subtype is a subset of the values denoted by the type. For this purpose the normalisation function Get_Subtype_Restriction is available.

Consider the simple example:

```
subtype my_nat is (x:natural :: x < 100);
```

The result returned by Get_Subtype_Expression for the subtype my_nat corresponds to the logical expression:

```
for all x: integer => x >= 0 and x < 100
```

```
Normalise_Subtype: TP_PROPERTY_DESCR x TP_THEORY --> TP_PROPERTY_DESCR;

Normalise_Expression: TP_PROPERTY_DESCR x TP_THEORY --> TP_PROPERTY_DESCR;

Get_Subtype_Restriction: UNIQUE_NAME --> THEORY --> EXPR_DESCR;

Extract_Subtype: UNIQUE_NAME x TP_THEORY --> TP_PROPERTY_DESCR;

Extract_Expressions: TP_THEORY --> TP_PROPERTY_DESCR_LIST;

Generate_Membership_Predicate: LOGICAL_EXPRESSION x TP_THEORY --> LOGICAL_EXPRESSION;
```

Figure 4.2.28: Normalisation Functions

It should be noted that there are no explicit normalisation functions for generics. The instantiation of generics is performed via attribute computation. Only the subsequent normalisation of the generic instantiation is required.

As another example take again the specification of NSTACK in Figure 4.2.29. The un-normalised representation of the local theory of stack is given in the first part. The normalisation for the axiom components, excluding those normalisation for the natural components of the axioms, are given in the second part.

The theory in this example is relatively simple, however it serves to illustrate the way in which a specification must be elaborated in order to achieve a representation which is close to the kernel language. In a full decomposition into the kernel language, all references to natural would be replaced by integer with associated normalisations corresponding to the subtype restriction.

By eliminating the order sortedness of specifications as they are represented in the local theory, we have effectively increased the size of the specification. All types are denoted with respect to their base types. Additionally, all axioms contained in the local theory reflect the decomposition of the specification into the respective base types.

The strictness, versus non strictness, of functions is still an issue to be considered from the point of view of theorem proving.

Furthermore, for PA^{nn}dA-S the interpretation of higher order functions in a first order framework is required. Currently the local theory is currently restricted to deal with first order functions and generics only. The local theory must be extended to represent the higher order parts of the PA^{nn}dA-S language in parallel with the extension of the proof system with higher order rules of inference.

```
with STACK;
package P is
   package NSTACK is new STACK( natural);
   subtype natural_stack is NSTACK.stack;
   sum: natural_stack --> natural;
   axiom for all s: natural_stack; i: natural =>
      sum( empty) = 0,
      sum( push( i, s)) = i + sum(s);
end p:
```

```
sum( empty) = 0,

for all s: stack; i: natural =>
   sum( push( i, s)) = i + sum(s);

for all s: stack; i: natural =>
   not(isestack(push(i,s))) -> top( push( i, s)) = i ;

for all s: stack; i: natural =>
   not(isestack(push(i,s))) -> pop( push( i, s)) = s;
```

Figure 4.2.29: Un-normalised and Normalised Representation of Expressions

4.2.E.4. Structure of the Local Theory

The local theory contains information on the current compilation unit as well as any transitively used units. The information on used units is fixed and will never change, in contrast to the content of the local theory for the current package, which occasionally may be updated, e.g. when entering a quantified expression. As a consequence, the local theory is split into two distinct parts: a descriptor for the current unit together with a list of descriptors for imported units (see Figure 4.2.30).

```
with basic_types, pannda;
package theory is
   type TP_THEORY is private;
   type TP_UNIT_THEORY_LIST is private;
   type TP_UNIT_THEORY is private;
   type TP_PROPERTY_DESCR is private;
   type TP_PROPERTY_DESCR_LIST is private;

   mk_Theory: TP_UNIT_THEORY # TP_UNIT_THEORY_LIST --> TP_THEORY;
   current_unit: TP_THEORY --> TP_UNIT_THEORY;
   used_units: TP_THEORY --> TP_UNIT_THEORY_LIST;
   axiom for all A: TP_THEORY; E1: TP_UNIT_THEORY; E2: TP_UNIT_THEORY_LIST =>
         A = mk_Theory( E1, E2) -> current_unit(A) = E1,
         A = mk_Theory( E1, E2) -> used_units(A) = E2;

   empty_Unit_Theory_List: TP_UNIT_THEORY_LIST;
   mk_Unit_Theory_List: TP_UNIT_THEORY # TP_UNIT_THEORY_LIST --> TP_UNIT_THEORY_LIST;

   mk_Unit_Theory: TP_KEY # (e2, e3, e4, e5, e6: TP_PROPERTY_DESCR_LIST)  --> TP_UNIT_THEORY;
   unit_key: TP_UNIT_THEORY --> TP_KEY;
   type_descriptors: TP_UNIT_THEORY --> TP_PROPERTY_DESCR_LIST;
   subtype_descriptors: TP_UNIT_THEORY --> TP_PROPERTY_DESCR_LIST;
   object_descriptors: TP_UNIT_THEORY --> TP_PROPERTY_DESCR_LIST;
   generic_descriptors: TP_UNIT_THEORY --> TP_PROPERTY_DESCR_LIST;
   expression_descriptors: TP_UNIT_THEORY --> TP_PROPERTY_DESCR_LIST;
   axiom for all A: TP_UNIT_THEORY;
                 E1: TP_KEY;
                 E2, E3, E4, E5, E6: TP_PROPERTY_DESCR_LIST =>
         A = mk_Unit_Theory( E1, E2, E3, E4, E5, E6) -> unit_key(A) = E1,
         A = mk_Unit_Theory( E1, E2, E3, E4, E5, E6) -> type_descriptors(A) = E2,
         A = mk_Unit_Theory( E1, E2, E3, E4, E5, E6) -> subtype_descriptors(A) = E3,
         A = mk_Unit_Theory( E1, E2, E3, E4, E5, E6) -> object_descriptors(A) = E4,
         A = mk_Unit_Theory( E1, E2, E3, E4, E5, E6) -> generic_descriptors(A) = E5,
         A = mk_Unit_Theory( E1, E2, E3, E4, E5, E6) -> expression_descriptors(A) = E6;

   mk_Entity_Descr: TP_KEY # TP_KEY # DECLARATION --> TP_PROPERTY_DESCR;
   mk_Expr_Descr: TP_KEY # TP_KEY # EXPRESSION --> TP_PROPERTY_DESCR;
   entity_key: TP_PROPERTY_DESCR --> TP_KEY;
   enclosing_entity: TP_PROPERTY_DESCR --> TP_KEY;
   entity_declaration: TP_PROPERTY_DESCR --> DECLARATION;
   entity_expression: TP_PROPERTY_DESCR --> EXPRESSION;
   axiom for all A: TP_PROPERTY_DESCR; E, E2: TP_KEY;  E3: DECLARATION; E4: EXPRESSION=>
         A = mk_Entity_Descr( E1, E2, E3) -> entity_key(A) = E1,
         A = mk_Entity_Descr( E1, E2, E3) -> enclosing_entity(A) = E2,
         A = mk_Entity_Descr( E1, E2, E3) -> entity_declaration(A) = E3,
         A = mk_Expr_Descr( E1, E2, E4) -> entity_key(A) = E1,
         A = mk_Expr_Descr( E1, E2, E4) -> enclosing_entity(A) = E2,
         A = mk_Expr_Descr( E1, E2, E4) -> entity_expression(A) = E4;

   empty_Property_Descr_List: TP_PROPERTY_DESCR_LIST;
   mk_Property_Descr_List:
         TP_PROPERTY_DESCR # TP_PROPERTY_DESCR_LIST --> TP_PROPERTY_DESCR_LIST;

end theory;
```

Figure 4.2.30: Structure of Local Theory

The relevant information of a compilation unit is contained in a unit theory (TP_UNIT_THEORY). Each unit theory contains the following information: the unique key of the compilation unit; descriptors for subtype declarations; descriptors for type declarations; descriptors for objects; descriptors for inner generic packages; and a list of descriptors for the axioms given within the compilation unit. The descriptors are all of the type TP_PROPERTY_DESCR_LIST.

A property descriptor (TP_PROPERTY_DESCR) is either a descriptor for declarations, or a descriptor for logical expressions. The descriptors for declarations contains the unique key associated with the declaration, the unique key of the enclosing construct, and the declarations itself.

The descriptors for expressions contain similar information: a unique key of the logical expression; the unique key of the associated enclosing construct; and the abstract syntax fragment representing the logical expression.

Efficient retrieval of information from the local theory has been a major goal behind its design. This goal has been reached through its design in combination with various functions that narrows the search space. Generally the access functions are on the form:

```
Get_Theory: UNIQUE_NAME--> THEORY--> TP_PROPERTY_DESCR_LIST;
```

Efficient retrieval of information from the local theory, is accomplished on the first hand by a function that narrows the search space to the enclosing compilation unit. Generation of unique names of entities has been performed in a way such that the unique key of the enclosing compilation unit can be encoded from the unique name of any entity declared within that unit by the function Compilation_Unit_Key (see Figure 4.2.31). Given the unique key of the enclosing compilation unit, it is a simple task to retrieve the associated unit theory from the set of unit theories within the local theory.

When the relevant unit theory is retrieved, the search space is further narrowed by the kind of (or say nature of) entity being looked for. Unique names of entities contains information on the kind of entity denoted, e.g. whether it is a subtype, a type, a function or say a generic package. On basis of the function Nature_Of the search space can be further limited to one of the lists of property descriptors given in a unit theory. The final search is then accomplished by comparing keys of property descriptors, with the key of the entity, using the function Key_Of. For retrieving the logical expressions giving the semantics of a specific object, the auxiliary function Occurs_In is provided. This function constitutes the basis for filtering the result of Get_Function_Theory and Get_Type_Theory to those axioms relevant for the given type or function.

During the design of the local theory it has been considered whether to use hashing techniques or not. In particular, it has been discussed whether to provide a hashtable from package, function and type names to the relevant expression descriptors. Incorporation of a hash table would make the retrieval functions faster, whereas the synthesis of the local theory would be significantly slower. Since the hash table adds to the complexity of the local theory, and the advantages of such a hash table are questionable, it has been decided not to include it in this very first implementation of the local theory. More experimentation is needed within that area.

```
Compilation_Unit_Key: UNIQUE_NAME --> KEY;
Nature_Of: UNIQUE_NAME --> TP_NATURE;
Key_Of: UNIQUE_NAME --> TP_KEY;
Occurs_In: UNIQUE_NAME --> TP_PROPERTY_DESCR --> BOOLEAN;
```

Figure 4.2.31: Implementation Functions for Narrowing the Search Space

4.2.E.5. Design of the Attribute Grammar

The attribute grammar has been designed in accordance with the two main requirements concerned: to provide the basis for synthesizing normalised expressions, and to provide the basis for an efficient search of properties in the local theory.

The denotation of the local theory is basically synthesized by two attributes associated with e.g. declarations and list of declarations: dlt_in and dlt_out. The attribute dlt_in contains the local theory for declarations in scope immediately before the declaration itself; the attribute dlt_out is defined as dlt_in enriched with an entity descriptor for the current declaration. The relationship between the two attributes for e.g. function declarations and axioms are illustrated in Figure 4.2.32. The functions Add_Declaration and Add_Expressions enriches the current unit theory with the relevant property descriptors. Add_Expressions additionally performs a flattening of the quantified expressions in the sense that each logical expression of a quantified expression is given a property descriptor of its own.

Neither the attribute dlt_in, nor the attribute dlt_out contain a full description of the local theory since they only contains descriptors for entities within scope of the current declaration. The denotation of the complete local theory itself is declared as an inherited attribute dct and associated to all nodes of PA^{nn}dA programs. The attribute dct contains the complete local theory for declarations and equations declared within a compilation unit, i.e. all equations and declarations declared within the given compilation unit apart from a few reasonable exceptions:

- descriptors for objects declared in domains, e.g. formal parameters of functions and quantified variables of quantified expressions, will only be part of the current theory iff the current part of the program is within the scope of the object (that is, within the innermost enclosing function declaration or axiom),
- descriptors for entities declared within a generic package will only be part of the local theory within the generic package itself. Generic packages are templates and it makes therefore no sense to reason about the content of a generic package outside the package itself.

In any other cases, the declarations of all types and functions within a compilation unit will be used in forming the local theory as it is contained in the attribute dct. Forming the denotation of the complete theory for a quantified expression is established as defined by the attribute equation in Figure 4.2.32.

The attributes dlt_in, dlt_out and dct are not sufficient in the case of generic instantiations. For generic instantiations a substitution of formal parameters with actual parameters must be performed as described in (Ada 83). The mapping of formal parameters to actual parameters is modelled by two attributes associated with e.g. declarations and list of declarations: gmap_in and gmap_out. These attributes initially contains a map

attribute name	**kind**	**type**	**nodes**
dlt_in	inherited	TP_THEORY	all
dlt_out	synthesized	TP_THEORY	all
dct	inherited	TP_THEORY	all

attribute equations

```
Mk_Object.dlt_out = Add_Declaration( UNIQUE_NAME,DECLARATION, Mk_Object.dlt_in)
Mk_Axiom.dlt_out = Add_Expressions( EXPRESSION_LIST, Mk_Axiom.dlt_in)
Mk_Quantified.EXPRESSION_LIST.dct = Add_Local_Declarations(DECLARATION._LIST.dlt_out, $$.dct)
```

Figure 4.2.32: Attributes for Synthesizing the Local Theory

from formal parameters to actual parameters of the generic instantiation. This initial map is enriched for each local declaration of the generic package. The instantiated package is thus obtained by various synthesized attributes declared for nearly all nodes. For unique names, the instantiation is simply obtained by looking up in the inherited map of formal to actual parameters (see Figure 4.2.33)

attribute name	**kind**	**type**	**nodes**
gmap_in	inherited	TP_GENERIC_MAP	all
gmap_out	synthesized	TP_GENERIC_MAP	all
inst	synthesized	DECLARATION	declarations
inst	synthesized	EXPRESSION	expressions
inst	synthesized	UNIQUE_NAME	names

attribute equations

```
UNIQUE_NAME.inst =
   if  Is_In_Map(UNIQUE_NAMEUNIQUE_NAME.gmap_in) then
       Lookup_New_Name(UNIQUE_NAME,UNIQUE_NAME.gmap_in)
   else
       UNIQUE_NAME
```

Figure 4.2.33: Attributes for Generic Instantiations

4.3 Completion Subsystem

Hubert Bertling[1]*, Harald Ganzinger*[2]*, Renate Schäfers, Universität Dortmund*
Robert Nieuwenhuis, Fernando Orejas, Universitat Politécnica de Catalunya

4.3.1 Introduction

This section describes the use of CEC as a specialized transformer within PA^{nn}dA-C. CEC is a system for conditional equational completion. We assume familiarity with well known notions in the term rewriting area e.g. signature, term over a signature, (conditional) term rewrite rule, applicability of a rewrite rule, . . . , cf. e.g. [Huet, Oppen 80], [Kaplan 84] and I.2 of this book. The concepts are discussed only as far as needed to allow a meaningful interaction with the system. Theoretical foundations of the concepts implemented in CEC are not discussed. Hints to the literature will be given whenever such concepts are introduced.

4.3.2 An Example Session

For an overview of the main capabilities of CEC, we describe the completion of a quicksort algorithm on lists of natural numbers.

4.3.2.1 The Specification of Quicksort

The hierarchy of modules for the specification of quicksort on lists of natural numbers is given in the following diagram:

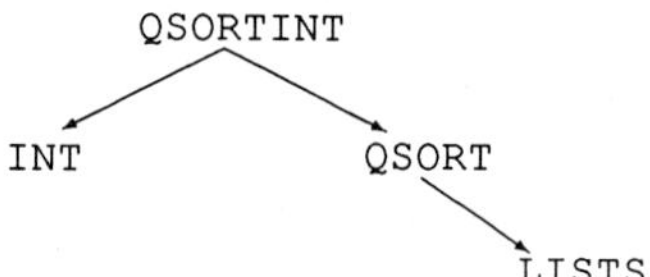

The package `qsort` describes the quicksort algorithm:

```
with LISTS;
generic
   type ELEM is private;
   "<=": ELEM # ELEM --> BOOLEAN;
   axiom for all e1, e2, e3: ELEM =>
         (e1 <= e1) = true,
         (e1 <= e2) = false -> (e2 <= e1) = true,
         (e1 <= e2) = true and (e2 <= e3) = true ->
               (e1 <= e3) = true,
         (e1 <= e2) = true and (e2 <= e1) = true -> e1 = e2;
package QSORT is
   package LIST is new LISTS(ELEM);
   type pairs is private;
   sort: LIST.list --> LIST.list;
   split: ELEM # LIST.list --> pairs;
   pair: LIST.list # LIST.list --> pairs;
   axiom for all e1, e2: ELEM; l, l1, l2: LIST.list =>
     sort(empty) = empty,
     split( e1, l) = pair( l1, l2) ->
          sort(cons( e1, l)) = append( sort(l1),
                                       cons( e1, sort(l2))),
     split( e1, empty) = pair( empty, empty),
     (e2 <= e1) = true and split( e1, l) = pair( l1, l2) ->
          split( e1, cons( e2, l)) = pair( cons( e2, l1), l2),
     (e2 <= e1) = false and split( e1, l) = pair( l1, l2) ->
          split( e1, cons( e2, l)) = pair( l1, cons( e2, l2));
end QSORT;
```

[1]*Author's present address*: Ges. f. Software-Qualitätssicherung, Aachener Straße 197–199, D-5000 Köln 41
[2]*Author's present address*: M.-Planck-Inst. f. Informatik, Im Stadtwald, D-6600 Saarbrücken

The axioms in the formal parameter part of QSORT are an approximation of the usual first-order axioms for total orders in a *Horn clause* setting. QSORT can be instantiated with specifications that contain a boolean function <= satisfying the given axioms. QSORT is based on the package LIST which is an instance of the generic package LISTS.

```
generic
  type ELEM is private;
package LISTS is
  type list is private;
  subtype nelist is list;
  empty: list;
  cons: ELEM # list --> nelist;
  first: nelist --> ELEM;
  tail: nelist --> list;
  append: (l1: list) # (l2: list) --> (l3: list) ::
              l1 in nelist or l2 in nelist -> l3 in nelist;
  axiom for all e: ELEM; l, l1: list =>
        first(cons( e, l)) = e,
        tail(cons( e, l)) = l,
        append( empty, l) = l,
        append( cons( e, l), l1) = cons( e, append( l, l1));
end LISTS;
```

empty denotes the empty list, cons adds an element at the beginning of a list. first and tail are the corresponding selection functions. append concatenates two lists.

An actual parameter candidate for QSORT is the following specification of integers:

```
package INT is
  type integer is private;
  subtype natural is integer;
  subtype inatural is integer;
  subtype positive is natural;
  subtype negative is inatural;
  subtype zero is (i:integer :: i in natural and i in inatural);
  0: zero;
  succ: natural --> positive;
  "-": (i1: integer) --> (i2: integer) ::
        i1 in positive -> i2 in negative;
  "<=": integer # integer --> BOOLEAN;
  axiom for all n, m: natural; p: positive; i: integer =>
        - 0 = 0,
        - (- i) = i,
        (0 <= n) = true,
        (p <= 0) = false,
        (succ(n) <= succ(m)) = (n <= m),
        (- n <= m) = true,
        (n <= - p) = false,
        (- n <= - m) = (m <= n);
end INT;
```

This specification makes intensive use of the *subtype* feature. The integers are constructed using 0, s and –. qsortint instantiates QSORT with INT, binding the formal parameter element ELEM to INT.integer and <= to INT."<=":

```
with QSORT, INT;
package qsortint is
  package qsortinteger is new QSORT( INT.integer, INT."<=");
end qsortint;
```

This completes the specification of our example. In the following sections we will show how to transfer this specification to CEC, how to complete it and how to compute with the completed specification.

4.3.2.2 Establishing a connection to CEC

Selecting the option **CEC commands** in the **Commands** menu from a PAnndA-S transformer, you can access a submenu with some basic CEC-commands. Starting a CEC process and connecting it to the

PAnndA-S editor is achieved by the command **connect**. This causes the creation of a new window with a new CEC process:

```
        CEC Version 1.5 (Quintus-Prolog 2.x)
           saved on Feb 15, 1990 at 22:02

  Copyright: PROSPECTRA group, University of Dortmund
       e-mail: hg@informatik.uni-dortmund.de

To obtain help, type  "??<space>.<return>"
```

We will call this window the *CEC window* in the following. This process is terminated by selecting **kill** (PAnndA-S will not terminate the process automatically on **exit**).

4.3.2.3 Transfering specifications

You have to transform your specification to AS2 before transferring it to CEC. To transfer a specification use the CEC-command **transfer**. It will prompt for the name of an order specification. The default is `noorder`, which should be used if no file containing an order specification is available. Simply click on the start button to transfer the specification:

Transfering the `LISTS` specification results in

```
------------ transfer ------------
[collecting garbage...]
[evaluating base of lists.eqn with noorder...]
 [thawing standard.q2.0 into user...]
 [storing to standard.noorder...]
[reading body of lists.eqn...]
[analyzing axioms...]
[collecting garbage...]
Specification accepted
```

on your CEC window.

4.3.2.4 Displaying specifications

By invoking the CEC-command **show** you can display the result of the translation of the package `LISTS` into a CEC-specification:

```
------------ show ------------

Current order-sorted equations

  1     first(cons(e,l)) = e
  2     tail(cons(e,l)) = l
  3     append(empty,l) = l
  4     append(cons(e,l),l1) = cons(e,append(l,l1))


Current order-sorted rules



Current order-sorted nonoperational equations



Some axioms may be reducible.
Some superpositions may be nontrivial.
```

This representation hides the fact that within CEC order-sorted specifications are represented in many-sorted form. The internal CEC-command `showms` makes it possible to look at the many-sorted version of the axioms. Access to the internal CEC-commands is provided by the CEC-command **goal** (→ 4.3.3).

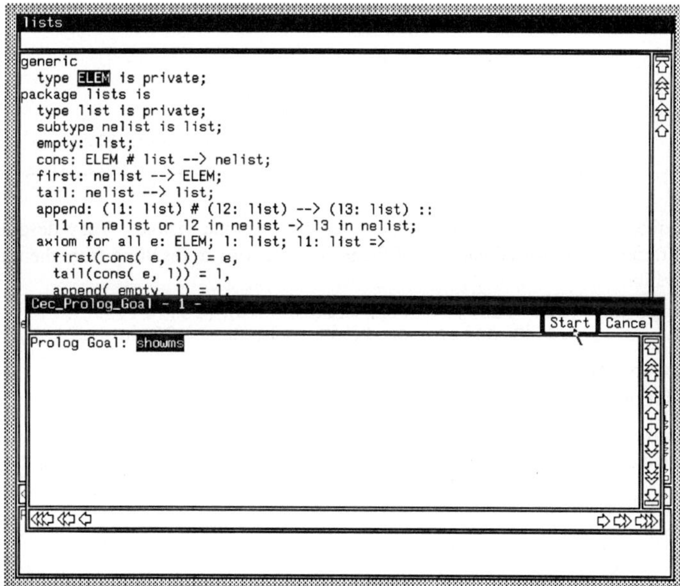

goal allows to send prolog goals, and CEC-commands in particular, to the CEC-system. For `showms` this results in:

```
------------ goal ------------

[[showms]]

Current equations

  1     first(cons(e:elem,l:list)) = e:elem
  2     tail(cons(e:elem,l:list)) = l:list
  3     append(empty,l:list) = l:list
  4     append(cons(e:elem,l:list),l1:list) =
            cons(e:elem,append(l:list,l1:list))


Current rules

  1     append(X2:list,list(X1:nelist)) =
            list(append(X2:list,X1:nelist))
  2     append(X2:nelist,list(X1:nelist)) =
            append(list(X2:nelist),X1:nelist)
  3     append(list(X2:nelist),X1:list) =
            list(append(X2:nelist,X1:list))
  4     append(list(X2:nelist),X1:nelist) =
            append(X2:nelist,X1:nelist)
  5     append(X2:nelist,list(X1:nelist)) =
            append(X2:nelist,X1:nelist)


Current nonoperational equations

  1     list(X1:nelist) = list(X2:nelist) =>
            X1:nelist = X2:nelist
  2     integer(X1:natural) = integer(X2:natural) =>
            X1:natural = X2:natural


The following rules may be reducible: [1,2,3]
The following superpositions may be nontrivial:
R4xR4; R5xR5; R1xR1; R1xR3; R2xR2; R2xR5; R3xR1; R3xR3; R5xR2
```

Now some additional rules and nonoperational equations become visible. They describe the relation between the different many-sorted variants of the operator `append`, resulting from the translation of the operator declaration

```
append: (l1: list) # (l2: list) --> (l3: list) ::
          l1 in nelist or l2 in nelist -> l3 in nelist;
```

and the subtype declaration

```
subtype nelist is list;
```

respectively, into equivalent many-sorted specification fragments.

By using **goal** and the internal CEC-command `sig` one can display the signature of the specification:

```
------------ goal ------------

[[sig]]

Signature :

cons true         : bool.
cons false        : bool.
op $inj           : (nelist -> list).
op empty          : list.
op cons           : (elem * list -> nelist).
op first          : (nelist -> elem).
op tail           : (nelist -> list).
op append         : (list * list -> list).
op append         : (nelist * list -> nelist).
op append         : (list * nelist -> nelist).
op append         : (nelist * nelist -> nelist).
op $inj           : (natural -> integer).
op <              : (integer * integer -> bool).
```

All identifiers in uppercase are changed to lowercase and some identifiers have been renamed. For more about this translation process see chapter 5 of volume 1.

4.3.2.5 Completion of hierarchical specifications

CEC stores specification modules in *specification variables.* Whenever a specification is transferred, CEC tries to load any imported specification from a specification variable. Specifications are stored when they are transferred or when you use the internal CEC-command `store` (→ 4.3.4). Hierarchical specifications should be completed in a bottom-up fashion, starting from the primitive basic modules. After successful completion the final state of the specification should be stored. CEC will then use the completed specification and not complete it again when it is imported as part of a larger specification. The internal CEC-command `load` (→ 4.3.4) allows to load the current state from a specification variable. You may use specification variables freely to load and store specifications, e.g., you may want to store your specification before taking some critical decision during completion. The `specifications`-command will list all currently defined specification variables.

If CEC doesn't find a specification variable it tries to read a file containing a *frozen state.* This is very similar to a specification variable, but instead of an internal variable the specification is stored in a file. The commands are `freeze` to write and `thaw` to read a frozen state.

Completing `LISTS`

Assume that the specification `LISTS` has been transferred previously. Now we start the completion process using the CEC-command **complete**. For ordered completion the construction of a termination ordering is required. For the first three equations there is only one possible choice of orientation for any termination ordering. CEC can orient these equations into rules without requesting user interaction.

```
------------ c ------------

rule deleted:
              2     append(X2:nelist,list(X1:nelist)) =
                    append(list(X2:nelist),X1:nelist)

new rule      6     append(empty,l:list) = l:list .

new rule      7     first(cons(e:elem,l:list)) = e:elem .

new rule      8     tail(cons(e:elem,l:list)) = l:list .
```

For the fourth equation, both directions are terminating and the user is asked for a decision:

```
Trying to orient equation
        append(cons(e:elem,l:list),l1:list) =
        cons(e:elem,append(l:list,l1:list))
into a reductive rule:

Consider the terms
        append(cons(e,l),l1)
and
        cons(e,append(l,l1)).

This pair can be ordered in both directions.
For which  direction would  you like to have precedence
suggestions ?
                    1.   ----->
                    2.   <-----
your choice?(#.): 1.
```

Since the default termination ordering used by CEC is `neqkns`[3] (except if the specification contains associative and commutative operators demanding the use of `poly`), the user is asked to define or extend some precedence ordering on the operators. CEC suggests possible ordering directions and precedence definition. In this example we choose to orient the equation from left to right and, therefore, have to accept the precedence `append` > `cons`.

```
Trying to orient equation
        append(cons(e:elem,l:list),l1:list) =
        cons(e:elem,append(l:list,l1:list))
into a reductive rule:

Consider the terms
        append(cons(e,l),l1)
and
        cons(e,append(l,l1)).

To order this pair you have to extend the precedence as
follows:

    Direction   Suggestions
    ---------   -----------
 1.    -->         'append' > 'cons'
 n.      no choice
your choice?(#.): 1.
```

Now the equation is turned into a rule and the system starts to compute superpositions to ensure confluence of the system.

[3] `neqkns` stands for the recursive path decomposition ordering after Kapur, Narendran and Sivakumar ("`kns`") without allowing equivalences between operators ("`neq`").

```
new rule  9     append(cons(e:elem,l:list),l1:list) =
                cons(e:elem,append(l:list,l1:list)) .

[16 superpositions yet to be considered.]

instance  5     X1:nelist = append(empty,X1:nelist)
of        1     append(X2:list,list(X1:nelist)) =
                list(append(X2:list,X1:nelist))
by superposing
          6     append(empty,l:list) = l:list
on the left side.

new rule 10     append(empty,X1:nelist) = X1:nelist .

[7 superpositions yet to be considered.]

instance  6     cons(e:elem,list(append(l:list,X1:nelist))) =
                append(cons(e:elem,l:list),X1:nelist)
of        5     append(X2:nelist,list(X1:nelist)) =
                append(X2:nelist,X1:nelist)
by superposing
          9     append(cons(e:elem,l:list),l1:list) =
                cons(e:elem,append(l:list,l1:list))
on the left side.

new rule 11     append(cons(e:elem,l:list),X1:nelist) =
                cons(e:elem,list(append(l:list,X1:nelist))) .

[2 superpositions yet to be considered.]

3 superpositions have been computed.
Time used: 4.51601 sec.

yes
```

The resulting system is

```
Current order-sorted equations



Current order-sorted rules

   6     append(empty,l) = l
   7     first(cons(e,l)) = e
   8     tail(cons(e,l)) = l
   9     append(cons(e,l),l1) = cons(e,append(l,l1))


Current order-sorted nonoperational equations



All axioms reduced.
All superpositions computed.
No more equations, the system is complete.

yes
```

4.3.2.6 *Specifying the ordering*

The first part of our example session showed how to build the ordering by querying the user during completion. Nevertheless, it is often more convenient to use a file, especially if the same module has to be completed more than once. For `LIST` an appropriate ordering would be

```
order neqkns for lists.
greater([[append/2,tail/1,first/1,cons/2,empty/0]]).
status([append/2:lr]).
```

`greater` takes as its argument a list of lists of operators, where each sublist specifies that its elements are in descending order. Note that the example ordering is total. The ordering between operators usually reflects how some operations are built on top of others. `status` specifies for an operator how its argument terms are to be compared: as a multiset (`ms`), from left to right (`lr`) or from right to left (`rl`), respectively. In most cases `ms` will suffice. However, if in some recursive rule the left subterm decreases, while the right one increases, `lr` should be used.

Unfortunately the termination ordering method `neqkns` is not appropriate for proving the termination of the quicksort algorithm. We will need `poly3` to do this. Because orderings `neqkns` and `poly` cannot be mixed it is required that all termination proofs in specifications imported from `QSORT` or given as formal parameter instantiation of `QSORT` use a polynomial ordering.

It is possible for polynomial orderings to specify them during completion, although we suggest in this case to prepare order specifications in advance. To use `poly3` for `LISTS` you will need to create a file `lists.poly3.ord`[4]. Our file looks like this:

```
order poly3 for lists.
setInterpretation([
   cons(x,y)                               : [3*x+y+1,x+y,x+y],
   empty                                   : [2,2,2],
   tail(x)                                 : [2*x,2*x,2*x],
   first(x)                                : [2*x,2*x,2*x],
   append(x,y)                             : [x+y,x+y,2*x+y],
   'append-list-list-list'(x,y)            : [x+y+4,x+y+1,x+y+1],
   'append-nelist-list-nelist'(x,y)        : [x+y+2,x+y+1,x+y+1],
   'append-nelist-nelist-list'(x,y)        : [x+y+3,x+y+1,x+y+1],
   'append-nelist-nelist-nelist'(x,y)      : [x+y+1,x+y+1,x+y+1],
   '$inj-list-nelist'(x)                   : [x+1,x+1,x+1]
]).
```

Each operator is interpreted by a tuple of polynomials. To order terms, the terms are evaluated to triples and their components are then compared lexicographically, from left to right. In most cases a single polynomial will suffice (in which case the square brackets may be omitted). The polynomials must contain each variable at least once and may not contain negative coefficients. Constants must be interpreted with 2 or greater.

You can load the information contained in this file using the `loadOrder`-command, or you can transfer the package LISTS as described in section 4.3.2.3 and enter `poly3` as order name. CEC then automatically reads the order specification, and is able to complete the specification without any further user interaction.

We store the completed specification in the specification variable `lists.poly3`.

Completing `QSORT`

The next step is the completion of the `QSORT` specification. We supply the order specification

```
order poly3 for qsort using poly3 for lists.
setInterpretation([
   <=(x,y)     : [x+y+5, x+y+5, x+y+5],
   sort(x)     : [2*x, 2*x, 2*x],
   split(x,y)  : [x+y+1, x+2*y, x+2*y],
   pair(x,y)   : [x+y, x+y, x+y]]).
```

and transfer the specification. Not only the equations concerning the operations `sort` and `split` are completed, but also the equations of the formal parameter part. This is done in arbitrary order, so the completion procedure starts with

[4] If CEC is invoked via a remote shell, its working directory is your home directory on the other machine. Otherwise it is the directory where you invoked the PAnndA-S editor. To read order specifications from files it is necessary to set the working directory. Use the CEC-command **goal** to execute `cd` *'directory'*, where *directory* contains your order specifications.

```
new rule  12     sort(empty) = empty .

new rule  13     split(e1:elem,empty) = pair(empty,empty) .

new rule  14     e1:elem<=e1:elem = true .
```

Then the system discovers that it is unable to orient the clause stating the totality of =>:

```
Checking reductivity constraints for rule
        e1:elem<=e2:elem = false => e2:elem<=e1:elem = true:
The current ordering fails to prove
[e2:elem<=e1:elem]  >  [e1:elem<=e2:elem,false].
At this point you may take any of the the following actions:
a. for assume to be proved
p. for postpone
n. for considering equation as nonoperational
   Please answer with a. or c. or p. or n.
   (Type A. to abort) > n.
```

We want to consider this equation as nonoperational and hence entered "`n.`" above.

Conditional equations become useless for the equational theory, and hence in fact nonoperational, if they are superposed on at least one of their conditions by all rewrite rules. This may yield new conditional equations which, when taken together, define the same equational theory as the original equation. However, they may have better operational properties than the equation they have been generated from. Equations which cannot be oriented into a reductive rule must either become redundant eventually or considered nonoperational.

Checking the redundance of conditional equations requires to compare certain instances different applications of equations and rewrite rules with respect to the given termination ordering. The comparison of an instance of an equation is performed by comparing its literals. The *status* of an equation determines the order in which the literals of the equation should be inspected. The status `ms` means that the literals are compared as a multiset. Instead of `ms` the user can choose an arbitrary sequence of the literals by entering a permutation of `[0,..,`n`]` where n is the number of conditions (→ [Ganzinger 88]). A good rule of thumb is to use `[0,..,`n`]` whenever two literals are equal up to variable renaming or replacing `true` by `false` or vice versa, and otherwise to use `ms`.

Thus we want to use `[0,1]` here:

```
In which order should the literals of the equation be
inspected when comparing proofs that use this equation?
Please enter ms (for multiset ordering) or a permutation
of [0 .. 1]
(0 stands for the consequent,
 i>0 for the ith condition). > [0,1].
```

The other two equations concerning <= can be handled in the same way.

Clauses with extra variables in the condition or in the right side of the consequence, like the recursive cases of `split` and `sort`, are usually considered not reductive. The standard definition of reductivity requires that the left side of the conclusion contains all variables of the clause and that it is greater than the right side and the conditions. All rules have to be reductive to ensure that rewriting and the evaluation of conditions terminate. CEC relaxes reductivity to quasi-reductivity, where conditions are oriented and deterministic goal solving is used to evaluate them. I.e., the left side of an oriented condition is rewritten to its normal form and then matched against the right side, which may bind some variables. The conditions for an equation to be quasi-reductive ensure that variables are bound before they are used and that the sizes of the actual instances created during rewriting are smaller than the left side of the conclusion. With this definition rewriting also is guaranteed to terminate (→ [Ganzinger 91]).

The above mentioned clauses for `split` and `sort` are quasi-reductive in this sense. CEC automatically detects this and orients them into rules.

For the quicksort specification, four nontrivial superposition instances are computed. For any nontrivial equation with at least one condition generated, CEC will ask the user to decide if this equation should be oriented, postponed or declared as nonoperational. Here we decide to declare these consequences as "nonoperational" and choose the first equation of the condition for superposition.

Completing `INT`

The completion of the `INT` specification is straightforward using the following order specification:

```
order poly1 for int.
setInterpretation([
        '$inj-integer-natural'(x)          : x + 1,
        '$inj-integer-inatural'(x)         : x + 2,
        '$inj-natural-positive'(x)         : x + 3,
        '$inj-inatural-negative'(x)        : x + 3,
        '$inj-natural-zero'(x)             : x + 4,
        '$inj-inatural-zero'(x)            : x + 4,
        0                                  : 2,
        succ(x)                            : x + 5,
        -x                                 : x + 9,
        '--integer-integer'(x)             : x + 8,
        '--negative-positive'(x)           : x + 6,
        <=(x,y)                            : x + y + 5]).
```

Completing `QSORTINT`

Transfering `QSORTINT` requires the instantiation of the formal parameter of `QSORT` with `INT`. Under the CEC paradigm of modules this simply implies the renaming of `ELEM` into `integer` and the (textual) combination of the `QSORT`- and `INT`-specifications. Checking the consistency of the axioms for <= in the actual parameter and in the formal parameter is achieved through completion.

4.3.2.7 Using the completed specification

Transfering objects from CEC to PAnndA-S

You may transfer equations, rules and nonoperational equations from CEC back to PAnndA-S with the command **get object**. Select a `DECLARATION_LIST` in your specification and call the transformation `CEC_Completion`. Then execute the command **get object**

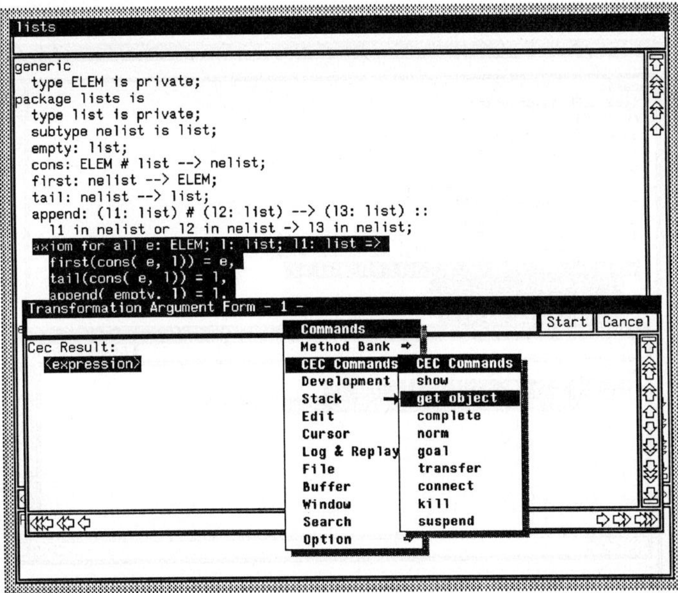

Then a second form will pop up and ask you for the kind and number of the object you want to transfer. Here we want to transfer rule 9 of the completed specification of LISTS:

After clicking on the start button rule 9 will be transferred from CEC to PAnndA-S and will be displayed in the Transformation Argument Form:

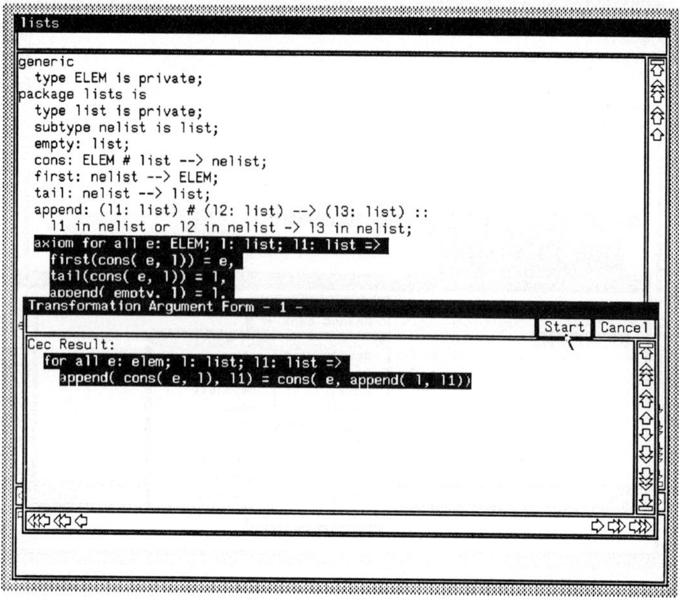

You may then insert the transferred equation or rule after the DECLARATION_LIST by clicking on the start button.

Normalizing

A completed specification enables CEC to normalize expressions in your specification by rewriting with the rules generated during completion. Select an expression in your specification and invoke the transformation CEC_Normalisation. Then use the CEC-command **norm** to normalize the expression:

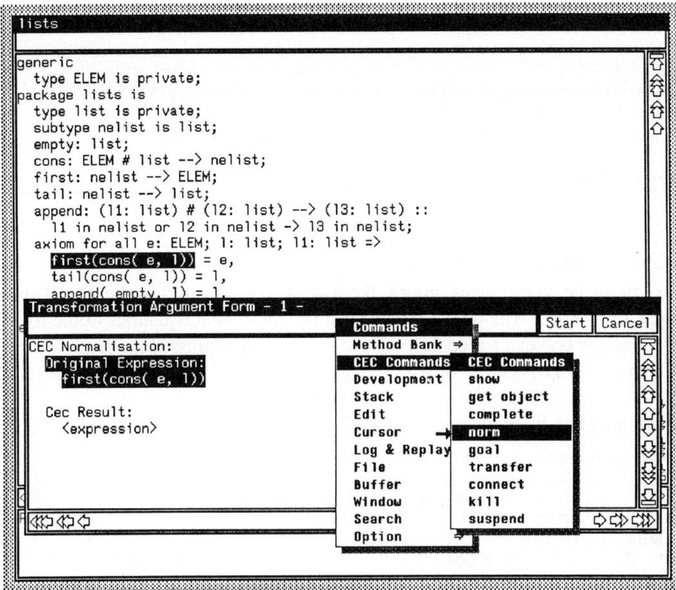

The expression is then transferred to CEC and normalized, the result is transferred back to PAnndA-S and displayed. By pressing the start button you may replace the original expression by the normalized one in your specification.

You may normalize terms which don't appear in your specification with **goal** and `norm`. As a final example we sort the list `[3,0,1]` using qsortint:

The result is indeed the list [0,1,3]:

```
------------ goal ------------

[[norm(sort(cons(s(s(s(o))),cons(o,cons(s(o),empty)))))]]
The normalform of
     sort(cons(s(s(s(o))),cons(o,cons(s(o),empty))))
is
     cons(o,cons(s(o),cons(s(s(s(o))),empty))) .
```

4.3.2.8 The Clausal Completion Subsystem

In this section we describe, via some examples, the way in which restricted equality clausal specifications are treated in the CEC system. The input axioms must be conditional equations of the form $T \Rightarrow t = t'$ or simply T, where T is any boolean sorted term. These axioms are expressed internally by restricted equality clauses of the form $(t = t')\vee l_1 \vee \ldots \vee l_n$ or $l_1 \vee \ldots \vee l_n$, where $l_1, \ldots, l_n$ are positive or negative non-equality literals.

This is an example of an input clausal specification:

```
module(natmax).
cons 0 : nat.
cons s : ( nat -> nat ).
op =<  : ( nat * nat -> bool ).
op  max : ( nat * nat -> nat ).
(0 =< x)          = true.
(s(x) =< 0)       = false.
(s(x) =< s(y))  =  (x =< y).
(x =< x)          = true.
(x =< s(x))       = true.
(x =< y) = true => (x =< s(y)) = true.
(x =< y) = true => max(x, y) = y.
(x =< y) = false => max(x, y) = x.
(x =< max(x, y)) = true.
(y =< max(x, y)) = true.
```

And this is the internal representation of the axioms before clausal completion:

```
1 )  B=<max(C,B)
2 )  B=<max(B,C)
3 )  B=<B
4 )  B=<s(B)
5 )  B=<B
6 )  - (s(B)=<s(C)) V B=<C
7 )  s(B)=<s(C) V - (B=<C)
8 )  - (s(B)=<0)
9 )  0=<B
10 )  - (B=<C) V B=<s(C)
11 )  max(B,C) = C V - (B=<C)
12 )  max(B,C) = B V B=<C
```

After reading an input specification (using as in the standard conditional case the **in**-command), we can start the completion procedure in order to transform the specification into a complete set of rules. For example, the previous specification could be completed as follows:

```
| ?- cr_kb.
Current clauses:

 1 )   B=<max(C,B)
 2 )   B=<max(B,C)
 3 )   B=<B
 4 )   B=<s(B)
 5 )   B=<B
 6 )   - (s(B)=<s(C)) V B=<C
 7 )   s(B)=<s(C) V - (B=<C)
 8 )   - (s(B)=<0)
 9 )   0=<B
 10 )   - (B=<C) V B=<s(C)
 11 )   max(B,C) = C V - (B=<C)
 12 )   max(B,C) = B V B=<C

  Reducing the clause:  B=<max(C,B)
  New c-rule:
   1 )   (B=<max(C,B)) --> true
  Reducing the clause:  B=<max(B,C)
  New c-rule:
   2 )   (B=<max(B,C)) --> true
  Reducing the clause:  B=<B
  New c-rule:
   3 )   (B=<B) --> true
  Reducing the clause:  B=<s(B)
  New c-rule:
   4 )   (B=<s(B)) --> true
  Reducing the clause:  B=<B
  Reducing the clause:  - (s(B)=<s(C)) V B=<C
  New c-rule:
   5 )   - (B=<C) => (s(B)=<s(C)) --> false
         complement  - (B=<C)
  Reducing the clause:  s(B)=<s(C) V - (B=<C)
    c-rule no. 5 modified.
  New c-rule:
   6 )   - (B=<C) => (s(B)=<s(C)) --> false
         B=<C => (s(B)=<s(C)) --> true
  Reducing the clause:  - (s(B)=<0)
...
  Reducing the clause:  B=<C V s(B)=<C V s(C)=<s(B)
  Reducing the clause:  B=<C V s(B)=<C V s(C)=<s(B)

  Computing critical pairs with c-rule  16 ) s(B)=<0 --> ...

Completion successfully terminated.

Final system of c-rules:

   3 )   (B=<B) --> true
   8 )   (0=<B) --> true
   9 )   B=<C => (B=<s(C)) --> true
         complement  B=<C
  11 )   B=<C => (max(B,C)) --> C
         - (B=<C) => (max(B,C)) --> B
  13 )   - (B=<C) => (s(B)=<C) --> false
         complement  - (B=<C)
  14 )   - (B=<C) / - (s(B)=<C) => (s(B)=<s(C)) --> false
         - (s(B)=<C) / B=<C => (s(B)=<s(C)) --> true
         complement  - (s(B)=<C)
  15 )   (B=<C V C=<B) --> true
  16 )   B=<0 => (s(B)=<0) --> false
         complement  B=<0
time spent: 16.617 sec.
yes
```

Clausal Completion, being a refutationally complete procedure, can also be used to detect inconsistencies in specifications. For example, if we try to complete another specification describing binary numbers (where the last axiom provokes an inconsistency):

```
module(ibinbase).
cons 0 : bin.
cons 1 : bin.
op(o,200,yf)  :  (bin -> bin).
op(1,200,yf)  :  (bin -> bin).
op <    : (bin * bin -> bool).
op \== : (bin * bin -> bool).
0 o = 0.
0 1 = 1.
(0 < 1) = true.
(a < b) = true => (a o < b o) = true.
(a < b) = true => (a o < b 1) = true.
(a o < a 1) = true.
(a < b) = true => (a 1 < b o) = true.
(a < b) = true => (a 1 < b 1) = true.
(a < b) = true and (b < a) = true => true = false.
(a < 0) = true => true = false.
(a < a) = true => true = false.
(a < b) = false and (b < a) = false => (a \== b) = false.
(b < a) = true  => (a \== b) = true.
(a < b) = false => (a \== b) = true.
```

we obtain the following result:

```
| ?- cr_kb.

Current clauses:

 1 )  B o<B 1
 2 )  0<1
 3 )  0 1 = 1
 4 )  0 o = 0
 5 )  - (B<C) V B o<C o
 6 )  - (B<C) V B o<C 1
 7 )  - (B<C) V B 1<C o
 8 )  - (B<C) V B 1<C 1
 9 )  - (B<C) V - (C<B)
 10 )  - (B<0)
 11 )  - (B<B)
 12 )  B<C V B\==C
 13 )  - (B<C) V C\==B
 14 )  B<C V C<B V - (B\==C)

  Reducing the clause:  B o<B 1
  New c-rule:
   1 )  (B o<B 1) --> true
  Reducing the clause:  0<1
  New c-rule:
   2 )  (0<1) --> true
  Reducing the clause:  0 1 = 1
  New c-rule:
          .
          .
          .
  Reducing the clause:  B<B

 Inconsistency detected: empty clause deduced.

yes
```

After completing a specification, clauses may be proved (or disproved) by clausal rewriting. For instance, after completing the "natmax" module seen above, we can try to prove the following clauses:

```
| ?- cr_prove([ (max(a,b) =< max(b,a) )]).

Proving the following theorem:

max(a,b)=<max(b,a)

  Theorem proved.

yes

| ?- cr_prove([ (max(a,b) =< max(b,b) )]).

Proving the following theorem:

max(a,b)=<max(b,b)

  Theorem disproved. Set of normal forms follows:
a=<b
yes

| ?- cr_prove([ (max(b,b) =< (max(a,b)))]).

Proving the following theorem:

max(b,b)=<max(a,b)

  Theorem proved.

yes
```

4.3.3 The CEC-commands

complete

calls the Knuth-Bendix completion procedure for the current specification. The procedure executes a fixed strategy of applications of the "completion inference" predicates `cp`, `orderEq`, `redRule`, `redEq`, `redNOpEq` and `superpose`. The PAnndA-C editor does not wait for a result or return code and the editor session can be continued immediately.

A manual guidance of the process is possible. Use **goal** for calls to the predicates mentioned above or use **suspend** to give control to CEC.

Completion — manual or automatic — can always safely be restarted after any abortion caused by answering "**A.**" to some query of the system. Because "**A.**" results in the execution of an `abort` command, the connection between PAnndA-S editor and CEC process is suspended and you must type "`serve.`" in your cec window to reestablish the connection, before you can restart the completion using the CEC-command **complete**.

The resulting system is not necessarily a reduced system. In the conditional case it is anyway not clear what a reduced equation is. On the other hand, a user may always call any of the `red`-predicates after completion to force reduction of the axioms. This may, however, lead to an incomplete system.

connect

Starts the CEC process and connects it to the PAnndA-C editor. If you use an editor version for windows, the CEC-system is called automatically in a new window, else for connecting the editor with the CEC-system, you have to invoke the CEC-sytem on demand of the editor (after the **connect**-command in the editor) with two arguments : the hostname of your computer and the port number which is displayed by the editor.

Warning: If the connection is interrupted (e.g., by executing an `abort` command), it is necessary to reconnect the two processes with the `serve` command in the cec window. **Warning:** Do not start any CEC related commands at the PAnndA-C editor while the connection is interrupted (otherwise the PAnndA-S editor will wait for a respond that will not occur until the connection is reestablished).

get object

Out of the parameter editor window resulting from the transform command "CEC_Completion" on DECLARATION_LIST you can call **get object**. It asks for an "Object kind", which is `rule` or `equation` or `nonoperational equation`, and a number. The object kind (default is `rule`) can be altered with transform commands. The number is typed in. The command **get object** returns the corresponding object from the CEC system to the parameter editor. Provided that an expression is RETURNed, and you click on the "Start" button, its translation to AS2 is inserted after the DECLARATION_LIST.

goal

The user can enter any prolog goal and send it to the CEC system. If the goal contains any uninstantiated variable `X` whose value should be output in the cec window, it is necessary to add a `write(X)` command to the goal you want to send, as there is no default output. **goal** is primarily intended for use with internal CEC-commands like `store` and `load`, that have arguments (e.g. filenames) that are not part of a specification, but expect no answer from the user. A list of all internal CEC-commands is given in chaper 4.3.4.

kill

Terminates the CEC process.

norm

Out of the parameter editor window resulting from the transform command "CEC_Normalisation" on EXPRESSION you can call **norm**. The command **norm** returns the normalized value (using the current set of rules in the CEC system) to the parameter editor. Provided that an expression is RETURNed, and you click on the "Start" button, its translation to AS2 replaces the EXPRESSION.

show

Starts the CEC command `show`, that diplays the current specification in the CEC system (see also the internal CEC-commands `sig`, `show` and `showms` in chapter 4.3.4).

suspend

Temporarily disconnects from the CEC process, which will take any further input from the terminal. To reconnect type "**serve.**" in the cec window.

Warning: Do not start any CEC related commands at the editor while the connection is interrupted.

transfer

Transfers the current specification in the PAnndA-C editor buffer to the CEC system. Only valid in buffers having phylum "Local_State" or "PROGRAM" and containing a PAnndA program. It prompts for an "order name" ($\rightarrow$ order_specification in CEC). The default is `noorder.` If you have no files containing order specifications simply click on the start button.

4.3.4 Listing of all internal CEC commands

If the commands are used in the cec window (after **suspend**), they must be followed by a full stop '.'. The full stop must be omitted if the commands are used as arguments for the CEC-command **goal**.

`??`<space>

lists the available CEC commands and refers to the `?`-command for further informations.

`??`*Keyword*

Lists only topics which contain *Keyword* as a substring. *Keyword* must be a Prolog atom, e.g. if it contains any special characters it must be enclosed in single quotes.

`?` (*Function*)

prints a short description for the CEC command *Function*. `?` is specified as prefix operator.

`applyRule`(*Term*, *RuleIndex*, *ReducedTerm*)

attempts to apply the rule with the given index once to the given term. Different redexes are tried upon backtracking. If successful, the reduced term is computed.

`c`

calls the Knuth-Bendix completion procedure. This executes a fixed strategy of applications of the "completion inference" predicates `orderEq`, `cp`, `superpose`, `redRule`, `redEq` and `redNOpEq`. A manual guidance of the process is possible by explicitly calling these predicates. The `repeat` predicate can be used to execute a predicate repeatedly until no more instances of it can be applied. An arbitrary interleaving of manual and automatic completion is supported. Also, completion — manual or automatic — can always safely be restarted after any abortion caused by answering "**A.**" to some query of the system. The resulting system is not necessarily a reduced system. In the conditional case it is anyway not clear what a reduced equation is. On the other hand, a user may always call any of the `red`-predicates after completion to force reduction of the axioms. This may, however, lead to an incomplete system.

`cr_kb`

Calls the contextual or clausal completion procedure. The axioms loaded into the system are translated into clauses (disjunctions of literals) with at most one equality literal which must be positive. If there is no translation into this language, the `cr_kb` procedure will stop with a corresponding message. The completion procedure consists of a fair application of the following inference rules:

1. Orienting an axiom. This is done by orienting the equality literal (if any), considering the rest of the literals as condition and checking for reductivity. If there is no equality literal, then the set of maximal literals of the clause is used as left hand side, true as right hand side and the rest of them as condition. The rules obtained that have the same left hand side are grouped together into c-rules. These c-rules contain also the set of complementary conditions with respect to the rules they contain.
2. computing contextual and resolution critical pairs between two c-rules.
3. simplifying axioms and c-rules.
4. deleting the trivial axiom "true".

Orientation is performed by using the current ordering. Completion can always safely be restarted after any abortion caused by answering "**A.**" to some query of the system.

`cr_prove (`*Clause*`)`

This command takes as argument a clause in list form. This clause may not have any negated equality literals. The system will try to prove the theorem to be deducible from the current system of c-rules. This proof process is performed by contextual rewriting.

`cr_show`

Shows the current system of c-rules. In each c-rule, first the reductive rules are displayed and below the complementary contexts.

cResume

restarts the completion procedure after the completion process was aborted by answering "**A.**" to some query of the system.

`cd (`*Path*`)`

Changes, as the cd command in UNIX, the directory for all following file-related commands. It is declared as prefix operator.
The path is given in form of a Prolog-atom, hence don't forget the quotes, if the path contains '`/`', '`.`', and '`..`' and other special characters.

`cd` does not implement file name generation using patterns. Hence, '`*`', '`?`' and '`[`' do not receive any special treatment.
Without an argument `cd` resets the current directory to the one in which the CEC-system was invoked initially.

`combineSpecs (`*StateName1*`,` *StateName2*`,` *CombinedSpec*`)`

The specifications stored (→ `store`) in specification variables *StateName1* and *StateName2* will be combined, if possible, by forming the union of the signature, axioms and pragmas. If *CombinedSpec* ≠ `user`, the result will be stored in *CombinedSpec*, and the current specification will not be affected. Otherwise, the combined specification becomes the new current specification.

`compile`

compiles the current set of rewrite rules into `compiled` Prolog. The compiled rules are used when calling `eval`. Later changes to the set of rewrite rules have no effect on `eval` unless a new call to `compile` is performed. The predicate `norm` always uses the current set of rewrite rules.

`compileRules (`*File*`)`

compiles the current set of rewrite rules to Prolog and writes the Prolog clauses into the file *File*`.rules`. *File*`.rules` may later be consulted or compiled (cf. `loadRules`) to produce a new definition of `eval`, cf. `compile`.

`cp (`*RuleIndex1*`,` *RuleIndex2*`)`

computes all critical pairs of rule *RuleIndex1* on rule *RuleIndex2*. The predicate fails, if no non-redundant critical pair can be found.

`constructor`

asks the user to enter an operator and declares this operator to be a constructor, if this is consistent with the current specification.

`delete` (*ModuleName*, *OrderName*)

deletes the specification variable named *ModuleName*.*OrderName*. If `delete` is used only with argument `ModuleName`, the specification stored under this name is deleted.

`enrich` (*ModuleName*, *OrderName*)

reads in additional parts of a specification from the specification file *ModuleName*.`eqn` and the order file *ModuleName*.*OrderName*.`ord` after saving the current state for later checks for consistency of the enrichment. These additional parts must form an enrichment (cf. chapter 3 of [Bertling et al. 89]). *ModuleName* and *OrderName* can be arbitrary Prolog atoms. Leaving out *OrderName* or even both arguments yields the same effect as for `in`.

`equal`

asks the user to enter a list of the following form:

[[*a*,*b*,*c*, ...], [*g*,*h*,*i*, ...], ...]

and declares operators to have equivalent precedences — only allowed for `kns`.
Meaning: $a = b = c = \ldots$ and $g = h = i = \ldots$.

`eval` (*Expression*)

computes the normalform of a expression using the most recently compiled set of rewrite rules. `eval` fails, if `compile` has not been called yet, cf. `compile`. The trace mechanism applies also to `eval`.

`forget`

forgets the complete undo history.

`freeze` (*ModuleName*, *OrderName*)

writes the state of the current specification to the file *ModuleName.OrderName*.`q2.0` and updates the content of the specification variable *ModuleName.OrderName*. If freeze is used without *OrderName* the state is just written to *ModuleName*.`q2.0`. If freeze is used without any argument the module name of the current specification is used for *ModuleName* and the current order name is used for *OrderName*. In the last two cases the specification variable determined by the current module name and the current order name will be updated (If current order name is `noorder` the specification variable associated with the current module name and the current termination ordering will be updated too). The specification may later be reused by thawing it from this file, cf. the `thaw`-command. The state of CEC remains unchanged by this operation.

`greater`

asks the user to enter a list of the following form:

[[*a*,*b*,*c*, ...], [*g*,*h*,*i*, ...], ...]

and adds ordered pairs of operators to the precedence.
Meaning: $a > b > c > \ldots$ and $g > h > i > \ldots$

`in(`*ModuleName*`,` *OrderName*`)`

reads in a specification from the file *ModuleName*`.eqn` and the associated order specification from the file *ModuleName*`.`*OrderName*`.ord`. As log-files are "enriched" order specifications, any log-file can be used as an order file. If not stated otherwise these files are assumed to be in the current directory. Before the specification is read in, CEC will be re-initialized, e.g. the current specification will be deleted. Specifications saved in variables will not be affected. *ModuleName* and *OrderName* must be Prolog atoms. *OrderName* becomes the current order name for the specification.
`in(`*ModuleName*`, noorder)` has the effect that no order specification is consulted. The termination ordering for the new specification will be initialized to a default value (`neqkns` or `poly1`, depending on the presence of AC-operators). Using `in` only with the parameter *ModuleName* yields the same effect. *ModuleName* = `user` expects input from terminal.

`interpretation`

displays all operator interpretations, provided `poly<N>` is the chosen termination ordering and asks the user if he wants to change any. If so all rules will be turned back into equations.

`load(`*ModuleName*`,` *OrderName*`)`

loads the system which is currently the value of the variable *ModuleName*`.`*OrderName*, cf. the `store`-command. If `load` is used only with argument *ModuleName*, this actual parameter completely specifies the name of the variable. Specification variables remain unchanged. *StateName* = `'$initial'` re-initializes the system.

`loadLog(`*ModuleName*`,` *OrderName*`)`

reads in the file *ModuleName*`.`*OrderName*`.@.ord`. If the completion process is started again, questions whose answers are already contained in *ModuleName*`.`*OrderName*`.@.ord` will be suppressed. If `loadLog` is used without the argument *OrderName* the information will be taken from the file *ModuleName*`.@.ord`. If `loadLog` is used without any argument the name of the current specification together with the current order name will be used.

`loadOrder(`*ModuleName*`,` *OrderName*`)`

reads in the file *ModuleName*`.`*OrderName*`.ord`. This file should contain information concerning the termination ordering. If `loadOrder` is used without the argument *OrderName* the information will be taken from the file *ModuleName*`.ord`. If `loadOrder` is used without any argument the name of the current specification together with the current order name will be used.

`loadRules(`*File*`)`

compiles the set of rewrite rules which has been stored previously in the file *File*`.rules`, cf. `compileRules`.

`moduleName`

displays the name of the current specification.

`nopEq(`*EquationIndex*`)`

declares equation with index *EquationIndex* as nonoperational. The predicate fails if equation *EquationIndex* does not exist or if the equation is trivial.

`norm` (*Expression*)

normalizes the input expression *Expression*. See also `eval`

`operators`

displays all operator precedences and stati in `kns` or `neqkns` or all polynomial interpretations in `poly`<N> respectively.

`order`

indicates the current termination ordering and asks the user whether he wants to change it. If a new ordering is selected and if the previous termination ordering is incompatible with the new ordering, all rules are turned back into equations and the completion must be repeated from the beginning.

`orderEq` (*EquationIndex*)

orients equation with index *EquationIndex*. The predicate fails if equation *EquationIndex* does not exist or if the equation cannot be oriented or turned into a nonoperational equation or if the equation is eliminated during reduction.

`orderName`

displays the name of the order specification associated with the current specification.

`polGreater` (*Interpretation1*, *Interpretation2*)

Only useful with ordering `poly`<N>. If it succeeds, *Interpretation1* > *Interpretation2* holds true (if > is the ordering on tuples of polynomials). Interpretations (i.e. tupels of polynomials) of terms can be generated via `polynomial`.

`polynomial` (*Term*, *Interpretation*)

yields the polynomial interpretation of *Term*. It fails, if the ordering is not `poly`<N>. If there are operators in *Term*, for which no polynomial interpretation is known, the user is asked for such an interpretation (and the given interpretation is stored).

`preregular`

succeeds if the current (order-sorted) signature is preregular, and fails otherwise. The preregularity condition is the regularity of Smolka/Nutt/Goguen/Meseguer 87 (→ [Smolka et al. 87]).

`prove` (*ConditionalEquation*)

proves or disproves the conditional equation *ConditionalEquation* by rewriting the conclusion to normalform, using the equations in the condition as additional rewrite rules. The method is incomplete for nonempty conditions and/or noncanonical systems.

`pwd`

prints out the current path.

`redEq` (*EquationIndex*)

reduces equation with index *EquationIndex*. The predicate fails if equation *EquationIndex* does not exist or if the equation cannot be reduced or if the equation is eliminated during reduction.

`redNopEq` (*NopEqIndex*)

reduces nonoperational equation with index *NopEqIndex*. The predicate fails if equation *NopEqIndex* does not exist or if the equation cannot be reduced or if the equation is eliminated during reduction.

`redRule` (*RuleIndex*)

reduces rule with index *RuleIndex*. The predicate fails if rule *RuleIndex* does not exist or if the rule cannot be reduced or if the rule is eliminated during reduction.

`regular`

succeeds if the current (order-sorted) signature is regular, and fails otherwise. The regularity condition is the one of Goguen/Meseguer 87 (→ [Goguen, Meseguer 87]).

`renameSpec` ([*OldSort1* <- *NewSort1*, . . . , *OldSortN* <- *NewSortN*,
OldOperator1 <- *NewOperator1*, . . . , *OldOperatorM* <- *NewOperatorM*])

renames the current specification according to the given lists of sort associations and operator associations. Only injective renamings of operators are allowed. Sorts may be renamed arbitrarily. Sorts and operators which are not mentioned remain unchanged.

`repeat` (*Predicate*)

causes repeated backtracking of *Predicate* until *Predicate* fails.

`resetOrient` (*Index*)

turns the rule Index back into an equation. If `resetOrient` is used without an argument, all rules are turned back into equations.

`restoreCEC` (*FileName*)

restores the CEC state (prolog state) in *FileName*.

`saveCEC` (*FileName*)

saves the whole CEC state (prolog state) in *FileName*. The CEC state can be used by simply invoking *FileName* instead of CEC or using the `restoreCEC`-command. If `saveCEC` is used without argument, the current CEC-name, i.e. the actual parameter for the last use of the `saveCEC`-command, is used for *FileName*. If no current CEC-name is known, the name `cec` will be taken (so be careful).

`setInterpretation`

asks the user to enter a list of the following form:

[*Operator(Arguments)* : *Interpretation*, . . .]

Provided `poly`<N> is the current termination ordering a new interpretation *Interpretation* for an operator *Operator* is added to the current state. The interpretation may be a polynomial over the variables in *Arguments* (if N = 1) or a list with N polynomials. The new interpretation must be compatible with all C- or AC-declarations in the current state.

`show`

shows the sets of equations, rules and nonoperational equations of the current specification in order-sorted notation. (Usually there exists more than one many-sorted representation of an order-sorted axiom.)

Rules $C \Rightarrow l \to r$ which are marked by an asterix $*$ have an associated auxiliary rule of form $C \Rightarrow l + X \to r + X$ where $+$ is the AC-operator at the top of l and X is a new variable of appropriate sort. Auxiliary rules are automatically generated when needed during completion modulo AC.

`show(`*SpecificationVariable*`)`

shows the sets of equations, rules and nonoperational equations of the specification which is stored in the variable *SpecificationVariable*.

`showCStatus`

displays the current completion status.

`showms`

shows the set of equations, rules and nonoperational equations of the current specification in many-sorted notation.

`sig`

displays the signature of the current specification.

`solve(`*Goal*`,` *Solution*`)`

tries to solve *Goal* and to return an answer-substitution if successful. The set of all answer-substitutions can be obtained by backtracking (enter ';'<return> at the user level).

Enter <return>, if no more solutions are wanted.

`sp(`*Index*`,` *NopEqIndex*`)`

same as `superpose(`*Index*`,` *NopEqIndex*`, left, condition(1))`.

`specifications`

lists the module and order names of all specifications that are currently saved in variables.

`status`

asks the user to enter a list of the following form:

`[`*Operator* : *Status*`, ...]`

and declares that the operators should have the desired stati provided `kns` or `neqkns` is the type of the current termination ordering. *Status* can be `lr` for *left-to-right*, `rl` for *right-to-left* or `ms` for *multiset*.

`store(`*ModuleName*`,` *OrderName*`)`

saves the current specification in a specification variable named *ModuleName*`.`*OrderName*. If `store` is used only with argument *ModuleName* the specification is saved in a variable with this name, if `store` is used without any argument, we take the names currently associated with the specification. For later restoring use the command *load*. The system remains unchanged except for this variable containing afterwards the current specification.

`storeLog` (*ModuleName*, *OrderName*)

creates the log-file. The name of the log-file is *ModuleName*.`@.ord`. It has the format of an order specification file which can be used with the `in`-command or the `loadLog`-command. If `storeLog` is used only with argument *ModuleName* the log-file is named *ModuleName*.`@.ord`, if `storeLog` is used without any argument, the log-file is named <moduleName>.<orderName>.`@.ord`.

`storeOrder` (*ModuleName*, *OrderName*)

creates a file named *ModuleName*.*OrderName*.`ord`. It has the format of an order specification file which can be used with the `in`-command or the `loadOrder`-command. If `storeOrder` is used only with argument *ModuleName*, the name *ModuleName*.`ord` is used. If the command `storeOrder` is used without any argument, the order specification file created is named <moduleName>.<orderName>.`ord`.

`superpose` (*RuleIndex*, *NopEqIndex*, *Literal*, *LiteralSide*)

superposes the left-side of the rule *RuleIndex* on the *LiteralSide*-side of the literal *Literal* of the nonoperational equation with index *NopEqIndex*. It fails if no non-redundant superpositions can be found, if any of the two axioms can be reduced, or if superpositions of the specified type need not be computed to achieve fairness.
To denote the *LiteralSide* `left` and `right` are used. *NopEqIndex* must be the index of a nonoperational equation. Considering superposition with $L_1 \wedge \ldots \wedge L_n \Rightarrow L$, we use `conclusion` to denote L, and `condition(`i`)` to denote L_i in *Literal*.

`superpose(reflexivity,` *NopEqIndex*, *Literal*, _)

tries to apply equality resolution (i.e., resolution with $x = x$) to the literal *Literal* of the nonoperational equation with index *NopEqIndex*. It fails if no non-redundant superpositions can be found, if any of the two axioms can be reduced, or if superpositions of the specified type need not be computed to achieve fairness.

`'superpose!'` (*RuleIndex*, *NopEqIndex*, *Literal*, *LiteralSide*)

same effect as `superpose`, except that the specified superposition will be performed in any case, even if not necessary for fairness of completion.

`thaw` (*ModuleName*, *OrderName*, *SpecificationVariable*)

This command is the inverse operation of `freeze` and restores the specification previously frozen in *ModuleName*.*OrderName*.`q2.0` into the *SpecificationVariable*. The current specification and other variables will be not affected by this operation. If `thaw` is used without argument *StateName* the current specification is overwritten by the thawed specification. Specifications saved in variables will still not be affected by this operation. If `thaw` is used only with argument *ModuleName* the frozen specification will be taken from the file *ModuleName*.`q2.0`.

`undo`

can be entered at the system's top level to set the system to the state before the last command that has caused a state change, if there was any. `undo` can be used repeatedly to undo several steps of state changes. It also undoes `undoUndo`-calls. There is no way, however, to backtrack from single decisions that have been taken while running the completion process.

`undoUndo`

allows to undo the last `undo`-command at the system's top level. Repeated use of this command undoes sequences of `undo`-commands. Chains of undo-calls begin at the last user interaction different from an `undo` or `undoUndo`.

The CEC-commands `equal`, `greater`, `status`, `setInterpretation` and `constructor` can be used as order pragmas, cf. chapter 2 of [Bertling et al. 89].

4.3.5 Syntax of the PA^{nn}dA-S-Subset, Suited for Completion

Only a subset of all Pannda specifications (and therefore only a subset of all Pannda-S specifications) can be translated to CEC specifications. In the following we describe the syntactical restrictions which must be fulfilled for any specifications that you want to transfer to CEC.

A special Pannda-S editor displaying warnings about specification parts that do not belong to this subset is available. It is called 'CEC subset checker' and is designed for checking (existing and currently edited) Pannda-S specifications. You can use a specification within the CEC system, if the checker displays no warning for it (the warnings of the CEC subset checker contain the string "*** CEC:"). It is possible to integrate this checker into other editor tools (a command to switch on/off the checker (i.e. display/suppress the warnings in Pannda-S editor buffers) is needed).

2.1 <graphic_character> ::= <letter>
| <digit>
| <space_character>
| <special_character>
| <format_effector>
<letter> ::= <upper_case_letter>
| <lower_case_letter>

Comments: Upper case letters, lower case letters and digits are defined as usual.
Special characters are: " & ' ( ) * + , - . / : ; < = > _ | ! $ % ? @ [\ ] ^ ` { } ~
Format effectors are horizontal tabulation, vertical tabulation, carriage return, line feed and form feed.

2.3 <identifier> ::= <letter> {[_] <letter_or_digit> }
<letter_or_digit> ::= <letter>
| <digit>

Changes: `list` and `optional` are not special identifiers in the CEC-system. Compare appendix 4.3.6 for a listing of the reserved words.

Comments: Identifiers differing only in the use of corresponding upper and lower case letters are considered as the same. The CEC-system distinguishes between lower-case and upper-case letters, so all identifiers will be transformed into the corresponding identifiers consisting only of lower-case letters.

2.4 <literal> ::= <string_literal>
| <integer_literal>

Changes: `others` and `undefined` are not special literals in the CEC-system.

2.5 <integer_literal> ::= <digit> {<digit>}

Changes: no underline character in integer literals

Comments: An integer literal will be translated into the corresponding `succ`-term (e.g.: 2 will be translated into `succ(succ(0)))` when transferring the specification to the CEC-system.

2.6 <string_literal> ::= " {<graphic_character>} "

Comments: If a quotation character value (") is to be represented in the sequence of character values, then a pair of adjacent quotation characters must be written at the corresponding place within the string literal. General strings are not implemented in the CEC-system, so strings are only allowed as operator symbols in a PAnndA-S specification.

2.7 <comment> ::= -- {<graphic_character>}

3.1 <declaration> ::= <private_type_declaration>
| <subtype_declaration>
| <function_specification>
| <package_specification>
| <generic_specification>
| <generic_instantiation>
| <axiomatic_annotation>
| <comment>

Comments: (Generic) Packages inside of packages are not implemented in the CEC-system. They will be flattened when transformed into a CEC-specification.

3.4 <subtype_declaration> ::=
`subtype` <identifier> `is` <name> `;`
| `subtype` <identifier> `is` `(` <designator> `:` <name restriction> `)` `;`

Changes: In PAnndA-S an identifier can be declared as a subtype of an arbitrary type expression with an arbitrary constraint. For the CEC-system the supertype can only be a type name and only a special kind of restriction is allowed.

Comments: A subtype in PAnndA-S is a type together with a constraint; a value is said to belong to a subtype of a given type if it belongs to the type and satisfies the constraint. Declaring a subtype in the CEC-system means that the set represented by the subtype is a subset of the set represented by the supertype. A restriction allowed in the CEC-system is a logical expression that restricts the subtype to be a subtype of an intersection of several types. This is the only possibility to declare that a type is a subtype (in the sense of CEC) of several types, e.g.: The type `zero` of the qsort-example is a subtype of the types `natural` and `inatural`. This will be specified in PAnndA-S in the following way:

```
subtype zero is (i:int :: i in natural and i in inatural);
```

Generally, the declaration that: s is a subtype of the types $t_1, t_2, \ldots, t_n$ $(n \geq 2)$ has to be written in PAnndA-S in the following way

`subtype` s `is (i:`t `:: i in` t_1 `and i in` t_2 `and ... and i in` t_n`);`

where t is a common supertype of $t_1, t_2, ..., t_n$ $(n \geq 2)$. This declaration is only possible if such a common supertype exists, otherwise we cannot declare s to be a subtype of $t_1, t_2, ..., t_n$ for $(n \geq 2)$.

3.5 <function_type_expression> ::=
<tuple_type_expression> --> <simple_type_expression> ;
<tuple_type_expression> ::=
<simple_type_expression> {# <simple_type_expression>}
<simple_type_expression> ::=
<name>
| (<domain>)

Changes: It is only allowed to use the weak function arrow in CEC-specifications, and there exist no higher-order functions in the CEC-system.

There exists no equivalence for extended types in the CEC-system.

Comments: There exist no higher-order functions in the CEC-system, so no function type or tuple type expression is allowed as result type or parameter type of a function.

4.1 <name> ::= <designator>
| <expanded_name>
<expanded_name> ::= <name> . <designator>

Comments: The feature of referencing designators by putting the name of the package in front of the designator is not implemented in the CEC-system. When transferring a specification to the CEC-system the prefix of the expanded names will be omitted.

4.3a
```
<logical_expression> ::=
        [<quantifier> <domain> {; <domain>} =>]
            <implication_or_comment> {[,] <implication_or_comment>}
<implication_or_comment> ::=
        <implication>
      | <comment>
<implication> ::=
        [ <expression> {and <expression>} -> ] <expression>
      | ( <logical_expression> )
<expression> ::=
        <boolean_expression>
      | <bool_or_simple_expression> = <bool_or_simple_expression>
<boolean_expression> ::=
        <relation>
      | <boolean_expression> <logical_operator relation>
<relation> ::=
        [not] <secondary> [<relational_operator> [not] <secondary>]
      | ( <boolean_expression> )
<bool_or_simple_expression> ::=
        <boolean_expression>
      | <simple_expression>
<simple_expression> ::=
        [<unary_adding_operator>] <term>
      | <simple_expression> <binary_adding_operator> <term>
<term> ::=
        <factor>
      | <term> <multiplying_operator> <factor>
<factor> ::=
        <secondary> [** <secondary>]
      | abs <secondary>
<secondary> ::=
        <primary>
      | <designator>
            [ ( <bool_or_simple_expression> {, <bool_or_simple_expression>} ) ]
<primary> ::=
        <identifier>
      | <name> . <designator>
      | ( <simple_expression> )
      | <literal>
```

Changes: exists, <->, and then, or else, in, defined and ^ are not allowed
no qualified expressions

Comments:

<logical_expression>

The ',' appearing as separator between implications of a logical expression corresponds to the operator and. There should not be any ',' after a comment in a logical expression.

<expression>

The short-circuit control forms and then and or else do not have semantic equivalences in the CEC-system, so they are not allowed in CEC-specifications. Expressions can only be boolean expressions, or equations between simple expressions.

<boolean_expression>

Boolean expression cannot include the equality relation.

<relation>
The membership test `in` cannot be used in logical expressions of axioms.

<factor>
The definedness test `defined` has no semantic equivalence in the CEC-system.

<secondary>
The function part of a function call must be restricted to a designator.

<primary>
A qualified expression is used to state which of a set of overloaded functions is meant or to constrain a value to a given subtype. Such expressions are not allowed in CEC-specifications.

There are no logical expressions inside of expressions allowed, so a primary can only be a parenthesized boolean or simple expression and not a parenthesized logical expression.

4.3b <logical_expression_for_restrictions> ::=
<implication_or_comment_for_restrictions>
{[,] <implication_or_comment_for_restrictions>}
<implication_or_comment_for_restrictions> ::=
<implication_for_restrictions>
| <comment>
<implication_for_restrictions> ::=
<expression_for_restrictions>
only for restrictions on supertypes
| <expression_for_restrictions> `->` <relation_for_restrictions>
only for restrictions on function types
| (<implication_for_restrictions>)
<expression_for_restrictions> ::=
<relation_for_restrictions>
| <expression_for_restrictions> `and` <expression_for_restrictions>
| <expression_for_restrictions> `or` <expression_for_restrictions>
only for restrictions on function types
| (<expression_for_restrictions>)
<relation_for_restrictions> ::=
<designator> `in` <name>
| (<relation_for_restrictions>)

Changes: Restrictions cannot be arbitrary logical expressions.

Comments: In PAnndA-S restrictions can be arbitrary expressions and they can occur at several points. In CEC-specifications restrictions are only allowed in subtype and function declarations and they are restricted to special forms.

```
4.5  <implicator>                  ::= ->
     <logical_operator>            ::= and | or | xor
     <relational_operator>         ::= > | >= | /= | < | <=
     <binary_adding_operator>      ::= + | -
     <unary_adding_operator>       ::= + | -
     <multiplying_operator>        ::= * | / | mod | rem
     <binary_high_prec_operator>   ::= **
     <unary_high_prec_operator>    ::= abs | not
     <binary_operator>             ::= <implicator>
                                     | <logical_operator>
                                     | <relational_operator>
                                     | <binary_adding_operator>
                                     | <multiplying_operator>
                                     | <binary_high_prec_operator>
     <unary_operator>              ::= <unary_adding_operator>
                                     | <unary_high_prec_operator>
```

Changes: `<->`, `&`, `defined`, `and then`, `or else` are not allowed,
= cannot be used as a relational operator in boolean expressions.

Comments: The operators above are given in the order of increasing precedence.

Because strings are not defined in the CEC-system there is no need for the string concatenation operator '`&`' in CEC-specifications.

The equivalence implicator '`<->`' cannot be used in CEC-specifications.

There exist no semantic equivalences for the short-circuit forms `and then` and `or else` and for the definedness test `defined` in the CEC-system.

```
4.11  <quantifier> ::= for all
```

Changes: `exists` not allowed

Comments: CEC-specifications do not include existential quantification.

```
6.1  <function_specification> ::=
             [--:] <designator> {, <designator>} : <function_type_expression restriction> ;
            | predicate <designator> {, <designator>} :
                  <tuple_type_expression> <restriction> ;
     <domain> ::=
             <designator> {, <designator>} : <name>
     <restriction> ::=
             :: <logical_expression_for_restrictions>
     <designator> ::=
             <identifier>
            | <operator_symbol>
     <operator_symbol> ::=
             <string_literal>
```

Changes: The restriction is moved from the domain to the function specification and subtype declaration.

Comments: The same function identifier or operator symbol can be used in several function specifications. The identifier or operator symbol is then said to be overloaded.

7.1 <package_specification> ::= `package` <identifier> `is` {<declaration>} `end`
[<*package*_identifier>] ;

7.2 <private_type_declaration> ::= `type` <identifier> `is` `private` ;

7.8 <axiomatic_annotation> ::= `axiom` <logical_expression> ;

10.1 <compilation_unit> ::= [<with_clause>] <library_unit> ;
<library_unit> ::= <package_specification>
| <generic_specification>
| <generic_instantiation>

10.2 <with_clause> ::= `with` <identifier> {, <identifier>} ;

12.1 <generic_specification> ::= <generic_formal_part> <package_specification> ;
<generic_formal_part> ::= `generic` {<generic_parameter>}
<generic_parameter> ::= <private_type_declaration>
| <function_specification>
| <axiomatic_annotation>
| <comment>

12.3 <generic_instantiation> ::=
`package` <identifier> `is`
`new` <*generic_package*_name> [<generic_actual_part>] ;
<generic_actual_part> ::=
(<generic_actual_parameter> {, <generic_actual_parameter>})
<generic_actual_parameter> ::=
<comment>
| <*function*_name>
| <*type*_name>

Changes: Generic actual parameters are restricted to function names and type names.

4.3.6 Predefined Operators in CEC

CEC operators	priority	fix	reserved	changable
=>	950	xfx	+	-
=	700	xfx	+	-
:	600	xfy	+	-
and	850	fy	+	-
@	50	fx	+	-
->	1050	xfy	-	-
cons, op	950	fx	-	-
in	935	xfy	-	-
let	910	fy	-	-
var	1100	fx	-	-
<	700	xfx	-	-
using	600	xfx	-	-
module, order	500	fx	-	-
+	500	yfx	-	-
for	400	xfx	-	-
*	400	yfx	-	-
:-, -->	1200	xfx	-	+
:-, ?-	1200	fx	-	+
public, multifile, mode, meta_predicate, dynamic	1150	fx	-	+
;	1100	xfy	-	+
,	1000	xfy	-	+
spy, nospy, \+	900	fy	-	+
not	900	fx	-	+
is, =.., ==, \==, @<, @>, @=<, @>=, =:=, =\=, >, =<, >=	700	xfx	-	+
-, /\, \/	500	yfx	-	+
|	500	xfy	-	+
-	500	fx	-	+
/, //, <<, >>	400	yfx	-	+
mod	300	xfx	-	+
^	200	xfy	-	+
?	200	fx	-	+

If an operator is *reserved*, it cannot me used in any signature. If an operator is not *changable*, it can be used in a signature, but its priority and fix may not be changed.

4.4. Proof Subsystem

Owen Traynor, University of Strathclyde[1]

This section describes the user interface of the PROSPECTRA proof subsystem. It also acts as a user manual. Justification is given for some design decisions made in the process of its construction. Further, the interface provided, which allows for the definition of tactics, is also defined.

4.4.1. Introduction

The proof system is interactive, based on the language manipulation facilities provided by the Cornell Synthesizer Generator (CSG) [Reps, Teitelbaum 88]. Conceptually the proof system is integrated with the PAnndA editors. No extension to the abstract syntax of PAnndA is required to represent the conjectures of the proof system; these are PAnndA-S logical formulae.

Proof derivations are represented by means of an abstract syntax. The proof abstract syntax is a means of structuring the development history of proven conjectures; the abstract form of this language is never manipulated directly by the user but is created as a side effect of applying inference rules to conjectures. The structuring of proofs via this abstract syntax also serves as a basis for reuse and replay.

In section 4.4.2 a definition of the basic inference rules used for PAnndA logic is given. Additionally some justification is given for pursuing the intuitionistic approach to deduction. Section 4.4.3 describes the interactive facilities available for using the system. In section 4.4.4 the basic schemes available for performing induction are detailed together with the treatment of equality and proof management facilities. In section 4.4.5 the facilities for defining tactics for the proof system are discussed and a few basic tactics are presented. Section 4.4.6 discusses some important aspects of the current version of the proof system, together with a description of the framework within which the proof theory for a particular specification is derived. Section 4.4.7 provides some examples, and section 4.4.8 gives a summary of system commands.

4.4.2. The Calculus

The inference rules used in proof are given below. All rules are presented in a top down manner with goal sequents on the bottom. Taking such an approach provides a closer correspondence with the transformation system; the goal directed application of a proof rule has a close correspondence with the application of a tactic. The rules are actually formulated as transformations within the PROSPECTRA system, this allows them to be composed in order to form proof strategies or tactics (as described in section 4.4.5). A sequent consisits of a set of assumtions (premisses) called the antecedent and a conjecture (goal) called a conclusion. The antecedent and conclusion of a sequent are separated by a turnstyle (|-). The inference system given here is based on Gentzen's Ga3 calculus (see [Kleene 62] and [Gentzen 69]). For justification of this formulation see [Schmidt 84] and [Ritchie 88] .

In the following,

x' - denotes new free variable, not already used in the sequent.

z - denotes term, appropriately selected so as to allow a successful conclusion to the proof.

§ - denotes a possibly empty list of premisses.

---

[1] present address: Universität Bremen

Rules

Immediate Validity	$\S, A \vdash A$
Duplication	$\dfrac{\S, A \vdash C}{\S, A, A \vdash C}$

Rules for Logical Connectives

Connective	**Antecedent**	**Consequent**
& (**and**)	$\dfrac{\S, A \& B \vdash C}{\S, A, B \vdash C}$	$\dfrac{\S \vdash A \& B}{\S \vdash A \quad \S \vdash B}$
v (**or**)	$\dfrac{\S, A \vee B \vdash C}{\S, A \vdash C \quad \S, B \vdash C}$	$\dfrac{\S \vdash A \vee B}{\S \vdash A} \quad \dfrac{\S \vdash A \vee B}{\S \vdash B}$
⇒(implication)	$\dfrac{\S, A \Rightarrow B \vdash C}{\S \vdash A \quad \S, B \vdash C}$	$\dfrac{\S \vdash A \Rightarrow B}{\S, A \vdash B}$
~ (**not**)	$\dfrac{\S, \sim A \vdash C}{\S \vdash A}$	$\dfrac{\S \vdash \sim A}{\S, A \vdash \text{contradiction}}$
⇔(iff)	$\dfrac{\S, A \Leftrightarrow B \vdash C}{\S, A \Rightarrow B, B \Rightarrow A \vdash C}$	$\dfrac{\S \vdash A \Leftrightarrow B}{\S, A \vdash B \quad \S, B \vdash A}$
∀(**for all**)	$\dfrac{\S, \forall x\, A(x) \vdash C}{\S, A(z) \vdash C}$	$\dfrac{\S \vdash \forall x\, A(x)}{\S \vdash A(x')}$
∃ (**exist**)	$\dfrac{\S, \exists x\, A(x) \vdash C}{\S, A(x') \vdash C}$	$\dfrac{\S \vdash \exists x\, A(x)}{\S \vdash A(z)}$

Examples of proofs performed using this calculus can be found in PROSPECTRA Report S.3.4-SN-12.0. Additionally some example proofs are given in section 4.4.7.

The motivation behind the choice of a sequent calculus for the proof system may, at first, seem somewhat arbitrary. However, under closer examination there are a number of advantages. Firstly, proofs are constructive. The tautology from classical logic,

A or not A,

does not hold. For such a conjecture to be proven a demonstration of A (or of ***not** A*) would have to be provided (of course the Excluded Middle axiom "*A **or not** A*" could be added as a premiss which would allow such classical tautologies to be proven). Thus proofs performed in an intuitionistic calculus are much more useful in the context of program synthesis or transformation synthesis since the framework provided by a constructive system is closer to a logic which would be employed in a program development context. Secondly, the system has a natural flavour, proofs can be read and abstracted. The sequent calculus provides a clean and elegant mechanism for interaction. Thirdly, the calculus is relatively efficient, providing a reasonable framework for automation.

4.4.3. Interacting with the Proof System

In this section, before detailing the way in which rules are invoked, a summary of the general structure of the proof system and its proofs is given. It is assumed that the reader is familiar with the interface facilities and capabilities of the Synthesizer-generated editors. For a more detailed account of the interface see [Reps, Teitelbaum 88]. For details regarding specifics of the PAnndA-S editor see part II chapter 3 of this publication. A summary of all the commands available for the manipulation of proof terms is given in section 4.4.8.

4.4.3.1. Structure of Proofs

Within the proof system all sequents are represented as logical formulae. A sequent is split into two parts: the antecedent (a set of assumptions) and a conclusion (what is actually to be proven given the assumptions). The major connective of all sequents, in terms of their representation as logical formulae, is the implies operator ("⇒"), this replaces the traditional "|–"[2] or turnstile. The antecedent of the sequent is a premiss list; a list of assumptions. The comma, which is normally used to signify the concatenation of assumptions, is replaced with a right associative conjunction, "***and***". There are no semantic anomalies introduced by giving "⇒" and "***and***" the interpretation of "|–" and "," respectively.

Each application of a primitive rule of the calculus causes a step or extension of the current proof tree. For example, a rule to remove an implication from the conclusion of a sequent would cause the fragment of the proof tree shown in (i) to be transformed to that shown in (ii).

(4.4.3-1) Extending the proof tree

(i)	>> (a **and** b) |– ((a **or** c) –> c)	by <step>
(ii)	>> (a **and** b) |– ((a **or** c) –> c)	by Implies Intro
	>> ((a **or** c) **and** (a **and** b)) |– c	by <step>

It should be obvious from the example how the application of a transformation rule to the sequent transforms the actual sequent and causes the proof tree to grow. More interesting are the rules which cause the current sequent to be split into two component sequents, both of which require to be shown or proven. These obviously cause the proof tree to be extended somewhat differently. For example, given (ii) above, applying a rule to remove the disjunction from the antecedent would cause the proof tree to be extended as shown in (iii).

---

[2] This is hidden from the user unless the trafo version of the proof system is employed. In this case "->" is the major connective and corresponds to the turnstile in sequents.

(4.4.3-2) Splitting the proof tree.

```
(iii)    >> ( a and b) |– ((a or c) –> c)           by Implies Intro
         >> ((a or c) and (a and b)) |– c           by Or Elim
            >> a and (a and b) |– c                 by <step>      (*)
     AND >> (c and ( a and b)) |– c PROVEN          by <step>      (*)
```

From the example it can be seen that the proof tree splits at the point of application of the rule into two subtrees. In the second subtree the sequent is obviously true since the term 'c' appears in the antecedent and the conclusion. In this case both subtrees, marked (*), are required to be proven for the proof to be complete.

All rules available in the proof system cause the proof tree to extend in one way or another. A synopsis of each rule is given in section 1.8. The approach taken in the formulation of the proof rules is a top down one, as can be seen by the presentation of the calculus for logical inference. However, the term 'top down' has been much abused and the phrase 'goal directed' is perhaps a better description.

4.4.3.2. *Creating a Proof*

There are a number of ways in which the proof system may be activated. Firstly, proof is associated with the development process. Therefore the proof system is integrated with the PAnndA transformer shell (see Vol II Chapter 4 of this publication).

Within the transformer shell the proof system can be invoked in the following ways:

- By selection of a Logical Expression and by calling the proof system directly for this expression.
- By applying a transformation which calls the proof system via the *verify* function. This is provided as a means of defining applicability conditions which require the verifier to ensure their correctness.
- By opening a browser with the PROOFROOT phylum as the buffer kind.

All of these activities result in a buffer being opened with the required logical formula as the conjecture of the proof. Different facilities are provided depending on the part of the proof term currently selected; these functions appear in the help pane.

In order to apply an inference rule a proof tree must be selected; in this context the appropriate component of the proof tree would be the placeholder <step>. When selected, a number of transformations become applicable. The active transformations correspond to those proof rules which are applicable in the current context. Selection of the desired rule will cause the proof tree to be extended accordingly. If a rule, which is not applicable in the context, is selected, then an error message is displayed highlighting the error. For example, given the proof object in (iv), if a rule for "not introduction" is selected the result would be as in (v).

(4.4.3-3) The initial proof

```
(iv)  Proof of <a –> (a or b)>
      >> empty |– a -> (a or b)          by <step>
      Not Proven
```

(4.4.3-4) An inappropriate rule application

```
(v)  Proof of <a -> (a or b)>
     >> empty |- a -> (a or b)        by Implies Elim
     >> a |- (a or b)                 by Not Intro  <-- Inappropriate Proof Rule
     >> a |- (a or b)                 by <step>
     Not Proven
```

As can be seen, the application has no effect on the sequent but the proof tree is extended. Generally, errors of this type will not occur unless manipulation of the initial conjecture somehow changes the applicability of the rules forming the proof tree. If the initial conjecture is modified, the attribute evaluation will propagate the change through the proof. If any rules are not applicable then they are highlighted as above. Generally, proof rules which would cause such immediate errors would not be available for application in an interactive context since only rules applicable to the current conjecture are available. However, the mechanism can be exploited as a means of parameterising proofs.

Some transformations, for example those which remove quantifiers from a sequent, require parameters. When interacting with the system, if a rule requiring a parameter is selected, a transformation parameter form appears. The appropriate parameter can then be entered in the form. After the proof tree has been extended by a transformation, the parameter will appear in the proof tree as a PAnndA phrase (which can be modified by invoking the parameter editor). For example, given a proof fragment as shown in (vi), by applying the rule for "for all elimination" the proof term would look like (vii).

(4.4.3-5) A universal quantification

```
(vi)  >> for all A:Int => A+(b+1)=A+b+1 |- F(y)+(b+1)=F(y)+b+)  by <step>
```

(4.4.3-6) Instantiation of a quantified variable

```
(vii) >> for all A:Int => A+(b+1)=A+b+1 |- F(y)+(b+1)=F(y)+b+1   by For All Elim with <F(y)>
      >> F(y)+(b+1)=F(y)+b+1 |- F(y)+(b+1)=F(y)+b+1               by <step>
```

The term *F(y)* in *italics* is an editable expression and can be modified, via the parameter editor, after the rule for "for all elimination" has been applied. The result of the modification will be propagated down the proof tree from that point[3].

At any point of a proof, if a subgoal is valid then the word PROVEN will appear in the proof after the appropriate sequent. When all the required subgoals of a proof are complete, the words "Not Proven" at the end of the proof will change to "QED". It should be noted that all the inference rules described in section 4.4.2 exist as transformations in the system. That is, each of the rules has a corresponding transformation in the proof system.

4.4.3.3. Backtracking

Backtracking is achieved by selecting the appropriate node of the proof tree and then progressing from that point again by transformation. Normally a subtree will be deleted, leaving a placeholder, from which point development continues.

3More generally, a predefined tactic for the instantiation of a quantified variable would be selected. Such a tactic would attempt to provide an appropriate instantiation for such quantified variables automatically.

Backtracking may take other forms. For example, where rules are parameterised, as in the case of removal of quantifiers, the parameters may be edited directly in the proof tree. Such modifications causes a recomputation of the proof with the new parameters. This provides the user of the interactive system with an interesting and powerful mechanism for backtracking. For instance, take example 4.4.3-6 above. If the wrong instantiation of the quantified variable, A, is given and the mistake is not discovered until some point later in the proof, then the proof developer need only navigate back up the proof tree and modify the editable parameter of the rule for universal quantifier elimination. The result of the modification is then propagated to all subsequent parts of the proof. This type of backtracking is particularly efficient since the proof development carried out after the initial (wrong) instantiation of the quantified variable is not wasted but is reused (reapplied) in the new context.

4.4.4. Induction, and Other Rules

For the proof system to be even remotely usable, a certain minimum number of additional or 'meta' facilities have been provided to ease interaction and proof development. Some extensions are also required to allow inductive theorems to be proven. In particular, efficient mechanisms for dealing with equality and performing induction are necessary. Additional facilities for manipulation of sequents are described towards the end of this section.

In the following section the induction rule available in version 3.0 of the proof system is described. A framework for induction, based on the technical work contained in [Duffy 89], is under construction and will be part of future versions of the proof subsystem.

4.4.4.1. Induction Rules

A relatively simple rule of induction is provided. It requires that the user specify an induction scheme for the type under analysis. This is then matched with the conjecture which is instantiated to the given scheme. Thus, given the conjecture (i) and the induction scheme (ii), the induction hypothesis (iii) is produced when inducting on 'c'. These steps are shown below as a fragment of a proof tree.

(4.4.4-1) The initial conjecture

```
(i)    >> empty |- a+(b+c)=(a+b)+c    by <step>
```

(4.4.4-2) Applying a rule of Induction

```
(ii)   >> empty |- a+(b+c)=(a+b)+c    by Schema Induction
          With <F(0) and (F(Ind) -> F(Ind+1))> on Vars <c>
(iii)  >> empty |- for all c:Integer => ( a+(b+0)=(a+b)+0 and a+(b+c)=(a+b)+c ->
                                     a+(b+(c+1))=(a+b)+(c+1) )  by <step>
```

Thus, this type of induction requires users to provide the scheme for the type upon which they wish to base the induction. Such general rules are similar in form to the homomorphic extension functionals described in [Krieg-Brückner 89]. Additionally this induction mechanism allows the user to induct on more than one variable. It should be noted that induction schemes are treated as axiomatic and, at present, there are no facilities provided for ensuring their correctness. Note, that the term 'F' above is a higher order variable and will match the inductive conjecture.

4.4.4.2. Other Induction Methods

A number of other rules for performing induction are possible. Computational and Fixpoint induction have been used in other transformational development systems (cf [Pepper 84]). Care should be taken when introducing such mechanisms into the transformation system, and their effect, in terms of the resultant proofs, should be gauged. Nevertheless, should such rules be required by the methodology, their inclusion in the proof system requires only their definition as transformation rules in PAnndA-S.

4.4.4.3. Dealing with Equality

In the context of PROSPECTRA, rules for dealing (comfortably) with equality are of paramount importance. Since most specifications (which provide the context in which proof will be performed) are equational, appropriate matching, instantiation, and rewriting facilities should be provided. To have to instantiate axioms by hand, and then use the substitutivity rule to apply them to a conjecture, is laborious in the extreme. Such an activity requires that axioms be treated as explicitly quantified formulae and that the instantiation of each quantified variable be deduced by inspection of the conclusion before the axiom may be applied as a rewrite rule. Given that definition from the local context will be used very frequently, insisting on such an activity from the user is ludicrous.

However, since the static semantic environment includes information regarding the declaration of the variable used in the current context, it is possible to extract the necessary information regarding quantifiers from the environment. This can be used to give implicit quantification to terms. This means that quantification need not be present in the axioms introduced for the local theory (unless the user wishes to manually instantiate the variables).

This then dispenses with the need to manually instantiate the variable of an axiom for the current proof or subgoal, and allows a term, whose major connective is the equality predicate, to be treated as a rewrite rule.

Given this information, the following facilities can be provided which are essentially shorthand for more laborious rule applications:

Rewrite — Apply, as a rewrite rule, a premiss, whose major connective is "=", to the conclusion.

Rewrite Premiss — Apply, as a rewrite rule, a premiss, whose major connective is "=", to the another premiss.

Instantiate — Attempts to instantiate a chosen premiss, by appropriate substitutions for 'variables', to match the conclusion. If this is successful it is added as a premiss to the antecedent.

The equality is strong equality: Transitivity, Symmetry, Substitutivity, and Reflexivity are embodied in transformations. It should be noted that the transformation for instantiation above can be used for terms whose major connective is not "=".

Conditional equations can be treated in a similar way. Such axioms cannot directly be treated as rewrite rules; instead a slightly different approach is taken. The left hand side of the axiom proper is matched with the object to be rewritten. The instantiation for the variables in the axiom which allows it to match are then applied throughout the axiom. The condition part is then separated from the axiom, via the implies elimination rule, and the remaining axiom is applied as a rewrite rule to the object. An example is given below, it should be noted that the rule for manipulation of conditional axioms is a composite rule which, in the proof subsystem, corresponds to a tactic. For this reason there is no single derivation to represent its application.

(4.4.4-3) A conditional equation in the antecedent

```
>> empty |- for all A, B: Natural => ((A > 0) -> B/A=(B-A) / A + 1) |- 2/1=1 + 1    by <step>
```

By applying the rule for application of conditional axioms we have

(4.4.4-4) Application of a composite rule for conditional equations

```
    >> for all A, B: Natural => (A > 0) -> B/A=(B-A) / A + 1 |- 2/1 = 1 + 1   by For All Elim with < 1 >
    >> for all B: Natural => (1 > 0) -> B/1=(B-1) / 1 + 1 |- 2/1=1 + 1        by For All Elim with< 2 >
    >> (1 > 0) -> 2/1=(2-1) / 1 +1 |- 2/1=1 + 1                               by Implies Elim
       >>.2/1=(2-1) / 1 +1 |- 2/1=1 + 1                                       by Rewrite with Premiss 1
       >> empty |- (2-1)/1 + 1=1 + 1                                          by <step>
AND >> empty |- 1 > 0                                                         by <step>
```

4.4.5. Other Rules for Proof Manipulation

There are a number of other rules for proof manipulation. These are relatively simple rules which perform such management tasks as deletion of a premiss from the antecedent. There are two main rules of this type provided. Firstly a rule to delete a premiss. This transformation is simply used to keep a proof manageable. In many cases it will be obvious that some of the premisses in a sequent are irrelevant. This rules serves as a primitive simplification mechanism.

The second rule allows the order of the premisses in a sequent to be changed. This rule is required because the rules of the calculus which manipulate the antecedent always act on the first premiss whose major connective causes the transformation to be applicable. Thus, in cases where there are two or more premisses in the antecedent with the same major connective, it may be necessary to change the order of these premisses.

4.4.5.1. Lemmas

In many cases when performing proofs, easily identifiable subgoals arise. In such situations it is convenient to assume the subgoal for the purposes of the current proof development. The assumed subgoal must, at some point, be proven and so an obligation to do so must be generated. Such a facility has been provided. The user assumes a lemma. The lemma is then introduced into the antecedent of the current sequent so it may be used in the proof. At the point of introducing the lemma the proof tree is split and an obligation to prove the used lemma is generated. Such a scenario is shown below.

(4.4.5-1) Bottom-up proof using lemmas

```
>> empty |- rev(conc(rev(make(x)),y)) = conc(rev(y),make(x))
      by Adding Lemma <rev(conc(X,Y)) = conc(rev(Y),rev(X))>
      >> rev(conc(X,Y)) = conc(rev(Y),rev(X)) |- rev(conc(rev(make(x)),y)) = conc(rev(y),make(x))   by <step>
AND >> empty |- For All X:Seq;Y:Seq => rev(conc(X,Y))=conc(rev(Y),rev(X))                            by <step>
```

Note that the derivation of the quantifications here requires information about the declarations of the functions rev and conc. Some of the issues associated with this are discussed in the next section. In some cases a weakening of the requirement regarding the obligation associated with the introduction of the lemma may be possible. Lemmas exist as a means of performing proof in a bottom up manner; proofs may be carried out by using only the lemma rule until we reach the situation where the only obligations left to prove correspond to axioms in the current theory.

4.4.5.2. *Tactics*

A facility for isolating and naming a subproof has been introduced. This serves two purposes:

- As a means of separating logically distinct parts of the proof.
- As a *hook* for the integration of the tactic system.

A number of benefits accrue from such separation/modularity. Firstly, alternate unparsing schemes can be used on the subproofs without effecting all other subsequent proof derivations. From the point of view of reuse, a named component is preferable to an anonymous subproof which requires some sort of positioning and addressing in order to determine its location in an abstract syntax tree. Traversal of the proof tree also becomes simpler; by using tactics the proof tree becomes broader and shallower. An example is shown below.

(4.4.5-2) Initial conjecture

```
>> empty |- (a or b) -> a and P(X,Y) = P(Y,X)   by <step>
```

By application of the tactic operation (and an appropriate proof) this results in:

(4.4.5-3) Application of a tactic

```
>> empty |- (a or b) -> a and P(X,Y) = P(Y,X)   by tactic "Commute"  Justified By <...>
>> empty |- (a or b) -> a                       by <step>
```

Here the <...> corresponds to a proof of the term P(X,Y) = P(Y,X) resulting in only the second part of the initial conjecture being left to prove. Additionally, the subproof is named by the label "Commute". Since the tactic is essentially the derivation part of a proof step, the result of the derivation is the result of the application of the tactic; the obligations which remain unproven after the application of the tactic.This means that, even if a tactic is only partially successful, it has still performed a useful function in the proof.

A facility also exists to extract a section of a proof and convert it to a modular, named subproof (a proof tactic). The user must provided the name for the subproof as a parameter to the function. This is illustrated in the example below; the section involved in breaking down the inductive conjecture and proving the base case of the induction is extracted and converted to a named module. The command is called "*Abstract_To_Proof*".

(4.4.5-4) Extracting a module (before)

```
Proof of <empty |- (rev( rev( X)) = X)>
empty |- rev( rev( X)) = X    by Schema Induction With (F( eseq) and (F( Ind) -> F( conc( make( d), Ind)))) on Vars X
>>empty |- for all X: Seq =>   rev( rev( eseq) = eseq and rev( rev( X) = X ->
                               rev( rev( conc( make( d), X))) = conc( make( d), X))
                                                  by For All Intro With y
>>empty |- rev( rev( eseq)) = eseq and (rev( rev( y)) = y) -> rev( rev( conc( make( d), y))) = conc( make( d), y))
                                                  by And Intro
    >>empty |- rev( rev( eseq)) = eseq            by By Adding <rev( eseq) = eseq>
    >>A0 |- rev( rev( eseq)) = eseq               by Duplicate P1
    >>A0 and A0 |- rev( rev( eseq)) = eseq        by Subst by P1
    >>A0 |- rev( eseq) = eseq PROVEN              by Immediate
    Proven
AND >>empty |- rev( rev( y)) = y -> rev( rev( conc( make( d), y))) = conc( make( d), y) by <step> -- rest of proof
QED
```

(4.4.5-5) Extracting a module (after)

```
Proof of <empty |- rev( rev( X)) = X>
empty |- rev( rev( X)) = X     by Schema Induction With (F( eseq) and (F( Ind) -> F( conc( make( d), Ind)))) on Vars X
>>empty |- for all X: Seq =>   rev( rev( eseq)) = eseq and (rev( rev( X)) = X ->
                               (rev( rev( conc( make( d), X))) = conc( make( d), X))
                            by Tactic "Base_Case" Justified by <...>
>>empty |- rev( rev( y)) = y -> rev( rev( conc( make( d), y))) = conc( make( d), y) by <step> -- rest of proof
QED
```

4.4.5.3. Adding a Theory

A mechanism which allows a completely developed theory to be added to the proof system has been defined. This allows proof to be performed in the context of a set of definitions (displayed in a theory browser). This theory may then be referenced during the proof. Axioms from this theory are introduced by indicating their label whenever their use is required in a particular proof rule.Figure 4.4.5-6. gives an example of an imported theory (for the previous example) would look like The axiom is then automatically imported from the theory into the proof.

(4.4.5-6) Part of the local theory for sequences

```
A01 - rev(eseq) = eseq
A02 - for all d:ITEM => rev(make(d)) = make(d)
A03 - for all x:seq, y: seq => rev(conc(x, y)) = conc(rev(y), rev(x))
```

Facilities are provided to match definitions from the local theory with the current conjecture of the proof system. Axioms are referenced via the *Apply_Axiom* rule. This selects the axiom for the local theory and does the following:

(1) If the axiom has a major connective which is the equality operator, the axiom is applied as a rewrite rule to the conjecture.

(2) If the axiom is a conditional equation, the left hand side of the equality is instantiated for the conclusion. Appropriate instantiations are made for variables in the rest of the axiom. The whole conditional axiom is then added as a premiss.

(3) For any other variables, an attempt is made to instantiate them in context. The result of this attempt is then added as a premiss; it may subsequently be applied using other proof rules.

(4) If no instantiation can be made, the axiom is added to the antecedent together with appropriate quantification of its variables. These variables may then be instantiated manually.

In order to browse the local theory, a buffer should be opened (called "**theory**"). During a proof the associated theory of the current proof can be displayed by causing the attribute containing this theory to be displayed in the theory buffer. The attribute used for this is **axiom**.

When the command show-attribute is executed, a parameter form will appear requesting the attribute and the buffer name. As described, these should be **axiom** and **theory** respectively.

An additional attribute, which shows only the axioms from the current theory which match in the context of the current proof, is also defined. It may be browsed in the same way as the axiom attribute. Its name is **Matched_Theory**.

An example of the local theory being used, in the context of figure 4.4.5-5, is shown below. The third axiom is seleted by reference to its label and is applied in the context of the proof. Note that the axiom being applied does not appear explicitly in the proof tree.

(4.4.5-7) Applying the local theory

```
Proof of <empty |- rev( rev( X)) = X>
empty |- rev( rev( X)) = X     by Schema Induction With (F( eseq) and (F( Ind) -> F( conc( make( d), Ind)))) on Vars X
>>empty |- for all X: Seq =>   rev( rev( eseq)) = eseq and (rev( rev( X)) = X ->
                               (rev( rev( conc( make( d), X))) = conc( make( d), X))
        by Tactic "Base_Case" Justified    by <...>
>>empty |- rev( rev( y)) = y -> rev( rev( conc( make( d), y))) = conc( make( d), y)     by Implies Intro
>> rev( rev( y)) = y |- rev( rev( conc( make( d), y))) = conc( make( d), y)            by Applying Axiom 3
>> rev( rev( y)) = y |- rev( conc( rev(y), rev( make( d)))) = conc( make( d), y)        by Applying Axiom 3
>> rev( rev( y)) = y |- conc( rev(rev( make( d))), rev(rev(y))) = conc( make( d), y)   by <step>  -- Rest of Proof
```

4.4.6. Defining Tactics

4.4.6.1. Why Tactics are a Good Idea

The description so far has mainly concentrated on interacting with the proof system. In the next section a "Programmers Interface" is described. The programmers interface provides the basic functions which can can be used to develop tactics for performing proof. There are two possibilities for writing tactics:

- Define all tactics as transformations on logical formulae.
- Define tactics as transformations on proof terms which implicitly encompass the constituent logical formulae representing the sequents.

Both of these approaches have merits and disadvantages. Probably the major requirement is that there is a clean, conceptual integration with the rest of the transformation system.

The initial advantages of the first approach are the following:

- The current transformation system can be used to describe tactics.
- TrafoLa-S and the associated conversion tools exists.
- Use can be made of the library of existing transformations for program development.
- The relationship between proof and transformation becomes 1:1; proof rules are simply transformations on logical formulae.

On the other hand the following are glaring disadvantages:

- The granularity of the transformation system is imposed on proof.
- Backtracking is cumbersome.
- It is not obvious how to intuitively represent development histories of proofs.
- The 'opening up' and analysis of composite transformations (or transformals) in the context of its failure is difficult.

Many of these problems are solved when the second approach described above is taken. There are also additional advantages:

- The structure of a proof is immediately obvious to the user.
- Backtracking is a trivial and intuitive procedure.
- Failed tactics can easily be opened up and the failed proofs examined.
- The transformational paradigm can still be usefully exploited in the creation of tactics and their application.
- Proof becomes an explicit part of the development process.
- Proof trees provide a constructive basis for program synthesis.
- There is no change in the requirements regarding access to environmental attributes.

There are, of course, disadvantages:

- Existing program transformations can still be used in writing tactics, however not to the same extent as the direct, transformational, method allows.
- The development of an the abstract syntax for proof objects is required; adding yet another language level to PROSPECTRA.
- The correspondence between the transformation system and the proof system is no longer 1:1. However, from a user point of view, they are still sufficiently close to allow each to benefit form the other.
- The purpose of a development history, at the level exploited by the transformation system, is subsumed by the proof tree. A development history is still important but not at the level of atomic refinements of proofs.

A system which has the benefits of both the situations described above is defined. Tactics are first defined in terms of logical formulae and then translated to equivalent tactics producing proof terms.

It is notable that the proof systems which have received most interest and focus in the literature are those which provide a two level interface to proof, e.g. LCF ([Gordon et al 79] and [Paulson 85]) and NuPrl [Constable et al 86] use the language ML as the meta language for describing complex proof derivations. As has been acknowledged by the developers of these systems, a powerful mechanism for meta development is of major importance. The ability to formulate generalised strategies for proof development (and store them for later use) provides the first building blocks from the reuse point of view.

Given that the basic proof system (calculus) is sound, the simplest extension to this would be a view where the each rule of inference was available as a function in a programming language. Other facilities, such as functions to determine the applicability of rules in a given context, would also be provided.

One possible approach is to formulate the proof system as a type in the specification language PAnndA-S and then introduce the inference rules of our calculus as functions on this type[4]. Language transformations directed towards proof are then written by creating a specification of the desired functionality in PAnndA-S. The tools developed under the PROSPECTRA project are then used to produce an executable version of the specification. These are language oriented transformations in the various structure editors (which can

[1] In this way the basic functions of the proof system are defined as over terms in the type corresponding to the PAnndA-S language.

be seen as the transformers of the PROSPECTRA system). The translation process is more fully described in part III sections 5.1 and 5.2.

A transformation in the proof system is essentially a named collection of the basic rules of the proof system composed in a 'consistent' manner. These named functions are termed 'logic transformers'. Given an expression corresponding to a conjecture in the proof system, these transformers will attempt to deduce 'true' by application of the various basic proof functions. They can be seen as a way of expressing basic proof strategies.

4.4.6.2. A System for Manipulating Concrete Proof Objects.

The tools of the PROSPECTRA system represent objects by their abstract syntax form. This is an efficient means of internally storing and manipulating objects. However, it is obviously tremendously tedious to specify operations on language constructs using such a notation. For this reason the use of concrete syntax paraphrasing (for the types being used in the specification of language-based transformations) is desirable. The problem is non trivial. PAnndA-S is being used to specify tactics; it is also the object language upon which many of the operations are specified. Obviously, conflicts and parsing problems will occur. By necessity, some method of distinguishing object expressions from specification language constructs and expressions is required. An editor which provides such facilities, where terms in an object language can be used within a specification directly, is called a *phrase* editor. The editor system which supports this type of language oriented specification is called the TrafoLa-S system. Technical details can be found in part II chapter 6.

Given that a formulation of the concrete and abstract syntax of proof terms (logical formulae) is given using the language transformation tools, it is then possible to generate, automatically, an editor which will allow specifications to be written using the concrete representations of the object language. The editor maintains the underlying abstract representation. It should be noted that since the object being specified is actually a valid PAnndA-S specification it can undergo the usual static semantic checking etc. associated with all objects specified in the PAnndA-S language. Some basic notation is outlined below.

Notation

Concrete terms of the object language, over which the specification is being formulated, are delimited by square braces.

```
[pop(empty)]
```

is equivalent to a PAnndA-S term, of type expression, with the following abstract form:

```
Mk_Call(Mk_Name(Mk_Unique_Name("pop", TP_KEY, TP_NATURE)),
Mk_Name(Mk_Unique_Name("empty", TP_KEY, TP_NATURE)))
```

A TrafoLa-S term (a canonical specification language term) within a concrete object is delimited by curly braces.

```
[pop(Gen_Param)]
```

is equivalent to

```
Mk_Call(Mk_Name(Mk_Unique_Name("pop",TP_KEY, TP_NATURE)),Gen_Param)
```

where GenParam is a variable in the PAnndA-S specification of type EXPRESSION (the second parameter to Mk_Call is an EXPRESSION, possibly a tuple, corresponding to the parameter list of the function).

Essentially, this is the only notation which is required to distinguish the concrete objects from the variables of the specification language and the abstract form of terms.

4.4.6.3. Logic Transformers in PROSPECTRA

Within the PROSPECTRA system the proof component deals solely with logical formulae. Therefore, the object language for expressing the transformers of the proof system focuses on the logical expression part of the PAnndA formalism.

Using the various tools of the PROSPECTRA system, together with a definition of the functions of the proof system itself (in PAnndA-S), transformers can be defined over the logical formulae part of the PAnndA language which may be translated to executable transformations. These transformations would then manipulate the basic entities of the proof system (sequents). Such transformations would not be used in the proof editor component of the system but would be employed in a similar, though less sophisticated tool, the logic transformer. The logic transformer does not have an explicit derivation history for proofs and so is effective for simple proof obligations only. Logical formulae are broken down or refined by application of the primitive rules of the proof system, applied as functions, or by applying logic transformers (composite functions). With a logic transformer, the development history corresponds to the concrete proof trees of the proof editor.

An example of the application of a simple logic transformer to a conjecture is given below. The logic transformer splits a conjecture containing an existential quantifier, disjunctions, and conjunctions into the component subgoals. It can be considered as a fragment of a general purpose simplification logic transformer.

(4.4.6-1) A logic transformer.

```
(Conj_Has_Exists(E) = true) and (Exists_Intro(E,Derive_E_Instance(E)) = A) -> Simplify(E) = Simplify(A),
(Conj_Has_Implies(E) = true) and (Impies_Intro(E) = A) ->                     Simplify(E) = Simplify(A),
(Conj_Has_Or(E) = true) and (Or_Intro(E) = [A or B]) -> Simplify(E) = [Simpify(A) or Simplify(B)]   -- BOOLEAN or
(Immediate(E) = true) ->                                Simplify(E) = [true],                       -- BOOLEAN true
```

(4.4.6-2) Application of the logic transformer.

```
exists X:integer => ((X > 1 and X < 4) -> X = 2 or X = 3)                          --Initial conjecture
```

by application of the above transformer we have (omitting out the last step of applying the immediate validity rule)

```
(2 > 1 and 2 < 4) -> 2 = 2      -- obviously true; immediate by reflexivity.
  or
(2 > 1 and 2 < 4) -> 2 = 3      -- False but since it is part of a disjunction it can be discarded.
```

4.4.6.4. The Tactic Writers Interface

In order to write logic transformers the transformation developer must be aware of the facilities which are available. In particular, since logic transformers must be defined in terms of the basic proof rules, the profiles of these rules, as well as a description of their semantics, must be available to the developer. In addition to the basic rules, applicability predicate for each rule should be provided. The profiles of these functions can be seen in the package below.

```
with Panndac
package Calculus is
   subtype Exp is EXPRESSION;
   subtype Literal is EXPRESSION;
   ForAll_Intro, Exist_Intro:     Exp × Exp —> Exp;
   Exists_Elim, ForAll_Elim:      Exp × Exp —> Exp;
   And_Intro, Or_Intro, Implies_Intro, Not_Intro, Iff_Intro:    Exp —> Exp,
   And_Elim, Or_Elim, Implies_Elim, Not_Elim, Iff_Elim:         Exp —> Exp,
   Induct, SInduct:               Exp × Exp —> Exp;
   Subst:                         Exp × Literal —> Exp;
   Lemma:                         Exp × Exp —> Exp;
   Instanciate:                   Exp × Literal —> Exp;
   Immediate:                     Exp —> BOOLEAN;
   Delete, PremissToFront:        Exp × Literal —> Exp;
   Add, Rewrite_Premiss:          Exp × Exp —> Exp;
   Rewrite_Premiss:               Exp × Exp —> Exp;
   Duplicate:                     Exp × Literal —> Exp;
   Ante_Has_ForAll, Ante_Has_Exists, Ante_Has_AndLeft,
   Ante_Has_Or, Ante_Has_Not, Ante_Has_Equal, Ante_Has_Iff:        Exp —> BOOLEAN;
   Conc_Has_ForAll, Conc_Has_Exists, Conc_Has_AndLeft,
   Conc_Has_Or, Conc_Has_Not, Conc_Has_Equal, Conc_Has_Iff:        Exp —> BOOLEAN;
   Is_Sequent:                                                     Exp —> BOOLEAN;
end Calculus;
```

When considering the semantics of these functions the developer needs to consider two things; the result of the application of the rule and any parameters, in addition to the basic conjecture, which the rule accepts.

4.4.6.5. Structure of Result Expressions

In terms of structure, there are four possible results of the application of a primitive proof rule. Note that the parameter to all proof rules is the object sequent to which the inference rule is being applied.

(1) A single sequent, for example, as a result of a rule for *not introduction.*

(2) True, as a result of the *immediate validity* rule successfully applied to the sequent.

(3) A disjunction of 2 sequents, as a result of the rule for *or introduction.*

(4) A conjunction, as a result of the rule for *implies elimination*, for example.

Most rules produce as a result a single sequent. It is the rules which produce a conjunction or disjunction of sequents which cause the tree structure in proofs.

4.4.6.6. Auxiliary Functions in Logic Transformers

Many of the function defined when describing logic transformers do not directly manipulate the conjectures which are the subject of such transformations. These functions can be considered as 'help' functions which compute some intermediate value for use in the transformation. For example, many of the rules in the conditional parts of an axiom merely determine the applicability of the rule and are not directly involved in the manipulation of the conjecture.

Other functions of this type are those which determine the parameters for those proof functions which accept a parameter in addition to the basic conjecture. For example, the *Exists_Intro* rule accepts an instantiation for the existentially quantified variable being eliminated. A 'help' function here would, perhaps, try to determine an appropriate instantiation for the variable. In fact this is the purpose of the function *Derive_E_Instance* in example 4.4.6-1. In this context the only restriction on such a parameter is that it is well typed in the context of the proof and that it is a well-formed PAnndA-S expression. Help functions, in general, may be any appropriate function defined in PAnndA-S which may be translated to an equivalent SSL function or operation.

4.4.6.7. Executing Transformation Specifications

A specification with the functionality of the desired tactic (or language-based transformation) can now be written in PAnndA-S. This specification, once translated to SSL and compiled with a transformer shell, is then available as a logic transformer within that editor[5].

There are, of course, restrictions on the forms of specification which can be compiled directly (without further development) to an equivalent, executable SSL specification. Essentially the equational specification of the tactic must correspond to an applicative program over the type of the object language. For further details see Vol III Chapter 6.2 of this publication.

4.4.6.8. Writing and Compiling Tactic Specifications

In defining tactics a number of problems occur. Firstly, tactics are defined on the PAnndA-S language (specifically the Expressions part). This means that tactics, as a result type, produce logical formulae and not proof terms. Thus tactics, aimed at the proof system, are actually transformations over PAnndA-S terms. These resultant 'logic transformers' are useful for simple theorem proving tasks; no derivation is associated with the transformation, only the end result of the application is visible. However, for any substantial proof development activity the tactics should be transformations over proof terms; it must be possible to record the application of a tactic in the same manner as the primitive rules of the proof system are recorded. Thus an instantaneous representation of developments is produced (the proof tree). The problem now is that two *distinctt* systems for meta development need to be developed; one for logic transformers and one for tactics.

In defining logic transformers the algorithms expressed are essentially those which would be desirable from the point of view of general proof development. That is to say, if tactics were to be specified over proof terms then, conceptually, these tactics would serve exactly the same function as the logic transformers, the difference being that the application of a tactic would produce, as a side effect, the derivation history of the transformation (a proof tree whose component steps are the primitive rules of the proof system).

The tactic writer, given such an interpretation of logic transformers, is freed from the unnecessary details of the representation of proof terms. Only the signatures of proof system functions need be familiar to the tactic writer (i.e. the set of functions which categorise the functionality of the proof system in terms of its basic inference rules and proof 'management' facilities).

One of the main aims is therefore to allow the tactics specified as logic transformers to be used directly in the proof editor as true proof tactics. When applied, they produce a proof tree as the result of the computation rather than a simplified logical expression.

---

[5]A language transformation exists which converts a PAnndA-S object, given an operational interpretation of the specification, into an equivalent specification in the language of the CSG (the synthesizer specification language: SSL).

4.4.7. Translating Logic Transformers to Tactics

Given an arbitrary specification over PAnndA-S logical formulae it is possible to analyse (statically) the specification in order to determine whether or not there exists an equivalent specification over proof terms (a tactic). If there is no equivalent specification then either the tactic does not have a representation as a applicative program or it is in some sense badly defined, i.e. uses functions other than those available in the calculus to define transformations.

There are a number of restrictions which must be imposed on the way in which the user defines the transformation over logical formulae if there is to be a reasonable possibility of translating this specification to an equivalent specification over proof terms. These are given below:

- The basic manipulation of logical terms must be via the primitive proof functions defined to represent the inference rules of the calculus.
- Axioms of the specification must have an operational interpretation as a functional program. In particular, any terms which appear on the right hand side of axioms must have binding occurrences in the conditional part of the axiom or be parameters (arguments of the left hand side). Essentially, axioms must be left-linear in form.

As already described, the PAnndA-S language itself is formulated as a type in PAnndA-S. The inference rules of the proof system are then defined as functions on this type.

In addition to these definitions, a type corresponding to the abstract syntax of proof terms is also provided. Given that a mapping exists between the application of rules of the basic calculus and proof trees, a language transformation can be defined which generates, from the definition of logic transformers, equivalent proof tactics. The transformation is described below:

Transformer: EXPRESSION —> EXPRESSION

$\Downarrow$ Lifting Transformation

Tactic: EXPRESSION —> Proofs

An Example of a simple logic transformer, used to instantiate a quantified variable in the antecedent of a sequent, is given below.

The example below defines a tactic which automatically removes a quantified variable from a term by replacing it with an appropriate instantiation.

(4.4.7-1) Instantiation of a quantified variable in a premiss

```
( (Ante_Has_ForAll(E) = true) and (ForAll_Elim(E,Get_V_Inst(E)) = B) ) -> (Rem_Quant(E) = B)
```

The translation to a proof tactic produces the term below.

(4.4.7-2) The equivalent proof tactic.

```
(Ante_Has_ForAll(E) = true) and (ForAll_Elim(E,Get_V_Inst(E)) = B) ->
  Pr_Rem_Quant(E) =
    mk_Proof( mk_Proof_Step( mk_derv_forall_elim(Get_V_Inst(E)), mk_Simple(mk_Proof(null_step)))
```

The above tactic has a more compaxt concrete representation in the TrafoLa-S style in example 4.4.7-3 below. There is no concrete representation of proofs available within the TrafoLa-S editor. This is not a serious problem since canonical proof terms will never be manipulated by the user but are produced by transformation.

(4.4.7-3) The equivalent proof tactic (concrete form).

```
(Ante_Has_ForAll(E) = true) and (ForAll_Elim(E,Get_V_Inst(E)) = B) ->
   Pr_Rem_Quant(E) = [>> E by Forall Elim with <Get_V_Inst(E)>
                              >> B by <step> ]
```

The proof tactic equivalent to the transformation in Example 2.1 is given below. In this example, TrafoLa-S style syntax is used in the tactic definition.

(4.4.7-3) Another proof tactic

```
(Conj_Has_Exists(E) = true) and (Exists_Intro(E,Derive_E_Instance(E)) = A) ->
   Pr_Simplify(E) = [ >> E by Exists Intro with <Derive_E_Instance(E)> Pr_Simplify(A) ],
(Conj_Has_Implies(E) = true) and (Implies_Intro(E) = A) ->
   Pr_Simplify(E) = [ >> E by Implies Intro Pr_Simplify(A) ] ,
(Conj_Has_Or(E) = true) and (Or_Intro(E) = [A or B]) ->
   Pr_Simplify(E) = [ >> E by Or Intro Pr_Simplify(A) OR Pr_Simplify(B) ],
(Immediate(E) = true) ->
   Pr_Simplify(E) = [ >> E by Immediate Proven ]
```

The general translation process is described below. It requires 4 stages.

- Translate the TrafoLa-S definition of the logic transformer to its canonical form.
- Synthesise from the definition of the logic transformer an equivalent computation structure which produces a proof term.
- Produce an SSL specification of the tactic (via the PAnndA-S to SSL translator).
- Compile (via CSG) this definition together with a definition of the proof system. This produces an editor with the tactic included as a proof language transformation.

The process of translating from the canonical form of the logic transformer to the canonical form of a proof transformer is the main step here (with respect to the proof system). The other translation steps are performed by other tools of the PROSPECTRA system.

It is obvious that there are two distinct levels at which it is possible to operate in order to define composite tactics or transformations for the proof system. The first is isomorphic to the language-based transformation system of PROSPECTRA which is used to develop program transformations. The second level can be considered somewhat differently, as a language for proof description. This language is used to describe the generation of proofs is such a way so as to be independent of the conjectures they prove. On the other hand the abstract structure of the proof tree is not seen by the user, nor should it be. Neither should the tactic writer need to know the details of proof representation in order to write effective tactics. Terms in the algebra of proofs are created either:

- interactively by the user as a side effect of applying basic proof rules to a sequent.
- as a result of the computation of a tactic (corresponding to the execution profile of that tactic).

The proof language then records each stage of the proof; each node of the proof tree corresponding to the application of one of the primitive rules of the inference system.

In this way the proof tree has a correspondence with the control language user as a means of recording the development history of specification or programs. The proof tree is different in that it is an instantaneous representation of developments. Modification of the tree will correspond to the redevelopment and replay of a whole part of the proof. In the proof system the replay is instantaneous since redevelopment is done automatically via attribute computation over the structure of a proof.

4.4.7.1. The Lifting Transformation

The algorithm for this transformation is outlined below. Note that the manipulation of proof terms in the specification is not direct; the transformation is designed to manipulate a PAnndA-S definition of a PAnndA-S transformation. This means that the object of the transformation is a PAnndA-S expressions which manipulates the canonical form of a PAnndA-S term.

Once the correct conceptual level for the modelling of the transformation has been fixed then the definition of the transformation is relatively straightforward. One only has to look at the definition of very simple TrafoLa-S terms to appreciate the value of such a tool for transformation description. For technical reasons the actual transformation from logic transformers to proof tactics has been formulated in SSL. Some parts of the definition would have been made much simpler had TrafoLa-S been used. A simple example illustrates. As a simple example, the TrafoLa-S term [A **or** B] is equivalent to the following canonical term.

(4.4.7-4) The canonical form of a simple TrafoLa-S term.

```
Mk_Call(Mk_Name(Mk_Unique_Name("or", TP_KEY, TP_NATURE)),
   Mk_Tuple(Mk_Expr_List(Mk_Name(Mk_Unique_Name("A", TP_KEY, TP_NATURE)),
      Mk_Expr_List(Mk_Name(Mk_Unique_Name("B", TP_KEY, TP_NATURE)), Empty_Expr_List()))))
```

The formulation of this as a pattern in SSL, which must actually be used if we wish to define transformations over SSL descritions of objects (transform transformation description), is still larger in equivalent ratio as the canonical form is to the concrete from, i.e. about a factor of ten.

The transformation from logic transformers to tactics is formulated in such a way. For many reasons, not least maintainability, it is necessary to re-formulate this transformation in TrafoLa-S. The basic algorithm for the synthesis of tactics from logic transformers is now described:

- Analyse the specification is order to determine all functions which are defined via kernel proof functions that do not have corresponding tactic definitions.
- Generate declarations for new equivalent functions whose result type will be **Proof** rather than **EXPRESSION**.
- For each axiom associated with the logic transformer generate an equivalent axiom implementing a tactic. This requires that the transformation from transformers to tactics understands the structure of the rules of the proof system (which rules require parameters, which result in disjunctions or conjunction of goals etc.) so as to facilitate the creation of an appropriate proof term.
- Add the new functions just synthsised to the set of kernel proof functions.
- Repeat the whole process until no new function definitions are generated.

4.4.7.2. Conclusion

A conceptually simple way of giving logic transformers an interpretation as tactics has been presented. The tactic writer needs no more information about the system than was necessary to create logic transformers. In particular the underlying model of proof trees need not be visible. The insulation of the developer form yet another level of language is then achieved.

Some restrictions as to the formulation tactic descriptions are necessary. In particular, the basic functions of the proof system (other than those employed as auxiliary functions) must be considered as kernel functions, in terms of which all tactic definition is expressed.

4.4.8. Editing Proof Objects

In a transformation system user input should be limited to guidance. There is an argument for requiring the user to perform all tasks by transformation. This approach disposes with the need to perform any actual typing other than to invoke commands. It is interesting to note which aspects of the proof system currently require that the user input information, which the system is required to parse in the context of the language being used, to perform proof. Parsing or structure editing within the system can occur in the following situations:

- When the initial conjecture is introduced.
- When axioms are added to the antecedent.
- When quantifiers are removed from the sequent (providing their instantiation).
- When rules requiring (numeric) stipulation of a premiss are invoked.

In the first two cases above it is easy to see how parsing (or editing) can be avoided. In the first case, proof terms are automatically generated from the applicability conditions associated with transformations. In the second case the provision of local theory information solves the problem since axioms are selected from the local theory.

Of the other two cases, the first is relatively easy to solve. For the purposes of removing universal quantifiers from the conclusion and existential quantifiers from the antecedent, the automatic generation of an unused free variable is sufficient. In removing existential quantifiers from the conclusion and universal quantifiers from the antecedent, simple matching could be used to determine instantiations for the quantified variables. The parameter editor may also be used in this context to define instantiations or edit existing ones.

In the final case, the problem is solved by the parameter editor; string and integer literals are always well typed (with respect to package STANDARD) and so require no additional context.

In general the editing of proof objects is inhibited. It is currently only possible to create a proof object by transformation. This will not change: the textual creation of proof objects and their subsequent parsing and checking by the system is not seen as a sensible or productive activity.

4.4.9. Some Examples

```
Proof of <not (not (a or (not a)))>
empty |- not (not (a or (not a)))                                          by Not Intro
>>not (a or (not a)) |- Contradiction                                      by Duplicate P1
>>not (a or (not a)) and not (a or (not a)) |- Contradiction               by Not Elim
      >>not (a or (not a)) |- a or (not a)                                 by Or Intro
      >>...
OR    >>not (a or (not a)) |- not a                                        by Not Intro
      >>a and not (a or (not a)) |- Contradiction                          by Not Elim
      >>a |- a or (not a)                                                  by Or Intro
      >>a |- a PROVEN                                                      by Immediate

      Proven
OR    >>...
QED
```

```
Proof of <a -> ((a -> b) -> (a -> b))>
>>empty |- a -> ((a -> b) -> (a -> b))                                     by Implies Intro
>>a |- (a -> b) -> (a -> b)                                                by Implies Intro
>>(a -> b) and a |- (a -> b) PROVEN                                        by Immediate
Proven
QED
```

```
Proof of <a or (not a)>
>>empty |- a or (not a)                                                    by Or Intro
      >>empty |- a                                                         by <Step>
OR    >>empty |- not a                                                     by Not Intro
      >>a |- Contradiction                        by Immediate   <-- Inappropriate Proof Rule
      Not Proven
Not Yet Shown
```

Now for some more interesting proofs:

```
Proof of < A + (B + C) = (A + B) + C>
>>empty |- A + (B + C) = (A + B) + C       by Schema Induction With (F(0) and F(Ind) -> F(Ind + 1)) on Vars< C>
>>empty |- A + (B + 0) = (A + B) + 0 and
         for all C: Int => A + (B + C) = (A + B) + C -> A + (B + (C + 1)) = (A + B) + (C + 1)   by And Intro
      >>empty |- A + (B + 0) = (A + B) + 0                                 by Adding <A + 0 = A>
      >>A0 |- A + (B + 0) = (A + B) + 0                                    by Subst by P1
      >>empty |- (A + B) = (A + B) PROVEN                                  by Immediate
      Proven
AND   >>empty |- for all C: Int => A + (B + C) = (A + B) + C -> A + (B + (C + 1)) = (A + B) + (C + 1)
                                                                           by For All Intro With <c>
      >>empty |- A + (B + c) = (A + B) + c -> A + (B + (c + 1)) = (A + B) + (c + 1)     by Adding
                                                                           <A + (B + 1) = (A + B) + 1>
      >>A0 |- A + (B + c) = (A + B) + c -> A + (B + (c + 1)) = (A + B) + (c +1)         by Implies Intro
      >>A + (B + c) = (A + B) + c and A0 |- A + (B + (c+1)) = (A + B) + (c+1)           by Duplicate P2
      >>A0 and A + (B + c) = (A + B) + c and A0 |- A+(B+(c+1)) = (A+B)+(c+1)            by Subst by P1
      >>A + (B + c) = (A + B) + c and A0 |- (A + ((B + c) + 1) = ((A + B) + c) +1       by Subst by P2
      >>A + (B + c) = (A + B) + c |- (A + (B + c)) + 1 = ((A + B) + c) + 1              by Subst by P1
      >>empty |- ((A + B) + c) + 1 = ((A + B) + c) + 1 PROVEN                           by Immediate
      Proven
   QED
```

```
Proof of <rev( rev( X)) = X>
>>empty |- rev( rev( X)) = X by Schema Induction With <F( eseq) and (F( Ind) -> F( conc( make( x), Ind)))>
                                                      on Vars <X>
>>empty |- for all X: Seq => rev( rev( eseq)) = eseq and ( rev( rev( X)) = X ->
                 rev( rev( conc( make( x), X))) = conc( make( x), X) )          by For All Intro With <y>
>>empty |- rev( rev( eseq)) = eseq and (rev( rev( y)) = y -> rev( rev( conc( make( x), y))) = conc( make( x), y) )
                                                                                by And Intro
    >>empty |- rev( rev( eseq)) = eseq                                          by Adding
                                                                              <(rev( eseq) = eseq)>
    >>A0 |- rev( rev( eseq)) = eseq                                             by Duplicate P1
    >>A0 and A0 |- rev( rev( eseq)) = eseq                                      by Subst by P1
    >>A0 |- rev( eseq) = eseq PROVEN                                            by Immediate
    Proven
AND >>empty |- rev( rev( y)) = y -> rev( rev( conc( make( x), y))) = conc( make( x), y)   by Adding
                                                            <rev( conc( X, Y)) = conc( rev( Y), rev( X))>
    >>A0 |- rev( rev( y)) = y->rev( rev( conc( make( x), y))) = conc( make( x), y)       by Duplicate P1
    >>A0 and A0 |- rev( rev( y)) = y -> rev( rev( conc( make( x), y))) = conc( make( x), y) by Subst by P1
    >>A0 |- rev( rev( y)) = y -> rev( conc( rev( y), rev( make( x)))) = conc( make( x), y)  by Subst by P1
    >>empty |- rev( rev( y)) = y -> conc( rev( rev( make( x))), rev( rev( y))) = conc( make( x), y)
                                                                                by Adding
                                                                              <rev( make( D)) = make( D)>
    >>A1 |- rev( rev( y)) = y -> conc( rev( rev( make( x))), rev( rev( y))) = conc( make( x), y)  by Duplicate P1
    >>A1 and A1 |- rev( rev( y)) = y -> conc( rev( rev( make( x))), rev( rev( y))) = conc( make( x), y)
                                                                                by Subst by P1
    >>A1 |- rev( rev( y)) = y -> conc( rev( make( x)), rev( rev( y))) = conc( make( x), y)   by Subst by P1
    >>empty |- rev( rev( y)) = y -> conc( make(x), rev( rev(y))) = conc( make(x), y)         by Implies Intro
    >>rev( rev( y)) = y |- conc( make( x), rev( rev( y))) = conc( make( x), y)               by Subst by P1
    >>empty |- conc( make( x), y) = conc( make( x), y) PROVEN                                by Immediate
    Proven
QED
```

4.4.10. System Description

In this section a description of the proof language is given for completeness. The language is the basis for structuring proofs and its formulation as a PAnndA-S type is used to express transformations over proof terms, synthesised when translating from logic transformers to tactics. It will never be directly manipulated by the user.

```
with panndac;
package proof is
  type PROOF_STEP is private;
  type DerResult is private;
  type Derivation is private;
  type PROOF is private;
-----------------------------------------------------------
  -- PROOF_STEP
  null_step:          PROOF_STEP;
  is_null_step:       PROOF_STEP —> BOOLEAN;
  mk_Proof_Step:      Derivation × DerResult —> PROOF_STEP;
  is_mk_Proof_Step:   PROOF_STEP —> BOOLEAN;
  EQ:                 PROOF_STEP × PROOF_STEP —> BOOLEAN;
```

```
-- DerResult
mk_Immediate:        DerResult;
is_mk_Immediate:     DerResult —> BOOLEAN;
mk_Simple:           PROOF —>DerResult;
is_mk_Simple:        DerResult —> BOOLEAN;
mk_And_Comb:         PROOF × PROOF —> DerResult;
is_mk_And_Comb:      DerResult —> BOOLEAN;
mk_Or_Comb:          PROOF × PROOF —> DerResult;
is_mk_Or_Comb:       DerResult —> BOOLEAN;
EQ:                  DerResult × DerResult —> BOOLEAN;
-- --Derivations: the scheme for derivations is given here.
-- --Two types of scheme are necessary, one for proof rules which require a parameter, in addition to the
-- --sequent being manipulated, an one for those that only accept the sequent as a parameter.
-- --The Schema are defined where X may be instantiated with each of the rules defined in section 4.4.2

-- --Basic null derivation (represents an incomplete proof)
null_derivation:              Derivation;
is_null_derivation:           Derivation —> BOOLEAN;
-- --Proof Rules with no additional parameters
mk_derv_X:                    Derivation;
-- --Proof rules with an additional parameter
-- -- Applicability predicate for each proof rule
   is_mk_derv_X:                 Derivation —>BOOLEAN;
end proof;
```

4.4.10.1. Command Summary

In this section a list of the transformations available in the proof system are given. Together with the command name there is a short summary of its purpose, the syntactic category to which it is applicable, and the parameters, if any, that it requires. Transformations are conditional, they only become active when it is sensible to apply them. For example the transformation for not elimination only becomes active when there is a negation which is the major connective of a premiss. Note that the transformation writer's interface has already been given in section 1.5.

Command Name:	Verify
Syntactic Category:	Built-in function
Synopsis:	Creates a browser with the a proof term. Returns the validity of the proof on exit.
Parameters:	Proof obligation, TP_ENV.

Command Name:	Immediate
Syntactic Category:	Proof_Step
Synopsis:	Determines if the current sequent is immediate, i.e that the conclusion is true or follows directly from a premiss.
Parameters:	None

Command Name:	OrElim
Syntactic Category:	Proof_Step
Synopsis:	Removes the **or** connective from a premiss, causing the proof tree to split into two, both subtrees then being obligations for the proof
Parameters:	None

Command Name:	AndElim
Syntactic Category:	Proof_Step
Synopsis:	A premiss list or antecedent is a right associated conjunction. This command converts any left associated conjunctions to right associated ones.
Parameters:	None.

Command Name: NotElim
Syntactic Category: Proof_Step
Synopsis: Removes a negation from a premiss, removing the premiss, stripping the negation from the formulae and then replacing the conclusion with the new formulae.
Parameters: None.

Command Name: ImpliesElim
Syntactic Category: Proof_Step
Synopsis: Removes an implication from the antecedent. Causes the proof tree to split. Both subtrees require to be proven.
Parameters: None.

Command Name: ForAllElim
Syntactic Category: Proof_Step
Synopsis: Removes a universally quantified variable from a premiss, replacing it with a term. The term should be well chosen to lead to a successful conclusion to the proof.
Parameters: An expression.

Command Name: ExistsElim
Syntactic Category: Proof_Step
Synopsis: Removes an existentially quantified variable from a premiss by substituting a free variable for the bound one.
Parameters: A variable not used anywhere in the sequent.

Command Name: AndIntro
Syntactic Category: Proof_Step
Synopsis: Removes a conjunction from the conclusion of a sequent. This causes the proof tree to split into two subtrees, both of which should be proven.
Parameters: None.

Command Name: OrIntro
Syntactic Category: Proof_Step
Synopsis: Removes a disjunction from the conclusion of a sequent. This causes the proof tree to split into two subtrees, either of which should be proven.
Parameters: None.

Command Name: ImpliesIntro
Syntactic Category: Proof_Step
Synopsis: Add the left hand formulae of an implication from the conclusion to the antecedent as a new premiss
Parameters: None.

Command Name: NotIntro
Syntactic Category: Proof_Step
Synopsis: Removes a negation from the conclusion. This causes the formulae with the negation removed to be added to the antecedent. The conclusion is then empty, i.e. there is a contradiction entailed.
Parameters: None.

Command Name: IffIntro
Syntactic Category: Proof_Step
Synopsis: Removes an equivalence connective (<–>) and produces a conjunction of subproofs requiring the proof of the component of implications.
Parameters: None.

Command Name: IffElim
Syntactic Category: Proof_Step
Synopsis: Removes an equivalence from the antecedent, replacing it with two implications.
Parameters: None.

Command Name: ForAllIntro
Syntactic Category: Proof_Step
Synopsis: Removes a universally quantified variable from the conclusion by substituting an arbitrary constant for the quantified variable.
Parameters: A constant, not used anywhere in the sequent.

Command Name: ExistsIntro
Syntactic Category: Proof_Step
Synopsis: Removes a existentially quantified variable from the conclusion, replacing it with a term. The term should be well chosen to lead to a successful conclusion to the proof.
Parameters: An expression.

Command Name: Sinduct
Syntactic Category: Proof_Step
Synopsis: Applies an induction scheme to the conclusion of the sequent.
Parameters: An appropriate induction scheme for the conclusion and the variable(s) upon which to induct.

Command Name: Delete
Syntactic Category: Proof_Step
Synopsis: Deletes a premiss from the antecedent.
Parameters: An integer specifying the premiss to be deleted. The premisses are numbered left to right starting from 1.

Command Name: Add
Syntactic Category: Proof_Step
Synopsis: Adds an axiom to the antecedent. The axiom is unparsed as a reference.
Parameters: The required axiom.

Command Name: Duplicate
Syntactic Category: Proof_Step
Synopsis: Duplicates a premiss.
Parameters: An integer specifying the premiss to be duplicated.

Command Name: PremissToFront
Syntactic Category: Proof_Step
Synopsis: Moves a premiss to the leftmost position in the antecedent.
Parameters: An integer specifying the premiss to be moved.

Command Name: Subst
Syntactic Category: Proof_Step
Synopsis: Applies, as a rewrite rule, an axiom from the premiss, whose major connective is "=", to the conclusion.
Parameters: An Integer specifying the premiss to be used.

Command Name: Premiss_Subst
Syntactic Category: Proof_Step
Synopsis: Applies, as a rewrite rule, an axiom from the premiss, whose major connective is "=", to another premiss.
Parameters: An Integer pair, specifying the two premisses to be used.

Command Name: Lemma
Syntactic Category: Proof_Step
Synopsis: Introduces a lemma, or assumption, into the current sequent, creating an obligation in the proof tree for the justification of the assumption.
Parameters: A lemma (a logical formulae)

Command Name:	Tactic
Syntactic Category:	Proof_Step
Synopsis:	Names the proof associated with this derivation. Applies the proof tree to the current conjecture and return the unproven part of the obligation.
Parameters:	A name for the subproof.

Command Name:	Apply_Theory
Syntactic Category:	Proof_Step
Synopsis:	Selects an axiom from the current theory by reference to its internal label (can be determined by viewing the **axiom** attribute in a theory browser).
Parameters:	An integer label.

Command Name:	Auto
Syntactic Category:	Proof
Synopsis:	Applies a very general strategy in order to try and prove tautologies. If it fails the incomplete proof tree is left for the user to manipulate or examine.
Parameters:	None.

Command Name:	ConcAuto
Syntactic Category:	Proof
Synopsis:	Automatically applies the appropriate rule to the Conclusion of the sequent.
Parameters:	None.

Command Name:	AnteAuto
Syntactic Category:	Proof
Synopsis:	Automatically applies the appropriate rule to the antecedent of the sequent.
Parameters:	None.

Command Name:	CondRewrite
Syntactic Category:	Proof
Synopsis:	Automatically applies the a conditional axiom from the antecedent as a rewite rule to the conclusion. An obligation to prove the condition is generated.
Parameters:	An integer label.

Command Name:	ProofModule
Syntactic Category:	Proof
Synopsis:	Converts the current selection to a named subproof.
Parameters:	A tactic name.

4.4.11 Index

5. Transformation Development

5.1. The TrafoLa-S Editor

José Luis Mañas, Pedro de la Cruz, Alcatel Standard Eléctrica S.A.
(Revised by Berthold Hoffmann, Universität Bremen)

This section describes the extensions to the PA^{nn}dA-S editor (see part III, section 4.1) for the editing of transformations in TrafoLa-S (see part II, chapter 6), the language for specifying transformations in PROSPECTRA.

5.1.1. Introduction

TrafoLa-S is the language for specifying transformations in PROSPECTRA. The TrafoLa-S editor is a full-screen language-based editor for TrafoLa-S, based on the PA^{nn}dA-S editor described in part III, section 4.1. It has been implemented using the Cornell Synthesizer Generator [Reps,Teitelbaum 88] with the extensions described in part III, chapter 6 and in [de la Cruz *et al.* 90].

The design of the language, and the implementation of the editor for TrafoLa-S have been guided by the insight that transformations are just functions over the abstract syntax trees of the object language (PA^{nn}dA in this case). Both abstract syntax trees and transformations can be specified algebraically, as described in [Krieg-Brückner 89] and in part II, chapter 6.

Thus PA^{nn}dA-S can be used as a language for specifying transformation as well, and the transformational approach to program development can be used to derive efficient implementations of transformations from their specification.

However, specifying transformations in terms of the constructors of the abstract syntax of a language is very cumbersome, as illustrated in part II, chapter 6. For this reason TrafoLa-S has been extended by *PA^{nn}dA phrases*, which allow to write PA^{nn}dA abstract syntax trees in their concrete form. The TrafoLa-S editor supports editing operations for phrases, and a transformation of phrases into the abstract syntax trees (called canonical representation).

This section describes only the extensions to the PA^{nn}dA-S editor included in the TrafoLa-S editor. For a general introduction to CSG-generated editors and the functionalities of the PA^{nn}dA-S editor, we refer to part III, section 4.1.

More specifically, the TrafoLa-S editor extends the PA^{nn}dA-S editor as follows:

- A package **pannda** defining the abstract syntax of phrases.
- Editing of PA^{nn}dA Phrases as a special kind of PanndA-S expressions.
- Editing of embedded TrafoLa-S expressions inside PA^{nn}dA phrases.
- Transformation to the canonical representation of PA^{nn}dA phrases.

These features are described in the following sections 5.1.2 to 5.1.5. Section 5.1.6 points to an implementation detail and mentions a deficiency of the present implementation.

5.1.2. The Predefined Abstract Syntax of PA^{nn}dA

The predefined package **pannda** defines the abstract syntax trees of PA^{nn}dA as an abstract data type. Sorts define the syntactic categories, and constructor functions correspond to syntactic rules of the language. These abstract syntax trees are called the *canonical representation* of PA^{nn}dA; the package is implicitely imported by every TrafoLa-S program.

Semantically, a PA^{nn}dA phrase is just a TrafoLa-S expressions over the constructors from the package **pannda**; its type corresponds to the sort for some syntactic category defined in that package.

In order to write properly typed transformation functions, the transformation developper has to know the definitions in the package **pannda**. This is also important to prevent him from accidentally hiding some sort or constructor definition by giving the same name to some local object. Since the PA^{nn}dA-S scope rules apply equally to TrafoLa-S and the package **pannda**, phrases of a hidden sort, or phrases containing such hidden constructors cannot be edited.

5.1.3. Phrases

A PA^{nn}dA phrase is a syntactically well-formed fragment of a PA^{nn}dA program, enclosed in square brackets, e.g. the text of a package body, a declaration, an axiom, an expression etc. Phrases denote patterns of PA^{nn}dA programs in the axioms specifying transformation functions; they can be edited in structural or in textual mode.

Structural Editing of Phrases

If a node of type *expression* is selected, the template-inserting transformation PAnndA_Phrase is available. When selected, the placeholder for phrases is displayed, and the *phrase editor* is entered.

At this placeholder, a set of templates is available, one for (almost) every syntactic category in the PA^{nn}dA syntax. So, the user can transform the phrase placeholder to obtain a placeholder term for any syntactic category of PA^{nn}dA phrases. Then a set of templates is provided for every syntactic rule so that every legal PA^{nn}dA construction can be inserted.

Textual Editing of Phrases

The syntactic category of a phrase is needed in order to check whether it is wellformed w.r.t. that cartegory. So textual editing of phrases is limited to the cases where this syntactic category of a phrase can be deduced from its context, by a mechanism called *context-sensitive parsing*. If the context information is not sufficient to resolve ambiguity, additional information has to be provided by the user, usually by qualifying the type of the phrase.

Semantic Checking of Phrases

The TrafoLa-S editor assures that PA^{nn}dA phrases are correct w.r.t. the *context-free syntax* of PA^{nn}dA. However, PA^{nn}dA phrases cannot be checked w.r.t. the static semantics of PA^{nn}dA because this depends on the context where the transformation is applied which is unknown when the transformation is edited.

5.1.4. Embedded Expressions

Embedded expressions are TrafoLa-S expressions occurring inside phrases. They are allowed for any syntactic category of a phrase. On the screen, embedded expressions are displayed in curly brackets unless they are just TrafoLa-S variables, in which case the brackets are ommitted. Embedded expressions can be edited in structural or textual mode.

Structural Editing of Embedded Expressions

When positioned at any placeholder term in a phrase (which is not a list phylum), there is a template TrafoLa-S_Expression which produces the completing term of a TrafoLa-S expression. Such an expression has exactly the same templates and static semantics as in PA^{nn}dA-S editor.

For the frequently occurring case that a TrafoLa-S expression is just a variable, there is a transformation ⟨Trafola-S_Variable⟩ at every resting place in the phrase editor (which is not a list phylum).

Textual Editing of Embedded Expressions

Textual editing of embedded expressions and variables inside phrases is allowed, though some context information must be present to direct the parsing. As for phrases, the expected type for the expression has to be extracted from the embedding phrase.

If the context information is not sufficient, the parser will suspend the parsing of the expression and return an error. Then the user can correct either the expression or its embedding phrase.

5.1.5. Transformation to the Canonical Form

The TrafoLa-S editor provides a global transformation Canonical form which is available when selecting the root of a TrafoLa-S program.

The transformation traverses the whole TrafoLa-S program and replaces every phrase by its canonical representation, i.e. a PA^{nn}dA-S expression over the functions of the abstract data type defining the PA^{nn}dA abstract syntax, leaving embedded TrafoLa-S expressions and TrafoLa-S variables as they are.

5.1.6. Conclusions

A major problem in implementing the TrafoLa-S editor has been the textual editing of phrases and embedded expressions: The goal of parsing is determined by a sort in the predefined package **pannda**, i.e. by an attribute value.

To this end, a method called *Context Sensitive Parsing* has been incorporated in the editor. Details concerning the use of this method in the TrafoLa-S editor are described in the report [de la Cruz *et al.* 90].

Deficiencies

It is straight-forward to assume that there is a transformation from canonical representatoions of phrases into their concrete form (the inverse to the transformation described in 5.1.5). However, such a transformation is very difficult to implement and is therefore still missing in the present implementation of the editor.

5.2. Translators from TrafoLa to SSL and TrafoLa-H

Bernd Gersdorf, Universität Bremen

This section describes the translator for transformations written in TrafoLa. There are two possible backends: The first produces output for the **C**ornell **P**rogram **S**ynthesizer (CPS) thas is a text following the rules for the CSG input language, the **S**ynthesizer **S**pecification **L**anguage (SSL). It can be used to generate new transformers using the CPS. Most of the existing transformations in the system are produced in this ways. The second backend produces TrafoLa-H output. Each transformer can execute TrafoLa-H transformations without any regeneration.

5.2.1. Normal Form for Transformations

Not all constructs in TrafoLa can be translated to SSL or TrafoLa-H, because TrafoLa is an extension of PAnndA-S, a specification language that joins algebraic, predicative and higher order concepts into one specifcation languages. SSL on the other hand is just a first-order applicative language.

The subset of TrafoLa-S that can be translated to SSL is therefore restricted. The backend to TrafoLa-H is even more restricted than the SSL backend. The normal form for the SSL backend is described in this chapter, the additional restrictions for TrafoLa-H at the end of chapter 5.

Transformations are either context-sensitive (CST) or context-free. Context-free transformations neither use information from the static semantic analyses nor from the local theory. However, the normal form for context-free transformations is much simpler. The next part describes context-free transformations with some hooks for context-sensitive transformations.

5.2.2. Syntax

The meta language for syntactic descriptions is an extended BNF. Italic parts in a nonterminal are only comments that can be ignored (e.g. "*type*_id" is the same as "id"). The syntax given is ambiguous; the editor may require additional parentheses around some of the constructs to build an abstract syntax tree that corresponds to a derivation of a term produced with the following syntax.

A compilation unit is a single package that contains a sequence of type, function and axiom declarations:

```
program::=
   'WITH' package_identifier { ',' package_identifier } ';'
   'PACKAGE' package_identifier 'IS'
       { declarations }
   'END' package_identifier ';'

declarations ::=
   [ '--:' ] function_identifier ':' function_type ';'
 | 'TYPE' identifier 'IS' 'PRIVATE' ';'
 | 'AXIOM' logical_expression ';'
 | 'PRAGMA' 'context_free_trafo' '(' function_identifier ','
       menu_string_literal ')' ';'
   'PRAGMA' 'module' '(' module_name_string_literal ')' ';'
 | pragma_decl
```

A type declaration introduces a new type. A function declaration can be a **help function**, a **constructor**, a **trafo-function** or a **CST-function** (Context-Sensitive Trafo-function). For each trafo-function, there is a pragma containing the string '*menu_string*_literal' that is used as the menu entry in the CPS. The function type has the form:

```
function_type ::=
    [ domain { '#' domain } '-->' ] identifier
  | context_sensitive_function_type

domain ::=
    formal_parameter_identifier ':' type_identifier
    [ '::' restriction_condition ]
  | type_identifier
```

A trafo-function declared with 'pragma context_free_trafo(...)' has one or two formal parameters. The first formal parameter is the fragment parameter. The fragment type is one of the types listed in the package containing the abstract syntax of PA^{nn}dA-S. The result type of the trafo-function is the same as the fragment type. An optional domain restriction should be given for partial trafo-functions. It will be translated into a conditional SSL transformation, where the restriction is evaluated before the transformation is displayed as applicable.

If a trafo-function has a second parameter, it is considered to be parameterised. The restriction given for this parameter will be evaluated when the user has provided a value for this parameter. The declaration

```
trafo: (X: EXPRESSION:: p(X); Y: EXPRESSION_LIST:: q(X,Y))
    --> Z:EXPRESSION:: t(X,Y,Z)
```

introduces a parameterised trafo-function "trafo". It will be displayed, if the logical expression *p(X)* is true. The parameter *X* in *p(X)* indicates that X can be used in the logical expression..The second parameter *Y* is the user input that will be checked by *q(X,Y)*. The result annotation *t(X,Y,Z)* will be ignored.

A help function may have zero or more formal parameters with optional domain restrictions. Restrictions for help functions are ignored during the translation process, which means that neither static nor dynamic check of these predicates will be done.

Logical expressions in axiomatic parts and in restrictions have the following form:

```
logical_expression ::=
    [ quantifier variable_declaration_list '=>' ]
        log_expression { ',' log_expression }

log_expression ::=
    f_call '=' expression
  | condition '->' log_expression
  | logical_expression

condition ::=
    condition ( 'AND' | 'OR' ) condition
  | 'NOT' condition
  | expression '=' pattern_expression
```

```
expression ::=
    f_call
  | expression bin_op expression
  | unary_op expression
  | identifier
  | literal

f_call ::=
    function_identifier '(' expression { ',' expression } ')'
```

Beside these purely syntactic conditions, there are lots of semantic restrictions that will be described in the next section.

5.2.3. Semantic Restrictions

There are several semantic restrictions that must be fulfilled for a translation to SSL. Beside static semantic restrictions like the well-typedness (checked by the TrafoLa editor), there are restrictions for the construction of equations. This allows e.g. the separation of functions into constructors and other functions. Semantically, each expression containing no variables and no partial applications (underparameterized function calls) can be assigned an element in a set. Each element of such a set can be represented as a unique *constructor expression*. This is an `expression` containing only literals, constructors and fully parameterized constructor applications. Furthermore, the constructors are *free* that is, each constructor expression can be assigned a unique element in this set. Constructor expressions can therefore be seen as the data itself (abstract syntax trees, input from the user,...).

Main equations

The syntax for `logical_expression` contains at least one `log_expression` of the form

```
f_call '=' expression
```

This "equation" will be interpreted from left to right as a rewrite rule for the function named with f_call. In the following, this equation will be called *main equation*. If there are no main equations for a declared function, this function will be interpreted as a (free) constructor. Main equations for functions that are not declared are simply ignored. The actual parameters of f_call are *pattern*_expressions. This means, they are expressions constructed over literals, variables and constructors. Here is a small example for a complete package with a single transformation written in TrafoLa:

```
with panndac, p_nature, p_ssl;
package EXAMPLE1 is
    twist: (X: EXPRESSION) --> EXPRESSION;
    pragma context_free_trafo(twist,"twist");
    axiom for all L: EXPRESSION; R: EXPRESSION =>
        twist([L and R]) = [R and L];
end EXAMPLE1;
```

After translation to PA^nndA-S this example looks as follows:

```
with panndac, p_nature, p_ssl;
package EXAMPLE1 is
   twist: X: EXPRESSION --> EXPRESSION;
   pragma context_free_trafo(twist,"twist");
   axiom for all L: EXPRESSION; R: EXPRESSION =>
         twist(Mk_Call(Mk_Name(Mk_Unique_Name("and","#Land",
               mk_Predefined_Op_Nature)),
                     Mk_Tuple(Mk_Expr_List(A,Mk_Expr_List(B,
               Empty_Expr_List)))))
         = Mk_Call(Mk_Name(Mk_Unique_Name("and","#Land",
               mk_Predefined_Op_Nature)),
                     Mk_Tuple(Mk_Expr_List(B,Mk_Expr_List(A,
               Empty_Expr_List))));
end EXAMPLE1;
```

Now the identifiers in italics are constructors of the abstract syntax of PA^{nn}dA-S. It is easy to see that the result is in the form described above.

Pattern Expressions

Variables introduced by quantified expressions must be *free* or *bound* in pattern expressions, and *bound* in other non-pattern expressions. The rules for variable bindings are:

- free variables on the left hand side of a main equation are bound on the right hand side and in the condition of that equation.
- in a condition, new variable bindings can be produced by an equation that contains free variables on the right hand side. These variables are bound in the rest of the conjunction that contains the equation (textually to the right) and in the right hand side of the main equation.
- if a condition contains a logical negation, all variables bound by the argument expression of the negation are unbound outside.

Here is an example with a condition:

```
package EXAMPLE2 is
   twist: X: EXPRESSION --> EXPRESSION;
   pragma context_free_trafo(twist,"twist");
   axiom for all L: EXPRESSION; R: EXPRESSION;
                  H: EXPRESSION =>
          X=[L and R] -> twist(X)=[R and L];
end EXAMPLE2;
```

The actual argument of “twist” will be bound to X first, then X will be matched against the pattern expression “[L and R]”, binding also L and R. The result is “[R and L]”, with all variables being bound.

The rules for bound variables also apply to `restriction_condition` (see `domain`). Here, the formal parameter variables for the fragment and for additional parameters are bound, and more bindings can be produced in the same way as for conditions of main equations.

Simplification of Logical Expressions

The combination of logical operations, tuple expressions and quantified expressions can lead to rather complex terms. For the translation, logical expressions are normalised in the following way:

```
e -> (e1, e2,...)       ⇒   (e -> e1), (e -> e2),...
(e1,e2,...) -> e        ⇒   (e1 and e2 and ...) -> e
e and (e1 or e2)        ⇒   (e and e1) or (e and e2)
(e1 or e2) and e        ⇒   (e1 and e) or (e2 and e)
(e1 or e2) -> e         ⇒   (e1 -> e), (e2 -> e)
not (e1 or e2)          ⇒   (not e1) and (not e2)
not (e1 and e2)         ⇒   (not e1) or (not e2)
e1 -> (e2 -> e)         ⇒   (e1 and e2) -> e
not (not e)             ⇒   e
```

There is also a rule for quantified expressions: It is assumed that each local quantifier can be removed by declaring the new variables on top of the axiom part, quantified "for all".

```
for all d1; d2;...
     => e1, e2,...      ⇒    e1, e2,...
```

The rules for variable bindings are extended to all expressions that can be normalized using these rules.

5.2.4. Transformation Modules

All transformations defined within a single package can be grouped into a **transformation module.** Transformations in such a module can be switched on and off inside a transformer. A package becomes a transformation module if it contains a pragma "module" as described in the syntax for "declaration". Transformation Modules are ignored in the TrafoLa-H backend.

5.2.5. A More Complex Example

Below is a more complex example that uses a lot of the constructs mentioned in the previous sections. The transformation function norm is a partial function that moves implications into premises

```
(e1, e2,...) -> e   ⇒   (e1 -> e), (e2 -> e),...
```

by calling a help function norm_h. The formal parameter of norm contains a domain restriction that also uses a help function with result type Res_t which is a user-defined type with the two constructor operations yes and no. All other types are imported from the package containing the abstract syntax types (by **with** pannda, p_basic;).

```
with pannda, p_basic;
package EXAMPLE3 is
pragma module("normalize_logical_expressions");
  type Res_t is private;
  yes: Res_t;
  no: Res_t;
  --: is_list: (X: EXPRESSION) --> Res_t;

  norm:
    (X: EXPRESSION :: exist E: EXPRESSION_LIST; E2: EXPRESSION; Op: UNIQUE_NAME =>
        (X = Mk_Call(Mk_Name(Op),
                     Mk_Tuple(Mk_Expr_List(Mk_Tuple(E), Mk_Expr_List(E2, Empty_Expr_List))))
          and is_list(Mk_Tuple(E)) = yes)
          and Op = Mk_Unique_Name("->", "#L->", mk_Predefined_Op_Nature)
     ) --> EXPRESSION;

  --: norm_h:  (X: EXPRESSION_LIST) # (E: EXPRESSION) --> EXPRESSION_LIST;
  axiom exist Impl: UNIQUE_NAME; X: EXPRESSION_LIST =>
    Mk_Unique_Name( "->",  "#L->",  mk_Predefined_Op_Nature) = Impl ->
      (for all C: EXPRESSION_LIST; E: EXPRESSION =>
      norm(
        Mk_Call(
          Mk_Name(Impl),
          Mk_Tuple(Mk_Expr_List(Mk_Tuple(C), Mk_Expr_List(E, Empty_Expr_List))))) =
        mk_Tuple(norm_h( C, E)),
      norm_h( Empty_Expr_List, E) = Empty_Expr_List,
      (exist H: EXPRESSION; L: EXPRESSION_LIST =>
        X = mk_Expr_List( H, L) ->
          (norm(
            Mk_Call(
              Mk_Name(Impl),
              Mk_Tuple(
                Mk_Expr_List(Mk_Tuple(L), Mk_Expr_List(E, Empty_Exp BOOL)))) =
            mk_Tuple(C) -> norm_h( X, E) =
            mk_Expr_List(
            Mk_Call(
              Mk_Name(Impl),
              Mk_Tuple(Mk_Expr_List(H, Mk_Expr_List(E, Empty_Expr_List)))),
            C),
          is_list(mk_Tuple(X)) = yes),
        not (exist H: EXPRESSION; T: EXPRESSION_LIST =>
          X = mk_Expr_List( H, T)) ->  is_list(mk_Tuple(X)) = no));
end EXAMPLE3;
```

5.2.6. Context-Sensitive Transformations and the Parameter Editor

A typical program transformation rule requires additional *contextual* information about the program fragment that must be transformed. E.g., the type of an expression can not be derived from the fragment alone since type declarations are normally not part of the fragment.

Therefore a CST-function has an additional parameter, containing all additional information available for the program fragment (called *context* or *environment* parameter).

```
context_sensitive_function_type ::=
   context_type_domain '-->' fragment_domain '-->'
   [ parameter_decls '-->' ] type_identifier
```

```
parameter_decls ::=
  domain
| dummy_identifier ':' '(' domain { '#' domain } ')' '::'
     parameter_restriction_condition
```

Here is an example for a valid declaration of a CST-function:

```
f1: EXPRESSION_CST --> (E: EXPRESSION) --> EXPRESSION;
```

The type name of "*context_type*_domain" can always be derived from the "*fragment*_domain" by appending "_CST" to the fragment type name.

When called directly as a transformation, the context-type parameter of a CST-function has a value consistent to the surrounding program (context) of the selected program fragment. Inside expressions, this context parameter can be used together with some predefined functions operating on context types. These operations can be classified as either *context update functions* or *attribute access functions*. Context update functions can be used to build new contexts from existing ones, e.g. for recursive transformations. Attribute access functions are functions for selecting specific information (e.g. type information) that can be useful for the definition of a transformation.

Since the use of context update functions is a rather complex and tedious work, there exists a short notation for the class of CST-functions that can be translated to SSL. This is the *hat notation* described below.

The syntax for function calls is extended to allow also curried function calls for CST-functions:

```
f_call ::=
  function_identifier expression expression
     [ '(' expression { ',' expression } ')' ]
```

Partial parameterisation is not allowed since higher order expressions will be translated into a first order function call.

A CST-function may have more parameters than just the fragment and context type domain. If the CST-function is a transformation, these additional parameters can be typed in (or copied in) using the *parameter editor*. Otherwise, it is assumed to be a help function that is context-sensitive. To enable a CST-function as a transformation that can be called from the outside, a pragma must be given:

```
pragma_decl ::=
  'PRAGMA' 'trafo' '(' function_identifier ','
     menu_string_literal { parameter_info } ')' ';'
parameter_info ::=
  ',' ( 'as1' | 'as2' ) ',' info_string_literal ','
     as2_default_expression ',' position_string_literal
```

The rules are the same as for trafo-functions except that for each additional parameter there must be a "parameter_info" in the pragma containing

- the specification whether a parameter must be edited (as1) or copied in, using the copy mechanism (as2) of the CPS,
- a string literal that will be displayed as an additional information when the user is asked for an input,

- a *default expression* as a standard answer to the question.
- a *position string* that refers to a so called *parameter pattern*

For each parameter, the parameter editor performs a static semantic check. The context information used for this check comes from a position within the fragment parameter that matches the parameter pattern. This position is given by the `position_string_literal`, which refers either to the root of the parameter pattern or to one of the variables within the parameter pattern.

A reference to the root is a string containing the name of the formal parameter of the fragment parameter. Such a reference can also be made if there is no parameter pattern. A reference to a variable in the parameter pattern is a string containing the name of that variable.

The parameter pattern is defined by a fragment restriction of the form

```
'exists' <variable_declaration_list> '=>'
    <formal_fragment_parameter_identifier> '='
        <parameter_pattern_expression>
',' <more_restrictions_log_expression>
```

The type of the variable refered to by the position string must be the same as the type of the corresponding additional parameter.

Here is an example:

```
testing:(CON: EXPRESSION_CST) -->
        (E:EXPRESSION
        :: exist ES: EXPRESSION_LIST; DS: DECLARATION_LIST;
        Q: QUANTIFIER =>
            E = Mk_Quantified( Q, DS, ES),
            DS /= Empty_Decl_List)
        --> (Dummy: (P1: EXPRESSION) # (P2: DECLARATION_LIST)
                :: P2 /= Empty_Decl_List)
        --> EXPRESSION;
   pragma trafo(testing, "testing-trafo",
        as2, "Copy EXPRESSION", Empty_Expr, "E",
        as1, "Type in DECLARATION_LIST", Empty_Decl_List, "DS"
   );
```

The parameter pattern is `Mk_Quantified(Q, DS, ES)`. The first additional parameter `P1` is checked inside the context of the root fragment expression (the position string is `"E"`, that is a reference to the fragment parameter) and the second parameter `P2` in the context of the declaration list of the quantified expression (position string `"DS"`).

The application of the transformation `testing` in a transformer opens a parameter window (Transformation Argument Form) with all menu strings inserted as specified by the pragma for `testing`::

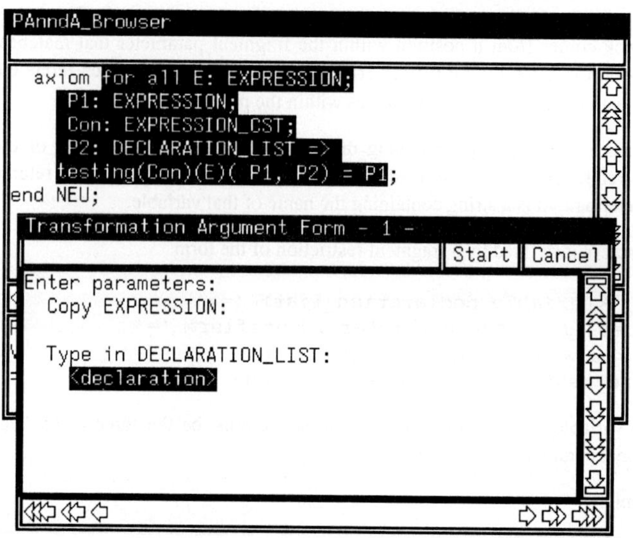

5.2.7. The Subset of Translatable CST Functions

The notation for CST-functions described so far is much larger than the class of CST-functions translatable to SSL. The reason is that that the context parameter in CPS generated transformers contains only a subset of the possible information of a context.

A idealised view of the context parameter is the following: The context is a term representing the *rest of the program* or, in other words, the program that surrounds the fragment term. Given this view of a context, each information about a fragment can be computed since the fragment can always be completed to a whole program.

The translation to SSL uses the following implementation: The context is a tuple of all inherited attributes valid for the fragment at the current place. This means, that the context information is frozen immediately before the transformation is applied. It is therefore illegal to access context information for new fragments constructed during the transformation. Here is an example::

```
axiom for all C: EXPRESSION_CST; A,B,X: EXPRESSION =>
    get_type C [X-A] = ...-> trafo C [A+B*X] = ...;
```

The attribute access function `get_type` is called here with the fragment `[X-A]` although the original fragment was `[A+B*X]`. Since the context `C` (tuple of inherited attributes) may change if the fragment changes, the call to 'get_type' may be inconsistent.

Given the idealised view of the context, this example makes sense: `get_type` returns the type of an expression `X-A` in a program derived from the original one by replacing `A+B*X` by `X-A`.

The remaining class of CST-functions therefore contains only those attribute access calls asking for values at different places *in the original program.* Given the view of attributes as it exists in the CPS, this means that all attribute values are frozen in the abstract syntax tree before a transformation is called. Each attribute access function returns a value computed from one or more frozen attribute values.

5.2.8. Updating the Context

Let us change the example above to::

```
axiom for all C: EXPRESSION_CST; A,B,X: EXPRESSION =>
    get_type C [B*X] = ...-> trafo C [A+B*X] = ...;
```

Now the function 'get_type' will be called for a subterm `B*X` of the original fragment `A+B*X`, but the context `C` may still be wrong since it contains the context for `A+B*X` instead of `B*X`. To correct this, *context update functions* can be used. Given the original context and fragment, the new context for a subterm of the fragment can be computed::

```
axiom for all C: EXPRESSION_CST; A,B,X: EXPRESSION =>
    get_type (bin_exp_2(C,[A+B*X])) [B*X] = ...-> trafo C [A+B*X] = ...;
```

Here, `bin_exp_2` is the context update function computing the new context for the second argument ('B*X') of the binary expression involving '+' as an operator. This update function is not defined in the system, but it can be constructed from a canonical set of update functions defined in the system. However, there is a simpler method to cope with context update functions that is described in the next section.

5.2.9. The Hat Notation Expansion

Instead of inserting the context update functions by hand, it is possible to use the **hat notation** as a short form. Each CST- or attribute access function call can be simplified by replacing the actual parameter for the context information by the symbol ^. The example then changes as follows::

```
axiom for all A,B,X: EXPRESSION =>
    get_type ^ [B*X] = ...-> trafo ^ [A+B*X] = ...;
```

This notation can be translated into pure PAnndA-S with context update function calls inserted automatically. To do this, the use of ^ must follow some conventions:

- in the *main equation*, the left hand side must be an f_call of the form
  ```
  cst_function_identifier ^ main_pattern_expression
      [ more_expression ]
  ```

- in the right hand side of the main equation and in the condition of a main equation, function calls of the following form are allowed:
  ```
  function_identifier ^ subpattern_expression [ more_expression ]
  ```

The function can be a CST-function or an attribute access function. The *`subpattern_expression`* is a subexpression of the *`main_pattern_expression`* of the main equation. The optional `more_expression` is used for additional parameters (help or parameterised trafo-functions).

Following these rules, the translation to pure PA^{nn}dA-S can be done with the hat expander implemented as a transformation `hat_expansion` in the TrafoLa-editor, just before the translation to SSL.

5.2.10. Partial Transformations

The hat notation can also be used in restrictions for formal parameters. For the fragment parameter, the restriction is the condition in the *fragment*_domain. For additional parameters, it is the restriction of the outermost domain. Using "p" and "q" for the restricting expressions of the fragment and the restriction for additional parameters, the declarations have the form:

```
f1: t_CST --> (X: t :: p(X)) --> t;
f2: t_CST --> (X: t :: p(X)) --> (P1: t1:: q(X,P1)) --> t;
f3: t_CST --> (X: t :: p(X)) --> (P: ((P1: t1) # (P2: t2))
              :: q(X,P1,P2)) --> t;
...
```

All three declarations declare CST-functions mapping fragments of type `t` to `t` with a restriction *p(X)*. The function `f1` has no additional parameters, `f2` has exactly one. For more additional parameters, a tuple must be used as in `f3`, but there there is still only one parameter restriction *q(X,P1,P2)* for all parameters.

In a restriction expression there is no main equation, and therefore no main pattern that could be used to derive context update function calls for occurrences of ^. To overcome this problem, there is an additional rule for *main pattern* in restriction expressions of the form

e1 **and** (*fragment*_identifier = *main_pattern*_expression) **and** *e2*

The *fragment*_identifier is the formal parameter identifier used in the declaration of the CST-function. The first equation in a conjunction with the fragment identifier on the left hand side will be used to define the main pattern. In the rest (textually to the right) of the conjunction (e2), expansion of hat's works as for conditions for main equations.

Here is a legal example:

```
trafo: EXPRESSION_CST --> (E: EXPRESSION ::
    exist A,B: EXPRESSION =>
          (E=[A+B] and (get_type ^ A) = get_type ^ B))
    or    (E=[A*B] and (get_type ^ B)=[Integer])
) --> EXPRESSION;
```

The function call `get_type` is an attribute selection that returns the type of the expression passed in as an argument (the name may change in the near future).

5.2.11. Other Restrictions

The translation process does not cope with all the semantic features of TrafoLa. Here is a list of known problems:

- If one uses help constructors with parameter types that are imported from the abstract syntax, one can run into the problem that the CPS has no attribution rules for the corresponding constructors. They must then be added by hand directly in SSL.
- Identifiers imported from one of the predefined packages are case-sensitive. Most of them are generated such that no problems occur.

5.2.12. Separate Compilation

Transformations can be split into several packages and compiled separately using the translator to SSL/TrafoLa-H. The visibility rules are the same as for PA^{nn}dA-S. The next section describes some predefined packages that can (or must) be used for the definition of transformations.

5.2.13. Predefined Operations and Types

The PA^{nn}dA-S environment for transformations is organized in several packages (families). The packages `pannda` and `p_basic` are sufficient for context-free transformations. They contain the abstract syntax of PA^{nn}dA-S and some useful operations that are available for base types.

For context-sensitive transformations, the packages `cst`, `cst_ops` and `cst_base` must be used. The package `cst` contains context type definitions, context update functions and some elementary context access functions. The package `cst_base` has additional type declarations for result types of the elementary attribute access functions, and `cst_ops` contains operations based on `cst` that can be useful in transformations.

5.2.14. Packages pannda and `p_basic`

All the constructor operations defined to build up an abstract syntax tree for a PA^{nn}dA-S program are listed in a package `pannda`. This package was constructed using the *SSL type scheme* of the PA^{nn}dA-S editor. The operations named "&" are generated for all list phyla to have an append operation available that corresponds to the SSL operations "::" (cons) and "@" (append). Only concatenation of two list parameters is supported.

There is additional support for patterns constructed using the "&" operation: If it is used in a way that one of the arguments is a call to a list constructor, then the type of the expression can be deduced locally. Having the type information, the expression will be converted into a "normal" pattern. This is of course only possible if all the arguments are patterns for lists have a constant length, except for the "rest" of the list. An example in TrafoLa-S is:

```
[p1,p2] & [] & p
```

Here, p1 and p2 are patterns denoting elements of a list and p any pattern of the list type (e.g. a variable). A typical use is

```
axiom for all H: EXPRESSION; T: EXPRESSION_LIST => ...[H] & T....
```

which will be translated to PA^{nn}dA-S first and then into

```
... Mk_Expr_List(H,T) ...
```

5.2.15. Using the Translator to SSL

The translator to SSL can be invoked as a transformation inside the TrafoLa-editor, or as a Unix command.

Use from the PROSPECTRA System

The normal way for writing transformations is to write them in the TrafoLa-editor. The translation of such transformations to PA^{nn}dA consist of three steps:

- elimination of TrafoLa-S phrases
- translation into abstract syntax for PA^{nn}dA (AS2 abstract syntax)
- hat expansion transformation

Then the translation to SSL is invoked by the "--> SSL" command on the library level of the TrafoLa-editor. The produced SSL output is saved in text form with the suffix ".ssl" in the file system.

For each package containing transformations, a single ".ssl" file will be produced. Before generating a transformer, the linker must be called by

```
( 'lpts' | 'lcpts' ) filename { filename }
```

The command 'lpts' can only be used for context-free transformations. The `filename` contains only the base name of the file name (without suffix ".ssl"). The list of file names should contain only files written by the user. Predefined packages (pannda, p_basic, ...) will be linked automatically. The result of the linker is a file "alltrafos.ssl" that is used by the shell command `make_transformer` that generates a library based tool containing all specified transformations.

Use from the UNIX Shell

Beside the translator in the TrafoLa-editor, there is a variant that can be called directly in a Unix shell. This translator produces error messages when applied to transformations having an illegal style. Therefore it should be preferred. It can be called by the shell command "pts" that requires only the base name of a file with suffix ".pc" that contains the PA^{nn}dA structure format of the transformation. This means, that the package containing the transformations must be saved (after the hat expansion) in *structure format* with a file name ending in ".pc".

5.2.16. TrafoLa-H Backend

The TrafoLa-H backend is only available inside the TrafoLa-editor. First, the translation proceeds as for SSL (including the translation to SSL!). Switching to "alternate-unparsing-style" will then produce TrafoLa-H output that must be saved with suffix ".trah".

The linker for TrafoLa-H is called "lhpts" and its usage is similar to "lpts".

There are some restrictions for TrafoLa-H:

- context-sensitive transformations are not supported
- parameterised transformations must have exactly one parameter.
- no transformation modules
- no user-defined constructors

5.3. TrafoLa-H Subsystem

Martin Alt, Christian Fecht, Christian Ferdinand, Reinhard Wilhelm
Universität des Saarlandes

The functional language TrafoLa-H, designed as a specification language for program transformations, has been implemented by an interpreter and a compiler. The compiler implementation is described in this section. A short introduction to the structure of the TrafoLa-H system and its use is followed by a detailed description of the implementation. State-of-the-art techniques in the implementation of functional and logical languages were used to arrive at an implementation of the required performance.

5.3.1. Introduction

This section describes a compiler for the transformation language TrafoLa-H that is defined in section 8 of part II. Earlier, the language designer Reinhold Heckmann had written an experimental interpreter for a nondeterministic variant of the language. The compiler presented here has been developed to increase run-time efficiency.

TrafoLa-H has been designed as an expressive functional language with powerful constructs for pattern matching. The implementation of TrafoLa-H thus required some deep analysis of its semantics and state-of-the-art implementation techniques for functional and logical languages.

The main efforts of the implementation of TrafoLa-H have been:

- support for over- and undersupply of arguments to functions,
- nondeterministic pattern matching with backtracking through sets of possible environments,
- efficient matching of large pattern using bottom-up tree automata (tree parsers),
- development of an efficient abstract machine based on optimized compiled graph reduction,
- development of a type inference algorithm.

In the following sections, the most interesting aspects of the TrafoLa-H implementation are described. Section 5.3.2 explains the structure and configuration of the system. Section 5.3.3 covers some algorithms for the analysis and transformation of source programs that simplify the translation into abstract machine code. Section 5.3.4 introduces the structure of the TRAMA, an abstract machine for compiled graph reduction. In section 5.3.5, the translation of TrafoLa-H to TRAMA code and the instruction set of the TRAMA are developed step by step. The translation is specified by a set of mutually recursive functions. Section 5.3.6 gives some optimizations of the translation functions. Finally, section 5.3.7 and 5.3.8 describe the techniques used for implementing TrafoLa-H pattern matching.

5.3.2. Compiler Structure

The TrafoLa-H compiler translates TrafoLa-H programs into code for the TRAMA, an abstract machine for the efficient execution of TrafoLa-H programs using compiled graph reduction. It consists of the following modules, all written or generated in C.

1. The *scanner* for the lexical analysis of TrafoLa-H was generated using the scanner generator FLEX.
2. The *LALR(1) parser* for TrafoLa-H was generated using the parser generator BISON.

3. The *type checker* implements an extension of the Hindley/Milner type inference algorithm. It is described in sections 8.6 and 8.7 of part II.

4. The *code generator* translates to abstract machine code. It includes the following optimizations:
   - algebraic simplifications
   - extraction of local functions
   - elimination of unused pattern variables
   - transformation of linear recursive into tail recursive functions
   - efficient code generation for tail recursion
   - exploitation of type information for better code generation
   - address assignment to variables according to their lifetime
   - short circuit evaluation of boolean expressions

5. A subclass of TrafoLa-H patterns can be transformed into a regular tree grammar, describing the values matched by the pattern. The *tree parser generator* transforms such a grammar into a fast tree parser. This is especially interesting for matching complex patterns and large values.

6. A *peep-hole optimizer* simplifies the abstract machine code.

5.3.2.1. System Configurations

The type checker and tree parser generator consume a considerable amount of time and space during compilation. So these parts of the compiler can be switched off (independently of each other) in order to increase compilation speed and reduce the compiler's space requirements, at the cost of generating less efficient code. On small computers, the tree parser generator should always be switched off because this component has high storage demands.

5.3.3. The Front End

Apart from scanning and parsing, the front end performs several analyses and transformations on the source. Occurrences of variables in TrafoLa-H programs are divided into different categories, which are to be stored in different memory areas. This allows for efficient variable access.

5.3.3.1. Free and bound variables

While translating expressions and programs, the compiler has to compute the set of free and bound variables of every language construct. Furthermore, it has to find the corresponding defining occurrence for every used occurrence of a variable. The sets of free and bound variables are defined similarly as in other functional languages. Some important differences are related to the patterns of TrafoLa-H. Patterns have a structure similar to, and as complex as that of expressions. 'Unbind' and 'Not' patterns introduce new scopes (see chapter 8 of part II for details). Patterns may also contain free variables. These are the 'Import' variables and the variables in the expression of 'Where' clauses not occurring in the pattern. The necessary information is computed by the following four functions. Most of the formal definition can be found in [?].

1. Var p
   computes the set of all the variables of the pattern p, except those that only occur free in p.

2. Bound p
   computes the set of the variables bound in pattern p; a variable v in a pattern p is bound if at least one occurrence of v in p is not enclosed in an 'Unbind'- or 'Not'-pattern.

3. Local p
   computes the set of local variables of pattern p; a variable v in a pattern p is local (or temporary) if at least one occurrences of v is enclosed in an 'Unbind'- or 'Not'-pattern.

4. Freepat p
   computes the set of free variables of pattern p; a variable v in a pattern p is free if p contains a subpattern $\%v$ ('Import'-pattern) or p contains a 'Where'-pattern (p' where e) with $v \in$ Freevar e and p' contains no defining occurrences of v.

Example 1: Bound, Local and Free variables in patterns
For the TrafoLa-H pattern p `(a&{a}&(c where c == a)::%v)` holds: Var p = {a,c}, Bound p = {a,c}, Local p = {a} and Freepat p = {a,v}. This TrafoLa-H-pattern shows the difficult semantics. The identification phase is more complex than in other languages. Furthermore, the compiler has to detect name clashes between local and bound variables in a declaration. Such an analysis can be omitted for patterns in normalform, simplifying the code generation.

Definition 5.3.1 (Normalform of TrafoLa-H Pattern)
Let p be a TrafoLa-H pattern. If for all different 'Not'- and 'Unbind' subpatterns p_1 and p_2 of p

1. *Bound $p_1 \cap$ Bound $p_2 = \emptyset$ (no clashes between subpatterns) and*

2. *Bound $p \cap$ Bound $p_i = \emptyset$ (no clashes between a subpattern and the whole pattern, $i \in \{1,2\}$)*

then p is in normalform.

To simplify the following definitions, the translator assumes all patterns to be received in normalform. The algorithm *remove* transforming a TrafoLa-H pattern into normalform is defined on the structure of a pattern. It is integrated into the analyzing phase.

5.3.3.2. Transforming a Pattern

TrafoLa-H supports nonlinear patterns. During pattern matching, the occurrences of a variable matched first will be treated differently from other occurrences of the same variable matched later. Therefore, the compiler has to determine some order of the occurrences of a variable in nonlinear patterns for code generation. Exploiting this information, it can produce more efficient code. Two restrictions on patterns currently exists.

1. Any subpattern p of a pattern p^* must not contain any pattern variable that is bound during matching.

2. Both subpatterns p_1 and p_2 of $(p_1 \mid p_2)$ have to contain the same pattern variables, i.e., Bound p_1 = Bound p_2.

These conditions are checked in the front end. The function *mark* annotates variable occurrences as being first or nonfirst. It is an extension of similar algorithms known from other funcional languages and depends on some compilation methods described later.

5.3.4. The Abstract Machine

In this section, we give a short introduction to the TRAMA. To explain this machine in full detail would exceed the scope of this section. The TRAMA is a compiled graph reduction machine based on the MaMa

[?], which is a variant of the G-machine [?]. Function application causes the creation of stack frames. Arguments and local variables are accessed through fixed relative addresses in these frames. According to the call-by-value semantics of TrafoLa-H, actual arguments of functions are evaluated and passed as values to the called function. The sets of binding environments resulting from nondeterministic pattern matching are elaborated by backtracking, using techniques of abstract machines for the implementation of Prolog ([?], [?]).

The important parts of the TRAMA are:

- the program store, PS, with access register PC
- three stacks
  - the evaluation stack, ST, with access registers SP, FP and MATCHNULL
  - the alternatives stack, AS, with access registers ALTNULL and AP
  - the trap stack, TS, with access register TP
- The heap, HP, with register HP_level

The Evaluation Stack

A stack cell can contain several objects:

- a basic object, like integers, booleans, constructors, or holes
- a pointer into the heap
- a pointer into the alternatives stack
- a pointer into the evaluation stack
- a pointer into the program store

The topmost stack cell is pointed to by the register SP (the stack pointer). The stack is divided into so-called stack frames, each frame corresponding to a function call. The topmost frame can be accessed by FP (frame pointer). A frame has the following structure:

- Cells for organization (activation record):
  1. The code address where – after returning from the function call – execution must be continued.
  2. A pointer to the previous frame.
  3. The global pointer of the previous frame. An array of global values is associated with each frame. This array, which is pointed to by the global pointer GP, contains the values of the free variables of the function corresponding to the frame.

  These three cells are installed by the caller. They serve to restore the right context after completion of the function call.
- A local environment (match environment) where the values bound to variables of the pattern of the called function are stored. The called function provides the space for this environment and fills it up during pattern matching.

- A local stack area:
  The evaluation of the body of the called function takes place here. This local stack is also used by the pattern matcher to perform a traversal through the object to be matched. Because of backtracking in pattern matching, the local stack has to be cleared in some way or rearranged when the matching of a subpattern has proved unsuccessful. For that reason, a special register MATCHNULL (only needed during pattern matching) is used to give access to the beginning of the match environment. This part of the frame is used only by the called function.

The local variables and the arguments can be adressed by SP or MATCHNULL.

The Heap

All values that can be analyzed by pattern matching and all objects whose lifetimes do not obey a stack discipline or that are too big to be stored in one stack cell are stored in the heap of the TRAMA. A call of the function $new(x)$ allocates an appropriate cell to hold an object x on the heap and returns a pointer to that cell.

The Alternatives Stack

The nondeterministic patterns of TrafoLa-H are implemented by backtracking. The backtrack points of the patterns are stored in the alternatives stack. A detailed description of the structure and the use of the alternatives stack is given in section 5.3.7.

The Trap Stack

The trap stack TS is needed to efficiently implement the expression operator '|'. $f_1 \mid f_2$, where f_1 and f_2 are functions, denotes the function which, when applied to an argument v, at first tries to apply f_1 to v, and on success returns the result, otherwise applies f_2 to v. The topmost cell of TS is pointed to by the TP (trap pointer). A cell of TS is structured in the following way:

- A code address pointing to a code sequence that contains the call of f_2 on v.
- The current values of FP and ALTNULL.

The code for $f_1 \mid f_2$ pushes a new cell onto the trap stack. When a match has failed, the content of the trap stack determines the following computation. If the trap stack is empty, a message is printed out and the machine halts. If there is a trap entry, the frame and stack pointers are set back and computation continues at the given address.

5.3.4.1. Representation of TrafoLa-H Values

All values that can be analyzed by pattern matching are stored in the heap of the TRAMA. The values are organized as records. The first component *tag* specifies the type of the record. All nonfunctional values are represented as directed acyclic graphs (see table 1).

FUNVAL objects need further explanations. Such an object represents a functional value. A FUNVAL object is a triple (fcp, fgp, fav). fcp points into the code array to the beginning for the code of the compiled function body. fgp is a pointer to a vector for the values of the global variables of the function. fav points to a vector of arguments for the function. When a function taking n arguments is applied to less than n arguments, the result of this application is a new function which has already consumed some of its n arguments. In this case a new FUNVAL object is built with the same code pointer and the the same global pointer and the already existing arguments are assembled into a vector pointed to by the fav entry

Value	tag	further components
Integer	INT	val: Integer number
Boolean	BOOL	val: True or false
Operators	CONST	val: Operator name
Strings	STRING	val: Chain of characters
Holes	HOLE	val: Hole number
Trees	TREE	oper: Pointer to operator son: Pointer to son
Lists	CONS	hd: Pointer to list element tl: Pointer to the remainder of the list
	NIL	-
Functions	FUNVAL	- *cannot be partitioned by pattern matching*
fail	-	- *is implemented by jumps*

Table 1: TrafoLa-H values

of the new FUNVAL object. To store the vectors of arguments or global variables, a heap object with tag VECTOR is used. An object of that kind is an array containing pointers to other cells.

5.3.5. The Translation of TrafoLa-H

5.3.5.1. Introduction

In this section, a simplified translation is given from TrafoLa-H to TRAMA code. The translation is described by mutually recursive code functions as in [?] or [?]. The code functions and their types are listed in Table 2.

Program_Code describes the translation of a TrafoLa-H program, which consists of a sequence of declarations and an expression. Decl_Code translates a sequence of declarations, where D_Code is used to decide whether N_Code (for nonrecursive declarations) or R_Code (for recursive declarations) is applied to a single declaration.

Expressions are translated with V_Code or B_Code. The execution of a result of B_Code produces a value on the evaluation stack, whereas the execution of a result of V_Code leaves a pointer on the topmost evaluation stack cell to a value in the heap. F_Code translates a TrafoLa-H function. The execution of a result of F_Code leaves a pointer to a FUNVAL object on the evaluation stack. The A_Code function is used by F_Code to translate a single function case (i.e., a pattern expression pair). O_Code describes the translation of the built-in operators of TrafoLa-H. Finally, P_Code describes the translation of patterns into TRAMA code.

There exist only two different places to store values, the heap and the evaluation stack. An efficient implementation prefers to store a value in the evaluation stack whenever possible. Nested if-then-else expressions are a good example with which to explain the dependency between the translation of an expression, the type of the expected result value, and the surrounding context and the attempt to keep the value on the evaluation stack as long as possible.

Code function	Type
Program_Code	definition* × expression ↦ $Trama^+$
Decl_Code	definition* × binding ↦ (binding,$Trama^+$)
D_Code	definition × binding ↦ (binding,$Trama^+$)
N_Code	definition × binding × binding × $\mathcal{Z}$ ↦ $Trama^+$
R_Code	definition × binding × $\mathcal{Z}$ ↦ $Trama^+$
V_Code	expression × binding × $\mathcal{Z}$ ↦ $Trama^+$
B_Code	expression × binding × $\mathcal{Z}$ ↦ $Trama^+$
F_Code	expression × binding ↦ $Trama^+$
A_Code	alternative × binding × **bool** ↦ $Trama^+$
O_Code	operator ↦ $Trama^+$
P_Code	pattern × binding × binding × $\mathcal{Z}$ ↦ $Trama^+$

Table 2: code functions; $\mathcal{Z}$ denotes the set of integers and $Trama^+$ a nonempty sequence of TRAMA instructions.

$$\textbf{dec}\ a = \underbrace{\textbf{if}\ \underbrace{\textbf{if}\ \underbrace{b_1}_{B\_Code}\ \textbf{then}\ \underbrace{e_1}_{B\_Code}\ \textbf{else}\ \underbrace{e_2}_{B\_Code}}_{B\_Code}\ \textbf{then}\ \underbrace{f_1}_{V\_Code}\ \textbf{else}\ \underbrace{f_2}_{V\_Code}}_{V\_Code}\ ;$$

The expressions e_1 and e_2 can be translated in a different context than f_1 and f_2. The translator can handle the innermost if-then-else more efficiently (i.e., B_Code), because both branches have to result in a boolean value that can be stored on the evaluation stack, whereas the values of f_1 and f_2 may be structured values (list, tuple, or tree) or functions that can not be stored in an evaluation stack cell.

Bindings and Environments

In TrafoLa-H, there are three ways to define a variable,

- global declarations
- local declarations in **let** expressions
- pattern variables on left hand sides of functional abstractions.

A major task of a compiler is to determine the valid definition for an applied occurrence of a variable. The correspondence between defining and applied occurrences is normally handled by environments. The TrafoLa-H → TRAMA compiler uses all information that can be statically computed from the source program in order to handle the run-time object as efficiently as possible.

Remark 1: (static information)
The following information is static:

- The number of arguments of a function and the number of its pattern variables
- The sets of free and bound variables of an expression
- The number of newly defined variables in a local or a global declaration

Definition 5.3.2 (Positions and environments)
A position of a variable is a pair consisting of the type of the binding, i.e., LOC, GLOB, ABS, or LOC_, and its address. The set of positions P is:

$$P = \{LOC,GLOB,ABS,LOC\_\} \times \textbf{integer}$$

An environment maps variables to positions. The set of environments B is:

$$B = \{f \mid f : V \rightarrow P\}$$

V denotes the set of variables.

The binding of a variable denotes the access mode to its storage location. The storage location and the binding type is chosen initially for every defining occurrence of a variable and may change in the process of further translation. With binding type ABS, the access is done relative to the beginning of the evaluation stack. The binding type GLOB gives access to the global variables of a function relative to the beginning of the global pointer (i.e. the storage location being referenced by the GP register). The binding types LOC and LOC_ have two different interpretations in the translation process, although the access mode is the same in all cases (relative to the top of the evaluation stack). Translating a global declaration the type, LOC describes the access mode to the newly defined variables. They immediately receive their storage location in the global environment. Conversely, redefined variables first receive a location at the top of the stack. When the old bindings are no longer used, they are overwritten with the new bindings, and the new bindings on the top of the stack can be popped off. Example 2 below describes this process.

The other meaning of the binding types LOC and LOC_ refers to the address mode of pattern variables in functions. Variables in 'Not' and 'Unbind' patterns receive the binding type LOC_ whereas the other variables get type LOC. After pattern matching, the bindings with binding type LOC_ are no longer used, and can be popped off the stack, as they reside on the top of the stack.

Stack Allocation and Management

One task in the implementation of a functional language is the efficient access to the parameters of a function. In a language like TrafoLa-H with the facility to under- and oversupply functions, this problem is much harder than in other programming languages. Usually, the access is possible relative to the stack frame pointer. The potential over- and undersupply of function applications prevents this solution in the TRAMA. The access, however, can be performed relative to the top of the stack, i.e., the content of the SP register (similar to the techniques of [?] and [?]). This is done by simulating the movement of SP in a new parameter (k_p) for every code function, which reflects the distance between the end of the local match environment at entry to the code for the expression and the actual stack height at run time.

5.3.5.2. The Code Functions

The Translations of the Program and the Program Expression

A program in TrafoLa-H consists of a declaration sequence and an expression, called the program expression. The result of the program is defined as the value of the program expression, evaluated in the environment produced by the declaration sequence.

Assume a TrafoLa-H program $p = d_1; \ \dots \ d_n; e;$ is given, with $d = d_1; \dots d_n;$ a sequence of declarations and e the program expression. We expect that after the execution of the code for p the stack cell referred to by SP contains a pointer to the value of e. Furthermore, the stack cells between the initial level and the present stack level should contain pointers to the values of the variables globally defined in $d_1, \dots, d_n$.

Program_Code d e = **let** (β, ϕ) = Decl_Code d [ ]
in ϕ
V_Code e β 0
halt

In the implementation there exist some predefined objects with special access names. In the real system, the environment containing these bindings is given to Decl_Code instead of the empty environment. The instruction **halt** stops the TRAMA and prints the representation of the result on the screen.

$$
\begin{array}{lcll}
\text{Decl\_Code } (d_1; d_s)\ \beta & = & \textbf{let} & (\beta_1, \phi_1) = \text{D\_Code } d_1\ \beta\ ; \\
 & & & \beta_2 = change\ (update\ \beta\ \beta_1)\ ; \\
 & & & (\beta_3,\phi_3) = \text{Decl\_Code } d_s\ \beta_2 \\
 & & \textbf{in} & (\beta_3, \\
 & & & \quad \phi_1 \\
 & & & \quad \phi_3 \\
 & & &) \\
\text{Decl\_Code } \epsilon\ \beta & = & (\beta, \epsilon) &
\end{array}
$$

let $d_1;\ldots;d_n$ in e_0 is an abbreviation for let d_1 in let d_2 in ... in e_0. The declaration sequence is compiled according to its syntactical order. *update* adds new bindings or replaces old bindings when they are redefined. *change* changes the binding type of the newly defined variables in the environment from LOC to ABS and computes the new addresses. So, the earlier produced environment is updated and given to the next declaration.

Definition 5.3.3 (update, change)
The following definition gives the algebraic description of *update*.

$$
(update\ \beta\ \beta_1)(v) = \begin{cases} \beta(v) & , v \in \mathcal{DOM}(\beta) \\ \beta_1(v) & , v \in \mathcal{DOM}(\beta_1) - \mathcal{DOM}(\beta) \\ undef & , \text{otherwise} \end{cases}
$$

$\mathcal{DOM}(\beta)$ denotes the argument domain of the environment β.

TOP β denotes the greatest absolute address in the environment β and NEW β is the number of newly defined variables. TOP and NEW can be defined by the following equations.

$$
\text{TOP } \beta = \max\{x \mid [v, (ABS, x)] \in \beta\} \qquad \text{and} \qquad \text{NEW } \beta = -\min\{i \mid [v, (binding\_type, i)] \in \beta\}
$$

$$
(change\ \beta)\ (v) = \begin{cases} \beta(v) & , \beta(v) = (\text{ABS}, n) \\ (\text{ABS}, (\text{TOP } \beta) + (\text{NEW } \beta) + 1 + n) & , \beta(v) = (\text{LOC}, n) \\ undef & , \text{otherwise} \end{cases}
$$

Example 2: Stack assignment

This example demonstrates how environments are handled during the execution of the code for declarations.

```
dec a = 1 and b = 1 and c = 2;
dec c = a and d = 4 and a = 5 and f = 7;
```

At runtime, after the execution of the code for the first declaration, the three topmost stack cells hold the references to the values for the variables a, b, and c. ρ denotes the global environment at this point. These variables are addressable absolutely from the bottom of the stack with addresses $n+2$, $n+1$, and n. This situation is described by picture (a) below.

During the execution of the code for the second declaration, the newly redefined variables c, d, a, and f are located in the four topmost stack cells, above the environment of the previous declarations. The local environment for the second declaration is denoted by β. In the topmost stack cells the redefined variables (these are the variables with a definition in a previous declaration) are stored. See picture (b).

After the evaluation of the expressions in the second declaration, the old values of the redefined variables a and b are no longer needed. Their locations are overwritten with the references to the new values to save stack space. The new global environment is described by ρ'. See picture (c).

This kind of stack management prevents holes and an expensive reorganization of the evaluation stack.

(a)

	⋮
$\rho(c) \mapsto$	(ABS,n)
$\rho(b) \mapsto$	(ABS,n+1)
$\rho(a) \mapsto$	(ABS,n+2)

(b)

	⋮
$\rho(c) \mapsto$	(ABS,n)
$\rho(b) \mapsto$	(ABS,n+1)
$\rho(a) \mapsto$	(ABS,n+2)
$\beta(d) \mapsto$	(LOC,−4)
$\beta(f) \mapsto$	(LOC,−3)
$\beta(a) \mapsto$	(LOC_,−2)
$\beta(c) \mapsto$	(LOC_,−1)

with the definition from above

$$\text{TOP } \rho \;=\; n+2 \qquad \textit{and} \qquad \text{NEW } \beta \;=\; 4$$

which gives the result.

(c)

	⋮
$\rho'(c)$	(ABS,n)
$\rho'(b)$	(ABS,n+1)
$\rho'(a)$	(ABS,n+2)
$\rho'(d)$	(ABS,n+3)
$\rho'(f)$	(ABS,n+4)

$$\rho'_f = \underbrace{n+2}_{TOP} + \underbrace{4}_{NEW} + 1 + \underbrace{(-3)}_{i} = n+4$$

$$\rho'_d = \underbrace{n+2}_{TOP} + \underbrace{4}_{NEW} + 1 + \underbrace{(-4)}_{i} = n+3$$

The Translation of Non-Recursive Declarations

The expressions and the left hand side patterns are evaluated in the global environment. For the pattern variables, unification semantics applies.

$$\text{D\_Code}\left(\text{dec}\begin{array}{c} p_1 = e_1 \\ \text{and} \\ \vdots \\ \text{and} \\ p_n = e_n \end{array}\right)\beta = (\beta_1,$$

```
teststack z
enter (newglobs + oldglobs + l)
N_Code (p1 = e1) β β1 0
⋮
N_Code (pn = en) β β1 0
assabs (getadr β v1)
⋮
assabs (getadr β v_oldglobs)
pop l)
```

Before evaluating the declaration, the available stack space is tested with the **teststack** instruction. The

Instruction	Semantics	Remark
enter n	SP + = n;	allocate space for the environment
assabs n	ST[n] = ST[SP]; SP− =1;	copying the value
pop n	SP − = n;	delete the environment

Table 3: The instructions **enter, assabs** and **pop**

number z is a upper bound to the really necessary stack space. The storage for the local environment is allocated from the evaluation stack by the instruction **enter**. The single declarations are translated in the same environment by the code function N_Code. The second environment of the function N_Code (β_1) contains the bindings of the global variables of $p_1, \ldots, p_n$, i.e., $\bigcup_{i=1}^{n}$ Freepat p_i. The sequence of **assabs** instructions moves the values of the previously defined variables to their storage locations, and the **pop** instruction removes the values of the local pattern variables from the evaluation stack.

Above, $v_1, \ldots, v_{oldglobs}$ are the existing variables, which are overwritten by the new declarations, $g_1, \ldots, g_{newglobs}$ the newly defined variables, and $h_1, \ldots, h_l$ the local pattern variables, i.e.

$$\{h_1, \ldots, h_l\} = \bigcup_{i=1}^{n} \text{Local } p_i$$

$$\{v_1, \ldots, v_{oldglobs}\} = \{w_i | w_i \in \mathcal{DOM}(\beta)\,, i \in \{1, \ldots, oldglobs + newglobs\}\}$$

$$\{g_1, \ldots, g_{newglobs}\} = \{w_i | w_i \notin \mathcal{DOM}(\beta) \wedge\ w_i \neq\ h_j, j \in \{1, \ldots, l\}\}$$

with $\{w_1, \ldots, w_{oldglobs+newglobs}\} = \bigcup_{i=1}^{n}$ Var p_i (all variables occurring in the patterns.)

According to the algorithms described in the front end section, these three sets are pairwise disjoint. β_1 is the local match environment and is defined by

$$\begin{array}{rcl} \beta_1 & = & \{v_i \mapsto (\text{LOC}_-, -i)\}_{i=1,\ldots,oldglobs} \\ & \cup & \{g_i \mapsto (\text{LOC}, -i - oldglobs - l)\}_{i=1,\ldots,newglobs} \\ & \cup & \{h_i \mapsto (\text{LOC}, -i - oldglobs)\}_{i=1,\ldots,l} \end{array}$$

Definition 5.3.4 (getadr)
This function extracts the position of a variable from an environment. It must be defined according to the representation of the environments. It extracts only absolute positions.

$$\begin{array}{rcl} getadr\ \beta\ v & = & \textbf{let}\ \ (art, pos)\ =\ \beta(v) \\ & & \textbf{in}\ \ pos \end{array}$$

The structure of the local match environment divides the stack into three different parts. In the first part, the newly defined variables are stored. Later, this allows the efficient modification of the global environment. The second part consists of local pattern variables, which will be popped off after pattern matching. This can be done by one instruction. The last part contains variables, for which storage on the evaluation stack is already available. The new values for these are stored in the old locations after pattern matching. This kind of assignment prevents holes in the evaluation stack.

The Translation of a Single Declaration

The code for a single declaration $p = e$ has to first produce the value of e. Then pattern matching analyses this value and stores the values of the variables of p into the local match environment. The code for a single declaration is divided into five parts.

- the match registers ALTNULL and MATCHNULL are saved on the evaluation stack if necessary. This can be determined by inspecting the expression and the pattern
- the expression e is evaluated
- the match environment is filled with the appropriate bindings
- the registers are restored if necessary
- local backtrack points are removed

$$
\begin{aligned}
\text{N\_Code } (p = e)\ \beta\ \beta_1\ k_p \quad = \quad & pushalt\ p\ e \\
& \text{V\_Code } e\ \beta\ (k_p + addkp\ p\ e) \\
& genalt\ p\ e \\
& \text{SP\_Code } p\ \beta\ \beta_1\ k_p \\
& clearalt\ p\ true
\end{aligned}
$$

The two match registers are only needed during pattern matching. Executing the code for pattern matching of a function alternative, they need not be saved. Nested pattern matching can only occur in 'Where' patterns and this case is handled by the patterns themselves (i.e., explicit storing of the match registers onto the evaluation stack). In single declarations however, the expression is evaluated after the initialization of the match registers. Sometimes (statically computable) the registers ha ve to be saved on the evaluation stack, if the evaluation of the expression might change the contents of ALTNULL and MATCHNULL. The static check of whether the match registers have to be stored on the evaluation stack is defined by the following auxiliary definitions.

Definition 5.3.5 (*pushalt*, *genalt* **and** *clearalt*)
test_enter computes, whether the two match registers may potentially be changed. It recursiveley tests the occurrences of an application, a **let** or a **case** expression. In unoptimized code (as presented here) the computation is exact, otherwise it is a safe approximation. The function *need_alt* checks whether the translation for p produces backtrack points. This happens in nondeterministic patterns and 'Not' patterns and can be computed from the abstract syntax tree. The functions *pushalt*, *genalt* and *clearalt* can be easily defined using these two auxiliary functions.

pushalt p ϵ = **if** *need_alt* p **and** *test_enter* e **then pushalt else** ϵ

genalt p ϵ = **if** *need_alt* p **and** *test_enter* e **then genalt else** ϵ

The registers have to be stored if the evaluation of the expression can change their contents *and* the pattern matching needs the registers. By storing the match registers, the simulated stack level increases by 2.

addkp p ϵ = **if** *need_alt* p **and** *test_enter* e **then** 2 **else** 0

pushalt stores the two match registers onto the evaluation stack and **genalt** restores them. This is necessary in some cases (and can be statically determined) because the evaluation of the expression e can require pattern matching and therefore change the contents of the match registers. If the match registers have been

Instruction	Semantic	Remark
pushalt	ST[SP+1] = ALTNULL; ST[SP+2] = MATCHNULL; SP + = 2;	pushes the match registers onto the stack
genalt	MATCHNULL = ST[SP-1]; ALTNULL = ST[SP-2]; SP − = 2; ST[SP] = ST[SP+2];	pops the match registers from the stack
clearalt	AP = ALTNULL;	remove local backtrack points

Table 4: **genalt,pushalt** and **clearalt**

saved onto the evaluation stack, the simulated stack level has to increase by two. The instruction **clearalt** removes the created backtrack points if the pattern has matched the value. The function *clearalt* will be defined later (see page 556), because it is also needed in code sequences for functional abstraction.

The Translation of Recursive Declarations

The translation of recursive declarations differs from that of nonrecursive ones in that references to objects not so far constructed have to be available. The solution is to assign storage for the objects in advance, such that the address is known for the translation of the whole construct. If the object is entirely available, the former location is overwritten with the created value.

$$\text{D\_Code}\left(\text{rec}\begin{array}{c} r_1 = f_1 \\ \text{and} \\ \vdots \\ \text{and} \\ r_n = f_n \end{array}\right)\beta = \begin{array}{l} (\beta_2, \ \textbf{teststack}\ z \\ \quad\ \ \textbf{dumfun}\ (newglobs + oldglobs) \\ \quad\ \ \text{R\_Code}\ (r_1 = f_1)\ \beta_2\ 0 \\ \quad\ \ \vdots \\ \quad\ \ \text{R\_Code}\ (r_n = f_n)\ \beta_2\ 0 \\ \quad\ \ \textbf{assabs}\ (\text{getadr}\ \beta\ v_1) \\ \quad\ \ \vdots \\ \quad\ \ \textbf{assabs}\ (\text{getadr}\ \beta\ v_{oldglobs})) \end{array}$$

$v_1, \ldots, v_{oldglobs}$ are the already defined variables and $g_1, \ldots, g_{newglobs}$ the newly defined variables. The address assignment is simpler than for non-recursive declarations because no local variables can occur.

$$\{v_1, \ldots, v_{oldglobs}\} = \{r_i | r_i \in \mathcal{DOM}(\beta), i \in \{1, \ldots, n\}\}$$

$$\{g_1, \ldots, g_{newglobs}\} = \{r_i | r_i \notin \mathcal{DOM}(\beta), i \in \{1, \ldots, n\}\}$$

β_1 denotes the environment for the variables $v_1, \ldots, v_n$ and is defined by

$$\beta_1 = \{v_i \mapsto (\text{LOC\_}, -i)\}_{i=1,\ldots,oldglobs} \uplus \{g_i \mapsto (\text{LOC}, -i - oldglobs)\}_{i=1,\ldots,newglobs}$$

and

$$\beta_2 = overlay\ \beta\ \beta_1$$

The previously defined variables receive binding type LOC_ separating them from the new global variables for efficient handling of the global environment. The instruction **dumfun** produces the dummy heap objects and *overlay* has the usual semantics. The environment β_1 overlays β.

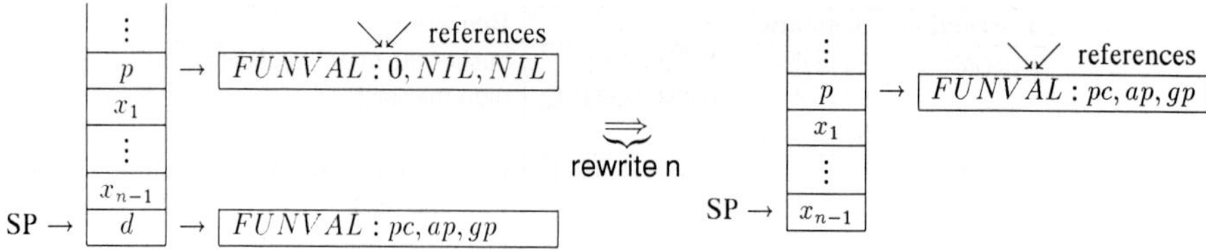

Figure 1: semantics of rewrite

The code for a single declaration creates a FUNVAL object and overwrites one dummy cell. A function f has to be supplied with the values of its global variables at declaration time, because TrafoLa-H has static binding.

R_Code $(r = f)\ \beta\ k_p$ = *pushfree* $\beta\ k_p\ fr$;
mkvec n;
mkfun l_1;
F_Code $f\ \beta_1$;
l_1 : **rewrite** $-(getadr\ \beta\ r)$

fr denotes the list of free variables of f. Access is performed relative to the GP register. These global variables receive the binding type GLOB.

$$fr = \{v_1, \ldots, v_n\} = freevar\ f$$

and

$$\beta_1 = \{[v_i, (\text{GLOB}, i-1)]_{i=1\ldots n}\}$$

$pushfree$ produces code to store the pointers to values of the global variables of f onto the evaluation stack. The instruction **mkvec** creates a heap object VECTOR with these pointers as content, and finally **mkfun** builds the desired heap object FUNVAL. **rewrite** moves the result to the appropriate place in the evaluation stack.

Definition 5.3.6 (pushfree)
The function $pushfree$ creates code for access to the global variables of the function. References to them are pushed onto the stack and are available to the following **mkvec** instruction.

$$pushfree\ \beta\ k_p\ \{v_1, \ldots, v_n\} = \begin{cases} getvar\ v_1\ \beta\ k_p \\ \vdots \\ getvar\ v_n\ \beta\ (k_p + n - 1) \end{cases}$$

Instruction	Semantics	Remark
dumfun n	**for** i = 1 **to** n **do** ST[SP+1] = newfun(0,Nil,Nil); SP+=1; **od**	creates a dummy FUNVAL object

Table 5: The instruction **dumfun**

Instruction	Semantics	Remark
mkvec n	ST[SP−n+1] = newvec(SP−n+1,n); SP− = n-1;	creates the global vector pops the superfluous cells
mkfun l	ST[SP] = newfun(PC+1,Nil,ST[SP]); PC = l;	creates a FUNVAL object jumps over the function code
rewrite n	HP[ST[SP-n]] = HP[ST[SP]]; SP−−;	overwrites the heap cell pops the local result

Table 6: **mkvec**, **mkfun** and **rewrite**

Instruction	Semantics	Remark
pushloc m	SP+ =1; ST[SP] = ST[SP−m];	relative (SP)
pushglob m	SP+ =1; ST[SP] = HP[GP][m];	relative (GP)
pushabs m	SP+ =1; ST[SP] = ST[m];	absolute

Table 7: The instructions **pushloc**, **pushglob** and **pushabs**

Definition 5.3.7 (Access to variables)
$getvar$ produces an instruction that gets the content of the (with v) associated location. The access can be either relative to SP or GP, or absolute in ST.

$$
\begin{array}{lcll}
getvar\ v\ \beta\ k_p & = & \textbf{let} & (kind, pos) = \beta(v) \\
 & & \textbf{in} & \textbf{case}\ kind\ \textbf{of} \\
 & & & \{LOC \quad => \quad pushglob\ (k_p - pos) \\
 & & & \#GLOB \quad => \quad pushglob\ pos \\
 & & & \#ABS \quad => \quad pushabs\ pos \\
 & & & \#LOC\_ \quad => \quad pushloc\ (k_p - pos)\}
\end{array}
$$

$getvar$ produces instructions depending on the binding type of v using either absolute addresses or addresses relative to SP or GP.

The Translation of Functions

The code for a function has to do all the tasks which are common to all right hand sides of functional abstractions, i.e., test for the availability of all actual parameters, the test for the availability of local memory and create the local match environment.

$$\text{F\_Code}\left\{\begin{array}{c} pl_1\texttt{=>[all]}e_1 \\ \vdots \\ pl_n\texttt{=>[all]}e_n \end{array}\right\}\beta = \begin{array}{l} \textbf{targ}\ m \\ \textbf{teststack}\ pos \\ \textbf{enter}\ anz \\ \text{A\_Code}\ (\ pl_1\texttt{=>[all]}e_1)\ \beta\ \text{false} \\ \text{A\_Code}\ (\ pl_2\texttt{=>[all]}e_2)\ \beta\ \text{false} \\ \quad\vdots \\ \text{A\_Code}\ (\ pl_n\texttt{=>[all]}e_n)\ \beta\ \text{true} \end{array}$$

where pos is the maximal stack space used by the function, and

$$\forall\, i \in \{1,\ldots,n\}\ :\ pl_i = p_{i1},\ldots,p_{im} \text{ and } anz = \max_{i=1\ldots n} \mid \text{Var}\ pl_i \mid$$

The function expects its arguments on the evaluation stack in reverse ordering supplying an efficient over– and undersupplying with arguments. The instruction **targ** tests the number of available arguments and produces a new FUNVAL object with nonempty argument vector in the undersupplied case, otherwise the instruction after **targ** is executed. Its semantics is described in Table 8, and the stack situation is shown in Figure 2.

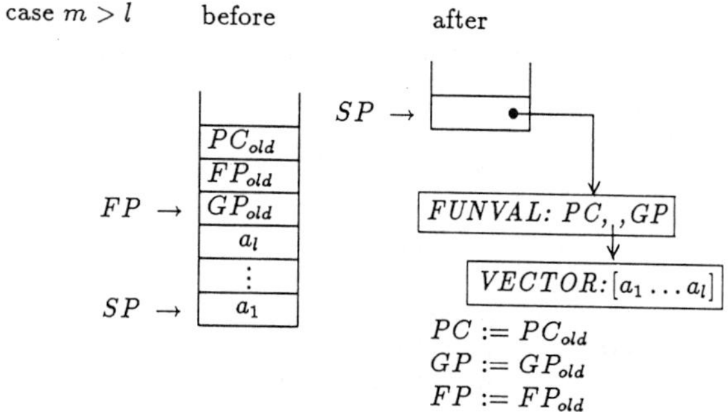

Figure 2: The **targ**–instruction discovers a partial application and creates a *FUNVAL*–object with the existing arguments.

An instruction **targ 1** can be removed because no possibility exists to write an application with fewer than one argument. This static computation allows a check at every function entry. The abstract machine would normally have to determine for every instruction increasing the stack, whether the stack space is sufficient. These checks can be collected into one. The check is done by an explicit instruction (**teststack**) at the beginning of the code for a function. The local stack space needed for the local match environment is allocated by the instruction **enter**. The definition of anz shows that the allocated stack space is the maximal stack requirement of the different alternatives of a function. The compiler handles the location clashes of variables occurring in different alternatives.

The Translation of Right Hand Sides

The code starts in a situation according to Figure 8. The local match environment has been created. The tasks of an alternative are mainly to test whether this alternative is appropriate to the value, i.e., pattern matching does not fail, and to construct the result value. Furthermore, the **=>all** function arrow has to be handled.

Instruction	Semantics
targ m	**if** SP−FP < m **then** /* undersupplied case */ h = ST[FP−2]; ST[FP−2] = newfun(PC−1,newvec(FP+1,SP−FP),GP); GP = ST[FP]; SP = FP−2; FP = ST[FP−1]; PC = h; **fi**

Table 8: The instruction **targ**.

$$
\begin{array}{lll}
\text{A\_Code } (pl\ arrow\ e)\ \beta\ last & = & setnext\ l_1\ last \\
& & allfun\ arrow\ last \\
& & \text{CP\_Code}\ pl\ \beta_m\ \beta\ 0 \\
& & \textbf{pop}\ l \\
& & allpush\ arrow \\
& & clearalt\ pl\ last \\
& & \text{V\_Code}\ e\ \beta_r\ (-l+a) \\
& & returngen\ arrow\ last\ (m+n-l+a) \\
& l_1: &
\end{array}
$$

with

$$\beta_m = create\_loc\_env\ pl$$

and

$$\beta_r = overlay\ \beta\ \beta_m \qquad a = \begin{cases} 2 & arrow = \texttt{=>all} \\ 0 & otherwise \end{cases}$$

$$m = |\ \beta_m\ | \qquad l = |\ \text{Local}\ pl\ | \qquad pl = p_1, \ldots, p_n$$

This code function produces many different code sequences and is therefore very complicated. To explain the different sequences, many auxiliary functions have to be defined. The local match environment is defined by

$$
\begin{array}{lll}
create\_loc\_env\ p & = & \textbf{let}\ \ [v_1, \ldots, v_z] = \text{Bound}\ p \\
& & \textbf{and}\ \ [w_1, \ldots, w_l] = \text{Local}\ p \\
& & \textbf{in}\ \ \{[v_i, (\text{LOC}, -i-l)]_{i=1\ldots z}\} \uplus \{[w_i, (\text{LOC}\_, -i)]_{i=1\ldots l}\}
\end{array}
$$

The normal form of p guarantees Bound' $p \cap$ Local' $p = \emptyset$. The auxiliary functions perform the following tasks:

- *setnext*
  Each alternative sets a backtrack point to the next alternative, except the last one.
- *allfun*
  `=>all` functions need a special startup sequence that initializes a special data structure to hold the partial result during the entire computation.
- *allpush*
  Intermediate storing of match register (if needed in the `=>all` case).

- *clearalt*
  Deletion of the local backtrack points.

- *returngen*
  End of an alternative, giving up the stack frame and copying the result onto the dynamic predecessor. For **=>all** functions, a special code sequence is created.

Definition 5.3.8 (*allfun, allpush, returngen, setnext*)
The **setnext** instruction creates a backtrack point (similar to the **setalt** instruction, see page 570).

setnext l last = **if not** *last* **then setnext** *l* **else** ϵ

allfun arrow last = **if** (*arrow* = **=>all**) **then if** *last* **then initall_last else initall else** ϵ

allpush arrow = **if** (*arrow* = **=>all**) **then pushalt else** ϵ

An **=>all** needs some initialization in the alternatives stack. This is done by **initall** or **initall_last.** The match registers always have to be saved onto the evaluation stack, if an **=>all** function is translated (**pushalt**).

returngen arrow last m = **if** (*arrow* = **=>all**) **then if** *last* **then fail else fail_last else return** *m*

Normally, a **return** instruction is created to perform the return_from_function mechanism. The **=>all** function has to be handled in another way, since it has to collect the results of the expression evaluation in all match environments in a list. If the last result is created, the stack frame can be removed. The **fail** and the **fail_last** instructions add the results of the function expression to the list of previously computed results until all possible match environments have been built.

clearalt p last = **if** *need_alt p* **or not** *last* **then clearalt else** ϵ

The alternatives stack and the match registers have to be reset if a pattern produces local backtrack points *or* the alternative is the last one.

The detailed description of the **=>all** implementation can be found in [Fecht 90]. The interface to the pattern code functions is defined by:

$$\text{SP\_Code}\ p\ \beta\ \beta_1\ k_p \quad = \quad \text{P\_Code}\ p\ \beta\ \beta_1\ k_p$$

In this description this code function is just a renaming, but in the current implementation it has a special meaning. It includes some optimizations of the pattern matching algorithms. The P_Code function is defined in the next section.

The function CP_Code translates a left hand side of a functional abstraction. The arguments are given one by one.

$$\begin{aligned}\text{CP\_Code}\ pl\ \beta\ \beta_1\ k_p \quad = \quad & \textbf{pushloc}\ (m+1);\\ & \text{SP\_Code}\ p_1\ \beta\ \beta_1\ k_p;\\ & \textbf{pushloc}\ (m+2);\\ & \text{SP\_Code}\ p_2\ \beta\ \beta_1\ k_p;\\ & \vdots\\ & \textbf{pushloc}\ (m+n+1);\\ & \text{SP\_Code}\ p_n\ \beta\ \beta_1\ k_p;\end{aligned}$$

with $m = \mid \beta \mid$ and $pl = p_1, \ldots, p_n$

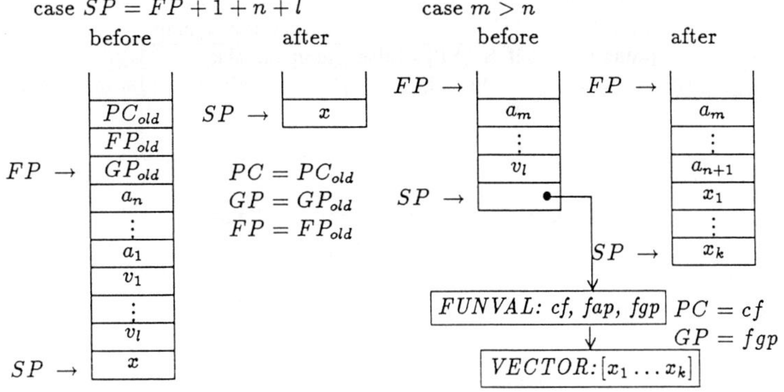

Figure 3: Two cases of the **return**–instruction; on the left side, the n-ary function has n arguments; here the stack frame is popped. On the right side, the function has more arguments than required and evaluates to a functional result. $v_1, \dots, v_l$, are the local match environment. If the result is a constructor and the function is oversupplied with one argument, a tree object has to be built. This would be a legal application. The untyped **return** instruction also handles this case. The typed version forbids such an application.

m is the size of the local match environment. It is needed to access the arguments of the function below the local match environment.

5.3.5.3. The Translation of Expressions

Expressions could all be translated by the V_Code function. Specializations are used to decrease the run time and the size of the object code. The code for an expression, translated by V_Code, creates a heap object. This is done by constructing the value bottom-up, according to the structure of the source expression. In the following, we assume that the instruction set of the abstract machine contains a special instruction for every TrafoLa-H operator. The problems with the alignment of storage or the representation of values are handled by the code generator. Keeping the size of different cases small, the translation is only partially given. Constants like integer are translated to instructions building the appropriate value in the heap and leaving a reference on the stack. Binary operators are handled according to the following pattern:

V_code (e_1 op e_2) β k_p = V_code e_2 β k_p
V_code e_1 β (k_p+1)
O_code op

The concept for translating if-then-else constructs is given formally below. The expression on predicate position is computed on the evalution stack, as the use of the B_code function shows.

V_code(**if** e_1 **then** e_2 **else** e_3) β k_p = B_code $e_1 \beta$ k_p
jfalse l_1
V_code e_2 β k_p
ujmp l_2
l_1: V_code e_3 β k_p
l_2:

The semantics of the operators **o** and '**|**' are defined as follows:

Instruction	Semantics	Remark
ujmp l	PC = l;	unconditional jump
jfalse l	**if** ST[SP] = **false** PC = l; **fi**; SP−−;	jump on false

Table 9: The instructions **ujmp** and **jfalse**

- Composition
  (f o g) (x) = { x => f(g(x)) }
- Alternative
  (f | g) (x) = { x => **if** f(x) = *fail* **then** g(x) **else** f(x) }

The translation or the abtract machine must realize these operators in an efficient way. In our system, this is done by two powerful machine instructions **composition** and **alternate**:

$$\text{V\_code } (e_1 \mid e_2)\ \beta\ k_p \;=\; \text{V\_code } e_1\ \beta\ k_p$$
$$\text{V\_code } e_2\ \beta\ (k_p{+}1)$$
alternate

$$\text{V\_code } (e_1 \circ e_2)\ \beta\ k_p \;=\; \text{V\_code } e_1\ \beta\ k_p$$
$$\text{V\_code } e_2\ \beta\ (k_p{+}1)$$
composition

alternate and **composition** produce a special kind of FUNVAL object, whereby the code sequences are the same for all alternatives (compositions). Therefore, these code sequences can be shared. So the two code arrays from table 10 are added to the TRAMA. The instruction **jsr** n in this table is an abbreviation for the two instructions **pushloc** n and **apply.**

The FUNVAL objects created by the code for $(f \circ g)$ or $(f \mid g)$ use the functions f and g as parameters. Figure 4 and 5 show the effects of the **composition** instruction. The implementation of the composition operator 'o' simulates the definition of an additional functional abstraction { x => f (g (x)) }. The code sequence for '|' needs further explanation. The instruction **eapply** places a negative continuation address onto the trap stack. In the successful case, this cell is deleted by the **popts** instruction. The other case is handled by the instruction **return_without**, which deletes the last created stack frame without copying the result and continues with the second alternative. Table 11 shows the semantics for the new instructions.

The translation of the functional abstraction in V_Code is defined equivalently to R_Code. It will be given in the next subsection.

The Translation of Local Declarations

Local declarations are similar to global ones, but a special stack management is needed. The expressions e_i and the patterns p_i have to be evaluated in the same environment and the expression e_0 has to be evaluated in the environment in which the new declarations overlay the old bindings. The result of the evaluation of e_0 is given to the surrounding expression as the result of the local declaration.

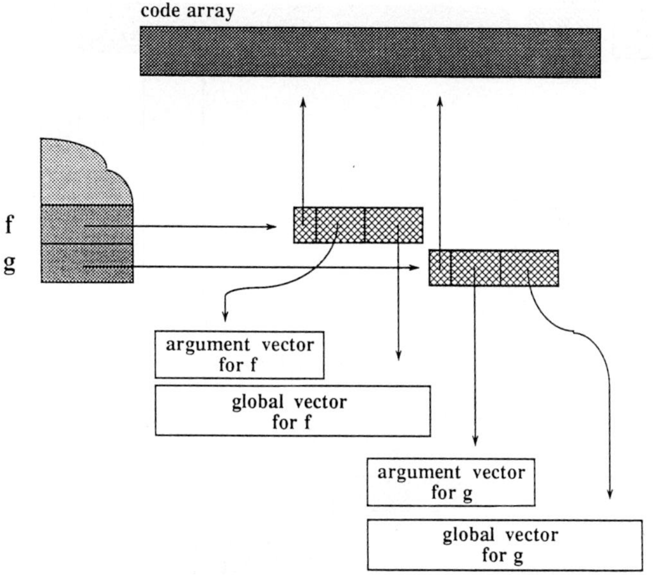

Figure 4: execution with code sharing before **composition**

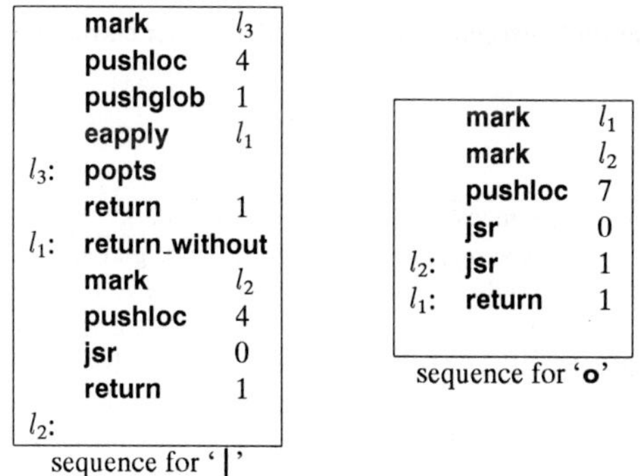

	mark	l_3
	pushloc	4
	pushglob	1
	eapply	l_1
l_3:	**popts**	
	return	1
l_1:	**return_without**	
	mark	l_2
	pushloc	4
	jsr	0
	return	1
l_2:		

sequence for '**|**'

	mark	l_1
	mark	l_2
	pushloc	7
	jsr	0
l_2:	**jsr**	1
l_1:	**return**	1

sequence for '**o**'

Table 10: predefined code sequences

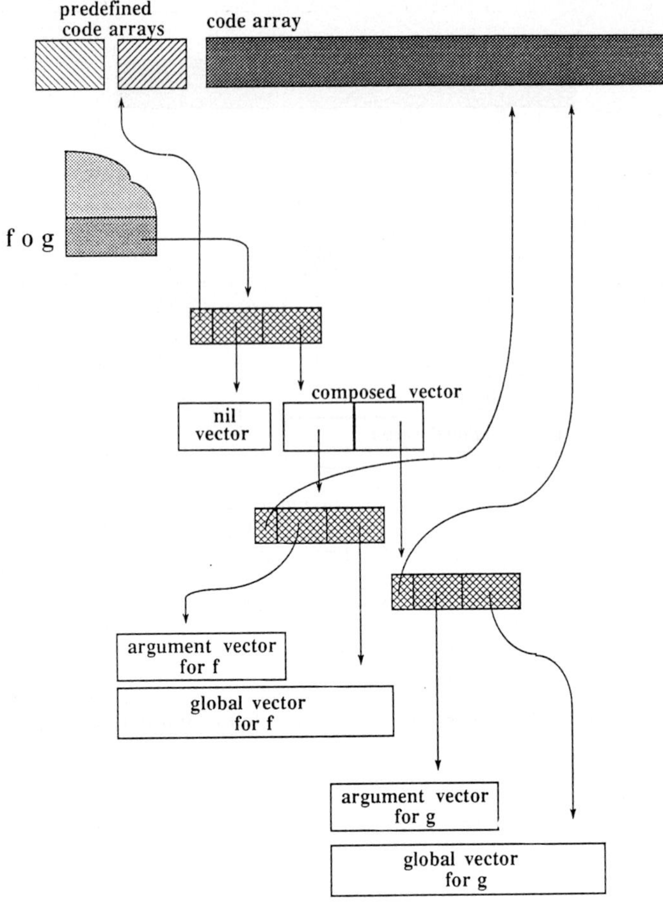

Figure 5: execution with code sharing after **composition**

instruction	semantics	remark
eapply l	*newtrap*(l,FP,ALTNULL); **apply**	new global backtrack point same code as for *apply*
popts	TS− =1;	delete a backtrack point
return_without	GP = ST[FP]; SP = FP − 3; FP = ST[FP−1];	old global pointer old stack level delete the unnecessary stack frame

Table 11: **eapply** , **popts** , and **return_without**; *newtrap* creates an item on the trap stack containing its three parameters.

$$\text{V\_Code}\left(\begin{array}{lcl} \text{let} & \begin{array}{c} p_1 = e_1 \\ \text{and} \\ \vdots \\ \text{and} \\ p_n = e_n \end{array} & \text{in } e_0 \end{array}\right) \beta\ k_p = \begin{array}{l} \textbf{enter } m \\ \text{N\_Code } (p_1 = e_1)\ \beta_1\ \beta\ (k_p + m) \\ \vdots \\ \text{N\_Code } (p_n = e_n)\ \beta_1\ \beta\ (k_p + m) \\ \textbf{pop } unbs \\ \text{V\_Code } e_0\ \beta_2\ (k_p + m - unbs) \\ \textbf{slide } l \end{array}$$

The address assignment is similar to that of the global declaration except that auxiliary variables do not arise. β_1 is defined by

$$\{h_1, \ldots, h_{unbs}\} = \bigcup_{i=1}^{n} \text{Local } p_i \text{ and } \{v_1, \ldots, v_l\} = \bigcup_{i=1}^{n} \text{Bound } p_i$$

$$\beta_1 = \{[v_i \mapsto (\text{LOC}, k_p + i - 1)]_{i=1,\ldots,l}\} \biguplus \{[h_i \mapsto (\text{LOC\_}, k_p + l + i - 1)]_{i=1,\ldots,unbs}\}$$

$$m = l + unbs \quad \text{and} \quad \beta_2 = overlay\ \beta\ \beta_1$$

In local declarations, the binding type LOC_ has a meaning different from global declarations. The local pattern variables have binding type LOC_ in local declarations. In global declarations, it is used to separate old from newly defined variables with the same name. The local pattern variables (i.e. $\bigcup_{i=1}^{n}$ Local p_i) will be popped after the evaluation of the patterns. In this case, the simulated stack level k_p has to be decreased in the translation of the expression e_0. After evaluation of the expression e_0, the result is given to the surrounding expression by the **slide** instruction. It also removes the local match environment.

The Translation of Recursive Local Declarations

That scheme is analogous to the translation scheme of the global recursive declaration.

$$\text{V\_Code}\left(\begin{array}{lcl} \text{letrec} & \begin{array}{c} v_1 = f_1 \\ \text{and} \\ \vdots \\ \text{and} \\ v_m = f_m \end{array} & \text{in } e_0 \end{array}\right) \beta\ k_p = \begin{array}{l} \textbf{dumfun } m \\ \text{R\_Code } (v_1 = f_1)\ \beta_2\ (k_p + m) \\ \vdots \\ \text{R\_Code } (v_n = f_n)\ \beta_2\ (k_p + m) \\ \text{V\_Code } e_0\ \beta_2\ (k_p + m) \\ \textbf{slide } m \end{array}$$

where $\beta_1 = \{[v_i \mapsto (\text{LOC}, k_p + i - 1)]_{i=1,\ldots,m}\}$ and $\beta_2 = overlay\ \beta\ \beta_1$. Note that the functions f_i and the expression e_0 are evaluated in the same environment.

Instruction	Semantics	Remark
slide n	ST[SP-n] = ST[SP]; SP −= n;	copying the result delete the match environment

Table 12: The instruction **slide**

The Translation of Applications

In the typed version, it is possible to distinguish function application and tree construction. In a similar way to other implementations ([Johnsson 84] [Wilhelm, Maurer 92]), the arguments are written onto the stack in reverse order. Over- and undersupply of arguments is handled by the function itself. The detailed mechanism can be found in [Fecht 90].

V_Code $(e_0\ e_1 \dots\ e_n)\ \beta\ k_p$ = **mark** l
(where $e_0 \neq e'\ e''$) V_Code $e_n\ \beta\ (k_p + 3)$
$\vdots$
V_Code $e_1\ \beta\ (k_p$+3+n−1)
V_Code $e_0\ \beta\ (k_p$+3+n)
apply
l:

The stack space used to store the organizational cells becomes visible in this translation. Since all arguments of an application are written into the same stack frame, they can be accessed efficiently. Figure 7 shows the semantics of the **apply** instruction.

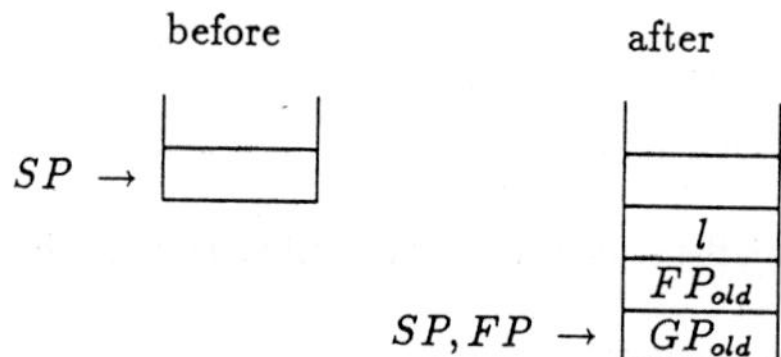

Figure 6: The **mark**–instruction creates a new stack frame and initializes the organizational cells.

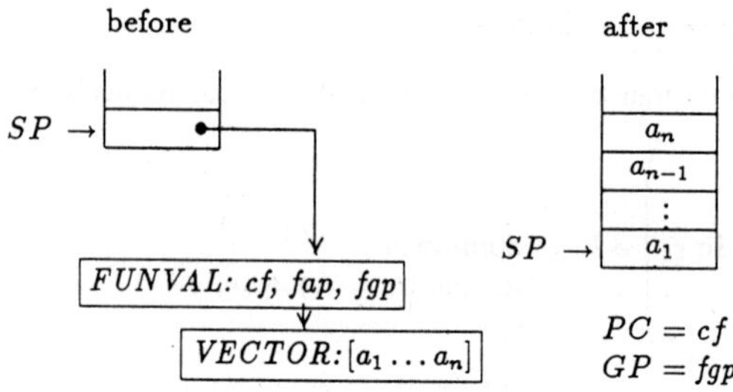

Figure 7: The **apply**–instruction starts the application of a function; it loads the references to existing arguments onto the stack, loads the pointer to the environment and then jumps to the function code.

The Translation of Structured Expressions

Most computer languages provide methods collecting a number of objects into a structured object such that it can be referred to as a whole. In TrafoLa-H, there are three kinds of structured expressions: lists, tuples, and trees.
In the typed TrafoLa-H version, the tuple expression had to be added for grouping expressions of different types. The tree datatype is divided into several distinct subtypes, which have to be defined by the user.

The Translation of Lists List values are built by repeatedly adding one element to the beginning of the already constructed tail of the list, thus working in constant stack space.

$$
\begin{aligned}
\text{V\_Code } [\epsilon_1, \ldots, \epsilon_n]\ \beta\ k_p \ = \ & \textbf{ldnil} \\
& \text{V\_Code } \epsilon_n\ \beta\ (k_p{+}1) \\
& \textbf{cons} \\
& \text{V\_Code } \epsilon_{n-1}\ \beta\ (k_p{+}1) \\
& \textbf{cons} \\
& \vdots \\
& \text{V\_Code } \epsilon_1\ \beta\ (k_p{+}1) \\
& \textbf{cons}
\end{aligned}
$$

For small lists, the translator uses a more efficient translation scheme, similar to the translation scheme of tuples (see below).

The Translation of Tuples

The results of the last sections also hold for tuple expressions, but here we assume that a tuple has less components than a list. Thus tuples are built in one step.

$$
\begin{aligned}
\text{V\_Code } (\epsilon_1, \ldots, \epsilon_n)\ \beta\ k_p \ = \ & \text{V\_Code } \epsilon_n\ \beta\ k_p \\
& \text{V\_Code } \epsilon_{n-1}\ \beta\ (k_p{+}1) \\
& \vdots \\
& \text{V\_Code } \epsilon_1\ \beta\ (k_p{+}\text{n}{-}1) \\
& \textbf{mktuple}\ \text{n}
\end{aligned}
$$

$$
\text{V\_Code } ()\ \beta\ k_p \ = \ \textbf{ldunit}
$$

The Translation of Trees

A tree expression looks like a function application with one argument. In the untyped TrafoLa-H version, the translator cannot statically decide to generate an **apply** for functions or a data construction instruction. This work has to be done by the **apply** instruction itself. In the typed version however, the type checker knows the meaning of the application expression. With this information, better code can be generated.

$$
\begin{aligned}
\text{V\_Code } (\epsilon\ \epsilon')\ \beta\ k_p \ = \ & \text{V\_Code } \epsilon\ \beta\ k_p \\
& \text{V\_Code } \epsilon'\ \beta\ (k_p{+}1) \\
& \textbf{mktree}
\end{aligned}
$$

Often, tree expressions have the form $c\ \epsilon$, where c is a constructor. In this case, the constructor need not be stored on the evaluation stack. A simpler translation scheme is used, which joins the construction of a heap object of type tree to a construction of a constructor value.

$$
\begin{aligned}
\text{V\_Code } (c\ \epsilon)\ \beta\ k_p \ = \ & \text{V\_Code } \epsilon\ \beta\ k_p \\
& \textbf{mkctree}\ c
\end{aligned}
$$

The instruction **mkctree** c is an abbreviation for the instruction sequence **mkconst_i** c; **mktree**.

5.3.5.4. The Translation of Simple Expressions

Values need not always be stored in the heap. Simple values can be stored on the evaluation stack, especially if they are only needed in local computations. They can be handled more efficiently than normal values. The translation scheme (B_Code) is a specialization of the V_Code function.

5.3.6. Optimizations of the Translation Functions

A primary objective of the optimizations is to use the stack as long as possible rather than the heap. The B_Code function is the first approach toward doing this. The following enumeration discusses most of the further optimizations of the TrafoLa-H compiler.

- Avoiding explicit matching
  The compiler sometimes has perfect information about the result of a pattern match. This information can be staticly computed from the pattern. If a pattern does not decompose a value and is linear, explicit matching is useless because it only performs a movement of the value into the match environment. The local match environment is not created and pattern matching is omitted in such a case. The access to the value is performed directly.

- Improvement of tail recursion
  Efficient handling of tail recursion is one of the main tasks for every efficient implementation of a functional language. The optimization should handle all staticly known cases. The general form of tail recursion optimization is not compatible with the avoidance of explicit pattern matching because the compiler has to determine that no argument of the function is overwritten before its last usage. Therefore, the combination of both optimizations requires additional analysis.

- Short circuit evaluation of boolean expressions
  The second operand of a conjunction (disjunction) need not be considered if the first evaluates to 'false' or 'true' respectively. This chance for optimization is handled in the programming language family in two ways. One way is to introduce two sets of boolean operators[1], whereas the other way is to perform either short circuit or normal evaluation in all cases. A problem arises whenever the short circuit evaluation changes the semantics. This happens if the second operand contains nonterminating computations, run time errors, side effects, or match failures. The TrafoLa-H system performs normal evaluation of boolean expressions. Short circuit evaluation can be switched on as a compiler option.

- Improvement of function calls
  Function calls are performed in the implementation by loading the functional object onto the evaluation stack, updating the GP register with the pointer to the vector of the global variables of the function, moving the argument vector to the evaluation stack, and jumping to the code of the function. Other implementations perform a direct jump to the code of the function, which is more efficient. A rather complicated analysis computes the cases to be handled this way. The optimization is even extended to mutually recursive functions.

- Resolution of local functions
  TrafoLa-H is implemented by an abstract machine, which handles local functions very efficiently. Implementations of other languages always raise local functions to the top level by introducing additional parameters (lambda lifting). If the local function does not contain global variables that depend on local parameters of the enclosing function, it may be extracted without any trouble. The other case, however, demands deeper analysis of the dependencies between the global variables of the local function and the local variables of the surrounding function. In [?], a heuristic is given solving the problem efficiently.

- Transformation of linear recursive functions into tail recursive ones
  This optimization also occurs in every efficient implementation of functional languages. The TrafoLa-H compiler extends the usual transformation (which only works for conditionals) to pattern matching. Furthermore, some special transformation schemes on functions to build list values are performed.

- Improvement with type information
  The type checker computes the most general type of every program construct (i.e., a polymorphic

[1]Example: **'or else'** and **'and then'** in Ada

type). Therefore, the type terms reflect the structure of the corresponding values at run time. With this information, the compiler can use optimized translation schemes for code generation. The typed TrafoLa-H version performs these optimizations.

- Code optimizations
  Most efficient code generators include a special kind of optimization unit, called peep-hole optimizer, working locally on the target program. Such a unit typically replaces an expensive machine instruction sequence by a cheaper one. Such a unit is of even greater importance for an abstract machine because its instructions can be regarded as macros for instruction sequences of real machines. The optimization also often decreases the size of the target program. A simple peep-hole optimizer is added to the TrafoLa-H system.

5.3.7. Pattern Matching with Backtracking

For reasons of simplicity, pattern matching is discussed only for untyped TrafoLa-H in the following.

5.3.7.1. The Concepts of the TRAMA

Nondeterministic patterns have more than one possibility of matching a value, which are investigated by *backtracking*. Earlier experience has shown that computing *sets of matches* does not lead to acceptable execution speed (see [Alt et al. 88] [Heckmann 88]).

To support backtracking search through a set of alternatives, the code for every nondeterministic subpattern creates a backtrack point that is stored on a special stack, the *alternatives stack.*

The alternatives stack AS has an alternatives stack pointer AP and an alternatives stack frame pointer ALTNULL. During a match, the additional evaluation stack pointer MATCHNULL is needed to mark the upper stack fragment used by pattern matching.

The Situation on the Evaluation Stack at the Beginning of Matching

At the beginning of matching, a reference to the value to be matched is stored on the stack. This value is partitioned according to the structure of the pattern. The references to parts of the value are also stored on the evaluation stack.

In the following, only pattern matching in functions is described. Pattern matching in *let* expressions and in top-level definitions can be handled analogously.

After the call of a function, a code sequence is executed that installs the static part of the function frame (see figure 8). This ensures that

- all arguments of the function lie fully above the auxiliary cells (activation record).
- the locations for the variables of the patterns (local environment) are established on the evaluation stack.
- the pointers SP and MATCHNULL point to the topmost cell of the stack.

The local variables and the arguments are addressable by MATCHNULL or SP.

Heap Organization

Pattern matching may require a large amount of heap space. In order to reduce these space requirements, the heap is organized as a stack. With every backtrack point (alternative), the actual value of HP_level is saved. The space for heap objects generated after the installation of the alternative is freed when this alternative fails. Therefore, garbage collection has to preserve the order of the heap objects within the heap.

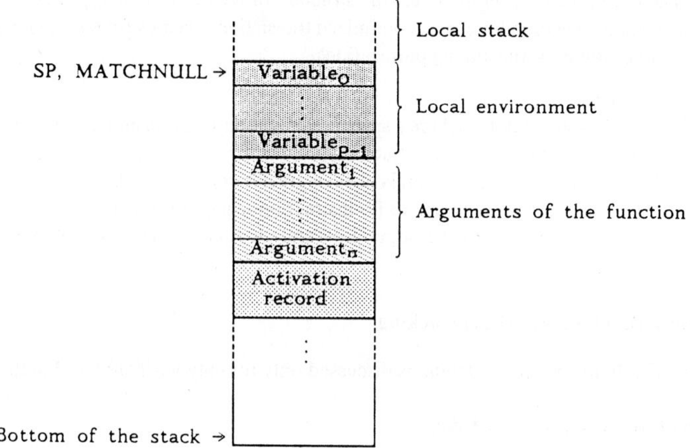

Figure 8: Situation on the stack after passing the initial code sequence of an n-ary function with p local variables. *Note*: The evaluation stack in this and all following figures is drawn reversed.

The Alternatives Stack

On the alternatives stack, all possible alternatives of the matching are stored to allow backtracking. Each element of the alternatives stack (called alternative) is a record with the following components:

pc: Contains the program address where pattern matching should resume.

stack: Contains the reference to a copy of the evaluation stack fragment above the pointer MATCHNULL. This stack copy is needed because the contents of the stack may change during pattern matching. This stack fragment contains references to subvalues that still have to be matched by subpatterns, and auxiliary values that are needed only during pattern matching.

heap: Here, the value of HP_level at which the alternative was generated is stored. This value is used to reset the heap if the alternative fails.

desc: 'Append' and 'Insert' patterns generally have more than one possibility of partitioning a value. To construct a new partition, the old one is stored in a special data structure called *descriptor*. The component *desc* contains a reference to a descriptor if the alternative is generated by an 'Append' or 'Insert' pattern.

The register ALTNULL is needed to mark the alternatives stack frame. At 'Where' patterns (p **where** e) the content of the alternatives stack has to be the same before and after the evaluation of the condition e. Therefore, a frame is installed for every 'Where' pattern before the condition is evaluated by setting ALTNULL to AP, because pattern matching may take place during this evaluation. At the beginning of a TrafoLa-H program, ALTNULL is set to zero.

5.3.7.2. Handling of Alternatives

Nondeterministic patterns lead to more than one possibility of matching a value. The following patterns may be nondeterministic:

'Or' pattern ($p_1|p_2$): Here, p_1 or p_2 may match.

'Append' pattern ($p_1 \cdot p_2$): Normally, there is more than one partition of a list value into a front and a back list.

'Insert' pattern ($p_1 \,\hat{}\, p_2$): Similar to 'append' patterns, there is more than one possible partition of a value.

For these patterns, the implementation must assure that backtracking finds all possible partitions.

The partitions are generated in a canonical order. 'Or' patterns always try to match the left subpattern first. The second subpattern is stored as an alternative on the alternatives stack. With 'append' patterns, the partition point of the list value moves from left to right. This means that the processing of an alternative on the alternatives stack extends the front list and shortens the back list by one element. With 'insert' patterns, the hole (@1) moves like an in-order-left-to-right walk over the value.

The whole match fails if a partial match fails and the alternatives stack is empty. Otherwise, the TRAMA is reset to the state in which the topmost alternative was installed. This means the evaluation stack and SP are reset, but in the following another matching possibility is tried. Furthermore, the heap space requested after installing this alternative can be freed.

In the case of 'or' patterns ($p_1|p_2$), the TRAMA jumps to the code for p_2 if the match of p_1 fails. The upper evaluation stack fragment (which contains references to subvalues, which still have to be analyzed by pattern matching), SP, HP_level, and the address of the code for p_2 are saved when installing the alternative. If a partial match fails, the alternative is removed from the alternatives stack after resetting the TRAMA.

'Insert' and 'append' patterns (($p_1 \cdot p_2$) and ($p_1 \,\hat{}\, p_2$)) compute a partition of the value to be matched. This partition has to be matched by the subpatterns p_1 and p_2. Each alternative has to "remember" which partitions have already been tested and generate the next partition in the order specified above. Therefore, the current partition is stored in the alternative. With this partition, it is possible to construct the next one.

These partitions and other information, like the path to a partition point in a tree value, are stored in data structures called *descriptors*, which are saved with the corresponding alternative. A processing of an alternative of an 'append' or 'insert' pattern has to reset the stack, SP, and HP_level and jump to the code for the subpatterns. This code has to generate a new partition and "remember" this partition, which means to update the descriptor. The alternative is popped from the alternatives stack if no further partitions can be generated.

A partial match may fail:

- when checking a syntactic class.
- when checking an individual value.
- when unification semantics is violated.
- when type properties are violated.
- if 'append' or 'insert' patterns cannot generate further partitions.
- if the subpattern *p* of a 'not' pattern *!p* matches.
- if the condition of a 'where' pattern returns false.
- if the lengths of a list pattern and a list value do not correspond.

The evaluation stack and the heap have to be reset and the continuation code has to be executed if a partial match fails. This is done by the following program fragment:

```
next_alt:
 if        AP > ALTNULL then
           reset(AS[AP].stack);
           HP_level = AS[AP].heap;
           PC = AS[AP].pc;
           AP = AP−1;              /* The alternative is used again if the alternative */
                                   /* was installed by an append or insert pattern. In */
                                   /* these cases, the code of the alternative will */
                                   /* increment AP immediately. */
           else
           /* Handling of the '|'-operator in expressions. */
           /* the continuation address is stored on the trap stack */
 fi
```

```
reset( (VECTOR: st[1],st[2], ... , st[n]))
      /* the argument of function reset is a vector */
      /* containing a copy of the evaluation stack */
      /* fragment above MATCHNULL. */
for   i=1 to n do ST[MATCHNULL + i] = st[i]; od;
SP = MATCHNULL + n;
```

5.3.7.3. Translating Patterns into TRAMA-Code

The code for a pattern has to test whether the pattern matches and to bind the pattern variables. The translation function for patterns is defined under the precondition that a reference to the value to be matched is at the topmost stack position. Furthermore, the code for a pattern consumes the reference to the value. After a successful match, the stack height is decreased by one. The other elements of the evaluation stack remain unchanged, except the local environment.

The code for a pattern with two immediate subpatterns ('cons', 'append', 'tree' pattern ...) pushes two references to the parts of the partition on the evaluation stack that are consumed by the code for the subpatterns.

The code function P_Code has four arguments: a pattern, the binding β (pattern variables), the binding β_1 (global variables) and the simulated stack level k_p. The binding β associates with each pattern variable an address relative to MATCHNULL in the local environment on the stack. Global variables are treated as in expressions.

Syntactic Classes

To match a syntactic class, it is sufficient to test the *tag* of the value. For each class, there exists an instruction of its own. Wildcards are translated into **pop** instructions, because the wildcard '_' matches all values.

P_Code NUM $\beta\ \beta_1\ k_p$ = **numpat**
P_Code STRING $\beta\ \beta_1\ k_p$ = **stringpat**

.
.
.

P_Code _ $\beta\ \beta_1\ k_p$ = **pop** 1

Instruction	Semantics
numpat	**if** HP[ST[SP]].tag = INT **then** SP = SP−1; **else goto** next_alt; **fi**

Individual Values

For each individual value, there exists an instruction which checks the type and the proper value.

P_Code i β β_1 k_p = **testnum** i
P_Code s β β_1 k_p = **teststring** s
P_Code c β β_1 k_p = **testconst** c
P_Code b β β_1 k_p = **testbool** b
P_Code @i β β_1 k_p = **testhole** i

Instruction	Semantics
testnum i	**if** HP[ST[SP]].tag = INT **and** HP[ST[SP]].val = i **then** SP = SP−1; **else goto** next_alt; **fi**

Pattern Variables

The translation of TrafoLa-H patterns allow to determine which occurrence of a variable is matched first (see section 5.3.3). According to the unification semantics of TrafoLa-H, these variables are translated into **assign** instructions binding the variable to the topmost value on the stack. For all later occurrences of a variable, a test has to be generated (**update** instruction) to compare the new value and the value already bound.

Example: List patterns are translated "left to right". The first occurrence of A in the list pattern [A,A,A] is translated into the instruction **assign** β(A). β(A) is the relative address of A in the local environment. For the other occurrences of A, an **update** β(A) is generated.

P_Code v β β_1 k_p = **assign** β(v)
for "first" occurrences of v.

P_Code v β β_1 k_p = **update** β(v)
otherwise.

Instruction	Semantics
assign i	ST[MATCHNULL−i] = ST[SP]; SP = SP−1;
update i	**if** *Equal* (ST[MATCHNULL − i],ST[SP]) **then** SP = SP−1; **else goto** next_alt; **fi**

Import variables are translated into a machine instruction which does a runtime equality check.

Cons Pattern

The pattern p_1 :: p_2 matches nonempty list values, whose heads are matched by p_1 and whose tails are matched by p_2.

$$\begin{array}{lcl} \text{P\_Code } (p_1 :: p_2)\ \beta\ \beta_1\ k_p & = & \textbf{initcons} \\ & & \text{P\_Code } p_1\ \beta\ \beta_1\ (k_p{+}1) \\ & & \text{P\_Code } p_2\ \beta\ \beta_1\ k_p \end{array}$$

If the value to be matched is a nonempty list (CONS cell), the **initcons** instruction replaces the reference to the value on the stack by references to the tail and to the head of the list. These references are consumed by the code for the subpatterns p_1 and p_2.

The translation of *list* and *tree* patterns is analogous. The *and* patterns ($p_1\&p_2$) have to test both p_1 and p_2. Therefore, the reference to the value to be matched is duplicated on the stack.

Or Pattern

The 'or' pattern ($p_1|p_2$) matches the union of the values matched by p_1 and p_2. p_1 is tried first, and p_2 is installed as an alternative on the alternatives stack. The continuation address (i.e., the code address for p_2), the value of HP_level, and a copy of the stack fragment above MATCHNULL are thereby stored. The *desc* component on the alternatives stack is set to nil because 'or' patterns do not need a descriptor.

The stack copies are generally small. They are realized as vectors in the heap of the TRAMA. But it is also possible to use a special stack only for stack copies. The stack fragment is copied after the value of HP_level is stored. The requested heap space of the stack copy is freed automatically if a partial match fails, and the alternative p_2 is tried out. (see figure ??).

$$\begin{array}{lcl} \text{P\_Code } (p_1|p_2)\ \beta\ \beta_1\ k_p & = & \quad\ \ \textbf{setalt } l_1 \\ & & \quad\ \ \text{P\_Code } p_1\ \beta\ \beta_1\ k_p \\ & & \quad\ \ \textbf{ujmp } l_2 \\ & & l_1\text{: P\_Code } p_2\ \beta\ \beta_1\ k_p \\ & & l_2\text{:} \end{array}$$

Append Pattern

The 'append' pattern ($p_1.p_2$) matches a list value if there is a partition into a front list matched by p_1 and a back list matched by p_2. The nondeterministic selection of a partition is simulated by backtracking. Thereby, the possible partitions are generated successively until p_1 and p_2 match. The partition point of the list value moves from left to right.

$$\begin{array}{lcl} \text{P\_Code } (p_1.p_2)\ \beta\ \beta_1\ k_p & = & \textbf{initdot} \\ & & \textbf{idot} \\ & & \text{P\_Code } p_1\ \beta\ \beta_1\ (k_p{+}1) \\ & & \text{P\_Code } p_2\ \beta\ \beta_1\ k_p \end{array}$$

The instruction **initdot** (see figure ??) creates an alternative with continuation address **idot** and computes the first partition (the empty list and the whole list). The following **idot** instruction is skipped. If a partial match fails, the next partition is generated by the **idot** instruction. The old partition is stored in an 'append' descriptor. An 'append' descriptor (see figure ??) has three components *first*, *last*, and *second*. *first* and *second* point to the front and back list of the partition. *last* is used to extend the front list. It points to the last CONS-cell of the front list. To compute the next partition, the front list is extended by the first element of the back list, and the back list is shortened by the first element (see figure ??).

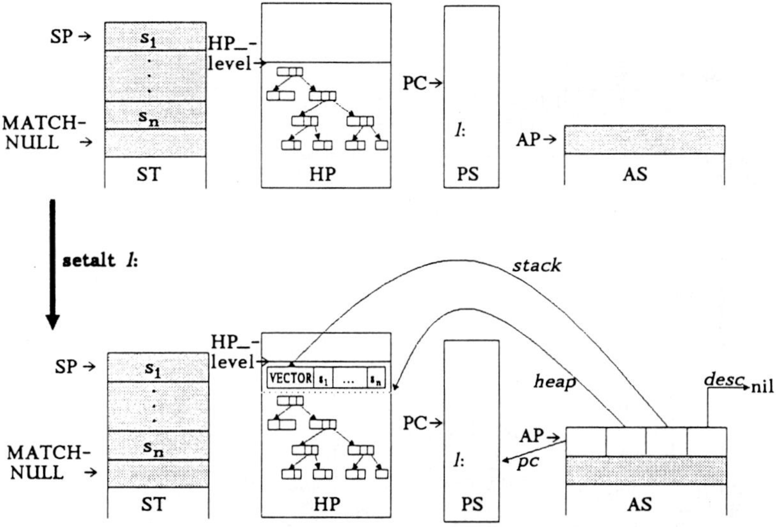

Figure 9: The **setalt** instruction

Sharing of values does not allow any changes in the original list value. Therefore, the CONS-cells of the front list have to be copied. The copying is done incrementally. Each processing of an alternative creates a new CONS cell. The back list is a true subvalue of the original list value, therefore no copying is needed.

Insert Pattern

The 'insert' pattern ($p_1 \frown p_2$) is the inversion of the *insert* operation on values. The *insert* operation in ($a \frown b$) replaces all occurrences of @1 in a by b and increments the hole numbers of the other holes in a by one. Holes (@1, @2, ...) are special placeholders. See chapter 8 of part II for a detailed description.

Example: @1⌢1 yields 1
[1,@1,3]⌢2 yields [1,2,3]
[1,@2,@1,@1,@3]⌢1 yields [1,@1,1,1,@2]
@1⌢@1 yields @1

The 'insert' pattern ($p_1 \frown p_2$) matches a value if there is a partition into an upper part a and lower part b such that a contains exactly one @1, and $a \frown b$ results in the original value. The possible partitions are generated successively and analyzed by the code for p_1 and p_2.

The possible lower parts are the whole value, sons of trees, and all list elements. To compute all possible partitions, the value to be matched is copied and the hole numbers of all holes in the copy are incremented by one. Then the original value and the copy are traversed synchronously. Whenever a TREE or CONS cell is found, the reference to the son or to the head in the copy is replaced by a reference to @1. Thereby, no side effects occur because sharing was eliminated by copying the value. The upper part of the partition is the upper part of the copy and the lower part of the partition is the corresponding subvalue in the original value. The copy is restored and the next partition is tried out if the subpatterns p_1 and p_2 do not match.

It is sufficient to copy the skeleton of the value (i.e., the TREE and CONS cells) because only TREE and CONS cells are changed.

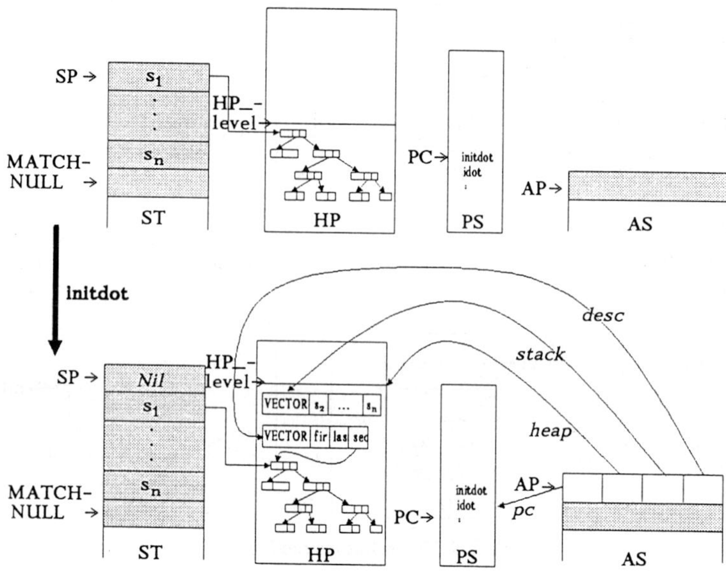

Figure 10: The instruction **initdot**

$$
\begin{aligned}
\text{P\_Code } (p_1 \hat{\ } p_2)\ \beta\ \beta_1\ k_p \quad = \quad & \textbf{inithat} \\
& \textbf{ihat} \\
& \text{P\_Code } p_1\ \beta\ \beta_1\ (k_p{+}1) \\
& \text{P\_Code } p_2\ \beta\ \beta_1\ k_p
\end{aligned}
$$

The instruction **inithat** (see figure **??**) creates an alternative with continuation address **ihat** and computes the first partition, namely @1 and the original value. The following **ihat** instruction is skipped and the code for the subpatterns p_1 and p_2 is executed.

If a generated partition is not matched, the TRAMA backtracks and resumes the computation at the **ihat** instruction (see figure **??**), which generates the next partition (the first execution of **ihat** provides a copy of the value with incremented hole numbers). The old partition is stored in an 'insert' descriptor. 'Insert' descriptors have the following components:

- *hstack:* Short stack to traverse original value and copy synchronously.
- *orig:* Pointer into the original value.
- *copy_root:* Pointer to the upper part of the copy.
- *copy:* Pointer into the copy.
- *copy_save:* Pointer to the lower part of the copy.

Kleene Pattern

The Kleene star pattern p^* is translated into a loop, which matches the pattern p against every element of the list value to be matched. In contrast to patterns p^+, the Kleene star patterns p^* are not allowed to contain variables.

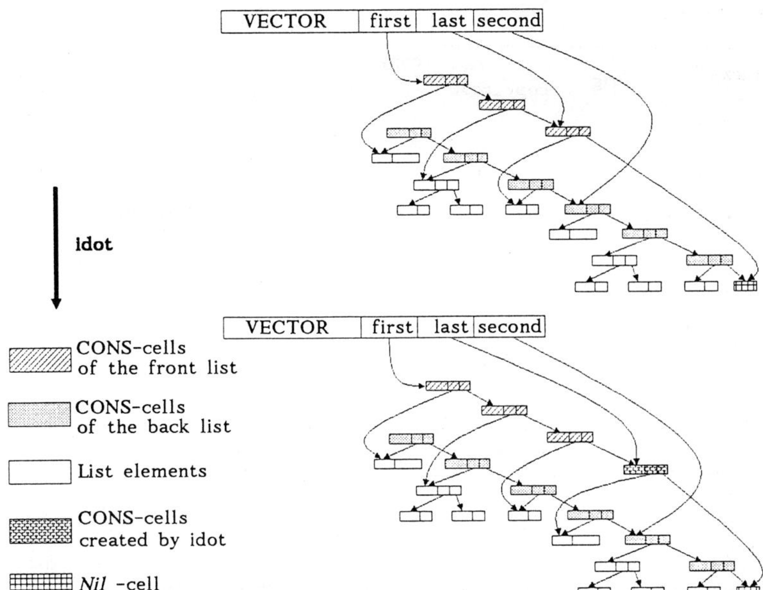

Figure 11: An 'append' descriptor

The code for p in Kleene plus patterns p^+ may be executed more than once. During the first execution, an access to a variable in p has to bind a value (**assign**). All other executions have to test whether the "old" and the "new" value are equal (**update**). p is therefore translated twice. The code function P_Code$_u$ generates **update** instructions for all occurrences of variables.

P_Code $(p^+)\ \beta\ \beta_1\ k_p$	=		**initcons**
			P_Code $p\ \beta\ \beta_1\ (k_p+1)$
			jumpnil l_2
		l_1:	**initcons**
			P_Code$_u$ $p\ \beta\ \beta_1\ (k_p+1)$
			jumpnotnil l_1
		l_2:	

Unbind Pattern

The result of an 'unbind' pattern { p } is the empty environment. The renaming of the variables in p ensures that the 'unbind' variables become invisible. To guarantee no more than one environment (important in **=>all** functions), the alternatives installed by p are removed from the alternative stack.

P_Code { p } $\beta\ \beta_1\ k_p$	=	**savealtstack**
		P_Code p $\beta\ \beta_1\ (k_p+1)$
		resetaltstack

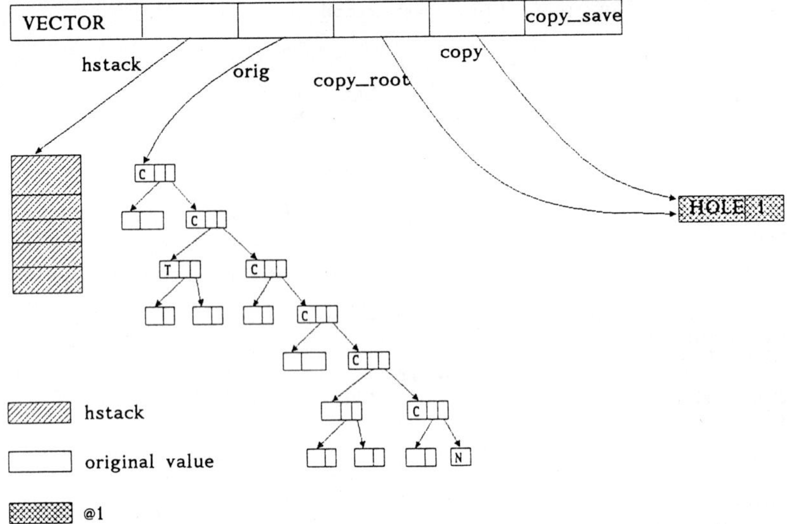

Figure 12: 'Insert' descriptor after the execution of **inithat** (first part).

Instruction	Semantics
savealtstack	ST[SP+1] = ST[SP]; ST[SP] = AP; SP = SP+1;
resetaltstack	AP = ST[SP]; SP = SP−1;

Not Pattern

A match of a pattern succeeds if the end of its code is reached. A 'not' pattern !*p* matches if the match of *p* fails. Therefore, an alternative is installed jumping behind the code for *p*, before the code for *p* is entered.

P_Code (!p) β β_1 k_p = **savealtstack**
setalt *l*
P_Code p β β_1 (k_p+1)
pnot
l: **pop** 2

Instruction	Semantics
pnot	AP = ST[SP]; **goto** next_alt;

Where Pattern

The 'where' pattern (*p where e*) allows the combination of patterns with expressions. Before the expression is evaluated, the match registers MATCHNULL, ALTNULL, and AP have to be saved because pattern matching may occur in *e*.

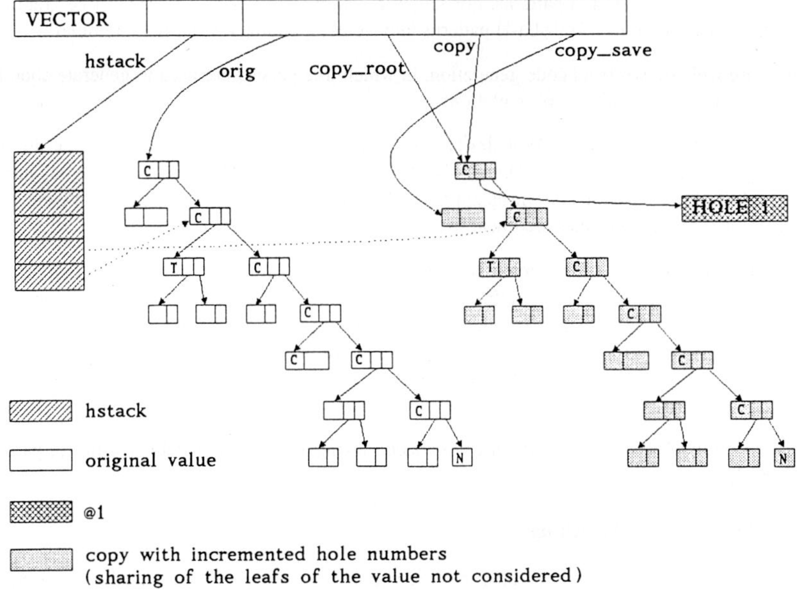

Figure 13: 'Insert' descriptor after the first execution of **ihat** (second part).

P_Code (p where e) β β_1 k_p	=	P_Code p β β_1 k_p **markwhere** V_Code e ρ (k_p+2) **where**

ρ denotes the binding of the global variables (β_1) overlayed with the bindings of the pattern variables of p.

Instruction	Semantics
markwhere	ST[SP+1] = MATCHNULL; ST[SP+2] = ALTNULL; ALTNULL = AP; SP = SP+2;
where	MATCHNULL = ST[SP-2]; ALTNULL = ST[SP−1]; **if** HP[ST[SP]].tag = BOOL **and** HP[ST[SP]].val = true **then** SP = SP−3; **else goto** next_alt;

5.3.8. Pattern Matching Using Tree Parsing

Matching a TrafoLa-H pattern against a value can be shown to be a NP-complete problem. Nevertheless, translating TrafoLa-H patterns into TRAMA code using some optimizations and heuristics (not presented here) leads in most cases to adequate execution times. However, a subclass of TrafoLa-H patterns can be matched without backtracking in times linear in the size of the value.

A TrafoLa-H pattern may be viewed as a medium to describe the language of the values matched by this pattern. For a subclass of TrafoLa-H patterns, this language can be described by a regular tree grammar. [?] describes the transformation of TrafoLa-H patterns into a corresponding regular tree grammar.

Tree grammars are well known from code generation, in which tree parsers are used to generate code for an expression tree in an intermediate representation.

For regular tree grammars, Weisgerber/Wilhelm [?] have described parser generators based on the tree pattern matching approach of Hoffman/O'Donnell [Hoffmann, O'Donnell 82] or Kron [?]. In our implementation of TrafoLa-H, we use the bottom-up approach, because bottom up tree analyzers have the great advantage that their analysis time costs are linear in the number of nodes of the subject tree.

These parsers compute a match set for every node of the subject tree (TrafoLa-H value), which can be used to determine the applicable grammar rules at this node. This information can be used to compute top-down all possible parse trees (tree grammars for nondeterministic TrafoLa-H patterns are ambiguous). Such a parse tree corresponds to exactly one possibility of matching the value. In the case of translating TrafoLa-H patterns, this information is used to bind the variables of the patterns during a top down traversal of the subject tree (i.e., the value to be matched).

A complete description of both pattern matching with backtracking and pattern matching with tree parsing can be found in [?].

5.3.8.1. Tree Parsing vs. Backtracking

Pattern matching with treeparsers is integrated into the compiler and is used automatically for complex TrafoLa-H patterns. Here, some heuristics are used to estimate the complexity of a pattern. With tree parsing, the matching times are nearly independent of the complexity of the patterns and depend only linearly on the size of the values to be matched. The sometimes impressive speed-up reached by using treeparsing compared with pattern matching using backtracking or coding as a function in the style of Hope, Miranda, or SML has to be paid with increasing compiling times and larger memory requirements. The problem of parser generation for a regular tree grammar corresponds to the construction of the deterministic bottom up tree automaton from a nondeterministic one, which is known to be exponential time hard. In order to speed up the compilation process, patterns can be translated optionally into code using the backtrack facilities of the TRAMA.

5.3.9. Conclusion

TrafoLa-H was implemented at the Universität des Saarlandes. The compiler, the abstract machine TRAMA, and a runtime environment with wide variety of debugging facilities (not discussed in this section) are embedded in a comfortable interactive programming environment. In this environment, TrafoLa-H is a universal functional language for every kind of symbolic computations and transformations. The powerful constructs of the language (i.e., nondeterministic patterns, exception handling, and a large set of predefined operators and system functions) allow for very short and suggestive formulation of algorithms.

The TrafoLa-H system is written completely in C, and is available on SUN workstations, DEC Vax series, and, in a restricted form, on a small Motorola 68000 personal computer. The abstract machine code is normally interpreted, but for Motorola 68000, a native code generator exists.

Despite the overhead required for the implementation of the powerful pattern language and transformation facilities, the overall performance of TrafoLa-H programs is comparable to that of Edinburgh SML. Particular strengths of the implementation are apparent in cases where the complexity of transformations lies in the pattern matching effort.

6. System Development Components

Juan Antonio de Miguel, ALCATEL SESA

Many of the PROSPECTRA system tools have been generated using the Cornell Synthesizer Generator (*CSG* for short, see [Reps, Teitelbaum 88]). CSG was created as a tool for implementing language-based editors, but its characteristics make it usable for generating other kinds of language-based tools as well. Particularly, in PROSPECTRA, CSG has been used as the generator for editors and transformers. However, standard CSG does not completely meet the requirements of the PROSPECTRA project, so an effort has been made to adapt CSG features to them.

This chapter explains those extensions, mainly from the user's point of view. It is divided in two sections. The first one includes those modifications needed for using CSG as the PROSPECTRA *Editor Generator*. The second one includes changes made in adapting CSG as the PROSPECTRA *Transformer Generator*. We assume that the reader has some familiarity with CSG.

6.1. Editor Generator

6.1.1. Log-and-Replay Facilities

CSG-generated editors have been extended by a mechanism to record editing operations in files (the *log* mechanism), and an associated facility to execute such records. Log files are written in a language (the *CSG Scripts Language*) which has been designed to express every possible action carried out during editing, such as typewriting text, executing editor commands, performing transformations over selections, changing selections using the mouse, etc. Furthermore, the language incorporates iteration and conditional constructs, parameterized functions, variables, expressions and types similar to those used in the editor specification language SSL (see [Reps, Teitelbaum 88]), and assignment of values to variables by pattern-matching, among other important features. As a consequence, the language has become expressive enough for users to write their own scripts.

This section will focus on how the user can access the facilities to record sessions or run scripts. For those interested in the details of the language, a complete description of the CSG Scripts Language can be found in the [de Miguel 90].

Generating CSG Scripts

There exist two possible ways to generate a CSG script for further replaying:

- By automatically recording a part of or a whole editing session.
- By writing it by hand in a text editor.

Obviously, both possibilities can be mixed: for example, a script can be generated by recording a session, and can be later modified by edition to include parameters for generalization.

To generate a script for a whole editing session, there is a command-line option (*-l*) for CSG editors. See 6.1.3 for details.

During a session, there exist two editor commands that allow the user to select a part of the session for recording. These commands are *start-log* and *stop-log*.

Both commands are present in the *File Operations* menu.

The *start-log* command allows the user to specify a name for a log file for recording the editing operations performed starting with the execution of the command following *start-log* up to the end of the session or to the execution of the next *stop-log* command. If the specified file already exists, the user is warned and asked whether he wants to append the following operations at the end of the file, or to overwrite the file.

The *stop-log* command allows the user to stop the recording of editing operations. This does not depend on how the log was started: either with the *-l* option, or with the *start-log* command.

Executing CSG Scripts

There are three ways to execute a CSG script:

1. By calling a CSG-generated editor with some particular options.

   There exists a number of command-line options that provoke the execution of a script during editing sessions. A detailed description can be found in 6.1.3.

2. By calling the CSG script as if it were a CSG command.

   CSG scripts can be called as CSG commands, with some little differences.

   CSG scripts can be called by typing their name in the command line of a CSG-generated editor or by writing it in other scripts. In both cases, the whole name of the script must be provided, in contrast with the case of command calls, where the shortest non-ambiguous prefix of the name suffices. With respect to this, it is important to remark that CSG-generated editors look first for commands, and then look for the name of scripts. Therefore, a script whose name coincides with the name (or a prefix) of a command cannot be called in this way.

   Furthermore, a CSG script cannot be called from a menu, unless it has been "installed" as if it were a command by means of the function *scr_open*. This function has been incorporated to CSG to override all the differences between script and command call mechanisms, including script incorporation to menus and the aforementioned problems with prefixes. See 6.1.6 for more information.

   Anyway, a CSG-generated editor behaves in a similar way after a script or a command call, be the called script installed or not:

   - Calling a parameterized script (or a script that has no header to tell it has arguments or not) just produces the opening of a form to enter the arguments. Such forms are described below. The script is actually run when the form is "started", or, in other words, when the *start-command* command is called. This is exactly what happens with a parameterized command: starting such a command causes the execution of an associated function, while starting a parameterized script causes its interpretation.
   - Calling a script which has no arguments forces its immediate interpretation. This reproduces again the behaviour of command calls.

   Script arguments are provided by filling in a form that includes a list phylum (each of its elements being an argument) with the following properties:

   - If the script has no header, and therefore it is impossible to know the type and number of the arguments it needs, arguments are parsed as if they belong to the phylum STR.
   - If the script has a header, the list of arguments is initialized as the list of completing terms associated to the phyla of the formal parameters of the script.

3. By calling the command *execute-batch-file*.

   Execute-batch-file is a command that allows script execution in editing sessions. It has three parameters:

(a) The name of the file that contains the script.

(b) The list of the script actual parameters

(c) The execution mode for the script (set by default to *continuous*).

This command allows the user to choose the mode of execution (see below) for a CSG script. It also allows calls to those scripts whose names coincide with a prefix of a transformation or a command.

Execution Mode for CSG Scripts

There are two modes of execution for CSG scripts: *continuous* or *step-by-step*.

Scripts in *continuous* mode are run without any user interaction. Once the script has started execution, there is no way to stop it other than aborting the whole editing session.

In *step-by-step* mode, execution stops each time a new action has to be carried out. For action we mean a command, script, or transformation call or an expression evaluation. Note that actions may have parameters and that these are actions too.

A message is displayed in the command line to show the stopping point. The editor waits for the user to send some information about what to do next. There are three possible answers to this request, each one associated with a different key:

- Run the next action (*s* key). If the next action is parameterized, it forces the opening of the corresponding form, and stops script execution in the first action to be undertaken inside the form. If the next action causes the beginning of a script execution, this answer allows the user to get into the called script and continue execution within it.

- Run the next action and, if it is parameterized, its parameters and the corresponding *start-command* command in the same step (*n* key). If the script is stopped in a script call, this forces the execution of the whole script in one single step. If it is stopped in a form command or a parameterized transformation, the arguments will be filled in and the form started at once.

- Quit the script (*q* key).

6.1.2. Buffer Modes

Each object being edited in a CSG-generated editor is held in a different *buffer*. Buffers in standard CSG editors are always opened in *read-and-write* mode, except the special buffers *CLIPPED* and *DELETED* which are always opened in *read-only* mode. This led to unsuitable situations in the context of the PROSPECTRA system, specially in the case of transformers, which are tools that must not allow arbitrary text edition. A new facility has been incorporated to CSG in order to associate a mode of edition to buffers. The user is asked for a mode every time a command is called that implies the opening of a buffer. Three different modes can be assigned:

- *Editor mode:* This is the default mode. A buffer that has been opened with this mode behaves exactly like standard editor buffers do: editing transformations, update commands and text input are enabled both in it and in every parameter form opened from it.

- *Transformer mode:* This mode restricts edition facilities: editing transformations, update commands and text input are prohibited in the buffer, but enabled in the parameter forms opened from it. So, in transformer mode, text cannot be edited arbitrarily and can only be modified by transformation.

- *Browser mode:* This mode forbids all kinds of edition. It only allows users to take a look at the contents of a buffer.

Users can set which commands are allowed in transformer mode and which are not (see 6.1.6) for the commands they define. They can group transformations in interactively selectable modules associated to each buffer as well (see 6.2.1).

As told above, one of the ways to associate a mode to a buffer is by means of a new argument that has been added to some commands. These commands are *new-buffer* and *switch-to-buffer*. The argument for the mode appears only in case the editor was not called with the *-t* option (see the next paragraph) and is initialized with the value that corresponds to the editor mode. If the user switches to a buffer that was already opened with a given mode, this mode cannot be changed using the *switch-to-buffer* command.

There is also a command-line option (*-t*) that allows to call an editor as if it were a transformer (see 6.1.3). If the editor was called with such option, every buffer is opened in transformer mode during the editing session.

6.1.3. New Command-Line Options

In standard CSG, editors could be invoked with a very limited set of options. This set has been enriched with some new possibilities that will be introduced in the coming lines.

Working Directory Option

A CSG-generated editor can now work in a default directory different from the one it was started from. If such directory is specified, data files, scripts etc. are taken from and written to it; otherwise, the current directory is used. The working directory can be specified on editor invocation (option *-W*) and changed in edition by means of a command.

The syntax for this option is:

editor_name [options] -W directory_name *[options] [file_name]*

The name of the aforementioned command is *change-working-directory*. This command shows the current working directory in a form and allows to change it. If an incorrect path is given, the command fails but the form window remains open so the path can be corrected. If the command is canceled, the working directory remains unchanged.

Log-and-Replay Options

CSG-generated editors have now a number of options related with the log-and-replay facilities incorporated by PROSPECTRA. These options fall into three groups:

- *Log Option*

  To generate a script of a whole editing session there is a command-line option (*-l*) that allows the user to specify a file where editing operations during the following session will be recorded. The syntax for the editor call is:

  editor_name [options] -l log_name *[options] [file_name]*

  where *log_name* is the name of the file where the session is going to be recorded.

- *Replay Options*

  There are four different options (*-r*, *-R*, *-i* and *-o*) that imply that script executions will take place at some moments after the editor has been called.

  The syntax of the editor call for these options is:

editor_name [options] [file_name] -option script_name [script_arguments]

where *option* stands for one of the mentioned options, *script_name* is the name of the script to be executed, and *script_arguments* is the list of arguments for the script. *script_arguments* must be a single string with arguments separated by commas. Note that the name of the file to be read must come before any of the replay options. Otherwise, it may be taken as a script argument instead of a file name.

Options *-r* and *-R* allow the replaying of sessions. When invoked with one of such options, the editor gives immediate control to the CSG script interpreter which executes the script. When the script is over, the editor is exited. The difference between these options is that the *-R* option runs the script in *step-by-step* mode, while the *-r* option runs it in *continuous* mode.

Options *-i* and *-o* can be used to define *prelude* (*-i*) and *postlude* (*-o*) scripts, which are executed just after the editor starts running, or just before it stops resp.

These four options are syntactically compatible with each other: they can all be present in the same editor call. In any case, the following rules hold:

1. The script associated with the *-i* option is always executed before any other one.
2. The script associated with the *-o* option is always executed after any other one.
3. Only the rightmost one of *-r* and *-R* options in the command-line is taken into account. No error or warning message is issued.

- *Search Path for CSG Scripts Option*

  Search paths for scripts can be specified when invoking a CSG-generated editor. The first directory of the path is always the *working directory*. The rest of the directories in the path are declared by means of the *-S* option.

  The syntax for this option is the following:

  editor_name [options] -S directory_name *[options] [file_name]*

  This option can appear as many times as desired in editor calls. Each time it appears, the associated directory is included in the last position of the path. Therefore, the leftmost directory is the first to be explored (after the *working directory*); the rightmost is the last.

Transformer Option

CSG was designed to generate editors. Transformations were a help in edition, not a goal on their own. This is not the case in PROSPECTRA. An option to force the called editor to work as a transformer has been provided.

The syntax for this option is:

editor_name [options] -t *[options] [file_name]*

When called with *-t* option, every buffer is opened in transformer mode during editor execution.

6.1.4. Read and Write with Attributes

In CSG Version 2.0, files could be read or written in two different formats: ***structured*** or ***textual***. In a structured file, a representation of a tree, not including the representation of its attributes values, was held, while a textual file contained plain text.

Now, a new facility to read and write files in a structured format, called *extended format*, that includes attribute representation too, has been incorporated to CSG. This feature saves time on reading since no attribute evaluation is needed after one of these files is read.

The format is thoroughly explained in [Hinojal 88]. A short introduction follows.

The extended format for files is quite similar to the standard CSG structured format. Files are divided in three parts:

1. *File type key:* A field that indicates the format of the file. This is to distinguish files that include structural representations from text files.

2. *Operators information:* This part includes information about the operator names that should appear in the term representations contained in the file. Beware that, in extended format, the terms to be represented include also attribute values, so the operator names are those used in building a syntactic tree plus those used in building the attribute values associated to it. This part begins with the keyword "$operators" and consists of an enumeration of operator names with other associated information.

3. *Terms representation:* This part includes a representation of the terms involved in an attributed tree. It begins with the keyword "$terms". The syntactic tree is represented in the same format used in structured files. The trees for attributes are represented in a way that takes into account that attribute values may be repeated, and so, references to values, instead of copies, should be kept when possible.

Access to this facility is provided by the following commands (both of them belonging to the *File Operations* menu):

- *write-with-attributes:* This command writes in extended format the contents of the current buffer to a file whose name is supplied by the user.

- *read-with-attributes:* This command reads a file in the current buffer if the file is in extended format. Otherwise it answers with an error message indicating the reason of the failure.

6.1.5. Context Sensitive Parsing

The addition of PA$^{nn}{}_{d}$A-C phrases to the TrafoLa-S editor generates a lot of parsing conflicts because of the LALR(1) nature of CSG-generated parsers. These conflicts could be solved by explicitly tagging PA$^{nn}{}_{d}$A phrases and embedded TrafoLa-S expressions and variables with some characters to denote their type. However, type information is held in environment attributes in every CSG editor, and so, the possibility to use it existed. *Context Sensitive Parsing* (CSP) is a general technique for delaying the parsing of phrases until attribute information is available, and for using this information to drive the parsing. CSP can be applied to any language sharing the characteristics of TrafoLa-S , namely, a language with phrases and embedded expressions in the sense of TrafoLa-S .

The technique consists in parsing phrases as plain text and then reparse them using context information. Embedded phrases and expressions are initially parsed without taking care of their type, and then, synthesized type information is used to build a term of the suitable phylum which is inserted in the right place of the abstract tree. This method is recursively applied until no more reparsing is needed.

Detailed information about the CSP implementation can be found in [de la Cruz *et al.* 90]. Information about its application in the TrafoLa-S editor can be found in the TrafoLa-S Editor Reference Manual (see part II, chapter 6).

6.1.6. Changes to the C-Interface

[Reps, Teitelbaum 88] gives little information about the C code used in the implementation of the system. Nevertheless, on Chapter 5 a description is made on how to use C functions in CSG editors. Furthermore, the profile of some C functions that editor designers may frequently use, like those to define new commands or those to reconfigure menues, are carefully described there. Information generated by the PROSPECTRA modifications to CSG that would be worth to include in such chapter is the subject of this subsection. These are the functions that have been changed or created:

- *co_open* is the only documented C function whose interface has varied. *co_open* is an operation that creates an entry in the editor's command table to inform the editor kernel of the properties of the new command. Now, it has a fifth argument to indicate whether the command can be applied or not in a buffer running in transformer mode. The values that specify this new property are CO_VALID_IN_TRANSFORMER and CO_INVALID_IN_TRANSFORMER. An example of a call to *co_open* would be:

```
co_open(
    "operation-name",
    operation_command,
    CO_WITHOUT_PARSE,
    CO_VALID_IN_FORM,
    CO_VALID_IN_TRANSFORMER
    );
```

- *scr_open* is a new C function that "opens" CSG scripts as if they were commands. The pieces of information that must be provided are: the name of the script, its precedence with respect to parsing, its validity in forms and its validity in buffers under transformer mode. A CSG script opened with this function can be, from then on, used exactly as a command, i.e.: it can be incorporated to command menus.

6.1.7. Syntax Error Reporting

In standard editors users did not get much information when an attempt to enter a syntactically incorrect text was made. In such case, only a message saying "*syntax error*" was raised. A better error reporting has been included in the PROSPECTRA version of CSG: the name of the wrong token found and the name of the possible valid tokens are displayed in consecutive lines of a form window. Editing cannot be resumed until the form is started or canceled.

6.2. Transformer Generator

6.2.1. Transformation Modules

In the PROSPECTRA version of CSG, transformations can be grouped into ***modules*** to allow users to selectively enable or disable sets of transformations while edition is taking place. This means that the availability of a transformation in a given moment does not only depend on the fact that its associated pattern matches the selection, but also depends on whether the transformation belongs to one of the currently enabled modules. This mechanism facilitates a way for users to work with a restricted set of transformations depending on their current goal.

Transformation modules are declared in SSL specifications, and so, SSL has been extended to allow modules declaration. Its syntax is shown in the next figure:

```
module ident
    { decl_list }
end ident
```

decl_list contains any declaration but other module declarations (nested modules are forbidden). Identifiers coming after the module and end keywords must be the same. An error is issued and generation is stopped if two modules with the same name are found in the editor specification. Note that not only transformations but any declaration can be embedded in modules, though this has no special meaning up to now.

Conceptually, there is still another module besides the declared ones: the one that includes all the transformations that are defined out of modules. The transformations it contains are considered to be *editing transformations*, and can be never directly disabled or enabled by the user.

Transformation modules are associated to *buffers*: each buffer has its corresponding set of enabled transformation modules. When a buffer is opened (including form buffers), the set contains only the editing module, if the buffer mode is *editor*, or nothing, if it is *transformer*.

To modify the status of modules, a new command, *trafo-modules-info*, has been made available. It is included in the *Edit Operations* menu. *Trafo-modules-info* shows the status of modules and provides a mechanism to change it. It displays the list of user defined modules telling whether they are enabled or not. Module information can be changed over the list, though it is not actualized until the command is started. If it is canceled, modifications to the list are not recorded.

6.2.2. Extended Transformations

SSL transformations were not expressive enough for PROSPECTRA purposes. Language facilities to specify semantic conditions for the application of transformations and to include parameters in the result expression, and associated mechanisms to enter them, have been included in the PROSPECTRA version of CSG. Most of the information supplied here is based upon [González 88], so the reader is referred to this document for further reading.

Conditional Transformations

The inner pattern matching mechanism of CSG just allows the specification of syntactic conditions in the definition of patterns. Frequently, a transformation should be applied only if some semantic conditions hold. In order to deal with this problem, the syntax of SSL has been extended to permit the association of an optional boolean expression to transformations.

In editing, only those transformations whose pattern matches the current selection and whose boolean condition, if defined, evaluates to true, become enabled transformations of the buffer. The conditional expression is evaluated in the same environment as the result expression, that is, pattern-variables and their attributes can be referenced in it.

Parameterized Transformations

Most useful transformations need some information at the moment the user applies them. A language facility to define a parameter and to use it in the result expression, plus a mechanism to enter the parameter on transformation invocation have been added to CSG. Additionally, the possibility to check a validity condition for the transformation over the set of pattern-variables and the parameter has been included in transformation definitions.

The parameter is defined in SSL by giving an identifier and a phylum name for it. Optionally, an initialization expression can be supplied.

The parameter is entered in edition by filling in a form that shows up after the transformation has been called. Canceling the form is like never having called the transformation. The parameter phylum is used for typechecking purposes on generation time, and to provide the proper template for the form. The initialization expression is used to initialize the form. Pattern-variables can be referenced in it.

The validity condition definition comes after the parameter definition. Pattern-variables and the parameter can be referenced in it. In edition, the condition is checked right after the actual parameter has been entered. If it evaluates to true, the transformation is applied. Otherwise, a warning message is displayed in the command-line of the form, and the user is allowed to correct the parameter or to cancel the transformation.

It is important to remark that, while the current selection and, so, its associated pattern-variables, are attributed terms, the parameter is merely a term, hence no parameter's attributes can be referred to either in the validity condition or in the result expression.

6.2.3. Parameter Stack

There are restricted facilities for cutting and pasting tree fragments among buffers in standard CSG. This is particularly inconvenient when filling complex transformation parameters.

To overcome these situations, a stack of buffers to keep tree fragments, with a set of associated commands to manage it, has been included in PROSPECTRA CSG.

The stack is composed of a parallel collection of buffers which are accessed by other means than conventional buffers. For example:

1. Edition is impossible for stack buffers.

2. Stack buffers are not listed when the command *list-buffers* is invoked.

A set of commands is associated to the stack to push selections to it, to extract a given element from it, to automatically fill a tree with the elements of the stack etc. Copies to or from stack buffers are implemented as commands *copy-to-clipped* and *copy-from-clipped* are with respect to the buffer CLIPPED. A copy to the stack fails if an attempt to copy a placeholder is made. Copies from the stack fail when the selection of the tree is not a placeholder, or when the selection and the element phyla are not compatible.

The stack is designed as a facility to fill in parameters, so copies from the stack are not allowed out of form browsers.

The set of commands is the following:

- *push-to-stack:* It pushes the current selection onto the stack. It assigns a number to the copied element, so it can be later accessed by another stack command. Number 1 is given to the first entered element (the one over the bottom of the stack), number 2 is for the next one and so on.

- *fill-in-from-stack:* It traverses the tree under edition copying an element from the stack into the tree each time a placeholder is found. Elements are copied beginning in element number 1 up to the top of the stack. Elements are popped out from the stack after being copied. If a copy fails, the element that produced the failure is not eliminated from the stack, and the command terminates, leaving this element at the top of the it. If the bottom of the tree is reached, or if there are no more elements in the stack, the command terminates leaving an empty stack.

- *copy-from-stack:* It copies a given element of the stack in the current selection (if it is a placeholder). A form browser is displayed to ask for the number of the element. It does not modify the stack. It cannot be invoked but in form browsers.
- *pop-and-copy-from-stack:* It copies the tree at the top of the stack over the current selection and removes it from the stack. If copy fails, the stack remains unchanged. Only callable in form browsers.
- *pop-and-delete-from-stack:* It eliminates the uppermost element from the stack.
- *delete-from-stack:* It deletes a given element from the stack. It has an associated form for the user to supply the number of the element.
- *list-parameters:* It lists the current elements of the stack, giving its number and the phylum of the root of its subtree as information.

6.2.4. Transformer-Verifier Interface

Every new CSG feature described so far has involved changes to the source code of the system. The *Transformer-Verifier Interface* is a C function that allows communication between PROSPECTRA transformers and the PROSPECTRA Proof Editor, and whose implementation has not required further modifications to the system. Instead, it has been built using the facilities the PROSPECTRA CSG gives. Therefore, it might not be completely correct to include its description in this chapter, but the fact that the interface can be seen as a first attempt to have a general mean to communicate CSG editors justifies it.

The name of the C function that provides the interface is *Verify*. Usually, *Verify* is called for verifying semantical applicability conditions for transformations (see 6.2.2). *Verify* has two arguments:

1. A term of phylum *EXPRESSION*.
2. A term of phylum *TP_ENV*.

Verify returns a boolean value indicating if the *EXPRESSION* has been proven true or false with such *TP_ENV*.

The proof is done interactively. Thus, *Verify* opens the Proof Editor in a form window, initializes it with the given values, and passes control for the user to operate over the editor. When the form is started, the value of an attribute (*proven*), which is a flag that informs of success in a proof, is returned. If the form is canceled, a *false* value is returned to indicate the proof has been aborted.

PROgram Development by SPECification and TRAnsformation

Part IV

Literature

Annotated Bibliography of the PROSPECTRA Project

Berthold Hoffmann, Hui Shi, Universität Bremen

The publications of the PROSPECTRA Project are listed according to the areas of the project's work plan.Within each area, documents are listed according to their dates of (first) appearence.

M.1.1. Development by Transformation

[1] Bernd Krieg-Brückner, Harald Ganzinger, Manfred Broy, Reinhard Wilhelm, Ulrich Möncke, Beatrix Weisgerber, Andrew McGettrick, Ian G. Campbell, Georg Winterstein: *PROSPECTRA Project Summary*. **Date:** 85-00-00.
Summary: Objectives of the PROSPECTRA Project are described, and its compliance with the ESPRIT programme explained. The project plan, and the contributions of the partners to the project are summarized.
Superseded by [10]
PROSPECTRA Report [M.1.1.S1-R-1.0]

[2] Bernd Krieg-Brückner: *Systematic Transformation of Interface Specifications (Applicative to Imperative Style, Exceptions, Monitors).*
Date: 85-10-21.
Summary: The relationship between different styles of interfaces in Ada and their formal specifications in Anna is defined by transformation rules: applicative packages with axiomatic specifications of Abstract Data Types, imperative packages with pre- and post-conditions, and stand-alone packages with an internally hidden state. The introduction of exceptions for such packages, or the transition to monitor tasks in the concurrent case is derived from the notion of partial functions. In all these cases, the original axiomatic algebraic ADT specification is retained.
Superseded by [5]
In: H.-J. Kreowski (ed.): Recent Trends in Data Type Specification. Proc. 3rd Workshop on Theory and Application of Abstract Data Types, Informatik-Fachberichte 116, Berlin-Heidelberg-New York: Springer (1986), 156-170.

[3] Bernd Krieg-Brückner: *A Little Example of PROgram Development by SPECification and TRAnsformation*. **Date:** 86-03-05.
Summary: To illustrate the methodology of PROgram development by SPECification and TRAnsformation, a little example, division and modulo of natural numbers, is carried through all phases of program development: formal specification, initial implementation, verification of correctness, development by transformation, variation of implementation, revision of specification. The interaction between Anna as the specification language and Ada as the implementation language is discussed.
Superseded by [9]
PROSPECTRA Report [M.1.S1-SN-4.2]

[4] Bernd Krieg-Brückner, Harald Ganzinger, Manfred Broy, Reinhard Wilhelm, Ulrich Möncke, Beatrix Weisgerber, Andrew McGettrick, Ian G. Campbell, Georg Winterstein: *PROgram Development by SPECification and TRAnsformation in Ada/Anna*. **Date:** 86-05-06.
Summary: This paper gives an overview of the ESPRIT Project PROSPECTRA, carried out jointly by Universität Bremen, Universität Dortmund, Universität Passau, Universität des Saarlandes, University of Strathclyde, SYSECA Logiciel and SYSTEAM KG. The project shall provide a rigorous methodology for developing Ada software that is correct w.r.t. a formal specification in Anna, and a comprehensive support system. This paper is a compact revised version of [M.1.1.S1-R-1.0].
Superseded by [10]
In: P. Wallis (ed.): Ada: Managing the Transition, Proc. Ada Europe Conf.'86, May 6-8 1986 at Edinburgh. Ada Companion Series, Cambridge University Press 1986. 249-258.

[5] Bernd Krieg-Brückner: *Systematic Transformation of Interface Specifications: Applicative Style to Imperative Style, Exceptions*. **Date:** 86-05-10.
Summary: This paper is an extended version of [M.1.1.S1-R-3.1].
In: H. Partsch (ed.): Program Specification and Transformation, Proceedings of the IFIP TC2 Working Conf., April 86, Bad Tölz. Amsterdam: North-Holland (1986). pp. 269-291

[6] Bernd Krieg-Brückner: *PAnndA-S, its Canonical Syntax and Alternative Paraphrasings.* **Date:** 86-02-25.
Summary: The subset PAnndA-S of PAnndA (PROSPECTRA Ada/Anna) may be used for the development of Ada/Anna specifications and initial implementations at the early stages of a PROSPECTRA program development. A *Canonical Syntax* describes the kernel of this language which contains all semantically necessary concepts. *Alternative Paraphrasings* define (by transformation rules) equivalent notations based on the kernel in order to enhance the usability of the language.
PROSPECTRA Report [M.1.1.S1-R-7.2]

[7] Bernd Krieg-Brückner: *Informal Specification of the PROSPECTRA System.* **Date:** 86-03-04.
Summary: The informal specification of the PROSPECTRA system is sketched. A global view of the user activities is given in order to help with the formulation of more precise system requirements.
PROSPECTRA Report [M.1.1.S1-SN-9.1]

[8] Stefan Kahrs: *PAnndA-S Standard Types.* **Date:** 86-10-29.
Summary: The Ada standard types to be included in PAnndA-S are specified. In the Canonical Syntax of PAnndA-S, these types and type constructors will be considered as (generic) packages which are specified as Abstract Data Types.
PROSPECTRA Report [M.1.1.S1-SN-11.2]

[9] Bernd Krieg-Brückner: Integration of Program Construction and Verification: The PROSPECTRA Methodology. **Date:** 87-03-10.
Summary: A methodology for PROgram development by SPECification and TRAnsformation is described. Formal requirement specifications in Anna are the basis for constructing *correct* and efficient Ada programs by gradual transformation. The methodology is illustrated by a few examples.
In: Montanari,U., and Habermann,A.N. (eds.): Innovative Software Factories and Ada, Proc. CRAI International Spring Conference, Capri, LNCS 275.(1987) pp. 173-194

[10] Bernd Krieg-Brückner, Berthold Hoffmann, Harald Ganzinger, Manfred Broy, Reinhard Wilhelm, Ulrich Möncke, Beatrix Weisgerber, Andrew McGettrick, Ian G. Campbell, Georg Winterstein: *PROgram Development by SPECification and TRAnsformation.* **Date:** 86-09-01.
Summary: This paper gives an overview of the ESPRIT Project PROSPECTRA, carried out jointly by Universität Bremen, Universität Dortmund, Universität Passau, Universität des Saarlandes, University of Strathclyde, SYSECA Logiciel and SYSTEAM KG. The project shall provide a rigorous methodology for developing Ada software that is correct w.r.t. a formal specification in Anna, and a comprehensive support system.
This paper is a compact revised version of [M.1.1.S1-R-5.1].
In: Proc. ESPRIT Conf. 86 (Result and Achievements). North-Holland (1987) pp. 301-312.

[11] Qian, Zhenyu: *Sufficient Condition for Confluent and Terminating Term Rewrite System and its Extension to Recursively Presented Term Rewriting.* **Date:** 86-11 -05.
Summary: Recursive presentation of term rewriting is a technique developed to describe some equational specifications which in the conventional approach can only be described by infinite many equations. It is found out that this technique is also useful in simulating some conditional equations with the advantage that the syntactical structures are fully revealed. Therefore an efficient implementation can be derived from it. This paper considers the confluence and termination of a recursive presentation. To do this, we extend the O'Donnell's sufficient condition for confluence and termination to cover a larger class of TRS's. The extended approach allows the co-existence of two rewrite rules which have almost the same structure except each of them rewrites different leaves.
PROSPECTRA Report [M.1.1.S1-SN-16.2]

[12] Qian, Zhenyu: *Recursive Presentation of Program Transformation.* **Date:** 86-09-25.
Summary: This paper discusses a new technique, which we call *recursive presentation*, to describe equivalence relation of terms. This kind of technique allows us to treat some non-finitely based equations without introducing any auxiliary function symbols. It is shown that the technique can be widely used not only for purely equational algebraic specifications, term rewrite systems and program transformations, but also for conditional cases of them. The relationship of this technique to the conventional notations is also discussed.
PROSPECTRA Report [M.1.1.S1-SN-17.1]

[13] Bernd Krieg-Brückner: *Korrekte Software mit PROgrammentwicklung durch SPECification and TRAnsformation* (in German). **Date:** 86-09.
Summary: The PROSPECTRA project aims to provide a technological basis for developing correct software: a rigorous methodology based on formal methods and a comprehensive support system. Formal requirement specifications in *Anna* are the basis for constructing efficient *Ada* programs by gradual transformation.
PROSPECTRA Report [M.1.1.S1-SN-20.0]

[14] Qian, Zhenyu: *An Example of Recursively Presented Transformation (Program Transformation of Functions into Procedures).* **Date:** 86-11-10.
Summary: A program transformation is described by recursively presented rules. The rule, when applied, attemps to transform in a program a function declaration and all its calls into corresponding procedure ones in one step.
PROSPECTRA Report [M.1.1.S1-SN-21.0]

[15] Bernd Krieg-Brückner: *The PROSPECTRA Methodology: A Course in 20 Lectures, Part B: Development Methodology.* **Date:** 1986-12.
Summary: This document contains the transparencies of a course given at SESA in November, 1986. It will be the basis of a more detailed documentation of the PROSPECTRA Methodology.
Part A: Formal Specification is contained in PROSPECTRA Report [M.2.2. S1-R-2.0]
PROSPECTRA Report [M.1.1.A3-R-22.0]

[16] Qian, Zhenyu: *Structured Contextual Rewritin.* **Date:** 86-12-00.
Summary: In this paper, we develop a mechanism, which we call structured contextual system, to deal with some non-finitely-based algebraic specifications. The sufficient condition for confluence and termination of this kind of systems is also considered, based on a generalization of the approach by O'Donnell.
This paper is a compact revised version of part of [M.1.1. S1-SN-16.1], [M.1.1.S1-SN-17.1] and [M.1.1.S1-SN-21.0]
In: Proc. of 2nd International Conference on Rewriting Techniques and Applications, May, 1987, Bordeaux, France, in Springer Verlag's LNCS 256. pp. 168-179.

[17] Bernd Krieg-Brückner: *Formalisation of Developments: an Algebraic Approach* **Date:** 87-07.
Summary: In the context of ESPRIT Project #390, PROSPECTRA (PROgram development by SPECification and TRAnsformation), a uniform treatment of algebraic specification is proposed to formalise data, programs, transformation rules, and program developments.
Superseded by [19]
In: M.W.Rogers (ed.) Proc. of the ESPRIT Conference'87. Brussels. North-Holland. (1987) pp. 491-501..

[18] Wei Li: *Implementing First Order Logic in Modula-2 Using an Intuitionistic Approach*
Date: 87-08-15
Summary: A variant of Martin-löf's type theory is given using extended Modula-2 constructs, and a subset of first order logic is interpreted by certain type constructors of this theory. Under this theory, given a formula of the form for all x find a y such that R(x,y) as a specification, program sythesis amounts to proving the truth of the formula. During the proof a Modula-2 program is extracted automatically which meets the specification. *PROSPECTRA Report [M.1.1.A3-R-27.0]*

[19] Bernd Krieg-Brückner: *Algebraic Formalisation of Program Development by Transformation.*
Date: 88-02.
Summary: A uniform treatment of algebraic specification is proposed to formalise data, programs, transformation rules, and program developments. It is shown by example that the development of an efficient transformation algorithm incorporating the effect of a set of transformation rules is analogous to program development: the transformation rules act as specifications for the transformation algorithms.
In: H.Ganzinger (ed.): Proc. ESOP'88 (European Symposium On Programming) LNCS 300. (1988) pp. 34-48

[20] Bernd Krieg-Brückner: *The PROSPECTRA Methodology of Program Development.*
Date: 88-01.

Summary: A methodology for PROgram development by SPECification and TRAnsformation is described. Formal requirement specifications in Anna are the basis for constructing correct and efficient Ada programs by gradual transformation. As an example, the development of a monitor for priority queues is included.
In: Zalewski (ed.): Proc. of IFIP/IFAC Working Conf. on Hardware and Software for Real-Time Process Control. (Warsaw, 1988) North-Holland.

[21] Bernd Gersdorf: *Context Sensitive Transformations in Applicative Style.* **Date**:88-09.
Summary: For realistic transformations it is necessary to have access not only to the subtree that is matched by the left hand side, but also to informations in the rest of the program, the context information. In the traditional transformation area this access is done using attributes. Some methods to cope with context information in applicative languages will be discussed.
PROSPECTRA Report [M.1.1.S3-DP-41.0]

[22] Zhenyu Qian: *Relation-Sorted Algebraic Specification with Built-in Coercers: Parameterisation and Parameter Passing.* **Date:** 88-09.
Summary: A notion of relation-sorted (algebraic) specification (with built-in coercers) has been introduced recently in [KQ 88]. A relation-sorted specification SPEC consists of a signature, a set of equations and an arbitrary relation on the sorts. If two sorts are related: s → s', then a function C: As → As' is assumed as a component of a relation-sorted SPEC-algebra A.
The parameterisation of the relation-sorted specifications can be considered as a simple extension of the many-sorted parameterisation by ADJ-group. For the parameter passing, we introduce a notion of coordinate parameter passing, which considers the union of single parameter passings of the same parameterised specification and extends the sort relation conservatively and monotonically as much as possible. Conservativity means that the relation extension introduces no new →* path from sorts in the actual parameter specification to new generated sorts. Monotonicity means that each relation extension s → s' is made only when the sorts constructing s are related by →* path to the sorts constructing s'. For discussing the semantics of coordinate parameter passing considering multiple declarations of functions, the notion of regular parameterised specification is introduced.
The results obtained here can also apply to order-sorted specification by Goguen et al., since our notion of specification is more general than that of the order-sorted specification.
PROSPECTRA Report [M.1.1.S3-SN-43.0]

[23] Hans-Jörg Kreowski, Zhenyu Qian: *Relation-Sorted Algebraic Specification with Built-in Coercers: Basic Notions and Results.* **Date:** 88-12.
Summary: A relation-sorted specification SPEC with built-in coercers is, syntactically seen, quite similar to an order-sorted specification in the sense if Goguen et al., i.e. SPEC consists of a signature, a set of equations and an arbitrary relation → on the sorts. But our notion of SPEC-algebras is more general. In particular, if two sorts are in the sort relation: s → s', then we assume that, in each SPEC-algebra A, the corresponding carriers As and As' are related by an operator c: As → As', which is considered as a component of A, rather than by inclusion As ⊆ As', as required in order-sorted algebras. This allows us to map a sort into a sort and simultaneously forget about some aspects as it occurs in object-oriented programming. Although our approach is more general than order-sorted specification, we get similar results, e.g. concerning the construction of initial algebras and a complete deduction system. Our approach provides a general foundation for considering subtypes not only as subsets, but also as subclasses as they occur in the areas of object-oriented, higher-order and algebraic process specifications.
In: Proc. 7th Symposium on Theoretical Aspects of Computer Science, Springer LNCS 415. (1990) pp. 156-176.

[24] Zhenyu Qian: *Relation-Sorted Algebraic Specification with Built-in Coercers: Parameterisation and Parameter Passing.* **Date:** 88-09.
Summary: A notion of relation-sorted (algebraic) specification (with built-in coercers) has been introduced recently in [M.1.1.S3-R-44.0]. A relation-sorted specification SPEC consists of a signature, a set of equations and an arbitrary relation → on the sorts. If s → s' for two sorts s,s', then an operator c: As → As' is assumed in any relation-sorted SPEC-algebra A.
While the parameterisation for relation-sorted specifications can be considered as a simple extension of that for many-sorted specifications, a notion of coordinate parameter passing is for the parameter passing. Coordinate parameter passing considers the greatest conservative, monotonic extension of the relation between the sorts of different value specifications of the same parameterised specification. Conservativity

means that the extension introduces no new →* path from sorts in the actual parameter specification to new generated sorts. Monotonicity means that each relation extension s → s' is made only when the sorts constructing s are related by →* path to the sorts constructing s'. For discussing the semantics of coordinate parameter passing considering multiple declarations of functions, a notion of regular parameterised specification is introduced.
The results obtained here can also apply to order-sorted specification by Goguen et. al., since our notion of specification is more general than that of the order-sorted specification.
In: H. Ehrig, H. Herrlich, H.-J. Kreowski, G. Preuß (eds.) Proc. Categorical Method in Computer Science with Aspects from Topology, Berlin, Sept. 1988. Springer LNCS 393, (1989), pp.244-260

[25] Bernd Krieg-Brückner: *Transformational Meta Program Development.* **Date:** 88-12.
Summary: The ESPRIT project PROgram development by SPECification and TRAnsformation is based on the CIP approach. Its most distinguishing feature is perhaps the use of algebraic specification and the transformational development paradigm not only for program but also for meta-program development, in fact to formalised the program development process itself. Transformation rules and their applicability conditions act as requirement specifications for transformation algorithms.
The extension of algebraic specification by higher order functions leads to a considerable increase in abstraction, avoiding much repetitive development effort. Homomorphic extension functionals, in particular, allows a concentration on the essential basic functions. Compared with classical functional programming, the algebraic properties allow reasoning about correctness and optimisation; the recursive schema of homomorphic extension acts as a program development strategy and as an induction schema for proofs.
In: Festschrift zum 65. Geburtstag von F.L. Bauer, Springer-Verlag Berlin-Heidelberg-New York. For an extended version of this document, see [26].

[26] Bernd Krieg-Brückner: *Algebraic Specification and Functionals for Transformational Program and Meta Program Development.* **Date:** 88-12.
Summary: The methodology for PROgram development by SPECification and TRAnsformation is described. Formal requirement specificaitons are the basis for constructing correct and efficient programs by gradual transformation.
A uniform treatment of algebraic specification is presented to formalise data, programs, transformation rules, in fact the program development process itself. It is shown by example that the development of meta programs, for example an efficient transformation algorithm incorporating the effect of a set of transformation rules, is analogous to program development: the transformation rules act as specifications for the transformation algorithms, and the negation of their applicability conditions as development goals.
The paper focusses on the combination of functional programming and algebraic specification and reasoning, leading to a considerably higher degree of abstraction, avoiding much repetitive development effort. the use of homomorphic extension functionals, homomorphic properties for reasoning about correctness and optimisation, and the recursive schema of homomorphic extension acts as a program development strategy and as an induction schema for proofs.
In: Proc. TAPSOFT '89 (Barcelona), LNCS 352, Springer. (1989) pp. 36-59.

[27] Bernd Krieg-Brückner: *Algebraic Specification with Functionals in Program Development by Transformation.* **Date:** 89-06.
Summary: The methodology of PROgram development by SPECification and TRAnsformation is described. Formal requirement specifications are the basis for constructing correct and efficient programs by gradual transformation. The power of compact development methods using the transformational approach, as supported by the PROSPECTRA system, is illustrated by an example. The algebraic specification language is then described, focussing on its extension by higher order functions. The functional programming paradigm leads to a considerably higher degree of abstraction and avoids much repetitive development effort, in particular through the use of homomorphic extension functionals. The combination with algebraic specification not only allows reasonsing about correctness but also permits direct optimisation transformations.
In: Proc. ESPRIT Conf.'89 (Brussels) 1989.

[28] Bernd Krieg-Brückner (Editor): *PROgram development by SPECification and TRAnsformation: Part I-The Methodology.* **Date:** 90-04.
Summary: This is a tutorial introduction to the methodology used in the PROSPECTRA Project, in fact an introduction to the whole project.

Part I of this volume.
PROSPECTRA Report [M.1.1.S3-R-55.4]

[29] Bernd Krieg-Brückner (Editor): *PROgram development by SPECification and TRAnsformation: Part II-The Language Family.* **Date:** 90-04.
Summary: This is an overview of the PROSPECTRA language family. It gives a rationale for the relationship between the languages explains briefly what they are there.
Part II of this volume.
PROSPECTRA Report [M.1.1.S3-R-56.4]

[30] Bernd Krieg-Brückner (Editor): *PROgram development by SPECification and TRAnsformation: Part III-The System.* **Date:** 90-04.
Summary: This is an overview of the PROSPECTRA System. It gives a rationale for the structure, explains briefly what the components do and why they are there.
Part III in this volume.
PROSPECTRA Report [M.1.1.S3-R-57.4]

[31] Zhenyu Qian: *Higher-Order Order-Sorted Algebras.* **Date:** 89-09-00.
Summary: The aim of this paper is to provide a simple algebraic semantics for programming or specification languages. Compared with the well-known framework of order-sorted algebras, this semantics has the extra features of parametric polymorphism and higher-orderedness. Compared with the well-known framework of lambda-calculus-based models for type systems, this semantics has the extra features of higher-order equational deduction, type construction and partial functions. The new approach unifies higher-orderedness, ad hoc, parametric and subtype polymorphism, equational deduction, type constructions and partial functions in a single consistent framework.
In Proc. 2nd Conference on Algebraic and Logic Programming, Nancy, France, LNCS 463, (1990), pp. 86-100.

[32] Bernd Gersdorf: *Translating Context-Sensitive Transformations into SSL* **Date:** 89-12-12.
Summary: This document describes the style of transformations written in PAnndA-S that can be translated to SSL using the translator of the PROSPECTRA system release of the final review. It is a self contained update of a paper that can be found in the reference list ([1]). The new things are an extension that allows context sensitive transformations ([2]), an interface to the parameter editor, a support for transformation modules and overloading.
Superseded by [30], Chap. 6.2
PROSPECTRA Report [M.1.1.S3-R-64]

[33] Yulin Feng, B.Krieg-Brückner: *Conceptual Modelling for Software Requirements Analysis*
Date: 89-00-00.
Summary: The methodology of conceptual modelling is introduced in this paper to validate the requirements specification during the early stage of software development . A conceptual model gives insight into the applications and captures the main characteristics of user´s needs. This paper contributes to propose a kind of model description language which is subtle to understand, and to illustrate the conceptual modelling approach having the following features: (1) it can be used to describe the real world semantics incrementally by communicating between the developer and the user. (2) it has a mathematical basis for validating qualitative features, such as consistency, safety and liveness poperties etc. (3) it can be considered as a start point in formal development of software engineering. It has been proved that the conceptual modelling approach could be elegantly applied for the requirements analysis so as to narrow the gap between an informal problem statement and the development based on formal specification and transformation.
PROSPECTRA Report [M.1.1.S3-R-65.0]

[34] Yulin Feng, Junbo Liu : *Temporal Approach to Algebraic Specifications .* **Date:** 90-02-00.
Summary: The paper is contributed to make connections between models for algebraic and temporal specifications. It brings a different viewpoint for classical algebras and algebraic specifications. Every algebra we concern here is finitely generated and associate with an implicit transition structure. The operators in the algebra may be partially defined. The class of algebras could be used as Kripke semantic models to interpret the temporal, so that we can do temporal reasoning about system behaviours such as safety and liveness properties. The unification of notions in algebraic and temporal secifications has many

advantages for system developments. We may use a formal temporal deduction system to verify some dynamic properties from premises of algebraic specifications; or a temporal requirement specification may be used to develop system in the style of top-down refinements. The nation of C-algebras has been crucial all along this work. We in this paper present the concepts, definitions and some basic theorems on C-algebras. Moreover, there exists a minimally defined algebra which is the initial one for each partially defined specification. An example of lift controller is finally used to illustrate how to reason about tomporal behaviours from an algebraic specification.
In: Proc. of Theories of Concurrency: Unification and Extention, LNCS 458, (1990), pp.216-229.

[35] Bernd Krieg-Brückner: *PROgam development by SPECification and TRAnsformation.* **Date:** 90-00-00.
Summary: The methodology of PROgram development by SPECification and TRAnsformation is described. Formal requirement specifications are the basis for constructing correct and efficient programs by gradual transformation. The power of compact development methods using the transformational approach, as supported by the PROSPECTRA system, is illustrated by an example. The algebraic specification language is then described, focussing on its extension by higher order functions. The functoinal programming paradigm leads to a considerably higher degree of abstraction and avoids much repetitive development effort, in particular through the use of homomorphic extension functionals. The combination with algebraic specification not only allows reasoning about correctness but also permits direct optimisation transformations.
In: Technique et Science Informatiques Special Issue on Software Engineering in ESPRIT (1990), pp. 136-149.

[36] Einar W. Karlsen,Bernd Krieg-Brückner, Owen Traynor: *The PROSPECTRA System: A United Development Framework.* **Date:** 91-00-00.
Summary: In the PROSPECTRA System, any kind of activity is conceptually and technically regarded as a transformation of a "program" in one of the system components. This provides for a uniform user interface, reduces system complexity, allows the construction of system components in a highly generative way, and is the basis for generalisation of specification, transformation, proof and development tactics, command language, even library access, and system configuration and development, into a single, unified framework. *To appear in: Theoretical Computer Science (Special Issue on the AMAST Conference).*
PROSPECTRA Report [M.1.1.S3-R-68.0]

M.1.3 Deductional Methodes

[37] Harald Ganzinger: *Ground Term Confluence in Parametric Conditional Equational Specifications.* **Date:** 86-08-18.
Summary: We consider the problem of Knuth-Bendix completion for specifications with conditional equations for the restricted case of proving confluence on ground terms. Inductive theorems about the initial model of the given specification will be used for proving the convergence of critical pairs. The theorems may have the form of arbitrary first-order formulas, allowing for expressing properties of the theory that could otherwise not be specified equationally. A Knuth-Bendix completion procedure will be given and demonstrated to be useful on examples which previous approaches fail to handle. Finally, an application of these ideas to parameterized specifications will be indicated.
In: Proc. of 4th Annual Symposium on Theoretical Aspects of Computer Science, Passau, F.R.G. LNCS 247, pp. 286-298, 1987.

[38] Harald Ganzinger: *A Completion Procedure for Conditional Equations: Proof of Correctness and Applications.* **Date:** 86-00-00.
Summary: The paper gives a proof of correctness for a Knuth-Bendix-like completion procedure for conditional equations. Due to the notion of contextual rewriting, a generalized form of conditional rewriting, more specifications can be completed. Moreover, a variant of the procedure which makes use of additionally given covering constraints (disjunctions of equations) ground-completes specifications. Applications include modular completion of structured specifications and a complete decision procedure for an interesting class of conditional equations.
Superseded by [41].
PROSPECTRA Report [M.1.3-SN-2.0]

[39] Hubert Bertling, Harald Ganzinger: *A Collection of Examples to demonstrate CEC.* **Date:** 86-00
Superseded by [44]
PROSPECTRA Report [M.1.3-SN-3.0]

[40] Hubert Bertling, Harald Ganzinger, Renate Schäfers: *CEC - A System for Conditional Equational Completion - User Manual (Version 0.5).* **Date:** 87-10.
Summary: CEC is a rewrite rule laboratory for conditional equations. This manual describes its use assuming the user to be familiar with the basic notions in conditional term rewriting.

Superseded by [43]
PROSPECTRA Report [M.1.3-SN-4.0]

[41] Harald Ganzinger: *A Completion Procedure for Conditional Equations.* **Date:** 88-11-28.
Summary: The paper presents a new completion procedure for conditional equations. The work is based on the notion of the reductive conditional rewriting. The procedure has been designed to also handle nonreductive equations that are generated during completion. The paper in particular presents techniques for simplification of conditional equations and rules, so that the procedure terminates on more specifications. The correctness proofs which form a substantial part of this paper employ recursive path orderings on proof trees, an extension of the ideas of Bachmair, Dershowitz and Hsiang to the conditional case.
In: Proc. 1st Int' l Workshop on Conditional Term Rewriting, Orsay, LNCS 308, pp. 62-83, 1987.
A revised version to appear in: Journal of Symbolic Computation

[42] Harald Ganzinger: *Completion with History-Dependent Complexities for Generated Equations.*
Date: 88-03 .
Summary: The paper presents a new system of inference rules for the completion of conditional equations. Nonconvergent conditional equations that are generated during completion can either be oriented into reductive rewrite rules or considered as nonoperational. Rewrite rules are, as usual, subject to critical pair computation. Nonoperational equations are superposed by the rewrite rules on one of their conditions. A conditional equation can be eliminated if there is also a proof of the equation which is simpler than the equation itself. The purpose of this paper is to present a technique for convergence proofs in which the origin of an equation defines the complexity bound which alternative proofs must respect. This technique is shown to be particularly useful in the conditional case, making the completion process terminate on a number of nontrivial specifications which it would fail to terminate otherwise.
In: Proc. " Recent Trends in Data Type Specification", D. Sannella, A. Tarlecki (Eds.) LNCS 332. pp. 73-91, 1988.

[43] Hubert Bertling, Harald Ganzinger, Renate Schäfers: *CEC: A System for Conditional Equational Completion-User Manual (Version 1.0).* **Date:** 88-03 .
Summary: This user manual corresponds to the new version 1.0 of the CEC system. It is a new version of [M.1.3-SN-4.0] that incorporates all changes to the CEC - Version 0.5 and the new features of CEC - Version 1.0. The theoretical foundations of version 1.0 can be found in [M.1.3-SN-5.0] and [M1.3.-R-6.0]. *PROSPECTRA Report [M.1.3-R-7.0]*

[44] Hubert Bertling, Harald Ganzinger, Renate Schäfers: *A Collection of Specifications completed by CEC-system.* **Date:** 88-03 .
Summary: This report contains a collection of explained examples, which cover most of the CEC (Version 1.0) offered features.
PROSPECTRA Report [M.1.3-R-8.0]

[45] Harald Ganzinger: *Order-Sorted Completion: The Many-Sorted Way.* **Date:** 88-09.
Summary: Order-sorted specifications can be transformed into equivalent many-sorted ones by using injections to implement subsort relations. In this paper we first improve some of the results of Goguen / Jouannaud / Meseguer on the subject. In particular we prove that to any sort-decreasing and canonical system of order-sorted conditional rewrite rules there exists an equivalent canonical system of rewrite rules over the corresponding many-sorted signature. We then review the latest techniques in completion of many-sorted conditional equations and demonstrate how these can be successfully applied to systems obtained from translating order-sorted sources. In particular we show that this way one can overcome the problems with non-sort-decreasing rules in some cases. In other cases, completion will not terminate due to the unability of proving a complex type property at completion time. For these cases we prove that any non-

sort-decreasing rule can be replaced by a sort-decreasing rule with one additional condition without changing the initial algebra of the specification. The additional condition transfers the type check from completion-time to rewrite-time. The new rules also have extra variables on the right side of the consequent. Yet, an appropriately tailored completion procedure guarantees that rewriting will still be efficient.
In: Proc. TAPSOFT '89 (Barcelona), LNCS 351, pp. 244-258 Springer 1989.

[46] Marisa Navarro, Fernando Orejas, Jean-Luc Remy: *Contextual Rewriting as a sound and complete method for conditional LOG-Specifications.* **Date:** 88-09.
Summary: We present a class of conditional specifications, named LOG-specifications, that increase the expressive power of usual conditional ones, while they do not imply a loss of implementability of the associated deductive tools. Associated to the class of models of these specifications, we introduce the deductive system L, proving its soundness and completeness. Then, we present contextual rewriting as the adequate rewriting method for LOG-specifications, since we show that, under adequate assumptions of confluence and finite termination, contextual rewriting is a complete deductive method for this class of specifications.
PROSPECTRA Report [M.1.3b-R-10.1]

[47] F. Orejas, A. Sanchez, M. Navarro, P.Nivela, M.Peña: *Term rewriting methods for partial specifications.* **Date:** 88-09.
Summary: Transparencies of the presentation at the 6th workshop on Abstract Data Types (West Berlin). A procedure for computing definedness of terms for partial specifications with existential equality is presented. Problems when dealing with explicit definability and conditional equations are shown. A solution to these problems is sketched.
PROSPECTRA Report [M.1.3b-R-11.0]

[48] H. Bertling, H. Ganzinger: *Completion-Time Optimization of Rewrite-Time Goal Solving.* **Date:** 88-12.
Summary: Completion can be seen as a process that transforms any proof in an initially given equational theory to a rewrite proof in an equivalent final set of rewrite rules. Rewrite proofs can be regarded as the normal forms of proofs under these proof transformations. The purpose of this paper is to provide a framework in which one may further restrict the normal forms of proofs which completion is required to construct, thereby further decreasing the search space for proofs in completed systems.
PROSPECTRA Report [M.1.3-R-12.0]

[49] Pilar Nivela, Fernando Orejas, Ricardo Pena, Ana Sanchez: *Term rewriting techniques for positive partial specifications.* **Date:** 89-02-05.
Summary: Deduction by means of term rewriting it is studied for positive partial specifications, i.e. partial conditional specifications with existential equations on conditions and strong and existential equations on consequences. It is shown that the usual rewriting techniques work without problems for partial specifications, as far as some method for computing definedness is available. Then, a completion like method for aims is developed, showing its completeness.
PROSPECTRA Report [M.1.3-R-14.0]

[50] Harald Ganzinger, Renate Schäfers: *System Support for Modular Order-Sorted Horn Clause Specifications.* **Date:** 89-09.
Summary: This paper presents an overview of CEC --- a rewrite rule laboratory for order-sorted specifications with conditional equations. CEC differs from related systems such as OBJ-3 in that it can check, or achieve by completion, the semantic prerequisites for correct operational execution of specifications by conditional term rewriting.
CEC supports the modular structure of specifications in two ways. Its specification browser allows to access, edit and administrate the modules of a specification through a highly interactive user interface. The completion procedure, apart from transforming a specification into executable rewrite code, will find the inconsistencies, if any, between the formal and actual parameters of generic specifications. CEC can handle a large class of conditional equations with extra variables in the condition without having to resort to inefficient goal solving methods at rewrite-time.
In: Proc. of the 12th International Conference on Software Engineering, Nice, France, IEEE Computer Society Press, pp. 150-163, 1990

[51] Hubert Bertling, Harald Ganzinger: *Knuth-Bendix Completion Of Horn Clause Programs For Restricted Linear Resolution And Paramodulation.* **Date:** 90-02.
Summary: We present a Knuth-Bendix completion technique which is able to transform a given Horn clause program so that restrictions of the linear resolution/paramodulation calculus may become refutation complete. A class of restrictions for which completion succeeds in any case will be characterized. For other restrictions it may fail. We distinguish two kinds of refutation completeness, completeness w.r.t. the theory and completeness w.r.t. the ground theory of a specification. Dependent on what kind of completeness we want to achieve we apply different completion methods which we call completion and ground completion, respectively.
To appear in: Proc. of the 2nd International Workshop on Conditional and Typed Rewriting Systems, Montreal, 1990
PROSPECTRA Report [M.1.3-R-17.0]
[52] M.Navarro, F.Orejas: *Parametrized Conditional Log-Specifications: Proof Theory and Correctness.* **Date:** 89-04-00.
Summary: Conditional LOG-specifications extend standard conditional specifications in that the booleans are considered to be built-in. Formally, there is an initial constraint on booleans in every specification. It is shown that this allows to handle situations that could not be dealt within the standard approach. Moreover, it is shown that the usual techniques and results, including proof-theoretical characterizations, for usual parameterized specifications translate without problems to LOG-specifications, though the proofs are often quite different. To end, it must be said that in a previous paper it was proved that contextual rewriting provides a complete proof method for conditional LOG-specifications assuring the applicability of the approach.
PROSPECTRA Report [M.1.3b-R-17.0]

[53] Hubert Bertling, Harald Ganzinger, Renate Schäfers: *CEC A System to Support Modular Order-Sorted Specifications with Conditional Equations", User Manual (Version 1.5).* **Date:** 89-09.
Summary: This is a new CEC user manual which differs from the old one in two major aspects: it documents new features of the CEC-system as there are, completion of order-sorted specifications, quasi-reductive rewrite rules, a module concept, system interaction modi, etc. Additionally, the readability of the manual is improved: Instead of small examples, the manual contains now the specification of a quicksort algorithm and a protocol of its completion.
PROSPECTRA Report [M.1.3-R-18.0]

[54] Navarro, M., Nivela, P. Orejas, F., Sanchez, A.: *On Translating Partial to Total Specifications -- With Application to Theorem Proving for Partial Specifications.* **Date:** 89-09.
Summary: In this paper it is shown how partial specifications (with strong equations) can be translated into total ones. This translation is proven to be sound and complete, in the sense that a theorem is valid for all models of the partial specification if and only if its translation is valid in all models of the total one. Specifications are assumed to include the booleans built-in.
The results obtained allow to use contextual rewriting as a proof method for partial specifications in which conditional equations are restricted to have in the premises only boolean terms or definedness conditions. The general case can only be handled with a generalization of contextual rewriting not yet developed. The results, applied to PAnndA-S, allow to handle the use of domain predicates with both weak and strong interpretations.
PROSPECTRA Report [M.1.3b-R-18.0]

[55] Leo Bachmair, H. Ganzinger: *On Restrictions of Ordered Paramodulation with Simplification.* **Date:** 90-02.
Summary: We consider a restricted version of ordered paramodulation, called strict superposition. We show that strict superposition (together with equality resolution) is refutationally complete for Horn clauses, but not for general first-order clauses. Two moderate enrichments of the strict superposition calculus are, however, sufficient to establish refutation completeness. This strictly improves previous results. We also propose a simple semantic notion of redundancy for clauses which covers most simplification and elimination techniques used in practice yet preserves completeness of the proposed calculi. The paper introduces a new and comparatively simple technique for completeness proofs based on the use of canonical rewrite systems to represent equality interpretations.
In: Proc. of the 10th International Conference on Automated Deduction, Kaiserslautern, West Germany, LNCS 449, pp. 427-441, 1990

[56] Leo Bachmair, H. Ganzinger: *Completion of First-order Clauses with Equality by Strict Superposition.* **Date:** 90-02.
Summary: We have previously shown that strict superposition, a restricted version of ordered paramodulation, is not refutationally complete for first-order clauses with equality. This was the motivation for two moderate, complete enrichments of the strict superposition calculus. In this paper we show that strict superposition when appropriately re-defined according to a slightly different ordering on clauses is in fact complete. The paper also presents an abstract framework for simplification and elimination of clauses. The framework gives general criteria for when simplification and elimination does not destroy the refutation completeness of an inference system. It allows to modularize the completeness proof for theorem proving procedures based on strict superposition and related calculi. Having powerful simplification mechanims available makes it possible that closing nontrivial sets of clauses under strict superposition terminates after a finite number of steps. The result is what is called a *complete* set of clauses. Refutation or solving of *goals* for complete sets of clauses is simpler than for arbitrary sets of clauses. The results which we will give here contain as special cases or generalize many known results about about ordered Knuth-Bendix-like completion of equations, of Horn clauses, of Horn clauses over built-in Booleans, and about contextual completion of first-order clauses.
To appear in: Proc. of the 2nd International Workshop on Conditional and Typed Term Rewriting, Montreal, 1990

[57] R.Nieuwenhuis, F. Orejas, A. Rubio: *A system for theorem proving by Clausal rewriting.*
Summary: Clausal rewriting is a deduction method for a subset of first order logic, called restricted equality clauses: general clauses without negative equality literals and with at most one positive one. Rewriting with complete systems of clausal rewrite rules provides a decision procedure for restricted equality clauses, whereas the clausal completion procedure is itself a refutationally complete proof procedure. Here the system implementing clausal rewriting and clausal completion is described.
PROSPECTRA Report [M.1.3b-R-19.0]

M.1.4 Development Examples

[58] Pedro de la Cruz: *An Algebraic Specification of the ABRACADABRA Protocol Using PAnndA-S.* **Date:** 88-10-25
Summary: A temptative algebraic specification of the FULL ABRACADABRA protocol, including user interaction, timeouts, and two-way simultaneous data tranfers, is presented. The specification is based on algebraically defined stream processing functions, and carried out using PAnndA-S, an algebraic specification language being developed as part of the ESPRIT project PROSPECTRA.

Superseded by [63]
PROSPECTRA Report [M.1.4.A1-R-1.0]

[59] Pedro de la Cruz: *A Comprehensive Example of PROSPECTRA.* **Date:** 88-11-06
Summary: An attempt to apply PROSPECTRAmethodology to a comprehensive example is presented, and some preliminary results reported. The selected example is a real-life system that exhibits concurrency, distribution and real-time communication. The main objectives of the project are gaining experience in application of PROSPECTRA to medium-to-large sized problems, investigating the adequate profile of a PROSPECTRA developer, and obtaining some insight into the kind of tools that could be useful in each phase of development. A partial first specification attempt is presented, some problems reported, and future work is outlined. The need of some methodology to decompose large specifications seems to the main result for the moment.
PROSPECTRA Report [M.1.4.A1-SN-2.0]

[60] Pedro de la Cruz: *Another Algebraic Specification of the ABRACADABRA Protocol Using PAnndA-S.* **Date:** 88-03 .
PROSPECTRA Report [M.1.4.A2-R-3.0]

[61] Pedro de la Cruz, Bernd Krieg-Brückner, Angel Perez Riesco: *From Algebraic Specifications to Correct Ada Programs: the ESPRIT Project PROSPECTRA.* **Date:** 88-03 .

Summary: The ESPRIT project PROSPECTRA is developing a methodology and an integrated support system for transforming axiomatic specifications into efficient Ada programs in a stepwise, reliable and reusable way.
In: A. Alvarez (Ed.): Proc. Ada Europe Conf.'89, Ada Companion Series, Cambridge University Press. (1989)

[62] J. M. Pinilla: *An Initial Specification of a Representation of 3D Object Topologies* **Date:** 90-03.
Summary: This document introduces an initial specification of a representation of 3D-object topologies. It presents the objects to be modeled and reviews ways to represent them. A requirements specification and a model specification is initiated that can be related to the requirements one. This specification has exercised the PROSPECTRA methodology and comments and critiques to it are also included.
PROSPECTRA Report [M.1.4.A2-PM-5.1]

[63] P.de la Cruz: *The ABRACADABRA Protocol Revisited.* **Date:** 90-04.
Summary: The specification of the ABRACADABRA Protocol in [M.1.4.A2-R-1.0] has been improved by using non-strict functions and infinite streams.
PROSPECTRA Report [M.1.4.A2-R-6.0]

M.2.1 Semantic Foundation of the Methodology

[64] Michael Breu, Manfred Broy, Thomas Grünler, Friederike Nickl: *PAnndA-S Semantics.*
Date: 89-06-30.
Summary: This document contains the definition of the PROSPECTRA specification language PAnndA-S which may be used at the early stages of a PROSPECTRA program development. It is a revised version of the PAnndA-S semantics which includes predicates and higher order functions.
Superseded by [29], Chap. 3.
PROSPECTRA Report [M.2.1.S1-SN-1.4]

[65] Friederike Nickl, Manfred Broy, Michael Breu, Frank Dederichs, Thomas Grünler: *Towards a Semantics of Higher Order Specifications in PAnndA-S.* **Date:** 88-09-07.
Summary: The semantics of first-order PAnndA-S is extended in order to specify higher order and nonstrict functions. Some theoretical foundations on higher order algebras are given.
Superseded by: [29], Chap. 3.
PROSPECTRA Report [M.2.1.S2-SN-2.0]

M.2.2 Algebraic Specification

[66] Manfred Broy: *The PROSPECTRA Methodology: A Course in 20 Lectures, Part A: Formal Specification.* **Date:** 86-11-24.
Summary: This document contains the transparencies of a course given at SESA in November, 1986. It will be the basis of a more detailed documentation of the PROSPECTRA Methodology.
Part B: Development Methodology is contained in PROSPECTRA Report [M.1.1.A3-R-22.0].
PROSPECTRA Report [M.2.2.S1-R-2.0]

[67] Thomas Grünler: *Basic Types for PAnndA-S.* **Date:** 88-03-31.
Summary: This paper is to serve as a reference for some often used abstract data types. It is also shown how one can prove formulas from the axioms.
PROSPECTRA Report [M.2.2.S2-SN-7.0]

[68] Frank Dederichs, Thomas Grünler: *Specifying Higher Order Functions: Some Examples.*
Date: 88-09-01.
Summary: Some examples are given to demonstrate the use of higher order functions in PAnndA-S.
PROSPECTRA Report [M.2.2.S2-SN-8.0]

[69] Friederike Nickl, Frank Dederichs, Manfred Broy, Michael Breu, Thomas Grünler: *Towards a Semantics of Higher Order Specifications in PA^{nn}dA-S* . **Date:** 88-09-07 .
Outdated. PROSPECTRA Report [M.2.2.S2-SN-9.0]

[70] Thomas Grünler: *Transformation of Terms Built up by Binary Infix Operators and Represented as Trees into Postfix Notation Represented as Sequences and their Evaluation.* **Date:** 89-01-20.
Summary: As an example for the stepwise development in PAnndA we translate a recursive evaluation procedure on trees into an equivalent interative one for sequences. In order to do so we first convert trees into sequences and refine the straightforward axioms lateron step by step.
PROSPECTRA Report [M.2.2.S3-SN-10.0]

[71] Michael Breu: *The PROSPECTRA Implementation Relation and Implementation Development* .
Date: 90-02-08.
Summary: Program development in the framework of PROSPECTRA is done by a stepwise transformation of specifications. A transformation is valid, if the resulting specification is in the implementation relation w.r.t. the starting specification. The implementation on the model level is defined via the existence of a weak homomorphism between algebras. Weak homomorpnisms are generalized to weakening homomorphisms that allow functions in the source algebra to return more defined results. This leads to the notion of robust implementations. A further generalization is the implementation of higher order algebras and specifications. In the methodological part, a development mothod from an abstract specification to an implementing speciification using weak homomorphisms in the framework of PAnndA-S is shown. The same method is then generalized to develop robust implementations, first by allowing more defined functions, then by using arbitrary weakening homomorphisms. The main aim in the presented methodology is the ability to carry out the development and the required correctnmess proofs in the framework of PAnndA-S.
Superseded by [28], Chap. 2.2
PROSPECTRA Report [M.2.2.S4-R-11.0]

72] Thomas Grünler: *Algebraic Specification in PAnndA-S.* **Date:** 90-02-08.
Summary: This paper describes the approach to algebraic specifications within the PROSPECTRA project. It serves as an introduction to the semantic concepts of PAnndA-S. We try to motivate the specialities of this specification language with the application of these features to examples.
Superseded by [28], Chap. 2.1
PROSPECTRA Report [M.2.2.S4-R-12.0]

M.2.3 Concurrency

[73] Frank Dederichs: *An Exercise in the Design of a Distributed System using PAnndA-S : The Lift Example.* **Date:** 89-01-23.
Summary: A general methodology for the design of distributed systems is described. By means of a specifc example it is shown, that it is not possible to follow this approach using PAnndA-S as specification language. The basic problems are named, some proposals for their solution are made.
PROSPECTRA Report [M.2.3.S3-SN-2.0]

[74] Thomas Grünler, Frank Dederichs: *Transforming Stream Processing Functions into Ada.*
Date: 89-08-24.
Summary: We demonstrate two methods for the transformation of stream processing functions, specified in a special form in PAnndA-S, into Ada tasks and illustrate these approaches by their application to the lift example and the example of the bounded buffer respectively.
PROSPECTRA Report [M.2.3.C1-SN-3.2]

[75] Rainer Weber: *Specifying Distributed Systems in the PROSPECTRA Project - An Introduction.*
Date: 90-02-08.
Summary: We show how distributed systems can be described on different levels of abstraction using the specification languages developed in the PROSPECTRA project. The underlying formalisms are streams and stream processing agents. In particular we treat the question how to use these description formalisms in a methodological sound way.

Superseded by [28], Chap. 1.3
PROSPECTRA Report [M.2.3.C1-R-4.0]

M.3.1 Basic Transformation Rules

[76] Stefan Kahrs: *From Constructive Specifications to Algorithmic Specifications*. **Date:** 86-11-05.
Summary: The term "specification" means algebraic specifications with conditional equations. Algorithmic specifications are very close to applicative programs but still without operational semantics. A specification is said to be constructive iff it can be transformed into an algorithmic specification by a given set of transformation rules. The problems are: (1) What is the target of the transformation process? (2) How can we approach the target step by step? (3) What are the applicability conditions for each step? (4) What is the transitive closure of applicability conditions? The answer to the last question gives the class of constructive specifications. The motivation for this kind of transformation is to approach the class of programs that are executable in ALGOL-like languages. The algorithmic specifications can be understood as applicative programs, so these transformation rules transform specifications to their prototypes.
PROSPECTRA Report [M.3.1.S1-SN-1.2]

[77] Bernd Gersdorf: *A Functional Language for Term Manipulations*. **Date:** 87-11-09.
Summary: This document describes a small functional language *ExTra* designed in the context of term transformation, where terms represent abstract syntax trees of programming languages. Some of the properties of this language are partial functions producing sets of solutions, special treatment of sequences and a (restricted) second order pattern matching with additional operators for building complex patterns.
PROSPECTRA Report [M.3.1.S1-SN-2.0]

S.1.1 Parser Generator

[78] Reinhold Heckmann: *An Efficient ELL(1) Parser Generator*. **Date:** 85-00.00.
Summary: The generation of table-driven predictive parsers from extended context-free grammars (containing abbreviation operators for expressing iteration, alternatives etc.) is described. Efficiency of the generation process and the generated parsers is investigated.
In: Acta Informatica 23, (1986) pp. 127-148

[79] Reinhold Heckmann: *Manual for the ELL(2) Parser Generator and Tree Generator Generator*.
Date: 86-08-26.
Summary: Regular right part grammars, extended by tree generator specifications, are interpreted by a combined parser generator and tree generator generator that produces an ELL(2) parser. This parser is able to translate programs of the specified language into abstract syntax trees according to the tree specifications in the generator input.
In: Tech. Bericht Nr. A 05/86, Fachbereich 10, Univ. of Saarland

S.1.2 System Data Structures

[80] León Treff, SYSTEAM: *The PROSPECTRA Tree Manager: Analysis and Specification*.
Date: 85-10-23.
Summary: The functional and structural aspects of the languages involved in the PROSPECTRA system are summarized. An overview is given on those tools of the PROSPECTRA system which will use the operations of a tree manager.
PROSPECTRA Report [S.1.2-R-1.2]

[81] Dolores Hinojal: *Read/Write Extended Format for CSG*. **Date:** 88-05-00.
Summary: This is the first version of the read and write extended format. The format is explained below. Some improvements have been done since the preliminary version in relation with the performance and it has been assured that the reevaluation of the attributes is not done.
PROSPECTRA Report [S.1.2.C1-SN-1.1]

S.1.3 Attribute Evaluator Generator

[82] Peter Badt, Ulrich Möncke, Peter Raber: *Attribuation Schemata for List-Structured Nodes.*
Date: 85-10-16.
Summary: If the abstract syntax trees to be manipulated by the OPTRAN system shall be extended to contain list-structured nodes, the conventional attribute grammar concept must be extended to cope with these nodes. A proposal is made, basing on the work of Jüllig. *Outdated.*
PROSPECTRA Report [S.1.3-R-1.0]

[83] Ulrich Möncke: *Grammar Flow Analysis.* **Date:** 86-03-01. **Date:** 87-01.
Summary: The theoretical basis for the implementation of different generators of the OPTRAN system is described. Grammar flow analysis transports the techniques of data flow analysis to the meta level of compiler construction. The analogon to the states in data flow analysis are the syntax trees and the information which is associated with trees by propagation functions. An example is the association of characteristic graphs, another example the association of sets of matching tree patterns.
PROSPECTRA Report [S.1.1-R-2.2]

[84] Ulrich Möncke: *Production-local Attributes.* **Date:** 86-03-01.
Summary: Local attributes (which are associated to productions instead of nonterminals) may be useful to describe the semantic dependencies and offer some chances for optimization of the attribute evaluation process. It is shown that local attributes fit nicely into the pass-oriented attribute evaluation scheme, as proposed by Ablas.
PROSPECTRA Report [S.1.3-SN-3.0]

[85] Peter Lipps, Ulrich Möncke, Matthias Olk, Reinhard Wilhelm: *Attribute (Re)evaluation in OPTRAN.*
Date: 87-01-29.
Summary: A transformation of a tree decorated according to some attribute grammar may leave the tree containing attribute inconsistencies. An attribute reevaluation algorithm computes new attribute values for affected attribute instances. It has to guarantee, that never an inconsistent attribute value is accessed. Reps' algorithm performs this task in time O(|affected region|). It is *data driven* as changed values trigger recomputations of attribute instances dependent on them. After each transformation, a complete update of the effected instances is performed. Reps' algorithm is compared with the data driven reevaluation scheme used in OPTRAN. It uses the same strategic information in the initial attribute evaluation and the reevaluation process. Furthermore, we present a *demand driven* scheme for attribute reevaluation. It does not have the linear time complexity for each update after one transformation but, depending on the situation, often compares favourably with the data driven scheme for series of transformations. In addition, the linear time complexity of the data driven reevaluation algorithm needs fast convergence using an equality test between old and new attribute values. It is thus necessary, to keep the attribute values at (almost) all instances. The demand-driven reevaluator does not need all the old attribute values. It can flexibly trade time for space. We also describe the handling of space consuming attributes, e.g. tables, lists, and trees, in the reevaluation algorithm. An integrated version of data driven and demand driven reevaluation using these features has been implemented in the OPTRAN system.
In: Acta Informatica 26, pp. 213-239, 1988.

[86] Peter Lipps, Ulrich Möncke, Reinhard Wilhelm: OPTRAN - *A Language/System for the Specification of Program Transformations: System Overview and Experiences.* **Date:** 88-10 ..
Summary: OPTRAN is a batch-oriented system for the generation of compilers that support program transformations. The specification language OPTRAN allows for a static and declarative description of tree transformations. Given such a specification, the system will automatically generate the transformation system, mainly consisting of an attribute evaluator and reevaluator, as will as a tree analyzer and transformer. The paper presents an introduction to the description mechanisms together with an overview of the system, showing the interaction of several generators. The main goal of the system is the usage of precomputation methods wherever possible. This generative approach is explained. The static view of transformations makes it possible to generate highly efficient transformers but also has its limitationsm which we mention.
In: D.Hammer(Ed.) Proc.Workshop on Compiler-Compilers and Highspeed Compilation, 1988, Springer-Verlag, LNCS 371, pp. 52-65.

[87] Andreas V. Hense, Reinhard Wilhelm: *Evaluation of Applicative Style Attributes Using Lazy Memo Functions.* **Date:** 89-01-29.
Summary: Attributes are defined in an applicative style, separated from the grammar definition. It is shown, how applicative style attributes can be evaluated efficiently. A modification of lazy memo functions is used for that purpose.
PROSPECTRA Report [S.1.3-DI-6.0]

S.1.4 Paraphraser (Generator)

[88] Hubert Bertling, Harald Ganzinger: *Paraphrasing in the PROSPECTRA System.* **Date:** 86-03-13.
Summary: A *paraphraser* is a function mapping internal program representations to the corresponding external representation on a display. This function is described as consisting of two parts: (1) Mapping the internal representation into a representation by boxes, (2) mapping boxes into terms over a signature of displayable objects. A framework for automatically composing these parts is proposed so that both parts can be modified independent of each other.
Outdated. PROSPECTRA Report [S.1.4-R-1.0]

S.1.5 Editor (Generator)

[89] Hubert Bertling, Harald Ganzinger: *A Structure Editor Based on Term Rewriting.* **Date:** 85-10-00.
Summary: An approach to structure editing based on the single concept of term rewriting is described. It is demonstrated that important editor functions such as *undo* can be easily provided in such a setting. It is furthermore argued that the algebraic approach to semantics has some nice consequences w.r.t. incremental re-evaluation of semantic values.
In: Proc. of the 2nd ESPRIT Technical Week, Cambridge University Press (1986), pp. 455-466.

[90] Rafael Gonzalez: *Conditional and Parameterized Transformations with CSG.* **Date:** 88-05-24.
Summary: A major difficulty defining transformations in SSL is the unsupported capability to specify semantic condintions on transformation patterns. Even more, for some complex transformations it is necessary to give some extra information at the application moment. This short note shows some aspects about the recently implemented conditional and parameterized transformations with CSG.
PROSPECTRA Report [S.1.5.C2-SN-2.0]

[91] Pedro de la Cruz, Rafael Gonzalez, M. Dolores Hinojal: *Conditional and Parameterized CSG Scripts.* **Date:** 88-09.
Summary: Until now, CSG scripts allowed recursive replay, but otherwise the execution of actions was entirely sequential. Also, CSG scripts were not parameterized. A facility for conditional branching and parameterized invocation has been added to CSG scripts. Also, syntax has been modified to make it closer to that of a functional language, and a facility for error recovery has been included.
PROSPECTRA Report [S.1.5.C2-SN-3.0]

[92] J.A.de Miguel: *CSG Scripts Language Reference Manual* **Date:** 90-03.
Summary: This is the Reference Manual for the CSG Scripts Language (CSL), designed and implemented in the course of the PROSPECTRA Project. CSL is a language to write batch command programs that work over CSG editors. CSL characteristics are carefully described here for users to have a quick and complete reference on language items.
PROSPECTRA Report [S.1.5.C2-R-9.0]

[93] P. de la Cruz, D. Hinojal, J. L. Mañas, J. A. de Miguel: *Context Sensitive Parsing in CSG Editors* **Date:** 90-03.
Summary: The inclusion in the syntax of TrafoLa-S of PAnndA phrases and embedded TrafoLa-S expressions produces a lot of parsing conflicts, because of the LALR(1) nature of the CSG parser. In [S.1.5.C2-SN-4.0] a method was presented to solve these problems by using attribute information. This document presents a new version of context sensititve parsing in CSG generated editors. The method has not changed from the one used in the first version. There are changes only at the implementation level and

in the way editors must be specified.
PROSPECTRA Report [S.1.5.C2-R-10.0]

S.1.6 Transformer Generator

[94] Michael Schmigalla, Alois Schütte, Beatrix Weisgerber: *OPTRAN Manual (in German).*
Date: 84-00-00.
Summary: The OPTRAN (OPtimizing TRANsformation) system generates attributing tree transformers for a specification of attributed trees and a set of transformation rules. The input language of the system is specified.
Superseded by [96].
PROSPECTRA Report [S.1.6-R-1.1]

[95] Ulrich Möncke, Beatrix Weisgerber, Reinhard Wilhelm: *Generative Support for Transformational Programming.* **Date:** 84-10-00.
Summary: The generative approach to programming is motivated, and the generators available in the OPTRAN system are described. Different levels of transformation descriptions are presented, ranging from single transformation rules to transformation scripts (with possibly complex interaction of rules). Solutions to implementation problems, and limitations are investigated.
In: Proc. of the 2nd ESPRIT Technical Week, Cambridge University Press (1986), pp. 511-528.

[96] Michael Greim, Stefan Pistorius, Monika Solsbacher, Beatrix Weisgerber: *POPSY and OPTRAN Manual* .**Date:** 87-01.
Summary: The current kernel of the PROSPECTRA Basic System, as available under Berkeley Unix 4.2 on the VAX is described: POPSY is a preprocessor for the generation of string-to-tree (LALR(1)) parsers, OPTRAN a generator for transformers of attributed trees. This description includes Interactive OPTRAN.
PROSPECTRA Report [S.1.6-R-3.1]

[97] Peter Badt, Ulrich Möncke, Peter Raber: *Specification of Recursive Patterns.* **Date:** 86-03-00.
Summary: The language OPTRAN (OPtimizing TRANsformations) shall be extended by recursive transformation rules in order to increase the comfort of the system and meet requirements of the PROSPECTRA methodology.
PROSPECTRA Report [S.1.6-SN-4.0]

[98] Ulrich Möncke: *Simulating Automata for Weighted Tree Reductions.* **Date:** 87-01-00.
Summary: Application of tree reduction are considered, where the Church-Rosser property cannot be expected to hold. Typically, each reduction rule applied has a cost associated with it. The cherpest reduction sequence for each given tree is looked for. In our approach, we allow the use of input and output patterns with parameters, leading to complex competition between patterns, and output patterns may be of arbitrary size.The main idea is to support the reduction time process as far as possible by generating efficient automata. *PROSPECTRA Report [S.1.6-SN-5.0]*

[99] Reinhold Heckmann: *A Proposal for the Syntactic Part of the PROSPECTRA Transformation Language.* **Date:** 87-02-17 .
Summary: After a short introduction into the problems of the current OPTRAN system, we shall propose more powerful patterns with type constraints and wild card to match tuples of arbitrary length and tree fragments (contexts) of arbitrary height. Then a syntax for a functional transformation language is proposed and finally, a complex transformation (removal of function calls) is described.
Superseded by [102]
PROSPECTRA Report [S.1.6-SN-6.0]

[100] Reinhold Heckmann: *Notes on TrafoLA, II, The Objects of the Transformation Language and the Operations upon Them.* **Date:** 87-05-19
Summary: This note tries to treat formally several features introduced in the Study Note "A Proposal for the Syntactic Part of the PROSPECTRA Transformation Language", referred to as [1] in the sequel. At first we consider values and the operations on them. The term fragments of the study note contained exactly one hole, this will be generalized. Different kinds of syntactic insertions (inserting values into holes of another

value) will be introduced, and their algebraic properties will be investigated. At last, we shall consider the number of partitions of a given term into an upper and a lower fragment.
At the end of this document, we give a summary of all definitions and theorems contained in it as a quick reference.
Superseded by [103] Also: Tech. Bericht Nr. A 08 / 87, Fachbereich 10, Univ. of Saarland.

[101] Reinhold Heckmann: *Notes on TrafoLA, III, Semantics of Patterns* **Date:** 87-06-03
Summary: In this note, we shall make a proposal for the syntax and semantics of patterns in the transformation language TrafoLa. First, we shall define and investigate semantic damains for patterns, and consider semantic equivalence of patterns. Finally, some subclasses of patterns e.g. linear patterns, will be introduced.
Also: Tech. Bericht Nr. A 09 / 87, Fachbereich 10, Univ. of Saarland
Superseded by [103]

[102] Reinhold Heckmann: *Notes on TrafoLA, IV, Revision of the Previous Work* **Date:** 87-10-05 .
Summary: Now our view of TrafoLa has been more consolidated, and we are able to revise some of the concepts introduced in the previous papers [1,2,3]. This paper contains the recent changes of the design of TrafoLa and the reasons for them. "New" TrafoLa is presented in another paper.
Superseded by [103]
PROSPECTRA Report [S.1.6-SN-9.2]

[103] Reinhold Heckmann: *Notes on TrafoLA, V. Syntax and Semantics of TrafoLa.* **Date:** 87-10-05
Summary: In this paper, syntax and semantics of some part of TrafoLa are formally presented.
PROSPECTRA Report [S.1.6-SN-10.0]

[104] Jürgen Börstler, Ulrich R. Möncke, Reinhard Wilhelm: *Table Compression for Tree Automata.*
Date: 87-11-10.
Summary: The compression of bottom up tree automata and their representations as implemented in the OPTRAN tree transformation system is described as a four step process. First, the vertically working tree automata traversing one generation in one step are replaced by horizontally working automata splitting this step into arity(operator). This replaces the matrix of dimension arity(operator) by a tree of depth arity(operator). A second step replaces this tree by a shortened DAG, i.e. a DAG where "equivalent" states of the tree are identified and paths in the tree with no gain in information are condensed. The structure of the automaton is not changed. The third step embeds the DAG, which is naturally represented by 2-dimensional tables into a linear array using row displacement and row columns schemes. In addition, this step compresses strings of consecutive identical entries which occur often in this type of automaton. The last step exploits the memory structure and addressability of the target machine. Using automata and table sizes the most efficient storage representation is selected. The data structures and access functions are generated as C objects and functions, resp. Numbers about the effects of the different steps are given.
In: ACM Transaction on Programming Languages and Systems 13(3), 295-314, 1991.

[105] Reinhold Heckmann: *A Functional Language for the Specification of Complex Tree Transformations.*
Summary: Transformations of trees and rewriting of terms can be found in various settings e.g. transformations of abstract syntax trees in compiler construction and program synthesis. A language is proposed combining features of a general purpose functional language with special means to specify tree transformations. Atomic transformations are considered first order functions and described by pattern matching. The pattern specification language allows for partitioning trees by arbitrary vertical and horizontal cuts. This goes beyond what is possible in similar languages (HOPE, ML, and Miranda). High order functions and functional combinators are used to express strategies for the controlled application of transformations.
In: Ganzinger (Ed.) ESOP'88, Springer-Verlag's LNCS 300, 1988.

[106] Reinhold Heckmann: *Language Reference Manual of TrafoLa-H, Version 1.5.* **Date:** 88-09-05.
Summary: Relational TrafoLa-H is a language where each expression may have several or even infinitely many values, and each 'function' may produce many results. Its functional predecessor was developed to ease the specification of complex tree transformations starting from a usual functional language similar to HOPE or ML. The non-determinism resulting from its complex patterns was the reason to turn the

functional language into a relational one.
Superseded by [110]. PROSPECTRA Report [S.1.6-R-14.0]

[107] Reinhold Heckmann: *User Manual for the TrafoLa-H-ML System ,Version 1.5.* **Date:** 88-09-05.
Summary: The backtracking version of TrafoLa-H is a relational language where each expression may have several or even infinitely many values, and each 'function' may produce many results. An interpreter for this language was written in Standard ML with a front end in C. This paper describes the usage of the interpreter. *Superseded by [110].*
PROSPECTRA Report [S.1.6-R-15.0]

[108] Martin Alt, Christian Fecht, Christian Ferdinand: *Design of a TrafoLa Compiler.* **Date:** 89-01.
Summary: Experiences with the two existing Trafola-H interpreters [Alt: A Prototype Of A Transformation Language..., Heckmann: User Manual for the Trafola-H-ML System] have shown the need for a compiler to efficiently implement the language. The compiler generates code for an abstract machine based on the MaMa (Maschine Maurer) [Maurer,Wilhelm: MaMa]. This machine - Trama - differs from MaMa in the evaluation mechanism (Trafola uses call-by-value) and supports pattern matching for Trafola patterns. A typechecker will help to debug programs and enables the generation of optimized code (no runtime typechecking). The compiler includes a tree parser generator for efficient matching of special complex patterns.
PROSPECTRA Report [S.1.6-R-17.0]

[109] Georg Sander: *Proposal for a Type Discipline in Trafola-H, Types and their Semantics.*
Date: 89-01.
Summary: A type discipline for TRAFOLA-H is developed. It is based on Milner's theory of type polymorphism. This theory is extended with respect to the complex operations and patterns provided by TRAFOLA-H: a new type constructor is introduced to deal with insertion and extraction of subtrees; the concept of type versions leads to a new kind of polymorphism. A formal semantics of the type system is given together with proofs of basic properties.
PROSPECTRA Report [S.1.6-R-18.0]

[110] Reinhold Heckmann: *Updates and Extensions to the Description of the TrafoLa-H-ML System, Version 1.7.* **Date:** 89-02-16.
Summary: This paper describes changes of the TrafoLa-H-ML system since the review at Madrid in Sept. 1988 (version 1.5) up to version 1.7.
PROSPECTRA Report [S.1.6-R-19.0]

[111] Reinhold Heckmann: *Integration of CSG generated editors with the TrafoLa-H interpreter.*
Date: 89-02-17
Summary: Now, it is possible to join the TrafoLa-H interpreter (version 1.7) with CSG generated editors. Transformations written in TrafoLa-H may be called from within the editor and applied to the selected subterm. The TrafoLa-H interpreter completely runs in the background. Its interactions with the external world are all controlled by the editor.
PROSPECTRA Report [S1.6-R-20.0]

[112] Reinhold Heckmann: *Inversion of Functions.* **Date:** 89-03-13.
Summary: Finding an algorithm for the inverse of an explicitly given function is important for program and data type development. We informally present a method to derive an algorithm for the inverse from algorithms for given functions.
PROSPECTRA Report [S1.6-SN-21.0]

[113] Georg Sander: *Type Checking in TrafoLa-H: General View.* **Date:** 89-09-13.
Summary: This paper is the description of the current type checker of TRAFOLA-H. It is not the finalized version (that will be perhaps more efficient in time and space), but is implemented in one of our actual TRAFOLA systems. The type discipline is based on Milner's theory of type polymorphism. This theory is extended with respect to the complex operations and patterns provided by TRAFOLA-H (fragment type and type versions). The paper presents a general view of the type checker and its implementation.
PROSPECTRA Report [S1.6-DI-21.0]

[114] Martin Alt, Christian Fecht, Christian Ferdinand: *The Trafola-H Compiler.* **Date:** 89-09-13.
Summary: The following paper is a short description of the Trafola-H compiler developed at the Universität des Saarlandes. It contains a guide how to install the compiler and describes the current version of the Trafola-H language, i.e. the concrete syntax, system commands, known bugs and so on. At last, we present an abstract machine for the implementation of Trafola-H and an alternative way for pattern matching using a tree pattern matcher.
PROSPECTRA Report [S1.6-SN-22.0]

[115] Reinhold Heckmann: *Set Domains.* **Date:** 90-01-30,
Summary: Set domains are intended to give semantics to a data type of sets together with a wide range of useful set operations. The classical power domain constructions are shown to be inappropriate for this purpose. Lower and upper domain do not support quantification, whereas Plotkin's domain does not contain the empty set. This is an immense defect, since the empty set is not only interesting in its own, but is also needed to define operations such as filtering a set through a predicate. Two constructions, the big and the small set domain, are proposed that support the desired set operations. The big domain is bounded complete, whereas the small one only respects Plotkin's SFP-property. Both constructions are free with respect to suitable algebraic theories.
In: Proc. European Symposium on Programming (ESOP), LNCS 432, Springer-Verlag, pp. 177-196

[116] Reinhold Heckmann: *Power Domains and Second Order Predicates.* Date: 90-02-07,
Summary: The Plotkin power domain over some ground domain D and two more recent power domain constructions, the big and the small set domain, are all isomorphic to subdomains of the space of continuous second order predicates over D. The big set domain is isomorphic to the space of those predicates that are linear wrt. disjunction. The isomorphic images of the remaining two domains are characterized by additional axioms concerning conjunction and negation.
PROSPECTRA Report [S.1.6-SN-25.0]

[117] Reinhard Wilhelm: *Tree Transformations, Functional Languages, and Attribute Grammars.*
Date: 90-09.
Summary: The role of attribute grammars and functional programming languages in program transformation tools is studied. Starting from our own experiences with designing and implementing two such tools, the OPTRAN transformer generator and the finctional language TrafoLa, we compare those with other systems, e.g. the Cornell Synthesizer Generator and the Flagship tuples environment. Some design hints are derived from this comparison.
In: P.Deransart, M. Jourdan(Eds.), Proc. Attribute Grammars and their Application (WAGA 90), LNCS 461, Springer-Verlag, pp. 116-129.

[118] Christian Ferdinand: Pattern Matching in a Functional Transformation Language using Treeparsing.
Date: 90-08. .
Summary: This article descrinbes the techniques used for the implementation of pattern matching in TrafoLa-H, a functional tarnsformation language. TrafoLa-H was designed to allow for very short and suggestive formulations of program transformations. Therefore, TrafoLa-H has a very powerful pattern language. There exist `distributed` patterns matching a set of subterms without fixed distances; patterns can match at arbitrary distance from the root of the whole term and anywhere in lists. These powerful language constructs requires special inplementation techniques. By transforming TrafoLa-H patterns into regular tree grammars, and generating fast bottom-up parsers, it is possible to match even complex patterns in times linear to the size of the term to be matched. After a short introduction of TrafoLa-H, the translation of patterns into possibly ambiguous regular tree grammars is presented, and the mechanism of variable binding is demonstrated.
In: P. Deransart, J. Maluszynski (Eds.), Proc. Programming Language Implementation and Logic Programming (PLILP 90), LNCS 456, Springer-Verlag, pp. 358-371

S.3.1 Ada/Anna Front End

[119] Steen Lynenskjøld: *PROSPECTRA System, A Guided Tour.* **Date:** 90-01-12.
Summary: This document is an update of the document used during ESPRIT technical week. The remaining parts of the system are included in the examples (proof, cec, trafolah, controla, method bank)

and the example (divmod) will be carried through with the transformation rules available (this was not the case at ESPRIT technical week, as we had to derive some `specialised' transformation rules in order to be able to show the development). I am currently writing the text which is to be in the document, but the examples can not be finalised before I have the remainding parts of the system. The document you will receive next week will therefore contain <placeholders> where I still have dependencies to the system. *PROSPECTRA Report [S.3.1.I-R-1.2]*

[120] Steen Lynenskjøld: *PROSPECTRA System, Maintenance Guide.* **Date:** 90-00-00.
Summary: Actually, this document is a revision of the "Guide to System Integration" document; but instead of containing guides of how to do it - it describes how it was done. Anyway, the actual contents will look a lot like the old document. This document can also only be finalised after the system has been frozen, since it will have to contain the actual choice of logical grouping, directory structure, etc. A draft version will be send next week.
PROSPECTRA Report [S.3.1.I-R-3.0]

[121] Steen Lynenskjøld: *PROSPECTRA System, Installation Guide.* **Date:** 1990
Summary: Describes how to install the PROSPECTRA System. This document will be approximately 4-5 pages, and exists currently as ASCII files which are delivered as part of the system. However, this document has to describe the relations to externally developed products (CSG, yacc ?!, prolog, ...) in some details. *PROSPECTRA Report [S.3.1.I-R-4.0]*

S.3.3 Transformers

[122] A. Lopez: *A Transformation from Arbitrary Logical Expressions to Clausal Form* . **Date:** 90-03.
Summary: This transformation is intended to be a first step for producing axiomatic design specifications from predicative requirement specifications. It takes an arbitrary logical expression, possibly including nested existential quantifiers, and produces a set of universally quantified general clauses by skolemization.
PROSPECTRA Report [S.3.3.C4-R-3.1]

[123] P.de la Cruz: *A transformation from PAnndA-S Axioms to TrafoLa-S Transformations.*
Date: 89-09.
Summary: It is impossible to write in TrafoLa-S, transformations corresponding to algebraic laws of user-defined abstract data types, because they must specify the keys of the involved functions, and these are in general unknown. This transformation takes a PA^{nn}dA-S package with axioms stating algebraic properties of the functions of a data type and produces a TrafoLa-S package containing transformations that perform the substitutions corresponding to the algebraic laws.
Superseded by [125].
PROSPECTRA Report [S.3.3.C4-SN-5.0]

[124] A. Lopez: *A Transformation from Specifications to Programs: Package Body generation.*
Date: 90-04.
Summary: Some specifications may be translated into imperative programs. This document explains which are the conditions the specification must fulfill and what is the resulting program.
PROSPECTRA Report [S.3.3.C4-R-6.1]

[125] P.de la Cruz: *Update to the transformation from PAnndA-S Axioms to TrafoLa-S Transformations.*
Date: 90-04-16.
Summary: The "Axiom-to-Trafo" transformation has been updated to use the "TP_NATURE" field in UNIQUE_NAME's for distinguishing among quantified variables and function names, instead of carrying a "mini-environment" along the transformation.
PROSPECTRA Report [S.3.3.C4-SN-7.1]

[126] A. Lopez: *Transformations on Logical Expressions.* **Date:** 90-03.
Summary: This document contains some transformations on PAnndA Logical Expressions.
PROSPECTRA Report [S.3.3.C4-R-8.0]

[127] A. Lopez: *Some Transformations on Prospectra Standard Types.* **Date:** 90-03.
Summary: Some transformations on Boolean and Integer expressions have been developed using the "Axiom-to-Trafo" transformation.
PROSPECTRA Report [S.3.3.C4-R-9.0]

S.3.4 Verifier

[128] David Duffy, Owen Traynor, Andrew D. McGettrick: *Specification of Requirements for the PROSPECTRA Verifier.* **Date:**88-10-31.
Summary: In this document we look at the types of theorem proving which will generally be undertaken within the confines of the PROSPECTRA development methodology. We them go on to consider the tools currently available to perform such theorem proving. We give a general description of the PROSPECTRA verifier and attempt to categorise its functionality, highlighting those areas which we feel will be most problematic.
PROSPECTRA Report [S.3.4-R-6.1]

[129] Xiaoyu Chen, Owen Traynor: *A Proof Editor For PAnndA-S Theories.* **Date:** 88-04-07.
Summary: In this document a prototype Proof system for PAnndA-S specifications is described. A mechanism by which PAnndA-S specifications can automatically be converted to theories for a Proof editing system is given. The Proof editing system used is the Interactive Proof Editor (IPE) developed at Edinburgh University.
PROSPECTRA Report [S.3.4-R-7.0]

[130] Owen Traynor: *A specification for a Cornell based proof editor for PROSPECTRA.* **Date:** 88-09.
Summary: This document gives a detailed description of a proof editor, based on the Cornell Synthesiser generator, for the PROSPECTRA system. The proof editor will be closed integrated with the program development system. An abstract syntax for proof is given together with a justification for its existence. The attributes required for proof computation are defined as is the calculus for the logic. This is developed within the transformation system as a transformation. Comments are made regarding the suitability of the specification language for defining an object such as a proof editor.
PROSPECTRA Report [S.3.4-SN-10.0]

[131] Owen Traynor: *Integrating Completion based proof generators into an interactive proof editor.* **Date:** 88-09.
Summary: This paper describes an approach to the integration of completion based proof generators into a structure proof editor framework. A complete representation mechanism is out lined for the incorporation of simplification, existential and inductive proofs into the editor framework. This is done by expressing the proofs performed by the completion based proof gederators in terms of the primitive inference rules of the calculus of the proof editor. Methods for the structuring of these proofs are discussed as is the possibility pf using the completion mechanism to synthesise induction schemes. The advantages of the independence of the representation mechanism with respect to tools for analysis of proofs with a view to generalisation, analogy etc. are pointed out.
PROSPECTRA Report [S.3.4-SN-11.0]

[132] Owen Traynor, David Duffy: *Some Examples of Proofs Done in a Sequent Calculus Framework.* **Date:** 88-09.
Summary: In this document a number of example proofs using a sequent calculus [Ge 69] are performed. The methods of performing proof in the sequent calculus framework are outlined. Examples, starting with the propositional case, moving through equational to examples where induction is required are given. Guidelines for constructing Induction schemes for the new theories are presented.
PROSPECTRA Report [S.3.4-SN-12.0]

[133] David Duffy: *A Program Transformation by Induction and Completion.* **Date:** 88-09-10.
Summary: This note describes a program transformation performed on the Boyer-Moore theorem prover.

This is composed with the same transformation performed using the Knuth-Bedix completion procedure.
PROSPECTRA Report [S.3.4-SN-13.0]

[134] David Duffy: *A New Approach to Induction in Equational Theories.* **Date:**89-09-02.
Summary: This paper disscusses an approach to " inductionless induction" which does not depend upon the ground confluence and termination properties of a term rewrite system. Instead it uses ground "coverings" and an ordering on the terms involved in the induction based upon their meaning given by the initial axioms. This contrasts with previous approaches which depend upon the ordering implicitly imposed by the termination ordering on the rewrite system. Some strategies are discussed for the pracitical application of the method in the context of the Knuth-Bendix completion procedure. Furthermore, for the case where the original set of axioms may be expressed as a srt of rewrite rules, a proposal is made for reducing the requirement for a "semantic" ordering to a set of syntactical conditions. The analogy between the method of inductive proof to be described and program transformations is almost immediate. It is illustrated and discussed in the later sections of the paper.
PROSPECTRA Report [S.3.4-SN-14.0]

[135] Owen Traynor *A User Manual for the PROPSECTRA Proof Editor Version 2.0.* **Date:** 89-09.
Summary: This document describes the user interface of the PROSPECTRA proof system. It also acts as a user manual. In addition, justification is given for some design decisions made in the process of construction. Further, the interface provided which will allow the definition of tactics, is described. The final part of the document is devoted to outlining the influences that the development of contextual attributes will have on the system.
PROSPECTRA Report [S.3.4-R-15.1]

[136] David Duffy. *A New Approach to Induction in Equational Theories.* **Date:** 89-01.
Summary: This paper discusses an approach to "inductionless induction" which does not depend upon the ground confluence and termination properties of a term rewrite system. Instead it uses ground "coverings" and an ordering on the terms involved in the induction based upon their meaning given by the initial axioms. This contrasts with previous approaches which depend upon the ordering implicitly imposed by the termination ordering on the rewrite system. Some strategies are discussed for the practical application of the method in the context of the Knuth-Bendix completion procedure. Furthermore, for the case where the original set of axioms may be expressed as a ground canonical set of rewrite rules, a proposal is made for reducing the requirement for a "semantic" ordering" to a set of syntactical conditions.
The analogy between the method of inductive proof to be described and program transformation is almost immediate. It is illustrated and discussed in the later sections of the paper.
PROSPECTRA Report [S.3.4-SN-16.0]

[137] David Duffy: *A Review of Automated Theorem Proving Techniques.* **Date:** 89-01.
Summary: This work is a review of methods for automatically performing proofs in first order logic on the computer. The systems studied range from those for full first-order logic to those that treat only equations. The techniques studied range from those that are heuristic and "natural" in nature to those that are completely machine oriented. The intention of the thesis is to serve both as a discussion of the most prominent approaches to automatic theorem proving and as a guide to current work on the subject. In particular, three chapters concern the application of automatic proof methods to two important topics: logic programming and proof by induction.
PROSPECTRA Report [S.3.4-SN-17.0]

[138] David Duffy. *An Alternative to an Abstract Syntax for Proofs.* **Date:** 89-01.
Summary: This paper describes an alternative to an abstract syntax for proofs for an intuitionistic logic. For a standard sequent calculus there is a critical non- determinism associated with the application of the inference rules at each stage of the proof. The application of the wrong rule may lead the proof astray and make it necessary to backtrack. One way to deal with this problem is to develop the proof tree as the proof proceeds and to allow the user/system to move around this tree at will. In this paper an alternative approach is described which uses an indexing mechanism to keep track of the current information and their interconnections at each stage of the proof. This ensures that no backtracking is required. The indexing is quite straightforward and most importantly follows from the semantic definition of consequence for the logic.
The fundamental motivation for this approach to theorem proving in PROSPECTRA is that the analogy between (top-down) proofs and transformations is enhanced because proofs now consist of a

transformation (of a theorem to "true") and a development history (a sequence of reductions). On the other hand, an important problem with the approach is that it is not obvious, from the indexed proof, what the actual (standard) proof should be; thus the indexed "development history" is thus essentially useless. However, a method is indicated for solving this problem by reconstructing an appropriate derivation without resorting to backtracking.
PROSPECTRA Report [S.3.4-SN-18.0]

[139] Owen Traynor: *Tactics for the PROSPECTRA Proof Editor.*
Summary: The relationship between the language transformation system of PROSPECTRA and the tactic development component of the proof system is described. In particular, the way in which logic transformers, defined within the transformation system of PROSPECTRA, are given an equivalent interpretation as proof tactics is detailed. An outline of the mapping from logic transformers to tactics is given. The limitations of the system are also presented together with a definition of the various PAnndA-S description of system languages required to facilitate the translation. Some examples of logic transformers and their corresponding tactics are included.
PROSPECTRA Report [S.3.4-SN-20.0]

P Project Management

[140] Berthold Hoffmann, Hui Shi: *Publication List of the PROSPECTRA Project.* **Date:** 1989-04-12.
PROSPECTRA Report [P.M3-MM-17.10]

Author Index for PROSPECTRA Publications

References

[Ada 83] Reference Manual for the Ada Programming Language. ANSI/MIL.STD 1815A. US Government Printing Office, 1983. Also *in:* Rogers, M. W. (ed.): *Ada: Language, compilers and Bibliography.* Ada Companion Series, Cambridge University Press, 1984.

[ADJ 78] J. A. Goguen, J. W. Thatcher, E. G. Wagner, An Initial Algebra Approach to the Specification, Correctness and Implementation of Abstract Data Types, in: R. T. Yeh (ed.): Current trends in programming methodology, Vol. 4, Data structuring, Prentice-Hall, Englewood Cliffs (1978) 80-149.

[Alt 90] M. Alt, *Ein Übersetzer für die funktionale Sprache TrafoLa.* Diplomarbeit, Universität des Saarlandes, 1990.

[Alt et al. 88] M. Alt, C. Fecht, C. Ferdinand, G. Sander,*A Prototype Of A Transformation Language.* PROSPECTRA Report S.1.6-R-16.0, 1988.

[Ammann 81] U. Ammann, *Code Generation of a Pascal-Compiler.* in D.W. Barron (ed.): Pascal — The Language and its implementation, Wiley 1981.

[Anna 87]: D.C Luckham, F.W. von Henke, B. Krieg-Brückner and O.Owe, ANNA, A Language for Annotating Ada Programs - Reference Manual, LNCS 260, Springer Verlag, 1987.

[Appel 87] A. W. Appel, Garbage Collection Can Be Faster Than Stack Allocation.*Information Processing Letters* 25 (1987) 275-279.

[Arsac, Kodratoff 82] J. Arsac, Y. Kodratoff. Some Techniques for Recursion Removal from Recursive Functions. *ACM Transaction on Programming Languages and Systems, 4,2* (1982) 295-322.

[Ashcroft 77] E.A. Ashcroft, W.W. Wadge: Lucid, a Nonprocedural Language with Iteration, *CACM 20,* (1977) 519-526.

[Aubin 79] R.Aubin. Proving Theorems by Structural Induction. *TCS 9*

[Bauer 79] Bauer, F.L.: Program Development by Stepwise Transformations - The Project CIP. *in:* Bauer, F. L., Broy, M. (eds.): Program Construction. *LNCS 69* (1979).

[Bauer et al. 85] Bauer, F. L., R. Berghammer, M. Broy, W. Dosch, F. Geiselbrechtinger, R. Gnatz, E. Hangel, W. Hesse, B. Krieg-Brückner, A. Laut, T. Matzner, B. Möller, F. Nickl, H. Partsch, P. Pepper, K. Samelson, M. Wirsing, H. Wössner: *The Munich Project CIP, Volume I: The Wide Spectrum Language CIP-L. LNCS 183,* Springer 1985.

[Bauer et al. 87] Bauer, F.L., Ehler, H., Horsch, B., Möller, B., Partsch, H., Paukner, O., Pepper, P.,: *The Munich Project CIP, Part 2: The Transformation System CIP-S. LNCS 292,* Springer 1987.

[Bauer et al. 89] Bauer, F.L., Möller, B., Partsch, H., Pepper, P.: Formal Program Construction by Stepwise Transformations - Computer-Aided Intuition-Guided Programming.*IEEE Trans. on SW Eng. 15: 2* (1989) 165-180.

[Bauer, Wössner 82] Bauer, F.L., Wössner, H.: *Algorithmic Language and Program Development.* Springer 1982.

[Beierle, Voß 87] C. Beierle, A. Voß, On Implementations of Loose Abstract Data Type Specifications and their Vertical Composition, STACS 87, *LNCS 247* (19872) 45-258.

[Bergstra, Klop 86] J.A. Bergstra, J.W. Klop: Process Algebra: Specification and Verification in Bisimulation Semantics. In: M. Hazewinkel, J.K. Lenstra, L.G.L.T. Meertens (Eds.): CWI Monograph 4, North-Holland, Amsterdam (1986) 61-94.

[Bertling et al. 89] H. Bertling, H. Ganzinger, and R. Schäfers. *CEC — A System to Support Modular Order-Sorted Specifications with Conditional Equations.* User Manual (Version 1.5), PROSPECTRA Report M.1.3-R-18.0, Universität Dortmund, FB Informatik, 1989.

[Bird 89] Bird, R.: Lectures on Constructive Functional Programming. *in*: Broy, M. (ed.): *Constructive Methods in Computing Science.* NATO ASI Series F55, Springer (1989) 151-218.

[Bird, Wadler 88] Bird, R., Wadler, Ph.: *Introduction to Functional Programming*. Prentice Hall, 1988.

[Bochmann, Sunshine 80] G.K. v. Bochmann, C.A. Sunshine: Formal Methods in Communication Protocol Desing. *IEEE Trans. Communications. Vol. COM-28, No. 4* (1980) 624-631.

[Böhm, Berarducci 85] Böhm, C., Berarducci, A.: Automatic Synthesis of Typed Lambda-Programs on Term Algebras. *Theoretical Computer Science 39* (1985) 135-154.

[Boyer, Moore 88] R.S. Boyer, J.S. Moore. *A Computational Logic Handbook.* Academic Press.

[Breu et al. 89] M. Breu, M. Broy, T. Grünler, F. Nickl, PA^{nn}dA-S Semantics, PROSPECTRA Study Note M.2.1.S1-SN-1.4, Universität Passau (see also part II chapter 3).

[Brock, Ackerman 81] J.D. Brock, W.B. Ackerman: Scenarios: A Model of Non-deterministic Computation. In: J. Diaz, I. Ramos (Eds.): Foundations of Programming Concepts, Intern. Coll. Peniscola, Spain, *LNCS 107* (1981) 252-259.

[Broy 85] M. Broy: Extensional Behaviour of Concurrent, Nondeterministic Communicating Systems, in: M. Broy (ed.): Control Flow and Data Flow: *Concepts of Distributed Programming*, Springer, 1985.

[Broy 87a] M. Broy: Specification of a Railway System. Technische Berichte der Fakultät für Mathematik und Informatik, Universität Passau, 1987, MIP-8715.

[Broy 87b] M. Broy: Some Algebraic and Functional Hocus Pocus with Abracadabra. Technische Berichte der Fakultät für Mathematik und Informatik, Universität Passau, 1987, MIP-8717.

[Broy 87c] M. Broy: Algebraic and Functional Specification of a Serializable Database Interface. Technische Berichte der Fakultät für Mathematik und Informatik, Universität Passau, 1987, MIP-8718.

[Broy 87d] Broy, M.: Predicative Specification for Functional Programs Describing Communicating Networks. *Information Processing Letters 25:2* (1987) 93-101.

[Broy 87] Broy, M.: Equational Specification of Partial Higher Order Algebras. In: M. Broy (ed.): Logic of Programming and Calculi of Discrete Design, *Proc. International Summer School 1986, Marktoberdorf, NATO ASI Series F36,* Springer (1987) 185-243.

[Broy 88a] M. Broy: An Example for the Design of Distributed Systems in a Formal Setting: The Lift Problem. Technische Berichte der Fakultät für Mathematik und Informatik, Universität Passau, MIP-8802, (1988).

[Broy 88b] M. Broy: Nondeterministic Data Flow Programs: How to Avoid the Merge Anomaly. *Science of Computer Programming 10* (1988) 65-85.

[Broy 89a] M. Broy, Implementierung in SPECTRUM (unpublished)

[Broy 89] Broy, M.: Towards a Design Methodology for Distributed Systems. *in:* Broy, M. (ed.): *Constructive Methods in Computing Science.* NATO ASI Series F55, Springer (1989) 311-364.

[Broy 90] M. Broy: Functional Specification of Time Sensitive Communicating Systems. In: J.W. de Bakker, W.-P. de Roever, G. Rozenberg (Hrsg.): Stepwise Refinement of Distributed Systems. *LNCS 430* (1990) 153-179.

[Broy, Nickl 87] Broy, M., F. Nickl: *PA^{nn}dA-S Semantics*. Technische Berichte der Fakultät für Mathematik und Informatik, Universität Passau, 1987, MIP-8701.

[Broy, Streicher 87] M. Broy, T. Steicher: Specification and Design of Shared Resource Arbitration. Technische Berichte der Fakultät für Mathematik und Informatik, Universität Passau, 1987, MIP-8721.

[Broy, Wirsing 82] Broy, M., Wirsing, M.: Partial Abstract Types. *Acta Informatica 18* (1982) 47-64.

[Broy et al. 86] Broy, M., Möller, B., Pepper, P., Wirsing, M.: Algebraic Implementations Preserve Program Correctness. *Science of Computer Programming 7* (1986) 35-53.

[Broy et al. 87] Broy, M., Pepper, P., Wirsing, M.: On the Algebraic Definition of Programming Languages. *ACM TOPLAS 9* (1987) 54-99.

[Burstall, Darlington 77] R.M. Burstall, J. Darlington. A Transformation System for developing Recursive Programs, *JACM 24, 1* (1977) 44-67.

[Burstall et al. 80] R. Burstall, D. MacQueen, D.Sannella, *HOPE: An Experimental Applicative Language*. Report CSR-62-80, Computer Science Dept., Edinburgh, (1980)

[Clocksin, Mellish 81] F.W. Clocksin, C.S. Mellish, *Programming in Prolog*, Springer (1981).

[Constable et al. 86] R. Constable et al.: *Implementing Mathematics with the Nuprl Proof Development System*. Prentice Hall, New Jersey 1986.

[Dederichs 89] F. Dederichs: An Exercise in the Design of a Distributed System using PA^{nn}dA-S: The Lift Example. PROSPRECTRA Study Note M.2.3.S2-SN-2.0, Universität Passau, January 1989

[Dederichs, Grünler 88] Dederichs, F., T. Grünler: *Specifying Higher Order Functions: Some Examples*. PROSPECTRA Study Note M.2.2.S2-SN-8.0, Universität Passau, Passau 1988.

[Dershowitz 83] Dershowitz, N.: Applications of the Knuth-Bendix Completion Procedure. Technical Report, Office of Laboratory Operations, The Aerospace Corporation, 1983, ATR-83(8478)-2.

[de la Cruz 1991] P. de la Cruz, Abstract and Concrete Syntax of PAnndA Phrases. Alcatel Stándard Eléctrica S.A., Madrid, 1991.

[de la Cruz et al. 90] P. de la Cruz, D. Hinojal, J. L. Ma´nas, *Context-Sensitive Parsing in CSG-Editors*. PROSPECTRA Report [S.1.5.C2-R-10], Alcatel Stándard Eléctrica S.A., March 1990.

[de Miguel 90] J.A. de Miguel, *The CSG Scripts Language Reference Manual*. PROSPECTRA Report, Alcatel Stándard Eléctrica S.A., February 90.

[Dijkstra 76] Dijkstra, E. W.: *A Discipline of Programming*. Prentice Hall 1976.

[Duffy 88] D. Duffy. A Program Transformation by Induction and Completion. PROSPECTRA Study Note: S.3.4-SN-12.0, University of Strathclyde, 1988.

[Duffy 89] David Duffy, A New Approach to Induction in Equational Theories, PROSPECTRA Study Note-[S.3.4.SN.14.0], University of Strathclyde, February 1989.

[Ehrich et al. 89] Ehrich, H.-D., M. Gogolla, U. W. Lipeck: *Algebraische Spezifikation abstrakter Datentypen*. Teubner, Stuttgart 1989.

[Ehrig, Mahr 85] Ehrig, H., B. Mahr: *Fundamentals of Algebraic Specification 1: Equations and Initial Semantics*. Springer, Berlin 1985.

[Ehrig et al. 82] H. Ehrig, H.-J. Kreowski, B. Mahr and P. Padawitz, Algebraic Implementation of Abstract Data Types, *TCS 20* (1982) 209-263

[Fecht 90] C. Fecht, *TRAMA: Eine Abstrakte Maschine zur Implementierung der funktionalen Programmiersprache TrafoLa*. Diplomarbeit, Universität des Saarlandes, 1990.

[Feijs et al. 87] Feijs, L.M.G., Jonkers, H.B.M, Obbink, J.H., Koymans, P.P.J., Renardel de Lavalette, G.R., Rodenburg, P.M.: A Survey of the Design Language Cold. *in: Proc. ESPRIT Conf. 86 (Results and Achievements).* North Holland (1987) 631-644.

[Ferdinand 90a] C. Ferdinand, *Pattern Matching in a Functional Transformation Language using Treeparsing.* **in** Déransart, Maluszynski (Eds.): Proceedings of the Workshop: Programming Language Implementation and Logic Programming 90, *LNCS 456* (1990) 358-371.

[Ferdinand 90] C. Ferdinand, *Pattern Matching in TrafoLa.* Diplomarbeit, Universität des Saarlandes, 1990.

[Filman, Friedman 84] R.E. Filman, D.P. Friedman: *Coordinated Computing. Tools and Techniques for Distributed Software.* McGraw-Hill, 1984

[Ganzinger 83] H. Ganzinger, Parameterized Specifications: Parameter Passing and Implementation with Respect to Observability, *ACM TOPLAS* (1983) 318-354.

[Ganzinger 87] Ganzinger, H.: A Completion Procedure for Conditional Equations. Techn. Bericht No. 243, Fachbereich Informatik, Universität Dortmund, 1987.
also in: J. Symb. Comp 11 (1991) 51-81.

[Ganzinger 88] H.Ganzinger, Completion with History-Dependent Complexities for Generated Equations. *in* D.T. Sannella and A. Tarlecki, (eds.): Recent Trends in Data Type Specifications, *LNCS 332* (1988) 73-91.

[Ganzinger 91] H. Ganzinger, Order-Sorted Completion: The Many-Sorted Way. *Theoretical Computer Science*, Vol. 89 (1991) 3-32.

[Gentzen 69] G. Gentzen, Investigations into Logical Deduction. *in The Collected Papers of Gerhard Gentzen*, North-Holland (1969) 68-131.

[Gersdorf 1989] B. Gersdorf, *Context Sensitive Transformations in the PROSPECTRA Project.* PROSPECTRA Study Note [M.1.1.S3-SN-53.0], Universität Bremen, May 1989.

[Goguen, Meseguer 87] J.A. Goguen and J. Meseguer, Order-Sorted Algebra I: Partial and Overloaded Operators, Errors and Inheritance. Technical Report, SRI International, Computer Science Laboratory, 1987.

[González 88] R. Gonzàlez, *Conditional and parameterized transformations with CSG.* PROSPECTRA Report, Alcatel Stándard Eléctrica S.A., May 88.

[Gordon et al. 78] Gordon, M., Milner, R., Wadsworth, Ch.: Edinburgh LCF: A Mechanised Logic of Computation. *LNCS 78* (1978).

[Gries 81] Gries, D.: *The Science of Programming.* Springer 1981.

[Grünler 90] Grünler, T.: *Spezifikationen höherer Ordnung.* Dissertation, Fakultät für Mathematik und Informatik, Universität Passau, Passau 1990.

[Grünler, Broy 88] Grünler, T., M. Broy: *Theoretical Foundation of Algebraic Specification and Implementation in PA^{nn}dA-S.* PROSPECTRA Report M.2.2.S1-R-1.2, Universität Passau, 1988.

[Grünler, Dederichs 89] Th. Grünler, F. Dederichs: Transforming Stream Processing Functions into Ada. PROSPRECTRA Study Note M.2.3.C1-SN-3.2, Universitäat Passau, August 1989.

[Heckmann 87] R. Heckmann, *Semantics of Patterns.* PROSPECTRA Report S.1.6-SN-8.0, Universität des Saarlandes, 1987.

[Heckmann 88a] Heckmann, R.: A Functional Language for the Specification of Complex Tree Transformations. *in:* Proc. European Symposium On Programming '88, *LNCS 300* (1988) 175-190.

[Heckmann 88] R. Heckmann, *User Manual for the TrafoLa-ML System Version 1.5*. PROSPECTRA Report S.1.6-R-15.0, Universität des Saarlandes, 1988.

[Hindley 69] R. Hindley, The principal type-scheme of an object in combinatory logic. *Trans. Amer. Math. Soc.* 146 (1969) 29-60.

[Hinojal 88]D. Hinojal, *Read/Write Extended Format..* PROSPECTRA Report, Alcatel Stándard Eléctrica S.A., June 88

[Hoare 69] Hoare, C.A.R.: An Axiomatic Basis for Computer Programming. *CACM 12* (1969) 576-583.

[Hoare 72] Hoare, C.A.R.: Proofs of Correctness of Data Representations, *Acta Informatica 1* (1972) 271-281.

[Hoare 85] Hoare, C.A.R.: *Communicating Sequential Programs.* Prentice Hall, 1985.

[Hoffmann, O'Donnell 82] D.M. Hoffmann, M.J. O'Donnell, Pattern Matching in Trees. *JACM* 29,1 (1982) 68-95.

[Huet, Lang 78] Huet, G., Lang, B.: Proving and applying program transformations expressed as second order patterns. *Acta Informatica 11* (1978) 31-55.

[Huet, Oppen 80] G. Huet, D.C. Oppen, Equations and Rewrite Rules: A Survey. In R. Book, ed., *Formal Languages: Perspectives and Open Problems.* Academic Press, New York, 1980.

[Ichbiah et al. 79] Ichbiah, J.D., Barnes, J.G.P., Heliard, J.C., Krieg-Brückner, B. Roubine, O. and Wichmann, B.A.: Rationale for the Design of the Ada Programming Language. *SIGPLAN Notices 14:4B* (1979).

[INMOS 84] INMOS Ltd.: *OCCAM Programming Manual.* Prentice Hall, 1984.

[Jähnichen et al. 86] Jähnichen, S., Hussain, F.A., Weber, M.: Program Development Using a Design Calculus. *in:* Rogers, M. W. (ed.): *Results and Achievements,* Proc. ESPRIT Conf. '86 . North Holland (1987) 645-658.

[Johnsson 84] T. Johnsson, Efficient Compilation of Lazy Evaluation *SIGPLAN Notices*, 19, 6 (1984) 58-69.

[Kahn 74] G. Kahn: The Semantics of a Simple Language for Parallel Programming. *Information Processing 74,* North-Holland Publishing Company, 1974.

[Kaplan 84] S. Kaplan, Conditional Rewrite Rules. In *Theoretical Computer Science* 33 (1984) 175-193.

[Karlsen, Krieg-Brückner, Traynor 91] Karlsen, E.W., Krieg-Brückner, B., Traynor, O.: The PROSPECTRA System: A Unified Development Framwork. In: Nivat, Rattray, Rus, Scollo (eds.): *Algebraic Methodology and Software Technology (AMAST'91),* Springer (1992).

[Kleene 62] S.C. Kleene. *Introduction to Meta-Mathematics.* North Holland. (1962).

[Krieg-Brückner 87a] Krieg-Brückner, B.: Systematic Transformation of Interface Specifications. *in:* Meertens, L.G.T.L. (ed.): *Program Specification and Transformation,* Proc. IFIP TC2 Working Conf. (Tölz '86). North Holland (1987) 269-291.

[Krieg-Brückner 87b] Krieg-Brückner, B.: Integration of Program Construction and Verification: the PROSPECTRA Project. in: Habermann, N., Montanari, U. (eds.): Innovative Software Factories and Ada. Proc. CRAI Int'l Spring Conf. '86. *LNCS 275* (1987) 173-194.

[Krieg-Brückner 88a] Krieg-Brückner, B.: The PROSPECTRA Methodology of Program Development. *in:* Zalewski (ed.): Proc. IFIP/IFAC Working Conf. on HW and SW for Real Time Process Control (Warsaw). North Holland (1988) 257-271.

[Krieg-Brückner 88] Krieg-Brückner, B.: Algebraic Formalization of Program Development by Transformation. in: Ganzinger, H. (ed.).: Proc. European Symposium on Programming'88. *LNCS 300* (1988) 34-48.

[Krieg-Brückner 89a] Krieg-Brückner, B.: Algebraic Specification with Functionals in Program Development by Transformation. *in:* Hünke, H. (ed.): *Proc. ESPRIT Conf. '89*, Kluver Academic Publishers (1989) 302-320.

[Krieg-Brückner 89] Krieg-Brückner, B.: Algebraic Specification and Functionals for Transformational Program and Meta-Program Development. *in:* Diaz, J., Orejas, F. (eds.): Proc. TAPSOFT '89 (Barcelona) Part 2. *LNCS 352* (1989) 36-59.

[Krieg Brückner 90] Krieg-Brückner, B.: PROgram development by SPECification and TRAnsformation. *Technique et Science Informatiques* Special Issue on *Software Engineering in ESPRIT* (1990) 136-149.

[Krieg-Brückner 91a] Krieg-Brückner, B.: Transformational Meta Program development. *in:* Broy, M., Wirsing, M. (eds.): Methods of Programming; Selected Papers on the CIP-Project. *LNCS 544* (1991) 19-34.

[Krieg-Brückner 91b] Krieg-Brückner, B. (ed.): PROgram development by SPECification and TRAnsformation: Vol. I: Methodology, Vol. II: Language Family, Vol. III: System. PROSPECTRA Reports M.1.1.S3-R-55.3, -56.3, -57.3. Universität Bremen, 1990.

[Krieg-Brückner, Sannella 91] Krieg-Brückner, B., Sannella, D.: Structuring Specifications in-the-Large and in-the-Small: Higher-Order Functions, Dependent Types and Inheritance in SPECTRAL. Proc TAPSOFT '91, *LNCS* (1991) 313-336

[Krieg-Brückner et al. 91] Krieg-Brückner, B., Karlsen, E.W., Liu, J., Traynor, O.: The PROSPECTRA Methodology and System: Uniform Transformational (Meta-) Development. *in:* S. Prehn, W. J. Toetenel (eds.): VDM'91, Formal Software Development Methods, Proc. 4th Int'l Symp. of VDM Europe; Vol. 2: Tutorials. *LNCS 552* (1991) 363-397.

[Kron 75] H. Kron Tree Templates and Subtree Transformational Grammars PhD, University of California, Santa Cruz 1975.

[Lamport 83] L. Lamport: Specifying Concurrent Program Modules. *ACM Trans. on Programming Languages and Systems, 5:2* (1983) 190-222.

[Liu, Traynor, Krieg-Brückner 92] Liu, J., Traynor, O., Krieg-Brückner, B.: Knowledge-Based Transformational Programming. *in: Proc. 4th Intl. Conf. on Software Engineering and Knowledge-Engineering (Capri).* IEEE Computer Society Press (1992) 632-639.

[Loeckx, Sieber 84] J. Loeckx, K. Sieber: *The Foundations of Program Verification.* Wiley-Teubner, 1984.

[Luckham et al. 87] Luckham, D.C., von Henke, F.W., Krieg-Brückner, B., Owe, O.: *Anna, a Language for Annotating Ada Programs,* Reference Manual. *LNCS 260*, Springer (1987).

[Maher, Traynor 92] Maher, P.E., Traynor, O.: A Framework and Methodology for the Verification and Validation of Expert Systems. *in*: Proc. of the Intl. Conf. on Artificial Intelligence (Cancun). To Appear *LNCS* (1992).

[Manna, Waldinger 80] Z. Manna, R Waldinger. A Deductive Approach to Program Synthesis. *ACM TOPLAS 2:1*, 90-121.

[Mathis 90] Nicole Mathis, Weiterentwicklung eines Codeselektorgenerators und Anwendung auf den NSC32000 Diplomarbeit, Universität des Saarlandes, 1990.

[Milner 78] R. Milner, A Theory of Type Polymorphism in Programming. *Journ. Comp. Sys. Sci.* 17 (1978) 348-375.

[Milner 80] R. Milner: *A Calculus of Communicating Systems. LNCS 82,* 1980.

[Milner 85] R. Milner, The Standard ML Core Language, in: *Polymorphism* II, 2, (1985)

[Möller 85] Möller, B.: On the algebraic spacification of infinite objects- ordered and continuous models of algebraic types. *Acta Informatica 22* (1985) 537-578.

[Möller 87a] Möller, B.: Algebraic Specification with Higher Order Operators. *in:* Meertens, L.G.T.L. (ed.): *Program Specification and Transformation,* Proc. IFIP TC2 Working Conf. (Tölz '86). North Holland (1987) 367-398.

[Möller 87] Möller, B.: *Higher Order Algebraic Specifications.* Habilitationsschrift, Fakultät für Mathematik und Informatik, Technische Universität München, München 1987.

[Möller et al. 88] Möller, B., A. Tarlecki, M. Wirsing: *Algebraic Specifications of Reachable Higher-Order Algebras.* In: D. Sannella, A. Tarlecki (eds.): Recent Trends in Data Type Specification, Fifth Workshop on Specification of Abstract Data Types, Gullane, Scotland 1987, *LNCS 332* (1988) 154-169.

[Nickl et al. 88] Nickl, F., M. Broy, M. Breu, F. Dederichs, T. Grünler: *Towards a Semantics of Higher Order Specifications in PA^{nn}dA-S.* PROSPECTRA Study Note M.2.1.S2-SN-2.0, Universität Passau, Passau 1988.

[Nipkow 87] Nipkow, T.: Are Homomorphisms Sufficient for Behavioural Implementations of Deterministic and Nondeterministic Data Types? Proc. STACS 87, *LNCS 247* (1987) 260-271.

[Owe 85] Owe. O.: An Approach to Program Reasoning Based on a First Order Logic for Partial Functions. Research Report No. 89, Institute of Informatics, University of Oslo, 1985.

[Paige, Koenig 82] Paige, R., Koenig, S.: Finite Differencing of Computable Expressions. *ACM TOPLAS 4: 4* (1982) 402-454.

[Partsch, Steinbrüggen 83] Partsch, H., Steinbrüggen, R.: Program Transformation Systems. *ACM Computing Surveys 15* (1983) 199-236.

[Paulson 85] L. Paulson: Interactive theorem proving with Cambridge LCF: a user's manual, University of Cambridge Computer Laboratory, Technical Report no 80, 1985.

[Pepper 84] Peter Pepper, A Simple Calculus for Program Transformations (Inclusive of Induction), Technische Universität Munchen, TUM-INFO-07-84-IO9-280/1-FMA, 1984.

[Peterson 77] J.L. Peterson: Petri Nets. *ACM Computing Surveys 9:3* (1977) 223-252.

[Reps, Teitelbaum 88] T. Reps, T. Teitelbaum, *The Synthesizer Generator Reference Manual (3rd edition),* Text and Monographs in Computer Science, Springer 1988.

[Ritchie 88] B. Ritchie, The Design and Implementation of an Interactive Proof Editor. PhD Thesis, University of Edinburgh (1988).

[Sander 90] G. Sander, *Entwicklung und Implementierung eines polymorphen Typsystems für die funktionale Programmiersprache TRAFOLA.* Diplomarbeit, Universität des Saarlandes (1990)

[Sannella, Wirsing 83] D. T. Sannella, M. Wirsing, A Kernel Language for Algebraic Specification and Implementation, in: M. Karpinski (ed.): Coll. on Foundations of Computation Theory 11, *LNCS 158* (1983) 413-427.

[Schmidt 83] D. Schmidt. A Programming Notation for Tactical Reasoning. In Proc 7th Intl. Conf. on Automated Deduction, *LNCS 170* (1984).

[Schoett 87] O. Schoett, Data Abstraction and the Correctness of Modular Programming, Ph. D. Thesis, 1987, University of Edinburgh.

[Scott 81] Scott, D. S.: *Lectures on a Mathematical Theory of Computation.* Technical Monograph PRG-19, Oxford Computing Laboratory, Oxford 1981.

[Sharir 82] Sharir, M.: Some Observations Concerning Formal Differentiation of Set Theoretic Expressions. *ACM TOPLAS 4: 2* (1982) 196-226.

[Sintzoff 87] Sintzoff, M.: Expressing Program Developments in a Design Calculus. *in:* Broy, M. (ed.): *Logic of Programming and Calculi of Discrete Design.* NATO ASI Series, Part F36, Springer (1987) 343-365.

[Smith 85] Smith, D.R.: Top-Down Synthesis of Divide-and-Conquer Algorithms. *Artificial Intelligence 27:1* (1985) 43-95.

[Smith 91] Smith, D.R.: KIDS - a Knowledge-Based Software Development System. *in:* Lowry, M., McCartney, R. (eds.): *Automating Software Design,* Live Oak Press, Menlo Park (1991).

[Smith, Lowry 90] Smith, D.R., Lowry, M.R.: Algorithm Theories and Design Tactics. *Science of Computer Programming 14:*(1990) 305-321.

[Smolka et al. 87] G. Smolka, W. Nutt, J.A. Goguen, and J. Meseguer, *Order-Sorted Equational Computation.* SEKI Report SR-87-14, Universität Kaiserslautern, West Germany, December 1987. *Also in* Proc. Coll. on Resolution of Equations in Algebraic Structures, Austin.

[Streicher 87] Th. Streicher: A Verification Method for Finite Dataflow Networks with Constraints Applied to the Verification of the Alternating Bit Protocol. Technische Berichte der Fakultät für Mathematik und Informatik, Universität Passau, MIP-8706, 1987.

[Traynor 89] O. Traynor. Verification - its Methodology, Support and Integration into PROSPECTRA. Study Note [S.3.4 - SN - 16.0], University of Strathclyde, September 1989.

[Turner 85] D.A: Turner, *Miranda: a nonstrict Functional Language with Polymorphic Types. LNCS 201,* (1985)

[von Henke 76] von Henke, F.W.: An Algebraic Approach to Data Types, Program Verification and Program Synthesis. *in:* Mazurkiewicz, A. (ed.): Mathematical Foundations of Computer Science 1976. *LNCS 45* (1976) 330-336.

[Warren 83] D.H.D. Warren, *An Abstract Prolog Instruction Set.* Technical Report tn309, SRI, October 1983.

[Weber 91] R. Weber: Where can I get gas round here? - An Application of a Design Methodology for Distributed Systems. In: J.A. Bergstra, L.M.G. Feijs (Eds.): Algebraic Methods II: Theory, Tools and Applications. *LNCS 490* Springer (1991) 143-166.

[Weisgerber, Wilhelm 88] Beatrix Weisgerber, Reinhard Wilhelm: Two tree pattern matchers for code selection. *in* Hammer (ed.): Proc. Workshop Compiler Compilers and High Speed Compilation, *LNCS 371* (1988) 215-229.

[Wile 86a] Wile, D. S.: Program Developments: Formal Explanations of Implementations. *CACM 26:* 11 (1983) 902-911. *also in:* Agresti, W. A. (ed.): *New Paradigms for Software Development.* IEEE Computer Society Press / North Holland (1986) 239-248.

[Wile 86b] Wile, D. S.: Organizing Programming Knowledge into Syntax Directed Experts. Proc. Int'l Workshop on Advanced Programming Environments (Trondheim). *LNCS 244* (1986) 551-565.

[Wilhelm, Maurer 92] R. Wilhelm, D. Maurer, *Übersetzerbau — Theorie, Konstruktion, Generierung.* Springer Verlag, 1992.

[Wirsing 89] Wirsing, M.: *Algebraic Specification.* In: J. van Leeuwen (ed.): Handbook of Theoretical Computer Science, Elsevier (1990) 676-788.

[Wirsing et al. 83] M. Wirsing, P. Pepper, H. Partsch, W. Dosch, M. Broy, On Hierarchies of Abstract Data Types, *Acta Informatica 20* (1983) 1-33.

Springer-Verlag and the Environment

We at Springer-Verlag firmly believe that an international science publisher has a special obligation to the environment, and our corporate policies consistently reflect this conviction.

We also expect our business partners – paper mills, printers, packaging manufacturers, etc. – to commit themselves to using environmentally friendly materials and production processes.

The paper in this book is made from low- or no-chlorine pulp and is acid free, in conformance with international standards for paper permanency.

Printing: Weihert-Druck GmbH, Darmstadt
Binding: Buchbinderei Schäffer, Grünstadt

Lecture Notes in Computer Science

For information about Vols. 1–620
please contact your bookseller or Springer-Verlag

Vol. 621: O. Nurmi, E. Ukkonen (Eds.), Algorithm Theory – SWAT '92. Proceedings. VIII, 434 pages. 1992.

Vol. 622: F. Schmalhofer, G. Strube, Th. Wetter (Eds.), Contemporary Knowledge Engineering and Cognition. Proceedings, 1991. XII, 258 pages. 1992. (Subseries LNAI).

Vol. 623: W. Kuich (Ed.), Automata, Languages and Programming. Proceedings, 1992. XII, 721 pages. 1992.

Vol. 624: A. Voronkov (Ed.), Logic Programming and Automated Reasoning. Proceedings, 1992. XIV, 509 pages. 1992. (Subseries LNAI).

Vol. 625: W. Vogler, Modular Construction and Partial Order Semantics of Petri Nets. IX, 252 pages. 1992.

Vol. 626: E. Börger, G. Jäger, H. Kleine Büning, M. M. Richter (Eds.), Computer Science Logic. Proceedings, 1991. VIII, 428 pages. 1992.

Vol. 628: G. Vosselman, Relational Matching. IX, 190 pages. 1992.

Vol. 629: I. M. Havel, V. Koubek (Eds.), Mathematical Foundations of Computer Science 1992. Proceedings. IX, 521 pages. 1992.

Vol. 630: W. R. Cleaveland (Ed.), CONCUR '92. Proceedings. X, 580 pages. 1992.

Vol. 631: M. Bruynooghe, M. Wirsing (Eds.), Programming Language Impl[illegible]tation and Logic Programming. Proceedings, 1992. XI, 492 pages. 1992.

Vol. 632: H. Kirchner, G. Levi (Eds.), Algebraic and Logic Programming. Proceedings, 1992. IX, 457 pages. 1992.

Vol. 633: D. Pearce, G. Wagner (Eds.), Logics in AI. Proceedings. VIII, 410 pages. 1992. (Subseries LNAI).

Vol. 634: L. Bougé, M. Cosnard, Y. Robert, D. Trystram (Eds.), Parallel Processing: CONPAR 92 – VAPP V. Proceedings. XVII, 853 pages. 1992.

Vol. 635: J. C. Derniame (Ed.), Software Process Technology. Proceedings, 1992. VIII, 253 pages. 1992.

Vol. 636: G. Comyn, N. E. Fuchs, M. J. Ratcliffe (Eds.), Logic Programming in Action. Proceedings, 1992. X, 324 pages. 1992. (Subseries LNAI).

Vol. 637: Y. Bekkers, J. Cohen (Eds.), Memory Management. Proceedings, 1992. XI, 525 pages. 1992.

Vol. 639: A. U. Frank, I. Campari, U. Formentini (Eds.), Theories and Methods of Spatio-Temporal Reasoning in Geographic Space. Proceedings, 1992. XI, 431 pages. 1992.

Vol. 640: C. Sledge (Ed.), Software Engineering Education. Proceedings, 1992. X, 451 pages. 1992.

Vol. 641: U. Kastens, P. Pfahler (Eds.), Compiler Construction. Proceedings, 1992. VIII, 320 pages. 1992.

Vol. 642: K. P. Jantke (Ed.), Analogical and Inductive Inference. Proceedings, 1992. VIII, 319 pages. 1992. (Subseries LNAI).

Vol. 643: A. Habel, Hyperedge Replacement: Grammars and Languages. X, 214 pages. 1992.

Vol. 644: A. Apostolico, M. Crochemore, Z. Galil, U. Manber (Eds.), Combinatorial Pattern Matching. Proceedings, 1992. X, 287 pages. 1992.

Vol. 645: G. Pernul, A M. Tjoa (Eds.), Entity-Relationship Approach – ER '92. Proceedings, 1992. XI, 439 pages, 1992.

Vol. 646: J. Biskup, R. Hull (Eds.), Database Theory – ICDT '92. Proceedings, 1992. IX, 449 pages. 1992.

Vol. 647: A. Segall, S. Zaks (Eds.), Distributed Algorithms. X, 380 pages. 1992.

Vol. 648: Y. Deswarte, G. Eizenberg, J.-J. Quisquater (Eds.), Computer Security – ESORICS 92. Proceedings. XI, 451 pages. 1992.

Vol. 649: A. Pettorossi (Ed.), Meta-Programming in Logic. Proceedings, 1992. XII, 535 pages. 1992.

Vol. 650: T. Ibaraki, Y. Inagaki, K. Iwama, T. Nishizeki, M. Yamashita (Eds.), Algorithms and Computation. Proceedings, 1992. XI, 510 pages. 1992.

Vol. 651: R. Koymans, Specifying Message Passing and Time-Critical Systems with Temporal Logic. IX, 164 pages. 1992.

Vol. 652: R. Shyamasundar (Ed.), Foundations of Software Technology and Theoretical Computer Science. Proceedings, 1992. XIII, 405 pages. 1992.

Vol. 653: A. Bensoussan, J.-P. Verjus (Eds.), Future Tendencies in Computer Science, Control and Applied Mathematics. Proceedings, 1992. XV, 371 pages. 1992.

Vol. 654: A. Nakamura, M. Nivat, A. Saoudi, P. S. P. Wang, K. Inoue (Eds.), Parallel Image Analysis. Proceedings, 1992. VIII, 312 pages. 1992.

Vol. 655: M. Bidoit, C. Choppy (Eds.), Recent Trends in Data Type Specification. X, 344 pages. 1993.

Vol. 656: M. Rusinowitch, J. L. Rémy (Eds.), Conditional Term Rewriting Systems. Proceedings, 1992. XI, 501 pages. 1993.

Vol. 657: E. W. Mayr (Ed.), Graph-Theoretic Concepts in Computer Science. Proceedings, 1992. VIII, 350 pages. 1993.

Vol. 658: R. A. Rueppel (Ed.), Advances in Cryptology – EUROCRYPT '92. Proceedings, 1992. X, 493 pages. 1993.

Vol. 659: G. Brewka, K. P. Jantke, P. H. Schmitt (Eds.), Nonmonotonic and Inductive Logic. Proceedings, 1991. VIII, 332 pages. 1993. (Subseries LNAI).

Vol. 660: E. Lamma, P. Mello (Eds.), Extensions of Logic Programming. Proceedings, 1992. VIII, 417 pages. 1993. (Subseries LNAI).

Vol. 661: S. J. Hanson, W. Remmele, R. L. Rivest (Eds.), Machine Learning: From Theory to Applications. VIII, 271 pages. 1993.

Vol. 662: M. Nitzberg, D. Mumford, T. Shiota, Filtering, Segmentation and Depth. VIII, 143 pages. 1993.

Vol. 663: G. v. Bochmann, D. K. Probst (Eds.), Computer Aided Verification. Proceedings, 1992. IX, 422 pages. 1993.

Vol. 664: M. Bezem, J. F. Groote (Eds.), Typed Lambda Calculi and Applications. Proceedings, 1993. VIII, 433 pages. 1993.

Vol. 665: P. Enjalbert, A. Finkel, K. W. Wagner (Eds.), STACS 93. Proceedings, 1993. XIV, 724 pages. 1993.

Vol. 666: J. W. de Bakker, W.-P. de Roever, G. Rozenberg (Eds.), Semantics: Foundations and Applications. Proceedings, 1992. VIII, 659 pages. 1993.

Vol. 667: P. B. Brazdil (Ed.), Machine Learning: ECML – 93. Proceedings, 1993. XII, 471 pages. 1993. (Subseries LNAI).

Vol. 668: M.-C. Gaudel, J.-P. Jouannaud (Eds.), TAPSOFT '93: Theory and Practice of Software Development. Proceedings, 1993. XII, 762 pages. 1993.

Vol. 669: R. S. Bird, C. C. Morgan, J. C. P. Woodcock (Eds.), Mathematics of Program Construction. Proceedings, 1992. VIII, 378 pages. 1993.

Vol. 670: J. C. P. Woodcock, P. G. Larsen (Eds.), FME '93: Industrial-Strength Formal Methods. Proceedings, 1993. XI, 689 pages. 1993.

Vol. 671: H. J. Ohlbach (Ed.), GWAI-92: Advances in Artificial Intelligence. Proceedings, 1992. XI, 397 pages. 1993. (Subseries LNAI).

Vol. 672: A. Barak, S. Guday, R. G. Wheeler, The MOSIX Distributed Operating System. X, 221 pages. 1993.

Vol. 673: G. Cohen, T. Mora, O. Moreno (Eds.), Applied Algebra, Algebraic Algorithms and Error-Correcting Codes. Proceedings, 1993. X, 355 pages 1993.

Vol. 674: G. Rozenberg (Ed.), Advances in Petri Nets 1993. VII, 457 pages. 1993.

Vol. 675: A. Mulkers, Live Data Structures in Logic Programs. VIII, 220 pages. 1993.

Vol. 676: Th. H. Reiss, Recognizing Planar Objects Using Invariant Image Features. X, 180 pages. 1993.

Vol. 677: H. Abdulrab, J.-P. Pécuchet (Eds.), Word Equations and Related Topics. Proceedings, 1991. VII, 214 pages. 1993.

Vol. 678: F. Meyer auf der Heide, B. Monien, A. L. Rosenberg (Eds.), Parallel Architectures and Their Efficient Use. Proceedings, 1992. XII, 227 pages. 1993.

Vol. 679: C. Fermüller, A. Leitsch, T. Tammet, N. Zamov, Resolution Methods for the Decision Problem. VIII, 205 pages. 1993. (Subseries LNAI).

Vol. 680: B. Hoffmann, B. Krieg-Brückner (Eds.), Program Development by Specification and Transformation. XV, 623 pages. 1993.

Vol. 681: H. Wansing, The Logic of Information Structures. IX, 163 pages. 1993. (Subseries LNAI).

Vol. 682: B. Bouchon-Meunier, L. Valverde, R. R. Yager (Eds.), IPMU '92 – Advanced Methods in Artificial Intelligence. Proceedings, 1992. IX, 367 pages. 1993.

Vol. 683: G.J. Milne, L. Pierre (Eds.), Correct Hardware Design and Verification Methods. Proceedings, 1993. VIII, 270 Pages. 1993.

Vol. 684: A. Apostolico, M. Crochemore, Z. Galil, U. Manber (Eds.), Combinatorial Pattern Matching. Proceedings, 1993. VIII, 265 pages. 1993.

Vol. 685: C. Rolland, F. Bodart, C. Cauvet (Eds.), Advanced Information Systems Engineering. Proceedings, 1993. XI, 650 pages. 1993.

Vol. 686: J. Mira, J. Cabestany, A. Prieto (Eds.), New Trends in Neural Computation. Proceedings, 1993. XVII, 746 pages. 1993.

Vol. 687: H. H. Barrett, A. F. Gmitro (Eds.), Information Processing in Medical Imaging. Proceedings, 1993. XVI, 567 pages. 1993.

Vol. 688: M. Gauthier (Ed.), Ada - Europe '93. Proceedings, 1993. VIII, 353 pages. 1993.

Vol. 689: J. Komorowski, Z. W. Ras (Eds.), Methodologies for Intelligent Systems. Proceedings, 1993. XI, 653 pages. 1993. (Subseries LNAI).

Vol. 690: C. Kirchner (Ed.), Rewriting Techniques and Applications. Proceedings, 1993. XI, 488 pages. 1993.

Vol. 691: M. Ajmone Marsan (Ed.), Application and Theory of Petri Nets 1993. Proceedings, 1993. IX, 591 pages. 1993.

Vol. 692: D. Abel, B.C. Ooi (Eds.), Advances in Spatial Databases. Proceedings, 1993. XIII, 529 pages. 1993.

Vol. 693: P. E. Lauer (Ed.), Functional Programming, Concurrency, Simulation and Automated Reasoning. Proceedings, 1991/1992. XI, 398 pages. 1993.

Vol. 694: A. Bode, M. Reeve, G. Wolf (Eds.), PARLE '93. Parallel Architectures and Languages Europe. Proceedings, 1993. XVII, 770 pages. 1993.

Vol. 695: E. P. Klement, W. Slany (Eds.), Fuzzy Logic in Artificial Intelligence. Proceedings, 1993. VIII, 192 pages. 1993. (Subseries LNAI).

Vol. 696: M. Worboys, A. F. Grundy (Eds.), Advances in Databases. Proceedings, 1993. X, 276 pages. 1993.

Vol. 697: C. Courcoubetis (Ed.), Computer Aided Verification. Proceedings, 1993. IX, 504 pages. 1993.

Vol. 698: A. Voronkov (Ed.), Logic Programming and Automated Reasoning. Proceedings, 1993. XIII, 386 pages. 1993. (Subseries LNAI).

Vol. 699: G. W. Mineau, B. Moulin, J. F. Sowa (Eds.), Conceptual Graphs for Knowledge Representation. Proceedings, 1993. IX, 451 pages. 1993. (Subseries LNAI).

Vol. 700: A. Lingas, R. Karlsson, S. Carlsson (Eds.), Automata, Languages and Programming. Proceedings, 1993. XII, 697 pages. 1993.

Vol. 701: P. Atzeni (Ed.), LOGIDATA+: Deductive Databases with Complex Objects. VIII, 273 pages. 1993.

Vol. 702: E. Börger, G. Jäger, H. Kleine Büning, S. Martini, M. M. Richter (Eds.), Computer Science Logic. Proceedings, 1992. VIII, 439 pages. 1993.

Vol. 703: M. de Berg, Ray Shooting, Depth Orders and Hidden Surface Removal. X, 201 pages. 1993.

Lecture Notes in Computer Science

This series reports new developments in computer science research and teaching, quickly, informally, and at a high level. The timeliness of a manuscript is more important than its form, which may be unfinished or tentative. The type of material considered for publication includes

- drafts of original papers or monographs,
- technical reports of high quality and broad interest,
- advanced-level lectures,
- reports of meetings, provided they are of exceptional interest and focused on a single topic.

Publication of Lecture Notes is intended as a service to the computer science community in that the publisher Springer-Verlag offers global distribution of documents which would otherwise have a restricted readership. Once published and copyrighted they can be cited in the scientific literature.

Manuscripts

Lecture Notes are printed by photo-offset from the master copy delivered in camera-ready form. Manuscripts should be no less than 100 and preferably no more than 500 pages of text. Authors of monographs and editors of proceedings volumes receive 50 free copies of their book. Manuscripts should be printed with a laser or other high-resolution printer onto white paper of reasonable quality. To ensure that the final photo-reduced pages are easily readable, please use one of the following formats:

Font size	Printing area		Final size
(points)	(cm)	(inches)	(%)
10	12.2 x 19.3	4.8 x 7.6	100
12	15.3 x 24.2	6.0 x 9.5	80

On request the publisher will supply a leaflet with more detailed technical instructions or a TEX macro package for the preparation of manuscripts.

Manuscripts should be sent to one of the series editors or directly to:

Springer-Verlag, Computer Science Editorial I, Tiergartenstr. 17,
W-6900 Heidelberg 1, FRG

ISBN 3-540-56733-X
ISBN 0-387-56733-X